CLINICAL ASSESSMENT FOR SOCIAL WORKERS

Also available from Lyceum Books, Inc.

ENDINGS IN CLINICAL PRACTICE: EFFECTIVE CLOSURE IN DIVERSE SETTINGS, by Joseph Walsh

SOCIAL WORK WITH FAMILIES: CONTENT AND PROCESS, by Robert Constable and Daniel Lee

CASE MANAGEMENT: AN INTRODUCTION TO CONCEPTS AND SKILLS, 2E, by Arthur Frankel and Sheldon Gelman

"RAISE UP A CHILD: HUMAN DEVELOPMENT IN AN AFRICAN AMERICAN FAMILY", by Edith Hudley, Wendy Haight, and Margaret Miller

WORKING WITH CHILDREN, ADOLESCENTS, AND THEIR FAMILIES, 3E, by Martin Herbert and Karen Harper-Dorton

SOCIAL WORK PRACTICE: TREATING COMMON CLIENT PROBLEMS, edited by Harold Briggs and Kevin Corcoran

SCHOOL SOCIAL WORK: PRACTICE, POLICY, AND RESEARCH PERSPECTIVES, 5E, edited by Robert Constable, Shirley McDonald, and John Flynn

NAVIGATING THE HUMAN SERVICE ORGANIZATION, by Margaret Gibelman

TEAMWORK IN MULTIPROFESSIONAL CARE, by Malcolm Payne, foreword by Thomas M. Meenaghan

GENERALIST PRACTICE IN LARGER SETTINGS: KNOWLEDGE AND SKILL CONCEPTS, by Thomas Meenaghan and W. Eugene Gibbons

INTRODUCTION TO SOCIAL WORK: THE PEOPLE'S PROFESSION, 2E, by Ira Colby and Sophia Dziegielewski

MODERN SOCIAL WORK THEORY: A CRITICAL INTRODUCTION, 2E, by Malcolm Payne, foreword by Stephen C. Anderson

POLICY ANALYSIS AND RESEARCH TECHNOLOGY, 2E, by Thomas Meenaghan and Keith Kilty, and John McNutt

CLINICAL ASSESSMENT FOR SOCIAL WORKERS

Quantitative and Qualitative Methods
Second Edition

Edited by

CATHELEEN JORDAN
University of Texas, Arlington

CYNTHIA FRANKLIN
University of Texas, Austin

LYCEUM
BOOKS, INC.

5758 S. Blackstone Ave.
Chicago, Illinois 60637

DEDICATION

For Rick, Kate, Chris, Sharon, Mary, and Jan with all my love and gratitude.
To Jim Franklin my lifelong partner. The journey continues. . .

© Lyceum Books, Inc., 2003

Published by

LYCEUM BOOKS, INC.
5758 S. Blackstone Ave.
Chicago, Illinois 60637
773+643-1903 (Fax)
773+643-1902 (Phone)

Cataloging in Process is available

Library of Congress Cataloging-in-Publication Data

Jordan, Catheleen, 1947–
    Clinical assessment for social workers : quantitative and qualitative
methods / Catheleen Jordan and Cynthia Franklin.—2nd ed.
        p. cm.
    Includes bibliographical references (p.   ) and index.
    ISBN 0-925065-37-4 (paperback)
    1. Psychodiagnostics. 2. Psychiatric social work. 3. Needs
assessment. 4. Behavioral assessment. 5. Family assessment. I.
Franklin, Cynthia. II. Title.
    RC469.J67   2003
    361'.0068—dc21   2003011242

CONTENTS

TABLES

FIGURES

APPENDICES   407

INDEX   477

ABOUT THE EDITORS

Catheleen Jordan, Ph.D., is professor at the University of Texas at Arlington, School of Social Work. She is chair of the direct practice sequence and clinical supervisor in the School of Social Work Community Service Clinic. Professor Jordan teaches direct practice, family therapy, and philosophy of science. Professor Jordan's teaching and research interests include child and family treatment, work life issues, and program evaluation. Her numerous publications include *Family Practice: Brief Systems Methods for Social Work* coauthored with Cynthia Franklin, and *An Introduction to Family Social Work* coauthored with Don Collins and Heather Coleman of the University of Calgary. Professor Jordan is a licensed advanced clinical practitioner in social work.

Cynthia Franklin, Ph.D., is professor at the University of Texas at Austin, School of Social Work where she chairs the clinical concentration. Professor Franklin teaches courses on practice theories, family therapy, and research methods at doctoral levels. Professor Franklin specializes in clinical practice with children and families, and is known for her expertise in school social work and practice research integration. She has numerous publications on school social work practice, clinical assessment, the effectiveness of solution-focused therapy in school settings, and adolescent pregnancy prevention. Professor Franklin is author of several other books including Family Practice: *Brief Systems Methods for Social Work* coauthored with Catheleen Jordan. Professor Franklin is a clinical member of The American Association of Marriage and Family Therapy and holds practice licenses in clinical social work and marriage and family therapy.

Preface

Social workers and other helping professionals search for new and better ways to alleviate client problems. Early social workers like Mary Richmond urged professional social workers to use the scientific method and explore new methodologies. As social work has developed, so has our understanding of and appreciation for scientific methodology.

Clinical Assessment: Quantitative and Qualitative Methods will enable practitioners and students in the helping professions to learn more about assessment technology for children, families, and individual adults. We review available assessment models as well as some of the new advances in measurement and interviewing; we also integrate measurement and clinical assessment into a practice text.

We do not assume that the reader adheres to a particular theoretical orientation or epistemology. We believe assessment data can be collected using a variety of different formats. Having a repertoire of tools for performing assessment, derived from different perspectives, allows helpers more flexibility in data collection. For example, some clients might readily provide information by filling out a standardized questionnaire, whereas other clients might be happier sharing information through a genogram or an ecological map.

Clinical Assessment is designed for graduate and undergraduate social work students, as well as for social work practitioners and other related helping professionals—licensed professional counselors, marriage and family counselors, and psychologists. The book shows how to incorporate testing and measurement into practice and conduct empirically-based assessments on clients.

Every chapter in the second edition includes new and authoritative contributions from specialists. We have added more information about gay and lesbian families, mistreated children, and people with health-related problems. In an effort to assist the reader, chapter introductions, summaries, and review questions have been added. The book also includes extensive references, sample forms, samples of integrative skills assessments, and examples of standardized measures. Appendices in the first edition are now part of the chapters in the second edition.

Chapters 1 and 2 in the first edition have been combined in chapter 1 of the second edition to strengthen the tie between assessment theory and technology. The linking of assessment and intervention, including treatment planning information, has been strengthened and moved up to chapter 2, allowing the reader to get an overview of the assessment-to-treatment process from the beginning. The new chapter 11 adds information about the use of clinical research methodologies, which are so important in today's managed care environment. Chapter 6, "Children and Adolescents," and chapter 7, "Adults," now both end with a section on processing the movement from assessment to intervention, including treatment planning. Chapter 9, "Assessing Families who are Multi-stressed," includes new populations. The chapter also now reviews the assessment issues related to gay and lesbian families, mistreated children, and people with health-related problems such as substance abuse and HIV-AIDS. The new chapter 10, "Assessing Multicultural Clients," recommends alternative strategies for practice when the clientele is multicultural.

The authors would like to thank Meredith Hanson, Barry Ackerson, and Patricia Sherman for their insightful and helpful reviews of the manuscript. We want to thank Barbara W. White for her help in preparing the manuscript and Janie Hickerson for contributing a case study in chapter 9. We also wish to thank our publisher, David Follmer, for having confidence in us during the writing of the first book and for having patience with us during the writing of the second edition.

CHAPTER 1

An Integrative Skills Assessment Approach

Cynthia Franklin and Catheleen Jordan

This chapter provides a definition of social work assessment and a framework for understanding how to conduct a comprehensive social work assessment. Many facets of social work assessment are described. An integrative, theoretical basis is offered for what elements may go into a comprehensive assessment and is supported through the review of several social work practice models. Common features for current day assessment are highlighted through the convergent elements found in the diverse practice models. Finally, the authors use technical eclecticism to integrate assessment information across the models reviewed into an Integrative Skills Assessment Protocol that can be used by practitioners to guide assessment.

DEFINITION OF SOCIAL WORK ASSESSMENT

To date there is no unified definition of assessment in social work practice (Bisman, 1999). Levine (2002), however, offers a definition that covers most of the areas that are important to the assessment process and that is consistent with the philosophy of this book. Assessment in social work practice is:

> The process of systematically collecting data about a client's functioning and monitoring progress in client functioning on an ongoing basis. A process of problem selection and specification that is guided in social work by a person-in-environment, systems orientation. Assessment is used to identify and measure specific problem behaviors as well as protective and resilience factors, and to determine if treatment is necessary. Information is usually gathered from a variety of sources (e.g., individual, family members, case records, observation, rapid assessment tools and genograms). Types of assessment include biopsychosocial history taking, multiple dimensional crisis assessment, symptom checklists, functional analysis, and mental status exams. (p. 830)

As is reflected in Levine's definition, assessment is an ongoing process of understanding individual clients' characteristics such as their personality, problems, and strengths and related information about the social and interpersonal environments that are impacting clients. Multiple methods are often used to collect and evaluate ongoing information from clients. These methods are diverse and include face-to-face interviews with people, behavioral observations, review of written documents, and the use of measurement instruments.

Beyond the collection of information, the process of assessment also refers to ongoing analysis and synthesis of information about the client and his or her social environment for the purpose of formulating a diagnosis or coherent intervention plan for helping the client. Particular elements of an assessment are usually guided by practice theories and a case construction process that involves the cognitive appraisal of information, using diverse theories and clinical judgment, and the construction of that information into a written psychosocial study or report (Bisman, 1999).

THE NATURE OF THE ASSESSMENT PROCESS

The assessment of a client is a dynamic and context-driven process. Therefore, the most salient characteristics of a social work assessment may be decided by a practitioner's case construction process, the practice context, problems experienced by a client, and the practitioner's intervention models.

Case Construction Process

In order for a practitioner to develop an assessment he or she must use a case construction process that makes meaning out of disparate pieces of information that are received from the client, others, documents, and measurement instruments, for example. Analyzing and synthesizing this information requires cognitive and emotional intelligence as is found in analytical thinking, pattern recognition, and creativity. Practitioners combine deductive and inductive thinking processes, weave information into if-then propositions, and formulate logical hypotheses and conclusions. An example of the type of case construction process involving deductive and inductive thinking processes is provided by Bisman (1999).

> Deduction is moving from a theory's general propositions to application of these propositions for the purpose of offering an explanation of the specific case. The reasonableness of the hypothesis, the deduction depends on (1) the validity or truthfulness of the general theoretical propositions from which the hypothesis was deduced, (2) whether the specific case falls within the class of cases covered by the theoretical propositions, and (3) its capacity to guide the intervention hypothesis for this specific case. Do biological theories and social isolation explain depression? Is Mia Hanes' depression explained by her biology and social isolation? If the answer to either is no,

then the hypothesis that "Mia Hanes' depression is explained by and treated with medication and social supports" is neither logically deduced nor empirically supported.

In induction, observations lead to analyses of patterns out of which propositions emerge to explain those patterns. Steps for observations necessary in inductions include: 1) examine a representative sample of socially isolated persons who also have a genetic family history of depression for patterns of the relationships between depression with social support and genetic family history; 2) explore whether increased social support and medication results in reduction of depression for these persons. If the pattern indicates that there is a reduction, then we can formulate the induction: medication and social support help reduce depression. For the above situation we are ready for the "if-then" proposition. (p. 243)

As is illustrated above, when social workers gather assessment information, they find ways in their own minds of making sense out of that information. This is where the practitioner uses both deductive and inductive thinking to form conclusions. Part of this process involves asking questions to oneself and hypothesizing about what the information means. The practitioner draws on knowledge, practice experiences, and information obtained from the client. Armed with this information, the practitioner uses a process of inductive and deductive thinking to decide what is the most logical hypothesis for this case. This case construction is like a snapshot in time, it is a decision to construct the case according to what is known at that moment. The results of this process are often called the clinical impressions of the case. Of course, as the practitioner continues to gather information and think about that information, these clinical impressions or hypotheses might be updated or changed. The case construction process is not a onetime endeavor but an ongoing, ever changing process of gathering and synthesizing information. The practitioner must always be mindful that the process itself is not separate from his or her own viewpoints and biases as well. For this reason it is important to analyze information very carefully and to ask others, such as colleagues and a supervisor, their opinions about the information.

Improving Case Construction

Using multiple hypotheses and several sources of information may improve the case construction analysis. This is one reason why this text advocates using standardized measurement instruments; measures provide an objective source of information that the practitioner can consider hypotheses against. Of course measures are not without biases and weaknesses of their own. See Chapters 4 and 10 for a discussion of the strengths and weaknesses of standardized measures. An important set of thinking skills for assessment is hypothesis generation and flexible thinking. It is important for the practitioner to keep an open response set and to always focus on thinking of different possibilities when an idea seems right only to the practitioner. Some therapists refer to this process as *hypothesizing* or generating multiple ideas about the case. It is important to think in a flexible manner because, similar to clients, practitioners may develop thinking errors that keep them from performing good inductive and deductive thinking about a case. Cognitive errors like all-or-nothing thinking or black-and-white thinking may occur when considering information, for example. It is also common for humans to see client information through their own biased beliefs or perceptions, and this tendency may lead a practitioner to discount information or overlook helpful information or fail to consider other plausible ideas about a case (Gambrill, 1983). Being aware of one's own beliefs and perceptions helps a practitioner avoid response biases where he or she may fall into the trap of seeing all the information through the same lens.

A dialectic thinking process sometimes helps a practitioner consider different ideas about a case so that the practitioner does not get trapped into making cognitive errors during the case construction process. The dialectic process uses opposing ideas to challenge existing ideas. For this purpose, a practitioner may wish to develop a relationship with a colleague who has very different ideas about cases. It is possible, however, to coach yourself on thinking dialectically by using Socratic questions to challenge your own ideas. Some practitioners use a computer expert system or work in a setting that makes use of ongoing assessment reports with standardized measures that provide this feedback. See Chapters 4 and 7 for discussions of these types of assessment tools that are now being used in quality assurance. To be able to coach yourself, however, you must be self-reflexive and be able to observe yourself as if you were in an objective stance. This is also called meta-cognition—when you can think about your own thinking—and this is an important skill for engaging yourself in a dialectical process. For example, if you are certain that a client is depressed and that this explains his or her behavior, ask yourself, "What else could explain the client's behavior?" Press yourself for the answer and consider it. Strengths analysis may also help when making diagnosis and forming clinical impressions of a case. Because diagnosis is pathology oriented, the strengths analysis puts you in an opposite stance for viewing information. Ask yourself, "What are this client's strengths? How does this client cope with her pain? How come she does not have more of the *DSM* symptoms? In what ways is she doing well and performing symptom free, for example?"

Once a practitioner can consider different possibilities for a case, he or she can weigh those possibilities against the available data and evidence about the case. Information from the interviews and measurement instruments, for example, can be viewed against the multiple hypotheses to see which has the most evidence. It is important for the practitioner to stay close to the data and evidence from the client's life in making clinical decisions. Haynes, Leisne, and Blaine (1997), for example, developed a unique case formulation process from behavioral analysis that uses a vector graphing approach to help practitioners to pictorially graph relations between variables so that they can provide case formulations that are based on the data from the client's life. The picture and the tentative causal relationships that are drawn help the clinician to more accurately explain the client's behavior. It is not easy for a clinician to explain a client's behavior, and sometimes there are contradictions in information gathered. When these contradictions occur, the practitioner can use a functional analytic graphic approach to weigh the possible explanations against existing evidence. When applied in this manner, the case construction process is a recursive and reiterative thinking process that has its own checks and balances built in to improve the practitioner's abilities to accurately construct the case. The type of thinking skills needed to guide one in a valid and reliable case construction process are covered further in Chapter 5 on qualitative assessment.

Practice Environment

The practice environment, organizational structure, and community context in which social work practice is offered influence how treatment and assessment operate. Current practice environments, for example, usually offer short-term treatment sessions that are limited in number. Past studies suggest that clients rarely see practitioners more than six to eight sessions, regardless of therapeutic orientation (Koss & Shiang, 1994). Research in quality assurance and managed behavioral health care using large numbers of clients indicates that clients make the most change within six sessions, then the change tapers off, and it takes many other sessions to produce any more change. Other research indicates that although change is usually short term (6–14 sessions) it may take up to 40 sessions for some clients to maximize their change (Barkham et al., 2001; Lambert, Hansen, & Finch, 2001).

Today's practice sometimes follows a course of intermittent work similar to a primary care model in medicine. Working in this type of practice framework, practitioners would offer fewer sessions spaced over a long period of time (Cummings & Sayama, 1995). Other practice delivery systems are currently being used, such as intensive outpatient treatment, where clients are seen two to three times a week for a limited time period. Even single session therapies have been used (Talmon, 1990). In such a context, assessment must be short and include the most essential elements only. See box 1.1 for a list of twelve essential questions to ask in a brief assessment.

Box 1.1
Twelve Essential Questions to Be Asked in a
Brief Assessment Interview

---

1. Why is the client entering therapy now?
2. Are there any signs of psychosis, delusions, or thought disorders that would indicate that the client needs immediate medical/psychiatric treatment?
3. Are there signs of illness indicating the need for neurological or other medical treatment?
4. Is there evidence of depression or suicidal or homicidal ideations?
5. What are the presenting complaints?
6. What are the important antecedent factors of the client's problem?
7. Who or what is maintaining the problem?
8. What does the client wish to derive from therapy?
9. What is the client's preference for therapy style? How can you match that style?
10. Are there clear indications for a specific modality of treatment based on a person-environment assessment?
11. Can a therapeutic alliance be maintained or should the client be referred?
12. What are the client's positive attributes and strengths?

SOURCE: Adapted from Franklin, C., & Jordan, C. (1999a). The clinical utility of models and methods of assessment in managed care. In B. S. Compton & B. Galaway (Eds.), *Social work processes* (p. 289). Pacific Grove, CA: Brooks/Cole.

Clients Served

The clients whom social workers serve greatly influence the type of assessment that is completed. Some clients require more extensive neurological and medical evaluations, for example, such as those with Alzheimer's disease or severe eating disorders. Clients with chronic mental disorders such as schizophrenia may require assessment and monitoring of positive symptoms such as hallucinations and delusions, or assessment of medications by use of blood tests to ensure that their medications are not causing medical difficulties. These types of assessments, however, would not be routine or necessary with other clients.

Conversely, other clients might require more attention to their family, interpersonal, or developmental history such as those whose presenting problems include child, family, or couples problems; personality disorders; or sexual abuse. Still other clients may require considerable assessment of their immediate circumstances and living arrangements such as those who have lost jobs, receive public assistance, or may be homeless. In each situation, the client's current problems and circumstances determine what areas to spend the most time on in the assessment and direct the type of information that is needed. It is usually important to briefly scan all areas of the client's life to gain an understanding of his or her psychosocial history and social environment, but the more focused approach is guided by the client served and the presenting problems. Chapter 2 elaborates further on how to make clinical decisions about what areas to focus on in an assessment process.

PRACTICE MODELS OF THE PRACTITIONER

Perhaps the most salient influence on social work assessment is still the practice model or models used by the practitioner. The practice model of the practitioner dictates the type of information the practitioner gathers and how the practitioner thinks about that information and synthesizes that information into a conclusion. In this way, all practice models offer, to greater or lesser degree, their own case construction processes. In the next section, several models of social work intervention are described from the perspective of their unique contribution to social work assessment and their utility for performing current day assessments. Although the models are described in a distinct manner, it is common for practitioners to combine or integrate features from different models into their own unique way of thinking about client problems and what they need to be effective helpers. Franklin and Jordan (1995a, 1999a) and Mattaini (1990) provide previous reviews of the assessment features of prominent intervention models in social work practice. This current review draws heavily on those reviews. This review also focuses on several models that are unique to social work practice as well as models that originate in other disciplines but are frequently used by social work practitioners. It is not possible, however, to review every practice model that is important to social work, and the authors acknowledge that the space limitations of this text require that only a few well-known models be reviewed.

Psychosocial Assessment Model

Florence Hollis, Gordon Hamilton, and Helen Perlman are familiar names associated with the development of the psychosocial model (Woods & Robinson, 1996). Some of the other major contributors to the psychosocial and other ego approaches in social work include Perlman (1957, 1986), Parad and Miller (1963), Blanck and Blanck (1974), Maluccio (1981), Hollis and Wood (1981), and Goldstein (1986, 1988). The goal of the psychosocial approach, also sometimes called the diagnostic approach, is to determine a psychosocial diagnosis of the client. Factors such as history and developmental processes are taken into account in making this diagnosis and implementing the change efforts. The term *person-in-environment* originated with the thinking of this model. Ego psychology is the major theoretical basis of the psychosocial assessment

Figure 1.1   Areas for Assessment Using Biopsychosocial Framework

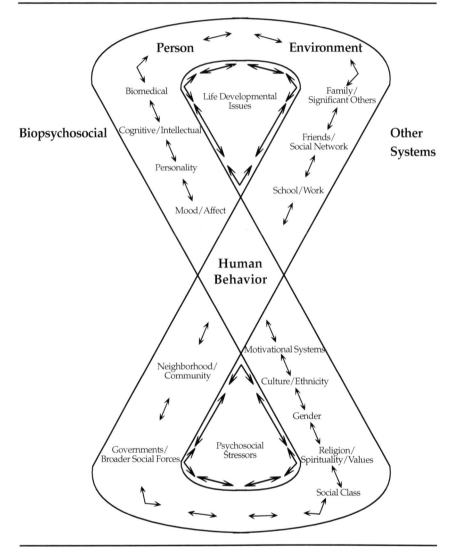

framework, but the added appreciation for the interplay of biopsychosocial processes is an inherent part of the model. See figure 1.2 for an overview of the areas of assessment to be covered when following a comprehensive biopsychosocial framework for assessment.

Over the years the psychosocial model has adapted, taking on variations of other models such as aspects of the shorter term functional case work model, which de-emphasized history and focused on solving problems in the here and now through the use of agency resources. Some of the outcomes of these adaptations include shortening the amount of history taken in a diagnostic interview and working more collaboratively with the client to solve problems (Woods & Robinson, 1996). Goldstein (1986) explains that, compared to the classical psychoanalytical thought that dominated early social work practice, ego psychology presented a more optimistic and sociocultural view of human behavior. Ego psychology concepts were used to refocus the study and assessment process on 1) the client's person-environment transactions in the here and now and particularly the degree to which he or she is coping effectively with major life roles and tasks; 2) the client's adaptive, autonomous, and conflict-free areas of ego functioning, as well as her ego deficits and maladaptive defenses and patterns; 3) the key developmental issues affecting the client's current reactions; and 4) the degree to which the external environment is creating obstacles to successful coping. One of the most recent explications of the psychosocial approach is provided by Goldstein (2002).

Unique Methods Used in Psychosocial Assessment. Turner (1988) suggested that psychosocial diagnosis is an ongoing process involved with the identification and labeling of problems, as well as with the recognition of client strengths. Detailed psychosocial interviewing has become a key component of assessment in the model. Specific assessment techniques include 1) classical psychiatric interviewing for the purpose of making a diagnosis; 2) the use of standardized and projective testing to aid accurate diagnosis; 3) psychosocial and developmental study to identify problem patterns; 4) observations and interpretations of the client-social worker relationship for the purposes of helping clients understand their problem patterns and providing a corrective emotional experience; and 5) using standardized interviews to obtain an accurate mental health diagnosis and further monitoring symptoms to make sure they are changed in treatment plans are important issues that the psychosocial model contributes.

Contributions to Today's Assessment Context. One of the strengths of the psychosocial assessment model for today's practice environments is that it matches well with the medical model that involves study, diagnosis, and treatment. Its focus on the biopsychosocial perspective makes it compatible with medically based behavioral health care settings that view people and their problems from this perspective. The psychosocial model also focuses on relationship building, social support, strengths, coping, problem solving, and a quick return to adaptive functioning. Finally, psychosocial assessment offers a person-in-environment framework that lends itself to comprehensive and diagnostic assessment. Today's practice environments require various types of diagnostic assessments and the use of the *DSM IV-TR* (Jarman-Rohde, McFall, Kolar, & Strom, 1997). Because the psychosocial model has historically focused on detailed study leading to a diagnosis, increasing the validity of these assessment activities may continue the best part of its traditions. Many diagnostic assessment measures are currently available to help practitioners make an accurate diagnosis. These instruments were developed to help provide a valid and efficient evaluation based on established diagnostic criteria. These measures involve semistructured interviews using standardized formats, some of the available measures are discussed in Part 2 of this book. In order for practitioners to make use of the best practices in clinical assessment, they must learn to identify and evaluate various standardized assessment tools based on their psychometric properties and clinical utility. This evaluation information is covered in detail in Chapter 4.

The person-in-environment perspective offered by the psychosocial model is perhaps one of the most popular ways to understand clients in social work practice. It has also influenced many other important social work models such as the problem-solving and task-centered models. Despite its infamy, the model actually has little research support other than the links that can be made to the medically based, biopsychosocial perspectives. More research on its unique contributions is definitely needed.

Problem-Solving Assessment Model

Helen Harris Perlman in the 1950s at the University of Chicago attempted to integrate the two prominent models of the day, the diagnostic and functional perspectives, into a framework known as the problem-solving social casework model. The diagnostic model integrated psychoanalytic theory into social casework, whereas the functional model, based on the work of Otto Rank, focused on growth and realization of potential and the agency function. Perlman (1986) stated that the problem-solving model is an eclectic construct. Johnson (1981) suggested that the problem-solving approach was theoretically eclectic, drawing upon ego psychology, symbolic interactionism, role theory, and Dewey's rational problem solving. This model is still taught in current practice texts and remains a popular model in social work practice (e.g., Compton & Galaway, 1994).

Unique Methods Used in Problem-Solving Assessment.   The goal of problem-solving assessment is to help the client cope; assessment is concerned with identifying the problem in the context of relevant intrapersonal issues (Johnson, 1981). Perlman (1957) suggested four P's—person, problem, place, and process—as a way of collecting and organizing assessment data from clients. Others have added further assessment criteria. Doremus (1976) added the four R's: roles, reactions, relationships, and resources; and Sheafor, Horejsi, and Horejsi (1988) added the four M's: motivation, meanings, management, and monitoring. Questions that practitioners may ask clients when collecting data on the four P's, four R's, and four M's are suggested by the authors as follows.

The four P's include, first, person or personality: What personality characteristics are important to the understanding of the problem? What is the interaction between the client's personality and other people or the environment? Second is the problem: What is the definition of the problem, and is the client's perception of the problem the same or different from others' perception? What are the specifics of the problem (frequency, magnitude, etc.), and is the situation a crisis? What other solutions have been attempted and with what outcomes? Third is place or agency: and What concerns and fears does the client have about being in contact with this particular agency? Is this agency setting the most helpful setting for this client with this particular problem? What barriers to helping the client can be attributed to the agency? Fourth is process: What type of helping process is the best for this particular client? What will be the consequences of the helping process for the client and his or her significant others?

The four R's include, first, roles: What roles must the client perform, and how well does he or she perform them? What do significant others report about the client's role performance? Second are reactions: What are the client's psychological, emotional, behavioral, and physical reactions to the problem? Third are relationships: Who are the client's significant others, and what is their relationship to the problem? What are the consequences of the problem for them? Fourth are resources: What resources does the client already have that may be utilized in this situation, and what resources need to be developed?

The four M's include motivation: How motivated is the client to change, and is the motivation to change promoted by discomfort or by optimism? Second are meanings: What is the client's perception of the problem, or what meaning does he or she attribute to the problem? What client beliefs and values are important for the practitioner to understand the problem? Third is management: How will the practitioner structure casework activity to work with this client? Fourth is monitoring: How will the problem be monitored and outcome evaluated? Who is available to help collect data?

Contributions to Today's Assessment Context. Problem-solving assessment is still very valuable in that it offers important questions and a framework for collecting and organizing information into a cohesive intervention plan. The main focus of this approach is the resolution of presenting problems, and the problem-solving model allows for a quick way to ascertain a client's resources for problem resolution. The model focuses on both client resources as well as environmental resources. It also helps the practitioner assess a client's motivation and readiness for change. Even though the problem-solving model is over thirty years old, it is very contemporary and matches well with other present-day integrative perspectives such as the transtheoretical model that also emphasizes client, context, and readiness to change (Prochaska & Norcross, 1999).

The problem-solving casework model, however, needs to work to establish its research basis and to identify itself as an effective means of helping clients solve their problems. To date, problem solving within social work is often seen as an effective means of engaging clients in a change process. The teaching of problem-solving skills to clients has a research base, but the problem-solving process of Perlman, however, has a minimal research basis. It is not known if coleading clients through a problem-solving process is helpful or not.

Cognitive Behavioral Assessment Models

Cognitive behavioral therapy focuses on clients' present functioning and attributes clients' problem behavior to learning processes, the formation of maladaptive cognitive schemas, errors in information processing, and proactive cognitive structures or meaning systems. Social workers who have integrated cognitive and behavioral techniques into social work practice include Gambrill, Thomas, and Carter (1971), Rose (1977, 1988), Stuart (1980), Gambrill (1983), Thyer (1983, 1985, 1987, 1988), Mattaini (1990), Shorkey and Sutton-Simon (1983), Brower and Nurius (1993), Berlin (1996), and Granvold, (1996). Rooted in the Cognitive Revolution that was ushered in by a 1956 symposium at MIT, cognitive therapy has moved to the forefront in psychotherapy and is one of the most widely applied and respected psychotherapies. Aaron Beck, a psychiatrist, is one of the main fathers of the field and has been the psychotherapist and researcher who is most responsible for developing the empirical basis of the cognitive model. Through his cognitive therapy institute (Beck Institute), Dr. Beck has invited diverse professionals including social workers to learn and contribute to this practice model (see http://www.beckinstitute.org). Cognitive behavior therapy has also become one of the most popular forms of brief psychotherapy (Turner, 1992). In addition, it is widely used in social work, through its integration into competency-based, problem-solving, and task-centered models, as well as the empirical practice model. Social work researchers Brower and Nurius (1993) have also integrated the latest knowledge from cognitive science into a new practice model, the cognitive-ecological model. Cormier and Nurius (2002) also integrate the cognitive behavioral perspective in their practice text.

The cognitive behavioral model is complex and includes numerous schools of therapy and practice models. For this reason cognitive behavioral therapy has become more of a school of thought than a unitary theory or set of practices. It has been influenced by diverse theoretical and philosophical positions, ranging from psychoanalytic to behavioral therapies. The approach has been associated most with behavior therapies, resulting in the term *cognitive behavior therapy*. The underlying theoretical base of the cognitive behavioral model is taken from experimental psychology—particularly, learning theories and work in cognition and memory, information processing, and social cognition. Recently, cognitive theory has also borrowed from developmental theories such as attachment theories and integrated newer systems theories such as complexity systems theory (Guidano, 1991; Mahoney, 1991, 1995). Meichenbaum (1993) describes how cognitive behavior therapy has changed over time by suggesting that there have been three metaphors that have guided the model.

1. Conditioning as a Metaphor—Cognitions viewed as covert behaviors subject to the same laws of learning as overt behavior in the conditioning paradigm.

2. Information Processing as a Metaphor—Mind as computer with the language of information processing and social learning theory (e.g., decoding, encoding, retrieval, attributional bias, cognitive structure, schemata, belief systems, cognitive distortion, and cognitive errors).

3. Constructive Narrative as a Metaphor—Constructivist perspective that humans construct their personal realities and create their own representational models of the world. Personal meanings, multiple realities, and consequences of cognitive constructions are emphasized. Therapist acts as coconstructor, helping clients alter their narratives and life stories. Therapist helps clients reframe stressful life experiences and emotions as normal. The focus is on strengths, resources, coping abilities, and narrative reconstruction.

Cognitive behavioral models are moving toward a focus on the complexity, interactional, circular, and self-perpetuating nature of behavioral and cognitive sequences. There is currently more of a focus on the understanding of schemas and how early schemas predispose people toward depression and other psychopathologies. Constructivism is a central theoretical construct for contemporary cognitive therapies, having become a guiding principle for theorists as diverse as Mahoney (1991), Meichenbaum and Fitzpatrick (1993), and Ellis. According to Mahoney (1991), constructivism

> 1) emphasizes the active and proactive nature of all perception, learning and knowing, 2) acknowledges the structural and functional primacy of abstract (tacit) over concrete (explicit) processes in all sentient and sapient experience; 3) views learning, knowing and memory as phenomena that reflect the ongoing attempts of body and mind to organize (and endlessly reorganize) their own patterns of action and experience—patterns that are of course, related to changing and highly mediated engagements with their momentary worlds. (p. 95)

Research into cognitive and social structures and processes provide support for many of the tenets discussed in newer cognitive therapies. Brower and Nurius (1993), for example, review emphirical research from the presprective of cognitive, personality, and social psychology, as well as ecological psychology, and describe the importance of the constructivist perspectives. For research in the following areas, please see the sources indicated: 1) memory (Brower & Nurius, 1993); 2) social cognition (Fiske & Taylor, 1984); 3) evolutionary epistemology [how humans construct knowledge] (Mahoney, 1991), 4) ecological psychology (Greenberg & Pascual-Leone, 1995); 5) narrative psychology (Van den Broek & Thurlow, 1991); 6) new social cognitive, applied developmental and learning theories (Prawat, 1993); and 7) complexity systems theory (Mahoney, 1995; Warren, Franklin, & Streeter, 1996).

Unique Methods Used in Cognitive Behavioral Assessment.   The goal of cognitive behavioral assessment is specification of the behavior (thoughts, feelings, or overt behavior) to be changed, along with its antecedents, consequences, and underlying cognitive mechanisms. From the nine-step behavioral assessment of Gambrill et al. (1971), behavioral assessment today has evolved into a multidimensional contextual model (Barth, 1986; Gambrill, 1983; Mattaini, 1990; Whittaker & Tracy, 1989). Gambrill (1983) identified sources of influence on clients' behavior, including the actions of others, thoughts, emotions, physiologic factors, setting, events, physical characteristics of the environment, ethnic and cultural factors, material and community resources, past history, societal factors, and developmental factors. Other influences include obstacles and opportunities, consequences of attempted solutions, environmental deficiencies, and motivations and/or inhibitions versus behavioral deficits. Specific assessment approaches used in the cognitive behavioral model include behavioral analysis theory, interviewing, identifying underlying cognitive schemas, logs, self-anchored scales, and standardized measures (Bellack & Hersen, 1988; Hudson, 1982; Kanfer & Schefft, 1988; Shorkey & Sutton-Simon, 1983).

In assessment systems, cognitive behaviorists focused on theoretically and experimentally based approaches for identifying and tracking specific behaviors and cognitions that needed to be changed. Now there is an increasing focus on putting people in their social contexts and understanding how clients' developmental history and attachment relationships have influenced their current schemas and automatic thoughts. Models like the ABC model that focused on tracking antecedents (A), self-talk, or automatic thoughts or beliefs (B), and behaviors and consequences of a particular problems (C) were among the popular earlier models. [Collecting data on the frequency and duration of cognitions and behaviors is important for observing the difficulties clients are experiencing and monitoring their changes.] Identifying automatic thoughts and their underlying schemas along with assessing behavioral deficits and excesses are at the center of current models. Self-observation, self-monitoring, and self-recording are hallmarks of assessment approaches, and these activities also become central to change efforts in newer constructivist models (Brower & Nurius, 1993).

Cognitive behavior therapists also have focused on developing standardized measures to assess maladaptive cognition and behavior (Clark, 1988). Beck and Beck (2002), for example, has developed measures for depression and suicide (http://www.beckinstitute.org). In general, cognitive behavior therapists have been forerunners in advocating valid and reliable methods for client assessment. For example, computerized assessment systems (Hudson, 1990; Jordan & Franklin, 1995; Nurius & Hudson, 1988) are used systematically to track behaviors using standardized measures. These types of systems are typified by the Hudson Clinical Assessment System (CAS) (Hudson, 1982, 1989). CAS provides approximately twenty scales such as generalized contentment and marital satisfaction, to measure intrapersonal and interpersonal client problems. These scales are discussed further in later chapters of this book. The CAS system is designed so that clients (or the practitioner) may enter and graph the data on computer for single system analysis. Expert systems are also endorsed by behavioral practitioners. These computer-based systems aim to help practitioners make clinical decisions. Systems have been developed for making decisions in child welfare and the mental health field (Mullen & Schuermann, 1990; Stein, 1990; Wakefield, 1990).

It is impossible to describe a full spectrum of cognitive behavioral approaches to assessment because of the increasing numbers of specific models and their unique features. Franklin (1995), for example, reports that there are currently over twenty approaches to cognitive therapy. One comprehensive assessment framework developed from the cognitive behavioral approach is multimodal assessment (Lazarus, 1989), and this model will be described here. See Vonk and Early (2002) for descriptions of other assessment frameworks used in cognitive behavioral therapy.

Multimodal Assessment

Using the multimodal assessment framework, practitioners evaluate client problems in great depth and detail across different modalities, including behavior, affect, sensation, imagery, cognitions, interpersonal relationships, and physiological factors of client functioning and their interactive effects (Lazarus, 1989). Lazarus (1991) developed a multimodal life history inventory to help practitioners gain information about the different modalities. Lazarus uses an acronym to describe the comprehensive components that go into a behavioral assessment: B = Behavior, A = Affect, S = Sensation, I = Imagery, C = Cognition, I = Interpersonal, and D = Drugs, which represents the broader biological realm.

The multimodal model helps practitioners formulate a brief, but comprehensive, assessment by developing a modality profile. A modality profile organizes information according to the BASIC ID assessment. Using the BASIC ID, the practitioner is able to make differential decisions about effective treatments. It is also possible to scale the modality preferences to see in which areas a client may show a more favorable response to treatment (Lazarus, 1981). For example, some clients may experience their difficulties through their behavior, whereas others have more difficulties with affects, or interpersonal relationships. Even a client with a presenting problem such as anxiety (an affect) may experience this problem in a way that responds to treatments that focus on another modality. For example, one of the authors had a client who experienced anxiety attacks mainly as physiological sensations (rapid pulse, tight muscles). The modality profile indicated that a treatment that focused on the sensation modality should be used as the first approach. As it turned out, the client difficulties were helped by teaching him progressive muscle relaxation exercises. Using the BASIC ID, it is possible for a practitioner to plan interventions systematically based on the client's assessment profile.

Contributions to Today's Assessment Context.   Cognitive behavioral assessment and treatment has considerable promise for work in today's practice environments. In fact, due to the inherent compatibility of cognitive behavior therapy with brief practice settings, some social workers have advocated that student training focus on cognitive behavioral methods (Jarmon-Rohde, 1997). Because cognitive behavioral therapies rejected Freudian psychology in favor of a more experimental and research-based approach to behavior, the model did not accept the idea of long-term treatment nor adapt a more pathological understanding of human behavior. Cognitive behavior therapies developed a different understanding of human behavior based on learning and cognitive theories, the importance of environmental modification, self-efficacy, and adaptive change. The principle of parsimony was adhered to in the models, and practitioners were taught to be pragmatic, efficient, and effective in their approach to solving human problems.

In cognitive behavior therapy, practitioners are active, and assessments are structured and goal directed. The relationship between the client and clinician is collaborative, with an emphasis on gathering evidence and exploring personal hypotheses to test out faulty ideas and personal coping strategies. There is an emphasis on developing a clear conceptualization of the case based on theory, and cognitive behavioral techniques are chosen according to the client's goals. Thus, cognitive behavior therapy offers its own case construction method that usually includes a brief listing of problems, thoughts and emotions associated with problems, and a possible hypothesis about the underlying schemas that may activate thoughts and emotions and contribute to the client's difficulties (Vonk & Early, 2002).

Four attributes of cognitive behavioral assessment make it especially useful:

1. Cognitive behavioral practice focuses on the rapid assessment and treatment of mental disorders. Cognitive behaviorists emphasize the resolution of the presenting problem; they work with history only as related to the client's current functioning. The main focus is to identify faulty learning and cognitive mechanisms that maintain the presenting problem and then to formulate assessment with specific goals and interventions.

2. Cognitive behavior therapies are the best researched of all psychotherapies. They provide a strong evidence base for the assessment methods that they use in practice. A network of researchers in academic psychology and psychiatry has supported the efficacy studies on cognitive behavioral therapies, and they have produced many impressive outcome studies on the effectiveness of cognitive behavioral approaches.

3. Cognitive behavior therapists also have provided detailed treatment manuals to guide assessment and practice. Treatment manuals exist to guide practitioners in assessing client problems such as depression, substance abuse, personality disorders, and posttraumatic stress disorders (e.g., Barkley, 1997; Beck & Freeman, 1990; Beck, Rush, Shaw, & Emery, 1987; Beck, Wright, Newman, & Liese, 1993; Linehan, 1993; Meichenbaum, 1994).

4. Finally, cognitive behavior therapies have a long tradition of advocating that practitioners use ongoing assessment to systematically monitor the effectiveness of their practices. Many of the early behavior therapists, for example, advocated the use of single case designs (Barlow & Hersen, 1984), which are discussed in more detail in Chapters 2 and 11.

Life Model Assessment

The life model for social work practice was developed by Germain and Gitterman of the Columbia School of Social Work. The authors suggest their approach is best described by the ecological metaphor. The underlying theory is ecological, concerned with interactions between people and their environments. Important concepts include stress, coping, and adaptation, as well as competence, autonomy, social networks, and organizations (Johnson, 1981). The goal of the life model assessment is for client and clinician to collaborate to understand the problem, then to set objectives and plan the intervention (Johnson, 1981). Germain and Gitterman (1996) explain assessment as concerned with "the interplay of dynamic forces within the life space, including the influence of the agency as a presence in the client's ecological context" (p. 633). The primary goal of assessment is to determine the problems in living formulation by examining three areas of the life space—life transitions, environmental pressures, and maladaptive interpersonal processes (Germain & Gitterman, 1996).

Gitterman (1988) identified five major aims of the life model. The first aim is to develop a perspective to give equal attention to people and to the environment. The second aim is to develop a model of practice to build bridges between the traditional specializations of casework, administration and planning, and family therapy. Third, the model aims to mirror life processes closely so that it is the social workers who fit in with clients; clients should not be required to fit in with social workers' theoretical orientations. The fourth aim is to build on people's strengths, rather than on their pathologies; labeling is seen as blaming clients for their problems. The fifth and final aim is to build bridges between treatment and social reform.

Unique Methods Used in Life Model Assessment.   Assessment techniques include the interview and ecomaps or social network mapping and standardized social support assessment instruments (Cheers, 1987; Hartman & Laird, 1983; Streeter & Franklin, 1992). The ecomap is one of the most important assessment tools to evolve from this model. See figure 1.2.

Use of the Life Model in Current Practice Environments.   Recently, Wakefield (1996a, 1996b, 1996c) provided a critique of the ecological systems theory, pointing out several weaknesses that are also especially important due to the theory's clinical utility for assessment in today's practice contexts. In particular, the ecological systems theory does not guide intervention selection very well. Warren et al. (1996) on the other hand suggest that some of the difficulties of the ecological systems theory mentioned by Wakefield can be transcended through the use of newer systems theories based on chaos and complexity systems theory. Evidence-based assessment tools that guide interventions may be developed in the future. The ecological systems theory has already proven to be an important tool for organizing complex interventions for youth who are adjudicated and are at risk for out-of-home placements. Henggeler et al. (1998), for example, has used the ecological model to develop the evidence-based therapy for youth and families known as multisystemic therapy. In this intervention, an ecological systems view is

Figure 1.2   Ecomap

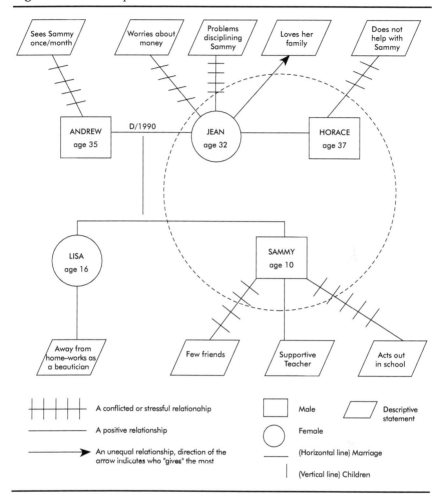

used to consider multisystemic (e.g., family, school, neighborhood, peers) risk factors, protective factors, client strengths, and points of intervention that are needed. The life model, like the multisystemic model, continues social work's tradition of focusing on both persons and their environments in assessment. Although the life model does not provide the impressive clinical trials on its effectiveness like other ecological models such as the multisystemic therapy, ecomaps appear to be an extremely useful assessment tool. Practitioners may, however, be restrained from using ecomaps by the amount of time available in various practice contexts. Computer software that allows practitioners to generate electronic ecomaps and genograms may make it more feasible for practitioners to use these assessment tools. (See for example the tools provided by WonderWare, Inc./301-942-3254, Software that Generates Genograms and Ecomaps, http://www.interpersonaluniverse.net)

Social support is another especially cogent assessment area that is important to the life model and can be linked empirically to improvements in social and mental health functioning (Streeter & Franklin, 1992). Tracy and Whittaker (1990) have improved on the information that can be obtained through a graphic approach like ecomapping by combining it with card sort techniques and an interview grid approach to perform clinical assessment of social network characteristics. This is an important area of investigation, but in its current form it is too cumbersome for use in brief therapy assessments. Future tools that help practitioners combine social network approaches with ecomaps and computerized expert systems may revolutionalize and revitalize the importance of life model assessment.

Ecobehavioral Assessment Model

The work of Mattaini (1990, 1992a, 1999) focuses on combining the ecological assessment model with specific, targeted interventions from the more empirical behavioral practice. It is an important step in assessment using an ecological systems framework and provides practitioners with useful computerized assessment tools for generating ecomaps and other graphic-based assessments. This model's main contribution is combining ecological systems theories with contemporary behavioral practice from behavioral analysis traditions. There is ongoing criticism from behavioral researchers and theorists that clinicians practicing behavioral therapies have not updated their knowledge about the new learning theories. Thus, the clinical practice does not keep abreast of the empirical and theoretical work that is going on in experimental psychology (e.g., Plaud & Eifert, 1998). The ecobehavioral model, however, does make use of knowledge from newer learning theories. Contemporary behavioral practice addresses overt behaviors and private experiences such as cognition and emotion and focuses on the social environment and the major systems that shape humans (Mattaini, Lowery, & Meyer, 2002). The structure and function of language (verbal behavior) is also given consideration in this model.

The new behaviorism is guided by three major developments. 1) the questioning of a mechanistic view of clients: Mechanistic stimulus and response, simple contingency analysis (i.e., antecedents and consequences), and mediation models were determined to be limited in explaining human behavior. 2) the development of contextual behavioral models that argue in favor of holism and a full contextual analysis for the understanding of behavior: Contextual-behaviorists believe that no type of human responding (e.g., overt behavior, cognition, emotion) can be separated from its contexts. This includes all forms of interacting such as thinking, feeling, doing, and verbal behavior (rule governed) and the environmental contexts in which these behaviors take place. Simple cause-and-effect relations are rejected by contextual-behaviorism because psychological events cannot be explained by one area of observation, such as behavior or cognition, but must be analyzed in their full context, which includes all domains of responding. This is a systemic view, contextual behaviorists are interested in the functions of behavior across contexts and why a behavior is occurring. This means they see both the history of the client and his or her current situation as important. 3) research on human verbal behavior (rule governed) and on how humans derive bidirectional relations in learning. This research has led to an understanding of the importance of indirect contingencies for behavior. In experiments it has been shown, for example, that once humans learn one set of assumptions or a distinct pattern, they can transfer that pattern to another similar pattern without any further direct learning (Hayes, Follette, & Follette, 1995).

Humans may also learn through observation learning and verbal associations instead of direct experience. This means that they can learn by watching others and can also talk themselves into responding a certain way in the present based on a past association. Indirect contingencies also often mediate more direct contingencies. This means the internal meanings and expectations dictate responses to current experiences. So, what aversive for one person may not be responded to in the same way by another person. Psychological problems such as phobias, for example, are usually learned indirectly through rule-governed behavior and not through direct experiences. Research on rule-governed, verbal behavior has led contemporary behaviorists to use more covert psychological events such as valued elements (the potency of private reinforcers), differing expectations (rules), and different meanings (equivalence relations) for understanding the functional analysis of a behavior (Hayes et al., 1995; Mattaini, 1999).

Like most contemporary behavioral models, the ecobehavioral model is much broader than behaviorism was in the past, and it is very integrative in that the model shares features with other models. For example, it shares many features with the cognitive-ecological model described by Brower and Nurius (see above), the life model, and the psychosocial model. The ecobehavioral model also incorporates knowledge and research from culture-analytic theory to help practitioners better assess and intervene with groups of people such as families. Using culture-analytic theory, the practitioner becomes acquainted with how culture shapes reinforcers, or rules for behavior, and sets the stage for individuals to form different meanings associated with experiences (Mattaini, 1999).

Unique Methods Used in Ecobehavioral Assessment. The eco-behavioral model assumes that human behavior is complex and highly interconnected and that the best way to understand human behavior is to assess it using an ecological framework. Assessment is understood as the process of the practitioner defining the difference between a client's current state and his or her goal state. This method is similar to the method used in solution-focused therapy (to be reviewed below) in that the focus is on change, goals, and new behavior and not on past pathology. The assessment process involves engagement, assessing the difference in goal state and current state, envisioning how the client wants a situation to change, and intervention planning. Assessment is completed in a framework of collaboration or shared power between the client and the practitioner (Mattaini, 1999). The ecobehavioral model is useful with individuals, families, groups, communities, and organizations but has been better developed for microbased practice than macrobased practice.

The ecomap is viewed as an essential assessment tool along with other graphic methods that allow practitioners to map the context and relations of behavior. Mattaini (1993) has provided detailed instructions and computer-based tools for graphing. (They are available at NASW Press at this website: http://www.naswpress.org/publications/books/clinical/1000_words/2243toc.html.) He has also provided a framework and outline for conducting assessment within the ecobehavioral model. See box 1.2.

Behavioral principles are used as analytical tools to map the exchanges between individuals, families, and their environment. For example, in the ecobehavioral model practitioners would use graphic tools or maps to help them understand the ecoscan (mini-psychosocial history). This involves the identification of focal issues and contingency analysis to understand the consequences of both overt and covert behavior that may be reinforcing that behavior. The practitioiner also seeks to determine who is involved in the issues and the motivating antecedents that may be triggering a behavior in the present. The final goal is to move to the intervention tasks that are desirable.

Family Systems Assessment Models

Over the past thirty years, the family therapy field developed multiple methodologies for assessing families as a system. These new methods focus on "whole systems" functioning and assess the interactional, interpersonal, and systemic functioning of family groups. Assessment of whole systems family functioning is based on systems theory and assumes that the interactions of a family group take on measurable and/or observable behavior patterns and characteristics that extend beyond the individual behaviors of each of its family members (Franklin & Jordan, 1999b).

Box 1.2
Ecobehavioral Assessment

I. Ecobehavioral Scan

I'd like to ask you a few questions so that we can develop a clear picture of your situation together and so that I can be sure I understand your life as it is now. (The social worker may wish to draw a transactional ecomap with the family during this stage.)

   a. Let's start with what's going right. What areas of your family life are currently going the best?
   b. What about connections you have outside the immediate family? How much contact do you have with relatives or extended family? On a scale of 0 (not at all) to 5 (a lot), how much satisfaction do you get from those contacts? Are there any struggles with those folks? On a scale of 0 to 5, how much pain do those struggles cause? (Use a similar scale with each of the following areas that appears particularly relevant.)
   c. Do you have many friends? How often do you see friends? How are those relationships going? Anyone else?
   d. What about work and school? What's going well there? So on our 0 to 5 scale, are there things that aren't going so well? About a __ on our scale?
   e. Tell me a little about where you live. How satisfied are you with your home and neighborhood?
   f. Any religious or church affiliation? Are you active?
   g. Is anyone in the family active in other groups or organizations?
   h. Any legal involvement?
   i. How is everyone's health? Any problems there?
   j. How much alcohol do people in the family use? Anyone take medication or drugs?
   k. Now let's turn to your family itself. What's going right in the family? Who gets along best with whom? Who have more struggles getting along? (Elaborate and quantify as necessary to explore the relationships within the family.)
   l. Does anyone else live in your home? How do you all get along? (Explore both positive and negative exchanges, and quantify if possible.)
   m. What would you like to do more of in your family? What would you like to do less of? (Suggest self-monitoring or observational measures to expand data.)

II. Identification of Focal Issues

(Remember that focal issues may involve the behavior of only one person; however, to the extent possible, try to shift toward transactional definitions. Also, remember that focal issues need not involve only family members, but may involve transactions with other people or systems.)

   a. So, out of all of this, where would you like to begin? What's most important to you?
   b. I notice that you seemed to struggle a bit with ___. Is that one thing we should pay attention to?

Box 1.2   *Continued*

---

 c. What do you think would be a realistic goal here? (Expanding with specifics, but build on the envisioning that occurred earlier.)

 d. Do you think that there is anything else we should work on at this point?

 e. So, specifically, one of our goals right now is (Explicate in behavioral terms.)

III. Contextual Analysis of Focal Issues

Now, let's see if we can get a really clear picture of our first goal (or focal issue), which is. (The general flow is from current undesirable situation to goal state; this kind of analysis should occur for each identified focal issue, although all may not be done at the same time. Focal issues left aside for later should be clearly stated and written down, however, so that the family knows they will be addressed later.)

 a. As near as you can tell, how did this problem start?

 b. When was that?

 c. Does this problem behavior ever pay off in any way for anyone? Does it ever produce any advantages for anybody?

 d. Who else acts a little like this sometimes?

 e. Who or what supports the current pattern?

 f. What are the costs? What other problems does it cause?

 g. What seems to trigger the problem? Are there times when it does not happen? (Identify occasions.)

 h. Are there some times when this is not a problem? Tell me about those times. When is the problem most likely to come up? (Search for motivating antecedents.)

 i. What do you think it would take to get from where you are to where you want to be? (Explore resources, including tangible, personal, and social.)

 j. Who would be willing to help you achieve this goal or resolve this problem?

 k. Who or what might stand in the way?

 l. How important is this to you? Why? How will reaching this goal enrich your lives? How quickly do you think that will happen? (Build motivation.)

IV. Identification of Interventive Tasks

(This part of the assessment process needs to flow from the information provided in earlier stages, and it should emphasize tasks that will address the areas identified in the contextual analysis. It should explore interventive options for mobilizing the resources and addressing the obstacles discussed in that analysis. Identify approaches with the best empirical support in the context of the family situation. Careful specification of the multiple steps required to work toward the goal may be required. Explore possible reinforcers to be used along the way as well.)

SOURCE: Mattaini, M. (1999).

Family systems assessment focuses on the systemic or relational network characteristics of family functioning and associated presenting problems. Systemic functioning specifically refers to the circular, patterned way in which family groups are believed to behave. Behavior patterns in family systems are nonlinear and recursive and operate in a repetitive, circular, and reflexive manner (Becvar & Becvar, 1988; de Shazer, 1982; Hoffman, 1981; O'Hanlon & Wilk, 1987; Palazzoli, Boscolo, Cecchin, & Prata, 1980; Tomm, 1987).

Some family clinicians believe that systemic family patterns have meaning or serve a function for the family system, such as helping the family to stay intact or to avoid marital conflict (Haley, 1990; Madanes, 1984; Palazzoli, Cirillo, Selvini, & Sorrentino, 1989). Other clinicians focus more on the behavioral aspects of the systemic functioning or on the self-reinforcing nature of the pattern and make few interpretations about its meaning or function (Cade & O'Hanlon, 1993; Fisch, Weakland, & Segal, 1982; Watzlawick, Weakland, & Fisch, 1974). Yet other practitioners focus on the longitudinal nature of these relational patterns across generations of a family. Regardless of one's theoretical orientation, in order to effectively assess family systems clinicians must use assessment methods that can focus on the interactive sequences and relational network characteristics of the entire family. Practitioners should view assessment as serving dual functions. Assessment is both a way to discover how a family system is functioning and a method for intervening into the patterns of a family system. The processes of assessment and change interventions are not distinct but interactive and circular, allowing for assessment methods to serve functions as information-gathering strategies and interventive methods (Tomm, 1987). Viewing assessment as intervention blurs the boundaries between methods that are for the purposes of assessment and of change.

Unique Methods Used in Family Systems Assessment.   In a family assessment practitioners use specialized questioning techniques to gather information and to introduce information into a family system. Techniques such as circular questions; conversational/therapeutic questions; hypothesizing, circularity, and neutrality; tracking problems, solutions, and/or exceptions to problems; and pretherapy change assessment are used. Graphic methods such as genograms are also used to assess longitudinal emotional and behavioral patterns in families. See figure 1.3. Finally, empirically derived assessment models and standardized measures are used in family assessment. These methods are derived from research on the classification and assessment of family systems functioning. Chapter 9 in this text reviews and illustrates several family systems assessment methods.

Figure 1.3　Renew of Family Systems Assessment Methods

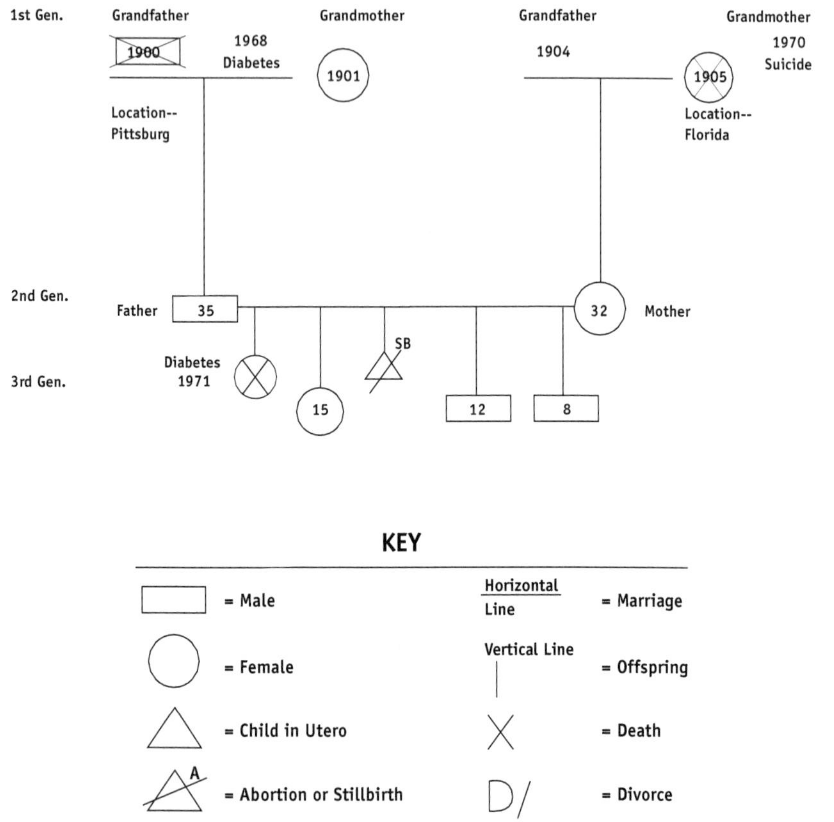

1st Gen.　Grandfather　　　　Grandmother　　　　Grandfather　　　　Grandmother

1900　1968 Diabetes　1901　1904　1970 Suicide　1905

Location--
Pittsburg

Location--
Florida

2nd Gen.　Father　35　　　　32　Mother

3rd Gen.　Diabetes 1971　SB　15　12　8

KEY

☐ = Male		Horizontal Line = Marriage	
◯ = Female		Vertical Line | = Offspring	
△ = Child in Utero		✕ = Death	
△ᴬ = Abortion or Stillbirth		D/ = Divorce	

SOURCE: Foley, V. (1989). Family therapy. In R. Corsini & D. Wedding (Eds.), *Current Psychotherapies* (4th ed.). Itasca, IL: Peacock.

Use of the Family Systems Assessments in Current Practice Environments. Because family assessment methods focus on introducing rapid change, they seem especially suited for current-day practice settings. Family therapy, like cognitive behavioral practice, has always been a shorter term method, and the brevity of this approach adds to its utility for brief therapy and managed behavioral care settings. One caveat to this approach, however, is the fact that all the interventions are based on systems theory. The theory maintains that if we alter the functioning of the whole system, the presenting problem will also resolve. Although some family approaches such as the MRI and solution-focused therapy specifically aim to resolve the presenting problem, not all approaches follow this goal-directed orientation. It may be easy to understand the importance of relationship functioning when family relationships are an important target of intervention or when the client's difficulties are primarily interpersonal in nature (e.g., marital conflict, battering). This is harder when the problem is more an individual's focused on an individual's mental health issues (e.g., depression, psychosis) (Franklin & Jordan, 1999b).

Fortunately, however, there is a body of research literature pointing to the importance of relationship problems to such areas as depression (Jacobson & Christensen, 1997; O'Leary & Beach, 1990), and there is growing research support for the effectiveness of family therapy with a variety of mental health disorders (Franklin & Jordan, 2002; Pinsof & Wynne, 1995). It is important for family researchers and practitioners to continue to develop research on the efficacy of family systems models with different problem areas.

Task-Centered Assessment Model

The task-centered model was developed in the 1960s from a psychoanalytically oriented short-term model (Reid, 1988, 1992, 2000). Today it appears more closely akin to the cognitive behavioral practice than the psychosocial model. The focus is on developing outcomes that could be researched empirically (Johnson, 1981). The theoretical base of task-centered casework was designed to be open to integration from various theoretical and technical orientations (Reid, 1988). Important ideas originally presented were that casework is a problem-solving process (Perlman, 1957) and that the client's task is the focus (Studt, 1968). Theory and techniques were borrowed from crisis-intervention literature. More recently, theory and techniques from behavioral theory, cognitive and learning theory, and structural family therapy have been integrated into the task-centered model.

Unique Methods Used in Task-Centered Assessment.   The goal of assessment is to specify target problems and their desired outcomes. Reid & Epstein (1972) and Reid (1988, 2000) explain the assessment and task-planning process. The first activity is the initial problem formulation. The clients' perception of the problem is important, though it is recognized that clients may need help expressing or even acknowledging the full range of problems. Practitioners may help in this process by exploring, clarifying, and specifying the problem(s). In the case of clients who are required to seek services (e.g., in the case of child abuse), practitioners begin with the problem that brought them to the service provider. After the problem has been formulated, it is then placed in the context in which it occurs. This context includes problem-maintaining conditions, resources, and interpersonal and intrapersonal systems. Standardized instruments may be used. Assessment continues into intervention and monitors case progress. In summary, the task-centered process includes task planning, implementation, and review (Reid, 1988).

The task-centered approach is a useful approach for ensuring that assessment moves to specific intervention planning. The structure of the model has been shown to be helpful for both voluntary and nonvoluntary clients. It has been used in case management and clinical services with much success (Reid & Fortune, 2002). Task-centered assessment is prescriptive in that specification of tasks and problems leads to specific implementation plans. Tasks are usually defined by client and clinician through a collaborative process in a face-to-face interview. Specific forms and contractual agreements may be used to write down the problems, tasks, and goals. The client and clinician often sign these agreements. Task-centered assessment offers a tremendous amount of specificity on the desired outcomes of assessment as is illustrated by the resulting service contract. It is, however, unclear what specific tasks work best with what types of clients and client problems. The link between assessment and intervention appears to be left up to the collaborative process of the interview and to the practitioner's own clinical judgment.

Use of the Task-Centered Assessments in Current Practice Environments.   Task-centered assessments are very contemporary, and the release of Reid's (2000) Task Planner assures that the model will continue to have utility in today's practice contexts. Task-centered assessment matches very well with today's time-limited and outcome-oriented treatment situations. Task assessment focuses on a thorough investigation of target problems and goals from the client's perspective, the prioritizing of those problems and goals, and the development of a specific contract that details the problems, goals, interventions, and time frame for interventions to be delivered. The contract would say both how long it would take to accomplish a specific goal so that the problem would be solved and what both the client and practitioner would do to make this happen. This type of approach is similar to the types of intervention contracts and plans required for today's fast-paced, practice settings that emphasize accountability in service delivery. Chapters 2 and 11 of this text explain and illustrate intervention planning and accountability for today's practice. Finally, the task-centered model has also established a respectable, although not definitive, research basis, and the model has always emphasized the importance of outcome research in its effectiveness.

The Strengths Perspective in Assessment

The strengths perspective in social work practice has been pioneered by Dennis Saleeby (1997). The essence of this model, however, is at the heart of social work's unique philosophical viewpoints on helping. Practicing from a strengths perspective incorporates a value system that encompasses belief in the dignity and worth of individuals, their self-determination, and the transformative power of humans and human relationships. Regardless of the model used, practicing with clients from a strengths perspective means viewing them through a humanistic lens that assumes *all clients can grow and change* (Early & GlenMaye, 2000).

A strengths perspective assumes that clients who come for help are more than their problems and circumstances dictate. All clients have competencies, knowledge, hidden resources, and resilience that may be used to reverse the misfortunes of their life struggles. Social workers practicing from a strengths perspective are convinced that clients have aspirations, motivation, untapped goals, and spiritual fortitude that they can muster against the impossible odds of their disabilities and social environment. Clients have self-determination, they are able to resist and shape their environments and utilize hidden resources within themselves and their environments.

The strengths-oriented practitioner empowers clients, treating them as equals in a collaborative relationship. He or she looks beyond the individual and the oppressive systems that marginalize and define realities toward the larger community and cultural contexts that help us understand clients and their life circumstances. The practitioner also moves away from pathologizing language and diagnostic schemes, such as mental health classifications systems like the *DSM IV-TR* in favor of broader, person-in-environment assessment for understanding client functioning. Saleeby argues that social work practice gives only lip service to strengths and that any strengths orientation has been obliterated by our continued practice within pathologizing, medical models. The importance of client strengths, however, can be traced to earlier models within social work such as the functional, psychosocial, cognitive behavioral, and systems perspectives.

Social workers practicing from a strengths perspective across different practice models know that their work with clients involves using their relationship with the client to enable and foster resilience. Research has shown that resilient children have the following characteristics: 1) social competence, including the abilities to be flexible, to communicate, to solution-build, and to have empathy for other perspectives; 2) autonomy, a sense of independence, and self-efficacy; and 3) a sense of purpose and future orientation, shown through the ability to set realistic expectations, goal directness, and persistence (Early & GlenMaye, 2000).

Unique Methods Used in Strengths Assessment. As a practice model, the strengths perspective shares more of a philosophical stance than a set of defining assessment and practice skills. However, some important practice skills do emerge in the writings. These assessment and practice skills mostly relate to the values and the therapeutic and helping stance of the practitioner. It is important, in assessment, for example, for the practitioner to give preeminence to clients' viewpoints of the problem and their subjective interpretations and experiences. It is equally important for the practitioner to establish a collaborative helping relationship with clients as a part of a dialogical, ongoing assessment. As a part of assessment, clients participate in the defining of their problems, goals, and ways of being helped. The practitioner uses the words and language of the client in order to establish rapport and mutual understanding. The practitioner avoids simplistic, black-and-white thinking and/or simple cause-effect relationships in favor of soliciting longer narratives and complex explanations that are laden with situational and contextual meanings (Franklin & Jordan, 1995b).

Finally, the practitioner focuses on assessing and defining competencies and uniqueness while avoiding blaming, pejorative labels, and debilitating diagnoses which serve to disable the clients (Cowger & Snively 2002). In this manner, many social work practitioners practicing from the strengths perspective steer away from prescriptive and normative approaches to assessment such as diagnostic and measurement approaches. These approaches are believed to be contrived and to produce limited options in their outcomes. Other practitioners, however, seek to find ways to integrate measurement approaches with the strengths perspectives. The type of context-driven and open-ended assessment most valued by strengths practitioners is consistent with qualitative and naturalistic approaches described in some detail in Chapter 5.

Use of the Strengths Assessments in Current Practice Environments. In recent years, most mental health disciplines have given attention to the importance of focusing on the strengths, competencies, and resilience of clients. Several standardized measures have recently been developed that assess strengths and competencies, for example. Some of these measures are covered in later chapters of this book. (See Chapters 4, 9, & 10). Although, as Saleeby (1997) points out, most of the work of practitioners continues to take place in mental health and other institutional settings that do not completely embrace an empowerment or strengths orientation to practice. Therefore, some blending between the medical model and strengths approaches is often required in practice. Although it is important to fully assess strengths, competencies, and protective factors of clients, it becomes equally important to assess psychopathology and risk factors. Graybeal (2001) offers an interview outline for how to incorporate a strengths assessment within a traditional psychosocial assessment. This outline is covered in more detail in Chapter 9.

Another challenge for the strengths perspective is the lack of research on its unique assessment and intervention methods. In current-day social work, preeminence is given to those practices that have considerable evidence and support through outcome studies. The strengths perspective as a critical perspective often challenges the veracity of assumptions that are inherent in these research perspectives. The gold standard of excellence for clinical practice across disciplines, however, is often judged by the amount of evidence-based support that the assessment and intervention model has produced for its effectiveness. The recent development of strengths-based, standardized measures that share the strengths perspectives' unique philosophical viewpoints will possibly help the model establish a more firm research basis. Later chapters in this text provide examples of strengths-based standardized measures that can be used in practice.

Brief Solution-Focused Therapy Assessment Models

In recent years, there has been an increasing emphasis on time-limited models in social work practice, resulting in a proliferation of brief practice models. It is now known that most clinical practice is brief because it is the preference of both clients and funders. Therapeutic practice sessions, for example, tend to last only four to eight sessions. The modal number for intervention sessions is one. Because one session is the natural way that a client involves himself or herself in therapy, clinicians have focused on practice approaches that can accommodate fewer and fewer sessions— even single session interventions (Talmon, 1990). The development toward brief practice has also been reinforced through reimbursement systems that will pay for only limited numbers of sessions (Corwin, 2002).

Several models of brief therapy exist, but this text will cover only one here and that is the brief, solution-focused therapy, which has gained a considerable amount of popularity within social work practice in recent years. Brief, solution-focused therapy is a strengths-based therapy model developed over the past twenty years by two social work practitioners, Steve de Shazer and Insoo Kim Berg and other associates at the Brief Family Therapy Center in Milwaukee, Wisconsin (Franklin & Moore, 1999). All brief therapy approaches, including solution-focused therapy, share similar assumptions.

Assumptions of Brief Therapies

1. Work in the present to help the client discover options for coping, new learning, and behavior.
2. Change is something that can happen quickly and can be lasting. Effective practitioners utilize presession change and facilitate the client's rapid change.
3. Small differences may cause major life changes.
4. Defining problems is not necessary for change. It is more important to focus on defining solutions and to coconstruct with the client a new vision for future behavior.
5. Long-term therapy has no advantages over time-limited approaches. Focusing on the past is not very helpful. It is more helpful to focus on the present and the future.

6. Brief therapists focus on exceptions to problems and client strengths.

7. Pragmatic and effective practitioners recognize that what happens in a client's life is more important than what happens in a social worker's office. Change can happen more quickly and be maintained when practitioners utilize the resources that exist in the client's environment.

8. Brief therapists focus on concrete goal construction and help the client take small steps to achieve those goals.

9. Change is viewed as hard work and involves focused effort and commitment from the client. There will be homework assignments and following through on tasks.

10. Once change is started, it will continue without the aid of the practitioner (Berg, 1994; Berg & De Jong, 1996; De Jong & Berg, 2001; de Shazer, 1991, 1994; Hoyt, 1995; Hoyt, Rosenbaum, & Talmon, 1992; Koss & Shiang, 1994).

Unique Methods Used in Brief, Solution-Focused Assessment. Much like the family systems models described above, the solution-focused model does not separate assessment and intervention; assessment is seen as a part of the intervention process. One of the unique features of this model is that it suggests that practitioners assess who in a particular case is motivated to change. This assessment is guided by a unique case construction process that helps practitioners think about who in the case is the *customer, complainant,* or *visitor*. The *customer* is viewed as the person who is willing to make a commitment to the change process. The *complainant* is the person who is complaining the most and must be satisfied that a change has occurred but does not usually view himself or herself as a part of the problem. The *visitor* is someone who is not very invested in the change process but is willing to be peripherally involved and may provide needed information. Solution-focused, brief therapists use their assessment of who is the customer, complainant, and visitor to develop goals and intervention strategies that can work for a particular case. The brief, solution-focused model also suggests that not all clients are customers and should not be treated in that manner by practitioners. The solution-focused model offers a wealth of information for assessing and working with "mandated," or involuntary, clients who are forced to seek services by other agencies such as the child protection system, schools, and legal authorities (De Jong & Berg, 2001).

In working with a mandated client, the practitioner is advised to change his or her relationship stance toward the client. It is not always necessary, for example, for the practitioner to engage in a completely mutual, trusting relationship when the client is at a point of change in order to begin the change process or to form a contract for the purposes of working with the client. Instead, practitioners may follow these principles summarized by Franklin (2002) in assessment and practice with mandated clients.

1. Use nonjudgmental acceptance to investigate the client's problem. Use reflective listening skills and hear the client's version of the story. Let the client tell you how others view him or her. Listen to the explanation for how the client was referred. Empathize with the client's perceptions.

2. Increase motivational congruence by making the fit between what the client genuinely wants and the services the practitioner provides as congruent as possible. Thus, the practitioner must seek to find out what the client wants and to define roles in accordance with this purpose. For example, if the client wishes to have children returned from child protective services, then the practitioner discusses with the client ways that treatment can help this happen if the client wishes to cooperate. Utilize reframing to help the client view his or her motivations and the system's or referral sources motivation as similar. For example, say to the client "So you and the child protective services both want to get your child back home as soon as possible."

3. Emphasize the client's choices when possible. Mandated clients often feel forced and helpless, like they have no choice but to come to see you. Practitioners should emphasize that clients do have choices and point out areas where such choices exist. For example, clients do not have to come to sessions; they can choose to take the consequences.

4. Educate clients about what to expect during intervention. Clients who are mandated may not know what to expect and may be very fearful of the situation. Their angry responses may be exacerbated by their fears. Practitioners should take care to inform clients about what to expect and to teach novice clients about the social services and legal systems.

5. Develop specific contracts and goals with the client. The contract can and should be different from the one developed with other systems. You can define what others expect differently than what you expect. It should involve your role and what the client agrees on with you.

6. Define for the client what is nonnegotiable from the standpoint of the referring agencies. Offer or point out incentives for the client to comply with behavioral demands with which he or she does not agree. Here is an example of an effective explanation: "When Charles insults you, hitting Charles is not acceptable to the school. They want you to go to this dumb conflict resolution person instead. You do not agree with that idea and neither does your dad. You think it is a dumb prac-

tice that does not fit into being a man or staying alive in your neighborhood. However, if you go to the conflict person, you can keep from being sent to the alternative school. Right? You said that you do not want to go to that place because you do not get to play basketball or leave school early. So, perhaps it is worth doing something dumb to avoid being sent to the alternative school. Anyway, I guess you have a choice on which way to go."

7. Use the client's goal of getting the system off his or her back as a way of getting compliance. For example, as you could say, "As you see it, your teachers have it in for you and it is difficult to get them to see you any differently. However, you have got to find a way to get them off your back so that they do not continue to call your mom every other day. So, are you willing to work on a few things they want just so you can get them off your back?"

Another advantage of brief, solution-focused therapy is that the model also offers a wealth of questioning techniques that can help facilitate client assessment and change. Brief, solution-focused therapists are interested in clients' perspectives on their lives and on facilitating and co-constructing with clients' solution-building conversations (Berg & De Jong, 1996; De Jong & Berg, 2001). Practitioners therefore focus on exceptions to problems, strengths, and competencies of clients instead of on their weaknesses and pathologies. In particular, practitioners work with clients to coconstruct specific goals that can move them in small steps toward their solutions. Some of the questioning techniques used in solution-focused assessment are briefly described in box 1.3.

Use of the Brief Solution-Focused Assessments in Current Practice Environments. Even though brief, solution-focused therapy existed prior to the advent of managed behavioral health care, this model has flourished under the auspices of practice contexts that require brief therapies. Solution-focused therapy has become a popular and frequently used model in social work and marriage and family therapy. A recent national survey of marriage and family practitioners found that solution-focused therapy was the fourth most frequently used model that was named in the survey, for example (Northey, 2002). Brief, solution-focused therapy, however, faces some of the same challenges that the strengths perspective does. It has to balance its focus on strengths and resources with work within mental health systems that are more problem focused. Brief, solution-focused therapy, like the strengths perspective and other models that originated from social work practitioners, also has to work diligently to establish its evidence base through clinical research. In the past seven years, the brief, solution-focused model has been working to develop studies on its effectiveness. Over twenty outcome studies on the effectiveness of

Box 1.3
Questions Used in a Solution-Focused Assessment

Tracking solution behaviors or exceptions to the problem. The therapist identifies times when the problem does not occur, effective coping responses, and the contexts for the absence of the problem. The therapist says something such as, "Even though this is a very bad problem, in my experience, people's lives do not always stay the same. I bet that there are times when the problem of being sent to the principal's office is not happening or at least it is better. Describe those times. What is different? How did you get that to happen?" The therapist gathers as many exceptions to the problem pattern as possible by repeatedly asking the client, "What else . . .? What other times . . .?" Once an exception has been identified by the client, the therapist uses prompts, such as "tell me more about that," to help the client describe in detail the exceptions. The therapist also uses his or her own affects, tone, and intense attention to the client's story to communicate to the client that he or she is very interested in those exceptions. Such nonverbal gestures as nodding, smiling, leaning forward, and looking surprised are used. The therapist also may say something such as "how about that," "I am amazed," or "Wow!" as social reinforcement to the client. This encourages the client to talk on and to develop in more detail the exceptions story.

Scaling the problem. This approach uses scaling questions to assess the problem and to track progress toward problem resolutions. The therapist says, "On a scale of 1 to 10, with 1 being that you are getting in trouble everyday in class, picking on Johnny and Susi, getting out of your seat and being scolded by your teacher, and 10 being that instead of fighting with Johnny and Susi you are doing your work, and that you ask permission to get out of your seat, and your teacher says something nice to you, where would you be on that scale now?" With children, often smiley and sad faces are also used to anchor the two ends of the scale.

Other uses of the scaling technique in the therapy process include the following: 1) asking questions about where the client is on the scale in relationship to solving the problem; 2) using the scaling experience to find exceptions to problems, such as saying "How did you get to the 3?" or "What are you doing so you are not a 1?"; 3) employing scales to construct "miracles" or to identify solution behaviors. For example, the therapist inquires as to where the client is on the scale (with 1 representing low and 10 representing high). The therapist then proceeds to ask the client how he or she will get from a 1 to a 3. Or, the therapist inquires how the client managed to move from a 4 rating to a 5 rating, for example, by asking, "How did you get that to happen? What new behaviors did you implement or what was different in your life that made the changes?" Solution-focused therapists may also express surprise that the problem is not worse on the scale as a way of complimenting the client's coping behavior or as a

Box 1.3 *Continued*

way to use language to change the client's perception of the intractable nature of the problem.

Using coping and motivation questions. This is a variation on the scaling question that helps the therapist assess the client's motivation for solving the problem as well as how well the client perceives that he or she is coping with the problem. The therapist says something like, "On a scale of 1 to 10, with 10 being that you would do anything to solve this problem, and 1 being that you do not care so much for solving it, where would you say you are right now?" Or the therapist may say, "On a scale of 1 to 10 with 1 being that you are ready to throw in the towel and give up ever doing well in school, and 10 being that you are ready to keep on trying, where would you rate yourself right now?" After asking coping and motivation questions, the therapist should be able to determine the following:

a) If the problem that has been defined is too overwhelming to the client. If the problem is too overwhelming, then the problem needs to be broken down into smaller steps and redefined for the client.

b) How much self-efficacy and hope the client possesses toward the problem resolution. If the client does not believe the problem can be solved, steps must be taken to change this belief. Here, the exception questions can be empowering.

c) What is the degree of commitment to work on the problem. If the client is not interested in committing to working on the problem, then the problem must be redefined to muster some degree of commitment.

d) If the problem that has been defined is the one that really interests the client and if it is a priority for him or her.

Asking the miracle question. This type of question seeks to assess the client's priorities and to develop solutions. The therapist says, for example, "Let's suppose that an overnight miracle happened, and your problem disappeared; but you were sleeping and did not know it. When you woke up the next day, what would be the first thing that you would notice?" The therapist proceeds to help the client envision how things could be different. An extreme amount of detail is elicited to help develop a set of solution behaviors that are concrete and behaviorally specific. The miracle question helps the therapist to assess a detailed description of the client's perception of what life would be like without the problem. It also helps the therapist coconstruct with the client's input a specific set of behaviors, thoughts, and feelings that can be substituted for problem patterns. Ultimately, the therapist can assess what is most important to the client and others concerning which changes the client perceives will solve the problem.

SOURCE: Franklin, C., & Moore, K. (1999). Solution-focused therapy. In C. Franklin & C. Jordan, *Family practice: Brief systems methods for social work.* Pacific Grove, CA: Brooks/Cole.

brief, solution-focused therapy now exist, and most of these studies have been reviewed by Gingerich and Eisengart (2000). One particular area in which this therapy has shown promise is in working with classroom management and school-related behavior problems (Franklin et al., 2001; Franklin & Moore, 1999). All research studies to date are promising, but more research studies with better designs must be completed before solution-focused therapy is fully recognized as an evidence-based practice.

COMMON FEATURES OF SOCIAL WORK ASSESSMENT MODELS

Current-day social work assessment models share many features with the previous definition of social work assessment as offered by Levine (2002). All models reviewed in this chapter share the following features.

1. Social work assessment emphasizes both individuals and their social environments: Viewing clients in their contexts of families, groups, and communities is the preferred approach to assessment.

2. Social work assessment includes the strengths and resilience of clients: It is equally important to assess competencies and strengths as it is to address problem areas and pathologies. The goals of most approaches include increasing the self-efficacy of clients, restoring or supporting their inherent problem-solving capacities, and returning clients to their best adaptive functioning.

3. Most social work assessment models are integrative and rely on more than one underlying theory: The theory base of social work practice is extremely eclectic. Social work models combine multiple theories in their assessment and practice focuses. Social work is interprofessional by nature, and social workers usually are employed in host settings. Knowledge from several fields is also integrated into social work assessment and practice.

4. Assessments de-emphasize long history taking: Overall, history for the sake of history taking has been de-emphasized, even in models such as the psychosocial that traditionally focused on this information. Instead, only relevant history is used in a more strategic manner to understand presenting problems and needed interventions.

5. Assessments are organized around task-centered planning or goal orientations: The purpose of assessment across models is to resolve presenting problems or to move clients toward desired goals. Assessments across social work models focus mostly on the present contexts and future behaviors that clients desire.

6. Social work assessments share common types of information: Even though different tools and methods are used across models for gather-

ing information from clients, social work models appear to share in common the types of information that are valued in constructing assessments. Problem definitions, identified strengths, specific goals, intervention planning or solution building, and outcome monitoring are shared by all models.

7. Social work assessments use a collaborative process between client and practitioner: Social work models all show a preference for collaborative work with clients in gathering information and goal construction. Shared power and client-centered perspectives are important to the clinical assessment process. This stands in contrast to more authoritative approaches where the practitioner is seen as the only expert on the client and his or her problems.

8. Assessments in social work emphasize brief, time-limited prespectiaves: The preference for brevity and short-term assessments and interventions is acknowledged by all practice models reviewed. This is perhaps driven by the current-day realities of the practice environments in which practitioners work as well as the applied and human problem-solving nature of social work practice.

INTEGRATING THE COMPONENTS OF PRACTICE MODELS FOR SOCIAL WORK ASSESSMENT

Similar to social work assessment models, this text takes an integrative approach to assessment. The integration of theory is a common approach to assessment and intervention in social work practice, as can be seen from the diverse practice models reviewed. The authors agree with Lazarus's (1981) technical eclecticism that assumes that practice methods from different underlying theoretical models may be used together. Lazarus believes that it is not necessary to embrace the theory to borrow techniques compatible with one's own theoretical and practice approach. Rather than choosing techniques based on one's theoretical philosophy, choice is based on research support for the technique or the best available practice wisdom. Although there are some limitations to a pragmatic approach like technical eclecticism, such as the lack of overarching or defining theory to guide practice, technical eclecticism allows for integration and a more experimental and problem-solving approach that tests different assessment methods without limiting one's self to one school of thought or set of practice methods. It is also assumed that it is important for the practitioner to evaluate assessment techniques with practice evaluation methods (Franklin & Jordan, 1995a). Box 1.4 integrates the major assessment issues covered in the models reviewed and shows the major elements that may be used in a comprehensive social work assessment.

Box 1.4
Integrative Skills Assessment Protocol

I. Identifying Information
  1. Name
  2. Address
  3. Home phone number
  4. Work phone number
  5. Date of birth
  6. Family members living at home
     a. Name
     b. Age
     c. Relationship
  7. Occupation
  8. Income
  9. Gender
  10. Race
  11. Religious affiliation
  12. Briefly describe the presenting problem or symptom(s)
II. Nature of Presenting Problem(s)
  1. List all of the problems identified by the client and/or practitioner
     a. What is the specific problem(s)?
  2. Specification of problem(s)
     a. History
        i. When did the problem first occur?
        ii. Is this a long-standing, unresolved problem? A recently established one?
     b. Duration
        i. How long has the problem been going on?
     c. Frequency
        i. How often does the problem occur?
     d. Magnitude
        i. What is the intensity of the problem?
     e. Antecedents
        i. What happens immediately before the problem occurs?
     f. Consequences
        i. What happens immediately after the problem occurs?
     g. Exceptions to the problem
        i. What exceptions to the problem exist?
        ii. How often have exceptions occurred?
        iii. When was the last time an exception happened?
        iv. What was different in the situation in which the exception occurred than in situations in which the problem happens?
        v. Who was involved in making the exception happen?
     h. Reason for seeking help
        i. What makes the client seek help now and not before?
     i. Prior efforts to solve problem(s)
        i. How has the client sought to solve the problem previously, including other therapy?
        ii. With what results?

Box 1.4 *Continued*

---

j. Client motivation
   i. What is the level of motivation for solving the problem?
   ii. Use scaling question to identify client motivation: "On a scale of 1 to 10 with 10 being you would do anything to solve this problem and 1 being that you do not care so much for solving it, where would you say you are right now?"
k. Client resources/strengths
   i. What are the client resources available for solving the problem?
   ii. Use scaling question to assess coping: "On a scale of 1 to 10, with 1 being that you are ready to throw in the towel and give up and 10 being that you are ready to keep on trying, where would you rate yourself right now?"
l. Other
   i. Are there other difficulties associated with or in addition to the problem?

3. Prioritize problems and goals
   a. Through negotiations with the client, prioritize problems in terms of severity.
   b What are the client's goals? Goals should be something he or she is motivated to accomplish.
   c. What is a small, obtainable goal? What can the client do toward the goal immediately and before the next session?
   d. What, when, how, and with whom is the behavior to happen?
   e. What will the client do instead of the problem behavior?
   f. Does the client understand that the goal is the first step and not the end to solving the problem?
   g. Is the goal something the client can do in the context of his or her life?
   h. Does the client understand that the goal is hard work and that effort must be put forth? Is the client committed to do so?
   i. Use the miracle question to prompt the client to set a goal or to envision a solution to the problem: "Let's suppose that an overnight miracle happened and the problem you are having disappeared, but you were sleeping and did not know it. When you woke up the next morning, what would be the first thing you would notice? Guide the client in discussing what life would be like without the problem.

III. Client
1. Intrapersonal issues
   a. Cognitive functioning
      i. What is the client's perception of the problem and its solution?
      ii. What are the client's most common upsetting thoughts?
      iii. What underlying beliefs and schemas support the client's upsetting thoughts and subsequent emotions and behaviors? Identify maladaptive cognitive schemas as the central focus of intervention.
2. Maladaptive schemas around autonomy
   a. Dependence (on others for support, fear one can't take care of self)
   b. Subjugation (sacrifice of one's own needs to satisfy others' needs)
   c. Vulnerability to harm or illness (fear of disasters)
   d. Fear of losing self-control (over own mind, behavior, impulses, body, etc.)

Box 1.4 *Continued*

---

3. Maladaptive schemas around connectedness
   a. Emotional deprivation (expectation own needs won't be met)
   b. Abandonment/loss (fear of losing significant others and of being isolated forever)
   c. Mistrust (expectation of others to willfully hurt, abuse, cheat, lie, manipulate, or take advantage)
   d. Social isolation/alienation (feels different from others, not part of)
4. Maladaptive schemas around worthiness
   a. Defectiveness/unlovability (feels inwardly defective, flawed, unlovable)
   b. Social undesirability (feels outwardly undesirable, ugly, of low status, dull)
   c. Incompetence/failure (believes self cannot perform)
   d. Guilt/punishment (believes self morally or ethically bad and deserving of punishment or harsh criticism)
   e. Shame/embarrassment (believes one's inadequacies are totally unacceptable to others)
5. Maladaptive schemas around limits and standards
   a. Unrelenting standards (relentless striving to meet extremely high expectations of oneself at the expense of happiness, pleasure, health, satisfying relationships)
      i. Trace antecedents, beliefs, and consequences of upsetting thoughts and behaviors.
      ii. What are the "hot cognitions," or those cogntions that are related to underlying emotions and schemas?
      iii. What is the client's view of self, others, and the world?
      iv. What evidence is there for problem-solving capacity?
      v. In what ways has client solved problems in the past?
      vi. Is there clear evidence of rational vs. irrational thoughts?
6. Emotional functioning
   a. Describe the client's affect and mood
   b. Can the client express a range of emotions?
   c. Is there evidence of appropriate vs. inappropriate emotions such as extreme anger, elation, or depression?
   d. Is there evidence that the client's cultural group or primary reference group views the client's affect or mood as being outside the norm?
7. Behavioral functioning
   a. Physical appearance
   b. Mannerisms
   c. Speech
   d. Abilities and disabilities
   e. Antisocial or acting-out behavior
   f. Behavioral deficits or excesses such as lack of social skills or addictions
8. Physiological functioning
   a. Has the client been seen medically during the past year?
   b. If so, with what results?
   c. Is there any evidence of drug and alcohol usage?
   d. Are any medications taken?
   e. Describe diet, caffeine, alcohol, and drug usage.

Box 1.4 *Continued*

---

  9. Client mental status
    a. Disturbances in appearance, dress, posture, etc.
    b. Disturbances in thoughts (hallucinations, delusions, etc.)
    c. Disturbances in level of awareness (memory, attention, etc.)
    d. Disturbances in thought processes (logic, intelligibility, coherence)
    e. Disturbances in emotional tone (deviations in affect or discrepancies in verbal reports of mood and client affect)
    f. Degree to which the client seems aware of the nature of the problem and the need for treatment
10. Ethnic/cultural/gender considerations
    a. What is the client's ethnic group?
    b. What is the degree of acculturation?
    c. What is the client's perception of how ethnic/cultural/gender group identification has helped or not helped?
    d. Are the sources of conflict related to ethnic/cultural/gender issues?
11. Motivation
    a. What stage of change is the client in?
    b. Is the client unaware of a need for changes?
    c. Is the client currently contemplating a need to change but has not made a full commitment to the change process?
    d. Has the client fully embraced the idea of change and is ready to move forward?
    e. Has the client already made some recent changes and needs help maintaining those changes?
    f. Has the client changed the problem behavior in the past but has since relapsed?
    g. What are factors that may contribute to client motivation, either causing client discomfort or causing client to have hope for the future?
12. Client roles and role performance
    a. What roles does the client perform (wife, mother, etc.)
    b. What are the client's issues related to role performance?
    c. What are the client's issues related to satisfaction or dissatisfaction?
    d. What are the client's gender issues?
    e. Are there of social and economic injustices?
13. Developmental considerations?
    a. Trace the birth, developmental history of the client (the mother's pregnancy, developmental milestones, illness, trauma, etc.)
    b. Is there an "identified patient"? If so, whom?
    c. What is each family member's perspective of the problem(s)?
14. Marital status
    a. What is the client's sexual dating and/or marital history?
    b. What is the quality of the client's intimate relationships?
    c. How long has the client been married?
    d. How many times has the client been married?
15. Interpersonal: Family structure
    a. Quality of the client's family interactions
    b. Family boundaries
    c. Family alliances
    d. Family power structure

Box 1.4 *Continued*

---

      e. Family communication patterns
      f. Family stories and narratives
      g. Family strengths
  16. Interpersonal: Work or school
      a. Occupation or grade in school
      b. Satisfaction with work/school
          i. Are there indicators of successful achievement in this setting?
          ii. What are issues related to grades, pay, promotions, etc?
          iii. Describe relationships with colleagues/peers
      c. Effect of problem(s) on work/school
          i. Does the problem(s) occur in this setting? If so, how does the client get along with peers, teachers/bosses, other authority figures?
          ii. What is the academic/work history?
          iii. Any evidence of antisocial behavior?
  17. Interpersonal: Peers
      a. Satisfaction with number of peers/friends?
          i. Who are the client's friends and what is the quality of these relationships?

IV. Context and Social Support Networks
  1. Agency considerations
      a. Does the agency setting have an effect on the problem/client (i.e., does the client have negative feelings about seeking services at this agency? Is the agency located too far away to be accessible to the client? Does the agency have the resources to deal with the client's problem in terms of worker time, interest, etc.?)
      b. Would referral be best for the client, and if so, what is the best referral source?
  2. Client's environmental context
      a. What environmental resources does client have? (adequate housing, transportation, food/clothing, recreation, social supports, educational opportunities, etc.)
      b. What environmental resources exist that the client is not currently utilizing (access to family or peer support, support from agencies in the neighborhood, etc.)
      c. What environmental resources do not exist and need to be developed? What gaps in resources exist for this client?

V. Measurement (use global and/or rapid assessment instruments)
  1. Family functioning
  2. Marital (or significant other) functioning
  3. Individual functioning
  4. Social supports
  5. Strengths, resources, and protective factors

VI. Summary
  1. Practitioner impressions
      a. Summarize areas for presentation to the client. List concerns of highest priority to the client. What is the goal? Generate a list of exceptions to the problem and a list of client strengths. Obtain client feedback.
      b. *DSM* diagnosis
      c. Problem(s) or solutions to be targeted for immediate intervention

---

Box 1.4 *Continued*

---

      2. To be negotiated with client and prioritized
         a. What are some progress indicators?
         b. What are desired outcomes?
         c. What is the baseline?
         d. What are the results of either pretest or repeated measurement of targeted problems and strengths?
VII. Treatment Plan
      1. Problem(s):
         a.
         b.
      2. Definition(s):
         a.
         b.
      3. Goal(s):
         a.
         b.
      4. Objective(s) (measurement):
         a.
         b.
         c.
         d.
      5. Intervention(s):
         a.
         b.
         c.
         d.

SUMMARY

This chapter provides a definition of social work assessment and a framework for understanding how to conduct a comprehensive social work assessment. The authors lay a foundation for an integrative, technically eclectical approach to assessment. A theoretical basis is offered for what elements may go into a comprehensive assessment; this basis is supported through the review of several well-known social work practice models. Common features for current-day assessment are highlighted through the convergent elements found in the diverse practice models. Finally, the authors integrate assessment information across the models reviewed into an Integrative Skills Assessment Protocol that can be used by practitioners to guide assessment.

STUDY QUESTIONS

1. What are the major issues covered in social work assessment?
2. Describe the features of practice context, clients served, and practice model and explain how these features impact social work assessment.

3. Name and describe the common assessment features that are found across social work practice models. What impacts do these features have on our work with clients?

4. What is the underlying eclectic theory behind the Integrative Skills Assessment Protocol?

5. Practice using the protocol by interviewing a friend.

REFERENCES

Barkham, M., Margison, F., Leach, C., Lucock, M., Mellor-Clark, J., Evans, C., Benson, L., Connell, J., Audin, K., & McGrach, G. (2001). The CORE-OM and benchmarking: Towards practice-based evidence in the psychological sciences. *Journal of Consulting and Clinical Psychology, 69*, 184–196.

Barkley, R. A. (1997). *Defiant children: A clinician's manual for parent training.* New York: Guilford.

Barlow, D., & Hersen, M. (1984). *Single case experimental designs: Strategies for studying behavior change.* New York: Pergamon.

Barth, R. (1986). *Social and cognitive treatment of children and adolescents.* San Francisco: Jossey-Bass.

Beck, A., & Freeman, A. (1990). *Cognitive therapy of personality disorders.* New York: Guilford.

Beck, A., Rush, J., Shaw, B. F., & Emery, G. (1987). *Cognitive therapy of depression.* New York: Guilford.

Beck, A., Wright, F. D., Newman, C. F., & Liese, B. S. (1993). *Cognitive therapy of substance abuse.* New York: Guilford.

Beck, J. S., & Beck, A. T. (2002). *Beck youth inventories of emotional and social impairment.* San Antonio, TX: The Psychological Corporation.

Becvar, D. S., & Becvar, R. J. (1988). *Family therapy: A systemic integration.* Needleham, MA: Allyn & Bacon.

Bellack, A. S., & Hersen, M. (1988). *Behavioral assessment: A practical handbook* (3rd ed.). Elmsford, NY: Pergamon Press.

Berg, I. K. (1994). *Family based services: A solution-focused approach.* New York: W. W. Norton.

Berg, I., & De Jong, P. (1996). Solution-building conversations: Co-constructing a sense of competence with clients. *Families in Society, 77*(6), 376–390.

Berlin, S. B. (1996). Constructivism and the environment: A cognitive-integrative perspective for social work practice. *Families in Society, 77*(6), 326–335.

Bisman, C. D., (1999). Social work assessment: Case theory construction. *Families in Society, 80*(3), 240–246.

Blanck, G., & Blanck, R. (1974). *Ego psychology in theory and practice.* New York: Columbia University Press.

Brower, A. M., & Nurius, P. S. (1993). *Social cognition and individual change: Current theory and counseling guidelines.* Newbury Park, CA: Sage.

Cade B., & O'Hanlon, W. H. (1993). *A brief guide to brief therapy.* New York: Norton.

Cheers, B. (1987). The social support network map as an educational tool. *Australian Social Work, 40,* 18–24.

Compton, B., & Galaway B. (Eds.). (1994). *Social work processes* (5th ed., pp. 283–300). Pacific Grove, CA: Brooks/Cole.

Cormier, S., & Nurius, P. S. (2002). *Interviewing and change strategies for helpers* (5th ed.). Pacific Grove, CA: Brooks/Cole.

Corwin, M. (2002). *Brief treatment in clinical social work practice.* Pacific Grove, CA: Brooks/Cole.

Cowger, C. D., & Snively, C. A. (2002). Assessing client strengths. In A. R. Roberts & G. J. Greene (Eds.), *Social workers desk reference* (pp. 221–225). New York: Oxford University Press.

Cummings, N. A., & Sayama, M. (1995). *Focused psychotherapy: A casebook of brief, intermittent psychotherapy throughout the life cycle.* New York: Brunner/Mazel.

De Jong, P., & Berg, I. K. (2001). Co-constructing cooperation with mandated clients. *Social Work, 46,* 361–374.

de Shazer, S. (1982). *Patterns of brief family therapy: An ecosytemic approach.* New York: Guilford.

de Shazer, S. (1991). *Putting differences to work.* New York: W. W. Norton.

de Shazer, S. (1994). *Words were originally magic.* New York: W. W. Norton.

Doremus, B. (1976). The four Rs: Social diagnosis in health care. *Health and Social Work, 1,* 121–139

Early, T., & GlenMaye, L. F. (2000). Valuing families: Social work practice with families from a strengths perspective. *Social Work, 45,* 118–130.

Fisch, R., Weakland, J. H., & Segal, L. (1982). *Tactics of change: Doing therapy briefly.* San Francisco: Jossey-Bass.

Fiske, S. T., & Taylor, S. T. (1984). *Social cognition.* New York: Random House.

Franklin, C. (1995). Expanding the vision of the social constructionist debates: Creating relevance for practitioners. *Families in Society, 76*(7), 395–407.

Franklin, C. (2002). Becoming a strengths fact finder. *AAMFT Magazine.* Washington DC: The American Association of Marital and Family Therapists (pp. 39–46).

Franklin, C., Biever, J. L., Moore, K., Clemons, D., & Scamardo, M. (2001). The effectiveness of solution-focused therapy with children in a school setting. *Research on Social Work Practice, 11,* 411–434.

Franklin, C., & Jordan, C. (1995a). *Clinical assessment for social workers.* Chicago: Lyceum Press.

Franklin, C., & Jordan, C. (1995b). Qualitative assessment: A methodological review. *Families in Society, 76*(5), 281–295.

Franklin, C., & Jordan, C. (1999a). The clinical utility of models and methods of assessment in managed care. In B. Compton & B. Galaway (Eds.), *Social work processes* (5th ed., pp. 283–300). Pacific Grove, CA: Brooks/Cole.

Franklin, C., & Jordan, C. (1999b). *Family practice: Brief systems methods for social work.* Pacific Grove, CA: Brooks/Cole.

Franklin, C., & Jordan, C. (2002). Effective family therapy: Guidelines for practice. In A. R. Roberts & G. J. Greene (Eds.), *Social workers desk reference* (pp. 256–262). New York: Oxford University Press.

Franklin, C., & Moore, K. C. (1999). Solution-focused brief therapy. In C. Franklin & C. Jordan (Eds.). *Family practice: Brief systems methods for social work* (pp. 105–141). Pacific Grove, CA: Brooks/Cole.

Franklin, C., & Nurius, P. (1998). Constructionst therapy: New directions in social work practice. *Families in Society, 77*(6), 323–325.

Gambrill, E. (1983). *Casework: A competency based approach.* Englewood Cliffs, NJ: Prentice-Hall.

Gambrill, E., Thomas, E., & Carter, R. (1971). Procedure for sociobehavioral practice in open settings. *Social Work, 16,* 51–62.

Germain, C., & Gitterman, A. (1996). *The life model approach to social work practice: Advances in theory and practice.* Storrs, CT: University of Connecticut.

Gingerich, W. J., & Eisengart, S. (2000). Solution-focused brief therapy: A review of outcome research. *Family Process, 39,* 477–498.

Gitterman, A. (1988, March). *Alternative practice explanatory frameworks: A debate.* (With E. G. Goldstein & S. Rose). Presentation at the annual program meeting, Council on Social Work Education, Atlanta, GA.

Goldstein, E. G. (1986). Ego psychology. In F. J. Turner (Ed.), *Social work treatment* (3rd ed., pp. 375–405). New York: Free Press.

Goldstein, E. G. (1988, March). *Alternative practice explanatory frameworks: A debate.* (With A. Gitterman & S. Rose). Presentation at the annual program meeting, Council on Social Work Education, Atlanta, GA.

Goldstein, E. G. (2002). *Object relations theory and self-psychology in social work.* New York: Free Press.

Granvold, D. K. (1996). Constructivist psychotherapy. *Families in Society, 77*(6), 345–357.

Graybeal, C. (2001). Strengths-based social work assessment: Transforming the dominant paradigm. *Families in Society: The Journal of Contemporary Human Services, 82*(3), 233–242.

Greenberg, L., & Pascual-Leone, J. (1995). A dialectical constructivist approach to experiential change. In R. A. Neimeyer & M. J. Mahoney (Eds.), *Constructivism in psychotherapy* (pp. 169–191). Washington, DC: American Psychological Association.

Guidano, V. F. (1991). *The self in process.* New York: Guilford.

Haley, J. (1990). *Problem solving therapy.* San Francisco: Jossey-Bass.

Hartman, A., & Laird, J. (1983). *Family centered social work practice.* New York: Free Press.

Hayes, S. C., Follette, W. C., & Follette, V. M. (1995). Behaviorism: A contextual approach. In A. S. Gurman & S. B. Messer (Eds.), *Essential psychotherapies: Theory and practice* (pp. 182–225). New York: Guilford.

Haynes, S. N., Leisne, M. B., & Blaine, D. D. (1997). Design of individualized behavioral treatment programs using functional analytic clinical case models. *Psychological Assessment, 9*, 334–348.

Henggeler, S. W., Schoenwald, S. K., Borduin, C. M., Rowland, M. D., & Cunningham, P. B. (1998). *Multisystemic treatment of antisocial behavior in children and adolescents.* New York: Guilford.

Hoffman, L. (1981). *Foundations of family therapy.* New York: Basic Books.

Hollis, F., & Wood, M. E. (1981). *Social casework: A psychosocial therapy* (3rd ed.). New York: Random House.

Hoyt, M. F. (1995). Brief psychotherapies. In A. S. Gurman & S. B. Messer (Eds.), *Essential psychotherapies: Theory and practice* (pp. 441–487). New York: Guilford.

Hoyt, M. F., Rosenbaum, R., & Talmon, M. (1992). Planned single-session therapy. In S. H. Budman, M. F. Hoyt, & S. Friedman (Eds.), *The first session in brief therapy* (pp. 59–86). New York: Guilford.

Hudson, W. W. (1982). *The clinical measurement package.* Homewood, IL: Dorsey Press.

Hudson, W. W. (1989). *Computer assisted social services manual.* Tempe, AZ: Walmyr.

Hudson, W. W. (1990). Computer-based clinical practice: Present status and future possibilities. In L. Videka-Sherman & W. J. Reid (Eds.), *Advances in clinical social work research* (pp. 105–117). Silver Spring, MD: NASW Press.

Jacobson, N. S., & Christensen, A. (1997). *Integrative couple therapy.* New York: Norton.

Jarman-Rohde, L., McFall, J., Kolar, P., & Strom, G. (1997). The changing context of social work practice: Implications and recommendations for social work education. *Journal of Social Work Education, 33*, 29–46.

Johnson, L. (1981). *Social work practice: A generalist approach.* Boston: Allyn & Bacon.

Jordan, C., & Franklin, C. (1995). *Clinical assessment for social workers: Quantitative and qualitative methods.* Chicago: Lyceum Books.

Kanfer, F. H., & Schefft, B. K. (1988). *Guiding the process of therapeutic change.* Champaign, IL: Research Press.

Koss, M. P., & Shiang, J. (1994). Research on brief psychotherapy. In A. E. Bergin & S. L. Garfield (Eds.), *Handbook of psychotherapy and behavior change* (4th ed., pp. 664–700). New York: Wiley.

Lambert, M. J., Hansen, N. B., & Finch, A. E. (2001). Patient-focused research: Using patient outcome data to enhance treatment effects. *Journal of Consulting and Clinical Psychology, 69*, 159–172.

Lazarus, A. (1981). *Multi-modal therapy.* New York: McGraw-Hill.

Lazarus, A. (1989). *Multimodal therapy.* In R. Corsini and D. Wedding (Eds.), *Current psychotherapies* (4th ed., pp. 503–544). Itasca, IL: Peacock.

Lazarus, A. (1991). *The multi-modal life history inventory.* Champaign, IL: Research Press.

Levine, E. R. (2002). Glossary. In A. R. Roberts & G. J. Greene (Eds.), *Social workers desk reference* (pp. 829–849). New York: Oxford University Press.

Linehan, M. (1993). *Skills training manual for treating borderline personality disorders.* New York: Guilford.

Madanes, C. (1984). *Behind the one-way mirror: Advances in the practice of strategic therapy.* San Francisco: Jossey-Bass.

Mahoney, M. J. (1991). *Human change processes.* New York: Basic Books.

Mahoney, M. J. (1995). Continuing evolution of cognitive sciences and psychotherapy. In R. A. Neimeyer & M. J. Mahoney (Eds.), *Constructivism in psychotherapy* (pp. 39–68). Washington, DC: American Psychological Association.

Maluccio, A. N. (Ed.). (1981). *Promoting competence in clients: A new/old approach to social work practice.* New York: Free Press.

Mattaini, M. A. (1990). Contextual behavioral analysis in the assessment process. *Families in Society, 7*(4), 236–245.

Mattaini, M.A. (1992a). *More than a thousand words: Graphics in clinical practice.* Washington, DC: NASW Press.

Mattaini, M. A. (1993). Misdiagnosing assessment. *Social Work 38*(2), 231–233.

Mattaini, M. A. (1999). *Intervention with families.* Washington, DC: NASW Press.

Mattaini, M. A., Lowery, C. T. & Meyer, C. H. (2002). *Foundations of social work practice* (3rd ed.). Washington, DC: NASW Press.

Meichenbaum, D. (1993). Changing conceptions of cognitive behavior modification: Retrospect and prospect. *Journal of Consulting and Clinical Psychology, 61,* 202–204.

Meichenbaum, D. (1994). *A clinical handbook/practical therapist manual for assessing and treating adults with post-traumatic stress disorder (PTSD).* Waterloo, Ontario, Canada: University of Waterloo, Institute Press.

Meichenbaum, D., & Fitzpatrick, D. (1993). A constructivist, narrative perspective on stress and coping: Stress inoculation applications. In L. Goldberger & S. Breznitz (Eds.), *Handbook of stress: Theoretical and clinical aspects* (2nd ed., pp. 706–723). New York: Free Press.

Mullen, E. J., & Schuermann, J. R. (1990). Expert systems and the development of knowledge in social welfare. In L. Videka-Sherman, & W. J. Reid (Eds.), *Advances in clinical social work research* (pp. 67–83). Silver Spring, MD: NASW Press.

Northey, W. F. (2002) Characteristics and clinical practices of marriage and family therapists: A national survey. *The Journal of Marital and Family Therapy, 28*(4), 487–494.

Nurius, P. S., & Hudson, W. W. (1988). Computers and social diagnosis: The client's perspective. *Computers in Human Services, 5*(1–2), 21–36.

O'Hanlon, W. H., & Wilk, J. (1987). *Shifting contexts: A generation of effective psychotherapies.* New York: Guilford.

O'Leary, K. D., & Beach, S. R. H. (1990). Marital therapy: A viable treatment for depression and marital discord. *American Journal of Psychiatry, 147*(2), 183–186.

Palazzoli, M. S., Boscolo, L., Cecchin, G., & Prata, G. (1980). Hypothesizing circularity-neutrality: Three guidelines for the conduct of the session. *Family Process, 19*, 3–12.

Palazzoli, M. S., Cirillo, S., Selvini, M., & Sorrentino, A. M. (1989). *Family games: General model of psychotic processes in the family.* New York: Norton.

Parad, H. J., & Miller, R. (Eds.). (1963). *Ego oriented casework.* New York: Family Service Association of America.

Perlman, H. (1957). *Social casework: A problem solving process.* Chicago: University of Chicago Press.

Perlman, H. (1986). The problem solving model. In F. Turner, (Ed.), *Social work treatment* (3rd ed., pp. 00–00). New York: Free Press.

Pinsof, W. M., & Wynne, L. C. (1995). The efficacy of marital and family therapy: An empirical overview, conclusions and recommendations. *Journal of Marital and Family Therapy, 21*, 585–613.

Plaud, J. J., & Eifert, G. H. (1998). *From behavior theory to behavior therapy.* Boston: Allyn & Bacon.

Prawat, R. S. (1993). The value of ideas: Problems versus possibilities in learning. *Educational Researcher, 22*, 5–16.

Prochaska, J. O., & Norcross, J. C. (1999). *Systems of psychotherapy* (4th ed.). Pacific Grove, CA: Brooks/Cole.

Reid, W. J. (1988). Brief task-centered treatment. In R. A. Dorfman (Ed.), *Paradigms of clinical social work* (pp. 196–219). New York: Brunner/Mazel.

Reid, W. J. (1992). *Task strategies: An empirical approach to clinical social work.* New York: Columbia University Press.

Reid, W. J. (2000). *The task planner.* New York: Columbia University Press.

Reid, W. J., & Epstein, L. (1972). *Task-centered casework.* New York: Columbia University Press.

Reid, W. J., & Fortune, A. E. (2002). The task-centered model. In A. R. Roberts & G. J. Greene (Eds.), *Social workers desk reference* (pp. 101–104). New York: Oxford University Press.

Rose, S. (1977). *Group therapy: A behavioral approach.* Englewood Cliffs, NJ: Prentice-Hall.

Rose, S. (1988, March). *Alternative practice explanatory frameworks: A debate.* (With A. Gitterman & E. G. Goldstein). Presentation at the annual program meeting, Council on Social Work Education, Atlanta, GA.

Saleeby, D. (1997). *The strengths perspective in social work practice* (2nd ed.). New York: Longman.

Sheafor, B., Horejsi, C., & Horejsi, G. (1988). *Techniques and guidelines for social work practice.* Boston: Allyn & Bacon.

Shorkey, C. T., & Sutton-Simon, K. (1983). Reliability and validity of the Rational Behavior Inventory with a clinical population. *Journal of Clinical Psychology, 39*(1), 34–38.

Stein, T. J. (1990). Commentary: Issues in the development of expert systems to enhance decision making in child welfare. In L. Videka-Sherman & W. J. Reid (Eds.), *Advances in clinical social work research* (pp. 84–87). Silver Spring, MD: NASW Press.

Streeter, C. L., & Franklin, C. (1992). Defining and measuring social support: Guidelines for social work practitioners. *Research on Social Work Practice, 2*(1), 81–98.

Stuart, R. (1980). *Helping couples change: A social learning theory approach to marital therapy.* New York: Guilford.

Studt, E. (1968). *C-unit, search for community in prison.* New York: Russell Sage Foundation.

Talmon, M. (1990). *Single session therapy.* San Francisco: Jossey-Bass.

Thyer, B. A. (1983). Behavior modification in social work practice. In M. Hersen, P. Miller, & R. Eisler (Eds.), *Progress in behavior modification* (Vol. 15, pp. 173–226). New York: Academic Press.

Thyer, B. A. (1985). Textbooks in behavioral social work: A bibliography. *The Behavior Therapist, 8,* 161–162.

Thyer, B. A. (1987). Contingency analysis: Toward a unified theory for social work practice. *Social Work, 32,* 150–157.

Thyer, B. A. (1988). Radical behaviorism and clinical social work. In R. Dorfman (Ed.), *Paradigms of clinical social work* (pp. 123–148). New York: Brunner/Mazel.

Tomm K. (1987). Interventive interviewing. *Family Process, 26*(2), 167–183.

Tracy, E. M., & Whittaker, J. K. (1990). The social network map: Assessing social support in clinical practice. *Families in Society, 71*(8), 461–470.

Turner, F. (1988). Psychosocial therapy. In R. Dorfman (Ed.), *Paradigms of clinical social work* (pp. 106–122). New York: Brunner/Mazel.

Turner, R. (1992). Launching cognitive behavioral therapy for adolescent depression and drug abuse. In S. H. Budman, M. F. Hoyt, & S. Friedman (Eds.), *The first session in brief therapy* (pp. 135–155). New York: Guilford.

Van den Broek, P., & Thurlow, R. (1991). The role and shucture of personal narratives. *Journal of Cognitive Psychotherapy, 5*(4), 257–274.

Vonk, M. E., & Early, T. J. (2002). Cognitive-behavioral therapy. In A. R. Roberts & G. J. Greene (Eds.), *Social workers desk reference* (pp. 116–120). New York: Oxford University Press.

Wakefield, J. C. (1990). Commentary: Expert systems, Socrates, and the philosophy. In L. Videka-Sherman & W. J. Reid (Eds.), *Advances in clinical social work research* (pp. 92–100). Silver Spring, MD: National Association of Social Workers Press.

Wakefield, J. C. (1996a). Does social work need the ecosystems perspective? Is the perspective clinically useful? (Part 1). *Social Service Review, 70*(1), 1–32.

Wakefield, J. C. (1996b). Does social work need the ecosystems perspective? Does the perspective save social work from incoherence? (Part 2). *Social Service Review, 70*(2), 183–213.

Wakefield, J. C. (1996c). Does social work need the ecological perspective: Reply to Alex Gitterman. *Social Service Review, 70*(3), 476–481.

Warren, K., Franklin, C., & Streeter, C. L. (1996). *New directions in systems theory: Chaos and complexity.* Unpublished manuscript, University of Texas at Austin, School of Social Work.

Watzlawick, P., Weakland, J. H., & Fisch R. (1974). *Change: Principles of problem formulation and problem resolution.* New York: Norton.

Whittaker, J., & Tracy, E. (1989). *Social treatment: An introduction to interpersonal helping in social work practice* (2nd ed.). New York: Aldine de Gruyter.

Woods, M. E., & Robinson, H. (1996). Psychosocial theory and social work treatment. In F. J. Turner (Ed.), *Social work treatment* (4th ed., pp. 555–580). New York: Free Press.

Linking Assessment and Intervention

Catheleen Jordan and Cynthia Franklin

An Integrative Skills Assessment Protocol, introduced in Chapter 1, is based on the assumptions that assessment must be empirically based and systems oriented and that multiple measures should be employed to help the accountable professional evaluate practice activities. (Accountability is an especially important topic for practitioners in the current practice climate of managed care and third-party payments.) This protocol is used in the final chapters of this book to assess various client populations including children and adolescents, adults, families, and special populations. Chapter 2 moves the reader from assessment to intervention. Clinical decision making, problem monitoring, and treatment planning are addressed.

CLINICAL DECISION MAKING

What happens in the assessment phase of treatment affects interventions selected at a later stage of treatment. The assessment information collected helps the practitioner focus on problems to be targeted for intervention and to specify the most helpful type of intervention for those problems. Various treatment planning manuals can help the practitioner select appropriate interventions for problems specified during the assessment phase (see for example Reid, 2000; Roberts & Greene, 2002). Three important decisions must be made by the social worker during assessment: how much and which data to collect, which assessment tools to use, and what specific problem to target.

Collecting Data

Elsewhere we have recommended performing assessment from a multidimensional perspective; now, we would like to propose limits to data collection in assessment. Gambrill (1983) suggests that a thorough assessment should consider interpersonal and intrapersonal issues related to client functioning but also that the assessment data collected should be relevant. When performing brief assessment, one should consider who requested the assessment and for what purpose. For instance, if Child Protective Services is requested to perform an assessment and provide a report to the court, the judge may require a thorough assessment that includes every detail of the child's life and environmental situation. However, if the assessment is performed in a managed care setting and the client requests time-limited help with a child management problem, only information about the parent-child relationship might be relevant.

The Integrative Skills Assessment Protocol presented in Chapter 1 and used throughout the text to guide case example also may be used to perform a brief assessment, that is, not all the information requested on the protocol is necessary for every case. Figure 2.1 provides the clinician with a checklist that guides the selection of relevant information. Note that the checklist asks the practitioner to consider the various areas that might be included in the assessment, such as client intrapersonal issues, client family issues, or client work issues. Those areas pertinent to the client are to be checked, and only those areas checked are addressed when completing the Integrative Skills Assessment Protocol.

Choosing Assessment Tools

Just as doing a brief assessment and collecting only relevant data is important to improving the assessment process, choosing the correct tools can make the assessment a more efficient endeavor. Meyer (1993) defines assessment as a five-step process. Different assessment tools and technologies may be required at each step, ranging from unstructured, qualitative methodologies to structured, standardized measurement instruments. The five stages and a description of each follow.

Stage one: *What are the facts?* This step of the assessment process is concerned with the observation of the raw data, or concrete evidence, of the case. Meyer asserts that there is little room for disagreement among observers about this data, as it is the description of the external and structural features of the case. For example, demographic information is collected in an intake, or face sheet, in the exploration/study phase of assessment. Other assessment tools that can give a global picture of the client problem in its environmental context are useful here. For example, genograms and other maps, sculpting, standardized measures, or a combination of these may be used to get an overall picture of client functioning. The orientation and perceptions of the observer are important issues at this level of assessment. According to Meyer (1993), "a case is 'built,' through selecting, ordering, and patterning the revealed case data" (p. 32).

Stage two: *What is the matter?* The inference stage, or second stage of assessment, requires that observers move their thinking to a new level of educated insight. In step one, the raw data is observed and recorded. In step two, the observer must infer the meaning of the data. There is less

Figure 2.1   Checklist for Brief Assessment with the Integrative Skills
Assessment Protocol

Instructions: Check off the sections below as they apply to the client and/or to
the client's problem(s). (Note: Check all sections required for all
clients.) Next, go to the Integrative Skills Assessment Protocol and
complete only the sections checked here.

    I. Identifying information
____   1–12
   II. Nature of presenting problem
____   1. List all problems
____   2. Specification of specific, discrete problem(s) behavior(s)
____   3. Prioritize problem(s)
  III. Client
____   1–14. Intrapersonal issue
____   15. Interpersonal - family
____   16. Interpersonal - work or school
____   17. Interpersonal - peers
  IV. Context and Social Support Networks
____   1. Agency consideration
____   2. Client's environmental context
    V. Measurement
____   1. Family functioning
____   2. Marital (or significant other) functioning
____   3. Individual functioning
____   4. Social Supports
____   5. Strengths, resources, & protective factors
  VI. Summary
____   1. Practitioner impressions
____   2. Priorities
 VII. Treatment Plan
____   1. Problem
____   2. Definitions
____   3. Goals
____   4. Objectives (measurements)
____   5. Interventions

---

consensus in this second phase of assessment than in the preceding one.
Observers make interpretations of the data based on the evidence presented as well as on the consistency and the logic of the evidence. Theories and empirical studies come into play here in helping the observer
find explanations for what is going on in the case.

Stage three: *How is the client functioning?* This stage involves evaluation. After inferring the meaning of the data, the observer must then answer questions about the strengths and limitations of the client in the face
of his or her problems. This step in assessment helps the observer to in-

dividualize the case. For example, two clients come to the observer reporting problems with depression; however, one client may be coping better than the other due to having more social and family supports. During stages two and three, measures that provide specific, quantified data are most helpful. Schemas to observe or count behaviors, thoughts, or feelings give the practitioner specific information to operationalize the problem.

Stage four: *What is doable?* The desired outcome from the assessment process is to define the problem or problems to be targeted for change and to negotiate these problems with the client. This stage of assessment calls for a focusing of the treatment process on specific problems for intervention. It is important at this phase to start where the client is and to focus on those problems that are doable, that is, problems that the client is willing to address. Data collected in the preceding phases may be presented to clients in order to increase their awareness of the problem.

Stage five: *What is the contract?* This stage leads the practitioner to intervention and treatment planning. It assumes that the first four stages of assessment "have been solidly based upon the client's story, and have included 'correct' or at least amenable interpretations of his or her affect, cognitive stance, and behavior, and the interacting role of environmental factors" (Meyer, 1993, p. 40). Intervention choices are carefully planned, contracted with the client, and based on collection of supporting evidence, inference, evaluation, and problem definition.

As stated throughout this text, use of multiple measures and methodologies ensures that the assessment information obtained provides the clinician with both qualitative and quantitative data. The clinician collects qualitative data to gain a depth of understanding of the client's problem and a description of the context in which the problem occurs. Quantitative measures allow the clinician to collect specific, operationalized information to determine the extent and severity of the problem. This information also helps with monitoring and evaluating treatment progress.

Sattler (1992) recommends matching client style and preference to the type of assessment tools used, which requires practitioners to have a wide repertoire of qualitative and quantitative assessment tools at their fingertips. In the first two stages of assessment, observation and inference, a broad range of qualitative and quantitative measures can be utilized depending on client preference. For example, some clients might feel more comfortable sharing information by completing a genogram with the practitioner, whereas other clients might prefer to complete a standardized global assessment instrument such as Hudson's Multi-Problem Inventory (Hudson, 1993). In the next two stages of assessment, problem definition and evaluation, more specific quantitative measures are most helpful. The goals here are to specify the problem(s), learn their extent and severity, and track them throughout the course of the treatment. Rapid assessment instruments are helpful in these later phases of assessment and in treatment, as are other ways of measuring specific problems, such as behavioral coding schemas and self-anchored scales.

Specifying Problems

Different types of qualitative and quantitative tools may be chosen for the assessment. At least one of the data collection methods should provide the practitioner with numerical information to assist in quantifying the client's problem(s) and, later, in monitoring outcomes. Bloom, Fischer, and Orme's (1999) single subject framework provides relevant guidelines at this stage of practice.

This framework begins by specifying the problem, which corresponds with Meyer's problem definition phase of assessment. The assumption here is that the practitioner has collected information by using some combination of qualitative and quantitative measures in order to have a clear picture of specific problems targeted for change. Problem definition follows from this assessment process and requires operationalizing (or defining in measurable terms) problems to be the focus of intervention. Problems might be overt or covert behaviors including individuals' thoughts and feelings; problems also might be conceptualized at the environmental level, such as a lack of needed resources. The clinician then uses quantitative-type measures to ascertain the existence, extent, severity, and duration, of the problem(s) targeted for intervention. These quantitative measures can be standardized measures, behavioral observations, self-anchored scales, to name a few.

PROBLEM MONITORING

After the assessment—brief or otherwise—produces problems targeted for change, the issue becomes monitoring the problems over the course of the therapeutic process. Quantitative data collection provides the clinician with information to determine the extent and severity of the problem during assessment. The clinician also can use this information to monitor the problem over the course of treatment. The recommended monitoring system for evaluating practice activities is single subject design. This evaluation design is different from traditional group research design where preintervention and postintervention information are compared. Rather than measuring the client's problems at only two points in time, single subject methodology requires repeated measurement of the problem over the course of assessment and treatment of the client. Therefore, the practitioner has a more in-depth look at the client's progress throughout the course of case activity. Single subject data provides information during the case so that changes may be made at any point during treatment if necessary. For example, if the data reveals that behavioral therapy is not making the expected difference in a client's level of depression, the decision might be made to change to a different intervention such as cognitive therapy.

Bloom et al. (1999) describe the stages involved in single subject design. Measures are administered repeatedly, usually weekly or daily. Data may be collected by the client, significant others, the practitioner, or a combination of these interested parties. The data is collected systematically over the course of the treatment, using the same measurement instruments at all phases of the case. The baseline phase of the case refers to the time when measurements are made before the formal intervention is begun. The baseline phase may last anywhere from a few days to a few weeks, and the data collected here is later compared with intervention phase data to observe changes in the problems.

Single subject evaluation incorporates phases for collecting data, specifically the baseline, intervention, and follow-up phases. Comparisons are made between the baseline and intervention phases and are used to make judgments about the success or failure of the treatment being implemented. A clear definition of intervention is required with this approach, and the practitioner must operationalize the intervention selected. It is important to know when the intervention is being applied and when it is not so that judgments about the effectiveness of the treatment can be made.

Finally, the data is analyzed. Single subject data is often analyzed simply by eyeballing or by observing the level, trend, and stability of the data in the different phases. However, there are some simple statistics that may be used when the data appears confusing to the eye. The Shewart Chart and the Celeration Line are two examples of statistical procedures used with single subject data. (Bloom et al., 1999)

Single subject designs provide many advantages for clients, according to Bloom et al. (1999). Using measurement to track problems allows clients to know the practitioner's view of the problem. If the client is responsible for recording some of the data about his or her problems, the recording process can help the client to be more aware of them. The single subject approach empowers clients by encouraging their participation in selecting goals and objectives, by operationalizing intervention, and by involving clients in the evaluation of their treatment. Single subject data gives clients anticipatory feedback and is a step toward encouraging clients to take charge of their lives and gain independence from therapy.

A single subject approach provides advantages for practitioners as well, including the collection of data to facilitate assessment of clients as well as to track and monitor problems during intervention. Practitioners collect data to help quantify client problems, including information on frequency, duration, and intensity of the problems. After problems are targeted for change, practitioners may continue to use single subject procedures to monitor progress, changing the intervention if necessary. Also, practitioners may use the data collected to show their treatment success rates to supervisors.

Administrators also benefit from use of single subject design to evaluate practice activities in agency settings. Administrators may aggregate the data collected and obtain averages on types of problems, types of interventions, and the levels of success of different interventions with specific problems and types of clients. Moreover, supervision is enhanced and evaluation of practitioners is facilitated by use of single subject design to evaluate all cases. Administrators also receive data on overall agency performance. This is especially important in these days of increasing managed care, in which practitioners have to be accountable for interventive outcomes. Accountability is also an issue for agencies seeking money from external funding sources, and single subject evaluation methods can help agencies establish a record of effective service. For more information about single subject designs, see Chapter 11.

TREATMENT PLANNING: MOVING FROM ASSESSMENT TO INTERVENTION

Treatments should follow logically from and be related to the problems targeted for change. This section presents guidelines for ascertaining the proper time to move from the assessment phase to the intervention phase and for selecting the proper intervention. Finally, a case example illustrates the tie between the problems targeted in assessment and the selection of corresponding treatments.

Cormier and Cormier (1985) provide five guidelines to help the practitioner move from the assessment phase to treatment, that is, to time the beginning of intervention. The first guideline or indicator of readiness for treatment is the quality of the therapeutic relationship. The client-practitioner relationship should be strong before intervention begins. The client should be able to trust the practitioner as well as feel supported by and cared for by the helper. Secondly, indicators of the quality of the relationship are 1) the client's statements that he or she feels understood by the practitioner; 2) the client's willingness to be in counseling as evidenced by homework assignments, self-disclosure, attendance, expression of feelings, and so forth; 3) the removal of barriers to open communication between client and practitioner (for example, a difference in ethnic background has been discussed); and 4) the practitioner feels comfortable with the client (for example, the practitioner can confront the client).

A third guideline is to perform an adequate assessment. An assessment that thoroughly evaluates the problem(s) to be targeted for treatment should be completed before moving to intervention. Cormier and Cormier (1985, p. 296) recommend asking the following questions as a way of evaluating the adequacy of the assessment:

1. Do I know why the client is here?
2. Is the client's presenting concern all, or only part, of the problem?
3. Do I know the problem behaviors and situations for this person?
4. Can I describe the conditions contributing to the client's problem?
5. Am I aware of the present severity and intensity of the problem?

Fourth, developing counseling goals is an essential step. The treatment should be a strategy that realistically may result in the desired outcomes. For example, if the goal or desired outcome is to increase a specific behavior such as school attendance, a realistic intervention might be an operant treatment approach such as a reward system for attending school.

A fifth guideline refers to client readiness. Clients must be ready and willing to commit to the treatment before intervention will be successful. The authors recommend moving slowing into intervention so as not to scare clients away by trying to push them along too quickly. Beginning intervention slowly and setting up interventions that are likely to give the client some small, quick successes encourage clients to continue in treatment. Other indicators that clients will continue in treatment are verbal admissions from clients saying they are thinking about the treatment between sessions, that they are doing their homework, and that they are looking forward to the positive changes treatment will bring.

Baseline data collection is an important part of problem specification, as mentioned in the previous section on single subject design. By analyzing the baseline data collected, the practitioner gains insight into the extent and severity of the problems specified for intervention, as well as some indicator of the desired outcomes or goals. For example, a client scores 40, 42, and 41 on weekly baseline measures of depression on a standardized measure that has a cutting score of 30—meaning that scores of 30 and below are the desired range, and scores above 30 indicate depression. The practitioner now has an outcome indicator, that is, the goal is to reduce the client's level of depression to a score of below 30 on the depression scale. Further, Cormier and Nurius (2003) elaborate on the importance of the working alliance between client and therapist. The working alliance consists of client-treatment agreement on therapeutic goals and tasks, as well as an emotional bond between client and therapist (pp. 73–74).

Criteria of Sound Interventions

Choosing interventions requires criteria to assess their soundness. Cormier and Cormier (1985, p. 297) suggest that the following apply to effective interventions. They:

- are easy to carry out
- match the unique characteristics and preferences of the client
- match the characteristics of the problem and related factors
- are positive rather than punitive
- encourage the development of self-management skills
- strengthen the client's expectations of personal effectiveness or self-efficacy
- are supported by the literature
- are feasible and practical to implement
- do not create additional problems for the client or significant others
- do not burden the client or significant others with too many things to do
- do not require more of the counselor than the counselor is able to give or is responsible for giving
- do not repeat or build on previous, unsuccessful solutions.

In addition to these characteristics of effective interventions, Cormier and Nurius (2003) and Cormier and Cormier (1985) present seven criteria for selecting an intervention: 1) Counselor characteristics and preferences should be considered. 2) Practitioners should use interventions that fit their level of expertise and their values and that are evidence based. The informed practitioner is continually learning new techniques so that he or she has a wide repertoire of skills that may be used to fit the needs of diverse clients. The skills may be learned in the context of necessary supervision, training, or consultation with experts and in consultation with the latest research. The more skills that the practitioner has for intervening with various types of clients or client problems, the more helpful he or she is likely to be. Clients may be given the choice between two different types of techniques that may be effective with their problem, thus increasing the likelihood of greater motivation toward and involvement in their treatment. For instance, a mother and child in treatment to resolve their fighting at home may choose an intervention such as communication training using a videotape, rather than a family system-oriented intervention in which all family members are included.

3) Documentation about strategies can provide empirical information about the effectiveness of specific interventions under consideration. However, other factors to consider in selecting an intervention are 4) the client's feelings about the intervention and 5) any issues related to implementation. For instance, an intervention that requires specific materials or an environment not readily available to the practitioner would not be a practical choice.

As mentioned above, environmental factors in the counseling setting may prohibit use of certain interventions. In addition to materials or equipment, time, cost, or personnel required for implementation of the intervention might be prohibitive. For example, long-term insight-oriented counseling strategies may be unrealistic in settings requiring shorter therapy. The new trend toward managed care has required time-limited, brief therapies, often only eight or so sessions per year are allowed by insurance plans.

6) The nature of the client problem and of the response systems involved, as identified in the assessment, gives the practitioner direction in selecting an intervention. For instance, consider a client whose problem is assessed as depression, and the response systems involved are identified as behavioral, emotional, and physiologic. (Note: Another client with depression might experience discomfort in only one or two response systems.) Different treatment strategies may be required to intervene with the different response systems—cognitive therapy for the emotional component of the problem, a behavioral intervention for the behavioral component, and so forth.

7) The nature of outcome goals effects the selection of the intervention. Choice and change goals require different treatment strategies. Choice issues are best treated with educational and training approaches such as vocational counseling, redecision work, and dialoguing. Change issues that specify some overt or covert behavioral change goal require more action-oriented techniques such as structural or strategic family therapy techniques. For overt and symptom-based problems, behavioral strategies are recommended; if problems are covert, cognitive techniques are more appropriate.

Considering the client's characteristics and preferences in selecting an intervention assumes that the client is an informed consumer who participates in selecting the treatment, consents to treatment, and has rights and choices in the therapy process. In keeping with this philosophy, according to Cormier and Cormier (1985, p. 300) it is important that clients are offered the following information about the intervention:

- a description of all relevant and potentially useful treatment approaches for this particular client with this particular problem
- a rationale for each procedure

- a description of the therapist's role in each procedure
- a description of the client's role in each procedure
- a discomforts or risks that may occur as a result of the procedure
- benefits expected to result from the procedure
- the estimated time and cost of each procedure. Further client characteristics to take into account include client functional impairments, coping style, and resistance level.

Diagnostic cues and patterns exhibited by the client may help in matching techniques to the client and to his or her identified problems. Shaffer (reported in Cormier & Cormier, 1985) describe eight major diagnostic cues and their corresponding interventions (see table 2.1). For example, a client needing to increase specific behaviors would be treated by operant or other traditional behavioral techniques; the client with errors in cognitive appraisals would be treated with interpretive or cognitive therapies.

In addition to these suggestions for selecting interventions, Gambrill (1997) offers guidelines for selecting interventions. In order to evaluate an intervention's feasibility, the practitioner should look at environmental resources and constraints, both in the office or agency setting and in the client's natural environment where the impact of the intervention is desired. For instance, are there reinforcers in the natural environment to ensure that homework assigned will be completed? Also, what are the client's resources and/or limitations in regard to implementation of a specific intervention. For example, for a congitively unsophisticated client like a small child, a behavioral intervention to modify misbehavior may be more appropriate than an insight-oriented approach.

Interventions differ in terms of their probable efficiency and effectiveness. When evaluating an intervention, look to the literature for reported success of the treatment with specific types of clients and client goals. For example, the outcome literature on treatment of sexual dysfunctions documents the effectiveness of behavioral interventions whereas treatment of other types of client problems is not as well documented in the literature.

The intrusiveness of the intervention refers to the degree to which the treatment alters the client's natural environment. Select the least intrusive or restrictive plans. This is an issue in a setting such as Child Protective Services where decisions must be made about whether or not to treat the child in his or her own home or to remove the child to a substitute care setting. The latter treatment option would obviously be more intrusive to the client and to the family and is the less desired option if treatment can safely be provided in the client's own home.

Table 2.1   Eight Categories of Diagnostic and Treatment Modalities

Diagnostic Cues	Corresponding Treatment
1. Low self-esteem. High, generalized anxiety. No acting out.	Rogerian/relationship approach.
2. Focal anxiety. Intact client. Gradient of anxiety.	Desensitization, other counterconditioning and anxiety reduction approaches.
3. Need to increase or decrease three or fewer specific behaviors.	Operant treatment and traditional noncognitive behavioral techniques.
4. Role discrepancy. Lack of information about self in relation to educational or vocational environments.	Educational/vocational counseling; decision making and problem solving; other "choice" strategies such as Gestalt dialogue, NLP reframing, TA redecision work.
5. Inability to introduce change. System rather than client is causing the problem. Therapist can get entry into the system.	Organizational or systems intervention.
6. Rigidity. More than three behaviors to change. Prior attempts to change behavior have failed. Nonpsychotic client.	Group work
7. Lack of cognitive sophistication. Errors in cognitive conceptualizations or appraisals. High degree of cognitive involvement.	Interpretive and cognitive therapies.
8. Therapist's belief that someone else can handle the case better owing to training, skills, values, time, cost, convenience, or availability.	Referral

* Used with permission from W. Cormier & L. S. Cormier (1985).

Treatments have associated side effects that may be positive or negative. Obviously an intervention's potential side effects should be considered before the intervention is selected, and those treatments with negative side effects should be avoided or at least discussed with the client. For instance, consider the couple coming to treatment for marital problems. The couple reports having a traditional marriage for the past twenty-five years, with wife as homemaker and husband as breadwinner.

The practitioner observes the wife to be meek and reluctant to express her opinion and the husband to be somewhat overbearing and critical. The couple reports boredom with the marriage over the past couple of years. The practitioner might consider an assertiveness training intervention for the wife; however a negative side effect for the husband might be the disruption of the traditional nature of their relationship.

Intervention plans should be acceptable and even motivating and exciting to clients. Even if an intervention meets the criteria for acceptability, but the client does not want to do it, it probably will not work. Some interventions involve more discomfort for clients than do other plans. For example, some cognitive desensitization procedures involve the client imagining scenes that cause them to feel nauseous. Any discomforts likely to be created by the intervention should be discussed with the client.

An intervention that has a positive rather than punitive focus is desirable. For example, it is better for parents to increase children's prosocial behaviors by rewarding and praising them rather than by using a punishing procedure like spanking. A punitive procedure like spanking may teach children to solve their problems by using force; also, the child may experience negative emotional reactions toward the punishing parent. On the other hand, use of positive procedures to increase prosocial behaviors has the expected side effect of decreasing undesirable behaviors. Intervention strategies with specific steps offer greater clarity to the client about what is required to move toward change. This approach also facilitates measurement of client outcomes at each step.

Another issue to consider that is related to outcome is the degree to which the intervention encourages generalization and maintenance. Does the plan help clients to generalize changes made in the treatment setting to their natural environment and will the changes last over time? Gambrill (1997) offers sources of error when practitioners are selecting interventions: Faulty problem structuring, incomplete assessment, overlooking client strengths or important cultural differences, overlooking opportunities to rearrange the physical environment, a "one size-fits-all" approach not being familiar with or ignoring the scientific literature, trying to do too much, and not involving clients and significant others in planning (p. 455).

Treatment Planning Framework

Jordan and Franklin (2002) present an evidence-based framework for treatment planning with families. Steps include problem selection, problem definition, goal development, objective construction, intervention creation, and diagnosis determination.

TREATMENT PLANNING CASE EXAMPLE: TOM AND JULIE

The case of Tom and Julie was first discussed by Jordan and Cobb in *101 Interventions in Family Therapy* (1993). They are a dual career couple, committed to their jobs and to their family life. Their difficulties presented in treatment were about how to balance these two very demanding worlds. Their case shows the link between assessment and intervention. A summary of the assessment on Tom and Julie is presented next. Following the assessment summary is a list of problems targeted for intervention, measurements to be used for case monitoring, and a brief discussion of the interventions selected.

Assessment Summary

Tom and Julie are spouses with promising careers in banking and merchandising, respectively. In addition to a commitment to their jobs and to each other, they also have an 18-month-old daughter, CeCe. They came to therapy to resolve issues related to their busy lifestyle. Julie reported that Tom disagrees with her about who should be responsible for household chores, resulting in screaming fights between the couple. They also argue about who should take on the primary caretaking role for CeCe. The little girl is enrolled in a day school, but the parents disagree about who should deliver her and pick her up from school, as well as about who should take her to the doctor or to other necessary appointments during the day.   Both Tom and Julie report feeling "stressed out" most of the time. They feel like their relationship is suffering from their lack of time and their many jobs.

Problem selection

The following problems were identified by the practitioner as areas of concern for this couple:

1. poor communication
2. stress

Problem definition

Tom and Julie's problems were defined as:

1. poor communication = communication style characterized by angry arguments with yelling and screaming; disagreements remain unresolved.

2. stress = feelings of tension from inability to get jobs done; no time for important activities.

The results of the assessment and the targeted problems were presented to Tom and Julie, and the couple was asked for their feedback. Both Tom and Julie agreed that communication and stress were the two major problems for them; they expressed a desire to continue in treatment to work on both of these problems.

Goals

Goals for the treatment were:

1. Improve couple's communication.
2. Reduced couple's stress.

Objectives

During the assessment phase, the two measures listed below were used to assess the extent and severity of Tom and Julie's problems. These are also used to describe the objectives. Note that the practitioner continued to collect data from Tom and Julie using these same measures over the course of treatment as a way of monitoring outcomes. The objectives are:

1. Improve communication as measured by an improvement on the Primary Communication Inventory (Navran, 1967)
2. Reduce stress as measured by the Stress Arousal Checklist (Mackay, Cox, Burrows, & Lazzerini, 1978)

Interventions selected

The practitioner offered two types of intervention approaches to Tom and Julie: family therapy using a human validation process model and skills training. After hearing a brief description of each intervention, the couple chose the skills training approach, which involved the following two components.

Communication training: The therapist focused on teaching the couple both verbal and nonverbal communicating skills. Verbal skills included the use of "I" statements to communicate needs, active listening, correct timing of message delivery, expression of feelings, and editing of unproductive communications. Nonverbal tools included appropriate facial expressions to match verbal content, posture, voice, and physical proximity to partner. In addition anger control techniques like recognizing escalating anger, taking a time-out, admitting one's own part in the argument, and problem solving were also taught to the couple.

Stress management training: The practitioner helped each partner to identify and analyze their stressors. Two considerations in analyzing stress were whether it came from lack of organization or from overwhelming responsibilities. Four components of stress management were then designated as appropriate interventions for Tom and Julie: self-monitoring, daily relaxation exercises, cognitive restructuring of unproductive irrational beliefs contributing to stress, and environmental alteration.

SUMMARY

Chapter 2 moves the reader from the issues surrounding clinical decision making and problem monitoring in the assessment phase of treatment to the linkage of the assessment phase with treatment planning and the selection of intervention strategies.

A decision that must be made in the assessment phase is how much data to collect. Brief assessment guidelines were presented for selecting the relevant areas for focus on the Integrative Skills Assessment Protocol. Clinical decisions must be made about which assessment tools and methodologies to use in any given case. These different assessment technologies add information at five stages of the assessment: 1) exploration/study, 2) inference, 3) evaluation, 4) problem definition, and 5) intervention/treatment planning. Qualitative and quantitative methods are equally important in the data collection process.

The important goals of assessment are to specify problems for intervention, and concomitantly, to specify a problem-monitoring system. Single subject design technology was recommended for these purposes, and its steps are here reviewed: 1) specify the problem, 2) measure the problem, 3) repeat measures, 4) determine the baseline, 5) select a design, 6) define the intervention, and 7) analyze the data. Advantages of single subject design for clients, practitioners, and administrators also have been described along with the trend toward managed care and its effects on efficient and effective service provision to clients.

The assessment information collected guides the practitioner to problems targeted for intervention and to the preferred intervention. Guidelines for moving from assessment to intervention, for selecting sound interventions, and for evaluating intervention plans have been thoroughly reviewed. Mistakes practitioners are likely to make also were identified. Finally, a case example was presented using the steps of treatment planning with families: problem selection, problem definition, goal development, objective construction, intervention creation, and diagnosis.

A final word from the authors: In the writing of this book and in our practice activities we assume a broad approach to assessment and treatment planning. We believe that to limit ourselves to only one method of collecting information about our clients due to theoretical narrowness is a disservice to our clients and to ourselves. We believe that a broad approach that uses creative ways to obtain quantitative and a qualitative client information helps us to know and be sensitive to our clients. We encourage practitioners to use the technologies presented here while always thinking about the client's needs, style, and willingness to participate. It is when we put the client first in our practice, that we can be of the most help.

STUDY QUESTIONS

1. Describe the five stages of assessment. Discuss the use of quantitative or qualitative methods in each stage as appropriate.
2. How does single subject technology inform assessment and treatment? Describe the steps.
3. How has managed care impacted assessment and treatment?
4. Discuss how you would choose the appropriate intervention and how you would time the movement from assessment to intervention?
5. Use a case example and design a treatment plan.

REFERENCES

Bloom, M., Fischer, J., & Orme, J. (1999). *Evaluating practice: Guidelines for the accountable professional* (3rd ed.). Boston: Allyn & Bacon.

Cormier, W., & Cormier, L. S. (1985). *Interviewing strategies for helpers.* Pacific Grove, CA: Brooks/Cole.

Cormier, S., & Nurius, P. S. (2003). *Interviewing and change strategies for helpers* (5th ed.). Pacific Grove, CA: Brooks/Cole.

Gambrill, E. (1983). *Casework: A competency based approach.* Englewood Cliffs, NJ: Prentice-Hall.

Gambrill, E. (1997). *Social work practice: A critical thinker's guide.* New York: Oxford University Press.

Hudson, W. (1993). *Multi-problem inventory.* Tempe, AZ: Walmyr.

Jordan, C., & Cobb, N. (1993). Treating dual career couples. In T. Nelson & T. Trepper (Eds.), *101 Interventions in family therapy* (pp. 10–11). New York: Haworth Press.

Jordan, C., & Franklin, C. (2002). Treatment planning with families: An evidence-based approach. In A. Roberts & G. Greene (Eds.), *Social worker's desk reference* (pp. 252–255). New York: Oxford University Press.

Mackay, C., Cox, T., Burrows, G., & Lazzerini, T. (1978). An inventory for the measurement of self-reported stress and arousal. *British Journal of Social and Clinical Psychology, 17*, 283–284.

Meyer, C. (1993). *Assessment in social work practice*. New York: Columbia University Press.

Navran, L. (1967). Communication and adjustment in marriage. *Family Process, 6*, 173–184.

Reid, W. J. (2000). *The task planner*. New York: Columbia University Press.

Roberts, A., & Greene, G. (2002). *Social worker's desk reference*. New York: Oxford University Press.

Sattler, J. (1992). *Assessment of children*. San Diego: Sattler Publications.

CHAPTER 3

Quantitative Clinical Assessment Methods

Cynthia Franklin and Kevin Corcoran

Quantitative clinical assessment methods involve operationally defining client behavior, affect, and cognition (including attitudes) to obtain an objective assessment of an aspect of the client's functioning. Quantitative methods are simply numerical indicators of a particular aspect of client functioning. Scores on a quantitative assessment are used as observable referents of the client's behavior, affect, or cognition. Such measurements require practitioners to devise or use already established assessment tools for assigning numerical indicators to problems or goals. Practitioners may use scales for assessing client problems (e.g., depression), or require the client to keep a record of the behavior that is the focus of treatment (for example, a frequency count of the number of times a child has temper tantrums). Empirically sound objective indicators may also be used to measure client behavior, for example, the practitioner may examine the prevailing interpersonal themes or latent traits of a client using projective measures.

Quantitative clinical measurement includes categorizing client characteristics, assigning diagnostic labels, developing behavior profiles and ratings, and systematically tracking problem behaviors, to observe change over the course of treatment and afterward. Measurements contribute to the practitioner's subjective and intuitive domains (practice wisdom) and add specificity and concreteness. In keeping with empirical and evidence-based practice, objective assessments help the practitioner provide a quantifiable and verifiable assessment of a client.

Measurement, therefore, assists practitioners in defining client problems and attributes, and in observing them over the course of treatment, as discussed in Chapters 2 and 11. In accordance with the person-in-environment approach of social work assessment, clinical quantitative measurement may also help practitioners define the client's environmental context by ascertaining situation-specific behaviors across settings. Examples include the rate of disruptive behavior in the school, home, and community, the functioning of social systems (such as families and friends), the quality of interpersonal interactions (such as peer relationship and classroom behaviors), available resources (such as finances and special assistance programs), and support networks (such as clubs, kin groups, close friends). In short, measurement helps practitioners to objectively assess clients and their situation and serves as a basis for translating this assessment into a plan of action.

This chapter provides a rationale for the inclusion of quantitative assessment methods in social work and summarizes the most frequently used measurement methods for assessing client behavior. These measurement methods are:

1. Client self-reporting and monitoring
2. Self-anchored and rating scales
3. Questionnaires
4. Direct behavioral observation
5. Role play and analogue situations
6. Behavioral by-products
7. Psychophysiological measures
8. Goal attainment scaling
9. Standardized measures
10. Projective measures

These methods of measurement are discussed and illustrated in relationship to clinical assessment and treatment planning. Finally, because there will be times when you simply cannot find a quantitative assessment tool that is right for your client's circumstances, this chapter provides guidelines for developing a more "homemade" instrument.

RATIONALE FOR INCLUDING QUANTITATIVE MEASURES IN ASSESSMENT

Clinical assessment is designed to provide a portrayal of client functioning that is as complete as possible. The complexity of causes, the client's actual condition, and the social environment in which the condition arises are gathered into a clinical understanding that facilitates the social work intervention. As part of an assessment, social work practitioners usually develop a social assessment report (Sheafor, Horejsi, & Horejsi, 1988). This report is a narrative summary of the client's history and current life functioning. The report defines the presenting problem, tells the client's story, summarizes the major strengths and weaknesses of the client, and provides a formulation for treatment. Quantitative assessment can facilitate much of this because the client's concern and the accuracy of assessing the client's problem, behavior, and attribute are foremost in the social worker's mind.

Historically, the social assessment report has been based on the social work practitioner's conceptual formulation of client problems and characteristics observed during an interview with the client and significant others. The interview process is important and the judgment of trained clinical practitioners is invaluable to the assessment process. The judgments and opinions of practitioners, however, may be subject to bias and to misformulations of client problems. Including quantitative measures as a part of the social assessment helps practitioners verify their opinions and provide objective, multiple sources of data, that is, instruments can help erase some of the likely bias.

The use of multiple sources of information is particularly important in obtaining accurate assessments (Hepworth & Larsen, 1989). For example, in the case of a child with school problems, practitioners may interview the client (child), the parents, and child's teachers and also collect quantitative information from the parents and school using a questionnaire. It might be useful in some circumstances to observe the youngster in the classroom using a child behavior rating scale.

There are four reasons for collecting quantitative measures on client behaviors as part of the assessment process:

Measuring client problems helps practitioners improve treatment. The objective assessment of client problems with measures improves treatment by increasing accuracy of the client problems. Monitoring client progress with measures allows treatment to be changed if progress is not being made (Barlow, Hayes, & Nelson, 1984).

Collecting client measures enables practitioners to contribute to clinical research. The clinical practice field needs new methods for client change. By collecting measurements of client problems across time, practitioners may also demonstrate the effectiveness of treatments and contribute to the clinical research literature. Single subject design methodology makes this possible (Barlow et al., 1984).

Collecting measures on client behaviors provides a basis for practice evaluation and accountability. Practice evaluation is essential to good service provision in today's managed care environment. Funding sources, such as federal agencies and insurance companies, demand that practitioners provide evidence of their accountability and effectiveness with clients. Managed care companies, for example, hire their own professional experts who require the social worker to monitor the progress of intervention, and consequently "certify" a certain number of sessions for payment. Measurement provides us with tools that may be incorporated in the assessment process and used as objective indicators of client problems and progress during the course of treatment (Barlow & Hersen, 1984).

In fact, Campbell (1988) found that clients overwhelmingly preferred to use some type of systematic data collection over reliance on practitioner opinion as the sole means of evaluating practice. Clients perceived practice that included measurement and single subject methodology as more satisfactory than practice that did not have these procedures.

Knowledge and skill in measurement increase practitioners' skills repertoire and broaden their client assessments and outcome evaluations. In today's practice environment, greater skill in assessment is needed; these skills will help social workers provide the same expertise in measurement that other counseling professionals have in conducting client assessments (Franklin & Jordan, 1992). If social workers are to function as independent practitioners with their own separate identity, it is important to conduct independent assessments of clients and, for this, measurement becomes a helpful tool. Competence in measurement will improve the status of social work and the ability of the profession to function autonomously. Measurement also provides an integral link between research and practice, which adds to the overall competence and effectiveness of the profession.

QUANTITATIVE METHODS OF MEASURING CLIENT BEHAVIOR

We have been discussing reasons for including quantitative measures as part of social work assessment practice evaluation. The remainder of this chapter summarizes several assessment methods for measuring client problems, behaviors, and goals. It also suggests guidelines for developing a measurement tool.

Client Self-Recording and Monitoring

Client self-recording and monitoring are the most common methods of observing clients. The client is asked to record his or her thoughts, feelings, and behaviors. Self-recording may be differentiated from self-monitoring by the manner in which the client is asked to collect the observations. In self-recording, the client is asked to report the information in a retrospective fashion (for example, record the number of times you thought about leaving your husband in the past week). In contrast, with self-monitoring, the client is asked to collect the observations every time the behavior occurs (for example, record each time you think of leaving your husband over the next week). Methods of self-recording and monitoring vary and include such techniques as client logs, diaries, journals, and structured forms of activities and behaviors.

Client self-recording and monitoring are useful clinical assessment tools and allow practitioners to obtain baseline measures of the client problems. When this baseline data shows that the client is similar to a clinical sample, or noticeably different from the general population, these measures tend to evidence treatment necessity (Corcoran & Boyer-Quick,

2002). Such information is particularly useful in managed care settings (Corcoran & Vandiver, 1996). For example, client may be asked to record the number of suicidal ideations they are experiencing and report the specific nature of the ideations in a log (see table 3.1). Social work practitioners may use such a log to explore the seriousness or magnitude of clients' suicidal intent and monitor any increase or decrease in the frequency or magnitude of suicidal ideations over the course of treatment. Figure 3.1 shows an anger diary of incidences of arguments between the client and the spouse. Deschner (1984) has used this method to collect clinical data on clients in treatment for anger control. Figure 3.2 shows a journal kept by a client seeking treatment because of recurring and obsessive thoughts of harm. Table 3.2 is a structured form for observations in this type of situation. Clients are asked to monitor their irrational be-

Table 3.1 Client Self-Recording, Self-Monitoring

	Time	Duration	Situation	Nature of Thoughts
Sunday	11:00 A.M.	2 hours	alone reading paper	Just wished I was dead, kept thinking about it, would like to be dead and not have to go through with my divorce.
	6:00 P.M.	2.5 hours	husband came by to get his files.	Thinking I would be better off dead than living alone. Didn't want to go on living without him.
Monday	4:30 A.M.	1.5 hours	alone, in bed at home	Don't want to face another day. Don't want to go to work, I'd be better off dead. I just want to go away.
Tuesday	4:15 A.M.	1.5 hours	same	same
Wednesday	4:15 A.M.	2 hours	same	Can't go on, its getting worse, I am sure I want to die rather than live. Surely it must be easier to be dead.
Thursday	5:00 A.M.	1 hour	same	same
Friday	6:00 P.M.	2 hours	husband called said he wanted to move the rest of his things on weekend.	I don't want to live. Maybe I will kill myself. I could take some pills or have a car accident.
Saturday	7:00 A.M.	3 hours	alone at home	same
	1:00 P.M.		at home with friend	same and might do it . . .

Figure 3.1   Anger Diary

Name: _____   Date: _____

How many arguments did you have this week? _____

How do you rate (0–10) your:

      Verbal: _____   Anger _____
                         Partner's Anger _____
                         Fear _____
      Physical _____   Anger _____
                         Partner's Anger _____
                         Fear _____

What were your internal signals when trouble began?

What signals came from your partner?

How many times did you call for time-out? _____

How many times did your partner call time? _____

Which steps did you use? (Answer Yes or No)

T sign _____   Exercise _____

Return of T _____   Error admitted _____

Leave quietly _____   Partner error _____

How long did you stay apart in time-out? _____

What happened afterward?

What other anger-control methods did you use?

	Practiced	Used in Real Life
Relaxation	_____	_____
Cognitive realignment	_____	_____
3-part assertion	_____	_____
Reflective listening	_____	_____
Diplomatic correction	_____	_____

Rate your happiness with this relationship if things go on just as they are (0–10):

Household responsibilities ____	General happiness ____	Spouse's independence ____
Rearing of children ____	Communication ____	Occupational progress ____
Money ____	Social life ____	Sex ____

Figure 3.2   Journal of Obsessive Thoughts of Harm and Compulsive Behaviors

---

Day and Date	Time of Day	Thought and Behavior
Monday, March 24th	9:15 P.M.	I probably didn't lock the door, a killer may come in, I better check. Got up and checked the door and returned to bed. Same thought recurred, got up and checked door again. This happened *seven* times.

Table 3.2 Structured Form for Observations

A (Activator)	*B (Belief)*			
Description of the activating event	Self-statement you made at the time	Emotional consequences	Cognitive restructuring activity	New emotional consequences
Negative event:	*Irrational belief about event:*	*How I felt:*	*1) Dispute your irrational belief:*	*Now I feel:*
Supervisor does not accept recommendation for a new project I want very much. States my recommendations are unrealistic.	#1 #2 #3	I feel inadequate, naive, embarrassed because this is a project I have boasted about. I feel depressed due to my project not being accepted. I must not be very intelligent. I am not a good employee.	My projects have been accepted in the past and complimented by my supervisor, therefore I am not inadequate, I should be proud of what I have done and not devastated because of this one nonacceptance. My supervisor still likes me even though he does not agree with this project. This project has its merits as well as its discredits 2) Now construct a positive statement	I am appreciated for my work. I feel I am a good employee. I feel disappointed that this project was not accepted, but I can improve on it to make it acceptable.
Positive event:	*Positive self-statement about event:*	*How I felt:*	*1) Improve on your positive self-statement or add another one to it:*	*Now I feel:*
After the staff meeting today, Susan came up and complimented me on my ideas for the new promotional project.	I do have worthwhile ideas to share.	I felt encouraged and more confident.	No one is right all the time but when I do have good ideas there are people that appreciate me. I do my best and even if I fail people will still like me.	I feel I am a valuable part of our staff team. I am happy about giving my input at the meeting.

liefs according to Ellis's (1985) rational emotional therapy, which uses cognitive restructuring as a primary vehicle for facilitating client change.

Client self-recording and monitoring have relevance for clinical assessment and the actual clinical intervention. Although they are not terribly rigorous scientific forms of quantitative measurement, they are appropriate tools for clinical observations of a client's thoughts, feelings, and behaviors. Self-recording and monitoring are a supplement to and never a substitute for clinical judgment; quantitative measures add another way to observe client change over the course of treatment. Self-recording and monitoring are compatible for use with other more rigorous measurement tools, such as standardized scales and provide useful validation information. Standardized measures are covered in detail in Chapter 4.

Self-Anchored and Rating Scales

Self-anchored scales are measures of client problems that the social worker and client construct together. This is often necessary when a standardized instrument is not available or when a particular subtlety of the client's problem or goal needs to be part of the assessment. These "do-it-yourself" scales, as they are sometimes called (Bloom, Fischer, & Orme, 2002), allow for the development of an assessment tool that represents the client's specific problem or concern. For example, a self-anchored rating scale may be constructed that measures a client's particular experience of depression which lasted for six weeks from Thanksgiving and is recurrent since her marriage. The dimensions of the scale range from the maximum severity of depression (such as, tired, loss of appetite, down in the dumps) to maximum improvement in the depression (e.g., energetic, feels alive and vibrant). These two extremes are called anchors and are used to describe the ends of a self-anchored rating scale. Clients are asked to complete the self-anchored scale regularly, say weekly or every other day or so (see figure 3.3). Scores on the self-anchored rating scale can be used to assess the client's depression and monitor its change over the

Figure 3.3   Self-Anchored Scale

Instructions: Circle the number that applies every day before 8:00 A.M.

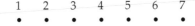

$$1 \quad 2 \quad 3 \quad 4 \quad 5 \quad 6 \quad 7$$

Energetic,		Tired, no energy
feel alive		feel like lying
and ready		down and never
to go to work.		getting up.

course of treatment. Scale scores are practical and relevant because they are additional referents of the client's experience. By constructing a self-anchored rating scale, practitioners help clients define the problems by identifying the extremes. They simply construct the scale by identifying the extreme of the least magnitude as "1" and the extreme of the greatest magnitude a "7" which we believe is the ideal scale range. It is important to capture sufficient deviations to reflect the client's experience, but not so many that the different intervals are not meaningful (Jordan, Franklin, & Corcoran, 2001). For example, say you construct a scale with 100 points, few clients would be able to meaningfully distinguish between 85 and 90 or 50 and 55. It is best to restrict the range of a self-anchored rating scale to five or seven intervals.

Self-anchored scales may be constructed on virtually any practice problem. They provide systematic ways for clients to observe their thoughts, feelings, and behaviors. Rating scales are similar to self-anchored scales in that they are constructed by the social worker and client to reflect the client's presenting problem. They differ in that rating scales are completed by person other than the client (see figures 3.4 and 3.5).

Figure 3.5 is an example of a rating scale used to track communication skills being taught in marital counseling. Franklin (1982) created this rating scale to use with couples in communication skills training based on the Gottman model (Gottman, Notavarius, Gonso, & Markman, 1976). It is possible to substitute the generalized anchors ("adequate" and "inadequate") with examples from the client's experience. For instance, on "use a stop action" the "inadequate" anchor could be substituted for "continues to insist and talk about difficulties after voices begin to rise," and the "adequate" anchor could be substituted for "calls a time-out when notices voice rising."

Figure 3.4   Rating Scale for Communication

	Inadequate									*Adequate*
Speak for self	1	2	3	4	5	6	7	8	9	10
Send I messages	1	2	3	4	5	6	7	8	9	10
Use a stop action	1	2	3	4	5	6	7	8	9	10
Ask for feedback	1	2	3	4	5	6	7	8	9	10
Give feedback	1	2	3	4	5	6	7	8	9	10
Listen	1	2	3	4	5	6	7	8	9	10
Summarize	1	2	3	4	5	6	7	8	9	10
Validate	1	2	3	4	5	6	7	8	9	10
Ask open questions	1	2	3	4	5	6	7	8	9	10
Build agenda	1	2	3	4	5	6	7	8	9	10
Check out	1	2	3	4	5	6	7	8	9	10

SOURCE: Franklin (1982).

Figure 3.5 is an example of a rating scale developed to assess the level of conflict avoidance of a couple in marital therapy. Rating scales allow the practitioner to obtain observations of client behavior from an outside observer, such as a spouse, a social worker, a teacher, or a member of a therapy group. These observations are helpful in that clients do not always observe themselves accurately; rating scales broaden the perspective on client functioning and substantiate progress in treatment.

Rating scales and self-anchored scales may be used together as measures of client problems and behavior for even a broader scope and more accurate input.

Self-anchored and rating scales also provide opportunities for the practitioner and client to quantify the presenting problem in ways that are clinically meaningful to both. Similar to the client self-recording method described above, these scales are not rigorous, scientifically valid, or reliable. They are useful only as a self-referenced comparison of the client's performance relative to the same client's previous performance. Despite their limitations, these measures often represent the best or only instrument available for your client's particular problem.

Questionnaires

Questionnaires are another useful way to collect assessment information about clients. They provide clients with opportunities to report a large repertoire of behaviors and background information. Questionnaires are flexible; many are designed to solicit both specific, detailed information from the client and more global, comprehensive material. Although many questionnaires are available through commercial publishers and the professional literature, they may also be designed by the social work practitioner to meet the demands of particular practice situation. For example, the Multimodal Life History Inventory assesses clients on several dimensions: behavior, affect, sensation, imagery, cognition, interpersonal relations, drugs, and biology (Lazarus, 1991). This instrument provides com-

Figure 3.5   Rating Scale for Conflict Avoidance

	1	2	3	4	5	6	7
	•	•	•	•	•	•	•

Changes the
subject, leaves
the room, and
refuses to talk
about conflictual
issues.

Stays on the topic
and engages in
conversation
regarding
conflictual issues.

prehensive assessment data to use in conjunction with multi-modal treatment. Another questionnaire is the Cassata History Questionnaire, which is designed for use with youngsters who are considering dropping out of high school (Franklin, McNeil, & Wright, 1990; Franklin & Streeter, 1992). See appendix 3A for a portion of this questionnaire.

The chief advantage of questionnaires is that they are useful clinical tools for providing assessment information on clients in a simplified and straight-forward manner. They are not particularly useful for monitoring clinical change but are helpful in formulating treatment plans and may guide our diagnosis and placement decisions. They may also point out to the social worker the need for a more specific measurement tool for a client problem.

Direct Behavioral Observation

Behavioral observation is one of the most direct and effective measures of client behavior. Behavior is observed in terms of its frequency, duration, or both called interval (Bloom et al., 2002). To gauge frequency, it is first necessary to operationalize the behavior to be observed and to decide if it is to be observed constantly (continuous recording) or on different occasions (time sampling recording). Observers must be trained in the behavior to look for and how to recognize it when it occurs.

Using more than one observer at a time makes it possible to establish interobserver agreement, that is, the occurrences of observed behaviors between the observers may be compared so that we will know if they are both recording the same behavior. Interobserver agreement allows us to calculate a reliability statistic for our observations to determine if the ratings are consistent. Eighty percent or higher agreement is believed to be acceptable for most clinical situations.

Direct behavioral observation using more than one rater is a very effective measurement strategy. It has been used frequently in research on clinical practice (Polster & Dangel, 1989). Direct behavioral observation, however, is time-consuming, expensive, and impractical for many practitioners to use. In practice settings, it is best utilized in residential and institutional settings. For example, in a hospital setting, a mental health aide and a nursing staff member may be trained to observe a client behavior such as "withdrawal into the patient's room." Both staff may independently record the time the patient stays in his or her room for a work shift (duration measure). The two observers' recordings may then be compared to establish with greater confidence the actual occurrence of that behavior. Once we have established how often the behavior occurs, we may continue to count the number or times the patient withdraws during the hospital stay to see if the patient's hospital stay is improving his or her social interaction.

Sometimes it is possible to use only one observer. The social worker may be the observer or a significant other may be trained to observe the behavior. For example, a parent may be asked to record the amount of time a student studies during the week (duration measure). Behavioral observation using one observer lacks the scientific reliability of observation with two or more raters, but it remains an important measurement indicator in clinical assessments because it provides observations of the client's behavior in natural settings.

It is not always necessary to count every occurrence to gain a sense of the frequency of a certain behavior. Interval recording simplifies behavioral observations, which makes this measurement strategy more adaptable to clinical practice. In interval recording, a period of observation (e.g., twenty minutes) is chosen and divided into equal short (ten to twenty second) blocks (intervals). The social worker simply observes whether the client is performing the behavior (for example, off-task in the classroom) during that time interval. The behavior is recorded only once for that time interval no matter how many times it actually occurs (Bloom et al., 2002).

Interval recording is flexible in that almost any type of behavior can be recorded. It is also adaptable to clinical situations because it allows for more than one behavior to be observed at a time. Interval recording is particularly useful for behaviors that are difficult to record using other methods (for example, high-frequency behavior or behaviors of extended duration [Bloom & Fischer, 1982]). Interval recording can also easily be converted into percentages, by dividing the number of intervals during which the behavior occurs by the total number of intervals observed and multiplying by one hundred. Figure 3.6 is an example of an interval recording form used to monitor a child's behavior.

Direct behavioral observation of clients remains one of the most effective tools for measuring client behavior and, when used with two or more observers, meets the claim of scientific rigor. This makes direct behavioral observation a useful tool for both practice and research.

Role Play and Analogue Situations

Practitioners frequently use role playing and other analogue situations to assess client performance of a variety of behaviors. These allow the client to demonstrate certain behaviors in the social worker's office. Social workers create role plays or behavioral rehearsals in which clients may demonstrate a behavior and the social worker may observe. For example, a social worker may ask a client to play the role of a job applicant in a personnel interview. The observation serves as an assessment of potential skill and therapeutic feedback to facilitate goal attainment. In this example, the role play allows the social worker to assess the client's job

Figure 3.6   Interval Recording Form

Observer: _____ *School Social Worker* _____	Date: _____ *28/10/78* _____
Reliability observer: _____ *paraprofessional* _____	day month year
Teacher: _____ *Mrs. Graves* _____	
School: _____ *Pine Elementary* _____	Time stop: _____ *11:16* _____
Subject area: _____ *reading-seatwork* _____	Time start: _____ *11:09* _____
Referred pupil (R): _____ *Chelsea* _____ Age: _*8–6*_	Total time: _____ *:7* _____
Comparison pupil (C): _____ Age: _*8–5*_	
Class size: _____ *31* _____ Class type: *regular*	

Grouping Situation	*Teacher Reaction Code: (T)*	*Observation Recording Method*
R = student	T = teacher	(circle one)
C = student	AA = attention to all	(a) interval: size ___ 30" ___
X = behavior occurs	A+ = positive attention to	(b) time sample: _____
O = behavior does	pupil	(c) event count
not occur	A– = negative attention	(d) duration for "out of
(circle one)	to pupil	seat"
L = large group	Ao = no attention to pupil	(e) latency
S = small group	An = neutral attention to	
O = one-to-one	pupil	
I = independent	= _____	
F = free time	= _____	
= _____		

Explicit classroom rules in effect during observation: *1. work quietly 2. sit at desks 3. raise hand to ask question*

---

interviewing skills and provides data from which the social worker may coach the client to improve. Observing the job interview role play on several occasions over a period makes it possible for the social worker to monitor improvement. The social worker may devise a plan for documenting this improvement, such as providing an objective, scaled rating of client performance or recording the client's improvements in a log, thus combining measurement strategies. The improvements may also be documented through analogue methods such as videotaping or audiotaping the role plays, which help clients understand their own behavior. Videotapes and audiotapes also are used in clinical supervision and provide a measure of analogue behavior for direct observation by the social worker and others. Camera equipment is reasonably priced nowadays and is no longer an impediment to routine clinical practice.

Another analogue measure is the use of vignettes and other contrived behavioral situations. Vignettes are more structured than role plays in that they usually provide the client with a set of questions to which he or she is to respond. Clients may be asked to respond to a series of vignettes approximating various behavioral situations. For example, a social worker may assess, at least in a hypothetical sense, an adolescent's problem-solving behavior by presenting the adolescent with a series of problem-solving vignettes or situations and asking him or her to respond. As with role plays, this information can be used to help the adolescent improve his or her problem-solving skills, which could be further assessed through the use of other vignette situations.

Role plays and other analogue methods are useful assessment measures of client behavior. They represent both indicators of client performance and mechanisms for helping clients improve their behavior.

Behavioral By-Products

Behavioral by-products are specific items or evidences that may be collected or accumulated as indicators of client behaviors. For example, cigarette butts may be collected to assess clients in a smoking cessation program. Similarly, weight gained or lost may serve as an indicator of client health functioning. The weight of the client may be verified by a set of scales; the readings serve as a behavioral by-product measure. As another example, a client who is agoraphobic (afraid to go into public places) may be asked to keep theater ticket stubs and other paraphernalia indicating his or her attendance at social or recreational events.

Behavioral by-products serve as objective indicators of client behaviors. They are naturally associated with and represent the behavior the client wants to change. Behavioral by-products are also easier for some clients to collect than a log or other written assignment.

Psychophysiological Measures

Psychophysiological measures are represented by mechanical and technological indices of client behaviors. These measures assess the client's physiological performance as it relates to behavior. Several devices of clinical significance have been developed and are currently used in clinical practice. Psychophysiological measures are frequently used in three categories of disorders: psychophysiological disorders (for example, high blood pressure), anxiety disorders (for example, stress symptoms, panic attacks); and sexual disorders (such as pedophilia and other deviant arousal syndromes) (Barlow et al., 1984). Examples of psychophysiological measures for each of these categories follow.

Psychophysiological Disorder.   The sphygmomanometer, an instrument that measures blood pressure, is frequently used. Various clinical biofeedback measures such as the electromyographic activity (EMG, a measure of tension or muscular contraction) and galvanic skin response (GSR, a measure of skin conductance) are also used.

Anxiety Disorder. Biofeedback equipment may be used to assess clients' anxiety and stress. Technology has increased the sophistication of biofeedback measures for clinical practice. For example, Davacon now produces a computerized biofeedback system that has the capability of completing a full physiological assessment of clients, including heart rate, EMG, GSR, and other measures. This biofeedback program administers a stress test to the client in conjunction with the other measures. Appendix 3B presents an example of a psycho-physiological assessment profile performed on a client by a biofeedback assessment program (Shannon, 1990). Stress tests and the like are also available on the Internet.

Sexual Disorders. The most common psycho-physiological measure used for assessment and treatment of sexual disorders is the plethysmograph, a direct measure of penile circumference. In the clinical setting, males with sexual deviations (e.g., pedophiles) are exposed to both appropriate and inappropriate sexual stimuli and measures of penile arousal are obtained in conjunction with self-reports of sexual arousal. The plethysmograph makes it possible to measure deviant sexual arousal and is an aid to the assessment and treatment of clients with sexual disorders (Barlow et al., 1984).

Psycho-physiological measures are important indices of client behaviors. Technological and mechanical devices greatly increase our ability to make scientifically valid and reliable assessments of client functioning in this domain. These measures, therefore, have significance for both clinical practice and research.

Goal Attainment Scaling Measures

Goal attainment scaling (GAS) is a method used to measure change in client problems according to their treatment goals (Corcoran, Gingerich, Gingerich, & Briggs, 2001), and thus to evaluate practice. GAS has been used primarily by social workers to evaluate specific client or program outcomes (Jordan et al., 1992). It is useful to the monitoring functions of assessment because it allows practitioners and clients to operationalize and determine different levels of progress toward treatment goals. Outcomes or progress indicators range from "most unfavorable" to "best anticipated" (Jordan et al., 1992). Table 3.3 shows an example of a GAS used in a crisis intervention center where two problem areas are evaluated: education and suicide.

Goal attainment scaling is an effective method for assessing clinical change in clients. GAS is a relevant and adaptable form of measurement

Table 3.3   Goal Attainment Scaling

Check whether or not the Scale has been mutually negotiated between patient & CIC interviewer.	Scale Headings and Scale Weights
	Yes _____ No _____ Yes _____
	No _____

Scale Attainment Level (WI = 20)	Scale 1: Education (W2 = 30)	Scale 2: Suicide
a. Most unfavorable treatment outcome thought likely. (–2)	Patient has made no attempt to enroll in high school. X	Patient has committed suicide.
b. Less expected success w/treatment. (–1)	Patient has enrolled in high school, but at time of follow-up has dropped out.	Patient had acted on at least one suicidal impulse since her first contact w/ the CIC, but has not succeeded.*
c. Expected level of treatment success. (0)	Patient has enrolled and is in school at follow-up, but is attending class sporadically (misses an average of more than a third of her class during a week).	Patient reports she has had at least 4 suicidal impulses since her first contact with the CIC but has not acted on any of them.
d. More than expected success with treatment.	Patient has enrolled, is in school at follow-up, and is attending classes consistently, but has no vocational goal.*	
e. Best anticipated success with treatment. (=2)	Patient has enrolled, is in school at follow-up, is attending classes consistently, and has some vocational goal.	Patient reports she has had no suicidal impulses since her first contact with the CIC.

X = Level at Intake
* = Level at Follow-up

SOURCE: Reid, W. and Smith, A. (1981). *Research in social work*. New York: Columbia University Press.

that has a proven record of success in measuring client change across diverse clinical settings.

Standardized Measures

Standardized measures are ready-made instruments with proven records. They are unique in that their statistical and psychometric properties have been researched. Standardization refers to uniformity of procedures when scoring and administering the measure. Generally, social work practitioners can have confidence in these measures and in their ability to assess the client behaviors for which they were developed.

Standardized assessment measures assess a broad spectrum of client behaviors, such as personality, intelligence, marital satisfaction, self-esteem, and just about all aspects of human behavior (Corcoran & Fischer, 2000a, 2000b). Some standardized measures assess global behaviors such as personality (e.g., the Personality Inventory for Children [Lachar, 1982]), and specific behaviors such as level of dysphoric mood (for example, the Beck Depression Inventory II, [Beck, 1978]). Self-report standardized measures exist, as well as measures that may be completed by others, for example, parents, teachers, or some informed individual. Both rapid assessment instruments and lengthy, comprehensive measures are available. See figure 3.7 for an example of a rapid assessment instrument, the Index of Self Esteem (Hudson, 1989).

Standardized measures generally make use of two points of reference that aid in their interpretation: criterion referenced and norm referenced points. These methods may be combined, however. Criterion referenced measures interpret specific content to be mastered. Clients' scores are interpreted based on their ability to master a certain number of items on the measure (Anastasi, 1988). As an example, criterion referenced standardized measures are used frequently in education to measure educational achievement. Norm referenced measures are used for interpretation of a specific population. Client scores on the measure are compared to the scores of a normative group of persons who have taken the measure. Rather than criterion referenced measures, norm reference standardized measures are generally used in clinical situations, so that the normative characteristics of clients may be assessed. However, both types of measures may be used in clinical situations.

Standardized measures represent the most useful quantitative clinical measurement tools available to practitioners. Box 3.1 provides a list of reference sources where practitioners can discover and review standardized measures. Appendix 3C provides a list of selected sources for obtaining standardized measures. Because of their importance to clinical assessment, norm referenced, standardized measurement instruments are discussed in more detail in Chapter 4.

Projective Measures

Projective measures, used widely in clinical practice, are less structured than the other quantitative assessment tools we have discussed in this chapter. Projective measures typically assign a task that allows an unlimited variety of possible responses (Anastasi, 1988). For example, a client is given a partially completed sentence to finish or is shown a picture and asked to describe what is happening. The most famous of projective meas-

Figure 3.7   Index of Self-Esteem (ISE)

INDEX OF SELF-ESTEEM (ISE)

Name: _____   Today's Date: _____

Context: _____

This questionnaire is designed to measure how you see yourself. It is not a test, so there are no right or wrong answers. Please answer each item as carefully and as accurately as you can by placing a number beside each one as follows.

    1 = None of the time
    2 = Very rarely
    3 = A little of the time
    4 = Some of the time
    5 = A good part of the time
    6 = Most of the time
    7 = All of the time

---

1. ____ I feel that people would not like me if they really knew me well.
2. ____ I feel that others get along much better than I do.
3. ____ I feel that I am a beautiful person.
4. ____ When I am with others I feel they are glad I am with them.
5. ____ I feel that people really like to talk with me.
6. ____ I feel that I am a very competent person.
7. ____ I think I make a good impression on others.
8. ____ I feel that I need more self-confidence.
9. ____ When I am with strangers I am very nervous.
10. ____ I think that I am a dull person.
11. ____ I feel ugly.
12. ____ I feel that others have more fun than I do.
13. ____ I feel that I bore people.
14. ____ I think my friends find me interesting.
15. ____ I think I have a good sense of humor.
16. ____ I feel very self-conscious when I am with strangers.
17. ____ I feel that if I could be more like other people I would have it made.
18. ____ I feel that people have a good time when they are with me.
19. ____ I feel like a wallflower when I go out.
20. ____ I feel I get pushed around more than others.
21. ____ I think I am a rather nice person.
22. ____ I feel that people really like me very much.
23. ____ I feel that I am a likeable person.
24. ____ I am afraid I will appear foolish to others.
25. ____ My friends think very highly of me.

3, 4, 5, 6, 7, 14, 15, 18, 21, 22, 23, 25.

---

ures is the Rorschach (Exner, 2001). The majority of projective measures are designed to assess global personality functioning and uncover hidden or unconscious personality processes. Most of these measures are based on psychoanalytic concepts (Anastasi, 1988) and have been widely criticized

Box 3.1
Resources for the Review of Standardized Measures

Books

Corcoran, K., & Fischer, J. (2000a). *Measures for Clinical Practice: A sourcebook Vol. 1, Couples and Families and Children.* New York: Free Press.

Corcoran, K., & Fischer, J. (2000b). *Measures for Clinical Practice: A sourcebook Vol. 2, Adults.* New York: Free Press.

Hudson, W. W. (1997). *Walmyr Assessment Scales.* Tallahassee, FL: Walmyr Publishing.

Keyser, D. J., & Sweetland, R. C. (Eds.). *Test Critiques, Vol. 8.* Austin, TX: Pro Ed.

McCubbin, H. I., Thompson, A. I., & McCubbin, M. A. (1996). *Family Assessment: Resilience, Coping, and Adaptation. Inventories for Research and Practice.* Madison, WI: University of Wisconsin Press.

Murphy, L. L., Plake, B. S., Impara, J. C., & Spies, R. A. (2002). *Tests in Print VI.* Lincoln, NE: Buros Institute of Mental Measurement.

Olin, J. T., & Keatinge, C. (1998). *Rapid Psychological Assessments.* New York: Wiley.

Plake, B. S., Impara, J. C., & Spies, R. A. (2003). *The fifteenth mental measurements yearbook.* Lincoln, NE: Buros Institute of Mental Measurement.

On-line Location Services and Reviews of Tests and Measures

See the comprehensive list and critical reviews of most commercially available tests and measures available on-line at Buros Institute http://www.unl.edu/buros.

Review tests through the ERIC TEST LOCATOR http://ericae.net/test-col.htm.

Find all kinds of test and measures located and reviewed at All the Tests.Com http://www.allthetests.com.

Review psychological tests at The American Psychological Association website http://www.apa.org/science/faq-findtests.html.

Discover measures and reviews of fun measures at Barbarians On-line Test page. Take the fun Learning Styles Inventory measure and have it scored on-line http://www.wizardrealm.com/tests/index.html.

by researchers for their clinical inadequacies and their lack of psychometric properties such as reliability and validity (Anastasi, 1988; Fredman & Sherman, 1987; Leiter, 1989). From this perspective, they may not be quantitative measures at all, in the psychometric sense. (We cover psychometric properties in Chapter 4.) Furthermore, with the exception of certain psychoanalytic constructs such as defense mechanisms, projective measures are not useful in tracking client progress in treatment.

Despite these criticisms, however, projective measures continue to be a favorite clinical assessment and measurement tool for clinicians (Anastasi, 1988; Fredman & Sherman, 1987; Leiter, 1989). Their continued popularity may be because of their viability as a clinical technique for unraveling the intricacies and subtleties of client functioning. Clinicians prefer projective measures because they reach for latent or broad aspects of client functioning. These allow clinicians to make more global interpretations, rather than just narrow approaches to assessment, like the rapid assessment instruments. In this sense, they are similar to the clinical interview, for they rely on the interpretations and judgments of the interviewer. Although projective measures have several weaknesses as a quantitative measure, they may be useful in a comprehensive assessment to generate global hypotheses about client characteristics such as personality or intelligence. Because they are vastly popular as a clinical technique and also a measure of client attributes, a few commonly used projective measures are described here.

Incomplete sentence forms are one commonly used group of projective measures. Uncompleted sentences are presented to the client; these allow almost unlimited varieties of possible completions. "My mother never . . .," "What worries me . . .," and "My father . . .," are some examples of incomplete sentences. Incomplete sentences are used to solicit clinical themes, relevant personality, and affective characteristics of the client.

The Draw-A-Person test (DAP) and the Good-Enough Harris Drawing test (Harris, 1963) are some of the other frequently used projective measures. The latter first gained respect as a nonverbal measure of intelligence. A set of norms have been developed for its use as a measure of intellectual maturity in children (Harris, 1963). The norms are rather dated, though. In this measure, the child is instructed to draw the best picture he or she can, of him- or herself and a woman. Credit is given for the inclusion of individual body parts, clothing details, proportion, perspective, and similar features. A level of intellectual maturity score can be determined based on a standard score with a mean of one hundred and a standard deviation of fifteen demonstrating the quantitative aspect of the measure (Harris, 1963). See Chapter 4 for a discussion of standard scores. The DAP test has also been used to infer personality characteristics. There appears to be some support for the use of the measure in the assessment of intellectual maturity (Dunn, 1967; Harris, 1963). However, it has been widely criticized as a personality measure (Fredman & Sherman, 1987).

The inkblot technique known as the Rorschach (Rorschach, 1921/ 1942) and the **picture story technique known as the Thematic Apperception Test** (TAT [Murray, 1938]) are popular projective measures used in clinical practice. The Rorschach requires clients to respond to a series of ten cards on which an inkblot is printed. Five cards are black and have shades of grey, two cards have some red, and the remaining three cards are of assorted pastel colors. Personality functioning is inferred from what the person reports seeing in the inkblots. Over the years, clinical psychologists have worked to standardize the answers a client may give to an inkblot shape and to develop norms for the cards. The Exner interpretive system (Exner, 2001) for the Rorschach provides such a standardization and has been both praised and criticized for its success in making the Rorschach conform to the rigor of validity and reliability needed for making a psychiatric diagnosis (see Wood, Garb, Lilienfeld, & Nezworski, 2002 for a review of the criticisms of the Exner system). Two of the most glaring criticisms have to do with the way the Exner norms make many normal adults and children appear to have severe psychopathologies and how the Exner scoring system does not conform to *DSM* diagnostic categories. The Rorschach measure has also failed in areas of construct validity by showing little or no correlation with more objective, self-report measures. Most noteable for social work practice, the Rorschach may have little validity or reliability when used with ethnic minorities. Recent research studies have shown that the Exner system did not perform well with American minorities (Ephraim, 2000). See Chapter 10 for further discussions about the limitations of measurement instruments with American minorities.

The Exner system scores responses on a variety of dimensions such as color, shading, movement, and location on the inkblot (Exner, 2001). What is actually assessed is a person's characteristic style of dealing with stimuli. Through Rorschach assessment, it is possible to ascertain a client's unique response style toward affective, ideational, perceptual, and interpersonal content (Howard, 1989). A client's strengths and weaknesses, and a diagnostic profile may also be inferred. The Rorschach is a measure that requires a great deal of sophistication and training to administer and score. Howard (1989) documents progress toward developing an empirically based scoring system for the Rorschach. Scoring systems such as the one developed by Exner (2001) seek to add to the validity of the measure but have has failed to do so. The Rorschach is typically not administered by social workers or other counselors but remains a tool of clinical psychologists. See appendix 3D for a sample write-up from a psychological evaluation (Pharis, 1990). Background information on the client is also provided to focus the reader's attention on the salient characteristics of the case.

The TAT, widely used by a variety of counseling professionals, consists of nineteen cards with simple black-and-white drawings of people interacting, and one blank card (Anastasi, 1988). Clinicians frequently use ten or twelve cards for their assessment. The client is asked to make up a story to represent each picture. The clinician further instructs the client to describe what is happening at that moment in the story, the events leading up to the story, how the characters are feeling, what they are thinking, and the outcome of the story. A good amount of information is published concerning the typical response characteristics for each card. Clinical practitioners, however, usually rely on their own interpretations of the themes, roles, and affective characteristics expressed in the stories, to develop an understanding of the client's personality and psychological functioning (Anastasi, 1988). This measure has lagged behind in its cultural relevance and should be used with caution for ethnic minority groups (Velasquez, 1995). See appendix 3D for a write-up of a TAT from a psychological report (Pharis, 1990).

Projective measures are widely used in clinical practice and have become an entrenched part of clinical assessment. Regardless of their validity or reliability, they will continue to be used. Research indicates that projective measures as a quantitative measurement instrument have several weaknesses, but as a clinical technique they may be extremely valuable in generating global hypothesis about the client. Social workers should be skeptical, however, about what can be determined by these instruments and should view their interpretation with extreme caution. As measures, projective assessment tools are the weakest of all psychological measures.

GUIDELINES FOR DEVELOPING A MEASUREMENT SYSTEM FOR CLIENT ASSESSMENT

Thus far in this chapter we have discussed the need for using quantitative measurement as a part of assessment. We have also summarized ten methods of measuring client behaviors that may be used by practitioners. Table 3.4 presents a conceptual representation of these methods. With so many different methods for measuring client behaviors available, it may be difficult for social work practitioners to decide which methods to use in their assessment. This section offers guidelines to help practi-

Table 3.4   Measurement Method Summary

Ask & Interpret	Watch	Ask
Interpretive Report	Observe and/or obtain objective indicators from other sources	Self-Report and/or obtain objective indicators from the client
Projective Measures	Direct Behavioral Observation (frequency, duration, and interval), Rating Scales, Goal Attainment Scaling, Standardized Measures, Psychophysiological Measures, Role Plays/ Analogue Situations, Behavioral By-Products	Logs, Journals, Diaries, Structured Behavioral Report Forms, Goal Attainment Scaling, Standardized Measures, Role Plays/Analogue Situations, Behavioral By-Products

tioners develop a measurement system for client assessments. General guidelines are followed by specific suggestions for development of an assessment plan.

Practitioners should use multiple methods to measure client behaviors. Ideally, both a self-report and a report of another rater should be used. For example, a client reporting depression could be administered the Beck Depression Inventory, and also be assessed based on information provided by a relative regarding the specific behavioral symptoms of depression, such as crying, isolating herself, not going to work, and so forth.

Practitioners should develop baseline indicators of client functioning. Baseline data that is considerably different from a general population may be used to evidence treatment necessity, Alternatively, scores at the baseline that are similar to a clinical sample also suggest the need for treatment. All measures should be given on at least a pretest and posttest basis. Follow-ups are also desirable.

Practitioners should use at least one repeated measure. This means that clients' behavior should be measured on several occasions to monitor their progress during the course of treatment. This approach is consistent with the single subject design approach described in detail in Chapter 11.

Include both specific measures and global measures of client problems. Doing so increases the likelihood that you will capture changes in the client behaviors.

Following these general guidelines, an ideal measurement system for client assessment might include:

- A standardized measure or a client log or self-anchored scale (self-report)
- A behavioral observation (self-report)
- A standardized rating scale, or do-it-yourself rating scale (significant other-report)

In developing a measurement system, it is important to not overwhelm the client with too many measures, yet collect multiple and repeated measures of the client problems. Good measurement, like good practice, requires knowledge, creativity, and flexibility of the practitioner. Similar to other practice skills, clinical measurement is as much art as science. A clinical measurement system, therefore, should be as unique as clients and their situations dictate. Clients may also find scores useful as they self-monitor their change.

SUMMARY

Clinical quantitative measurement involves operationally defining client behavior and attributes to obtain an objective assessment. Quantitative measurement requires practitioners to devise or use methods for assigning numerical indicators and objective qualitative indicators to be-haviors or attributes. Including measures as part of the assessment pro-vides objective sources of data and helps practitioners verify their opin-ions and judgments concerning client functioning. Ten methods of measurement that may be used by practitioners were discussed: 1) client self-reporting and monitoring, 2) self-anchored and rating scales, 3) ques-tionnaires, 4) direct behavioral observation, 5) role play and analogue sit-uations, 6) behavioral by-products, 7) psycho-physiological measures, 8) goal attainment scaling, 9) standardized measures, and 10) projective measures. Examples of these methods of measurement were provided.

Guidelines for developing a measurement system for assessment were also provided. Four important guidelines are: 1) using multiple methods, 2) developing baseline indicators of client functioning, 3) using repeated measures, and 4) using both global and specific measures. An ideal measurement system for assessment was also discussed.

This chapter has provided a broad overview of quantitative assess-ment methods. In Chapter 4 we will discuss in more detail standardized norm referenced, assessment measures frequently used in clinical prac-tice. In addition, computerized assessment technologies and database systems will be described. These methods are singled out for discussion because of their long history, their increased use in clinical assessment, and the inadequate training workers receive in understanding these quantitative assessment tools. Chapter 4 will provide background infor-mation that is essential to the use and interpretation of standardized as-sessment measures. Computerized assessment technologies will also be summarized to familiarize practitioners with the increasing sophistica-tion and practice relevance of standardized assessment methods.

REFERENCES

Anastasi, A. (1988). *Psychological testing* (6th ed.). New York: Macmillan.

Barlow, D. H., Hayes, S. C., & Nelson, R. O. (1984). *The scientist practitioner: Re-search and accountability in clinical and educational settings.* New York: Pergamon.

Barlow, D., & Hersen, M. (1984). *Single case experimental designs; Strategies for studying behavior change.* New York: Pergamon.

Beck, A. (1978). *Beck depression inventory.* San Antonio, TX: Psychological Corpo-ration.

Bloom, M., & Fischer, J. (1982). *Evaluating practice: Guidelines for the accountable pro-fessional.* Englewood Cliffs, NJ: Prentice-Hall.

Bloom, M., Fischer, J., & Orme, J. G. (2002). *Evaluating practice: Guidelines for the ac-countable professional* (4th ed.). Englewood Cliffs, NJ: Prentice-Hall.

Campbell, J. A. (1988). Client acceptance of single-system evaluation procedures. *Social Work Research and Abstracts, 24*(2), 21–22.

Corcoran, K. & Boyer-Quick, J. (2002). How clinicians can effectively use assessment tools to establish treatment necessity and throughout the treatment process. In A. Roberts & G. Greene (Eds.), *Social work desk reference* (pp. 00–00). New York: Oxford University Press.

Corcoran, K., & Fischer, J. (2000a). *Measures for clinical practice: A sourcebook. Vol. 1 Couples, families, & children.* New York: The Free Press.

Corcoran, K., & Fischer, J. (2000b). *Measures for clinical practice: A sourcebook, Vol. 2 Adults.* New York: The Free Press.

Corcoran, K., Gingerich, W. J., & Briggs, H. E. (2001). Practice evaluation: Setting goals and monitoring change. In H. E. Briggs & K. Corcoran (Eds.), *Social work practice: Treating common client practice* (pp. 66–84). Chicago: Lyceum.

Corcoran, K., & Vandiver, V. L. (1996). *Maneuvering the maze of managed care: Skills for mental health practitioners.* New York: Free Press.

Deschner, J. P. (1984). *The hitting habit: Anger control for battering couples.* New York: Free Press.

Dunn, J. A. (1967). Inter- and intra-rater reliability of the new Harris-Goodenough Draw-A-Man Test. *Perceptual and Motor Skills, 24,* 269–270.

Ellis, A. (1985). Expanding the ABC's of rational-emotive therapy. In M. Mahoney & A. Freeman (Eds.), *Cognition and psychotherapy* (pp. 313–323). New York: Plenum.

Ephraim, D. (2000). Culturally relevant research and practice with the Rorschach comprehensive system. In R. H. Dana (Ed.), *Handbook of cross cultural/multicultural personality assessment.* Personality and clinical psychology series (pp. 303–327). Mahwah, NJ: Lawrence Erlbaum Associates, Inc.

Exner, J. E. (2001). *A Rorschach workbook for the comprehensive system* (5th ed.). Asheville, NC: Rorschach Workshops.

Franklin, C. (1982). *Gottman couples communication rating scale.* Unpublished rating scale.

Franklin, C., & Jordan, C. (1992). Teaching students to perform assessment. *The Journal of Social Work Education, 28*(2), 222–241.

Franklin, C., McNeil, J., & Wright, R. (1990). School social work works: Findings from an alternative school for dropouts. *Social Work in Education, 12*(3), 177–194.

Franklin, C., & Streeter, C. L. (1992). Social support and psychoeducational interventions with middle class dropout youth. *Child and Adolescent Social Work, 9,* 131–153.

Fredman, N., & Sherman, R. (1987). *Handbook of measurements for marriage and family therapy.* New York: Brunner/Mazel.

Gottman, J., Notararius, C., Gonso, J., & Markman, H. (1976). *A couple's guide to communication.* Champaign, IL: Research Press.

Harris, D. B. (1963). *Children's drawings as measures of intellectual maturity: A revision and extension of the Goodenough Draw-a-Man Test.* New York: Harcourt Brace Jovanovich.

Hepworth, D. H., & Larsen, J. A. (1989). *Direct social work practice: Theory and skills* (3rd ed.). Belmont, CA: Wadsworth.

Howard, J. C. (1989). The Rorschach Test: Standardization and contemporary developments. In S. Wetzler & M. M. Katz (Eds.), *Contemporary approaches to psychological assessment* (pp. 127–153). New York: Brunner/Mazel.

Hudson, W. W. (1989). *Computer assisted social services.* Tempe, AZ: Walmyr Publishing.

Jordan, C., Franklin, C., & Corcoran, K. (2001). Standardized measures. In R. M. Grinnell, Jr. (Ed.), *Social work research and evaluation* (6th ed., pp. 198–209). Itasca, IL: Peacock.

Lachar, D. (1982). *Personality inventory for children (PIC) revised format manual supplement.* Los Angeles: Western Psychological Services.

Lazarus, A. (1991). *Multi-modal life history inventory.* Champaign, IL: Research Press.

Leiter, E. (1989). The role of projective testing. In S. Wetzler & M. M. Katz (Eds.), *Contemporary approaches to psychological testing* (pp. 118–126). New York: Brunner/Mazel.

Murray, H. A. (1938). *Exploration in personality.* New York: Oxford University Press.

Pharis, M. (1990). *Sample write-up on the Rorschach and TAT.* Unpublished psychological report.

Polster, R., & Dangel, R. (1989). Behavioral parent training in family therapy. In B. A. Thyer (Ed.), *Behavioral family therapy* (pp. 31–77). Springfield, IL: Charles C Thomas.

Rorschach, H. (1942). *Psychodiagnostics: A diagnostic test based on perception* (P. Lemkau & B. Kronenburg, Trans.). Berne, Switzerland: Huber (U.S. distributor, Grune & Stratton). (Original work published 1921)

Shannon, C. (1990). Biofeedback stress analysis using the Davacon system. Unpublished report from private practice.

Sheafor, B., Horejsi, C., & Horejsi, G. (1988). *Techniques and guidelines for social work practice.* Newton, MA: Allyn & Bacon.

Velasquez, R. J. (1995). Personality assessment of Hispanic clients. In J. N. Butcher (Ed.), *Clinical personality assessment: Practical approaches* (pp. 120–139). New York: Oxford University Press.

Wood, J. M., Garb, H. N., Lilienfeld, S. O., & Nezworski, T. (2002). Clinical assessment. *Annual Review of Psychology, 53*, 519–543.

CHAPTER 4

Standardized Assessment Measures and Computer-Assisted Assessment Technologies

David Springer and Cynthia Franklin

Once thought to be the domain of psychologists, standardized measures and computer-assisted assessment technologies continue to gain popularity with social work practitioners and other counselors for assessing clients (Baird & Wagner, 2000; Bloom, Fischer, & Orme, 1999; Blythe & Tripodi, 1989; Corcoran & Fischer, 2000; Grove, Zald, Lebow, Snitz, & Nelson, 2000; Hudson, 1982). Standardized assessment measures have long been used by practitioners from cognitive-behavioral and empirical practice orientations. Recall from Chapters 1 and 2 that practitioners trained in the empirical practice models value scientific practice and single case designs as important parts of the assessment process. That is why standardized measures are often used by more empirically oriented practitioners. Unfortunately, many social workers have not been thoroughly trained in standardized assessment methodologies. So we have devoted this chapter to their uses in clinical assessment.

Standardized measures encompass a wide range of assessment tools, including but not limited to personality assessment instruments, behavior-rating scales, social attitude scales, measures of marriage and family functioning, achievement tests, measures of cognitive functioning, and aptitude measures (Anastasi, 1988; Corcoran & Fischer, 2000; Fredman & Sherman, 1987; Grotevant & Carlson, 1989; Jordan, Franklin, & Corcoran, 1997). Computerized assessment technologies have been developed for many standardized measures, and computers are increasingly being used to aid practitioners in making clinical judgments (Garb, 1998, 2000).

The goal of this chapter is to help practitioners become informed consumers in the selection, use, and interpretation of standardized measurement instruments. Major issues involved in the development, evaluation, and interpretation of standardized measures are explored, as are applications of standardized assessment systems that use computer technologies.

Standardization is essential to the development of useful measures for clinical practice; it is defined in different but related ways by several different authors (Jordan et al., 1997). All definitions share two characteristics that distinguish a standardized measure from a nonstandardized measure.

First, standardized measures have uniform administration and scoring procedures. Measurement conditions and outcomes are clearly and completely specified to ensure comparability of the results. The development of the measure provides detailed directions about how the measure is to be given, to whom it is to be given, and the exact meanings of the results. Detailed directions include such information as materials to be used, oral instructions to be given while administering the measure, preliminary demonstrations, exact ways of scoring the measure, and meanings of the scores. These directions are often reported in a measurement manual that accompanies the measure at its purchase. All directions in the manual must be followed precisely to reduce or eliminate the influence of factors extraneous to the characteristic(s) of the client that are being assessed (Anastasi, 1988; Bloom, 1986; Graham & Lilly, 1984; Reid & Smith, 1981).

Second, standardization entails a process of establishing norms for a measure. A measure is thought to be standardized if it has gone through technical development involving a standardization sample (a large representative sample of people) used to establish its normalization (statistical properties). The establishment of norms is essential to the scoring and interpretation of the measure. Norms make the measure comparable across client groups and empirically define the limits and practicalities of the measure. For example, norms establish such relevant information as the average score on the measure, the deviations necessary to fall outside the average, and the client groups for which the measure is appropriate (Anastasi, 1988; Bloom, 1986; Graham & Lilly, 1984).

For a measure to be standardized, it must go through a rigorous process of research and development aimed at empirically verifying the measure's characteristics and usefulness. The level of research and development for different standardized measures varies greatly from minimal, crude standardization (such as, testing on a small group of college freshmen) to state-of-the-art development (e.g., testing on a large, representative national sample). As a rule of thumb, only the best and most technically developed standardized measures should be incorporated into practice situations (Jordan et al., 1997).

The remaining sections of this chapter will summarize important considerations for evaluation and use of standardized measures. First, the assessment of reliability of measures will be discussed. Second, methods for determining measurement validity will be examined. Third, norms, scoring, and interpretation of standardized measures will be summarized, and frequently used standard scoring systems will be explained. Fourth, the availability of computer-assisted assessment technologies will be summarized and illustrated. Fifth, the calculation and accounting for measurement error will be explained. Finally, clinical and ethical issues concerning the use of measures will be covered.

DETERMINING RELIABILITY

Reliability refers to the consistency of a measure and to its dependability and stability (Bloom et al., 1999; Corcoran & Fischer, 2000; Graham & Lilly, 1984; Sattler, 1988). A tool is reliable to the extent that it performs consistently over repeated uses. Reliability is understood by examining the reliability coefficient or by the standard error of measurement (explained below). A measure cannot be trusted if its reliability coefficient is low (Sattler, 1988). Reliability coefficients indicate the degree of consistency in the measurement of test scores, and range from 1.00 (perfect reliability) to 0.00 (no reliability). High reliability is especially important for measures incorporated into practice situations that will be used to guide clinical decision making. As the reliability of a measure decreases, so should our faith in it.

From the available measures, social workers should try to choose the assessment tools with the highest reliability. Four prominent methods for establishing reliability of measures are described below: test-retest, alternate form, split-half, and internal consistency.

Test-Retest Reliability

Test-retest reliability is an index of a measure's stability. The same test is given to the same client groups (subjects) on two different occasions, usually within a relatively short time (one week to a month or two). The Pearson product–moment correlation (Pearson's r), which indicates the relationship between two interval or ratio variables, is applied to the scores (Bostwick & Kyte, 1988; Rubin & Babbie, 2000). The obtained correlation coefficient is an indicator of how consistent the measure performs over time (Bostwick & Kyte, 1988; Rubin & Babbie, 2000; Sattler, 1988). To the extent that both sets of responses correlate with one another, test-retest reliability is established.

One challenge of establishing this type of reliability is that too much time between administrations of the measure allows for real change to take place in the group of clients, whereas too little time raises the possibility that the second set of responses are based on memory of the first administration. In either case, the obtained correlation coefficients will be misleading. This type of reliability may be difficult to establish and accurately interpret for scales that measure highly variable emotional and interpersonal traits (e.g., depression, anxiety). For this reason, test-retest reliability is not as useful as sometimes implied (Springer, Abell, & Hudson, 2000).

Alternate Form Reliability

Also called equivalent or parallel form reliability, alternate form reliability is obtained by giving two different but equivalent forms of the same measure to the same group of clients (Bostwick & Kyte, 1988; Rubin & Babbie, 2000; Sattler, 1988). The two sets of scores are then compared by computing a correlation coefficient (for example, Pearson's r). If there is no measurement error, clients should score the same on both measures, thus yielding a high correlation coefficient. This type of reliability is most commonly encountered when a scale developer wishes to establish a shorter version of a scale, say from twenty-five items to ten items, so that it is less time-consuming for clients to complete. A correlation coefficient of roughly 0.90 is needed to comfortably argue for the presence of alternate form reliability (Springer et al., 2002).

Split-Half Reliability

Split-half reliability is obtained by dividing a measure into two equivalent halves (Bostwick & Kyte, 1988; Rubin & Babbie, 2000; Sattler, 1988). Basically, the split-half method consists of administering one form of a scale to a group of subjects. The developer then uses half the items to compute one total score, and the other half to compute a second total score. The developer then computes a correlation between the two sets of scores. To the extent that the two halves correlate, split-half reliability is established. To use this method, all items must measure the same construct.

There is a limitation to this method of establishing reliability. The developer must decide how to divide the items. For example, on a thirty-item scale, one could create one half by taking the first fifteen items to create one score and the second set of fifteen items to create a second score. A more common practice is to create two sets of scores by using all of the odd-numbered items and even-numbered items to create two scores. The possibilities are infinite. In fact, for a thirty-item instrument, there are seventy-seven million estimates for split-half reliability (Hudson, 1999). Rather than choosing one of these estimates to determine the internal consistency of a new measure, the next approach allows us to effectively compute the average of all seventy-seven million estimates.

Internal-Consistency Reliability

Cronbach's (1951) coefficient alpha computes the mean of all possible split-half reliabilities. It is a measure of the internal consistency of a measure and is based on the positive intercorrelations of the scale's items (Kuder & Richardson, 1937). Computing the internal consistency of a measure allows one to estimate how consistently respondents performed across items of a measure. The internal consistency of a measure also lends support for evidence of its content validity.

Cronbach's alpha is appropriate for use with equal-appearing interval level data (such as, Likert type responses). For measures with a dichotomous (for example, yes-no) item response format, the Kuder–Richardson formula 20 (an equivalent procedure) should be computed.

Reliability Standards

A satisfactory degree of reliability depends on how a measure is intended to be used. For scales that are used in large group research efforts or scientific studies, a reliability coefficient of 0.60 or greater is needed (Hudson, 1982). Group research is typically concerned with mean differences among groups of subjects (for example, experimental versus comparison groups), but in clinical work, a higher reliability coefficient is needed for scales that will be used to help guide clinical decision making with individual clients. The reason for this standard is that, when working with an individual, there is no opportunity to average out the inevitable measurement error contained in the scale, as there is in group research. Measurement tools used to guide decision making about an individual client should have a minimum reliability coefficient of 0.80. Springer, Abell, and Nugent (2002) provide the following guidelines for acceptability of reliability coefficients for use with individuals:

$<.70$ = Unacceptable

.70 to .79 = Undesirable

.80 to .84 = Minimally acceptable

.85 to .89 = Respectable

.90 to .95 = Very Good

$>.95$ = Excellent

These reliability standards can help social workers make decisions about a scale's degree of reliability. The greater the seriousness of the problem being measured (e.g., suicidal risk), and the graver the consequences of being wrong, the higher the standard should be held.

Reliability is a necessary but not solely sufficient condition for ensuring that a scale has solid psychometric properties. If an instrument measures something consistently (indicating reliability), but does not do so accurately (indicating validity), that measure lacks clinical utility.

DETERMINING VALIDITY

Validity is concerned with the target and method of measurement of a particular measurement tool, that is, a tool is valid to the extent that it measures what it purports to measure. The client characteristics assessed by a particular measure can only be defined and verified by examination of the "objective sources of information and empirical operations utilized in establishing its validity" (Anastasi, 1988, p. 139).

Any information gathered as part of the process of developing or using a measure becomes relevant to its validity. No one type of validity is appropriate for every measurement situation. Validity must be verified with reference to the specific intended use of a measure (Anastasi, 1988; Graham & Lilly, 1984; Sattler, 1988). So, regarding a measurement tool, social workers must continually ask what and for whom is it valid? The answers to these questions can be determined only through examining the validity studies of a particular measure. All procedures for establishing measurement validity are concerned with the relationship between performance on the measure and other independent empirical criteria (Anastasi, 1988). Four methods for establishing measurement validity are described below: content validity, criterion validity (concurrent and predictive), construct validity (convergent and discriminant), and factorial analysis.

Content Validity

Content validity refers to the evaluation of items on a measure to determine if the content contained in the items relates to and is representative of the domain that the measure seeks to examine (Anastasi, 1988; Bostwick & Kyte, 1988; Rubin & Babbie, 2000; Sattler, 1988). For example, to select a measure that assesses behavioral disorders in children, it is necessary to examine the item universe (total number of items) of the measure to determine if the items on the measure include representative samples of the behavior of children. If the items relate only to depression, (e.g., I feel sad), the measure would not reflect the representative behavior domain of children. Although depression may be one dimension of that behavior domain, such a measure could not be said to have content validity (Jordan et al., 1997).

A measure reflecting representative samples of behavior for assessing behavior disorders in children would necessarily be multidimensional (measuring several different traits or behaviors) rather than unidimensional (measuring one trait or behavior). For instance, the measure would include items covering hyperactive behavior, antisocial behavior, and anxious behavior as well as depression. Several measures of this caliber have been developed (e.g., the Revised Behavior Problem Checklist [Quay, 1987], the Achenbach Child Behavior Checklist (CBCL) [Achenbach & Edelbrock, 1983]), the Child and Adolescent Functional Assessment Scale (CAFAS) [Hodges, 1994]. Such measures are said to have good content validity because they reflect the domain of interest (behavior disorders of children) and include questions that reflect representative samples of the types of behavior that are to be measured (such as, hyperactivity—fidgets in seat, antisocial—fights with other children, etc. [Jordan et al., 1997]).

To ensure the representativeness of a measure and its subsequent content validity, items to be included in the measure must be chosen carefully. According to Hudson (1981), developing the content of an item is the single most important step in developing a measure or selecting one for use. Items should represent the specific characteristics one wishes to measure.

Two basic methods are used to determine inclusion of items on measures; these are the *rational-intuitive method* and the *empirical method* (Jordan et al., 1997):

The rational-intuitive method involves choosing items logically. For example, items might be generated from a group of experts (such as, clinical social workers) asked to suggest items for determining the presence of a high-risk behavior such as suicide. The items generated by the group of experts would be examined, and dissimilar items would be excluded. Following the rational-intuitive approach, once items are selected, they are arranged in groups that appear to logically measure the same concept. For example, in measuring risk for suicide, one group of items might relate to a client's level of impulse control (e.g., drug usage, temper tantrums, etc.) and another group might relate to immediate danger of suicidal action (for example, having a clear plan, availability of means, and so on [Jordan et al., 1997]).

The empirical method involves selecting items for a measure through research or statistical techniques. For example, in developing a battering severity scale, Deschner (1986) had college students rank order items (e.g., cries in front of partner, hits partner, kills partner) according to their perceptions of item severity in relationship to fighting between couples. Through this method it was possible to scale the items and empirically verify their significance. Hambleton (1980) has provided a method for ranking how well an item measures its intended construct. Using Hambleton's schema, an expert reviewer would rate each item on a scale (or domain of that scale) as follows: assign +1 if the item measures the construct, assign 0 if the reviewer is uncertain, and assign –1 if the item does not measure the construct.

Additional statistical methods, such as factor analysis, are commonly used for selecting items for measures. In the development of social work measures a combination of both the rational-intuitive and empirical methods is often used (Jordan et al., 1997). For example, in the development of the Adolescent Concerns Evaluation (ACE) (Springer, 1998) discussed later in the section on factorial analysis, items were first reviewed by experts (rational-intuitive method), but later tested using factorial analysis techniques (empirical method).

Hudson (1981) has proposed two rules for determining content validity of a measure: "A clear and unambiguous definition of the variable or construct to be measured should be available," and "Each item should represent some aspect of the variable or construct being measured" (p. 197). Hudson suggests that social workers examine the items of the measure and use the best possible wisdom, training, experience, insight, and intuition in determining if a measure has content validity.

Criterion Validity

Criterion validity relates to the scores on the measure in relationship to some type of criterion (Bostwick & Kyte, 1988; Rubin & Babbie, 2000; Sattler, 1988). Procedures for criterion validity help to establish a measure's accuracy in identifying client characteristics or predicting client performance on specific activities (Anastasi, 1988). The results are checked against an empirical criterion and must be measurable, free from bias, and relevant to the purposes of the measure (Anastasi, 1988; Sattler, 1988). Research is done to establish the correlations (relationships) between scores on the measure and the outcomes of these independent, empirical criteria. If appropriate relationships are found, then social work practitioners can be confident that the measure is a useful tool for categorizing or predicting behavior.

This confidence is based on the measure's ability to produce the same results as the independent, objective criterion. For example, if a team of mental health professionals evaluates the clients, and a psychiatric assessment measure constantly assigns the same diagnosis for clients, the measure is said to have good criterion validity.

The criterion that is used to validate the measure may be obtained at approximately the same time as the measure is given or at some future point. Authors often differentiate between *concurrent* and *predictive* criterion validity by these time relations (Anastasi, 1988; Bostwick & Kyte, 1988; Rubin & Babbie, 2000).

Concurrent validity is based on a current criterion or a criterion existing at the same time the measure is given and is useful for measures involved in diagnosis or assigning existing status (Anastasi, 1988; Bostwick & Kyte, 1988; Rubin & Babbie, 2000). The example given previously concerning a measure's ability to formulate a consistent psychiatric diagnosis in relationship to an independent criterion (diagnosis by mental health team) is an illustration of concurrent validity of a measure. There are two primary types of concurrent criterion validity: 1) known-instruments validity and 2) known-groups validity.

Known-instruments validity is established to the extent that one's new measure correlates highly with a pre-existing instrument that measures the same construct of interest. For example, a newly developed scale to measure clinical depression could be compared to an already existing scale that measured depression. If the scores from these two scales correlated, then known-instruments validity would be evidenced.

To the extent that this new depression measure was able to distinguish between groups of people that one would expect to be clinically depressed from those that one would not expect to be depressed, known-groups validity would be established, that is, a scale's ability to distinguish between groups of people who possess the construct being measured from those who do not demonstrates known-groups validity for that scale.

Predictive validity is based on a future, after-the-fact criterion, and is necessary if a measure is going to be involved in specialized selection or classification (Anastasi, 1988). For instance, college entrance exams are assumed to have a certain degree of predictive validity. To establish predictive validity, the scores on the measures are compared to a person's later college grade point average or other college performance criteria. High correlations between scores on the measure and subsequent behavior indicate that the measures have good predictive validity.

Construct Validity

Construct validity is the highest form of validity. It ensures that we are measuring the client behaviors under assessment. This type of validity is concerned with the degree of measurement of a theoretical construct or trait (Anastasi, 1988; Bostwick & Kyte, 1988; Rubin & Babbie, 2000; Sattler, 1988). A construct is a concept that has been invented for the purpose of inquiry. It is a variable that can be studied or measured and is believed to be important to the development of theories. Constructs derive from theories and are developed to explain and organize observed responses. Many measures are developed to assess various constructs.

Anastasi (1988) discusses six ways for establishing construct validity of a measure:

1. Research on the measure's ability to reflect developmental changes of clients. This is a traditional criterion for the construct of the intelligence quotient (IQ). Intelligence measures should reflect increases in IQ as children get older; that these developmental changes are reflected in the test scores is taken as evidence of the measure's construct validity.

2. Validation of new measures of related constructs; using other measures. An old measure with proven construct validity may be utilized to demonstrate the construct validity of a new measure. The trick here is for the measure to correlate only moderately highly with the old measure; if its correlation is too high, there may not be a good reason for developing the new measure. It should add something unique or different (for example, it may be shorter or more specific).

3. Factor analysis. This statistical technique is particularly relevant to establishing construct validity because it can be used to identify underlying dimensions of traits or behaviors as well as the common factors existing in or between measures. (This technique is discussed further later.)

4. Statistical techniques to demonstrate the internal consistency of a measure (see section on internal consistency reliability). In this method the criterion becomes the total score on the test itself. Sometimes an adaptation of the contrasted group method is used. Biserial correlations between pass-fail on each item representing the constructs and the total test score are also used (biserial correlations relate a continuous distributed variable with a dichotomous one). Only those items yielding significant item-total measure correlations are retained. A measure whose items were selected by this method can be said to show internal consistency. Each item differentiates among clients in the same direction as does the score on the entire measure. This adds to the measure's construct validity by ensuring consistency in all dimensions of the measure.

5. Establishment of convergent and discriminant validation of a measure. It is important in construct validation for a measure to be shown to correlate with measures of like constructs (convergent construct validity). It is equally important for a measure to be shown to not correlate with measures of dissimilar constructs (discriminant construct validity). For example, a measure of depression should correlate highly with other measures of hopelessness and depression and correlate negatively with a measure of expectancy or mood elation. To truly argue for the presence of construct validity, both convergent and discriminant validity must be established for the scale.

6. Experimental interventions. For example, to validate an anxiety measure, clients may be administered an anxiety measure and then subjected to some type of anxiety-raising stimuli (such as taking an examination under distracting circumstances). Clients may then be retested to see if their anxiety scores rise. If they do rise, this may be taken as evidence for the measure's ability to reflect current anxiety (pp. 152–158).

A measure that demonstrates construct validity is well developed and may be confidently used in practice situations as an indicator of the client characteristics under consideration.

Factorial Analysis

The purposes of factorial analysis are to examine the interrelationships of behavioral data such as scale items, to group items, and to make it possible to identify the underlying dimension or trait for a set of items (Anastasi, 1988). Simply stated, data can be simplified by reducing the number of items from many to the most relevant ones that best capture the construct of interest.

To illustrate the Adolescent Concerns Evaluation (ACE) (Springer, 1998) will be used. The ACE is a forty-item instrument that measures the degree to which a youth is at risk of running away from home. It consists of four separate-yet-interdependent domains: Family, School, Peer, and Individual. The Family domain is composed of twelve items; each of which clusters (correlates) more strongly with the Family domain than with the other domains, that is, together they create a domain of items that captures how an adolescent perceives his or her family life. In contrast, suppose items that were intended to measure school functioning loaded more strongly onto the Peer domain. The factorial structure of both the School and Peer domains would be called into question. However, for the ACE, the Family domain (twelve items), School domain (nine items), Peer domain (seven items) and Individual domain (twelve items) load onto (correlate) with the domain for which they were intended. Thus, there is evidence for the factorial validity of the ACE. Additionally, because the items load onto the factors for which they were intended, there is also support for the ACE's content and construct validity.

A detailed description of factorial analysis and its uses in measurement construction are beyond the scope of this chapter. For a more detailed exposition on this topic, see additional resources (cf. Anastasi, 1988; Crocker & Algina, 1986; Nunnally & Bernstein, 1994; Springer, Abell, & Hudson, 2002; Springer, Abell, & Nugent, 2002).

Validity Standards

One rule that has been proposed to interpret validity coefficients is to consider coefficients in the range of 0.40 to 0.60 as acceptable (cf. Downie & Heath, 1974). However, Springer, Abell, and Nugent (2002) caution against using a strict criterion to interpret validity coefficients. Validity coefficients for one scale must be viewed within the context of similar validity coefficients for other measures that measure the same construct and are intended for similar uses (such as clinical decision making with clients, research studies).

NORMS, SCORING, AND INTERPRETATION OF MEASURES

Understanding normative measurement and its related scoring systems will help social work practitioners to develop further competence in using measures. Norms provide information on the typical or average performance of a particular group of clients. They are needed because the raw scores of a measure do not tell us anything about what the client's score means. (Graham & Lilly, 1984; Sattler, 1988). Norms are developed by administering the measure to a large, representative sample of clients whose characteristics are known. It is then possible to calculate the mean (average score) and standard deviation (deviation from the mean) for the sample. This allows the client to be compared to the norm group, and so aids in our understanding of what other similar individual client scores may mean.

To give further meaning to raw scores, they are statistically converted into derived, or standard, scores and compared to the normatization group (standardization sample). *Standard scores* are evenly distributed along the normal curve (see figure 4.1) and make it possible to determine the client's standing in relation to the norm group. It is, therefore, possible to determine whether the client is scoring in the average range. Standard scores make measurements possible across clients and even across measures (Sattler, 1988). Some of the derived and standard scoring systems used in normative measurement include cutting points, Z-scores, T-scores, percentile ranks, and stanines (Anastasi, 1988; Hudson, 1982; Sattler, 1988).

Cutting points indicate when a client has moved from the normal to the critical range of performance on a measure. For example, on the Index of Self-Esteem (ISE), a measure introduced in Chapter 3, one of the measures developed as part of the Clinical Measurement Package (Hudson, 1982) the cutting point is 30 (+5). This indicates that a client score of 30 or higher on this measure may indicate clinically significant problems in the area of self-esteem. Percentile ranks are based on derived scores that indicate a client's position relative to the standardization sample. They present the relative standing of a client in a given distribution. A percentile rank is the point in the distribution at or below which a percentage of the normalization group falls in comparison to the client.

Z-scores are derived scores that translate into standard scores. A Z-score is a standard score with a mean of 0 and a standard deviation of 1. Z-scores are frequently transformed into other standard score systems to eliminate the plus and minus signs. *T-scores* have a mean (average score) of 50 with a standard deviation of 10. According to the properties of the normal curve, two standard deviations above or below the mean is considered to deviate outside the normal range of functioning. These clients scoring 70 or above, or 30 or below deviate into the critical range. T-scores are popular standard scores used to interpret many psychological and clinical assessment measures. For example, the Minnesota Multiphasic Personality Inventory (MMPI [Hathaway & McKinley, 1943]) is interpreted based on T-scores. *Stanines* have a mean of 5 and a standard deviation of 2.

Figure 4.1   Standard Scores

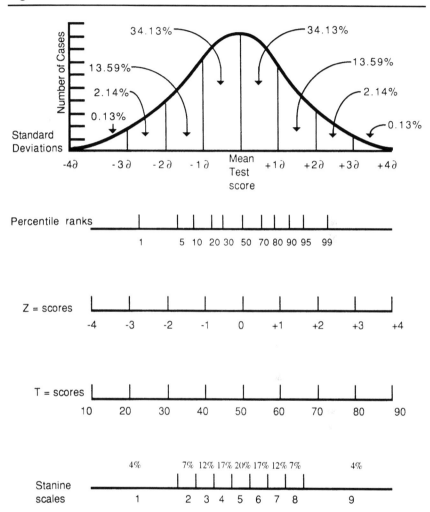

SOURCE: Adapted from Sattler (1988).

Several psychological and clinical measures are scored and interpreted using standard scoring systems based on properties of the normal curve. For example, the popular Weschler Intelligence Scales (WAIS-R and WISC-R) are interpreted based on a standard scoring system with a mean of 100 and a standard deviation of 15. The Stanford–Binet Intelligence test is interpreted similarly with a mean of 100 and a standard deviation of 16. Figure 4.1 illustrates several standard scoring systems discussed in relationship to the properties of the normal curve.

Norms are essential to standardized measurement and the development of measurement tools and should be considered in relationship to the characteristics of your particular client. Sattler (1988) provides the following three guidelines for evaluating the norms of a measure.

1. **Representativeness**. Norms are useful only if they share the characteristics of the client. For example, if minorities of color are being assessed using a particular measurement instrument that included no minorities in its normative sample, the available norms are not appropriate for comparison with your client.

2. **Size**. The larger and more representative the norm group, the better. As a general rule, at least one hundred of your clients should be included in a norm group before it is appropriate to use the norms for comparison.

3. **Relevance**. It is important to determine how relevant a particular norm group is to your client. Because many standardized measures have several different norm samples grouped by client characteristics (e.g., age), it becomes important to choose the norm group that best characterizes your client.

COMPUTER-ASSISTED ASSESSMENT TECHNOLOGIES

Research evidence from several empirical studies demonstrates the lack of reliability and validity of practitioner-based assessments (Briar, 1963; Daro, 1988; Garb, 1998, 2000; Grove et al., 2000; Lindsey, 1991, 1992; Schuerman & Vogel, 1986; Wolock, 1982). A meta-analysis of 162 studies on computers and prediction performed by Grove et al. confirms that computers perform well in making clinical judgments and setting tasks, and usually outperform clinicians who perform such tasks. Computers still need to improve in the areas of developing well-validated algorithms for making diagnosis and treatment decisions (Wood, Garb, Lilienfeld, & Nezworski, 2002).

Studies have repeatedly shown, however, that computers perform just as well as, or outperform, clinicians. The reasons for this are complex. First, practitioners lack the time and resources to check the reliability and validity of assessment information, analyze the important variables, and project their possible outcomes (Lindsey, 1992). Practitioners have to base their decisions on the information available at a given time, usually within the first or second contact with a client. Second, lack of standardization in the assessment process leads to inconsistencies in the data gathered and the conclusions drawn (Lindsey, 1992; Sicoly, 1989). Absence of standardized criteria for making assessment decisions prohibits setting priorities for treatment and development of normative data that may facilitate effectiveness in long-range treatment planning. In addition, a lack of criteria for organizing the existing data and making judgments about the available information makes it difficult for practitioners to accurately discriminate the critical from the less-critical variables in making treatment decisions (Lindsey, 1992). The best practice wisdom must be relied on. Third, lack of knowledge concerning community resources, availability of those resources, and the criteria for admission into those programs interferes with appropriate treatment decisions and long-term planning (Schwab & Wilson, 1989).

With the advent of computer technology, a variety of computer-assisted assessment procedures and measurement instruments have been developed. The cost-effectiveness and speed of personal computers makes this technology readily available and useful to practitioners (Nurius & Hudson, 1988). Several psychological and clinical measures are available in software that may be purchased from its respective publishers and marketers (see Chapter 3 for a list of sources). Some software examples are the Minnesota Multiphasic Personality Inventory (MMPI), a personality assessment measure; the Millon Clinical Multiaxial Inventory (MCMI and the recent MCMI II) (Millon, 1982), personality assessment measures; and the Child Behavior Checklist, a behavioral assessment measure for children (Achenbach & Edelbrock, 1983). See Chapter 7 for a review of the MMPI II.

These measures are administered, scored, and interpreted on the computer. Computer scoring and interpretation technologies produce client profiles based on the norms of the measure, narrative statements about client characteristics, and alternatives for treatment. See figure 4.2 for an example of a computer-generated profile and appendix 4A for an example of a computer-generated narrative from the MCMI.

The MCMI is a clinical personality assessment measure that parallels the *DSM*. The profile and narrative in the example are from the marital and family practice of one of the authors. The presenting problem of the female client used in the example that was assessed was marital distress. She had also experienced a severe career setback and some interpersonal difficulties on her job. She sought treatment at the insistence of her husband. As the example illustrates, computer-generated assessments can provide comprehensive information concerning client characteristics and recommendations for treatment. One caveat of these measurement computer-generated profiles, however, is that the reports tend to be "canned" and that little attention has been given over the last decade to examining the validity and reliability of the computer-generated scoring algorithms and accompanying narrative reports for popular measures like the MMPI II and MCMI II personality assessement measures. Butcher, Perry, and Atlis (2000) reviewed the literature and found only four validity studies on the popular personality measures, and two of these studies showed negative findings. Fortunately, however, there are good computer algorithms for predicting violence, child abuse and neglect, and recidivism among juvenile offenders. See the section on computer-generated, statistical decision-making, below.

Figure 4.2   Computer-Generated Profile

Scales	Raw BR		Profile of T Score					DSM (Millon) Parallels
			35	60	75	85	100	
1	5	12						Schizoid (Asocial)
2	3	15						Avoidant
3	12	46						Dependent (Submis)
4	18	82						Histrionic (Gregar)
5	25	76						Narcissistic
6	19	75						Antisocial (Aggressive)
7	30	72						Compulsive (Confor)
8	7	35						P. Aggressive (Negat)
S	2	23						Schizotypal (Schiz)
C	7	66						Borderline (Cycl)
P	13	75						Paranoid
A	9	87						Anxiety
H	8	72						Somatoform
N	18	58						Hypomania
D	7	71						Dysthymia
B	10	62						Alcohol Abuse
T	19	71						Drug Abuse
SS	5	55						Psychotic Thinking
CC	4	49						Psychotic Depression
PP	7	65						Psychotic Delusion

NOTE: "BR" stands for base rate. The left-hand column beneath BR is the raw score; the right-hand column beneath BR is the T-score.

SOURCE: NCS Assessments, P.O. Box 1416, Minneapolis, MN 55440.

In addition to software, many test publishers provide computerized scoring services for measures they market. These measures are administered in the practitioners' office and mailed to the publisher for scoring, which takes a week or less. The cost varies according to the measure and quantity given. Some examples of measures for which computerized scoring is available are the McMaster Family Assessment Device, a measure of family functioning (Epstein, Baldwin, & Bishop, 1982); The Hilson Adolescent Profile, a behavioral assessment measure for adolescents (Inwald, Brobst, & Morrissey, 1987); and the Couple's Pre-Counseling Inventory, a behavioral marital assessment measure (Stuart, 1987).

The trend in clinical assessment is to use such computer-assisted assessment technologies (Nurius & Hudson, 1988). These software programs are broader and more inclusive of intake and clinical assessment procedures than those described previously. For example, Walter Hudson has developed the Computer Assisted Social Services System (CASS) that includes a comprehensive assessment system for clients: social history forms, clinical questionnaires, mental status testing, unidimensional and multidimensional standardized measures, and more (Hudson, 1989; Nurius & Hudson, 1993). This program runs on a personal computer. The program administers measures to the client and scores them; most of the twenty-two scales in the CASS are scored in the same way and have the same clinical cutting score of 30. In addition, this program also graphs measurements taken on clients at different times and is compatible with single subject design methodology (see Chapter 11).

Use of Computerized Databases in Assessment

The development of computerized technologies has moved practice agencies to link assessment activities with computerized database systems (Franklin et al., 1993). A database system is a computerized information system that stores, organizes, and retrieves client information and the related information necessary for administrative office management. These technologies help standardize assessment methods and improve program evaluation in practice agencies.

Databases are used to manage client information, produce agency reports, and evaluate programs. The database, for example, makes it possible to produce client profiles, lists of the services provided to clients, and information on the effectiveness of these services. The latter assessment becomes particularly important to database technologies because assessment measures are used to identify the problems of clients and to track their progress clients during and after interventions. This tracking allows practitioners, agency administrators, and program funders to see tangible evidence of the impact their services are having on clients. (The use of assessment measures to evaluate the progress of clients in treatment is explained in more detail in Chapter 11.)

O'Hare (1991), for example, described a clinical administrative framework for developing and implementing an eclectic, empirically based model for assessing, monitoring, and evaluating brief clinical practice activities. The framework encompasses *empirical clinical assessments*, including checklists, scales, and other measures to be administered pre-

Box 4.1
Computerized Assessment Packages

Abbreviation Name	Description
ACHI	Assessment of Chemical Health Inventory Demo. IBM-PC, 1 disk. The ACHI is a 128-item, self-administered instrument designed to evaluate the nature and extent of adolescent and adult chemical use and associated problems.
ARES	At-Risk Evaluation System Demo. IBM-PC, 1 disk. The ARES is a battery of 20 individual surveys consisting of over 700 items designed to identify multiple risk factors, problems, issues, or personal concerns.
CAFAS	Child and Adolescent Functional Assessment Scale The CAFAS is a clinician-rated standardized instrument used to measure the degree of impairment in youth ages 7 to 17. The accompanying software program produces a client report and two administrative reports that aggregate data across clients. The program also collects additional information (e.g., demographic information, multiaxial diagnoses, risk factors, services rendered), functions as a MIS system, and can export data for analysis.
CASS	Computer Assisted Social Services system, 4 disks. 1. automated case notes 2. automated and fully relational structured forms, social histories, research and clinical questionnaires 3. automated bllling service 4. unidimensional and multidimensional assessment scales 5. mental status testing 6. graphics display of single case designs 7. complete program evaluation features at the client, worker, unit, section, office, or organization level
Decision-base	Demo of integrated mental health software. IBM-PC, 1disk.
DIS	Demo of client self-administered Diagnostic Interview Schedule generating *DSM* info. IBM-PC, 1 disk. The Diagnostic Interview Schedule (DIS) is a computerized structured interview used to obtain data required for most adult Axis I psychiatric diagnoses. The version of the DIS on this demo is designed so that the patient can take the interview with minimal assistance from the clinical staff.

Box 4.1   *Continued*

Abbreviation Name	Description
Hamilton Depression Assessment	Automates a modified Hamilton Depression Scale consisting of 19 questions. IBM-PC, 1 disk. Administers, stores, retrieves, scores, and prints the results.
MMPI	Minnesota Multiphasic Personality Inventory. IBM-PC, 1 disk. Provides a demo of MMPI report interpretation for adult and adolescent patients.
PsyMedications	Provides an easy-to-use guide to psychotropic medications, 2 disks. Includes condensed indications, adverse reactions, dosage, and visual identification information for over 130 medication definitions commonly needed by mental health professionals and others.
PSYSearch	Demo of a psychiatric diagnosis aide using a *DSM* type decision tree. 1 disk. Demo of an interactive diagnostic aid. Based on the users yes/no answers to questions, the software helps the user reach one of 70+ diagnostic conclusions.
The Psychiatric Assistant	Demo of a system to assist clinicians, 2 disks. Assists the clinician with writing progress notes and reports, making *DSM* diagnoses, storing and tracking literature abstracts, doing medical evaluations, etc. Although designed for psychiatrists, it can be customized for other clinicians.

and post intervention; *participation of the clinical staff* in designing or selecting practice-relevant assessment measures; *collaboration between clinician and clients* in defining specific, measurable, and achievable intervention goals; and the *collection of assessment and outcome information* for developing a database for program evaluation (Franklin et al., 1993). Computerized database systems may further be used to develop standardized and more effective assessment systems that aid the treatment decisions of practitioners. Such assessment systems, for example, have been used to improve assessments in the field of children's services.

Expert Systems and Computer-Assisted Statistical Decision Models

Computer-assisted assessment models and database systems have been suggested as methods to address the above issues, and to provide support to practitioners as they make treatment decisions (Baird & Wagner, 2000; Franklin, 1994; Mutschler, 1990; Nurius, 1990; Savicki, 1989; Sarrazin, Hall, Richards, & Carswell, 2002; Schwab, Franklin, & DiNitto, 1993; Schwab & Wilson, 1989; Sicoly, 1989). Some studies have demonstrated the superiority of the computer over practitioners in making assessment and treatment decisions. See Wood et al., (2002) for a recent review. The sum of these studies indicated that computers usually outperform practitioners by about ten percent. It has been demonstrated, for example, that the use of computer-based clinical assessment does not compromise the validity of responses among clients receiving substance abuse treatment, even when pending legal issues exist (Sarrazin et al., 2002).

Expert systems and statistical decision models have been discussed for more than fifty years as important methods for improving assessment and treatment decisions, and the advantages of integrating these approaches have also been suggested (Meddin, 1984; Savicki, 1989; Schuerman, 1987; Schwab, Bruce, & McRoy, 1985; Sicoly, 1989; Stone & Stone, 1983). Recent work in the area of quality assurance and in child welfare settings demonstrates that statistical decision models may be combined with standardized measures to greatly improve treatment (Baird & Wagner, 2000; Wood et al., 2002).

Expert systems, as used in social work, are rule-based or knowledge-based computerized programs that provide consultation on the problems practitioners are trying to solve (Gingerich, 1990; Mutschler, 1990). These computer programs operate on "if-then" and heuristic reasoning or "general rules." Practitioners ask the computer a set of questions about a case, and the computer applies the rules in its knowledge base to answer the questions. In this manner, the computer becomes the evaluator, by using assessment data fed to it by the practitioner to come up with a treatment plan. Computer-assisted statistical decision models rely on multivariate statistical techniques, predominately discriminant function analysis, and multiple regression, to predict the complexities that may exist in determining case outcomes (Sicoly, 1989). Psychologists have also combined these methods with normative-based benchmarks for improvement, actuarial data, and other methods that compare progress against what is expected from, normative-based data set. We discuss statistical decision models more thoroughly than expert systems, because their methodologies are substantive to linking computerized assessment methodologies to database systems and standardized assessment procedures. Statistical decision models are also frequently used in risk assessment in child welfare practice and have now become the leading method of client measurement in quality assurance systems.

Computer-based statistical decision models focus on predicting decisions concerning client placement, placement failure, risk assessment, and treatment progress. In child welfare services, for example, information given in an assessment is translated into a *risk assessment* or probability statement about how likely it is that a child will be maltreated by her parents. (Risk assessment is covered in more detail below). Risk assessment models help the social worker decide whether to remove the child from the home or to try to preserve a family through a different treatment approach.

Models have been developed to match the characteristics of youths with the type of treatments these youths need (Schwab & Wilson, 1989). A list of the characteristics of the youth and family is generated from case information that emerges in an assessment (Schwab et al., 1985, 1986). These characteristics are tested in a statistical model using case records and practitioner-based decisions to establish their criterion validity and to develop a list of predictor variables. (See the discussion on criterion and predictive validity, earlier in this chapter.) A normative database and statistical model are then generated for comparison with future cases.

To determine which variables can make accurate predictions, one uses discriminant function analysis, a statistical technique based on regression analysis that identifies relationships between qualitative criterion variables (e.g., referred second time for abuse: yes or no?) and quantitative predictor variables (e.g., age, emotional functioning). Accuracy in predictions has ranged from twenty-five percent to fifty percent (Sicoly, 1989). For example, Schwab et al. (1985) developed a model that can generate placement options within a system of care at an accuracy rate of slightly above fifty percent. Newer models using actuarial data and consensus-driven systems have even better success at predicting risk in abuse and neglect situations (Baird & Wagner, 2000).

An important feature of statistical decision models is their ability to make accurate long-term predictions about a case. Predict is precisely what practitioners are asked to do in an assessment: evaluate the characteristics of the client, family, and social context and prescribe a course of treatment that will be appropriate and effective. Of course, given the limits of human judgment (Faust, 1986), it is impossible for practitioners to know precisely what the future outcomes of a case will be (Lindsey, 1992). Computer-assisted statistical decision models provide a promising technology that can greatly assist social workers as they standardize the assessment process to more accurately predict the outcomes of treatment decisions, such as whether parents are likely to maltreat their child.

Child protection risk assessment is the process of identifying and recording relevant case information associated with child maltreatment and neglect or other types of violence to predict the likelihood of future occurence (Doueck, English, DePanfilis, & Moote, 1993; McDonald & Marks, 1991; Wood et al., 2002). Risk assessment models or systems "are

formalized methods that provide a uniform structure and criteria for determining risk" (Keller, Cicchinelli, & Gardner, 1988, p. 00). The use of
formalized risk assessment systems by child protection agencies is increasing. Most states use, or plan to use, some form of risk assessment
systems.

Risk assessment information is important for making a number of
critical decisions in Child Protective Services (CPS) during the investigation phase. It helps social workers determine: 1) whether the child is in
immediate risk of maltreatment; 2) what services or worker actions are
necessary to protect the child during the investigation; 3) whether the
child should be removed from the home for protection; and 4) what initial case plan will address the forces placing the child at risk (Holder &
Corey, 1987).

The term "risk assessment" refers both to a structured form of decision making and to the specific instruments that are used in this process.
A number of child welfare agencies and organizations have developed
models and instruments for assessing risk. The various systems being developed may be used to address one or all of the above decisions. Because
there is no standard definition or set of purposes ascribed to assessment,
there exists some confusion in the practice community. Yet risk assessment is being rapidly developed, aided in part by the increasing amount
of research and practice wisdom regarding which factors are associated
with various forms of child maltreatment.

Part of the rationale for using the statistical decision approach is that
1) workers can realistically assess only a small number of factors over the
phone or as part of the initial investigation; 2) the factors identified using
this method are assumed to be the same factors that predict first-time occurrences of maltreatment as well; and 3) often the CPS worker is inves-
tigating cases in which child maltreatment has already occurred and the
primary concern is whether the child will be maltreated again. The risk
factors that are identified are provided to the CPS intake personnel and,
in some cases, to CPS investigators to assist them in assessing the risk of
future maltreatment.

Statistical decision models are modeled after the risk studies conducted in the public health and juvenile corrections systems. The work in
juvenile corrections systems at predicting recidivism and in prison populations at prediciting violence is most promising (Douglas, Cox, & Webster, 1999; Wiebush, Baird, Krisberg, & Onek, 1995). Child welfare systems generally focus on identifying a small set of risk factors that are
most predictive of the recurrence of a problem behavior (e.g., caretaker
abused as a child, mother figure's parenting skills inadequate, presence
of more than one child in the home, how reasonable the mother figure's
expectations of the child are). Thus parent, family, or child characteristics
associated with child maltreatment are considered but not included in the

final set of risk factors unless they actually *predict* the recurrence of one or more types of child maltreatment.

The computerized statistical decision technologies used in child placement settings are based on systems theory; their utility may be demonstrated pragmatically. These technologies have been shown to lead to reduced placement failure in the foster care system and savings in the costs of children's services. Schwab et al. (1993) also predicted that some problems with the validity and reliability of the statistical decision models may be resolved in the standardization of the models, as more accurate databases from which to develop the decision models and define characteristics of clients and treatment options are established, that is, with adequate normative data on large samples, many problems in the statistical decision models could be resolved. He appears to be correct because many new systems within quality assurance (see the next section) have taken this approach and have developed systems with good validity and reliability that can also inform practice.

Computerized Quality Assurance Measures

Quality assurance measures are computerized and offer ongoing reports to the practitioner about the clinical outcomes of their clients. *The Jorunal of Consulting and Clinical Psychology* (2001, 69) ran a special issue on several quality assurance measures and reviews the strengths and weaknesses of many of the well-known measurement systems (see Beutler, 2001; Barkham et al., 2001; Kordy, Hannover, & Richard, 2001). These measurement systems are being used in the United States and Europe to study the effectiveness of psychotherapy and as alternatives to group-oriented, outcome studies on psychotherapy effectiveness (e.g., efficacy and effectiveness studies). Quality assurance systems use individual client data to provide feedback to clinicians on the therapy outcomes. They combine many of the methods previously discussed in this chapter such as computer algorithms used with standardized measures and actuarial and statistical decision methods to evaluate the outcomes of individual clients. Sophisticated statistical procedures are used to make decisions about client data, such as probit analysis, survival analysis, and hierarchical linear modeling. These methods help researchers to determine the progress and lack of progress of clients in treatment programs (Lambert, Hansen, & Finch, 2001). Similar to single case designs discussed in Chapter 11, these procedures focus on individual clients and can be used by clinicians in practice to evaluate the effectiveness of their practices. These client- or patient-focused measurement systems answer questions that are of interest to practitioners; such as, Is my client getting better? Is it time to stop treatment? Should I refer this client to someone else? (Lambert et al., 2001).

Quality assurance systems improve practice by using norms and standardized measures to define clinically significant change and the need for further treatment, and they can feed this information back to clinicians. Table 4.1 offers a comparative review of several measures. See Chapter 7 for more information on the computerized quality assurance measures and a review of one measure that is used, the Outcomes Questionnaire-45.2 (OQ-45.2).

LIMITATIONS IN STANDARDIZED ASSESSMENT MEASURES

Standardized assessment measures have many strengths: they are quick and efficient to use; they are easy to score and interpret; and they provide sources of data other than can be gained in a client interview, in that they measure or screen for specific client problems or characteristics. Yet these measures do have some practical weaknesses other than possible limitations in their psychometric properties (such as, validity, reliability, normatization, etc.). Five such limitations are covered below.

1. Standardized assessment measures are subject to demand characteristics or social desirability. Clients may answer the questions on the measure to cast themselves in a favorable or disfavorable light. Clients may seek to please the social worker or give incorrect information on purpose. Some measures include "lie scales" or "faking good scales" to try to correct for this limitation. A lie scale is a set of items that tests for false responses on the measure. The Personal Experience Screen Questionnaire, which assesses substance abuse in adolescents, has such a subscale, for example (Winters, 1988).

2. Measures present a narrow band of information; they are not able to assess the whole client picture. Some social workers have criticized standardized assessment methods for being unable to assess dynamic interactions or the systems complexities of the real world of clients (Mattaini & Kirk, 1991). These critics believe the measures have limited usefulness because they treat characteristics of clients as if they are static instead of forever changing in response to environmental contingencies. To these practitioners, the psychometric properties of the measures limit their usefulness. Many social workers who take this position object to trying to quantify client behavior. They believe that broader, qualitative methods are more useful for understanding the complexities of client behavior. (Qualitative assessment methods are covered in Chapter 5.) The argument that standardized measures cannot capture the complexities and dynamic, fluctuating interactions of client and environment appears to be true; such characteristics are beyond these measures' scope and current level of development.

Table 4.1 A Comparison of Five Computerized Quality Assurance Systems and Their Measures

Dimensions	Stuttgart-Heidelberg System	OQ-45	CORE-OM	COMPASS	Systematic Treatment Selection
Source of Information	Clinician and patient	Patient only	Patient only	Patient and four clinician questions	Clinician and patient
Length	Very long	Very short	Very short and Variable	Moderate	Variable
Flexibility of Questions	Very flexible	Nonflexible	Flexible	Nonflexible	Very flexible
Breadth	In-patient & out-patient	Out-patient	Out-patient	Out-patient	In-patient & Out-patient
Projected Response	Yes	Yes	No	Yes	Yes
Feedback	Graphic and narrative	Graphic and color codes	Graphic	Graphic	Graphic and narrative
Clinical Range	Yes	Yes	Yes	Yes (modified)	Yes
Signal Risk	Yes	Yes	Yes	Yes	Yes
Development and Availability	Center for Psychotherapy Research, Governmental agencies in Germany kordy@psyres-stuttgart.de	Brigham Young University, For fee, American Professional Credentialing Services www.oqfamily.com	Psychological Therapies Research Center, Leeds University, Public domain, United Kingdom m.barkham@leeds.ac.uk	Northwestern University, For Fee, lueger@Marquette.edu	Center for Behavioral Health Care Technologies STS4outcomes@aol. com

SOURCE: Adapted from Beutler, L. (2001).

3. Standardized measures have been criticized for focusing on client problems instead of strengths. In this regard, standardized methods are believed to pathologize clients without pointing to their unique motivation and capacities. Some assessment measures, however, have begun to include scales on coping abilities or problem solving. For example, the MMPI, the popular personality assessment measure, has an ego strengths subscale, and some family measures look at family strengths as well as problems. The Behavioral and Emotional Rating Scale (BERS) (Epstein & Sharma, 1998), summarized in box 4.2, is a notable exception. The BERS is a fifty-two item, strength-based instrument that measures functioning in youth across five different areas: interpersonal strength; involvement with family; intrapersonal strength; school functioning; and affective strength. A key feature that distinguishes the BERS from many other standardized tools is that it is truly based on a strengths perspective; the wording of the items reflects this perspective. Some sample items are as follows:

- *Maintains positive family relationships.*
- *Accepts responsibility for own actions.*
- *Pays attention in class.*
- *Identifies own feelings.*

Still, the unique characteristics or significant individual differences in a client's strengths and coping styles may be absent from the profiles produced by most standardized assessment measures.

4. Standardized assessment measures have been criticized for their inability to directly link between client problems to their interventions, that is, the measure does not prescribe a useful treatment plan, which is the main purpose of assessment. (In Chapter 11, we illustrate how to make decisions about treatment plans, based on assessments.) Developing a treatment plan involves practitioners using their own cognitive abilities to map out a set of tasks to undertake with the client. As standardized assessment measures have been combined with computerized assessment technologies, however, these technologies have begun to produce narrative client reports that do make recommendations for treatment. (See figure 4.2 and appendix 4A to this chapter, for examples of a narrative report.) Even so, they are still unable to present a complete treatment plan that is relevant to the client's unique experiences and environmental contingencies. The capabilities of standardized measures to help clinicians produce meaningful treatment plans is increasing with the use of the quality assurance measures and patient-focused measurement systems, as discussed above.

5. Standardized measures are subject to false positives and false negatives like any other standardized assessment procedure. For example,

BOX 4.2
Evaluation of the BERS

Name of measure: Behavioral and Emotional Rating Scale (BERS)
Authors: Michael H. Epstein and Jennifer M. Sharma
Date of publication: 1988
Purchase availability: Pro-Ed, International Publisher, 8700 Shoal Creek Blvd., Austin, Texas 78757 and other publishers of psychological measures.
Availability of manual: The manual is available from Pro-Ed and summarizes the following: description of the BERS, scoring and interpretation, reliability and validity, and its normatization.
Cost: $79.00 for complete kit (includes examiner's manual and 50 summary/response forms.
Time for administration: approximately ten minutes.
Ease of use: The BERS contains 52 strength-based items. It is designed for use by parents, teachers, counselors, or others with knowledge of the child. Scoring is easy and guidelines are provided to assist in interpreting results.
Clarity of directions: Directions are brief and easy to understand.
Scoring procedures: Each of the five subscales produces a total raw score. These raw scores can then be converted into percentile ranks and to standard scores. The sum of the subscale standard scores can be converted into the BERS Strength Quotient (a standard score with a mean of 100 and a standard deviation of 15).
Level of training needed: Little training is needed for use.
Purpose of the measure: The instrument was developed to measure the personal strengths of children and adolescents ages 5 to 18 years. It measures functioning in five areas: interpersonal strength, family involvement, intrapersonal strength, school functioning, and affective strength. It also provides a cumulative strength quotient.
Theoretical orientation: Based on a strength perspective, which is reflected in the wording of the items.
Standardization and appropriateness of norms: Norms are based on a nationally representative sample. Two sets of norma-

tive data are provided. One is based on children not identified with emotional or behavioral disorders (NEBD sample, N = 2,176) and one on children diagnosed with emotional or behavioral disorders (EBD sample, N = 861). Standard score for the NEBD sample = 17. Standard score for EBD sample = 20.
Evidence for validity: There is solid evidence for content validity. Criterion-related validity and construct validity: Known-instruments validity: When compared to several other measures of children's emotional and behavioral disorders (The Walker-McConnell Scale of Social Competence and School Adjustment-Adolescent Version; Self-Perception Profile for Children; and Achenbach's Teacher Report Form), the BERS had resultant coefficients large enough and in the direction hypothesized to demonstrate known-instruments validity. Mean standard scores and the ability of BERS to significantly discriminate between children with and without emotional and behavioral disorders demonstrate the known-groups validity of the BERS. Factorial validity is demonstrated as items load onto their respective domains.
Evidence for reliability: The BERS evidences a high degree of reliability. Coefficient alphas for the EBD sample on each domain are as follows: interpersonal strength (.92); family involvement (.89); intrapersonal strength (.85); school functioning (.85); affective strength (.84); overall strength quotient (.97). Coefficient alphas for the NEBD sample are even higher on average. Interrater reliability coefficients for each domain range from .83 to .96, with an interrater reliability coefficient of .98 for the overall strength quotient. The BERS possesses little test error as evidenced by low SEM values ranging from 0.8 to 2.6.
Evidence for clinical utility: The BERS is available at a reasonable cost and is easy to administer and score. It is able to distinguish between children and adolescents with and without emotional and behavioral disorders. The strength-based wording of the items makes it appealing to both parents and practitioners.

SOURCE: Review of BERS adapted from Epstein & Sharma (1998).

false positives and negatives are often found in tests used in medical practice. It may be necessary to give the test again to verify the results. A false positive or negative can be caused by errors in the administration of the test, errors in the scoring and interpretation of the test, and measurement error inherent in the psychometric properties of the test. Researchers have focused on reducing and accounting for measurement error in a standardized assessment measure. In the next section we will discuss in detail measurement error and its implications for interpreting and reporting results on standardized assessment measures.

MEASUREMENT ERROR

Unfortunately, there is no measurement instrument that can provide a perfect assessment of client characteristics. All measures, even computerized ones, are susceptible to certain errors that reduce their validity and reliability.

Reliability can be conceptualized as having two hypothetical components: a true score and an error score. Each person's observed score, O, contains both a "true" score, T, and a random error score, E. This relationship is depicted in the following equation (Nunnally & Bernstein, 1994):

$$O = T + E$$

These random errors prevent us from knowing the "true client score" for characteristics assessed by a measure. Errors of measurement are always present—we never have perfect conditions. Another way of conceptualizing this relationship is that a true score is that which reflects what the client is actually experiencing, and an error score is the gap between that actual experience and what is observed.

In this section, we will discuss types of measurement error, common sources of error, and how to account for measurement error. Although it isn't impossible to know the client's "true score" on a measure, it is possible to know approximately how close we might be to the "true score" (Jordan et al., 1997).

The statistic used to account for measurement error is known as the standard error of measurement (SEM), and is explained below.

Types of Errors

Two major types of errors occur in measurement, systematic and random:

Systematic error results in the measurements becoming biased in a singular or consistent direction. For example, the scores will either become consistently higher or lower (Guy, Edgley, Arafat, & Allen, 1987), and the error will be essentially the same for each client.

A common cause of this type of error is clients' attempts to produce desirable answers on the measure. Clients often try to guess what the measure is developed to assess and choose answers they think will show themselves in a more favorable light. This tendency of clients has been labeled *social desirability* (Crowne & Marlowe, 1964); clients consistently change their scores on the measure in a favorable direction. Social workers may also contribute to this type of error by using measures that cue clients about the construct and about the favorable direction of a measure. Social workers may also make erroneous judgments in observing behavior or interpreting a measure that makes the outcome correspond to their personal desires. For example, a social worker might provide a biased rating because of a desire to see improvement in the client.

Systematic error can be reduced by selecting measurement instruments that guard against social desirability; such measures have usually been well standardized. One technique to reduce error is to reverse items so that some items are worded in the positive direction and others are worded in the negative direction to guard against response set (a client answering all the items in the same direction). Some measures have actually been correlated with "social desirability scales" to evaluate their resistance to this construct. An example of such a measure is the Coopersmith Self-Esteem Inventory (Coopersmith, 1986), a standardized measure of self-esteem. In its development this measure was administered along with a social desirability scale. These two measures were correlated to test the Coopersmith's ability to measure the construct of self-esteem instead of social desirability. Other measures incorporate validity scales (items developed to detect lying or faking on the measure). Several standardized personality and behavioral measures have validity scales (exaples include the MMPI and the Hilson Adolescent Profile).

Social workers can further reduce systematic error by using standardized quality measures. An example of such measures developed by a social worker is the Hudson Clinical Measurement Package (Hudson, 1982). Through supervision of their observations and work, social workers can also reduce errors that originate from their own systematic biases.

Random error results in measurements becoming biased in a nonsystematic, fluctuating way. Some clients may score lower on the measure than their accurate score, whereas other clients score higher. These scores fall to either side of the range of the accurate score but in no predictable pattern. Random error may occur at any point of the measurement.

There are four common sources of error (Blythe & Tripodi, 1989; Guy et al., 1987). First, client characteristics like mood, reactions, and behavior may fluctuate day to day or even hour to hour. This sometimes makes it difficult to obtain a stable baseline measure of the client characteristics. Second, deficits in the measurement instrument always serve as the major contributor to error in any measurement situation. Measurements are essentially as accurate and reliable as the measures used. Selecting appropriate measures becomes the first rule for reducing measurement error. Third, a measure may be administered improperly; this can greatly reduce even an excellent measure's accuracy. Some important factors to remember in proper administration of measures are to present the exact instructions suggested in the measurement manual and to double-check that you are giving the right measure to the right client—some measures have several different versions and not all versions are appropriate for all clients. Being completely familiar with the measure is mandatory to administering it properly. To familiarize yourself with measures, you must study the manual or other relevant research and instructions. This requires devoting a great amount of time and commitment to the assessment situation. It may also be necessary to practice several times before giving the instructions and administering the measure to a client.

Finally, personal and situational factors are an additional source of measurement error. Personal results when clients read and respond to questions carelessly (Jordan et al., 1997). Errors may result when clients are tired, hungry, distressed, sick, or malingering. Such personal factors may greatly decrease measurement accuracy and contribute to measurement error. Being attentive to possible client distress can help reduce these errors. Environmental factors also may contribute to measurement error. It is important to provide an appropriate environment in which to administer the measure. Noise, uncomfortable room temperatures, and distractions will increase measurement error. Comfortable, quiet, and nondistracting surroundings are essential to the measurement situation. It is also important not to expect the client to respond to measures for overly long periods. Overwhelming the client with too many measures at once will unnecessarily stress the client and increase measurement error. The amount of time a client can respond to a group of measures without becoming stressed varies from client to client. As a general rule, however, extending assessment for longer than one to two hours is not recommended in most cases. Shorter periods are recommended when working with children or adolescents. Measurement error is an inevitable part of measuring client characteristics. In the next section, we discuss a way to systematically account for measurement error.

Accounting for Measurement Error

The standard error of measurement (SEM), or standard error of the score, is a special reliability statistic that allows us to estimate the amount of error that may be attached to a client's score on a measure (Hudson, 1981). A major advantage of the SEM over the regular reliability coefficient calculated for the measure is that its value is less influenced by the differences in the variance and standard deviation of a measurement tool from one sample or population to the next. The SEM is calculated to make more meaningful use of the reliability coefficient and is easy to compute (Hudson, 1981; Springer et al., 2002). The SEM is computed using the following formula:

$$SEM = SD \; \sqrt{1\text{-}r_{tt}}$$

where:

SEM = standard error of measurement
SD = standard deviation of observed scores
r_{tt} = coefficient Alpha

SD is multiplied by the square root of $1\text{-}r_{tt}$ to obtain the SEM. Social work practitioners should look for scales that have a small SEM and a large reliability coefficient. Springer et al. (2002) developed and recommend a general rule stating that the SEM should be approximately five percent (or less) of the range of possible scores. For example, many of Hudson's scales have a possible score ranging from 0 to 100, so an acceptable SEM for Hudson's scales would be 5.00 or less. With most standardized measures the SEM has already been calculated and reported in the measurement manual.

Measurement error is an inevitable part of the measurement process. Social work practitioners should do everything they can to reduce the sources of error. Thus far, we have been discussing technical considerations in measurement. The next section will focus on clinical and ethical uses of measures.

CLINICAL AND ETHICAL USES OF STANDARDIZED MEASURES

Earlier in this chapter the discussion has made it clear that standardized measures should be chosen based on their overall quality and purposes. In clinical practice, measures with excellent validity and reliability, and appropriate norms should be selected. Beyond these technical considerations, the clinical utility of the measure must also be considered. Clinical utility refers to the practical advantages of using a measure to assess clients, plan interventions, and obtain accurate feedback (Corcoran & Fischer, 2000; Streeter & Franklin, 1992). For example, does the measure tap a clinically relevant problem? Is it easy to administer and score? Does it make sense, given the particular practice situation? A measure may have excellent technical properties (e.g., validity, reliability) but be too lengthy to give in a crisis clinic where clients need rapid assessments and immediate assistance. Such a measure does not have clinical utility in this situation.

The clinical benefits of the measure in relationship to its cost should also be weighed. In many instances, measures may prove to be cost-ef-

fective and to provide rapid and objective assessments of client attributes. This is especially true with the availability of computerized assessment and measurement technology. For example, we discussed, earlier,
that statistical decision models and other computerized database systems
are cost-effective. The clinical benefits and utility of including standardized measures, however, should be considered in relationship to the
needs of the client. Measurement should exist to serve the needs of the
client. Does the standardized measure help us assess and serve the client
better? This should be the primary question all social work practitioners
ask before including a measure in their assessment.

To determine the appropriateness, clinical utility, and benefits of a
measurement instrument, it must be evaluated carefully. In box 4.2, a
form for evaluating measures for selection in clinical practice is provided;
here, the form has been used to evaluate the Behavioral and Emotional
Rating Scale (BERS) (Epstein & Sharma, 1998).

Ethical consideration are relevant to the clinical utility of measures.
For instance, social workers should use only measures they are competent to administer. Social workers must be trained in the administration,
scoring, and interpretation of the measures they use. This includes training in measurement theory and in evaluation of the quality of various
measurement tools, as well as training in scoring and interpretation of
measures. Several important issues related to measurement have been
summarized in this chapter. However, additional training in the application of these concepts may be needed before social work practitioners
may achieve competence in the administration of some measures.

Social workers receive training in measurement in their research
courses, which cover issues such as validity, reliability, item development, and norms. In recent years, there has also been a trend toward
training social workers to administer measures in their direct practice
courses, in the context of using single subject design methodology in
practice settings (Blythe & Tripodi, 1989; Corcoran & Fischer, 2000; Hudson, 1982). The training in measurement that most social workers receive
is adequate for the administration of several measurement instruments.
Unfortunately, some social workers receive only minimal training in tests
and measurement, which precludes their use of many excellent assessment tools. Test publishers are unwilling to sell measurement instruments to unqualified users. Therefore, social workers who want to use
these measures in practice may need to seek additional training. This
training is indispensable to clinical practitioners who work in settings
where measures are often administered. Even if social workers do not administer measurement instruments themselves as a part of their assessments, it is important for them to understand tests and measurement so
that they can evaluate other practitioners' work. In keeping with the current trends in clinical practice, schools of social work will undoubtedly

need to provide additional training in measurement as a part of their assessment and practice courses.

A second ethical consideration is to fully respect ethnic and cultural diversity when using measures in practice. Social workers have a long tradition of working with ethnically and culturally diverse client populations. Consistent with social work values and ethics, social workers should lead the way in ensuring that clinical assessments are not used to mislabel the attributes of ethnic minority clients. Standardized measurement instruments may be biased against certain ethnic and cultural groups. For example, Mercer (1979) has documented that African American children routinely scored ten points lower than European American children on the Weschler Intelligence Scale for Children, Revised (WISC-R). There appears to be cultural bias in the WISC-R and other normative-based standardized measures; they do not reflect the strengths of diverse populations. Mercer recommended applying a correction score to the WISC-R when administering it to African American children. Social workers should exercise cultural sensitivity in the selection and administration of measurement instruments and only administer measures that have been "normed" with these populations. In addition, social workers should be aware of any clinical caveats of a measure when applied to culturally diverse clients and make appropriate modifications, such as those described above. See Chapter 10 for more information on using standardized measures with American minorities.

A third ethical consideration concerns the responsible and appropriate use of measures. Measures should not be used as single indicators of client characteristics; rather, the use of multiple methods of assessment is recommended (Springer et al., 2002). It is appropriate for social work practitioners to use measures along with other sources of assessment information. For example, it would not be appropriate to use a measurement instrument as a substitute for a clinical interview and other behavioral observations of the client; the instrument should be administered in conjunction with other clinical assessment techniques. Measures can facilitate good assessments, but they are not an end in themselves. They should be used cautiously, responsibly, and appropriately in service of the client.

A fourth ethical consideration is that of confidentiality. Social workers should ensure clients confidentiality of measurement scores in the same way other client information is held confidential. Social workers should be aware that scores on standardized measures may be used to negatively label clients. They may also be used politically and legally against clients who are involved with government agencies. In reporting measurement scores, other client information should always be considered. In keeping with social work values, client strengths and resources should be focal to assessment reports.

In selecting standardized measures for use in practice, the technical considerations of the measure should be considered. Equally important is the clinical utility of the measure and ethical considerations regarding its use.

SUMMARY

Once thought to be the domain of psychologists, standardized measures are increasingly used among social work practitioners. Standardization means that every person to whom a particular measure is administered is treated in the exact same way. Standardization also means that research has been done on the measure, testing it against samples of people whose characteristics are known. The purpose of the research is to establish the statistical properties of the measure. These are essential to its proper use, scoring, and interpretation.

To guide social work practitioners in their evaluation and selection of standardized measures, three essential characteristics of standardized measures were discussed: reliability, validity, and norms. Reliability is related to the consistency of a measure, its dependability and stability. Reliability is understood by examining the reliability coefficient. A test cannot be trusted unless it has high reliability. Reliability coefficients of 0.80 or higher are desirable in practice situations. Three methods for establishing reliability of measures were discussed: the test-retest reliability method, the alternate form reliability method, and internal consistency reliability methods (split-half and Cronbach's coefficient alpha). Validity refers to what a particular measurement tool is measuring and how well it does so. Four different types of validity were examined: content validity, criterion validity, construct validity, and factorial validity.

Norms provide information on the typical or average performance of a group of clients. Norms are developed by administering the measure to a large, representative sample of clients and calculating the mean and standard deviation for this sample. Individual client scores may then be compared to the norm group. Client scores are routinely converted into standard scoring systems that aid in comparison of clients and measures. Some frequently used derived scores include cutting points, percentiles, Z-scores, T-scores, and stanines. Three guidelines for evaluating norm groups are representativeness, size, and relevance.

Use of computerized assessment and scoring systems is increasing. Many test publishers provide computer scoring services for a fee. The cost-effectiveness and time utility of computer-based assessment systems are likely to increase their future popularity and use in social work practice. Other computerized assessment technologies are also evolving and this chapter discussed several applications.

Measurement error is an inevitable part of the assessment of client characteristics. Two types of potential errors exist: systematic and random. Four common sources of measurement error were discussed: fluctuating client characteristics, deficits in the measurement instrument, administration of the measure, and personal and environmental factors. Computing the standard error of measurement (SEM) was presented as an estimate of how far the true score may lie from an observed score for an average respondent.

The clinical utility and benefit of employing a measure with clients should also be considered. Clinical utility refers to the practical applications of a measure and its implications in relationship to practice wisdom. Four ethical considerations relate to using standardized measures in direct practice. First, practitioners must be trained in the administration, scoring, and interpretation of measures. Second, social workers should lead the way in administering measures with respect for ethnic and cultural diversity. Third, measures should be employed responsibly with due caution and appropriateness to ensure good clinical assessments; multiple methods should always be used. Fourth, confidentiality of test scores should be maintained.

One final note is warranted. This chapter has focused on measurement instruments that are developed and validated using classical test theory, or the classical true score model. Spearman (1904) produced much of the original work on this model, which was later expanded upon by others (cf. Lord & Novick, 1968). The essence of the classical true score model is best captured in the equation presented in the section on measurement error:

$$O = T + E$$

where each person's observed score, O, contains both a "true" score, T, and a random error score, E.

Most of the instruments available to social workers (cf. Corcoran & Fischer, 2000) have been developed and validated using the classical true score model as a guiding framework. This model is very useful and has guided countless scale developers in their efforts to create new measurement tools. However, two new measurement theories, Item Response Theory (IRT) and Generalizability Theory (G-Theory), offer advantages that classical measurement theory does not (Nugent & Hankins, 1992; Nugent & Thomas, 1992). For example, IRT can inform us about how respondents at different levels of functioning on a specified trait have performed on an individual item. We need to begin using these two new theories in the development of measurement instruments (Springer, Abell, & Nugent, 2002).

Chapter 4 has focused on understanding and interpreting standardized assessment measures and computerized assisted assessment technologies. Standardized measures are quantitative assessment methods widely used in clinical assessment. It is important for social workers to comprehend how these assessment tools can be selected and appropriately utilized as quantitative assessment methods. In the next chapter, we will move away from our discussion of quantitative methods and review a set of distinct procedures known as qualitative methods, for collecting assessment information from clients.

STUDY QUESTIONS

1. What are the key features that distinguish standardized measures from nonstandardized measures?
2. What are the various methods of establishing the reliability and validity of a measure? In what ways are reliability and validity interrelated?
3. Choose a problem area that is of interest to you (e.g., depression, stress) and develop ten items that you think capture your construct of interest. Apply both the rational-intuitive method and the empirical method to examine the content validity of your new items. What advantages and disadvantages did you find for each approach?
4. What are the inherent advantages and challenges associated with practitioners using computer-assisted assessment technologies and standardized assessment measures?
5. Develop a case vignette in which a statistical decision model would potentially aid clinical decision making with a client system. Now develop a case vignette in which a statistical decision model would potentially hinder or complicate clinical decision making. Explore the advantages and disadvantages associated with practitioners using statistical decision models.
6. You have been asked by your agency administrator to select a measure to monitor client progress. What criterion would you use to select a measure to aid clinical decision making in practice with clients? Some possible criteria include: reliability and validity properties; norms; clinical utility; cost-effectiveness; and ethical considerations. Are any of these criteria more important to you than others? If so, which ones and why?

REFERENCES

Achenbach, T. M., & Edelbrock, C. S. (1983). *Manual for the child behavior checklist and revised child behavior profile*. Burlington, VT: Thomas M. Achenbach.

Anastasi, A. (1988). *Psychological testing* (6th ed.). New York: Macmillan.

Baird, C., & Wagner, D. (2000). The relative validity of actuarial- and consensus based assessment systems. *Children & Youth Services Review, 22,* 839–871.

Barkham, M., Margison, F., Leach, C., Lucock, M., Mellor-Clark, J., Evans, C., Benson, L., Connell, J., Audin, K., & McGrach, G. (2001). The CORE-OM and benchmarking: Towards practice-based evidence in the psychological sciences. *Journal of Consulting and Clinical Psychology, 69*, 184–196.

Beutler, L. (2001). Comparisons among quality assurance systems: from outcome assessment to clinical utility. *Journal of Consulting and Clinical Psychology, 69*, 197–204.

Bloom, M. (1986). *The experience of research.* New York: Macmillan.

Bloom, M., Fischer, J., & Orme, J. (1999). *Evaluating practice: Guidelines for the accountable professional* (3rd ed). Boston: Allyn & Bacon.

Blythe, B. J., & Tripodi, T. (1989). *Measurement in direct practice.* Newbury Park, CA: Sage.

Bostwick, G., & Kyte, N. (1988). Validity and reliability. In R. M. Grinnell, Jr. (Ed.), *Social work research and evaluation* (3rd ed., pp. 111–136). Itasca, IL: Peacock.

Briar, S. (1963). Clinical judgment in foster care placement. *Child Welfare, 2*, 161–169.

Butcher, J. N., Perry, J. N., & Atlis, M. M. (2000). Validity and utility of computer-based test intervention. *Psychological Assessment, 12*, 6–8.

Coopersmith, S. (1986). *The Coopersmith inventory.* Palo Alto, CA: Consulting Psychologists Press.

Corcoran, K., & Fischer, J. (2000). *Measures for clinical practice: A sourcebook* Vols. I & II (3rd ed.). New York: Free Press.

Crocker, L. M., & Algina, J. (1986). *Introduction to classical and modern test theory.* New York: Holt, Rinehart and Winston.

Cronbach, L. J. (1951). Coefficient alpha and the internal structure of tests. *Psychometrika, 16*, 297–334.

Cronbach, L. J., & Warrington, W. G. (1951). Time-limit tests: estimating their reliability and degree of speeding. *Psychometrika, 16*, 167–188.

Crowne, D. P., & Marlowe, D. (1964). *The approval motive: Studies in evaluative dependence.* New York: Wiley.

Daro, D. (1988). *Confronting child abuse: Research for effective program design.* New York: Free Press.

Deschner, J. (1986, July). *Measuring family violence with the Fighting Methods Inventory.* Paper presented at the annual convention of the American Psychological Association, Washington, D.C.

Doueck, H. J., English, D. J., DePanfilis, D., & Moote, G. T. (1993). Decision-making in child protective services: A comparison of selected-risk-assessment systems. *Child Welfare, 72*, 441–451.

Douglas, K. S., Cox, D. N., & Webster, C. D. (1999). Violence risk assessment: Science and practice. *Legal Criminologist Psychologists, 4*, 149–184.

Downie, N. M., & Heath, R. W. (1974). *Basic statistical methods* (4th ed.). New York: Harper and Row.

Epstein, N. B., Baldwin, M., & Bishop, D. S. (1982). *McMaster Family Assessment Device (FAD) manual (version 3).* Providence, RI: Brown University/Butler Hospital Family Research Program.

Epstein, M. H., & Sharma, J. M. (1998). *Behavioral and Emotional Rating Scale: A strength-based approach to assessment: Examiner's manual.* Austin, TX: Pro-Ed.

Faust, D. (1986). Research on human judgment and its application to clinical practice. *Professional Psychology: Review and Practice, 17,* 420–430.

Franklin, C. (1994). Assessment centers in children's services: A promise worth considering. In E. Gambrill & T. J. Stein (Ed.), *Controversial issues in child welfare services* (pp. 160–173). Boston: Allyn & Bacon.

Franklin, C., Nowicki, J., Trapp, J., Schwab, A. J., & Petersen, G. (1993). Developing a computerized assessment system for brief, crisis oriented youth services. *Families in Society: The Journal of Contemporary Human Services, 74*(10), 602–616.

Fredman, N., & Sherman, R. (1987). *Handbook of measurements for marriage and family therapy.* New York: Brunner/Mazel.

Garb, H. N. (1998). Recommendations for training in the use of the Thematic Apperception Test (TAT). *Professional Psychology—Research & Practice, 29*(6), 621–622.

Garb, H. N. (2000). Computers will become increasingly important for psychological assessment: Not that there's anything wrong with that. *Psychological Assessment, 12*(1), 31–39.

Gingerich, W. J. (1990). Expert systems and their potential uses in social work. *Families in Society, 71*(4), 220–228.

Graham, J. R., & Lilly, R. S. (1984). *Psychological testing.* Englewood Cliffs, NJ: Prentice-Hall.

Grotevant, H. D., & Carlson, C. I. (1989). *Family assessment: A guide to methods and measures.* New York: Guilford.

Grove, W. M., Zald, D. H., Lebow, B. S., Snitz, B. E., & Nelson, C. (2000). Clinical versus mechanical prediction: A meta-analysis. *Psychological Assessment, 12*(1), 19–30.

Guy, R., Edgley, C., Arafat, I., & Allen, D. (1987). *Social research methods.* Boston: Allyn & Bacon.

Hambleton, R. K. (1980). Contributions to criterion-referenced testing technology: An introduction. *Applied Psychological Measurement, 4*(4), 421–424.

Hathaway, S., & McKinley, J. (1943). *The Minnesota Multiphasic Personality Inventory.* St. Paul: University of Minnesota Press.

Hodges, K. (1994). *The Child and Adolescent Functional Assessment Scale self training manual.* Ypsilanti: Eastern Michigan University, Department of Psychology.

Holder, W., & Corey, M. (1987). *The child-at-risk field: A risk assessment/decision making model.* Charlotte, NC: Action for Child Protection.

Hudson, W. W. (1981). Development and use of indexes and scales. In R. M. Grinnell, Jr. (Ed.), *Social work research and evaluation* (1st ed., pp. 130–155). Itasca, IL: Peacock.

Hudson, W. W. (1982). *The clinical measurement package: A field manual.* Homewood, IL: Dorsey.

Hudson, W. W. (1989). *Computer assisted social services.* Tempe, AZ: Walmyr.

Hudson, W. W. (1999). *Measuring personal and social problems: Methods for scale development.* Unpublished manuscript. Tallahassee, FL.

Inwald, R. E., Brobst, K. E., & Morrissey, R. F. (1987). *Hilson adolescent profile.* Kew Gardens, NY: Hilson Research.

Jordan, C., Franklin, C., & Corcoran, K. (1997). Measuring instruments. In R. M. Grinnell, Jr. (Ed.), *Social work research and evaluation: Quantitative and qualitative approaches* (5th ed., pp. 184–211). Itasca, IL: Peacock.

Keller, R. A., Cicchinelli, M. F., & Gardner, D. (1988). *Comparative analysis of risk assessment models: Phase one analysis.* Denver, CO: Applied Research Associates.

Kordy, H., Hannover, W., & Richard, M. (2001). Computer assisted feedback driven active quality management for psychotherapy provision: The Stuttgart-Heidelberg Model. *Journal of Consulting and Clinical Psychology, 69,* 173–183.

Kuder, G. F., & Richardson, M. W. (1937). The theory of the estimation of test reliability. *Psychometrika, 2,* 151–160.

Lambert, M. J., Hansen, N. B., & Finch, A. E. (2001). Patient-focused research: Using patient outcome data to enhance treatment effects. *Journal of Consulting and Clinical Psychology, 69,* 147–149.

Lindsey, D. (1991). Factors affecting the foster care placement decision: An analysis of national survey data. *American Journal of Orthopsychiatry, 61,* 272–281.

Lindsey, D. (1992). Reliability of the foster care placement decision: A review. *Research on Social Work Practice, 2*(1), 65–80.

Lord, F. M., & Novick, M. R. (1968). *Statistical theories of mental test scores.* Reading, MA: Addison-Wesley.

McDonald, T., & Marks, J. (1991). A review of risk factors assessed in child protective services. *Social Service Review, 65,* 112–131.

Mattaini, N., & Kirk, S. (1991). Assessing assessment in social work. *Social Work, 36,* 260–266.

Meddin, B. (1984). Criteria for placement decisions in protective services. *Child Welfare, 63*(4), 367–373.

Mercer, J. (1979). *System of multicultural pluralistic assessment manual.* New York: Psychological Corporation.

Millon, T. (1982). *The Millon Clinical Multiaxial Inventory.* Minneapolis, MN: National Computer Systems.

Mutschler, E. (1990). Computer assisted decision making. *Computers in Human Services, 6*(4), 231–251.

Nugent, W. R., & Hankins, J. (1992). A comparison of classical, item response, and generalizability theories of measurement. *Journal of Social Service Research, 16,* 11–40.

Nugent, W. R., & Thomas, J. (1992). Validation of a clinical measure of self-esteem. *Research on Social Work Practice, 3,* 191–207.

Nunnally, J., & Bernstein, I. (1994*). Psychometric theory* (3rd ed.). New York: Mc-Graw-Hill.

Nurius, P. S. (1990). A review of automated assessment. *Computers in Human Services, 6*(4), 265–281.

Nurius P. S., & Hudson, W. W. (1988). Computer based practice: Future dream or current technology. *Social Work, 33,* 357–362.

Nurius, P. S., & Hudson, W. W. (1993). *Human services practice, evaluation, and computers: A practical guide for today and beyond.* Pacific Grove, CA: Brooks/Cole.

O'Hare, T. M. (1991). Integrating research and practice: A framework for implementation. *Social Work, 36,* 220–223.

Quay, P. (1987). *The revised behavior problem checklist manual.* Miami, FL: University of Miami.

Reid, W. J., & Smith, A. D. (1981). *Research in social work.* New York: Columbia University Press.

Rubin, A., & Babbie, E. (2000). *Research methods for social work* (4th ed). Pacific Grove, CA: Brooks/Cole.

Sarrazin, M. S. V., Hall, J. A., Richards, C., & Carswell, C. (2002). A comparison of computer-based versus pencil-and-paper assessment of drug use. *Research on Social Work Practice, 12*(5), 669–683.

Sattler, J. M. (1988). *Assessment of children* (3rd ed.). San Diego, CA: Author.

Savicki, V. (1989). Computers in the child and youth care field. *Child Welfare, 68*(5), 505–516.

Schuerman, J. R. (1987). Expert consulting systems in social welfare. *Social Work Research & Abstracts, 23*(3), 14–18.

Schuerman, J. R., & Vogel, L. H. (1986). Computer support of placement planning; The use of expert systems in child welfare. *Child Welfare, 65*(6), 531–543.

Schwab, A. J., Bruce, E. M., & McRoy, R. G. (1985). A statistical model of child placement decisions. *Social Work Research and Abstracts, 21*(2), 28–34.

Schwab, J. J., Franklin, C., & DiNitto, D. M. (1993, February). *Developing computer assisted assessment models that aid treatment and placement decisions in children's services.* Paper presented at the annual program meeting of the Council on Social Work Education, New York.

Schwab, J. J., & Wilson, S. S. (1989). The continuum of care system: Decision support for practitioners. *Computers in Human Services, 4*(1&2), 123–140.

Sicoly, F. (1989). Prediction and decision making in child welfare. *Computers in Human Services, 5*(3&4), 43–56.

Spearman, C. (1904). The proof and measurement of association between two things. *American Journal of Psychology, 15,* 72–101.

Springer, D. W. (1998). Validation of the Adolescent Concerns Evaluation (ACE): Detecting indicators of runaway behavior in adolescents. *Social Work Research, 22,* 241–250.

Springer, D. W., Abell, N., & Hudson, W. W. (2002). Creating and validating rapid assessment instruments for practice and research: Part one. *Research on Social Work Practice, 6,* 752–768.

Springer, D. W., Abell, N., & Nugent, W. R. (2002). Creating and validating rapid assessment instruments for practice and research: Part two. *Research on Social Work Practice, 6,* 752–768.

Stone, N. M., & Stone, S. F. (1983). The prediction of successful foster placement. *Social Casework: The Journal of Contemporary Social Work, 64*(1), 11–17.

Streeter, C. L., & Franklin, C. (1992). Defining and measuring social support: Guidelines for social work practitioners. *Research on Social Work Practice, 2,* 81–98.

Stuart, R. (1987). *Couple's pre-counseling inventory.* Champaign, IL: Research Press.

Winters, K. (1988). *Personal experiences screen questionnaire (PESQ) manual.* Los Angeles: Western Psychological Services.

Wolock, I. (1982). Community characteristics and staff judgments in child abuse and neglect cases. *Social Work Research and Abstracts, 18,* 9–15.

Wiebush, R. G., Baird, C., Krisberg, B., & Onek, D. (1995). Risk assessment and classification. In J. C. Howell, B. Krisberg, J. D. Hawkins, & J. J. Wilson (Eds.), *Serious, violent, and chronic juvenile offenders: A sourcebook* (pp. 171–212). Thousand Oaks, CA: Sage.

Wood, J. M., Garb, H. N., Lilienfeld, S. O., & Nezworski, T. M. (2002). Clinical assessment. *Annual Review of Psychology, 53,* 519–543.

CHAPTER 5

Qualitative Assessment Methods

Dorie J. Gilbert and Cynthia Franklin

Qualitative assessment methods are grounded in the need to understand and describe meaningful events in a client's life in the form of words, observations, and graphical depictions, rather than numbers. Accordingly, qualitative assessment methods differ distinctly in their philosophical, theoretical, and stylistic orientations to data gathering from the quantitative methods covered elsewhere in this book. The need for practitioners to emphasize qualitative observations in addition to quantitative measures for client assessments has been a much-debated topic in the field of psychological assessment over the past fifty years (Groth-Marnat, 2000).

Unlike quantitative assessment, qualitative assessment methods emphasize context and process through the gathering of detailed, case-by-case descriptions of the private meanings and interpretations of events by individual clients. These methods emphasize the complexities and fluctuating contexts in which problems exist. They typically give clinicians access to a client's frame of reference, personal beliefs, cognitive schemas, values, cultural realities, and personal motivations (Gilgun, Daily, & Handel, 1992; Landfield & Epting, 1987; Moon, Dillon, & Sprenkle, 1990; Polkinghorne, 1991).

In this chapter we will describe and show examples of qualitative assessment methods, including a discussion of their philosophical underpinnings and where they fit on the qualitative-quantitative continuum of methodological orientations. This chapter will help social workers understand the unique contributions of qualitative assessment methods. It will also discuss validity and reliability of qualitative data.

DEFINITIONS AND DESCRIPTIONS

Instead of relying on quantitative methods such as a measurement instrument to gather information about the client's problems, the social worker becomes the primary data gatherer when using a qualitative approach to assessment. That is to say, social workers rely on the conversations and interactions between the client and themselves to understand the client's problems. Qualitative assessment methods use words, pictures, diagrams, and narrative rather than numbers or operationalized concepts to tell the client's unique story. A clinician may describe the client verbally, use pictures or a diagram to demonstrate the client's life context, or use pictorial language, metaphors, or storytelling methods to describe the client and his or her problems (Borden, 1992; Guba, 1990; Moon et al., 1990; Neimeyer, 1993a; Taylor, 1993). This rich, in-depth description, sometimes referred to as "thick description," is used to provide enriching details about the client's experience to help clinicians gain a full understanding and appreciation for the complexity of a client's problem (Gilgun et al., 1992). For example, instead of labeling the client's marital arguments as severe because of a cutoff score on a quantitative measure or a record of the number of arguments a client has had in a week, the clinician would describe in detail using words, narrative, or pictures one or more of these arguments and expound on the impact of the fights on the couple's relationship. This is not to say that numbers may not be used in a qualitative assessment to describe the client's experience. When numbers are used, however, they are seen as just another method of description, generally as anchors along a continuum that represents the client's personal reality.

Thick description is believed to provide a method whereby clinicians can gain a better understanding of the context of problems because greater elaboration of the problems and situations is taken directly from the actual client reports. The client's own words, metaphors, and descriptions are reported verbatim or in edited form, and particular attention is given to making sure that the client's intended meanings are not altered. Clinicians may, for example, verify with the client their reporting of the client's stories in an assessment report, for example, (Yin, 1989). See appendix 5A for an excerpt from a narrative assessment report. Notice the rich detail, pictorial language, and descriptiveness of the information in the narrative assessment. This clinician frequently uses the client's own words or verbatim accounts and clearly differentiates between interpretations of client and clinician.

PHILOSOPHICAL UNDERPINNINGS

Qualitative methods differ from quantitative approaches in their ontological, epistemological, and theoretical orientations. Ontology has to do with one's view concerning the nature of reality. Epistemology refers to how we know what we know, or theories of knowing (Mahoney & Lyddon, 1988; Smith, 1989). The theoretical orientation of qualitative methods emphasizes theories that seek to describe how a group's meaning system is generated and sustained, as opposed to a theoretical orientation that consists of a logical, deductive system of interconnected definitions, axioms, and laws associated with quantitative methods (Neuman, 1994). The ontological, epistemological, and theoretical orientations of qualitative approaches are discussed in more detail below.

Qualitative methods are developed from a subjectivist ontology, rather than an empiricist or objectivist view. Subjectivists believe that realities are individual and socially constructed by the institutions and social order in which one lives: qualitative assessment methods seek to capture this subjectiveness of human experience. Their perspective is that human experience is subjective and contextually and culturally bound.

The epistemologies undergirding qualitative methods are constructivist. Constructivists believe that humans actively create and act on their own personal realities, and that there are no objective realities that can be known outside of one's own interpretations (Mahoney & Lyddon, 1988).

In contrast, quantitative assessment methods take the view that there is an objective reality that we should discover; even if we may only subjectively know it, we should try to ascertain this reality. Quantitative assessment methods prescribe to verification, quantification, and other methods to reduce subjectivity and verify observations made during assessment. This approach does not make sense to those who prescribe to qualitative assessment, because they do not believe that there are stable, knowable psychological or social realities of the client that can be assessed. Rather, they believe the way to know clients is to discover their own personal constructs or unique worldviews (Landfield & Epting, 1987; Neimeyer, 1993a). To make this discovery, the social worker must join the subjectivity of the client and engage the client in open-ended, individualistic, ideographic, and process-oriented assessments.

See table 5.1 for a comparison of the philosophical underpinnings of qualitative versus quantitative assessment methods.

QUALITATIVE VERSUS QUANTITATIVE ASSESSMENT METHODS: DISTINCT, BUT NOT INCOMPATIBLE

In his fifty-year review of psychological assessment, Groth-Marnat (2000) notes the classic work of Hunt (1946), who emphasized that clinical practitioners "should pay more attention to qualitative behavior during the testing situation and rework tests to yield a maximum amount of rich qualitative responses." In what has become a long-standing debate, critics and proponents of quantitative or qualitative methodologies tend to promote the data-gathering strategies consistent with their own philosophical allegiances (Atherton, 1993). Across social work and other disciplines, the contrast between qualitative and quantitative philosophies has generated considerable controversy (see, for example, Atherton, 1993; Hudson, 1982; Pieper, 1989; Raynor, 1984; Schuerman, 1982; Sheldon, 1984; Thyer, 1989a, 1989b; Tyson, 1992).

So, how does one decide whether to choose a quantitative or a qualitative assessment strategy? In this book, the authors take the view of technical, pragmatic eclecticism, that is, we support a synthesis approach

Table 5.1   Comparison of Philosophical Underpinnings

Issue or Area	Quantitative	Qualitative
Ontology (the nature of reality)	Realism: reality is singular, stable, and external.	Subjectivism: realities are individual and collective constructions of order in experience.
Epistemology (theories of knowing)	Objectivism: knowledge is authorized as valid by logic or reason; reality is revealed via the senses.	Constructivism: knowing is behavioral and emotional as well as cognitive; the validity of knowledge is less important than its viability; sensation is proactive.
Casual Processes (theories of causality or change)	Associationism: learning and change are linear chains of discrete causes and effects.	Structural Differentation: learning and development involve refinements and transformation of mental representations.
Axioms About	Quantitative/Posivitist Paradigm	Qualitative/Naturalist Paradigm
Nature of reality	Reality is single, tangible, and fragmented.	Realities are multiple, constructed, holistic.
Relationship of knower to known	Knower and known are independent, a dualism.	Knower and known are interactive, inseparable.
Possibility of generalization	Time- and context-free generalizations are possible (nomothetic).	Only time- and context-bound working hypotheses are possible (idiographic).
Possibility of causal linkages	There are real causes, temporally precedent to or simultaneous with their effects.	All entities are in a state of mutual simultaneous shaping, so it is impossible to distinguish causes from effects.
Role of values	Inquiry is value free.	Inquiry is value bound.

SOURCES: M. J. Mahoney & W. J. Lyddon. (1988). Recent developments in cognitive approaches to counseling and psychotherapy. *The Counseling Psychologist, 16*(2), 190–234. Y. S. Lincoln & E. G. Guba. (1985). *Naturalistic inquiry*. Beverly Hills, CA: Sage.

and agree with those who argue for a balance of both qualitative and quantitative approaches to data gathering as a response to the qualitative-quantitative debate (Moon, Dillon, & Sprenkle, 1991). There are many ways to know and empirically report a client's attributes and experiences, and the various assessment strategies can provide worthwhile and useful knowledge. What is important are the pragmatics and techniques of assessment (what the practitioner does to gather information about the client). The axiom followed throughout this text is: if an assessment method helps you obtain the type of information needed to help a particular client, then use it!

The authors take the position that qualitative and quantitative assessment methods, although distinct, are not incompatible, and both may be used in data gathering and formulating an assessment. From our perspective, all assessment methods, regardless of their distinct theoretical origins, may be used conjointly to improve the data gathered for an assessment. Multiple methods must be used to improve the reliability and validity of clinical information. In particular, qualitative methods add to the detail and thick description of a case assessment and may enhance the clinician's understanding of the context and process in which problems occur.

Unique Contributions of Qualitative Assessment

Qualitative assessment measures offer unique contributions to the assessment process. The ability of qualitative assessment methods to uncover perspectives and personal realities is grounded in the flexibility and emphasis on the context and process that clients present in the therapeutic relationship. Qualitative assessments range from behavioral observations, to verbal and written descriptions of a person's behavior or thoughts, biographical or autobiographical narratives, interviews, experiential exercises, and graphical depictions, all of which are well-suited for developing a holistic understanding of the client. The unique contributions that qualitative assessment measures bring to the assessment process and the helping relationship are discussed in the following sections.

Ability to Uncover and Corroborate Realities That Can Find and Confirm More Client Realities.   The depth and breadth of information that can be ascertained using quantitative approaches are limited. A major contribution of qualitative assessment is its ability to uncover social meanings of everyday behavior, the symbolic significance of an individual's behavior. In addition, qualitative assessments are often needed to corroborate and further elucidate the context of quantitative findings. An excellent example of this is provided by Layton and Lock (2001), who demonstrated the need for qualitative approaches to fully assess and confirm learning disabilities in students with low vision. The authors point out that the standardized measures used to assess learning disabilities in children rely on intake visual functioning and cannot be reliable when low-vision students use adaptations for visual impairments; they have not been normed on a low-vision student population. Instead, the authors use qualitative methods (informal testing to determine strengths and weaknesses in specific learning areas, behavioral observations and intensive observations of psychologically based mental actions and operations, interviews with parents and teachers, and sampling of students' work over time and across different environments) to provide a picture of students' daily performance. The qualitative data was then used to corroborate findings from the traditional, quantitative measure in what the authors term a "mixed methodology."

Adaptable to Assessing Diverse Populations.   Standardized instruments have been criticized for their limitations with people of color and other nonmajority or mainstream populations (Dana, 1998; Kutchins & Kirk, 1997). In making assessments across diverse populations, qualitative assessment measures have the advantage of being easily adapted to different populations that vary from the mainstream in ethnic or cultural identity, presence of disabilities, and any life experiences that separate them from the populations on whom tests are usually normed. For example, some Native American tribes do not espouse the concept of depression as a reaction to grief and loss, and thus, a standardized depression scale would not be appropriate with this population (Gilbert & Franklin, 2000).

The open-ended process-oriented style of qualitative assessment provides social workers with a window on clients' culturally based sociocultural and personal constructions. Certain Eurocentric values, such as of individualism and competition, which are central themes to many dominant theoretical perspectives, directly conflict with values of collectivism and cooperation that many nonmainstream populations hold. Qualitative assessments allow the social worker to explore cultural scripts and cultural meanings that would not be apparent in standardized assessments. The knowledge gained helps to place clients' experiences in a cultural context. This is especially important for identifying clients' strengths, even when their behavioral norms or beliefs do not match the values or norms of the majority culture.

Promoting the Social Worker's Self-Awareness.   The human-to-human interaction of a therapeutic relationship makes individualized assessment possible. The relationship further helps the social worker, as data gatherer, to capture unequivocal insights. Human-to-human assessments do not allow the social worker to maintain the type of objectivity that one might maintain in assessing a rock, for example (Peshkin, 1988; Smith, 1989). Rather, human-to-human assessment is subjective and experiential. When we are assessing our fellow humans, we are looking at ourselves. To understand the subjective human experience, both the social worker's and the client's, the social worker must develop a keen sense of self-awareness. Qualitative assessment requires social workers to be continuously cognizant that their own biases and beliefs may influence their clinical judgment (Gilgun et al., 1992). By developing self-awareness, clinicians are able to discern the differences between their interpretations and those of the client. It is essential that clinicians not force their reality or values on a client, because this will lead to misunderstandings of the client's problem and hamper the assessment process.

The Client-Social Worker Relationship Is Acknowledged.   Qualitative assessment methods allow for a more holistic, intimate, and cooperative relationship between the client and the practitioner. For example, soliciting recollections about early childhood experiences as an assessment strategy actively engages the client in the counseling process and reduces defensiveness while allowing the practitioner to interact empathetically in the counseling process (Clark, 2001). When conducting quantitative assessment, it may be easy to ignore the reality the social worker's presence has on the client. From the viewpoint of qualitative assessment, total objectivity and lack of reactivity is an illusion. Social workers as assessors must accept that their presence does affect the client-problem context and that this cannot be avoided. On entering into a relationship with a client, the social worker becomes a part of the *problem*; only by skillfully comprehending the client's problem definition and unique context may the social worker become a part of the *solution*. An example of comprehending a unique context would be understanding that the social worker's role and the system in which he or she works may be inadvertently maintaining a client's problem. Clients are more often aware of how the social welfare system negatively affects their lives than are social workers. To understand the subjectivity of the client, the social worker must use assessment methods that unravel the complexities of human thought and experience and allow the client to become the key informant and primary expert concerning his or her own problems (Crabtree & Miller, 1992). The social worker may then discover the context-bound, situational nature of the client's difficulties, as well as the relationship between process, context, and behavior.

Fits with Many Theoretical and Therapeutic Perspectives.   Qualitative assessments are well-suited for a number of commonly practiced therapeutic interventions. The diverse theoretical models that support qualitative methods range from family systems theories (second-order cybernetics) to ecological systems models, cognitive-constructivist therapies, and the strengths perspective. See Chapter 1 for a review of these perspectives. In addition, because qualitative methods emphasize process and acknowledge the subjectiveness of the client, these methods also fit well with cross-cultural perspectives, feminist theory, and Afri-centric theory—all of which emphasize the contextualized experiences of the client over traditional quantifiable ways of assessing a client. Many therapeutic approaches and personal construct therapies make use of qualitative assessment methods. These include cognitive-constructivist therapy, Adlerian therapy, and systemic family therapies (such as, solution-focused therapy) (Borgen, 1984; Jacob, 1987; Neimeyer, 1993a, 1993b; Polkinghorne, 1984, 1991).

Having so strongly emphasized the unique contributions of qualitative assessment methods, we need to reiterate that both qualitative and quantitative assessment methods are professionally sound and useful. In keeping with the rules for formulating comprehensive assessment, as discussed in Chapter 3, the practitioner should always use *multiple* methods to reduce errors in clinical judgment.

QUALITATIVE METHODS

Interviewing: Ethnographic Interviewing

Interviewing is the most frequently used method for assessing clients, and the face-to-face interview has been the cornerstone of social work practice. Qualitative assessment relies heavily on a form known as ethnographic interviewing (Berg, 1989; Fetterman, 1989; Taylor & Bogdan, 1984). The ethnographic interview demonstrates an abiding respect for context, language, and meaning for clients and their constructed reality (Crabtree & Miller, 1992; Fetterman, 1989). A formal discourse between client and social worker from which a negotiated view of one another is derived, ethnographic interviewing takes place in the context of building a relationship of mutual respect and cooperation with the client. The social worker treats the client as the expert and assumes a position of equality and collaboration.

Ethnographic interviewing entails speaking face-to-face and also mutual observation. Clinicians recognize that they become a part of the context of the interview and that there are restraints between the client and interviewer imposed by language. The social worker's questions may frame responses so that the role of translation between the client and social worker begins the process of constructing a joint reality.

Ethnographic interviewing is highly personal, interpretive, reflective, and elaborative. The interviewer tries to put away preconceived notions, diagnoses, and hunches about the client and starts out on a journey of understanding. To do so, social workers have to be reflexive and in touch with their own feelings, biases, and thoughts about the client. Clients become like teachers telling the social worker about their personal reality. But as every student knows, learning is not totally dependent on the teacher; learners have to be open, flexible, and receptive as well. They also have to be willing to interpret the ideas communicated within the context of the teacher and the concepts that are being taught. For example, if a student is a behaviorist and decides to study psychoanalytic theories, it will be necessary for that student to interpret those theories within his or her own linguistic and conceptual frameworks. If the student tries to interpret the psychoanalytic theories according to the concepts of behaviorism, the theories will never really be understood. The same is true for the social worker conducting ethnographic interviews; interpretations must occur within the client's own framework or worldview and not within the social worker's.

Ethnographic interviews may be structured, semistructured, or open-ended (Berg, 1989), although the latter two approaches appear to be more suitable to the explorative nature of the ethnographic approach (Fetterman, 1989). A structured interview has a previously formulated set of questions that the social worker asks the client; social workers do not deviate much from their list of questions. Semistructured interviews have a previously formulated set of questions, but the social worker may veer from that list as information emerges. Open-ended interviews have no previously formulated questions; the social worker just begins the interview and sees where it goes. In all three types of interviews, there usually is a guiding purpose that directs the interview: for example, to build rapport or assess whether abuse has occured.

Within the structure of different ethnographic interviews, various types of questioning techniques may be used to gather information from the client (Berg, 1989; Crabtree & Miller, 1992; Fetterman, 1989). Examples include the following:

Descriptive Questions are broadly open-ended. Grandtour descriptive questions attempt to elicit a rich story from the client. ("Describe your experiences at the high school after you became pregnant." "Tell me about life on the reservation." "Describe your future.") Minitour descriptive questions elicit smaller units of experience. ("What did your boyfriend do when he found out you were pregnant? Your teachers? mother?" "Tell me about your last experience at the sweat lodge.")

Structural Questions are inclusive and expand the focus of experience. ("Have you been married before?" "What does he do when he gets mad?")

Substituting Frame Questions take a term or phrase the client uses and substitute another question. (Note the sequence... Social Worker:

"Tell me what your mother is like." Client: "She comes across like she is cold and gripey." Social Worker: "What else does she comes across like?")

Contrast Questions are exclusive and expand experience. ("You said that you and Johnny had some good times together in the past; how has that changed now?" "You mentioned seeing a marital therapist in the past; how is your relationship different now?")

Rating Questions ask clients to give differential meaning to their experience. ("What is the worst experience you have had since you have been pregnant?" "What is the best thing someone did that really made a difference in your life?")

Circular Questions elicit information about transactions embedded in a system. ("How do mom and dad solve arguments between them?" "What do you think brother would say when dad doesn't pay attention to mom?")

These types of questions are not used exclusively with ethnographic interviewing but may be used in other forms of interviewing as well. In Chapter 8, for example, we cover how circular questions are used by systemic family therapists and give examples of such questions in that chapter's appendix.

Clinicians may use ethnographic interviewing to discover the personal meaning a client attributes to their problems, the therapy process, relationship patterns, or any other intrapersonal or interpersonal process. For example, Todd, Joanning, Enders, Mutchler, and Thomas (1990) used ethnographic interviewing to discover how the therapy process is perceived by clients. A semistructured interview was conducted for the purpose of keeping the clients focused on their experience. Following are examples of questions used in the ethnographic interview and a sample dialogue from one of the interviews. Todd et al., (1990, p. 56), provides these examples of questions:

> How do you refer to this place? What do you call what is done here? What do you feel is the role of a   ? It is important that the interviewer use the term used by the family (i.e., therapist, counselor, interviewer). Please describe the process you went through from the time you parked your car until now, please be as specific as possible. Does a "therapist" (whatever term the family uses) do the same things as other mental health professionals? What is the difference between mental health professionals such as therapists, counselors, psychologists, and psychiatrists? What makes a good "therapist"? (Use the term used by the family). How do you know if a "therapist" is or is not meeting your needs?
>
> It must be remembered that the interviewer should adopt the language of the family. In the example questions, the term *therapist* was used, but if the family continually referred to the therapist as a counselor, the term *counselor* should be substituted. Furthermore, each question may facilitate a response from a family that the interviewer may want to investigate in more detail, and he/she should improvise and do so.

A case example of an ethnographic interview by Todd et al. (1991, pp. 57–58) follows:

EI: (Ethnographic Interviewer): I would like to talk to you about what it is like for you to come into counseling. I would like to hear your perceptions, your story of what it is like to come here as if you were talking to another couple. . . . Fill me in briefly on what you would tell someone else about your experiences.

PHILIP: To start with . . . a little scary . . . I didn't know what they would say about me, didn't know if I'd be judged wrong, everything I was doing and saying. I've gotten to the point where I'm not scared to come here and say what I'm feeling. If they want to knock, that's their privilege. I want to get off my chest what I'm feeling.

EI: You moved from a place to come and be somewhat afraid because you might be blamed and jumped on to a place where you can get things off your chest?

PHILIP: Yeah.

EI: (to Marge): O.K., how about you?

MARGE: I like having that third person out there that is supposedly trained to know . . . to be able to read between the lines instead of a friend who will either agree with you because they think that's what you want them to say or a family member who is too much involved in it or doesn't have an objective view.

EI: Read between the lines? That part I was a little fuzzy.

MARGE: (pause) Well maybe like at the second session when the therapist said that he observed the anger and hurt going on . . . we might realize that but not understand it or maybe not want to admit it, and when a third person says it, you go, yeah that's what's going on.

EI: The therapist helped you understand and admit things you felt?

MARGE: Yeah.

PHILIP: At home I see her get angry, but I don't realize that she was angry because she was hurt. At the time I felt she was mad at me and wanted revenge, but actually it's because she has been hurt and I know I do that too and she doesn't know I've been hurt.

EI: So being here has helped you see more clearly what you've been feeling?

MARGE AND PHILIP: Yeah.

(Later in the interview)

PHILIP: I think he's done a super job.

MARGE: He gets the idea going then backs off and lets you fill in the pieces.

PHILIP: Passes you the ball and lets you run with it.

EI: He gives you the ball to run with?

MARGE: He points things out, that's where reading-between-the-lines type thing comes in.

EI: His role is to point things out, read between the lines, give you a ball to play with then get out of the way?

MARGE: To be there.

As shown in this example, ethnographic interviewing asks clients to explain in their own words the meanings that they ascribe to processes. Social workers listen intently and probe to understand in more depth what the client is saying. In addition, social workers adopt the language and the meanings of the client when communicating with the client. This aids in their mutual understanding of the world. Ethnographic interviewers know that there are multiple realities and that all clients communicate from their own unique reality. In a sense, from this viewpoint, every individual stands alone and speaks a unique language. Individuals from similar ethnicities, religions, cultures, or social classes have a long history of interaction, however, and have built similar realities; they speak the same type of language and may have had equivocal or similar experiences. Ethnographic interviewing is therefore particularly useful for understanding different ethnicities, religions, cultures, and classes. In every interview situation, the ethnographic interviewer becomes like an anthropologist seeking to discover the culture and personal frames of reference of the client. Clients become the key informants and teachers about their social realities.

Mutual understanding of different cultures and religious beliefs is formed out of the negotiation and social consensus building that transpire as we openly encounter one another and find ways to communicate. See box 5.1 for an example of a pretherapy assessment form used to assess a client's personal frames of reference within the context of solution-focused family therapy (de Shazer, 1985; Todd, 1993). Notice that the questions focus on getting detailed descriptions of client's behavior and the meanings associated with those behaviors.

Narrative Methods

Narrative assessment methods take into account life stories and the meanings that humans assign to their experiences. Narrative may function as a root metaphor in efforts to understand how people think, perceive, imagine, and make moral choices. All reality is constructed through stories. Richardson (1990, p. 118) describes narrative as, "both a mode of reasoning and a mode of representation. People can apprehend the world narratively and people can tell about the world narratively." There are two primary cognitive modes for understanding the world: the narrative and the logico-scientific modes (Bruner, 1986; Richardson, 1990). Each mode has a distinctive way of ordering experience and constructing reality (Richardson, 1990).

According to Polkinghorne (1991), the logico-scientific mode, as a language conceptual system, is an artificial system created to link the grammar of mathematics and relational logic. It limits its categories to the propositional type, with closed boundaries. In practice, the categories are defined by measurement operations. Relationships among members, in-

Box 5.1
Pretherapy Assessment Form

1. What makes you think your family needs our services?
2. What do you expect to happen here that will be helpful to your family?
3. What will convince you that your family does not need to come here?
4. How many days per week does the problem occur? (please circle)
   1   2   3   4   5   6   7
5. How many hours per day is the problem present?
6. Please place an X indicating the severity of the problem.
   1 .... 5 10
   very mild   very severe
7. Who will be the first person to notice an improvement in the problem? What will he or she notice that will indicate an improvement?
8. What is one of the first things your family will be doing differently when they notice improvement?
9. When does your family NOT have the problem?
10. How do you explain when the problem does not happen?
11. How will you know when the problem is really solved?
12. What are you doing to keep things from getting worse?
13. What would tell you that things are getting better?

SOURCE: T. Todd. (1993). *Pretherapy assessment.* The Brief Therapy Institute of Denver. Westminster, CO: Author.

cluding the existence of perceived characteristics such as a problem, can be established by mathematical procedures (Polkinghorne, 1991). The narrative mode, on the other hand, uses ordinary language conceptual systems that are culturally evolved. Narratives encompass a variety of category types other than mathematical. Their categories are most often defined in terms of similarity to a prototype (Polkinghorne, 1991).

Humans are believed to organize their experiences by narrative structure or the stories by which they explain and ascribe meanings to behaviors (Borden, 1992). Humans link events narratively and explain to themselves how and why events connect. Narrative meaning is created by explaining that something is a part of something else, or that something caused something else (Polkinghorne, 1988).

For example, a client may explain that her son commits crimes because he is like his father, who is in prison. Or she may explain her son's behavior as occurring because she is a bad mother and did not raise him properly. Either explanation gives structure to the meaning of events and may set in motion other behaviors or events that are consistent with the explanation. If the mother believes the first explanation, she may see her son as hopeless and destined to a life of crime; she may not be inclined to try to keep this from happening. If the social worker believes the first explanation, he or she may label the son as having "antisocial personality disorder" and recommend he be sent to the juvenile correction system.

If the mother believes the second explanation, she may involve herself in guilt-ridden responses that repeatedly rescue her son from the consequences of his behavior and inadvertently make his behavior worse. If the social worker believes the second explanation, she may decide the mother is an incompetent parent and recommend the son be removed from the home and sent to a residential treatment center.

The narrative can be communicated in verbal or written form. The client usually communicates the narrative in verbal form but may also do so in writing. The social worker as assessor usually captures in written form the essence of the narrative as reported by the client but also may communicate it in a verbal report, as at a case conference. Written narratives make it possible for social workers to record and reflect on the client's meaning structures, as well as their own responses to those private meanings. Written narratives are also used to communicate to others the client's experiences in a manner that provides insight into human behavior and motivations. According to Richardson (1990, p. 117), "narrative displays the goals and intentions of human actors; it makes individuals, cultures, and historical epochs comprehensible as wholes; it humanizes time, and allows us to contemplate the effects of our actions, and to alter the directions of our lives."

Written narratives provide social workers with methods that enhance assessment of the client. Three narrative methods will be covered below, process recording, case studies, and self-characterizations.

Process Recording.   Process or narrative recording is an intricately detailed and specialized type of case recording in which social workers write down the process of an interview with a client using an "I said, then he said" format and keeping as close as possible to direct quotes. In addition, the process recorder identifies his or her feelings or personal reactions to what the client says. A supervisor typically also goes over the recording and makes other comments about the client-social worker interview (Wilson, 1976). Process recordings help teach social workers interviewing and assessment skills. They also bring to light many of the relational or process issues that may emerge in managing a case. Social workers may be able to observe from the process recording something they said wrong or how their attitudes or feelings toward the client caused them to misunderstand the client. Germane to clinical assessment, social workers may be able to observe emerging themes or patterns in the interview that they might have missed if a shorter, less process-oriented recording of the interview had been used.

Despite its usefulness, process recording is time-consuming and impractical for use in everyday agency practice. It is usually reserved for social work education. It may also be used in agency practice, within the context of educational supervision, when a clinician wants special help with a difficult or unusual case. Following are some guidelines for writing a process recording.

According to Wilson (1976, pp. 18–20), the following information should go into a process recording.

(1) Identifying information. The name of the worker or student, the date of the interview, and the client's name and/or identifying number are necessary. It may be helpful to state the number of the interview (such as "fourth contact with Mrs. Smith").

(2) A word-for-word description of what happened, as well as the student can remember. For example: I told Mr. Garcia, "In order to find out what kind of work you might be able to do, you will be seen by the psychiatrist as well as the physician." Mr. Garcia said, "Psychiatrist? What do you mean?"

This student had chosen to spell out "I told Mr. Garcia" and "Mr. Garcia said." An abbreviated style is preferred, using "W" for "worker" and "C" for "client." Quotation marks are not necessary:

W: In order to find out what kind of work you might be able to do, you will be seen by the psychiatrist as well as the physician.

C: Psychiatrist? What do you mean?

(3) A description of any action or nonverbal activity that occurred. For example:

I invited Mr. Garcia into my office and asked him to sit down. He did so slowly and just sat there staring at the floor.

W: How are you feeling today Mr. Garcia? It took him a long time to answer but he finally raised his head and looked at me and said,

C: I feel terrible.

Before I had time to say or do anything he rose up out of his chair, started pacing around the room and was shouting that there was nothing wrong with him mentally and that he "didn't need to see no psychiatrist."

(4) The student's feelings and reactions to the client and to the interview as it takes place. This requires that the recorder put into writing his unspoken thoughts and reactions as the interview is going on. In the interview with Mr. Garcia, for example, the next few sentences might read:

At this point I began to feel a little uneasy. Mr. Garcia seemed to be getting awfully upset and I didn't know why. I was a little frightened and wondered what he would do next and I didn't know what to say.

(5) The social worker's observations and analytical thoughts regarding what has been happening during the interview. "What should I do next? I wonder how it would affect the client if I said such-and-such? Why is he acting this way? I wonder what he really meant by that statement? That seems to contradict what he told me earlier. He said he felt happy but he certainly didn't look it." In process recording, all these silent thoughts are put into writing. If the example of the contact with Mr. Garcia were continued, the next few lines might read as follows:

I was a little puzzled and wondered what to de next. I didn't know whether I should let him shout and get it out of his system or whether I should try and calm him down. I was curious why he was getting so upset but I didn't dare ask him any questions because I was afraid of getting him even more upset. I finally decided I had better show some empathy since he would probably argue and disagree with most anything I said anyway about the psychiatrist.

W: I can see that something about the idea of going to a psychiatrist is very upsetting to you.

C: (Turning and looking straight at me): You bet it is. I've been to those headshrinkers before and I've had it with them.

As soon as Mr. Garcia said that a lot of questions came to my mind about his past history and I knew he had opened the door for me to talk with him about this.

Another example of the worker's analysis and observations during the process recording might be as follows:

I asked Mrs. Jones if she had any income other than what she gets from our financial assistance program. She said not. She seemed very nervous though as she told me this. She was sitting very uncomfortable on the edge of her chair; she had a scarf in her hands that she kept winding around her fingers and she couldn't seem to sit still. She seemed so nervous that it made me wonder if she was telling me the truth or not. I asked her again, "Are you sure you don't have any other income?"

(6) A "diagnostic summary" or paragraph on the "worker's impressions" at the end of the process recording. Here the worker should summarize his or her analytical thinking about the entire interview he has just recorded.

(7) A "social service plan," "casework plan," or "treatment plan" immediately following the diagnostic summary statement. It indicates the worker's and client's goals for further social service contracts.

Notice that, in the above guidelines the process recording is very relevant to assessing a case, and the information from the process recording is used to formulate an immediate intervention plan. Most process recordings are set up in a column format that provides a place for the different aspects of the recording. Appendix 5B provides an example of a process recording that was completed by a social work student, Teyla Haas, in an educational setting at the University of Texas at Austin, School of Social Work.

Case Studies.   Another narrative method of recording and assessment, case studies, assists social workers in assessing different aspects of the client's functioning and related variables that may affect client functioning. A case study may be defined as a systematic organization and presentation of information about an individual case; it is typically undertaken to elucidate a particular clinical entity or problem requiring reflection or intervention (Trepper, 1990).

Case studies can be completed on individuals, families, groups, or organizations (Feagin, Orum, & Sjoberg, 1991; Yin, 1989). They make use of multiple sources of information, including interviews, social histories, life histories, and observations to investigate and communicate relevant clinical data concerning a certain aspect of the case (Yin, 1989). Usually the case study focuses on some descriptively relevant aspect of the case that the practitioner wishes to investigate. The practitioner organizes case information into a narrative summary, to explore or describe the client functioning along certain dimensions. For example, the case study might elucidate the impact of early developmental history on the client's current relationship functioning, or discuss the impact of culture on the client's response to treatment.

Case studies have also been used to discuss treatment effectiveness and outcomes (Trepper, 1990). A practitioner may discuss or write a case study to demonstrate how a certain set of interventions led to the resolution of a client's problems.

Historically, case studies were the preferred method for clinical investigation in a number of fields, including social work (Trepper, 1990). The case study method, however, fell into clinical disrepute with the increased focus on empiricism in clinical science. Scientific control of explanatory variables became of great concern, and any treatment outcomes that could not be verified through quantitative measurement methods and statistical models were considered invalid. These attitudes led many to shy away from the case study as a useful method of inquiry (Trepper, 1990).

Recent years have witnessed a resurgence of interest in the case study among clinical researchers and practitioners. For example, proponents of single case study designs brought a new empiricism to the case study. (In Chapter 11, we discuss the use of single case designs.) At the same time, other qualitatively oriented practitioners continued to see the usefulness of case studies and continued to use case study methodologies in their traditional forms (Crabtree & Miller, 1992; Gilgun et al., 1992).

Throughout the years, the case study has remained a favorite methodology among clinical practitioners. Case studies are presented at conferences in narrative form and on video and are frequently reported in journals and books to illustrate different aspects of clients' functioning and their responses to treatments. To present case studies that are rich in detail and filled with thick description, practitioners must take copious notes of their interviews and observations of the client (Crabtree & Miller, 1992; Yin, 1989). As they must with all qualitative assessment methods, practitioners creating case studies must make sure they are reporting the empirical processes that emerge from the client's case.

Following are five guidelines for keeping detailed notes for a case study.

1. Record key pieces of information while interviewing and observing the client. This may be in the form of key words or jottings. Use exact phrases and differentiate clinical impressions from empirical observations when necessary.

2. Limit the time the practitioner comes into contact with the client. For example, limit home visits to one or two hours so that stimulus overload does not occur and you can keep track of the information.

3. Make notes about the sequence of events and context in which they occur.

4. Write up detailed case notes that include a narrative account of the interview, observations, and clinical impressions, immediately after or as close as possible to the client contact.

5. Write your case notes before sharing details of the case or your clinical impressions with anyone, such as a colleague or supervisor.

Copious notes lead to case studies filled with thick description and clinically useful insights. Without detailed case notes it is not possible to construct a meaningful case study. Once the case notes are written, the social worker must find a method for reflecting on them and interpreting them into the case study. The immersion/crystallization analysis method that is used in qualitative research serves as a useful method for examining the case notes to identify clinically relevant patterns and themes (Crabtree & Miller, 1992).

Immersion/crystallization analysis comes from the heuristic paradigm in clinical research that emphasizes self-reflection in the research experience.

Social workers using the immersion/crystallization analysis method would take the following steps in analyzing the case notes. First, as interpreters and reflectors, social workers enter (read) the text (case notes) with the intent of empathetically immersing themselves, until an intuitive insight/interpretation or crystallization of the text emerges. Second, social workers investigate and interpret the case notes through concerned reflection, intensive inner searching, and the yearning for insight. Clinical intuition is relied on to gain insights into the clinical themes and patterns present in the case notes. Third, a cycle of empathic immersion with the case notes and crystallization is repeated until an interpretation is found. Finally, the results may be reported as a part of the case study.

Appendix 5C presents an example of a case study on ethnic identity. This case study was presented to illustrate the response of an African-American adolescent girl to a predominantly white social service delivery system. The case study illustrates the damage done to the adolescent's sense of self (Williams, 1987).

Self-Characterizations.   Narrative methods may make use of written self-description by the client. In Chapter 3, we covered journals and diaries as quantitative clinical methodologies that make use of clients' written descriptions of themselves and their problems to assess the frequency, magnitude, and severity of these problems. In self-monitoring and self-recording, two other narrative methods covered in Chapter 3, clients accurately report in writing on the occurrences of their problems, and the events that surround those occurrences. The methods covered in Chapter 3 developed from the cognitive-behavioral therapies. Behavior therapists, in particular, use narrative information, such as self-monitoring, to perform a contingency analysis to help identify antecedents (stimulus events) and reinforcers that are maintaining a client's problems. Recall from Chapter 1 that we discussed some of the methods used in behavioral assessment.

Qualitative practitioners and constructivists also ask clients to record narrative data on themselves. In particular, many narrative recording methods have developed from George Kelly's personal construct psychology, one of the distinctive theoretical underpinnings of the qualitative and constructivist approaches (Landfield & Epting, 1987; Neimeyer, 1993a). Self-characterization is one such self-recording method developed within personal construct theory (Neimeyer, 1993a). Another personal construct assessment method, the repertory grid, will be described in the next section; however, an exhaustive discussion of assessment methods from personal construct psychology are beyond the scope of this text. Readers are referred to Neimeyer (1993a) for a thorough investigation of the constructivist assessment methods of George Kelly, his followers, and other constructivist psychologists.

The self-characterization assessment technique asks clients to write a description of themselves as if they were a principal character in a play (Neimeyer, 1993a). In writing their description, they are instructed to take the position of an intimate friend or a personal and empathetic confidant. The primary purpose of this description is to assess how clients cognitively construct the world in relation to the roles they feel they must maintain. The unique cognitive structures of clients and the clients' social roles can then be explored and changed in therapy (Neimeyer, 1993a).

Self-characterizations were developed for use with individual clients but have been extended for use with families (Feixas, Proctor, & Neimeyer, 1993). Feixas et al. (1993, p. 161) give the following example of how practitioners may give an instruction to family members to gather a "family characterization" from them. The couple and family are asked to take about fifteen minutes to write a characterization of the family: "Write a brief character sketch of the family. Write it from the perspective of someone who knows the family intimately and sympathetically, perhaps better than anyone else knows the family. You should write in the third person. For example, begin by saying, I know the Smith Family. . . ."

Repertory Grids

Repertory grids assess the personal meanings and cognitive constructions of clients, along a particular dimension; they have become the most popular and best researched of the personal construct psychology assessment methods. The grid has appeared in over 1,000 studies and is considered by some to be the MMPI or Rorschach of constructivist assessment (Neimeyer, 1993a). Repertory grids were developed by George Kelly and were designed to assess personal meanings in relationship to Personal Construct Theory. Repertory grids can be used as both as a quantitative and a qualitative assessment tool. In this section we will explore their strengths as a qualitative method, yet considerable work has also been done on perfecting the grid as a quantitative measure. Statistical analysis of the patterns within the repertory grid and computerization of the grid have progressed significantly in the past ten years (Sewell, Adams-Webber, Mitterer, & Cromwell, 1992). Repertory grids are an example of an assessment method that combines or integrates the qualitative and quantitative assessment paradigms much as the projective assessment measures discussed in Chapter 3.

According to Neimeyer (1993a), repertory grids may be defined procedurally as a method for eliciting a client's construction of some domain of experience. Typically the client is asked to compare or contrast representatives from that domain (e.g., family members, possible careers) and then to systematically describe each of them on her or his own "repertory" of dimensions of evaluation, or personal constructs. The grid may be administered as a formal interview, as a written assignment, or on a computer. Sewell et al. (1992) review several computer programs that have been developed to obtain repertory grids from clients. Computer technologies for qualitative methods such as the repertory grid are on the increase (Fielding & Lee, 1992).

The following suggestions are adapted from Neimeyer (1993a) and provide guidelines for developing a repertory grid.

1. Determine which of the client's experience (domain) to explore in depth; this will, in turn, determine the elements used in the grid method. For example, does the social worker want to know about the client's relationship to the opposite sex? Parenting skills? Family relationships? Any element of experience can be used in the grid method as long as it comes from the same domain of experience. Different domains of experience must not be mixed, because they may not be construed the same way by the client.

2. After the elements are chosen, elicit from the client the constructs of the grid, that is, the items from the client's experience that are represented as a construct or a polar opposite for that realm or experience in order to generate many core constructs.

You may invite the client to compare or contrast elements. For example, if the elements on the grid were intimate relationships, the client might be asked questions such as "How are your father and your mother alike?" "How are they different?" "How are you and your brother alike or different?" "How is your wife like your mother?" "How are they different?"

Or, as another example, the client might be given a set of three elements on the grid and asked to compare two of the elements and contrast them to the third. Based on the answers to these questions, constructs would emerge that would be represented as polar opposite experiences and could be put on the repertory grid as representations of the client's constructs concerning intimate relationships. For example, if the client said that his mother and father differed in that one was lenient and easygoing and the other was strict and harsh, these dimensions would become polar opposites of relationship experiences that would be put on the grid.

3. In keeping with the qualitative approach to the measurement of meaning, use the client's own words and representations in developing the grid. Constructs may also be developed by the therapist from the session material. For example, if the social worker had taken an extensive social and family history from the client, it might be possible to ascertain from that material some of the client's constructs. Standardized constructs might also be used to compare one client to a group of clients of similar characteristics. For example, it is believed that clients who have been sexually abused have similar experiences psychologically, and much research literature is available to describe their experiences. It might be possible to describe the relationship experiences of your client from that material. For example, constructs such as control versus lack of control, trust versus mistrust, or manipulation versus honesty might be used as constructs for the intimate relationship experiences of incest victims.

4. After eliciting several constructs from the client, possibly up to ten or twenty, ask the client to compare, contrast, rank, order, or rate each element according to the construct dimensions (side or pole of a cognitive structure) elicited.

5. Interpret results of grid assessments by focusing on the content and the structure of the client's constructions. At the content level, grids can be analyzed in a qualitative or impressionistic manner by considering the patterns or unique constructions of the elements and constructs on the grid. At a formal level of content analysis, grids can be coded for

their themes or intrapersonal or interpersonal content. For example, themes such as fear, forcefulness, violence, and dependency may emerge as clinically relevant material. The level of abstractness that suggests a client's cognitive abilities in construing others may also be considered in the content analysis. Analysis of themes or abstractness of content are similar methods of assessment, as described by the projective measures discussed in Chapter 3. Such methods apprise clinicians of the latent or hidden psychological characteristics of a client's interpersonal experience.

At the structural level, grids can be analyzed using quantitative measurement methods, by concentrating on the degree of differentiation within the client's construct system or among the elements on the grid. Specifically, relationships between the constructs and the elements and a host of more subtle structural features can be assessed by computerized grid scoring programs. Many of these computer programs provide interactive feedback during administration of the grid (Neimeyer, 1993a). Computerization of the repertory grid methods is yet another example of the innovations available through computer technologies discussed in some detail in Chapter 4.

Figure 5.1 presents an example of a repertory grid constructed on a client Nadine. Nadine had a heterosexual relationship with Carl, who has now re-entered her life. She is confused about her feelings and sexual orientation. Listed at the top are the elements of the grid (the persons); listed on the sides are the constructs elicited. The numbers in the boxes are Nadine's comparisons of elements and constructs: 1 means that the person is better described by the first pole, 2 means that the person is better described by the second pole, and 0 means that neither pole applies. Recall from the discussion above that there is more than one method for the client to make comparisons of the elements and constructs on a repertory grid.

Graphics Methods

Graphic assessment methods are qualitative assessment tools that make use of pictures, drawings, spatial representations, or images to assess the client. There are many graphic methods that may be used in social work assessment; a full coverage of those methods is beyond the scope of this chapter. Three graphic methods are summarized below. Readers are referred to Mattaini (1993) for a more-detailed coverage of the graphic methods of assessment.

One graphic method developed by a social worker to assess families is the ecomap (Hartman, 1978). Ecomapping was introduced in Chapter 1 and provides a pictorial representation of the family and its ecological context from a cross-sectional perspective. One of the advantages of this

Figure 5.1   Repertory Grid

	Mother	Father	Joe (brother)	Nancy (sister)	Nadine (self)	Paul (son)	Joy (former lover)	Beth (lover)	Carl (lover)	Therapist	
1. Someone I am sexually attracted to	0	0	0	0	0	0	0	2	1	1	Less sexually attracted
2. Feel commitment toward	0	0	0	0	0	0	0	2	1	1	Feel no commitment
3. Committed to family and friends	0	0	0	0	0	0	0	2	1	1	Out for self
4. Dependent	0	0	0	0	0	0	0	2	1	1	Self-reliant
5. Smart	0	0	0	0	0	0	0	2	1	1	Average
6. Introverted/shy	0	0	0	0	0	0	0	2	1	1	Outgoing/assertive
7. Sexy and playful	0	0	0	0	0	0	0	2	1	1	Boring and serious
8. Moves toward me when I hurt	0	0	0	0	0	0	0	2	1	1	Stays away when I hurt
9. Intense	0	0	0	0	0	0	0	2	1	1	Emotional
10. Meets my expectations for affection	0	0	0	0	0	0	0	2	1	1	Doesn't like to be close
11. Successful in job	0	0	0	0	0	0	0	2	1	1	Dependent on me for support
12. Always knows what wants	0	0	0	0	0	0	0	2	1	1	Indecisive
13. Trustworthy	0	0	0	0	0	0	0	2	1	1	Mysterious
14. Feel admiration for	0	0	0	0	0	0	0	2	1	1	Feel sorry for

approach is that it maps the family and the relationships among its members, and also the relationship of the family to other social systems, such as schools, social services, and work. See figure 1.2 in Chapter 1 for an example of an ecomap.

Another type of graphic assessment technique is the PIE method, which measures individuals' and family members' psychological commitment to the different roles in their lives. The PIE method was originally developed by Cowan (1988). Initially, it was used to assess a husband's and wife's feeling regarding their roles as they transitioned into parenthood, but it may be applied to whole families. The PIE is easy to use. Each family member is given a page on which is drawn a circle with an eight-inch diameter (it looks like a pie; hence the name). Family members are asked to list the main roles in their lives; roles such as husband, wife, parent, son, friend, and student are included (Cowan, 1988). The family members are then asked to divide their PIE so that the different sections reflect the importance of each role to them. The different sections of the PIE can be measured to determine what percentage of the PIE is allocated to each role. These scores are described as representing the psychological self of each family member.

The Self Concept and Motivation Inventory (SCAMIN) "What face would you wear?" is a graphic method developed for use with small children. It involves showing children different drawings of faces: one face with a happy smile, a second with a straight line for a mouth, and a third with a down-turned mouth. Children are asked to mark the face that best depicts their feelings about certain conditions, such as how they feel at home (Farrah, Milchus, & Reitz, 1968). This method is best for understanding the feelings of young children and for assessing depression in particular. Some clinicians have adapted the method for work with families, however, by asking family members to draw one of the three faces for each family member. Extended family members can be included also. Younger children can be included in this assessment technique by asking them which face belongs to each family member. See figure 5.2 for an example of a family SCAMIN drawing done by a female client.

Observational Methods: Participant Observation

Qualitative assessment makes use of specialized forms of observation called nonstructured and participant observation. *Nonstructured observation* allows the clinician to observe the client without having a specific preconceived plan to observe particular content. Information is reflectively recorded as it emerges in interactions with the client. This nonstructured method is in contrast to the structured behavioral observation methods described in Chapter 3. *Participant observation* takes the nonstructured method a step further, by encouraging the practitioner to purposefully observe the client in everyday life and even participate with the client in his or her daily routine, as nonintrusively as possible. This methodology, of course, requires clinicians to get permission from clients to observe them and assumes that a prolonged period of observation is being arranged.

Figure 5.2   Family SCAMIN

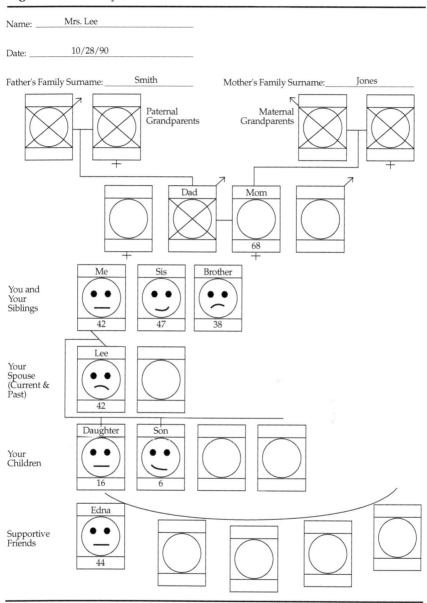

Name: _____Mrs. Lee_____

Date: _____10/28/90_____

Father's Family Surname: _____Smith_____   Mother's Family Surname: _____Jones_____

Paternal Grandparents

Maternal Grandparents

Dad   Mom
              68

You and Your Siblings

Me   Sis   Brother
42   47   38

Your Spouse (Current & Past)

Lee
42

Your Children

Daughter   Son
16   6

Supportive Friends

Edna
44

Participant observation is a humanistic methodology that is excellent
for studying processes and relationships among people (Jorgensen, 1989).
It emphasizes the insider's viewpoint of the participant's everyday life
experience. The participant observation methodology originated in the
research of social and cultural anthropologists and has been adapted to

social work research by family therapists and other clinicians (Gilgun et al., 1992). It also has clinical utility for social work assessment. Participant observation emphasizes the understanding of how the activities of groups and interactions of settings give meaning to certain behaviors or beliefs (Jorgensen, 1989).

Participant observation is most appropriate in the following situations:

1. The problems are concerned with human meanings (beliefs, values, etc.), contexts, and interactions that are best viewed from an insider's perspective.

2. The phenomenon to be assessed is an everyday life situation in a setting where the practitioner may observe or join the activities of the client (e.g., having dinner with a client family, observing a student in class, or participating in an activity within a day hospital).

3. The practitioner is able to gain access to a novel setting such as a crack or gang house.

4. The practitioner is trying to perform an in-depth case study.

5. The assessment information needed can be gained from the thick description obtained through the qualitative observation of clients.

As an assessment method, participant observation is especially useful when 1) little is known about the client; 2) there are important difference between outsider and insider view, as in the case of diverse cultures or economic conditions; 3) the phenomenon is usually obscured from outsiders, as in the case of family life; and 4) the phenomenon is intentionally hid from public view, as in the case of illegal behaviors (Crabtree & Miller, 1992; Jorgensen, 1989).

The following suggestions are provided for conducting a participant observation. First, clinicians must gain permission to enter and observe the everyday life of the client. They must decide where to start observing the client and gain supporters from the client's social network who will also agree to this observation. Clinicians must be prepared to reassure clients about concerns regarding their presence in everyday life activities. Second, clinicians must establish rapport and develop a trusting and cooperative relationship with those involved in the observation. They must fit in with the client's everyday life, be unobtrusive, and play down their evaluative role as an expert. Reflective listening and genuineness are critical skills to be used to gain rapport in participant observation settings.

Finally, clinicians should tell the truth about the purpose of their presence but not go into so much detail that the client is intimidated. The initial contact can make or break the observation period. Clinicians should try not to communicate the evaluative nature of their visits. They should, however, be honest if their observations could result in a decision or action that would affect the client's life, as in the case of an adoption study (Berg, 1989; Crabtree & Miller, 1992; Jorgensen, 1989).

Different types of observations are used in a participant observation. *Descriptive observation* is less systematic and represents a shotgun approach in which everything about clients and their situation is observed, to get an overall impression of their functioning. Focused observation is more focused and is based on the specific interests of the assessor. For example, if only the client's parenting style is of concern, the social worker might observe the client only in interactions with his or her children, perhaps at playtime, at dinnertime, or at bedtime. *Selective observation* enables clinicians to concentrate on specific characteristics or attributes. For example, if the social worker is interested in assessing only how the client disciplines his or her children, the social worker might observe specific situations between parent and child in which the parent attempts to discipline the children (Crabtree & Miller, 1992; Jorgensen, 1989).

Clinicians who use participant observation use case notes to keep track of what they are observing. A simple format will help the clinician keep case notes that may aid in the understanding of client behavior and its context. Notes on observations should be able to answer the questions: 1) Who is present? 2) What is happening? 3) When does the activity or behavior occur? 4) Where is the activity or behavior happening? 5) Why is the activity or behavior happening? 6) How is the activity or behavior organized? (Crabtree & Miller, 1992).

Recording structured case notes that answer the five questions above will help clinicians draw on their observations to formulate meaningful assessment of the client. Keeping track of the sequence of events and the emotions being expressed during these events may give the clinician further insights into what motivates the client.

Participant observations have many advantages over other qualitative assessment methods. As time passes in an observation within clients' everyday life, clients are less likely to alter their behavior because of the clinician's presence. Therefore, the practitioner may gain a more accurate picture of clients' behavior in an observation than in an interview. The longer the clinician observes clients in their everyday life, the more likely it is for the clinician to accurately distinguish between real and perceived behavior. Also, participant observation methods help clinicians learn effective ways to communicate with the client and therefore assist them in the reconstruction of client beliefs and behaviors (Crabtree & Miller, 1992; Jorgensen, 1989).

Combining Qualitative Methods Through Portfolio Assessment

Portfolio or performance-based assessments are multidimensional in nature and blend several types of evaluative approaches. These methods

have been particularly popular in educational settings where school social workers are employed but have applications to other types of clinical
assessments, as well. Wolf (1991, p. 36) defines portfolio assessment as a
"depository of artifacts" which at some point requires "a written reflection by the developer on the significance or contributions of those artifacts to the attributes of interest." The compilation of artifacts, or "portfolio," is an assortment of various documents, some of which may be
paper-and-pencil tests or classroom observations; others may be projects,
constructions, videotapes, audiotapes, poems, artwork, or stories produced by the student (Karoly & Franklin, 1996). Portfolios reflect a shift
in assessment from a behaviorist framework of learning involving the ac-
quisition of a sequence of component skills through drill and practice, to
a constructivist lens that regards learning as complex, contextual, and
collaborative. Portfolio assessment is culturally sensitive in that it recognizes a broad diversity in the pace and style of cognitive and learning development among children from various cultures.

Metacognition, a form of cognition that facilitates self-observation
and reflection, is a part of the assessment process. When portfolio assessment is used in educational assessments, students evaluate, in a systemic
way, how their learning is progressing on a particular assignment or
across a set of learning tasks (Karoly & Franklin, 1996). Reflections are
most often written but may also be oral presentations, remarks, or rumi-
nations supplemented by teacher annotations. Two assumptions underlie
the use of portfolio assessment in schools: 1) Judgments based on portfolios are more reliable and valid because of the comprehensive and inclusive nature of the samples, 2) Portfolios, when used as a supplement to
other methods of measuring learning, will improve the reliability and validity of the evidence (Karoly & Franklin, 1996).

Standards for evaluating performance-based assessments are usually
developed after portfolio work has been systematically collected; this
method is consistent with the qualitative approach to research and evaluation. This method is also in sharp contrast to traditional testing with standardized measures (discussed in Chapter 4), which sets specific criteria or
develops normative-based samples for comparison before students are
evaluated. The rationale for this approach is that standards should be locally (and realistically) established only after student work has been gathered. Portfolios cannot be reduced to numeric grades; they must be ap-
proached qualitatively, through a multidimensional evaluation. The case
study assessment at the end of the chapter further clarifies the usefulness
of the portfolio or performance-based methods of assessment.

DATA GATHERING IN QUALITATIVE ASSESSMENT

Both the qualitative and quantitative assessment methods intend to
ensure the accurate reporting of empirical observations of the clients. The

difference between the approaches is that qualitative assessment methods are concerned with ensuring that the clinician reports valid and reliable descriptions of client phenomenon from the perspectives of the client and other key informants. In this manner, qualitative assessments emphasize the understandings of private meanings, the context of behavior, and the individualized clinical significance of the results reported (Berg, 1989; Crabtree & Miller, 1992; Landfield & Epting, 1987; Taylor, 1993).

Because clinical assessment may be used to assign diagnostic labels that may, in turn, be used to assign people to differential roles (e.g., hospital patient, prisoner) by systems such as child welfare or mental health, it is also necessary to discern when a key informant may be misrepresenting information. That a client has misrepresented information would be particularly relevant to the assessment and would add to the clinician's understanding of the client's problems and their contexts. That is to say, the misrepresentation of facts would be viewed within its context and not just as a personal deficit of the reporter. In qualitative assessment, clinicians judge the accuracy of the data and are the expert interpreters of client problems and experiences as they are relayed by the client (Gilgun et al., 1992). Individualized personal exploration with the client, thick description from the case material, adherence to the client reports, and empirical observations of the clients are valued in the clinical interpretations.

In contrast, quantitative methods rely on numerical indices of observable client behavior, operationalization of verifiable descriptions, and quantitative measurement methods to establish the validity and reliability of the information gathered. The validity and reliability of data-gathering methods may be established without knowledge of the individual client's experience, and the client and social worker may not directly interpret the client's problems. For example, comparison with a normative sample may be used to judge whether the client is having a problem. See Chapter 4 for a discussion of validity and reliability of quantitative measurement, and Chapter 3 for a discussion of reliability of observational methods from the quantitative perspective.

Of course, clinicians using qualitative assessment methods do not rely exclusively on verbatim client descriptions, or representations of those descriptions such as pictures or diagrams. Nor do those using quantitative assessment rely exclusively on quantitative indices to assess the client. In any assessment situation, clinicians report their opinions and interpretations of what they saw and heard in their interactions with the client. Previous case records or reports from colleagues who have assessed the client may also influence the clinician's interpretations. In *qualitative* assessment, as in *quantitative* assessment, social workers are expected to report interpretations in a descriptive and empirical manner.

For example, clinicians would be explicit that these interpretations are their impressions and not what the client reported. Clinicians using qualitative assessment methods, however, give great credibility to client reports and clinical impressions, because the client is the main source of data and the clinician is the primary data gatherer and interpreter of clinical information.

Given the subjective nature of qualitative assessment, how does one evaluate the legitimacy of clinical impressions written in an assessment report or the validity and reliability of qualitative assessment information in general? In the next section, we will explore some common ways clinical impressions and other qualitative assessment data in the context of the assessment report.

Determining Validity and Reliability of Qualitative Data

Recall from our discussion in Chapter 4, that validity and reliability refer respectively to the accuracy and consistency of the assessment information. The evaluation of the validity and reliability of qualitative assessment data rests on the credibility, thoroughness, completeness, and consistency of the information within a narrative assessment report and the logical inferences and conclusions that the clinician draws from this information about the client. It may not be possible to know from an assessment report whether the clinician is reporting the client's story accurately. But it is possible to view the information in the report, with knowledge of the manner in which it was gathered, to evaluate the validity and reliability of the interpretations made by the clinician (Berg, 1989; Crabtree & Miller, 1992). Seven suggestions for evaluating the reliability and validity of qualitative assessment information follow.

1. Does the information tell a complete story, and do the conclusions drawn make sense in relationship to the client's story, as told? For example, are there big gaps in the information? Is the information too sketchy? Or does it skip around too much to make a clear connection with the clinician's interpretations?

2. Are there missing details or information that would put the clinician's interpretations in doubt? For example, does the clinician make a diagnosis that is not supported by the data in the report or fail to disqualify a differential diagnosis that is equally as plausible as the one given?

3. Are there any contradictions that may disqualify the clinical impressions, and if so does the clinician explain them in the interpretations? For example, if the clinician interprets that the client had a warm and secure upbringing, but the report gives only minimal information about the client's family history and specifically mentions that the family moved frequently because of personal and economic hardships, perhaps this interpretation should be questioned unless further explanation is provided.

4. Do the metaphors, pictures, or diagrams used make sense, and do you see the themes and patterns in them that the clinician interprets? All diagrams and pictures should be provided as a part of the results of the assessment report to give others an opportunity to verify the interpretations in the assessment. Although more than one clinical interpretation is possible using these methods, the clinical themes interpreted and reported by the clinician should be easy to discern from the data.

5. Did the clinician collaborate with the client in the formulation and interpretations of the client's problems? Did they check out their interpretations with the client? Qualitative assessment relies on the personal stories of clients and their private meanings. Clinicians should ensure the readers of the report that they are representing the client's life context appropriately and without undue interpretations or unsupported inferences. The client's own language should be used throughout, and clinicians should explicitly differentiate their interpretations from the client's report. Every interpretation should be backed up with empirical referents to what the client did and said. Every deviation from this format should be logically explained based on the clinician's experience or subjective impressions. If the report is not written in this manner, its conclusions should be questioned. Refer to appendix 5A.

6. Were multiple methods used to gather the information? Qualitative assessment relies on multiple methods to ensure the credibility of its data. Triangulation of data-gathering techniques (such as client's observation interview or sources of information such as client's and others' reports) is used to interpret assessment data. All methods and sources should be compared and contrasted to see if they point to the same conclusion. For example, are the client's interview data consistent with the clinical interpretation? Did the social worker's observations of the client agree with collateral sources' reports? If there was not agreement, was this inconsistency logically explained?

7. Has the clinician tried to disqualify his or her own interpretations? In qualitative assessment, clinicians should seek to prove themselves wrong by looking for other explanations for a client's behavior. For example, if the clinician believes a client has depression, the social worker would look for disconfirming evidence to see if this judgment holds up to further exploration and probing.

CASE STUDY: PORTFOLIO ASSESSMENT

The following case study was taken from Karoly and Franklin (1996) and involves a portfolio assessment of an African-American student in a school setting.

Background Information

The associate psychologist (AP) working in the Judson School District (near San Antonio) in Texas, conducted a routine re-evaluation of a special education student, following the guidelines mandated by the Texas Education Agency (TEA). Essentially, TEA requires that school districts assess special education students in specified domains primarily with psychometric instruments. The student evaluated was a 10-year-old African-American male, AM, who was being served in a self-contained Behavior Adjustment Class (BAC) for students with severe behavior problems. The evaluation included standard psychometric procedures including the Wechsler Intelligence Scale for Children, third edition; the Woodcock Johnson Psychoeducational Battery, the Holtzman Inkblot Technique, the Self-Report of Personality, and the Personality Inventory for Children. Additionally, the AP conducted a clinical interview and consulted teacher and parent information checklists developed by the school district.

AM had a long history of services in self-contained classrooms since the first grade for the purpose of managing his severe temper tantrums and aggressive behaviors. He was initially diagnosed by another school district as having dysthymia and overanxious disorder. After his placement in a self-contained classroom in the first grade, he was never assigned to a less restrictive mainstream setting with exposure to students who were not developmentally disabled. AM enrolled in the Judson School District in the middle of the 1992-93 school year where he was placed in a BAC class on his home elementary campus. He has an intact family, which includes his natural parents and two younger sisters. Both parents are blue-collar workers.

The results of the psychological assessment indicated that AM had average intellectual functioning and academic skills ranging from marginally average to below average. Information from this assessment identified specific deficits in AM's math and writing skills. Projective data suggested that AM perceives his environment as threatening, has difficulty with interpersonal relationships, and fantasizes excessively. There were some morbid themes in his inkblot responses including "evil people plotting to destroy the world," "evil fighting evil," and "people and animals who are dead or messed up." Parent and teacher checklists provided corollary information about AM, indicating frequent daydreaming, peer conflicts, periods of mood lability and explosive outbursts, and feelings of helplessness. The diagnoses of dysthymia and overanxious disorder were continued.

Presenting Problem

When the AP met with the teachers to conduct a planning meeting for AM's individual education plan (IEP), the AP anticipated that she would spend an extensive amount of time developing a discipline plan and that it was unlikely that AM would be mainstreamed. Contrary to the expectations, AM had been mainstreamed extensively in the regular classroom and he was also doing very well. His teachers anticipated a full-time placement in the regular classroom within a month. They related that AM was making B's in all subjects and his behavior was appropriate in the regular classroom, although still aggressive and disruptive in the BAC class. His BAC teacher, Mr. St. Romain, and his regular education teachers Ms. Haushall and Ms. Pruitt, had been coordinating a plan to assist AM in the transition from the self-contained to the regular classroom. Because of the discrepancy between the findings from the standardized assessment data and teachers reports, a portfolio assessment was undertaken with the help of the teachers, and the consultation of a school social worker.

Sources of Information

Three, ninety-minute observations were scheduled for AM, two in the regular classroom and one in the BAC classroom. Handwritten notes were taken during the observations, and field notes were later typed. Three, sixty-minute interviews were conducted with each of AM's teachers. These interviews were open-ended, loosely structured, and guided only by the topic of the student. The interviews were "conversational" and free flowing, encouraging the teachers to identify what they perceived as important issues about this student and his performance. The flexibility of the interviews facilitated the emergence of new and sometimes unanticipated information.

The Portfolio Assessment

The portfolio consisted of three notebooks of documents and several individual products that AM had designed and constructed. One aspect of AM's development in which we could see a progression of skills was his written composition. Many of the documents included early and final drafts of essays, themes, stories, and research projects that he had completed. When we examined the range of his writing samples, it was obvious that AM's writing skills had evolved from constructing simple ungrammatical sentences, to composing sentences with correct usage that were more elaborative and descriptive, to organizing ideas with the same topic into paragraphs. AM's compositions included both compound and complex sentences with appropriate verb and pronoun agreement. This is in marked contrast to his writing samples on the Woodcock Johnson, some of which included sentence fragments.

Included in the portfolio were several constructed items, including a pyramid, an Indian village, a wooden stool, a weathervane, a small race car that ran on a battery, and a terrarium. Each of these products demonstrated a multiplicity of skills and was accompanied by a written narrative by AM, describing the item and how it was constructed. We noticed that to construct the wooden stool and the pyramid, AM was required to make many math computations, which he illustrated on diagrams. All of the computations were done by hand (Ms. Pruitt would not permit calculators) and were on an illustration drawn to scale. Besides the hand tools AM used, he also described the use of a protractor for the pyramid and a level for the stool. It did not appear that he had much difficulty applying multiplication and division skills to design these products. The written description of the car with the battery included a discussion of electromagnetic principles. Ms. Haushall reported that this project was actually not assigned, but that AM had requested to work on "something" in his free time when they were studying a unit on electromagnetic energy. Very quickly, she and the class became interested in his project. She noted that AM had taught the children better about the concept of electromagnetism than all of her class presentation had.

Several of the portfolio documents included both written and illustrated book reports. In some, AM had drawn pictures depicting scenes from the books. The illustrations were completed in great detail. For example, a watercolor portrait of a scene from a children's book about King Henry VIII included a drawing of the Tower of London and beside it a guillotine dripping with blood. With other book reports, AM had drawn a series of comic strips in crayon to show consecutive sequences of events in the stories. One comic strip included in the final frame a drawing of AM himself saying, "I'm a Caldecott winner!" (The actual illustrator of the book AM was describing was awarded a Caldecott medal for his work.)

Other entries in the portfolio included several photo displays. One in particular showed the different stages of construction of props used in a class play about the Alamo. AM had been the "project manager" in designing an Alamo backdrop task, which he organized very well. An Alamo profile, a barracks scene, and a small chapel were all developed by AM's team. AM's photo history of the props was an item of great interest to the other children. AM was the photographer for all of the pictures included in the portfolio.

Finally, there was an assortment of quizzes and major exams in the portfolio. AM's performance on these items was variable, ranging from A's and B's on social studies, science, reading, English and math word-problem tests to C's and D's on math calculation and English usage exams. It was interesting that on the samples where AM made good grades, the content was complex and required the application of skills. The documents with low grades were tests of isolated skills that were not linked to a larger project or product.

Results of the Portfolio Assessment

AM's portfolio was evaluated jointly by the AP and the three teachers who gathered the samples. The products were judged using a hermeneutical framework grounded in a holistic interpretation by teachers who were familiar with the context in which the tasks were performed and whose interpretations evolved from a dialogue and debate among all of us. Therefore, unlike the psychometric evaluation, AM was truly being evaluated within the classroom milieu. True to the findings in the literature (Moss, 1994), there was some debate among us about the merits of certain products. All final decisions were the result of a consensus of the judgments of the four evaluators. Although, in contested cases, the opinions of the teachers usually prevailed because they were more familiar with the context in which the work was performed.

An interesting discovery that emerged from the observations and interviews conducted during the portfolio assessment concerned AM's fantasizing. AM's frequent fantasizing, which was regarded as pathological in the traditional assessment, was found to be an asset for him in his classroom. Ms. Haushall and Ms. Pruitt reported that AM usually "daydreams aloud" before his writing assignments. However, far from being off-task, this behavior seems to reflect his unique style of organizing a task and outlining his composition. Mr. St. Romain regards AM's rich fantasy life as a "coping" style for dealing with demands on him at school. AM keeps a journal in the BAC class that includes interesting anecdotes and reveals AM's internal reflections about important issues (e.g., Why do some kids hurt other kids' feelings? How come if someone hurts you, it's not OK to hurt him back? Mr. St. Romain and Ms. Pruitt reported that when AM is timed-out for misbehavior, he often "talks out" his problems aloud to characters in books, plays, and posters).

Another perceived strength of AM's is a combination of high intelligence and creativity. Despite the marginally average and below average scores AM earned on his Woodcock Johnson Psychoeducational Battery, AM is regarded by his teachers as above grade level and capable of producing unusual and high quality work. Ms. Haushall reported that AM earned a top rating on his TAAS writing sample (Texas Assessment of Academic Skills, a state-mandated achievement test) and described his compositions as full of elaboration and insight. For library week, he wrote a short story that was coherent and entertaining, and he has made numerous oral presentations in class about topics in social studies and science that were interesting and thorough.

Ms. Pruitt and Ms. Haushall both indicated that AM responds well to their correction in the classroom because he wants to "fit in" and "not stand out." All three of the teachers have observed that AM is also a "follower" who is greatly influenced by the peer models around him and who is highly susceptible to peer provocation. If others are working quietly and cooperatively, then he will follow suit. This observation was further supported by AM himself during a classroom observation in Ms. Pruitt's room when she was giving the students a fifteen minute timed test in math. Aware that AM has difficulty sitting still and concentrating for fifteen sustained minutes, Ms. Pruitt quietly called AM to her desk and asked him whether he needed "more time" to complete his test. AM replied that he preferred to take the test in the fifteen minute allotted period "just like everybody else." The two regular education teachers have also noted that the other students in AM's classes have extinguished some inappropriate behaviors simply by telling him to stop. This was evident during one observation in Ms. Pruitt's class when AM, while working in a group, got off-task and began drawing and coloring. A male classmate, who is a leader and an athlete, nudged him gently and said quietly, "Put that away and pay attention, man!"

All three teachers have built in both opportunities for movement for AM during their class periods and some choices about planning his work. They believe that both the movement and the power to make some decisions have made him more invested in his work at school. For behaviors that are very difficult for AM to demonstrate on a sustained basis (e.g., pay attention for the entire lesson, avoid impulsive comments), they ask for successive approximations of these behaviors such as attending for ten minutes and remaining quiet until the teacher stops talking. At the end of the day, both regular teachers "debrief" AM about the extent to which he has complied with their expectations.

Recommendations for Intervention

Findings from the portfolio assessment indicate that AM must see the task as one that reflects his membership in a regular classroom and as one that is part of a larger integrated whole, rather than just an isolated drill. This was well evidenced by AM's desires to "fit in" and "not stand out" in the regular classroom. The portfolio particularly illustrated that AM does well on work that he sees as either directed toward a purpose or producing a product. The work had to be meaningful to him in some fashion. For those assignments in which he was unable to see an immediate goal or outcome (including drills of facts or computations), he was poorly motivated to do well.

AM's general academic functioning, as evidenced by the portfolio documents, is characterized by higher level thinking skills, clear and coherent written expression, and an ability to read well and reflect on his readings. These results could not be identified by a psychometric assessment because it does not address contextual issues and is limited to sampling only isolated skills in a single session evaluation (Karoly & Franklin, 1996).

SUMMARY

In this chapter, we have discussed qualitative assessment methods, a distinct type of assessment methodology that has unique philosophical underpinnings. Qualitative assessment methods were defined and their philosophical underpinnings described and contrasted to the quantitative assessment methods covered in Chapters 3 and 4.

Specific methods for qualitative assessment were described, including ethnographic interviewing; narrative approaches such as process recording, case studies, and self-characterization; repertory grids; graphic methods; and participant observations. Finally, we further described the importance of validity and reliability in qualitative assessment and provided some guidelines for determining these.

STUDY QUESTIONS

1. Describe some ways that qualitative assessment methods differ from quantitative assessment.
2. How do qualitative assessment methods complement quantitative approaches to assessment?
3. Describe some benefits of case studies and how they have been used in clinical practice.
4. Describe a few of the helpful elements of a process recording. How do such methods aid work with clients?
5. Write a client note following the elements of good note taking in participant observation.

REFERENCES

Atherton, C. R. (1993). Empiricists versus social constructionists: Time for a cease-fire. Families in Society; *The Journal of Contemporary Human Services, 12,* 617–625.

Berg, B. L. (1989). *Qualitative research methods for the social sciences.* Boston: Allyn & Bacon.

Borden, W. (1992). Narrative perspectives in psychosocial intervention following adverse life events. *Social Work, 27*(2), 135-141.

Borgen, F. H. (1984). Reaction: Are there necessary linkages between research practices and the philosophy of science? *Journal of Counseling Psychology, 31*(4), 457–460.

Bruner, J. (1986). *Actual minds, possible worlds.* Cambridge: Harvard University Press.

Clark, A. J. (2001). Early recollections: A humanistic assessment in counseling. *Journal of Humanistic Counseling, Education, and Development, 40*(1), 96–105.

Cowan, C. P. (1988). Working with men becoming fathers: The impact of a couples group intervention. In P. Bornstein & C. P. Cowans (Eds.), *Fatherhood today: Men's changing role in the family* (pp. 276–298). New York: Wiley.

Crabtree, B. F., & Miller, W. L. (Eds.). (1992). *Doing qualitative research.* Newbury Park, CA: Sage.

Dana, R. H. (1998). Understanding cultural identity in intervention and assessment. *Multicultural aspects of counseling series, vol. 9,* Thousand Oaks, CA: Sage.

de Shazer, S. (1985). *Keys to solution in brief therapy.* New York: Norton.

Farrah, G. A., Milchus, N. J., & Reitz, W. (1968). *The self-concept and motivation inventory: What face would you wear? SCAMIN manual of direction.* Dearborn Heights, MI: Person-O-Metrics.

Feagin, J. R., Orum, A. M., & Sjoberg, G. (Eds.). (1991). *A case for case study.* Chapel Hill: University of North Carolina Press.

Feixas, G., Proctor, H. G., & Neimeyer, G. J. (1993). Convergent lines of assessment: Systemic and constructivist contributions. In G. J. Neimeyer (Ed.), *Constructivist assessment: A case book* (pp. 143–178). Newbury Park, CA: Sage.

Fetterman, D. M. (1989). *Ethnography: Step by step.* Newbury Park, CA: Sage.

Fielding, N. G., & Lee, R. M. (Eds.). (1992). *Using computers in qualitative research.* Newbury Park, CA: Sage.

Gilbert, D. J., & Franklin, C. (2000). Evaluation skills with Native American individuals and families. In R. Fong & S. Furuto (Eds.), *Cultural competent social work practice: Practice skills* (pp. 00–00). Needham Heights, MA: Allyn & Bacon.

Gilgun, J. F., Daly, D., & Handel, G. (Eds.). (1992). *Qualitative methods in family research.* Newbury Park, CA: Sage.

Groth-Marnat, G. (2000). Visions of clinical assessment: Then, now, and a brief history of the future. *Journal of Clinical Psychology, 56*(3), 349–365.

Guba, E. G. (Ed.). (1990). *The paradigm dialogue.* Newbury Park, CA: Sage.

Hartman, A. (1978). Diagrammatic assessment of family relationships. *Social Casework, 59*(8), 465–476.

Hudson, W. W. (1982). Scientific imperatives in social work research and practice. *Social Service Review, 56*(2), 246–258.

Hunt, W. A. (1946). The future of diagnostic testing in clinical psychology. *Journal of Clinical Psychology, 2,* 311–317.

Jacob, E. (1987). Qualitative research traditions: A review. *Review of Educational Research, 57*(1), 1–50.

Jorgensen, D. L. (1989). *Participant observation: A methodology for human studies.* Newbury Park, CA: Sage.

Karoly, J. C., & Franklin, C. (1996). Using portfolios to assess students' academic strengths: A case study. *Social Work in Education, 18*(3), 179–185.

Kutchins, H., & Kirk, S. A. (1997). *Making us crazy. DSM: The psychiatric bible and the creation of mental disorders*. New York: Free Press.

Layton, C. A., & Lock, H. (2001). Determining learning disabilities in students with low vision. *Journal of Visual Impairment and Blindness, 95*(5), 288–296.

Landfield, A. W., & Epting, F. R. (1987). The personal construct. In, *Personal construct psychology: Clinical and personality assessment* (pp. 13–29). New York: Human Sciences Press.

Mahoney, J. J., & Lyddon, W. J. (1988). Recent developments in cognitive approaches to counseling psychotherapy. *The Counseling Psychologist, 16*(2), 190–234.

Mattaini, M. A. (1993). *More than a thousand words*. Silver Spring, MD: National Association of Social Workers Press.

Moon, S. M., Dillon, D. R., & Sprenkle, D. H. (1990). Family therapy and qualitative research. *Journal of Marital and Family Therapy, 16*(4), 357–373.

Moon, S. M., Dillon, D. R., & Sprenkle, D. H. (1991). On balance and synergy: Family therapy and qualitative research revisited. *Journal of Marital and Family Therapy, 17*(2), 173–178.

Moss, P. (1994). Can there be validity without reliability? *Educational Researcher, 23*, 5–12.

Neimeyer, R. A. (1993a). Constructivist approaches to the measurement of meaning. In G. A. Neimeyer (Ed.), *Constructivist assessment: A case book,* (pp. 58–103). Newbury Park, CA: Sage.

Neimeyer, R. A. (1993b). An appraisal of constructivist psychotherapies. *Journal of Consulting and Clinical Psychology, 61*(2), 221–234.

Neuman, W. L. (1994). *Social research methods: Qualitative and quantitative approaches*. Boston: Allyn & Bacon.

Peshkin, A. (1988). In search of subjectivity: One's own. *Educational Researcher, 17*(7), 17–21.

Pieper, M. H. (1989). The heuristic paradigm: A unifying and comprehensive approach to social work research. *Smith College Studies in Social Work, 60*(1), 8–34.

Polkinghorne, D. E. (1984). Further extensions of methodological diversity for counseling psychology. *Journal of Counseling Psychology, 31*(4), 416–429.

Polkinghorne, D. E. (1988). *Narrative knowing and the human sciences*. Albany: State University of New York.

Polkinghorne, D. E. (1991). Two conflicting calls for methodological reform. *The Counseling Psychologist, 19*(1), 103–114.

Raynor, P. (1984). Evaluation with one eye closed: The empiricist agenda in social work research. *British Journal of Social Work, 14*, 1–10.

Richardson, L. (1990). Narrative and sociology. *Journal of Contemporary Ethnography, 19*(1), 116–135.

Schuerman, J. R. (1982). Debate with authors: The obsolete scientific imperative in social work research. *Social Service Review, 56*(1), 144–146.

Sewell, K. W., Adams-Webber, J., Mitterer, J., & Cromwell, R. L. (1992). Computerized repertory grids: Review of the literature. *International Journal of Personal Construct Psychology, 5,* 1–23.

Sheldon, B. (1984). Evaluation with one eye closed: The empiricist agenda in social work research. A reply to Peter Raynor. *British Journal of Social Work, 14,* 635–637.

Smith, J. K. (1989). *The nature of social and educational inquiry: Empiricism versus interpretation* (pp. 63–86). Norwood, NJ: Ablex.

Taylor, J. B. (1993). The naturalistic research approach. In R. M. Grinnell, Jr. (Ed.), *Social work research and evaluation* (4th ed., pp. 53–78). Itasca, IL: Peacock.

Taylor, S. J., & Bogdan, R. (1984). *Introduction to qualitative research: The search for meanings.* New York: Wiley.

Thyer, B. A. (1989a). First principles of practice research. *British Journal of Social Work, 19,* 309–323.

Thyer, B. A. (1989b). Letters to the editor: Exploring epistemologies; The debate continues. *Journal of Social Work Education, 25*(2), 204–210.

Todd, T. (1993). *Pretherapy assessment.* The Brief Therapy Institute of Denver. Westminster, CO: Author.

Todd, T. A., Joanning, H., Enders, L., Mutchler, L., & Thomas, F. N. (1990). Using ethnographic interviews to create a more cooperative client-therapist relationship. *Journal of Family Psychotherapy, 1*(3), 51–63.

Trepper, T. S. (1990). In celebration of the case study. *Journal of Family Psychotherapy, 1*(1), 5–13.

Tyson, D. B. (1992). A new approach to relevant scientific research for practitioners: The heuristic paradigm, *Social Work, 37*(6), 541–556.

Williams, B. E. (1987). Looking for Linda: Identity in black and white. *Child Welfare, 66*(3), 207–216.

Wilson, S. J. (1976). *Recording: Guidelines for social workers.* New York: Free Press.

Wolf, K. (1991). *The schoolteacher's portfolio.* Stanford, CA: Stanford University Press.

Yin, R. K. (1989). *Case study research: Design and methods.* Newbury Park, CA: Sage.

CHAPTER 6

Children and Adolescents

Catheleen Jordan and Janie Hickerson

The special issues of child and adolescent populations are the focus of this chapter. Assessment and measurement techniques are reviewed and a case example is presented. The important environmental interactions for this group occur in the school, at home, and with peers.

Experts generally agree that children can and do exhibit seriously deviant behavior, that developmental considerations and the environmental context are extremely relevant in child assessment, and that childhood deviance may lead to problems in adulthood (Bornstein & Kazdin, 1985; Harper-Dorton & Herbert, 1999). Childhood experts disagree on the appropriate method of diagnosing children's problems; thus, different diagnostic methods are described next, as well as the multicultural issues of child assessment.

DIAGNOSIS

Child diagnosis is done from three different perspectives: categorical, empirical, and behavioral (Bornstein & Kazdin, 1985; Harper-Dorton & Herbert, 1999).

Categorical Diagnosis

The most widely used categorical system for diagnosing children is the *Diagnostic and Statistical Manual of Mental Disorders* (*DSM* [American Psychological Association, 2000]). As discussed in Chapter 1, the categories in this type of system are clinically derived, based on the judgment of those thought to be experts in the field.

Categorical diagnosis simply describes client symptoms, and features such as age at onset, predisposing factors, and prevalence. Diagnostic criteria are also provided. These attempt to provide key symptoms, duration of dysfunction, and so on and are based on clinical judgment. It is believed that corrections are made as new data becomes available. Finally, the system is multiaxial, that is, it takes into account the presenting problem, as well as related issues. The most used categories for describing problems of children and adolescents are listed in box 6.1.

BOX 6.1
Child/Adolescent Disorders

Mental Retardation (Axis II)
317.00 Mild mental retardation
318.00 Moderate mental retardation
318.10 Severe mental retardation
318.20 Profound mental retardation
319.00 Unspecified mental retardation

Learning Disorders
315.00 Reading disorder
315.1   Mathematics disorder
315.2   Disorder of written expression
315.9   Learning disorder NOS

Motor Skills Disorder
315.4   Developmental coordination disorder

Communication Disorders
315.31 Expressive language disorder
315.31 Mixed receptive-expressive language disorder
315.39 Phonological disorder
307.0   Stuttering
307.9   Communication disorder NOS

Pervasive Developmental Disorders (Axis I)
299.00 Autistic disorder
299.80 Rett's disorder
299.10 Childhood disintegrative disorder
299.80 Asperger's disorder
299.80 Pervasive developmental disorder NOS

Attention-Deficit and Disruptive Behavior Disorders (Axis I)
314.   Attention-deficit/hyperactivity disorder
314.01 Combined type
314.00 Predominantly inattentive type
314.01 Predominantly hyperactive-impulsive type
314.9   Attention-deficit/hyperactivity disorder NOS
312.8   Conduct disorder
        Specify type: childhood-onset type/ adolescent-onset type
313.81 Oppositional defiant disorder

Feeding and Eating Disorders of Early Childhood
307.52 Pica
307.53 Rumination disorder
307.59 Feeding disorder of infancy or early childhood

Tic Disorders (Axis I)
307.23 Tourette's disorder
307.22 Chronic motor or vocal tic disorder
307.21 Transient tic disorder
        Specify: single episode or recurrent
307.20 Tic disorder NOS

Elimination Disorders
        Encopresis
787.6   With constipation and overflow incontinence
307.7   Without constipation and overflow incontinence
307.6   Enuresis (not due to a general medical condition)
        Specify type: nocturnal only/ diurnal only/nocturnal and diurnal

Other Disorders of Infancy, Childhood, or Adolescence (Axis I)
313.23 Selective mutism
313.89 Reactive attachment disorder of infancy or early childhood
        Specify type: inhibited type/ disinhibited type
307.30 Stereotype/movement disorder
        Specify: if with self-injurious behavior
309.21 Separation anxiety disorder
        Specify: if early onset
313.9   Disorder of infancy, childhood, or adolescence NOS

NOS = Not Otherwise Specified

One advantage of categorical diagnosis is that multiple aspects of the problem are considered. For example, if a child is being diagnosed for a language or speech disorder, the child's articulation as well as expressive and receptive language are considered. An additional advantage is that the system gives child helpers a common language to discuss child problems.

Limitations of categorical diagnosis include the continual inclusion of more and more categories with no supporting empirical evidence. The *DSM* has also been criticized for overstepping its boundaries and diagnosing child problems not traditionally thought of as being in the psychiatric domain; for example, developmental delays. The low reliability of the categories is also criticized; research to date on the childhood diagnostic categories has not been positive. Other criticisms suggest that the duration of dysfunction or age of onset for some disorders was included in some instances when there was either no evidence, or conflicting evidence, for such inclusions. Additionally, children's social functioning is not given enough attention in the *DSM*. Finally, there is no system for prioritizing, when children experience multiple problems.

Empirical Diagnosis

The development of empirically tested measures for diagnosis of child problems is called empirical diagnosis. Statistical procedures, such as correlational analysis and factor analysis, are used to identify the important features that should be included for a specific diagnostic category or concept. For example, three factors have emerged as significant predictors of child problematic behavior: conduct problems, personality problems, and inadequacy/immaturity (Quay & Peterson, 1987).

In addition to identifying groupings of symptoms or syndromes that have been empirically derived, empirical diagnosis uses multivariate classification (use of a number of different measures) to diagnosis a problem. Reviews of these multivariate studies show similarities.

Advantages of empirically derived diagnosis include utilization in conjunction with the *DSM* for a more inclusive diagnosis. The child gets evaluated across all areas (factors) included in the empirically derived test. Because testing provides an empirically derived score, children's problems can also be prioritized (unlike *DSM*). Finally, because tests provide interpretive data that enable the child's score to be compared with a normative group, empirically derived tests help to establish how children compare with their peers.

Limitations of empirically derived testing include variation in a given analysis resulting from such factors as rater reliability, appropriateness of the clinical sample, and item content. Furthermore, data collected are often from parent or teacher reports, rather than from observations of behavior. Such reports are not always verified by comparison with direct observation of the problem behavior.

Finally, parents may well suffer from their own marital or individual problems which may influence the ratings.

Behavioral Diagnosis

Characteristics of behavioral diagnosis include emphasis on a functional analysis of behavior, rather than reliance on a categorical system such as the *DSM*. Functional analysis seeks to identify or operationalize children's specific problematic behaviors and the controlling conditions that continue or promote those behaviors. These behaviors are, in turn, targeted for modification. For example, a functional analysis of a child with problems in the classroom reveals that the child initiates conversations with other children and leaves his seat without permission approximately three times per half-hour observation period. These incidents occur only in reading class, where the teacher has a somewhat authoritarian disciplinarian style that seems to elicit the disruptive behavior from the child. A second characteristic of behavioral diagnosis is the classification of behavior into broad categories, such as excesses and deficits. In the example above, the child is excessively out of his seat. Third, behavioral diagnosis relies on direct measurement of the specific problem behavior. The teacher might measure or count the number of incidents of disruptive behavior (number of times child left seat).

One advantage of behavioral diagnosis is that it is highly individualized. It provides an in-depth analysis of a specific child's problematic behavior, the controlling conditions, and the modifications necessary for change. Behavioral diagnosis provides information on specific problems targeted for change, facilitating an easy transition from assessment to treatment.

Limitations of behavioral diagnosis relate to the lack of a classification system, which hampers accumulation of knowledge. Also, because behavioral diagnosis is oriented toward assessing the problem in the present rather than looking into the past, relevant historical factors (such as onset, depth of dysfunction) may be overlooked. The behavioral literature does not reflect what types of clients have which types of problems.

In contrast to classifying children's problems according to diagnostic or other criteria, psychological theories explain how children acquire behavior, problematic or otherwise. The next section reviews prominent child developmental theories.

PSYCHOLOGICAL THEORIES

Barth (1986) suggests that children's problems may be time limited, because children often "outgrow" their problems. Stage theories of development, such as the theories of Piaget and Erikson, suggest that children go through fixed developmental stages. Given more credence in recent years, however, are theories that show the developmental process to be more flexible, that is, children must have the maturational readiness as well as learning opportunities in the environment, before they can move ahead. Therefore children develop at different rates. This also implies that all children can learn and change. The major child developmental theories can be grouped as cognitive, affective, or learning (Bloom, 1984).

Cognitive Theories

The cognitive theories of Kohlberg and Piaget describe development from the perspective of how one's mental processes perceive and affect one's experience in the world. The development of mental processes or structures is the focus of the theory. Information is believed to be assimilated into existing mental structures, which are represented as schemata; integration of new experiences occurs by accommodation. Four discrete stages described by Piaget explain this development.

The first stage, the sensorimotor period, describes cognitive development from birth to two years of age. During this period, the infant's contact with the world is through the senses, that is, by sucking, tasting, touching, hearing, and seeing. Piaget describes the essential tasks that infants have during this period: differentiation of self from others, called object permanence; recognition that external people or objects can be experienced through more than one sense; and beginning formation of cognitive schema through interaction with others or objects.

The second stage, the preoperational period, occurs from ages two to seven and is composed of two phases, egocentric and intuitive. Egocentricism describes the child who is tied to current experiences and environment, but, through language development, begins to develop more symbolic processing. This symbolic processing is continued in the intuitive phase.

The third stage, the period of concrete operations, lasts from ages seven to eleven. This stage is characterized by the development of logical thinking, classification, seriation, and conservation and is thus characterized by what Piaget calls decentering, or moving away from the previous egocentric view of the world.

The fourth stage is the period of formal operations and lasts from ages eleven to fifteen. In this, the highest form of cognitive development described by Piaget, children develop the ability to logically reason, both inductively and deductively.

Piaget described children's moral development as occurring in two stages: heteronomy and autonomy. The first stage is characterized by children's adherence to the fixed rules of others, particularly the parents. Children gradually move into the second phase, which is characterized by rules that can be negotiated and changed by mutual consent.

Kohlberg furthered the discussion of children's moral development by describing three levels of moral development: premoral, conventional, and postconventional. Each level has two stages, which describe the choices individuals have at each level.

The premoral phase coincides with the preoperational stage of cognitive development. The two stages are punishment and obedience, in which the child obeys the rules to avoid being punished, and instrumental behavior, in which the child obeys to be rewarded.

The conventional phase is reached after the period of concrete operations begins. The two stages are conformity, in which the child seeks approval and tries to avoid disapproval from others, and law and order, in which the child obeys because of a respect for law and order.

The postconventional level is reached after the formal operations stage is reached. The two stages are social contracts, in which the child makes rational decisions but the law is the final word, and the perception of universal ethical principles, in which the child bases moral decisions on his or her conscience.

The strongest research support for the cognitive model appears to be for the substages in the sensorimotor stage and for the concrete operational stage. Findings from studies on the other stages are less clear-cut. Both Piaget and Kohlberg have been criticized for the difficulty of replicating their research findings and by critics who believe that their view minimizes the role of the environment.

Affective Theories

The work of Freud has been extended and expanded by numerous theorists and practitioners concerned with personality development from the affective perspective. The affective perspective of child development is concerned primarily with the role of feelings in human behavior, rather than the rate of thought, as with the cognitive theories described above. Freud's work is described in five dimensions: dynamic, genetic, topographical, structural, and economic.

The dynamic dimension describes psychological energy located in the instincts, innate structures that direct behavior (for example, the libido, an unconscious force that is expressed sexually). Freud also described the pleasure principle, the child's tendency to seek pleasure and avoid painful experiences or tensions.

The genetic or developmental dimension describes stages or periods that Freud felt to be a part of every individual's history. First, the *oral period* is represented by the infant's mouth and taking in of food, and symbolically the taking in of other nourishment such as warmth. The developing child is then faced with the challenge of toilet training, leading to the second stage, which Freud called the *anal stage*. The child's ability to exert control over his or her bodily functions, and perhaps to be in conflict with parental demands, may contribute to problems that continue in the individual's adult life. The third stage is referred to as the *phallic period* and involves the child's developing awareness of his or her genitalia. The next stage, the latency period, is a time when sexual issues are suppressed by the child's entering school and becoming refocused on other issues. However, in the *genital period*, which begins in puberty, sexual issues again become important to the developing child. Children are believed to need to achieve mastery in each of these stages before they can successfully move on to the others. If mastery is not achieved, the individual can become fixated at any one point and will display signs of this lack of resolution.

In the topographical or depth dimension, Freud described three personality components believed to account for behavior: the unconscious, the conscious, and the preconscious. The *unconscious* component is outside of the person's awareness and believed to be mostly composed of the id. The *conscious* component is a smaller area of awareness, focused on something in the present. The *preconscious* is outside current awareness, but accessible. The material in the unconscious is believed to be accessible only through mechanisms such as a slip of the tongue, or somatically as in the case of phobias.

The structural dimension describes the personality, as divided into id, ego, and superego. The id is believed to be unconscious and represents the primitive portion of the personality, which operates based on the pleasure principle. The ego develops next and is the rational portion of the personality. It seeks to express id impulses in a more rational fashion. Finally, the superego is composed of the ego ideal, that is, the information about good and bad that the child learns from the parents, and the conscience, and the information about good and bad that the child learns from the parent's actions.

The economic dimension describes how children utilize their inherent energy. Psychic investment toward a specific object is called cathexis. External conditions may prohibit expending energy toward an object, which is anticathexis; in this case, the child forms internal mechanisms to block or delay the energy.

Erikson described eight psychosocial developmental issues: trust, autonomy, initiative, industry, identity, intimacy, generativity, and integrity. These issues correspond to eight stages of the life span, from infancy and early childhood, to old age. Like Freud, Erikson postulated that the child had to resolve the tasks of one stage before moving onto the tasks of the next stage.

Affective theories have been criticized for their lack of empirical evidence and for the difficulty involved in operationalizing the concepts. However, recent attempts to study psychoanalytic theory have provided some support for some of the concepts.

Learning Theories

So far, we have reviewed thinking and feeling theories of child development. Learning theories focus on acting, which is behavior itself. Three learning models are discussed here: respondent conditioning, operant conditioning, and social learning theory. These models share the common idea that behavior is learned.

Pavlov's **respondent, or classical, conditioning model** illustrates the learning process as follows. Pavlov found that food (a natural or unconditional stimulus) elicited a salivation response. He paired the natural stimulus with another stimulus, a bell. This second stimulus, after repeated pairings with the natural stimulus, also elicited the salivation response without the presentation of the food. The second stimulus is now called the *conditioned* stimulus and has the power to condition other stimuli. This conditioning process occurs with objects, persons, and verbal behavior as well; for example, a baby is comforted by his baby blanket, which was conditioned by pairings with mother and feedings.

Skinner's **operant conditioning model** proposes that behavior is learned as a consequence of the rewards or punishments that follow the behavior. If the behavior is positively reinforced, it is more likely to occur again; it will be less likely to occur again if the behavior is followed by an aversive experience. If the parent or teacher gives attention only when a child acts disruptively at home or in class, the child will continue to be disruptive. Schedules or contingencies of reinforcement determine how quickly behavior is learned and how well established it will be. Continuous reinforcement encourages behavior to be emitted more quickly; whereas intermittent reinforcement establishes behavior at a slower rate. Behavior reinforced intermittently maintains longer after cessation of reinforcement than behavior reinforced continuously. For example, if a child is rewarded with candy every time she carries her dishes to the sink, this behavior will be learned quickly but stop quickly if the reward is stopped. A child rewarded only some of the time will take longer to learn the behavior; however, once the behavior is learned, it will be maintained for a longer time, because the child thinks a reward will eventually be forthcoming.

Bandura's social learning theory elaborates on learning by respondent or operant mechanisms, contributing the idea of vicarious learning, that is, learning may occur by observation of a model and by observation of the consequences of the model's behavior. Bandura's studies on the vicarious development of aggressive social behavior has contributed to the debate on causes of aggressive behavior in children and others. Bandura showed that children viewing adults modeling aggressive behavior were more likely to exhibit the same aggressive behavior than children who did not view these adult models.

The learning theorists have contributed more empirical research to support their theoretical views than the cognitive or affective schools of thought. Bloom (1984, p. 312) recommends, however, that "Until such time as enough of the evidence is in to maintain or to discontinue use of one or another theory, the student is probably most wise to study their major representatives and try to become facile in all of them." Social theories, familial and environmental, are reviewed in the following section.

Social Theories

Child problems are not a symptom of individual pathology, but of a malfunctioning ecosystem, according to some (Barth, 1986; Harper-Dorton & Herbert 1999; Janzen, Harris, & Jordan, in press). These researchers assert that positive changes are longer lived when children's problems are assessed and treated in the broader context of the family and the environment. Next issues related to familial and environmental theories that affect child problems are reviewed.

Familial Theories

Children's problems are related to the number of stressful events experienced by the family. Also, as children grow, their normal developmental changes may lead to maladjustment. Isolated families are at a greater risk, because they lack access to community resources that could help them adjust to developmental changes (Barth, 1986). Family changes or transitions cause stress (Jordan & Cobb, 2001). The traditional family that consists of a father who goes out to work and a mother who stays home with the two kids is virtually nonexistent. New family styles, such as dual working couples, single-parent families, and remarried or blended families all have their associated stressors. Other family transitions, such as birth of a sibling, or children leaving for college, can also cause stress on the family system. Any family change may be expected to cause at least temporary discomfort for the parents and children, and any loss of money or status can be extremely devastating.

Physical or mental issues, or parent or family morale problems, may affect children (Jordan & Hoefer, 2002). Though more and more mothers work outside the home and share the role of provider, women still do the majority of the housework, with resultant fatigue, morale problems, and resentment. A mother's working outside the home may benefit the family by helping her to feel better about herself and by enhancing the family income. Problems may arise, however, when family members move from work or school to home life. Other parental job factors that may affect children's adjustment include parental job loss or transfer. Parent psychopathology, divorce, or spouse abuse can also affect children.

Environmental Theories

Parents' perception of their children's adjustment (or lack of it) is defined by their friendships and other external relationships (Barth, 1986). Parents learn what is "normal" and how their children stack up to other children by comparing to others in their neighborhood. Parents' social supports, friends, family, and neighbors all informally support parenting efforts. Some communities have more formal support systems, such as parenting classes and alcoholic support groups for parents.

The primary settings in which children are expected to perform are the home and the school (Barth, 1986). Studies show that children's personalities as well as their environments determine children's behavior. Some studies find that children behave differently at home than at school, but others find that children's behavior is consistent across settings. Children need social, cognitive, and self-management competencies to be successful at home and at school.

Social competencies include ability to accept influence, exert influence, learn from models, accept reprimands, negotiate with others, protect oneself from others, groom oneself, engage the company of others and avoid isolation, and resolve conflicts with strategies such as problem solving.

Cognitive competencies include cognitive skills for solving interpersonal problems: identifying the problem, generating alternative solutions, seeing the other party's viewpoint, seeing the consequences of the alternative solutions, evaluating the consequences, and choosing the best solution.

Self-management competencies include commitment, goal setting, arousal management, self-monitoring, evaluation, and self-administration of consequences (self-reinforcement).

The child's level of motivation—the interaction between individuals and their environments—is an important part of the environmental picture. A lack of motivation indicates that social or material incentives should be considered for the child. For example, the child can be rewarded with a point system for completion of homework assignments. The points may then be exchanged for toys, privileges, and so forth.

Finally, the child's culture is an important part of assessing the child's environment. It is important to know how the members of the child's culture and ethnic background define child problems, child discipline, and so forth, as discussed in the following section on children of color.

CHILDREN OF COLOR

Children and families of color require special consideration and should be assessed as framed by Erickson's developmental stages, ecological systems, and with a cross-cultural perspective (Gibbs & Huang, 1989; Janzen et al., in press). Canino and Spurlock (2000) discuss a multi-axial approach to assessment and intervention with children of color; this approach should be spearheaded by a culturally competent practitioner who is willing to consider ethnicity and immigration status in assessment, and also willing to advocate for change in larger systems, such as school and community, as part of the intervention process.

Psychosocial Adjustment

Individual psychosocial adjustment includes several special considerations. Low-income, minority children may suffer from the effects of malnutrition, leading to lack of energy and stunted growth; therefore, a physical exam may be indicated. Children's affect may be a product of cultural variation; for example, not making eye contact may indicate respect for adults rather than lack of respect. Self-esteem, interpersonal competence, achievement, and attitudes toward autonomy may be defined differently by particular ethnic groups; therefore, it is important to check one's assumptions and determine the norms for these ethnic groups.

Ethnicity and culture affect all aspects of a child's life. Migration and acculturation experiences vary among minorities and can be stressful events, especially if the youth emigrates from a war-torn country. Psychosocial adjustment should be carefully assessed within this context (Guarnaccia & Lopez, 1998). Achievement might be defined in ways other than the traditional majority-culture definition of educational achievement (Nurmi, 1993); if so, assessment should focus on the child's success in other areas, such as sports or music. Beliefs about development and behavior vary widely cross-culturally. Even the emergence of language is regarded uniquely according to ethnicity. Characteristics such as dependence and passivity are valued in some cultures, whereas independence and assertiveness are prized in others (Johnson-Powell, Yamamoto, & Arroyo, 1997). Ethnic groups have different methods of teaching children how to manage aggression and control impulses. Some may use guilt; others, shame. Finally, coping and defense mechanisms to protect the child from anxiety may be either externalizing (acting out or yelling, for example) or internalizing (withdrawing from social situations).

Relationships with Family

A second area for assessment is family relationships. Ethnicity and social class influence family size, structure, traditions, and so forth, all of which influence the child's role within the family. Some important characteristics that may prescribe norms or expectations for children include age, sex, birth order, physical characteristics, and personality traits. Families also differ in terms of parental authority, disciplinary practices, communication styles, and language fluency, all of which should be topics in the assessment. Recognizing the family beliefs, the level of acculturation, and the degree of involvement in neighborhood and community can provide important information in assessment, as can religion. In some cases, religion plays an important role in health issues as well as in the family value system. Acknowledging not only the parents but also extended family, and significant adults such as "healers" and religious leaders, can improve the prospects for successful intervention (Barona & de Barona, 2000; Canino & Spurlock, 2000).

School Adjustment and Achievement

School adjustment and achievement should be assessed from four perspectives: psychological adjustment, behavioral adjustment, academic achievement, and relationships with peers. Children from low-income, minority families have difficulty making the transition to school environment from homes that are different from the societal norm. Families may lack education and view the educational system negatively; they may be unfamiliar with school requirements; or they may have language and other difficulties. Therefore, a review of records, sensitive interviews with parents and children, and interviews with teachers can establish rapport and enlist needed support for intervention. Furthermore, expectations and cultural norms can emerge to direct the clinician in interpreting the assessment within the appropriate ethnic context. When assessing or testing a minority child, the practitioner may want to suspend some procedures. For example, use of time-limited standardized tests may work unnecessarily against the child (Armour-Thomas & Gopaul-McNicol, 2001).

Adolescents may fear school or fear the rejection they may suffer from being different. Minority children account for a proportion of students with behavior problems that result from their propensity to solve problems, or to cope with the environment, by acting out. Behavior problems, however, may be symptoms of other, more-worrisome problems, such as poor health from inadequate nutrition or health care. In addition, the social pressures of being a minority, of feeling disempowered, of chronic poverty and anxiety predispose these children and adolescents to depression (Roberts & Chen, 1995; Siegel, Aneshensel, Taub, Cantwell, & Driscoll, 1998). Minority students do not generally do as well in school as white students and have more problems with dropping out and being expulsed or suspended. Some of the problem may lie with inappropriate testing procedures; IQ and achievement tests may not be culturally sensitive. Also, children may have motivational deficits or lack of parental support. Study skills should also be assessed.

Peer Relationships

Peer relationships are an indicator of the minority child's well-being. Peer interactions, or lack thereof, and degree of involvement may be indicative of the child's perception of self in relation to the larger society. Peer group assessment should be done at the school and community level, as the child may have different experiences in the two settings. Peer interactions, and particularly opposite-sex relationships, may be an issue for biracial youth.

Adaptation to the Community

The child's overall community relationships should be assessed, as these may be indicative of the child's adjustment. Specific areas to look for include the child's group and community involvement, and special interests or abilities that could help the child develop a sense of competence. Gibbs and Huang (1989) stress that these assessment guidelines should serve as general guides to assessing children in their unique culture. They point out that there is variation within ethnic groups, and one should consider the uniqueness of each child.

One must always, also, be aware of the conditions by which the child arrived in the mainstream culture. Immigrant children have different issues, such as the trauma of hurriedly leaving a country torn by war or political upheaval, whereas children of color who were born into minority status may be fully acculturated. In all cases, children may experience a sense of belonging to both cultures (the minority and the majority cultures) or of belonging to neither culture. In assessing this factor, clinicians should consider, too, how willing the majority culture has been to confer equal status on these children and their families (Canino & Spurlock, 2000).

In summary, childhood assessment should cover four broad areas: diagnosis, psychological issues, social issues, and issues of children of color.

The following section reviews methodologies available to aid the assessment process.

ASSESSMENT METHODS

This section reviews some of the many assessment tools that are currently available to help in the assessment of children, categorized as global techniques and self-report techniques/scales.

Global Techniques

Global techniques for assessing children help to obtain a global picture of children's functioning and the problems they are encountering. The three techniques mentioned here are interviews, play, and sculpting/other family techniques.

Interviews. Interviews are the most commonly used technique for assessing children, parents, and teachers (Hughes & Baker, 1990; McConaughy, 1996). Sattler (1988) reviewed the use of interviews for gleaning information from children and their parents. Goals for the interview include establishing rapport, understanding the presenting problem, and obtaining information from a broad range of perspectives. In addition to the guidelines presented in Chapter 2 for the integrative skills protocol, important areas for the assessment of children for inclusion in the interview include interests, school, peers, family, fears or worries, self-image, mood or feelings, somatic concerns, thought disorders, aspirations, expectations, and fantasies. Additional topics for adolescents include heterosexual or homosexual relationships, sexual activity, and drug or alcohol usage.

Structured and semistructured interviews can elicit this wide range of information. Some structured interviews require lengthy time to administer and, in some cases, extensive training for the clinician; others may be conducted and scored by laypersons. Examples of structured interviews that do not require specialized training include the Diagnostic Interview Schedule for Children, Version 2.3 (Schaffer, 1992) and the Diagnostic Interview for Children and Adolescents–Revised (Reich & Welner, 1990). These instruments yield information that is easily codified for data analysis and for diagnosing mental disorders in children and adolescents. However, these instruments may not be as flexible as semistructured interviews, which provide not only standardized questions but also some adaptability for the age and personality of the child.

The Semistructured Clinical Interview for Children and Adolescents (SCICA) (McConaughy & Achenbach, 1994) was specifically designed for use with children aged six to eighteen years. This instrument allows the interviewer to adjust the order of questions to the natural order of the discussion with the child; it also provides information about a variety of facets in the child's life, including peer group and school, not just mental health status. The SCICA shows moderate to good test-retest reliability (0.54 to 0.89) for all of its subscales, and generally good concurrent validity (McConaughy, 1996). Social workers should be mindful that the reliability of all interviews rests solidly with the interviewer, in how careful the interviewer is to follow testing protocol, how prepared the interviewer is to work with the child, and how conscientiously the interviewer scores the data. In general, the reliability of interviews across time and sometimes across subjects (child and parent) can be questionable, particularly structured interviews with children under twelve.

Interviewing parents generates essential information in the assessment of and intervention with children and adolescents. Barkley (1990) recognized parent interviews as not only a source for diagnosis but also as the primary way to gauge the level of family distress and to understand more about the child's problems with relationships. In addition, interviewing the parents gives them the chance to express their concerns, their frustrations, and their systems for coping with these problems. This process establishes rapport with the parent that is fundamental to successful intervention or treatment later on (Jenson & Potter, 1990).

Parents should be asked about the referral problem; the ways they have attempted to deal with the problem; the child's medical, developmental, educational, and social history; family history; prior treatment for the problem; results of past treatment; and expectations about the evaluation. As with child interviews, parents can provide more comprehensive information through semistructured interviews that may include standardized rating scales such as the Child Behavior Checklist (CLBC) (Achenbach, 1991) or the Basic Assessment System for Children (BASC) (Reynolds & Kamphaus, 1992). A primary goal of interviews with parents is to define the child's problems in observable, discreet behaviors that will facilitate targeted intervention and measurable progress.

Teachers should also be interviewed when appropriate. It is appropriate to involve teachers when the child's problem is exhibited in the school setting. They should be asked about their view of the referral problem; the antecedents and consequences of the problem; any attempts that have been made to solve the problem; how others (teachers and students) react to the problem; school academic performance; their view of the family; and their expectations and suggestions for school-based interventions (McConaughy, 1996). Standardized teacher rating scales include BASC (Reynolds & Kamphaus, 1992), and the Behavior Evaluation Scale-2 (McCarney & Leigh, 1990). More-specific problems, such as attention and hyperactivity or social skills difficulty, are addressed by scales like the Conners' Teacher Rating Scale (Conners, 1990) and the School Social Behavior Scales (Merrill, 1993). Of course, personal interviews with teachers are useful, as well, and can uncover any negative feelings the teacher has toward the child or any underlying reasons for referral.

The family may also be interviewed as a whole. Information about the following subjects may be obtained by the social worker's observation of the family or through direct questioning: each member's view of the child's problem(s); family interactional patterns; family communication patterns; family social and cultural norms and values; and child's behavior individually, as compared with child's behavior in the family group. The Darlington Family Assessment System (Wilkinson, 2000) presents a thorough method for describing and assessing families by providing information from the child's point of view, the parents' point of view, and the total family point of view. This framework offers a semi-structured interview and rating scale with explicit directions about how to implement the system in clinical work with children and families. A fundamental advantage to this model is its adaptability to a variety of families and theoretical approaches.

Sattler (1988) gives guidelines for interpreting the assessment data and sharing it with the child and parents. Before meeting with the child and parents, synthesize the data gathered from the interview and evaluate your own feelings about it; look for common patterns or themes; try to account for any discrepancies you may find; look for indicators of the child's strengths and weaknesses, and resources for change or for coping. Then meet with the child to provide reassurance, verify your hypothesis concerning the problem(s), and present your findings. Meet with the parents to describe the child's problems and the plan for treatment and to address any parental issues or problems that may affect the child. Be sensitive to the parents' feelings while also protecting the child's right to confidentiality.

Play.   With the younger child, information may be gathered during games or other play activities more efficiently than in a formal interview session. Asking children to engage in unstructured play, such as drawing pictures of themselves or their family and then telling about what they've drawn, or making models of themselves out of clay, may help the social worker to establish rapport and learn valuable information. More-structured therapy games are also available (e.g., The Thinking, Feeling, Doing Game, 1973) and may serve the same purpose.

Sattler (1988) offers guidelines for interpreting children's unstructured play. These include how the child enters the room, initiates play activities, expends energy while playing, moves while manipulating the play materials, paces self during play, moves his or her body in play, verbalizes while playing, integrates play activities, exhibits creativity, utilizes products, and reflects attitudes about adults during play. Other important considerations in assessing children's play are the age appropriateness of the child's play, as well as the tone of play (hostile, impatient, etc.). Cross-culturally, children's play mirrors social role and family structure and may display symptoms of family problems such as uninvolved or neglectful parenting (Berk, 1999).

Sculpting/Other Family Techniques.   Older children may be assessed in the context of the family system by utilizing techniques such as sculpting (Frieson, 1985) or ecomapping (Sheafor, Horejsi, & Horejsi, 1988). Sculpting requires the child or other family member to address family members as if they were made of clay and mold them accordingly. The social worker might request that the child mold the family to depict a typical family scenario, such as when they have supper together. The child then places members in relation to each other and molds their faces to convey moods. The child would also place him- or herself in the picture. Then the family would be asked to talk about how it felt to be in the scene and whether they agreed with the depiction. Other members might then remold the family as they see it.

Ecomapping depicts the family in the larger community or societal system. It is done with paper and pencil and requires family members to identify external, environmental issues that affect each member (see figure 1.2 in Chapter 1). This form of assessment not only sets up collaboration between the clinician and the family but also encourages interaction among family members that may facilitate needed change. In addition, ecomapping allows parents to view their families more objectively, which may obviate defensiveness and resistance (Miley, O'Melia, & DuBois, 2001).

Other family techniques that might be helpful to children and their families are described by Frieson (1985). The family may be asked to construct a family floor plan. Each member draws his or her house floor plan and then answers questions about each room: What is the mood of the room? Smells, sounds, colors? Is there a special room? Are there issues of closeness, or privacy in the house? How does the house fit in with the neighborhood? Frieson also discusses using metaphors (such as animals or objects) to describe oneself or other family members.

Self-Report Techniques/Scales

Self-report techniques give children the opportunity to give information about themselves and their problems. The measures described here include standardized instruments, self-anchored and other rating scales, and self-observation. Because evaluating children is typically a multiaxial process, many standardized instruments have companion scales for parents and teachers.

Standardized Instruments.   The Depression Self-Rating Scale, identified by Corcoran and Fischer (1987), (figure 6.1) was designed by P. Birleson to measure the extent and severity of depression in children ages seven to thirteen. The scale asks questions about children's mood and thoughts, as well as physiologic or somatic problems. The test has fair reliability (alpha = 0.86 and 0.73, test-retest = 0.80) and good validity (correlation = 0.81) with the Children's Depression Inventory. The Children's Depression Inventory (CDI) (Kovacs, 1992) was created to determine depressive symptoms in children ages seven to seventeen. Based on the Beck Depression Inventory, the CDI requires that children identify statements that characterize themselves over the course of the previous two weeks on a scale of 0 to 2. Although the test-retest reliability of the CDI is in the moderate range (0.38 to 0.87), it has shown good internal consistency (Cronbach's alpha of 0.80), and it was normed on a sample of over 1,200 boys and girls from various ethnic and socioeconomic backgrounds.

Figure 6.1   Depression Self-Rating Scale

Please answer as honestly as you can by indicating at left the number that best refers to how you have felt over the past week. There are no right answers; it is important to say how *you* have felt.

1 = Most of the time
2 = Sometimes
3 = Never

____   1. I look forward to things as much as I used to.
____   2. I sleep very well.
____   3. I feel like crying.
____   4. I like to go out to play.
____   5. I feel like running away.
____   6. I get tummy aches.
____   7. I have lots of energy.
____   8. I enjoy my food.
____   9. I can stick up for myself.
____   10. I think life isn't worth living.
____   11. I am good at things I do.
____   12. I enjoy the things I do as much as I used to.
____   13. I like talking with my family.
____   14. I have horrible dreams.
____   15. I feel very lonely.
____   16. I am easily cheered up.
____   17. I feel so sad I can hardly stand it.
____   18. I feel very bored.

SOURCE: Used with permission of Peter Birleson, Royal Children's Hospital, Fleminton Road, Parkville, Victoria 3052, Australia.

The Hare Self-Esteem Scale, another commonly used scale, measures children's self-esteem in three settings, at home, at school, and with peers. Each of the three subscales comprises ten items; a total score is computed and higher scores indicate higher self-esteem. Reliability for the general scale is 0.74; validity was 0.83 with both the Coopersmith Self-Esteem Inventory and the Rosenberg Self-Esteem Scale (Corcoran & Fischer, 1987). The population sampled to norm the measures was fifth- and eighth-grade students including 41 blacks and 207 whites, 115 boys and 137 girls. The Multidimensional Self-Concept Scale (MSCS) [Bracken, 1992] was designed for use with children nine to nineteen. Comprising 150 items, this four-point Likert scale contains six subscales: social, compentence, affect, academic, family, and physical. The MSCS shows test-retest reliability coefficients ranging from 0.85 to 0.97 in the subscales, with higher coefficients for the total scale, ranging from 0.97 to 0.99. In addition, concurrent validity of 0.69 to 0.83 has been established with the Coopersmith Self-Esteem Inventory.

The Assessment of Interpersonal Relations (AIR) (Bracken & Kelley, 1993) was constructed to evaluate the interpersonal relationships between children and their peers, parents, and teachers. Children are asked to rate their level of agreement with the same thirty-five statements as they pertain to all three groups. Normed on 2,501 children and adolescents aged nine to nineteen, from across the United States, the AIR displays high test-retest reliability (0.93 to 0.96) and good discriminant validity across the subscales. This multidimensional instrument yields comprehensive information about the quality of relationships from the child's perspective.

The Impulsivity Scale (see figure 6.2) was designed by Hirschfield, Sutton-Smith, and Rosenberg and measures the child's tendency toward restlessness, rule breaking, and indulgence in horseplay. Reliability was good (test-retest = 0.85) and criterion-referenced validity was established by significant correlations with teacher ratings of children. The test was normed on 127 fifth- and sixth-graders.

Other children's scales include the Children's Action Tendency Scale, by Deluty; the Children's Cognitive Assessment Questionnaire, by Asher; the Common Belief Inventory for Students, by Hooper and Layne; and the Compulsive Eating Scale, by Kagan and Squires (Corcoran & Fischer, 1987). In their review of clinical measures for social workers, Corcoran and Fischer also included a number of family relationship scales appropriate for children to complete. The best example is the Hudson Family Scale Package, which measures the child's relationship with mother, father, and siblings, as well as the child's overall family satisfaction.

Self-Anchored and Other Rating Scales.   Children can rate the intensity of problems such as depression or anxiety on self-anchored scales (see figure 6.3). Children may be asked, for example, to develop "an-

Figure 6.2   Impulsivity Scale

Decide whether each statement is true as applied to you or false as applied to you. If a statement is True or Mostly True as applied to you, circle T. If a statement is False or Mostly False as applied to you, circle F.

T F   1. I like to keep moving around.
          (I don't like to keep moving around.)
T F   2. I make friends quickly.
          (I don't make friends quickly.)
T F   3. I like to wrestle and to horse around.
          (I don't like to wrestle and to horse around.)
T F   4. I like to shoot with bows and arrows.
          (I don't like to shoot with bows and arrows.)
T F   5. I must admit I'm a pretty good talker.
          (I must admit that I'm not a good talker.)
T F   6. Whenever there's a fire engine going someplace, I like to follow it.
          (If there's a fire engine going someplace, I don't usually like to
          follow it.)
T F   7. My home life is not always happy.
          (My home life is always happy.)
T F   8. When things get quiet, I like to stir up a little fuss.
          (I usually don't like to stir up a little fuss when things get quiet.)
T F   9. I am restless.
          (I am not restless.)
T F   10. I don't think I'm as happy as other people.
          (I think I'm happy as other people.)
T F   11. I get into tricks at Halloween.
          (I don't get into tricks at Halloween.)
T F   12. I like being "it" when we play games of that sort.
          (I don't like being "it" when we play games of that sort.)
T F   13. It's fun to push people off the edge into the pool.
          (It's not fun to push people off the edge into the pool.)
T F   14. I play hooky sometimes.
          (I never play hooky.)
T F   15. I like to go with lots of other kids, not just one.
          (I usually like to go with one kid, rather than lots of them.)
T F   16. I like throwing stones at targets.
          (I don't like throwing stones at targets.)
T F   17. It's hard to stick to the rules if you're losing the game.
          (It's not hard to stick to the rules even if you are losing the game.)
T F   18. I like to dare kids to do things.
          (I don't like to dare kids to do things.)
T F   19. I'm not known as a hard and steady worker.
          (I'm known as a hard and steady worker.)

SOURCE: Used with permission of Paul Hirschfield, Hirschfield and Associates, 529 Pharr Road, Atlanta, GA 30305.

Figure 6.3   Children's Self-Anchored Anxiety at Bedtime Scale

1 .... 2 .... 3 .... 4 .... 5 .... 6 7
Least Anxiety   Mid-level Anxiety   Most Anxiety

| Relaxed, sleeps peacefully through the night. | Falls asleep, wakes 1–2 times during the night, reports bad dreams in the morning. | Trouble falling asleep, sleeps fitfully, nightmares/wakes up screaming. |

chors" for a one-to-seven-point scale describing their depression from the lowest to the highest they could possibly imagine. Anchors are the specific behavioral indicators of depression for that child.

Another type of self-rating scale used with children measures their anxiety on a one-hundred-point scale (Jordan, Franklin, & Corcoran, 1993). The scale can be drawn to look like a thermometer, with a red center that moves up and down. When children push the red part all the way up (scale reads one hundred points) they are told this indicates that they are the most anxious they could ever imagine. When they lower the reading to zero, they are told that they are not anxious at all. Children are then instructed to move the red center to indicate their current amount of anxiety.

Self-Observation.   Children may be asked to observe their own behavior. One format is to make a simple problem checklist that asks children to check off the specific problems for which they would like help. This type of checklist can be made to reflect the types of problems for which the agency can provide services. An example of such a checklist developed for completion by children receiving social work services in a school setting appears in figure 6.4. Children may also be asked to collect data on their own or other's behavior using simple data-collection methods. For example, children can staple a three-by-five card to the inside of their school folder and keep a tally of the number of times they talk in class or the number of times they get out of their chair. Children may be asked to record information about family members or peer interactions using similar methods.

Ratings by Others

Parents and teachers are frequently asked to provide information about children's problems. Sometimes other professionals are asked to help in the assessment. One popular instrument is the Achenbach Child Behavior Checklist (CBCL) (Achenbach & Edelbrock, 1983). This is perhaps the most frequently used scale of its type. It has been shown to provide less accurate results for children who are mildly retarded, but it has

Figure 6.4   Problem Checklist

Name _____ Age _____ Grade _____
Who referred you to the social worker? _____

The following list are problems about which other kids at school have talked to the social worker. **Please check all of the following that are problems for you.**

____ New student adjustment
____ Failing grades
____ Lack of motivation in class
____ Disruptive classroom behavior
____ Truancy
____ Problems with a teacher
____ Excessive tardiness
____ Drug policy violation
____ Organization skills
____ Problems with peers
____ Conflicts with siblings-parents
____ Low self-concept
____ Poor social skills
____ Concern about friend
____ Depression
____ Withdrawn and isolated
____ Aggressive behavior
____ Failure to serve detention
____ Overweight or other physical problems
____ Physical abuse by parents
____ Other (please specify) _____

---

demonstrated clear accuracy for children of color when used in translation, identifying not only the impairment but also its severity (Bird, Gould, Rubio-Stipec, Staghezza, & Canino, 1991; Embregts, 2000). The CBCL was used to analyze premorbid behavioral differences among young adults diagnosed with schizophrenia and to analyze behavior functioning for children in foster care (Armsden, Pecora, Payne, & Szatkiewicz, 2000; Rossi, Pollice, Daneluzzo, Marinangeli, & Stratta, 2000).

Derived from the CBCL, the Child Behavior Checklist Depression Scale (CBCL-D) (Clarke, Lewinsohn, Hops, & Seeley, 1992) was designed to identify symptoms of depression as noted by both adolescents and parents. Each checklist has fifteen items. Although it possesses adequate criterion-related validity with diagnoses of depression from psychiatrists and acceptable concurrent validity with other measures of depression, the CBCL-D has demonstrated only moderate ranges of reliability (test-retest = 0.20 to 0.57; interrater = 0.35 to 0.59). It remains useful, however, as a general index of depression and for its adaptability across sources.

Another frequently used instrument is the Hilson Adolescent Profile (Inwald, Brobst, & Morrisey, 1988). A copy of the computer-generated report provided when the test is sent in for computer scoring is presented in appendix 6A. In addition to these specially designed instruments, parents, teachers, or other significant people in the child's environment may fill out the same self-report measures mentioned in the previous section. For example, if the child is asked to complete the Hare Self-Esteem Scale, the parent is also asked to fill out this measure for the child. This way, the social worker has two different perspectives on the child's self-esteem.

Parents and teachers, as well as social workers, may do direct observation and recording of children's behavior. Four types of recording are recommended. *Narrative recording* is a qualitative recording of an event. Special attention is given to the behavior as well as to the setting in which the behavior occurs. For example, a child may be observed while interacting in the classroom. The social worker might look for specific behaviors to occur, such as getting out of one's seat. Other, external conditions that might affect the child would also be observed and noted, such as actions of the teacher, actions of other students, and distracting aspects of the classroom setting itself. *Interval recording* is continuous, direct observation of the child during specified time periods divided into equal intervals. For example, the social worker may look to see if the child got out of his seat during a given interval. *Frequency recording* notes each occurrence of the behavior. For example, each occurrence of the child getting out of his seat would be counted. *Duration recording* is concerned with the length of each occurrence of the behavior. For example, how long the child was out of his seat would be recorded.

Child protective service department caseworkers may record information about children in a form such as the Children's Restrictiveness of Living Environments Instrument (figure 6.5). This instrument provides an indicator of factors related to out-of-home placement (Thomlison & Krysik, 1992). Magura and Moses (1985) have developed a set of scales to measure outcomes for child welfare services.

Standardized Tests.   Some of the tests utilized with children are designed to measure intelligence, achievement, or special problems or abilities. Social workers do not usually administer these tests but refer children to other trained personnel when appropriate. Social workers may administer screening inventories such as the Attention Deficit Hyperactivity Disorder Rating Scale (DuPaul, 1992), but comprehensive evaluations for ADHD or other complicated disorders require specialized training and skill. See appendix 6B for a listing of some of the commonly used tests of this type. When referring a child for testing, follow these guidelines: have a specific reason for referring a client; explain to the psychologist what questions you want answered; provide information you have collected to the psychologist; prepare the client for what to expect at the

Figure 6.5   Children's Restrictiveness of Living Environments Instrument

Children's Restrictiveness of Living Environments

Instructions for calculating the restrictiveness of children's living environments:
A. Complete the child and rating information.
B. On the right side of the items in column B, number the child's placements in sequential order and record the corresponding number of days in each placement, e.g., (1,30) indicates first placement, 30 days.
C. Record the corresponding Restrictiveness Score for each placement into the Restrictiveness Formula in column C, i.e., R_{p1}, represents the restrictiveness score of the child's first placement. Calculate the totals.
D. Record the corresponding per diem cost and the number of days in each placement in column D. Calculate the totals.

A. Child Name: _____   Rater Name: _____

   Child Birthdate: _____/_____/_____   Date Completed: _____/_____/_____
                   (year) (month) (day)   (year) (month) (day)

   Child Identification: _____

B. Restrictiveness Scores

1.51 Self-maintained residence
2.10 Private boarding home
2.18 Home of child's friend
2.33 Home of family friend
2.40 Home of relative
2.45 Home of biological parent
2.60 Homeless
2.66 Adoptive home
2.75 Supervised independent living
3.09 Independent living prep. group home
3.13 Regular foster care home
3.38 Family emergency shelter
3.48 Receiving foster care
3.57 Treatment foster family care home
3.58 Special needs foster home
3.61 Long-term group home
3.85 Youth emergence shelter
3.86 Receiving group home
4.00 Medical hospital
4.14 Private residential school
4.18 Wilderness camp
4.45 Ranch-based treatment center
4.60 Open youth correction facility
4.62 Adult drug/alcohol rehab. center
4.63 Cottage based treatment center
4.85 Psychiatric group home
4.97 Youth drug/alcohol rehab. center
5.13 Armed services base
5.40 Young offender group home
5.50 Psychiatric ward in a hospital
6.10 Psychiatric institution
6.40 Closed youth correction facility
6.56 Adult correction facility
6.58 Secure treatment facility

C. Restrictiveness Equation

R_{p1}_____ – R_{p2}_____ = _____
R_{p2}_____ – R_{p3}_____ = _____
R_{p3}_____ – R_{p4}_____ = _____
R_{p4}_____ – R_{p5}_____ = _____

Total _____

D. Cost Equation

T_{p1}_____ × C_{p1}_____ = _____
T_{p2}_____ × C_{p2}_____ = _____
T_{p3}_____ × C_{p3}_____ = _____
T_{p4}_____ × C_{p4}_____ = _____
T_{p5}_____ × C_{p5}_____ = _____

Total # Days   Total Cost
in Placement ___   of Placement ___

SOURCE: Used by permission of Barbara Thomlison (1992), Faculty of Social Work, The University of Calgary.

psychologist's office; do not have unrealistic expectations of what the testing will provide, because testing is only one tool for assessing the client; and ask the psychologist to explain any limitations of the specific tests that your client has been given (Sheafor et al., 1988). To further promote the process, social workers can learn more about testing instruments, their interpretation, and implications. Social workers can also help other professionals understand the parameters of social service and child welfare systems (Kayser & Lyon, 2000).

CASE STUDY

Identifying Information

Name: Anthony Estrada
Date of Birth: 11/09/93
Address: 1112 N. Clement Street, Mayfield, TX
Phone: 555.123.4567 (home), 555.890.1112
Family members living in the home:

Anthony Estrada	Client	Male	8 y.o.	Hispanic	2nd grader
Robert Estrada	Brother	Male	10 y.o.	Hispanic	3rd grader
John Estrada	Brother	Male	11 y.o.	Hispanic	5th grader
Lydia Estrada	Sister	Female	6 y.o.	Hispanic	1st grader
Hector Estrada	Father	Male	35 y.o.	Hispanic	Construction
Alina Estrada	Mother	Female	30 y.o.	Hispanic	Classroom Assistant

Family income: The family income is between $2,500 and $3,000 per month, depending on the mother's employment. She works part time at the elementary school during the school year.

Presenting problem: Anthony has been suspended from school for hitting a teacher while on the playground. He did not want to go inside at the end of recess and struck her in his frustration. His teacher complains that he's had a "bad attitude" all year, and the principal is suggesting placement for him in an alternative school.

Previous counseling: None.

Source of data: In-office assessment visit with Anthony and his parents. Additional information from the pediatrician, the teachers, and the school counselor.

Nature of Presenting Problem

In the last two years, Anthony has changed from an energetic, loving child to a moody, irritable child. Although Anthony has always been "busy and active," his mother reports that he has become more competitive with his older brothers and that he is easily frustrated if he cannot beat them at sports or other games. She reports that if Anthony loses a board game, he will sulk and say that he is "stupid" or that his brothers cheated. Often, he will cheat, himself, in an attempt to win. About a month ago, as the boys were playing soccer in their backyard, Anthony became so upset that he began to scream at his brothers and say that he wished he were dead. Shocked by this outburst, the mother tried to comfort Anthony, but she said that he resisted her effort and finally only calmed down at the urgings of his oldest brother. Since that incident, the family has tried to avoid making Anthony too angry.

Despite their efforts to mollify him, however, the mother reports that Anthony has become "sassy" and that, increasingly, she must discipline him for hitting his siblings and for not obeying her. She attempts to spank him, but she says that when she does that, he only tries to hit her back. More often, now, she sends him to his room. Although he obeys his father, who uses corporeal punishment, Anthony seems to ignore his mother's requests that he pick up his clothes and toys and that he complete his homework for school. She says that he is difficult to get up in the mornings and that he dawdles rather than dressing himself and gathering his supplies for school as his brothers do. She finds that she must spend as much time helping Anthony get ready in the mornings as she does his younger sister. Sometimes, they are all late for school because of Anthony's dilatory actions or because of one of his angry outbursts, when he feels that everyone is pushing him and causing *him* to be late.

With incomplete homework and, sometimes, incomplete work in school, Anthony's grades have suffered this year. The teacher says that Anthony is inattentive at school and that he bothers other children, often distracting them from their work and provoking them into confrontations with him. She believes that Anthony is smart enough to learn the material, but that he doesn't seem to want to. She reports that his work is careless and that he often leaves worksheets partially blank. In her exasperation, she enlisted help from the school counselor who assisted her in setting up a classroom behavior management plan of rewards and consequences for directing Anthony's behavior. Although Anthony responds to this system, the teacher says that the time she must spend managing Anthony's behavior takes away from class time that would normally be devoted to all of the children. She believes that Anthony should be transferred to a class for "emotionally disturbed" children, where his behavior can be monitored more closely in a smaller class of students.

The teacher reports that Anthony is able to play with peers most of the time, but she notes that his angry behavior alienates some children. In all competitive instances, he becomes frustrated and aggressive if he is unable to win or to perform as well as he wants to. The day of the playground incident, Anthony was playing in a group of children who were divided into teams for kickball. Anthony's team was behind, and when the teacher said that recess was over, Anthony was upset because he wanted to continue playing until his team could catch up. When the teacher refused to extend recess, he hit her in the back with his fist. She immediately took him to the principal who called Anthony's mother and suspended Anthony from school for three days. During the suspension, the principal and the teacher arranged to meet with Anthony and his parents to discuss appropriate ways to help him control his behavior and be more successful in school. The school social worker was asked to attend this meeting.

Anthony has several strengths. His parents are devoted to their family and are genuinely concerned for their son. They are willing to participate in recommended plans for intervention both at school and at home, but they strongly advocate for their son's continued placement in a regular classroom. Anthony's personal strengths include his ability to maintain focus on certain types of projects in school, his apparent ability to master second-grade work, and a stated understanding of why he has been suspended. He says that he is sorry for hitting his teacher.

The school prioritizes the problems (with 1 being the most severe) in the following order: 1) aggressive behavior, 2) distracting other students, 3) being unable to focus on schoolwork. The parents prioritize the problems similarly: 1) angry behavior, 2) being argumentative, 3) making poor grades.

Client Interpersonal Issues

Cognitive functioning: Anthony's school achievement tests indicate that he is capable of mastering second grade. He consistently scores in the fiftieth percentile, but his teacher thinks that he is capable of more. Neither his pediatrician nor his parents report any type of cognitive developmental delay. In fact, when he was young, his mother thought that he was exceptionally bright, because he could figure out how to get out of his crib and how to take apart most toys. Anthony has mastered all developmental tasks at age-appropriate times. The teacher reports that if she works with Anthony individually, he can learn anything, but he becomes easily distracted when she works with students as a group or when he must work alone.

Emotional functioning: During the assessment visit, Anthony seemed like a quiet child. He sat between his parents, closer to his mother, during most of the interview, showing appropriate anxiety about being in a meeting with adults. He warmed up quickly, however, to the interviewer and answered questions easily, although he did show some discomfort while discussing the playground incident. Only after about thirty minutes did he begin to fidget by swinging his legs against the chair, finally standing up and walking around the room as the adults continued to talk.

Behavioral functioning: Anthony exhibited no unusual behaviors during the assessment session. His impatience and need to move after thirty minutes were within normal limits for his age. In fact, he asked his father if he could stand up before he began to walk around. He sighed occasionally to display his boredom, but he did not interrupt the conversation by talking. His parents reported that Anthony has never enjoyed paperwork such as drawing and coloring; he prefers to climb, run, and jump. His parents recounted several events of inappropriate angry behavior over the last six months, but Anthony did not exhibit such behavior in this session. In fact, his behavior in this session indicated some strength in self-control and coping. His weakness in this area seems to be with coping in the classroom environment.

Physiologic functioning: Anthony's medical records reveal basically normal development. Anthony is in the fiftieth percentile for both height and weight, his immunizations are up-to-date, and he currently takes no medication. His illness history is not remarkable, although he did require minor surgery for repeated ear infections and ear tubes when he was three years old. Since that time, he has shown no delay in speech or hearing. He has only had minor colds and infections that have responded to conservative medical intervention. Although teachers complain about Anthony's handwriting, he does not demonstrate any unusual deficit in fine-motor skills. His drawings are not detailed, but they are not immature for his age. Anthony can dribble a basketball and throw a baseball within the appropriate range for his age. Neither the pediatrician nor the PE teacher reports any physical limitations, although the PE teacher says that he seems clumsy at times and that he needs to "run off steam" in PE.

Developmental considerations: Developmental milestones have been met within normal time ranges. Anthony's birth history reveals that he was delivered spontaneously and without complications at forty-one weeks gestation with an Apgar rating of nine, as reflected by the parents and the medical record. He weighed seven lbs, ten oz.

Client Interpersonal Issues: Family.   Anthony resides with his parents, his two older brothers, and his younger sister in a modest home in Mayfield. Anthony's parents are first-generation Mexican-Americans. Both sets of grandparents immigrated to Texas from northern Mexico. Anthony's mother grew up in a small border town where she says that she liked school, but that she often missed class to babysit for her younger siblings while her mother worked. She dropped out of high school in eleventh grade because she was somewhat behind in her studies, and she had found a good job as a seamstress. She later acquired her

GED by studying at night in an adult education class before her first child was born. Having the GED allows Mrs. Estrada to work as a classroom assistant for the elementary school Anthony attends. Anthony's father grew up in the same small border town, where he worked in fields from the time he was a boy. He reports that school was boring for him, that he preferred the physical activity of the fields, but that he stayed in school until high school. He dropped out after two years. He says that teachers sometimes called him inattentive and disruptive, too, because he found it hard to pay attention to things that did not matter to him. He currently works as a foreman for a local construction company. He says that he has always preferred being outdoors and working with his hands.

Mrs. Estrada has learned behavioral disciplining techniques, such as time-out, in her job, and she thinks these techniques work with her children when she is not too stressed to employ them. Mr. Estrada thinks these techniques are fine, but he prefers corporeal punishment because he thinks that it works best and that children should have a "healthy fear" of their parents. Mr. Estrada leaves much of the discipline to his wife, because she is with the children more than he is; but when he is home, he intervenes if he finds that the children are not responding appropriately to him or to their mother. He says that he has had to spank Anthony more than the other children lately, and he admits that the spankings seem to escalate Anthony's anger.

The other Estrada children, John, Robert, and Lydia, are healthy and developing normally. As a fifth-grader, John makes good grades and is well liked by his peers. He is in the highest performance groups for reading and math. Schoolwork appears to come easily for him, but his passion is baseball, where he is demonstrating talent as a pitcher. He is a confident and bright boy. Anthony seems closer to him than he is to Robert who is only 18 months older than he is. Robert is described as the "squeaky wheel" of the family. Like John, Robert performs well in school, but his parents and teachers describe him as competitive and, whiney although he has never displayed the anger problems that Anthony has. Robert excels in art. His drawings show dimensional depth and detail that are unusual for his age. Lydia is in first grade, where she seems to be on level. She is described as quiet and the "baby" of the family. The parents insist that the boys protect her and not tease or aggravate her.

Mrs. Estrada is with the children most of the time because her job allows her to leave for school and return with her children. In good weather, Mr. Estrada works many evenings and weekends. When he is home, he is often too tired to play with the children, but sometimes he throws the ball with the boys. Mrs. Estrada reports that all of the children want to spend more time with their father. Because the family depends heavily on Mr. Estrada's income, however, she acknowledges that he must work hard to maintain his job.

Client Interpersonal Issues: School. The school counselor reports that she observed Anthony's behavior in the classroom on several occasions, at the request of his teacher. The counselor found that Anthony was often off-task, playing with his pencil or talking to classmates, and that he seemed unable to follow directions that were spoken to the entire class. At times, the more he was corrected by the teacher, the more disruptive Anthony became.

The school counselor reports that Anthony responded well to the token economy system she set up for improving his focus in the classroom. She says that he was willing to work for the tokens and stayed on task better when he knew that his teacher would reward him. This focus, in turn, reduced his disruptive behavior with his peers and seemed to improve his schoolwork. Reviewing his test scores, she reported that she could see some disparity between Anthony's ability and performance scores, a disparity that continues in the classroom. She expresses some concern that if his school problems continue, he will fall behind in his schoolwork and lose interest completely. She recognizes that he must gain some control of his temper and his attention span if he is to succeed in the classroom.

Client Interpersonal Issues: Peers. Anthony and his parents report that he has some friends, but that sometimes people do not like to play with him because he gets so angry. The counselor reports that students in second grade try to stay out of trouble, and they fear that Anthony will get them in trouble with the teacher. Anthony is signed up for soccer this year, but the soccer season has not begun. His parents hope that sports will give him an outlet for his energy and that he will make friends.

Context and Social Support Networks. The family has been somewhat isolated since their move from the border two years ago where they left behind both sets of grandparents and a large extended family of aunts, uncles, and cousins. Mrs. Estrada stays busy with her work, her home, and her children. She does enjoy her colleagues at work, but she is busy the rest of the time meeting the needs of four active children. With his long work hours, Mr. Estrada is not often available to help with family and housekeeping tasks. He is, himself, exhausted with his labors. The children are each expected to do chores, but Mrs. Estrada admits that sometimes she does the work herself to ensure that it is done well and in a timely manner.

The family does attend a Catholic church nearby, but they have not become active in the church community, though all of their children have participated in first communion and will likely continue all of their religious education through confirmation.

Mr. and Mrs. Estrada are happy with their family and their circumstances. They believe that they have provided well for their children. Although they miss the support of extended family, they believe that the move has been beneficial financially and that they and their children will have more opportunity in Mayfield than in their home town.

Measurement

Individual Functioning: 1) Design a daily behavioral checklist so that Mrs. Estrada can record the number of Anthony's noncompliances, compliances, and angry outbursts.

Family Functioning: Administer the Hudson Index of Family Relations (Inwald et al., 1988), to assess overall family functioning.

BOX 6.2
Treatment Plan: Anthony Estrada

Problem: Child behavior problems; parental lack of skills

Definitions: Distractibility, inattentiveness, angry outbursts, and occasional aggression for child. Have skills deficit in parenting and use corporeal punishment instead of positive discipline, such as rewards.

Goals: 1. To improve attentiveness at home and at school
2. To eliminate angry outbursts and aggression
3. Improve overall parent-child relationship

Objectives:	Interventions:
1. Parents learn how to help Anthony stay on task, as measured by behavioral checklist.	1. Teach parents use of a reward system for child's staying on task. Teach parents to redirect inappropriate behaviors. Refer child for ADHD test.
2. Anthony learns to control his anger as measured by behavioral checklist.	2. Teach Anthony anger management skills, such as time-out, breathing, and focusing.
3. Improve family relationships, as measured by the Index of Family Relationships	3. Teach family to have family meetings and outings.

Diagnosis: Consider 314.01 Attention-Deficit/Hyperactivity Disorder, Combined Type

SUMMARY

This chapter described assessment of children and adolescents. The special issues important in assessing this population are diagnosis, psychological and social theories, and ethnicity. Childhood diagnosis is done from three different perspectives, categorical, empirical, and behavioral. Psychological theories explain child development from cognitive, affective, and learning perspectives. Development is assumed to occur at different rates for different children, depending on maturational readiness and environmental opportunities. Social theories explain children's behavior within the broader context of family and society. Issues that influence assessment of children of color include psychosocial adjustment, relationship with family, school adjustment and achievement, peers, and community.

Measures available for assessment of children and adolescents include global techniques such as interviews, use of play, and sculpting and other family techniques. Self-report measurement techniques include standardized instruments, self-anchored and other rating scales, self-observation, and ratings by others.

The case of Anthony, an eight-year-old boy with problems including distractability, inattentiveness, angry outbursts, and social agression is presented.

Next, Chapter 7 reviews the issues related to assessment of adults. Special attention is given to person-environment interactions.

STUDY QUESTIONS

1. Use psychological, social, and color guidelines from the chapter to assess a child you know. What are the strengths and weaknesses of each approach?
2. Using the same case example, design a measurement system that includes both qualitative (play or sculpting) and quantitative (standardized measures, self-anchored scales) techniques.

REFERENCES

Achenbach, T. M. (1991). *Manual for the youth self report and 1991 profile*. Burlington: University of Vermont, Department of Psychiatry.

Achenbach. T. M., & Edelbrock, L. (1983). *Manual for the child behavior checklist and revised child behavior profile*. Burlington, VA: Queen City Printers.

American Psychiatric Association. (2000). *Diagnostic and statistical manual of mental disorders (4th ed., rev.)*. Washington, DC: Author.

Armsden, G., Pecora, P. J., Payne, V. H., & Szatkiewicz, J. P. (2000). Children placed in long-term foster care: An intake profile using the child behavior checklist/4-18. *Journal of Emotional & Behavioral Disorders, 8*(1), 49–64.

Barkley, R. (1990). *Attention deficit hyperactivity disorder: A handbook for diagnosis and treatment.* New York: Guilford.

Barona, A., & de Barona, M. S. (2000). Assessing multicultural preschool children. In Bracken et al. (Eds.), *The psychoeducational assessment of preschool children* (pp. 282–297). Boston: Allyn & Bacon.

Barth, R. (1986). *Social and cognitive treatment of children and adolescents.* San Francisco: Jossey-Bass.

Berk, L. E. (1999). *Infants, children, and adolescents.* Boston: Allyn & Bacon.

Bird, H. R., Gould, M. S., Rubio-Stipec, M., Staghezza, B., & Canino, G. (1991). Screening for childhood psychopathology in the community using the child behavior checklist. *Journal of the American Academy of Child and Adolescent Psychiatry*

Bloom, M. (1984). *Configurations of human behavior.* New York: Macmillan.

Bloom, M., & Fischer, F. (1982). *Evaluating practice: Guidelines for the accountable professional.* Englewood Cliffs, NJ: Prentice Hall.

Bornstein, P., & Kazdin, A. (1985). *Handbook of clinical behavior therapy with children.* Homewood, IL: Dorsey Press.

Bracken, B. A. (1992). *Multidimensional self concept scale: Examiner's manual.* Austin, TX: PRO-ED.

Bracken, B. A., & Kelley, P. (1993). *Assessment of interpersonal relations.* Austin, TX: PRO-ED.

Canino, I. A., & Spurlock, J. (2000). *Culturally diverse children and adolescents: Assessment, diagnosis, and treatment* (2nd ed.). New York: Guilford.

Clarke, G. N., Lewinsohn, P. M., Hops, H., & Seeley, J. R. (1992). A self- and parent-report measure of adolescent depression: The child behavior checklist depression scale. *Behavioral Assessment, 14,* 443–463.

Conners, K. C. (1990). *Conners' rating scales manual.* North Tonawanda, NY: Multihealth Systems.

Corcoran, K., & Fischer, J. (1987). *Measures for clinical practice.* New York: Free Press.

DuPaul, G. J. (1992). How to assess attention deficit hyperactivity disorder within school settings. *School Psychology Quarterly, 7,* 60–74.

Embregts, P. (2000). Reliability of the child behavior checklist for the assessment of behavioral problems of children and youth with mild mental retardation. *Research in Developmental Disabilities, 21*(1), 31–41.

Frieson, J. (1985). *Structural-strategic marriage and family therapy.* New York: Gardner.

Gibbs, J., & Huang, L. (1989). *Children of color.* San Francisco: Jossey-Bass.

Gopaul-McNicol, S., & Armour-Thomas, E. (2001). *Assessment and culture: Psychological test with minority populations.* Academic Press, San Diego, CA.

Guarnaccia, P. J., & Lopez, S. (1998). The mental health and adjustment of immigrant and refugee children. *Child and Adolescent Psychiatric Clinics of North America, 7*(3), 537–553.

Harper-Dorton, K., & Herbert, M. (1999). *Working with children and their families* (2nd ed.). Chicago: Lyceum.

Hughes, J., & Baker, D. B. (1990). *The clinical child interview*. New York: Guilford.

Inwald, R. E., Brobst, K. E., & Morrisey, R. F. (1988). *Hilson adolescent profile*. Kew Gardens, NY: Hilson Research.

Janzen, C., Harris, O., & Jordan, C. (in press). *Family treatment in social work practice* (3rd ed.). Itasca, IL: Peacock.

Jenson, B. F., & Potter, M. L. (1990). Best practices in communicating with parents. In A. Thomas & J. Grimes (Eds.), *Best practices in school psychology-II* (pp. 183–193). Washington, DC: National Association of School Psychologists.

Johnson-Powell, G., Yamamoto, J., & Arrayo, W. (1997). *Transcultural child development*. New York: Wiley.

Jordan, C., & Cobb, N. (2001). Competency-based treatment for persons with marital discord. In K. Corcoran (Ed.), *Structuring change* (2nd ed.). Chicago: Lyceum.

Jordan, C., Franklin, C., & Corcoran, K. (1993). Development of measuring instruments. In R. Grinnell (Ed.), *Social work research and evaluation* (pp. 198–220). Itasca, IL: Peacock.

Jordan, C., & Hoefer, R. (2002). Work versus life: Family friendly benefits in nonprofit organizations. *National Social Science Journal, 17*(1), 16–25.

Kayser, J. A., & Lyon, M. A. (2000). Teaching social workers to use psychological assessment data. *Child Welfare, 79*(2), 197–222.

Kovacs, M. (1992). *Children's depression inventory*. Los Angeles: Multi-Health Systems.

Magura, S., & Moses, B. (1985). Outcome measures for child welfare services. Washington, DC: Child Welfare League of America.

McCarney, S. B., & Leigh, J. E. (1990). *Manual for the behavior evaluation scale-2*. Columbia, MO: Educational Services.

McConaughy, S. H. (1996). The interview process. In Breen & Fiedler (Eds.), *Behavioral approach to assessment of youth with emotional/behavioral disorders: A handbook for school-based practitioners* (pp. 00–00). Austin, TX: PRO-ED.

McConaughy, S. H., & Auchenbach, T. M. (1994). *Manual for the semistructured clinical interview with children and adolescents*. Burlington: University of Vermont, Department of Psychiatry.

Merrill, K. W. (1993). Using behavior rating scales to assess social skills and antisocial behavior in school settings: Development of the School Social Behavior Scales. *School Psychology Review, 22*, 115–133.

Miley, K. K., O'Melia, M., & DuBois, B. (2001). *Generalist social work practice*. Boston: Allyn & Bacon.

Nurmi, J. E. (1993). Adolescent development in an age graded context: The role of personal beliefs, goals, and strategies in the tackling of developmental tasks and standards. *International Journal of Behavioral Development, 16*, 169–189.

Quay, H., & Peterson, D. (1987). *Manual for the revised behavior problem checklist.* Coral Gables, FL: Authors.

Reich, W., & Welner, Z. (1990). *Diagnostic interview for children and adolescents-revised.* St. Louis, MO: Washington University, Division of Child Psychiatry.

Reynolds, C. R., & Kamphaus, R. W. (1992). *Behavior assessment system for children (BASC).* Circle Pines, MN: American Guidance Service.

Roberts, R. E., & Chen, Y. W. (1995). Depressive symptoms and suicidal ideation among Mexican-origin and Anglo adolescents. *Journal of the American Academy of Child and Adolescent Psychiatry.*

Rossi, A., Pollice, R., Daneluzzo, E., Marinangeli, M. G., & Stratta, P. (2000). Behavioral neurodevelopment abnormalities and schizophrenic disorder: A retrospective evaluation with childhood behavior checklist (CBCL). *Schizophrenia Research, 44*(2), 121–128.

Sattler, J. (1988). *Assessment of children* (3rd ed.). San Diego: Sattler.

Schaffer, D. (1992). *NIMH Diagnostic interview schedule for children, version 2.3.* New York: Columbia University, Division of Child and Adolescent Psychiatry.

Sheafor, B., Horejsi, C., & Horejsi, G. (1988). *Techniques and guidelines for social work practice.* Newton, MA: Allyn & Bacon.

Siegel, J. M., Aneshensel, C. S., Taub, B., Cantwell, D. P., & Driscoll, A. K. (1998). Adolescent depressed mood in a multi-ethnic sample. *Journal of Youth and Adolescence, 27*(4), 413–427.

The Thinking, Feeling, and Doing Game. (1973). Cresskill, NJ: Creative Therapeutics.

Thomlison, B., & Krysik, J. (1992). The development of an instrument to measure the restrictiveness of children's living environments. *Research on Social Work Practice, 2*(2), 207–219.

Wilkinson, Ian (2000). The Darlington Assessment System: Clinical guidelines for practitioners. *Journal of Family Therapy Special Issue: Empirical Approaches to Family Assessment, 22*(2), 211–224.

CHAPTER 7

Adults

Elizabeth C. Pomeroy, Lori K. Holleran, and Cynthia Franklin

Social work practice has built its uniqueness as a counseling profession on the belief that it is important to assess both persons and their environments, to plan appropriate treatment strategies for clients. Social work assessment has historically been plagued by endless dichotomies, with emphasis given to either individual clients or their social environment, but ignoring the interaction between them (Rodwell, 1987; Vigilante, & Mailick, 1988). The limitations inherent in adhering to various treatment models (such as psychoanalytic, social learning, and others) may have added to the proliferation of these dichotomies (Mattaini & Kirk, 1991). More recent literature on social work assessment emphasizes the need to draw on technical eclecticism and ecological systems theory to conceptualize and organize information relevant to the person-in-environment matrix (Allen-Meares & Lane, 1987; Cheers, 1987; Franklin & Jordan, 1992; Germaine & Gitterman, 1986; Mattaini, 1990). From this assessment perspective, clinicians should collect client data, such as developmental history, personality, mood, affect, cognitive abilities, judgment, coping, adaptation, and motivation. They could also collect information on the client's interactions with relevant social environments, such as family, school/work, community, neighborhood, friends/social network, and significant others.

This chapter provides a framework for assessing adult clients. It incorporates both the characteristics of person and environment dimensions, along with suggestions for the types of questions practitioners may use to gain information across the different areas. This framework draws on and is consistent with the integrative skills assessment protocol presented in Chapter 1. Next, several methods for assessing adult clients are presented. These methods are consistent with the types of assessment and measurement techniques described in Chapters 3, 4, and 5. Then, this chapter provides an example of a completed assessment report with an adult client; it demonstrates combining several of the assessment techniques. Finally, a case study offers an opportunity for readers to practice using the Person-In-Environment rating scale discussed in the chapter.

PERSON-IN-ENVIRONMENT RATING SCALE

The Person-In-Environment (PIE) rating scale, developed by Pomeroy & Holleran (2003), captures a systemic orientation to person and environment. A client's standing develops from numerous dynamic interactions between the intrapersonal/interpersonal and environmental domains. As shown in figure 7.1, the PIE assessment looks at the interactions between

Figure 7.1   Person-In-Environment (PIE) Testing Scale

For each category, first determine if it is a problem or a strength and then rate each for intensity from 1 to 5 below. In some cells, notes will be more useful.

	Personal	Family	Friends	School/ Work	Community	Social Work Intervention
Appearance						
Biomedical/organic						
Use of substances						
Developmental issues/transitions						
Coping abilities						
Stressors						
Capacity for relationships						
Social functioning						
Behavioral functioning						
Sexual functioning						
Problem solving/ coping skills						
Creativity						
Cognitive functioning						
Emotional functioning						
Self-concept						
Motivation						
Ethnic identification						
Cultural barriers						
Role functioning						
Spirituality/religion						
Other strengths						

C = concern   S = strength
N/A = not applicable

1 = minimal intensity
2 = mild intensity
3 = average intensity
4 = above average intensity
5 = significant intensity

aspects of the individual (along the vertical axis) and the environmental domains (along the horizontal axis).

When viewing the PIE rating scale dimensions, the biopsychosocial view of human behavior emerges with the goal of understanding the contributions of biological, psychological, and social-environmental factors and their interactions with a person's behavior (Saleeby, 1992; Simon, McNeil, Franklin, & Cooperman, 1991). In Chapter 1, the Integrative Skills Assessment Outline also provides a broad lens for looking at clients from a biopsychosocial and person-in-environment perspective. Chapter 2 suggests some ways to narrow the information for the purposes of assessment and clinical decision making and intervention planning. The PIE rating scale compliments the Integrative Skills Assessment Outline for client assessment. The overall assessment of a client can be designated on the PIE rating scale (1-minimal intensity to 5-significant intensity) to help practitioners focus on the areas that need the most attention first.

According to the rating scale, strengths as well as areas of concern are considered and ranked for client assessment. Strengths, such as coping skills, positive self-concept, and ethnic identity or spiritual beliefs, may assist the client in resolving existing difficulties (Saleeby, 1992). Concerns, on the other hand, are issues that hinder the client from functioning at optimal capacity. Concerns may be mild, moderate, or significantly intense. In many cases, setting the priority of specific concerns to be addressed is a collaborative effort between the social worker and the client, based on the intensity of the concern. Finally, there will be instances in which specific domains of the assessment do not apply to the particular individual; these times, use the "not applicable" (N/A) designation.

As indicated in figure 1, the area of assessments on the PIE are generic and reflect an eclectic theory base for understanding client functioning. The PIE model captures several dimensions of a person's behavior and environmental functioning. The PIE assessment places persons in their social context, similar to the psychosocial, and ecological systems perspectives that were covered in Chapter 1. Recall also from Chapter 1 that the breadth of social work assessment and the profession's preference for person-in-environment assessment causes social workers to draw on a large integrative theory base for assessing and intervening with clients. The integrative perspective is reflected in the assessment areas covered in this chapter and is also believed to reflect the current trends in clinical assessment, across disciplines.

To utilize the PIE assessment tool, do the following:

1. Have a copy of the chart (figure 1) on which to rate concerns and strengths, according to the instructions.
2. Attach several blank note pages on which to list the characteristics listed on the vertical axis.

3. Gather assessment information using the list of questions provided in box 7.1, to be discussed below.

Interview Questions for a Person-Environment Assessment

While the social worker is examining aspects of the individual's functioning, he or she must also keep in mind the complex interplay among the various personal issues being presented. For example, a client's culture and ethnicity have pervasive implications throughout all aspects of the client's life experience. Although some factors distinguish adult assessment from assessment of children and adolescents, it is important to note that, in cases of serious mental illness, boundary may be blurred depending on the client's level of functioning. In general, when assessing adults, it is important to recognize that 1) there is normally an extensive history of life experiences that affect the client's presentation, 2) coping mechanisms are more solidified and complex, and often less mutable, and 3) there are additional areas for inquiry, based on adult functioning and interactions. The goal of an assessment with an adult client is to gain a comprehensive profile of his or her present functioning in all areas of life.

The following is a list of questions (box 7.1) that a social worker must carefully explore, based on the particular needs of the client. These questions are designed to guide the social worker in developing his or her own questions to ask the client, that is, the social worker does not simply ask the client *these* questions—rather, he or she carefully chooses wording that is sensitive, culturally appropriate, and at the client's developmental and intellectual level.

ASSESSING CLINICAL PROBLEM AREAS IN ADULT CLIENTS

Recall from Chapter 1 that, even in a brief interview, it is important to find out about the presenting problems of clients and to assess clients for serious psychological difficulties, such as psychosis, mood disorders, anxiety disorders, and substance abuse. The practitioner must be aware of serious psychological impairments, such as psychotic behavior and suicide, that put the client and others at significant risk of harm. The PIE questions earlier in this chapter focus the practitioner on issues of concern, such as extreme moods, hullucinations, delusions, and other signs of thought disorders. Psychiatric classifications and assessment tools assess various psychopathologies and are useful for determining if a client has one or more major mental disorders. So it is important for the social work practitioner to have a thorough grounding in *nosological* assessment systems, such as the *Diagnostic and Statistical Manual for Mental Disorders*, fourth edition, text revision (*DSM-IV-TR*), and to learn how to give a

Box 7.1
Interviewing Questions

Appearance:
How is the client dressed (e.g., neatly, professionally, disheveled, colorfully, coordinated)?
What is the client's level of personal hygiene?
What is the client's physical appearance (e.g., overweight, underweight, marked physical anomalies)?

Biomedical/Organic:
What is the client's medical history?
What is the family medical history?
Are there any physical disabilities or limitations?
Are there any cognitive disabilities or limitations (such as, aphasia, ataxia, echolalia)?
Does the client take any prescribed drugs?
What are the client's eating patterns?
What are the client's sleeping patterns?
Has the client experienced any exposure to chemical or environmental toxins that may produce behavioral abnormalities?
How does the client describe his or her recent general state of health?
Has the client discovered any solutions to these concerns?
What is the impact of the above concerns regarding family, friends, school/work, or community?

Developmental Issues/Transitions:
Is the client experiencing any developmental or life transitions (such as, adolescent individuation, marriage, birth of a child, divorce, death of a family member, aging, retirement)?
How is the client being affected by the current life cycle tasks and demands?
Does the client have support systems available to help in these transitions?
Has the client discovered any solutions to these concerns?
What is the impact of the above concerns regarding family, friends, school/work, or community?

Problem Solving/Coping Skills:
What type of coping styles does the client demonstrate (e.g., problem solving, relational, avoidance, emotion-focused, task-focused)?
What type of coping skills does the client employ?
Does the client feel that his or her coping mechanisms are effective in dealing with problems?
Does it appear that the client's coping mechanisms are problematic?

Box 7.1
Interviewing Questions—(*Continued*)

Has the client discovered any solutions to these concerns?
What is the impact of the above concerns regarding family, friends, school/work, or community?

Stressors:
What are the primary stressors in the client's current life situation?
How long have these stressors been affecting the client?
Are the stressors internal or situational?
Is there a pattern of stress in the client's life (examples include, chronic, occupational, or relational problems)?
Are there any environmental or cultural stressors (such as, neighborhood violence, acculturation issues, minority status)?
Has the client discovered any solutions to these concerns?
What is the impact of the above concerns regarding family, friends, school/work, or community?

Relationship and Social Capacities:
Who are the client's significant others? With whom does he or she reside?
What are client's communication skills?
In what activities outside the home does the client participate?
How does the client perceive his or her level of social support?
Are there noteworthy relationship patterns?
Does the client appear to have the ability to form lasting relationships?
Does the client have the capacity for empathy toward others?
Does the client experience significant stress, fear, or anxiety concerning interpersonal contacts?
Is the client currently experiencing any relationship difficulties?
Has the client discovered any solutions to these concerns?
What is the impact of the above concerns regarding family, friends, school/work, or community?

Behavioral Functioning:
Does the client display any unusual behavioral characteristics (such as, tics, tremors, violence, hyperactive movements, responding to unobserved stimuli)?
Does the client appear to behave appropriately in the interview?
How comfortable is your interaction with the client?
Does the client report problems in psychosocial functioning because of behavioral issues?
Has the client discovered any solutions to these concerns?
What is the impact of the above concerns regarding family, friends, school/work, or community?

Box 7.1
Interviewing Questions—(*Continued*)

Sexual Functioning:
Does the client report any sexual difficulties?
If so, are the problems emotional, physical, or cultural in origin?
What is the duration of these problems?
Have the problems affected other areas of functioning?
Has the client discovered any solutions to these concerns?
What is the impact of the above concerns regarding family, friends,
    school/work, or community?

Cognitive Functioning:
(Use the Mini-Mental State Exam that follows to determine the possibility
of cognitive impairment.)

What are the results of the mental status exam?
What is the client's intellectual capacity and level of education?
Is there a history of cognitive/neurological problems in the client system?
Does the client display or report any delusional thinking (such as, para-
    noid ideations, grandiosity, delusions of reference)?
Does the client use bizarre expressions?
Is the client able to use language to express him- or herself clearly?
Does the client appear to have good judgment or "common sense" (i.e.,
    has a realistic plan for his or her life, recognizes risks and consequences
    of decisions, and is able to choose appropriate solutions to problems)?
Has the client discovered any solutions to these concerns?
What is the impact of the above concerns regarding family, friends,
    school/work, or community?

Emotional Functioning:
What is the client's general affective presentation (is it flat, manic, sad,
    content, anxious)?
Is the client's mood or affect stable or labile?
Is any lability situation-related?
Is the client's mood or affect appropriate to his or her current circumstances?
Is the client's mood or affect creating problems in his or her psychosocial
    functioning?
If so, what is the duration of these problems?
Has the client discovered any solutions to these concerns?
What is the impact of the above concerns regarding family, friends,
    school/work, or community?

Self-Concept:
Does the client view him- or herself as a valuable, worthwhile individual?
Does the client see him- or herself as competent?

Box 7.1
Interviewing Questions—(*Continued*)

Does the client have a reality-based perception of self?
Does the client report any problems with self-concept or self-esteem?
If so, has the client discovered any solutions to these concerns?
What is the impact of the above concerns regarding family, friends,
    school/work, or community?

Motivation:
Does the client report a desire to change?
How strong is the client's motivation to make changes?
What are the external and internal motivators?
Does the client have goals for him- or herself?
Can the client imagine ways of changing and visualize improvement?
What is the impact of the above concerns regarding family, friends,
    school/work, or community?

Culture and Ethnic Identification:
Does the client identify with particular cultural and/or ethnic group(s)?
Does the client gain strength from the identification(s)?
Does the client experience conflict related to his or her ethnic/cultural
    identity?
Does the client feel oppressed by membership in this group or population?
What cultural barriers are experienced by the client?
Has the client discovered any solutions to these concerns?
What is the impact of ethnic and cultural identity with regard to family,
    friends, school/work, or community?

Role Functioning:
What roles does the client currently fulfill?
How were these roles acquired (voluntarily or involuntarily)?
Is the client having difficulty with any of these roles or balancing these
    roles?
Has the client discovered any solutions to these concerns?
What is the impact of the above concerns regarding family, friends,
    school/work, or community?

Spirituality and Religion:
Does the client adhere to a particular spiritual belief system or religion?
Does the client view his or her spiritual or religious orientation as a
    strength?
Does the client view his or her spiritual or religious orientation as a prob-
    lem?

> **Box 7.1**
> **Interviewing Questions—**(*Continued*)
>
> If so, has he or she sought and/or discovered any solutions to these concerns?
> What is the client's sense of life purpose?
> Do the client's beliefs hinder his or her psychosocial functioning in any way?
> What is the impact of the above concerns regarding family, friends, school/work, or community?
>
> **Other Strengths:**
> Does the client identify any other strengths or talents?

client a mental status exam to assess the client's current psychological functioning and make an accurate diagnosis of a mental disorder, when appropriate to do so.

DSM-IV-TR

The *DSM-IV-TR* provides criteria that help practitioners decide if a client has one or more mental disorders or psychopathological syndromes. These diagnostic criteria are 1) widely accepted in practice settings, 2) descriptive in nature, and 3) not tied to any particular theoretical frameworks. The manual is organized according to mental/emotional disorders found in children, adolescents, and adults. Diagnoses are made according to five axes: Axis I, primary clinical disorder; Axis II, personality disorder or mental retardation; Axis III, medical problems; Axis IV, psychosocial issues; Axis V, global assessment of functioning (GAF). See appendix 7A for an outline of the five axes in the *DSM-IV-TR*. Although some mental disorders such as Alzheimer's disease require medical evaluation by a neuropsychologist and other doctors, most others can be assessed by master's level social workers who have a license to practice clinical social work.

The *DSM-IV-TR*, however, is a psychiatric textbook, and its credibility and use are somewhat controversial among social workers. As discussed in Chapter 1, for example, practitioners trained in the strengths perspective do not like the use of diagnostic labels, because it marginalizes the client. Other practitioners, such as those trained in brief, solution-focused and behavioral perspectives, prefer more functional ways to describe the problems of clients over diagnostic labels. They do not see diagnostic labels as helpful because these labels do not describe the specific behaviors of the client that are a problem for them and others. Neither do they specify change goals that are necessary for the client to solve his or her presenting problems. Practitioners also believe that the diagnostic labels used in the *DSM-IV-TR* pathologize clients instead of empowering them to overcome their psychosocial problems. Diagnostic labels, in fact, may be used by some clients to disempower, excuse dysfunctional behavior, and remove the personal incentives and self-determination necessary to change. Many therapists, including family therapists and others practicing from systems perspectives, brief therapists, cognitive constructivist therapists, and behaviorist practitioners, express some skepticism about the usefulness of *DSM* nosological system.

Specific Criticisms of the *DSM-IV-TR*

Beyond the critiques offered by social work practitioners and therapists working from differing models, the *DSM-IV-TR* has also been criticized for its lack of research into the validity and reliability of its diagnostic categories. Recall from Chapter 5, that it is necessary for a measurement instrument or a diagnostic assessment tool to demonstrate validity and reliability before it is useful to practitioners. Social work researchers Kutchins and Kirk (1997) have offered some of the most compelling criticisms of the research for the manual, showing that the categories lack reliability. Other practice-researchers have pointed to the political and social constructivist nature of the diagnoses in the *DSM-IV-TR* manual. These researchers demonstrate that the diagnoses are maintained or deleted from the manual based on social political processes instead of empirical research (Neimeyer & Raskin, 2000). Some social constructivists and advocates for the oppressed groups of mental health patients go so far as to say that the *DSM-IV-TR* manual is neither valid nor helpful to clients but serves instead to maintain the power of an elite group of psychiatrists and therapists. The social work profession in general does not prefer the categorical, noncontextual view of human behavior offered by the *DSM-IV-TR* manual. The National Association of Social Workers, for example, has published its own diagnostic assessment system, the Person-In-Environment (PIE) System, which is different than the PIE rating scale discussed in this chapter (Karls & Wandrei, 1994). The PIE System and classification manual are available from NASW Press at this web site: http://www.naswpress.org/publications/books/clinical/pie/2405A.html.

Over the years, the developers of the *DSM-IV-TR* have worked to address these criticisms; the current *DSM-IV-TR* manual offers more of a person-in-environment assessment for making a diagnosis. This is accomplished through the Axial system; in particular, Axis IV addresses psychosocial stressors. The manual also currently intergrates more material on culture and ethnicity. Future additions of the *DSM* are likely to continue to address current criticisms. Prospective reviews of the *DSM V* on what the future manual might look like suggest a major overhaul of the *DSM* in that revision. Diagnosis is likely to become less categorical, for example, and reflect more of a continuum or dimensional view of mental disorders (Widiger & Clark, 2000). It is not likely, however, that any revision will totally satisfy practitioners who have theoretical or epistemological concerns about the helpfulness of psychiatric diagnosis.

Use of the *DSM-IV-TR*

Despite the limitations of the *DSM-IV-TR*, it is important for social workers to learn and use the *DSM-IV-TR*. A recent national survey conducted by the Substance Abuse and Mental Health Services Administrations (SAMHSA) Board that social workers outnumber psychiatrists and psychologists two to one in working in mental health practice. The majority of practicing social workers are employed in mental health or school mental health services (O'Neil, 1999). The manual is constantly used in health and mental health services, in work with clients and insurance reimbursement, and other mental health professionals consider it to be the state of the art in mental health assessment. Because social workers often collaborate with other health care professionals, they need to be familiar with the content of the *DSM-IV-TR*, to communicate effectively about their clients with other professionals. The *DSM-IV-TR* delineates the symptoms, cultural factors, differential diagnoses, and prevalence rates that must be examined thoroughly in a complete psychosocial assessment. The social worker may gather the information in the PIE chart prior to making an initial diagnosis. Undoubtedly, the *DSM-IV-TR* is the state of art in mental health assessment and the most frequently used diagnostic system. For this reason, this chapter uses the diagnostic categories and their measurements for assessing and working with adult clients.

ASSESSING MAJOR MENTAL DISORDERS IN ADULTS

Social workers must be concerned that major mental disorders, such as schizophrenia and bipolar disorders, and serious neurological symptoms such as, delirium and dementia. It is important that practitioners be astute in diagnosing these symptoms in clients, to ensure that clients get the proper help and care. The mental status exam has long been used to help examine current mental functioning and to assess serious mental disorders. See appendix 7B for a list of criteria for diagnosing schizophrenia and other psychotic behaviors, bipolar disorder, delirium, and dementia in clients. Depression, anxiety disorders, and substance abuse are covered later in this chapter. Following are instructions for using the Mini-Mental State Examination to assess serious mental disorders.

Mini-Mental State Examanation

The Mini-Mental State Examination (MMSE), published by Folstein, Folstein, and Mchugh (1975), is a frequently used assessment tool designed to evaluate the mental state of clients in both clinical and research settings (Crum, Anthony, Bassett, & Folstein, 1993). It assesses cognitive impairments like dementia, delirium, and other thought disorders. The MMSE consists of brief and basic items that allow for a time-efficient and effective evaluation of various cognitive domains, including orientation, encoding, attention, recall, language, reading, writing, and drawing (Folstein et al., 1975). The eleven-item scale has a possible total of thirty points and requires less than ten minutes to administer. The MMSE has been widely used to detect cognitive difficulties in special populations, such as the elderly, head-injured clients, and individuals with severe mental illness (Lezak, 1995).

When using the MMSE, a cutoff score of twenty-three/twenty-four is generally accepted, to separate patients with cognitive impairment from those who are cognitively intact (Anthony, LeResche, Niaz, von Korff, & Folstein, 1982; DePaulo, Folstein, & Gordon, 1980). Research indicates that a cutoff score of twenty-three for clients with mental health issues is considered acceptable (Folstein et al., 1975). However, some studies have suggested a lower sensitivity level for those clients with less education, certain ethnicities, or older clients (Fillenbaum, Heyman, Willians, Prosnitz, & Burchett, 1990; Launer, Dinkgreve, Jonker, Hooijer, & Lindeboom, 1993; Murden, McRae, Kaner, & Bucknam, 1991).

The MMSE is published in the *Journal of Psychiatric Research*; thus it is in the public domain. The following describes the procedure for using the MMSE in practice.

Orientation. This refers to individual's grasp of time and place. By asking the client to note the year, season, day, or month, the social worker can ascertain the client's level of temporal awareness. Then, by asking about location, such as state, county, or agency, the worker can assess the client's spatial awareness. Clients who are disoriented as to time and/or place may need further evaluation for serious cognitive impairment.

Registration. This section evaluates how much repetition is necessary for a client to recognize and understand (i.e., "register") a concept. If a client takes considerable time or cannot register concepts, this may be an indication of a thought disorder or organic illness.

Attention and Calculation. By asking a client to count backward by seven, a social worker can assess the person's ability to focus and reformulate a concept. This indicates a level of reasoning ability that is necessary for normal cognitive functioning.

Recall/Memory. By asking the client to recall three items identified earlier in the exam, the social worker can assess the client's ability to retain information. If the client is not able to remember, this may indicate a cognitive deficit associated with such disorders as amnesia, stroke conditions, dissociative disorders, head trauma, dementia, or other neurological conditions.

Amnesia, the absence of memory, can be partial or complete, or have an emotional or organic basis. *Disassociative amnesia* is a highly selective loss of memory involving emotionally charged events (such as, a childhood sexual assault, ritualistic abuse, or other trauma). In the case of a stroke, *anterograde amnesia,* loss of memory for recent events, is usually progressive and somewhat characteristic of arteriosclerotic cerebral degeneration (hardening of the arteries). *Retrograde amnesia* involves long-past events and is usually not progressive. A *fugue state* is a severe and abrupt personality dissociation involving amnesia and actual physical flight (during the period of amnesia) from the area of ostensible psychological conflict. Assumption of a new identity during the fugue is common.

Language. This portion of the exam determines a client's capacity and fluency with verbal expression, literacy, and writing skills. For example, can the client write a simple sentence that you say orally? It also assesses the client's ability to 1) comprehend and follow instructions and 2) make the complex series of recognitions necessary to complete this simple task (e.g., "Take a paper in your right hand, fold it in half, and put it on the floor"). Thus, motor tasks are concurrently assessed with cognitive understanding.

This section will also elucidate bizarre thinking patterns and disruptions in communication. For example, punning and rhyming to an extreme can occur in those with mania and occasionally with schizophrenia (disorganized type). Mutism (refusal or simply the inability to speak) frequently accompanies severe psychosis. Verbigeration (word salad), the stringing together, in a seemingly meaningless way, of words and phrases repetitively, occurs in certain kinds of schizophrenia (notably disorganized type, occasionally other types). Aphasia (loss of some of the faculty for language comprehension or production) may indicate lesions in certain parts of the brain.

The MMSEs have to be taken in context and in concert with other information.

ASSESSING COMMON PROBLEMS IN ADULT CLIENTS USING STANDARDIZED MEASURES

Two of the most prominent types of problems that adult clients experience are depression and anxiety. Other frequent problems are substance abuse and substance dependence. To develop accurate assessments of these disorders, a social worker should utilize a set of rapid assessment instruments specific to the particular diagnoses. In the following sections, some of the prominent rapid assessment tools recommended for assessment purposes are introduced. Recall from Chapters 3 and 4 that these standardized measures are meant to offer quick, valid, reliable assessments of a client's characteristics. As screening tools, rapid assessment measures can provide one part of the information necessary to make a diagnosis. If the client scores are clinically significant on one of these rapid assessment measures the practitioner can follow up with more thorough diagnostic interviews and procedures to see if the person qualifies for the diagnosis. The measures are also helpful in outcomes monitoring. See Chapters 2 and 11.

Major Depressive Disorder

In practice, a social worker is likely to encounter clients with a variety of mood or affective disorders. According to the *DSM-IV-TR*, there are several basic types of depression in adults. *Major depressive disorder* is characterized by one or more depressive episodes over a two-week period, which are evidenced by five or more of the following symptoms nearly every day:

- Depressed mood most of the day
- Diminished interest and/or pleasure in activities
- Significant weight loss or gain
- Insomnia or hypersomnia nearly every day
- Psychomotor agitation or retardation
- Fatigue
- Feelings of worthlessness or inappropriate guilt
- Diminished ability to concentrate or think
- Recurrent thoughts of death

Dysthymic disorder, on the other hand, can be defined as a protracted, less severe form of depression that is characterized to a lesser extent by many of the same symptoms as major depressive disorder. These include poor appetite, insomnia or hypersomnia, low energy, low self-esteem, poor concentration, and feelings of hopelessness (APA, 1994). For a diagnosis of dysthymia, the symptoms must be present for the majority of the time over a two-year period.

Depression may be an accompanying symptom in other disorders (such as, adjustment disorder with depressed mood). To appropriately diagnose major depression and dysthymia, some examples of appropriate screening instruments include the following:

Beck Depression Inventory—The mostly widely known and extensively utilized assessment instrument for ascertaining depressive symptomatology in adults is the Beck Depression Inventory II (BDI-II) (Beck, Steer, & Brown, 1996). First developed in 1961 by Aaron Beck, M.D., the Beck Depression Inventory consists of twenty-one items rated on a four-point scale ranging from 0–3 to assess the intensity of depression in adult clients. The current version, the BDI-II, was revised from earlier versions in order to be congruent with the *DSM-IV-TR*. The self-administered instrument takes between five and ten minutes to complete and should be filled out in the presence of a doctoral-level clinician trained in the use of the instrument. It has excellent reliability with a test-retest coefficient of 0.90. Hundreds of research studies have been conducted using the BDI over the past forty years attesting to its concurrent and criterion validity. A score of 0–13 indicates normal levels of depressive symptoms, 14–19 indicates mild to moderate levels of depression, 20–28 indicates moderate to severe levels of depression, and 29–63 indicates extremely severe levels of depression. The social worker needs to be able to comprehend these scores provided by the doctoral-level administrator in order to facilitate treatment strategies for the client.

The Hamilton Rating Scale for Depression—The Hamilton Rating Scale for Depression (Hamilton, 1967), unlike the Beck Depression Inventory, is an assessment instrument completed by the interviewer. It is normally used when the interviewer has some knowledge of the client's affective status and strong evidence of symptoms of depressive disorder. The scale has eighteen items measured on a five-point Likert scale. It addresses the issues of depressed mood, suicide, anxiety, general somatic symptoms, and loss of interest in work and recreational pursuits. It has been widely used in clinical research studies as well as in practice with adult populations including the elderly, adults with HIV/AIDS, adults with sexual disorders, and adults with minor depressive disorders.

Center for Epidemiological Studies-Depression Scale, Revised (CES-D-R)—Another commonly used instrument to assess depression is the Center for Epidemiologic Studies-Depression Scale (CES-D) (Radloff, 1977). This self-report scale consists of twenty items. This scale is found to be highly reliable with populations of varying ages, ethnicities and cultures (Beals, Manson, Keane, & Dick 1995; Garrison, Addy, Jackson, McKeown, & Walker, 1991; Radloff, 1977; Radloff & Terri, 1986). However, some studies have found the CES-D may not be as valid an instrument when administered to minority clients (Prescott et al., 1998). Studies utilizing this scale confirm the finding that females report depressive symptoms more frequently than males in the general population in the United States (Berganza & Agular, 1992; Radloff & Rae, 1981; cf.; Gjerde, Block, & Block, 1988; Kessler et al., 1994).

Anxiety Disorders

In addition to depression, clients often encounter problems with anxiety. There is growing evidence of a strong relationship between depression and anxiety disorders. Clients often qualify for both diagnoses, for example. The *DSM-IV-TR* defines an anxiety disorder as worry and "apprehensive expectation" for the majority of time during a six-month period (APA, 2000). Other symptoms might include restlessness, concentration difficulties, sleep problems, tension, and irritability. According to the *DSM-IV-TR*, the variety of anxiety disorders includes panic disorder, agoraphobia, obsessive-compulsive disorder (OCD), posttraumatic stress disorder (PTSD), phobias, and anxiety disorders of varied etiologies (e.g., from a general medical condition, substance-induced, etc.). Anxiety can be measured utilizing psychosocial instruments, such as the PIE assessment and standardized measurement tools. Following are some examples: (See appendix 7B for criteria for assessing anxiety disorders using the *DSM-IV-TR*).

State Trait Anxiety Inventory—The State Trait Anxiety Inventory (STAI) is a standardized two-part, self-report instrument. Both the State section and the Trait section contain twenty items, rated by the respondent from "not at all" to "very much so" on a scale of 1 to 4. The scale has been validated and shown to have coefficient alpha reliability coefficients ranging from 0.86 to 0.95 (Spielberger, 1983). Several of the items are reverse scored. Examples of items include "I feel tense," "I feel upset," and "I feel secure."

Trauma Symptom Checklist—The Trauma Symptom Checklist (TSC-33), a thirty-three item instrument, has been used in clinical research as a measure of traumatic effect (Briere & Ruentz, 1989). It has been used relative to the long-term effects of childhood physical and sexual abuse. It can be used in the assessment of PTSD in adults. The scale has been shown to have internal consistency with an alpha of 0.89 (Briere & Ruentz, 1989). The respondent rates a list of thirty-three items from 0 = never to 3 = very often. Examples of the items include "insomnia," "feeling isolated from others," and "trouble getting along with others."

Fear Questionnaire (FQ)—The Fear Questionnaire (FQ) is a twenty-four item instrument designed to assess symptoms for treatment with phobic individuals (Fischer & Corcoran, 1994). In addition to general fears, the scale can target specific phobias. The instrument includes fifteen questions and has subscales that assess agoraphobia, blood injury phobia, and social phobia. Items are rated from 1 to 8 with higher scores reflecting greater severity of symptoms. The instrument has an alpha of 0.82 for the three subscales and 0.92 for the main target phobia. Some examples of the items on the scale include "going into crowded shops," "large spaces," and "speaking or acting to an audience."

Panic Attack Symptoms Questionnaire (PASQ)—The Panic Attack Symptoms Questionnaire (PASQ) is a thirty-three item instrument measuring the severity of symptoms the client experiences during a panic attack (Clum, Broyles, Borden, & Watkins, 1990; Fischer & Corcoran, 1994). Items are rated from 0 to 5 with 0 = "Did not experience this" to 5 = "protractedly (1 day to 2 days or longer)." The instrument has good reliability with an alpha of 0.88. The scale can be used to differentiate between individuals who have panic attacks and those who do not have panic attacks.

Personality Disorders

Personality disorders are one type of psychopathology about which the social worker may be concerned. Clients with personality disorders often have difficulty functioning in work and social settings. Some examples from the *DSM-IV-TR* include antisocial personality disorder, paranoid personality disorder, borderline personality disorder, and obsessive-compulsive personality disorder. These disorders tend to require extensive therapeutic intervention, and the clients may be at risk for harming themselves and others, as is the case with clients who have antisocial and borderline diagnoses. A social worker needs to be careful not to fall into the trap of labeling confusing clients with certain personality diagnoses without also validating the disorder with standardized measurement instruments and appropriate developmental history. One method a social worker may use to ensure an appropriate diagnosis is to rely on standardized, structured interviews for assessing psychopathology. Interviews such as the Structured Clinical Interview for Diagnosis (SCIDII) can improve the reliability and validity of diagnosis among clinicians. (See, for example, Garb, 1998). In a review of this literature Wood, Garb, Lilienfeld, & Nezworski (2002) report that numerous studies that compare clinician-alone diagnosis to structured interviews indicate that practitioners both overrate and underrate diagnoses in clients, and that clinical judgment in general does not perform as well as standardized, structured interviews.

A social worker may use other standardized measures to assess a client's personality, such as a personality assessment measure. The client may be referred to a psychologist for a more-formal personality assessment if there is a suspicion that the person may have some underlying personality disorder. Psychologists may administer objective and projective measures such as the Millon and Rorschach ink blots. As discussed in Chapter 3, however, the Rorschach is not a very accurate measure. Social workers should use themselves and also ask psychologists to use more-objective, standardized personality assessment measures.

Standardized, objective measures, covered in Chapter 4, are the best self-report assessment tools for measuring personality functioning. Box 3.1 in Chapter 3 lists both books and Internet sources for identifying and reviewing standardized measures for assessment of personality and other psychological functioning. Personality assessment measures, such as the Minnesota Multiphasic Personality Inventories (MMPI and MMPI II), are based on the original work of Hathaway & McKinley, 1943. In recent years, the MMPI II was updated with the help of James Butcher and others. The short version of the MMPI II includes 370 items; the measure also offers longer versions with additional scales for assessing clients in forensic and correctional populations. See appendix 7C or a list of the scales of the MMPI II.

The MMPI and MMPI II are some of the most popular measures in psychology practice and have held this position for decades. See the web site of Pearson, NCS Assessments for more information about the MMPI II and its revision. http://assessments.ncspearson.com/assessments/tests/mmpi_2.htm).

Other standardized personality assessment measures may also be used by social workers and other clinicians. See, for example, the Millon Clinical Multiaxial Inventory III (Millon, 1997) and the California Psychological Inventory (McAllister, 1996). The Millon was discussed and illustrated in Chapter 3. More information about the Millon and how to purchase the instrument can be obtained from the NCES Assessments web site http://assessments.ncspearson.com/assessments/tests/mcmi_2.htm. Another measure that helps to diagnose antisocial personality and predict the aggression and violence these individuals are at risk of committing is the Hare Psychopathy Checklist-Revised (Hare, 1991; Hemphill, Hare, & Wong, 1998). This measure is helpful for use in forensic settings, where clinicians are asked to diagnose antisocial personality and psychopathy, and to present and predict a person's profile for violence. The original version of the Hare is a long instrument to use, taking two-three hours. There is, however, a shorter screening version of the measure that reduces the time to ninety minutes. See the web site for Psychological Assessment Resources http://www.parinc.com/product.cfm?ProductID=324 for more information about the Hare. To use personality assessment measures, the practitioner should have adequate training in testing and measurement and should be familiar with the scoring and interpretation of the particular measure being used.

Substance Abuse

When assessing adults, it is important to consider the possibility of substance-related disorders, which consist of substance use, abuse, and/or substance dependency. This chapter does not detail individual substances. However, it should be noted that for many years alcoholism has been recognized by professional medical organizations as a distinct, primary, chronic, progressive, and often fatal disease. More than seven percent of the population ages eighteen years and older—nearly 13.8 million Americans—have problems with drinking, including 8.1 million alcoholics. Almost three times as many men (9.8 million) as women (3.9 million) are problem drinkers; prevalence is highest for both sexes in the eighteen to twenty-nine-years-old age group (National Institute of Alcoholism and Addiction, 1994). There were 3.1 million Americans—approximately 1.4 percent of the population ages 12 and older—received treatment for alcoholism and alcohol-related problems in 1997; treatment peaked among people between the ages twenty-six and thirty-four (SAMSA, 1997).

The *DSM-IV-TR* offers a detailed way to diagnose alcoholism, various drug dependencies, and polysubstance (at least three of the eleven substances in a twelve-month period) dependencies. This aspect of adult diagnosis is extremely tricky, because 1) it is hard to differentiate chemically induced symptoms from symptoms of mental illness, 2) many clients have dual diagnoses, and 3) a major presenting issue of substance abuse is denial (i.e., a mechanism for minimizing and avoiding an issue). This section explores these complications and provides mechanisms for accurately diagnosing substance disorders.

First, as noted, the symptoms of substance use and abuse often mimic symptoms of other mental illnesses, and vice versa. For example, almost all addicts have "mood swings" between periods of elation and apparent depression (e.g., restlessness, irritability, and discontentment); however, only some addicts may actually be diagnosed with bipolar disorder.

Many adults with diagnoses other than addiction use substances as a mechanism of "self-medication." Still others can be diagnosed with concurrent illnesses. Such comorbidity is also referred to as "dual diagnoses" and in twelve-step recovery realms, "double trouble." Dually diagnosed individuals have complicated, multiproblem presentations in treatment; inpatient and longer-term services may need to be provided to such individuals.

The other major complicating factor in diagnosing substance problems is the tendency for the user to minimize and deny the problems. Chemically dependent individuals are often aware that their use and subsequent behaviors are socially unacceptable. Therefore, they often become adept at hiding their use, and manipulating and lying to cover up their actions. They also may try to minimize consequences and find ways to deceive others, especially the people who care about them, who, in turn, "enable" or perpetuate the problem through care taking.

Substance abuse is a pattern of substance use that results in recurrent and significant adverse consequences associated with the frequent use of substances. This pattern can significantly impair all aspects noted on the PIE chart. Substance dependence refers to a cluster of cognitive, behavioral, and physiological symptoms indicating the person continues to use the substance despite substantial substance-related problems (Munson, 2000). A repeated pattern of self-administration usually results in tolerance, withdrawal, and compulsive drug use.

Substance abuse causes a wide variety of medical and psychiatric symptoms and diseases. Therefore, all patients presenting to the health care system should be considered for the diagnosis. However, certain organ systems and problems have such a high prevalence of underlying substance abuse that they must be viewed with an even higher index of suspicion.

Common medical symptoms of substance abuse include vitamin deficiency, malnutrition, dyspepsia, upper GI problems, peptic ulcer, hepatitis, pancreatitis, hypertension, new-onset arrhythmia, cardiomyopathy, seizures, peripheral neuropathy, and AIDS. Trauma of any kind should arouse suspicion during an interview, especially accidents at work, single-car crashes, and domestic violence. Substance abuse also manifests in the following behavioral, emotional, and cognitive problems: stress, insomnia, anxiety, depression, suicidality, acute psychotic states, impaired cognition, and violent behavior. Perhaps the most subtle aspects of substance abuse are the associated social problems. Substance abusers are at high risk for marital and family problems, legal difficulties, loss of employment, and financial deterioration. Special consideration should be given to patients who are homeless, involved in prostitution, and those in the criminal justice system.

Substance abusers are at particularly high risk for HIV/AIDS. During the course of an assessment, social workers must be alert to symptoms that may be related to HIV infection (Fisher & Harrison, 2000). According to Barthwell & Gilbert (1993), these signs and symptoms may include complaints of swollen lymph nodes, severe abdominal pain, diarrhea, visual changes, and severe dermatological conditions or rashes. In addition, a mental status exam may reveal AIDS-related cognitive impairments.

The primary distinguishing characteristics between a person who *uses* substances and one who is *dependent* on the substance are as follows: 1) the phenomena of craving, which is a psychological and biological drive, experienced by addicts, to use more substances regardless of consequences; 2) the need for more and/or stronger substances for the same effect; 3) progression, or increasing problems and consequences of use over time; and 4) the eventual fatality of the illness if untreated. These aspects are the grounds for the characterization of substance abuse and dependence as a disease. Following are the clinical criteria for diagnosis of substance dependency.

CRITERIA FOR SUBSTANCE DEPENDENCE (*DSM-IV-TR* CRITERIA)

A maladaptive pattern of substance use, leading to clinically significant impairment or distress, as manifested by three (or more) of the following, occurring at any time in the same twelve-month period (APA, 2000):

1. Tolerance, as defined by either of the following: (a) a need for markedly increased amounts of the substance to achieve intoxication or desired effect or (b) markedly diminished effect with continued use of the same amount of the substance

2. Withdrawal, as manifested by either of the following: (a) the characteristic withdrawal syndrome for the substance or (b) the same (or a closely related) substance is taken to relieve or avoid withdrawal symptoms

3. The substance is taken in larger amounts or over a longer period than was intended

4. A persistent desire or unsuccessful efforts to cut down or control substance use

5. A great deal of time is spent in activities necessary to obtain the substance (e.g., visiting multiple doctors or driving long distances), use the substance (e.g., chain-smoking), or recover from its effects

6. Important social, occupational, or recreational activities are given up or reduced because of substance use

7. The substance use is continued despite knowledge of having a persistent or recurrent physical or psychological problem that is likely to have been caused or exacerbated by the substance (e.g., current cocaine use despite recognition of cocaine-induced depression, or continued drinking despite recognition that an ulcer was made worse by alcohol consumption)

   Once substance abuse or addiction is suspected, a worker must assess a client for physical withdrawal symptoms which can be life threatening. Many workers are surprised to learn that alcohol withdrawal is one of the most potentially fatal detoxifications, while cocaine withdrawal (although very uncomfortable) is virtually harmless. The best evaluative tool for withdrawal symptoms is the CIWA test. The Clinical Institute Withdrawal Assessment for Alcohol Based on DSM-IV-R (CIWA-AD) is an 8-item scale for clinical quantification of the severity of the alcohol withdrawal syndrome. Its origins stem from the 15-item CIWA-A and the more recent revised 10-item CIWA-

AR (Sullivan et al. 1989). It is a reliable, brief, uncomplicated and clinically useful scale that can also be used to monitor response to treatment. This scale offers an increase in efficiency over the original CIWA-A scale, while retaining clinical usefulness, validity, and reliability. It can be incorporated into the usual clinical care of patients undergoing alcohol withdrawal and into clinical drug trials of alcohol withdrawal.

There are a variety of assessment instruments that can be used to determine the presence, nature, and treatment directions with regard to clients with potential substance abuse problems. For an extensive list of assessment tools, particularly for alcohol problems, clinicians can access the Internet site of the National Institute on Alcohol Abuse and Alcoholism (NIAAA) at http://www.niaaa.nih.gov/publications/assinstr. htm. The following are two of the most commonly utilized and widely accepted assessment tools:

CAGEii – This test was developed by Dr. John Ewing, founding director of the Bowles Center for Alcohol Studies, University of North Carolina at Chapel Hill (Mayfield, McLeod, & Hall, 1994). CAGE is an internationally used assessment instrument for identifying alcoholics and other substance abusers. It is particularly popular with primary care givers. CAGE has been translated into several languages. The patient is asked four questions:

1. Have you ever felt you ought to **C**ut down your drinking (or drug use)?
2. Have people **A**nnoyed you by criticizing your drinking (or drug use)?
3. Have you ever felt bad or **G**uilty about your drinking (or drug use)?
4. Have you had a drink (or used drugs) first thing in the morning (**E**ye opener) to steady your nerves or get rid of a hangover?

Affirmative answers to two or more questions is a positive screen and should prompt further history.

The MAST – (Selzer, 1971) is a written, twenty-five item screening test that may be given to a patient initially, or in follow-up to another screening test, such as the CAGEii. Its brevity makes it useful as an outpatient screening tool. Cutoff scores correlate well with more extensive diagnostic tests for alcohol disorders. The MAST has been modified for drug abuse (i.e., DAST).

M A S T (Revised): *Michigan Alcohol Screening Test*

The MAST is a simple test that helps assess if you have a drinking problem.

1. Do you feel you are a normal drinker? ("normal"—drink as much or less than most other people)
   Circle Answer: YES NO

2. Have you ever awakened the morning after some drinking the night before and found that you could not remember a part of the evening?
   Circle Answer: YES NO

3. Does any near relative or close friend ever worry or complain about your drinking?
   Circle Answer: YES NO

4. Can you stop drinking without difficulty after one or two drinks?
   Answer: YES NO

5. Do you ever feel guilty about your drinking?
   Circle Answer: YES NO

6. Have you ever attended a meeting of Alcoholics Anonymous (AA)?
   Circle Answer: YES NO

7. Have you ever gotten into physical fights when drinking?
   Circle Answer: YES NO

8. Has drinking ever created problems between you and a near relative or close friend?
   Circle Answer: YES NO

9. Has any family member or close friend gone to anyone for help about your drinking?
   Circle Answer: YES NO

10. Have you ever lost friends because of your drinking?
    Circle Answer: YES NO

11. Have you ever gotten into trouble at work because of drinking?
    Circle Answer: YES NO

12. Have you ever lost a job because of drinking?
    Circle Answer: YES NO

13. Have you ever neglected your obligations, your family, or your work for two or more days in a row because you were drinking?
    Circle Answer: YES NO

14. Do you drink before noon fairly often?
    Circle Answer: YES NO

15. Have you ever been told you have liver trouble such as cirrhosis?
    Circle Answer: YES NO

16. After heavy drinking have you ever had delirium tremens (D.T.'s), severe shaking, visual or auditory (hearing) hallucinations?
    Circle Answer: YES NO

17. Have you ever gone to anyone for help about your drinking?
    Circle Answer: YES NO

18. Have you ever been hospitalized because of drinking?
    Circle Answer: YES NO

19. Has your drinking ever resulted in your being hospitalized in a psychiatric ward?
    Circle Answer: YES NO

20. Have you ever gone to any doctor, social worker, clergyman, or mental health clinic for help with any emotional problem in which drinking was part of the problem?
    Circle Answer: YES NO

21. Have you been arrested more than once for driving under the influence of alcohol?
    Circle Answer: YES NO

22. Have you ever been arrested, even for a few hours because of other behavior while drinking?
    Circle Answer: YES NO
    (If Yes, how many times _____)

Scoring for the MAST: Please score one point if you answered the following

1. No
2. Yes
3. Yes
4. No
5. Yes
6. Yes
7 through 22: Yes

Add up the scores and compare to the following:

0–2 No apparent problem

3–5 Early or middle problem drinker

6 or more problem drinker

In summary, substance abuse disorders are complex problems with a variety of etiologies and outcomes. Social work practitioners can use the above-noted instruments to assess substance abuse disorders. If you, as a social worker, have a large clientele of substance users/abusers, special training will be valuable and important.

SPECIAL ISSUES IN WORKING WITH OLDER ADULTS

With increasing advances in medical technology during the past two decades, there has been a corresponding increase in the number of older persons in the population. Nearly one third of the population today is over sixty-five years old. Older adults experience many of the same emotional problems that younger adults experience. For example, older adults can be diagnosed within any of the adult categories for mental disorders found in the *DSM-IV-TR*. On the other hand, depression and dementia are two psychobiological and emotional problems that are prevalent in the older adult population. In addition, medical or physical problems may be confounding factors for older adults and may mask emotional symptoms that older adults experience. In the older adult population, it is also important to be able to differentiate between what is an emotional or medical problem and what is a normal result of aging. Therefore, assessment instruments that specifically focus on the problems confronting older adults have been developed to address the psychological and medical issues that are prevalent in this population.

One of the most common emotional disorders experienced by older adults is depression. Like other adults, older persons display symptoms of sadness, hopelessness, fatigue, loss/increase of appetite, difficulty sleeping, and other symptoms outlined in the *DSM-IV-TR*. However, in addition to these symptoms, older adults may also experience memory loss and cognitive impairment when depressed. These symptoms mimic dementia and can often be confused by practitioners for more serious cognitive impairment when, in fact, the problem is depression (Yesavage et al., 1983). This condition is known as "pseudodementia." Other symptoms that may be present in depressed, young adults, such as a decline in sexual interest and other somatic complaints, may be normal signs of aging in older adults and not an indication of depression. Because of these differences in psychological symptomatology among older adults, specific scales have been designed to measure depression in the elderly, such as the Geriatric Depression Scale.

The Geriatric Depression Scale (GDS) is a well-known instrument designed to assess depressive symptoms in older adults (Brink, Yesavage, Lum, Heersema, Adley, & Rose, 1982). It is available in versions with thirty, fifteen, ten, and four items, as well as version with one item. With the exception of the one-item version of the GDS, all of the shorter versions are highly correlated with the original thirty-item version (D'Ath, Katona, Mullan, Evans, & Katona, 1994). The GDS has high internal consistency and has been validated in a large number of studies. Because depression in older adults is often first assessed in a physician's office, it is helpful to have a questionnaire that requires only a short time to complete. The GDS is often used as an initial screening tool to diagnose depressive symptoms in the elderly. If an elderly person scores above the cutoff point on this scale, it is likely that significant depressive symptomatology exists and a fuller assessment should be pursued. Social workers who have elderly clients can use this instrument during an initial interview or at any time the client appears to be displaying depressive symptoms. The original version of the long form of the scale and instructions for scoring are presented in box 7.2. The scale is in the public domain and can be used by practitioners without permission from the authors.

Box 7.2
Geriatric Depression Scale (Long Form)

1. Are you basically satisfied with your life?
2. Have you dropped many of your activities and interests?
3. Do you feel that your life is empty?
4. Do you often get bored?
5. Are you hopeful about the future?
6. Are you bothered by thoughts you can't get out of your head?
7. Are you in good spirits most of the time?
8. Are you afraid that something bad is going to happen to you?
9. Do you feel happy most of the time?
10. Do you often feel helpless?
11. Do you often get restless and fidgety?
12. Do you prefer to stay at home, rather than going out and doing new things?
13. Do you frequently worry about the future?
14. Do you feel you have more problems with memory than most?
15. Do you think it is wonderful to be alive now?
16. Do you often feel downhearted and blue?
17. Do you feel pretty worthless the way you are now?
18. Do you worry a lot about the past?
19. Do you find life very exciting?
20. Is it hard for you to get started on new projects?
21. Do you feel full of energy?
22. Do you feel that your situation is hopeless?
23. Do you think that most people are better off than you are?
24. Do you frequently get upset over little things?
25. Do you frequently feel like crying?
26. Do you have trouble concentrating?
27. Do you enjoy getting up in the morning?
28. Do you prefer to avoid social gatherings?
29. Is it easy for you to make decisions?
30. Is your mind as clear as it used to be?

This is the original scoring for the scale: One point for each of these answers. Cutoff: normal-0–9; mild depressives-10–19; severe depressives-20–30.

1. no	6. yes	11. yes	16. yes	21. no	26. yes
2. yes	7. no	12. yes	17. yes	22. yes	27. no
3. yes	8. yes	13. yes	18. yes	23. yes	28. yes
4. yes	9. no	14. yes	19. no	24. yes	29. no
5. no	10. yes	15. no	20. yes	25. yes	30. no

SOURCE: Brink, T. L., Yesavage, J. A., Lum, B., Heersma, P., Adey, M., et al. (1982). Depressive symptoms and depressive diagnoses in a community population. *Archives of General Psychiatry*, 45, 1078–1084.

Functional Status of Older Adults

Another important factor to consider in assessing older adults is their functional status. Functional status refers to the person's ability to take care of self, to perform physical activities, and to participate in activities of daily living. Older adults who have difficulties in their functional status may require additional community resources, such as home health services, meals on wheels, visiting nursing services, or housekeeping assistance. Elderly persons can range from mildly to severely impaired in their ability to perform functional activities. There are numerous assessment scales designed to measure an older person's abilities to perform activities of daily living. One example of a functional activities questionnaire is presented in figure 7.2.

Quality Assurance and Brief Assessment Screening and Outcome Measures for Adults

Rapid assessment tools like the ones covered in the sections on depression and anxiety provide a general screening for specific problem areas. More comprehensive assessment measures like the MMPI II covered in the section on personality disorders provide a comprehensive screen of major mental health diagnosis and psychological characteristics but are time-consuming and expensive to use in practice. In today's fast-paced, managed-care, practice settings it is not always desirable or cost-effective to perform a comprehensive assessment or to give a client a long measure like the MMP II or the Millon measure described earlier. In fact, surveys of psychologists indicate that the whole field of psychological assessment is being challenged to change and is evoluting because of managed care. Psychologists are using standardized measures less and less, for traditional psychological assessment batteries (Wood et al., 2002). Standardized, brief screening and outcomes measurement instruments, and quality assurance systems that provide specific feedback on individual clients for treatment planning and outcomes monitoring, are replacing traditional psychological assessment batteries (Beutler, 2001). In Chapter 4, the authors introduced computerized quality assessment systems and their measure. These measurement systems are able to assess client functioning quickly (like rapid assessment instruments) but include several problem areas instead of one specific area like depression. They also give specific feedback on high-risk areas, such as suicide and violence, and provide both graphic and narrative reports that can be used by practitioners in treatment planning and outcome monitoring.

When used in a quality assurance systems, brief screening instruments can provide an assessment of several problem areas and measures either acting as a screen of several different areas or making it possible for clinicians to combine rapid assessment questions as needed from different test item banks or measurement tools. Some systems even allow the

Figure 7.2   Functional Assessment: Self Maintaining and Instrumental Activities of Daily Living

The purpose of this instrument is to evaluate the functional ability of elderly persons on different levels of competence, in particular, autonomy in ambulatory, physical, and "instrumental" activities of daily living.

A. **ABILITY TO USE TELEPHONE**
  1 1. Operates telephone on own initiative
  1 2. Dials a few well-known numbers
  1 3. Answers telephone but does not dial
  0 4. Does not use telephone at all
B. **SHOPPING**
  1 1. Takes care of all shopping needs independently
  0 2. Shops independently for small purchases
  0 3. Needs to be accompanied on any shopping trip
  0 4. Completely unable to shop
C. **FOOD PREPARATION**
  1 1. Plans, prepares, and serves adequate meals independently
  0 2. Prepares adequate meals if supplied with ingredients
  0 3. Heats, serves, and prepares meals, or prepares meals, but does not maintain adequate diet
  0 4. Needs to have meals prepared and served
D. **HOUSEKEEPING**
  1 1. Maintains house alone or with occasional assistance
  1 2. Performs light daily tasks such as dishwashing or bedmaking
  1 3. Performs light daily tasks but cannot maintain acceptable level of cleanliness
  1 4. Needs help with all house maintenance tasks
  0 5. Does not participate in any housekeeping tasks
E. **LAUNDRY**
  1 1. Does personal laundry completely
  1 2. Launders small items by self
  0 3. All laundry must be done by others
F. **MODE OF TRANSPORTATION**
  1 1. Travels independently
  1 2. Arranges own travel via taxi, but does not use other modes of transportation
  1 3. Travels on public transportation when accompanied by others
  1 4. Travels limited to full assistance by others
  0 5. Does not travel at all
G. **RESPONSABILITY FOR MEDICATIONS**
  1 1. Is able to take medications in correct dosages at correct time
  0 2. Takes medications if they are prepared in advance in correct dosages
  0 3. Is not capable of dispensing own medications
H. **ABILITY TO HANDLE FINANCES**
  1 1. Manages financial matters independently
  1 2. Manages day-to-day purchases but needs help with banking, major purchases, etc.
  0 3. Incapable of handling money
  _____ **Total**

Completed by _____

Adapted from: M. P. Lawton and E. M. Brody. (1969). Assessment of older people: self-maintaining and instrumental activities of daily living. *Gerontologist, 9,* 179–186.

clinician to add client data from more traditional instruments such as the MMPI or Millon. The latter choices give clinicians more flexibility in assessment and can be individualized for client need. Quality assurance measurement systems generally provide:

1. A screen of several problem areas that is completed in a short time and is directly linked with treatment planning
2. Clinically significant scores based on normative data
3. A risk assessment profile
4. A projection for client outcome
5. An ongoing monitor of treatment effectiveness through the completion of repeated measures
6. A signal for the practitioner, if treatment is not progressing
7. A clinical change score and reliability of change index for showing client improvement
8. Graphic displays and/or narratives that can be used by the practitioner

See table 4.2 in Chapter 4 for a review of several quality assurance systems and their measures.

These types of measurement tools meet all the criteria and common themes identified in Chapter 1 as being important for social work assessment. Problem identification, task planning, and treatment monitoring, for example, are inherent in these quality assurance measurement systems. These types of measurement systems are also easy to use in single case designs and practice evaluation, as discussed in Chapter 11. One shortfalling of many of the quality assurance measurement systems, however, is that they often rely exclusively on client self-reports. Recall from the earlier chapters in this text that it is best to include more than one source of data in building valid and reliable assessments of clients. Some quality assurance systems correct for this possible information bias by including practitioner and other persons' perspectives, as well.

The Outcomes Questionnaire-45.2 (OQ-45.2) is discussed. It is used with adult clients in outpatient settings. This measure has also shown promise in working with more severely disturbed clients. The OQ-45 is also one of the first quality assurance measures to demonstrate in research that feeding outcome information back to practitioners can make a difference in the treatment outcomes of clients (Lambert & Finch, 1999; Lambert, Hansen, & Finch, 2001).

The Outcome Questionnaire-45.2 (OQ-45.2) is a brief, forty-five-item, self-report outcome/tracking instrument designed for repeated measurement of client progress through the course of therapy and following termination. It can be completed in five minutes and is inexpensive to use, costing less than one cent per administration. This makes it cost-effective and suitable for agency-based practice. It offers measures of social functioning and appears to have excellent potential for social work practice.

The OQ-45.2 measures functioning in three domains: 1) subjective distress/symptom dysfunction (items loaded for depression and anxiety); 2) interpersonal functioning; and 3) social role, enabling the practitioner to assess functional level and change over time. The OQ-45.2 contains risk assessment items for suicide potential, substance abuse, and potential violence at work. This questionnaire is available in a Windows-based and web-based versions, graphically reporting treatment progress in real time. It has decision support features, and numerous standard reports. Each item on the measure is rated on a five-point Likert scale. 0 = never, 1 = rarely, 2 = sometimes, 3 = frequently, and 4 = almost always. The overall score is recommended for tracking progress in treatment, because the number of items on the individual scales is small.

The OQ-45.2 provides a signal detecting system that alerts clinicians to the status of client's treatment and the need to make adjustments in the treatment plan. White feedback (dots appearing on reports) indicates that the client is functioning in the normal range and may be ready for termination. Green feedback suggests that the change the client is making is in the normal range and everything is okay; no change in treatment plan is needed. Yellow feedback indicates that the change the client is making is less than expected and that some adjustment in treatment plan is needed. Red feedback tells the practitioner that the client is not making progress and may terminate prematurely with no benefit from therapy (http://www.oqsystems.com).

The validity and reliability of the OQ-45.2 are acceptable, and it is one of the better measures in the quality assurance area. It has a large national normative base and good internal consistency reliability ($r = 0.93$). The test-retest reliability after three weeks ($r = 0.84$) is acceptable. The measure has also demonstrated construct validity in factor analytic studies showing a three-factor solution. Studies into concurrent validity have been done with acceptable results, and it has been shown to be sensitive to clinical change. A reliable change index has also been calculated and was found to be fourteen points. Clients whose scores change fourteen points or more are regarded to have made reliable change during treatment (Lambert et al., 2001).

LEARNING TO PERFORM ASSESSMENT WITH THE PIE CHART

Several other chapters in this text provide examples of assessment reports using elements of the Integrative Assessment Protocol or specific assessment approaches. This chapter approaches assessment differently. To provide practice using the PIE assessment rating scale, the following case example is presented. It follows the categories described in the PIE chart but has not been written-up in a formal assessment report. Before you read the case study, make a copy of the PIE chart. Using the information in the case study, complete the PIE assessment in its chart format. You may also want to practice writing up the information in the format of the protocol in Chapter 1. You may wish to consult Chapters 6, 8, and 9 for completed examples of assessments using the Integrative Skills Assessment Protocol.

To make use of the case study as a learning tool:

1. Develop a psychosocial assessment report including diagnosis on all *DSM-IV-TR* axes and social work intervention recommendations (following the categories in the PIE assessment).
2. Fill out the ratings on the PIE assessment chart in this chapter.
3. Decide which measures covered in this chapter would be most suitable for this client.
4. To develop an intervention plan considering the following:
   - Identify symptoms that may require referral to other professionals (i.e., physician, psychologist, psychiatrist, career counselor).
   - Identify availability of client resources (e.g., social support systems, transportation, housing, finances, recreational outlets, etc.)
   - Prioritize what are the most pressing issues for this client and what needs to be done first to help. What needs to be done second and third.
   - Identify what types of contract and treatment goals you might be able to form with this client, and project what how the client might suggest his or her main goals.
   - Decide which measurement tools you will use in outcomes monitoring

CASE STUDY

Christopher T. Hager, a 62-year-old, Caucasian male, appeared for the first interview wearing a wrinkled cardigan, blue jeans, and plaid shirt. He was unshaven and appeared to have just gotten out of bed. His hair was uncombed, and he had dark circles under his eyes. Chris was slightly underweight and had a subtle tremor in his hands.

When asked about his medical history, he reported that he recently had gone to the doctor for headaches. In addition, Chris reported that the doctor found no physiological reason for the pain he was experiencing.

He also remarked, "My headaches really made it hard to eat, so I've lost some more weight. I think I really need to gain a few pounds." Chris stated that there had been no prominent family history of illness, though he noted having an uncle who had committed suicide. He reported having tried Advil, Tylenol, and Aspirin for the headaches but has taken no other prescribed medication on a regular basis to alleviate the chronic pain. He also stated that he sometimes has a "nightcap" to help him fall asleep, which has become more difficult lately.

The client was referred to this Behavioral Health Center by his family physician who felt that he needed a psychological assessment. Chris readily agreed to make an appointment at BHC because his daughter, a graduate student in social work, supported the physician's recommendation.

Chris was employed for thirty years at a well-known, high-tech, computer corporation as an electronics engineer. He recently took early retirement because of the company's cutbacks in employees and their offer to provide a compelling severance package. Chris stated that he missed the routine of getting up and going to work every morning, although he did not miss the pressure of trying to "keep up with young, new college grads."

Chris noticed that after being out of work for approximately one month, he felt more lethargic and was having difficulty pursuing activities that he normally enjoyed. He mentioned that he often felt bored and "didn't know what to do with myself at times." Another difficulty that he encountered was that he no longer saw friends from work—for lunch or for weekend activities. When asked about solutions to this dilemma, he said, "I don't really have the energy to make plans with the guys." He reports that his daughter, Catherine, has been urging him to get out of the house and socialize. However, Chris states that he "just can't get going on anything these days."

Throughout the course of this assessment, Chris seemed to be using avoidance coping strategies to deal with his current problems. Rather than asserting himself on his own behalf, Chris tends to passively wait for others to initiate activities and solutions. When asked if he felt his coping mechanisms are effective, he answered, "No, but I don't know what else to do."

In addition to his headaches and the loss of his job, Chris stated that he was divorced from his wife, Connie, approximately five years ago and that he is still disturbed by the divorce. When this worker probed further, Chris revealed that his wife had left him after twenty-eight years of marriage. He stated angrily, "She was fed up with the whole thing." He also felt that Catherine had been caught in the middle, which prompted her to go to school in another state. Following the divorce, Chris moved from his comfortable, four-bedroom home in the suburbs to a small apartment downtown. Despite the manageable size of his present residence, he is reportedly still having difficulty adjusting to taking care of the apartment and other skills of daily living (e.g., laundry, cleaning, and self-care).

Chris has weekly phone contact with his twenty-four-year old daughter, Catherine, who is currently in graduate school. She is his only child. He no longer is in contact with his former wife, except on rare occasions. His primary companion is his bloodhound named Blue. The worker has assessed that Chris is quite committed to his dog, as he spoke at length about Blue's pedigree and how he takes Blue for long walks late at night. He constantly made references to Blue throughout the conversation (for example, "Blue and I had macaroni and cheese for dinner" and "Blue and I like to walk to the grocery store and get coffee in the mornings.")

Chris noted that "in his day," he was an eloquent speaker, a member of a large social network (primarily through playing golf), and a good communicator. However, he laments that he no longer feels like he is a part of a community, as he was when he was working. He states that he lost many of his golfing partners, because they were guys at work and they would make plans to golf at the end of the day. He also said that he was a member of several engineering organizations but that he'd lost interest in those functions following his job layoff. He also indicated that he used to play a lot of bridge when he was married but that, since the divorce, he had no one to partner with. He said he was embarrassed to go to bridge tournaments by himself. Chris stated that he not only felt like he was robbed of his professional title but that he also lost his role as a husband. He stated that he had been married for so long that he didn't know how to function as a single person. He did, however, mention one person, Mack, who played golf with him occasionally and who also went out to dinner with him at times.

Throughout the interview, Chris appeared sad when discussing his divorce and loss of job. He seemed engaged in the conversation and showed no signs of psychotic behavior. He did appear to have a slight trembling in both hands but made no mention of this problem during the session.

When asked about romantic interests, Chris laughed and responded, "Are you kidding? I haven't even LOOKED at a woman since my wife left me." On inquiry, Chris noted that although his first few years married to his wife were "romantic and fun," approximately five years prior to his wife leaving, the couple began sleeping in separate rooms. He noted in a defensive tone, "I snore pretty loudly." Chris was vague in response to questions about his sex life, but he did add, "I'm not what I used to be, if you know what I mean."

The worker administered the Mini-Mental State Exam to Chris prior to the interview. Chris scored within the normal range on this scale. He showed no signs of cognitive impairment, loss of memory, or thought disorder. He reported no history of cognitive problems. His thinking appeared to be clear, focused, and well-organized, and he had no difficulty engaging in conversation with the worker. Although he seemed to have some difficulty in finding solutions to his present life problems, he appeared to have good judgment and decision-making capacities.

Chris consistently had a flat affect during the assessment. Even his sporadic laughter at his own jokes was forced. He has a tendency toward sarcasm and a pessimistic attitude, as evidenced by his statement, "Even though I want things to be different, I am what I am. Guess you can't expect me to change after all these years." When asked if he has times when he feels good, he states, "There are times when I feel a bit better or worse, but I don't really ever feel like myself since my wife left." He adds that retirement is a challenge to a "workaholic like me." When asked about the impact of his mood on others, he expressed his belief that his daughter avoids spending time with him because she feels frustrated about his situation.

Although it was apparent that Chris viewed himself as a valuable worker and father, his self-esteem seemed to have diminished since he left his job. His relatively recent divorce also seems to have deflated his sense of self-worth. Although he did not offer a great deal of information about his marriage and the causes for the divorce, it was evident that the divorce was a traumatic event in his life. He appeared to be feeling somewhat hopeless about developing new relationships with others. His low self-esteem also seems to be preventing him from seeking out friends and other social supports with whom he could be involved.

Although Chris' low self-esteem and sadness appear to be preventing him from finding solutions to his present difficulties, he verbally expresses a strong desire to make changes in his life. For example, he stated that, "I just don't want to continue living this way" and "something's got to change in my life." Catherine seems to be strong support and motivator for Chris to resolve his feelings of loss. He obviously respects her opinions and acknowledges that she "knows a whole lot more about this type of thing (e.g., feelings) than I do." When asked by the worker about any goals he may have for the future, Chris stated that it is all he can do to get through a day and that he doesn't think beyond that very much. However, he stated that he used to always set goals and was a fairly "driven" person when he was employed. When the worker asked if he could imagine ways things could improve, Chris stated that he thought he might be drinking more than usual and that he needed to cut down on his alcohol consumption. "I think it may be clouding my vision, right now." Chris exhibits some ambivalence about the work involved in making some of these changes. "One day I tell myself I'm going to stop drinking and start finding some healthy outlets for myself, and the next day, I can't get out of bed. Two days last week, I never got out of my pajamas and Blue and I just spent the day watching videos and eating popcorn."

When asked about his culture and ethnicity, Chris reports that he is "Irish-Catholic." He jokes, "No wonder I am the way I am, right?" When asked to elaborate, he notes that he comes from a long line of "stoic, hardworking, hard-drinking" men. He states that his grandparents came to the United States when his parents were children. He did not know any more details about the family history. When asked about strengths and solutions that have come from his ethnic culture, he noted that he attributes his sense of humor, determination, and "realistic expectations" to his Irish heritage.

As referred to above, the client considers himself Catholic. He reports that he used to go to church, at least on holidays, but that he has not gone since his divorce. He believes that God punishes people for "sins." Through further inquiry, it became clear that Chris feels that because of his divorce, drinking, and what he feels is a lack of general contribution to society, there is "no way I can squeeze my way through the 'pearly gates.' " When asked about his life purpose, Chris responded, "At this point, just getting through the day." When pressed, he noted gaining strength from his belief that "I'm really Blue's 'higher power,' I suppose. He needs me."

Chris is apparently experiencing some role transition and confusion. He has lost his former roles of professional and husband. He has been having a great amount of difficulty transitioning to other roles in his life. He seems to enjoy the role of caretaker for his dog; however, he appears to need other roles to gain a sense of self-fulfillment. It does not appear that Chris is ready to accept the role of retired person and may perhaps need to find another part-time position or volunteer in the nonprofit sector to gain a sense of self-worth.

When asked if he had anything to add to this assessment, he noted that he used to be an avid woodworker. He told the worker that he made much of the furniture in his home. He expressed some pride in his work but noted that it has been so long since he has done such work, he does not even know where his tools are at present.

SUMMARY

This chapter describes a framework for assessing adult clients that integrates the person-in-environment perspective with clinical diagnostic criteria. In addition, several methods of assessing adults using standardized and clinical psychosocial instruments are provided. A case study provides an opportunity for the reader to apply the PIE assessment technique to an actual client situation. Assessment of adults from a strengths-based, systems perspective is a crucial component in the social worker's repertoire of skills. Using the suggested framework, tools, and techniques described in this chapter, social workers can improve their assessment skills to become competent practitioners.

STUDY QUESTIONS

1. How is the *DSM-IV-TR* used in practice?
2. Name three criticisms of the *DSM-IV-TR*.
3. Describe three measures for depression and anxiety.
4. What are two specific considerations in assessing older adult clients?
5. Name nine characteristics of quality-assessment measurement systems that are used in managed care.

REFERENCES

Allen-Meares, P., & Lane, B. A. (1987). Grounding social work practice in theory: Ecosystems. *Social Casework, 68*(9), 515–521.

American Psychiatric Association. (1994). *Diagnostic and statistical manual of mental disorders* (4th ed.). Washington, DC: Author.

American Psychiatric Association. (2000). *Diagnostic and statistical manual of mental disorders* (4th ed.). Washington, DC: Author.

Anthony, J. C., LeResche, L., Niaz, U., von Korff, M. R., & Folstein, M. F. (1982). Limits of the mini-mental state as a screening test for dementia and delirium among hospital patients. *Psychological Medicine, 12,* 397–408.

Barthwell, A. G., & Gilbert, C. L. (1993). Screening for infectious diseases among substance abusers. *Treatment improvement protocol (TIP) series, No. 6.* Rockville, MD: US Department of Health and Human Services.

Beals, J., Manson, S. M., Keane, E., & Dick, R. W. (1995). Factorial structure of the Center for Epidemiologic Studies Depression Scale among American Indian college students. *Psychological Assessment, 3,* 623–627.

Beck, A. T., Steer, R. A., & Brown, G. K. (1996). *Manual for the Beck Depression Inventory* (2nd ed.). San Antonio, TX: The Psychological Corporation.

Berganza C. E., & Agular, G. (1992). Depression in Guatemalan adolescents. *Adolescence, 27,* 771–782

Beutler, L. (2001). Comparisons among quality assurance systems: From outcome assessment to clinical utility. *Journal of Consulting and Clinical Psychology, 69,* 197–204.

Briere, J., & Ruentz, M. (1989). The TSC (TSC-33): Early data on a new scale. *Journal of Interpersonal Violence, 4,* 151–163.

Brink, T. L., Yesavage, J. A., Lum, O., Heersema, P., Adley, M. B., & Rose, T. L. (1982). Screening tests for geriatric depression. *Clinical Gerontologist, 1,* 37–44.

Cheers, B. (1987). The social network map as an educational tool. *Australian Socal Work, 40,* 18–24.

Clum, G. A., Broyles, S., Borden, J., & Watkins, P. L. (1990). Validity and reliability of panic attack symptoms and cognition questionnaire. *Journal of Psychopathology and Behavioral Assessment, 12,* 233–245.

Crum, R. M., Anthony, J. C., Bassett, S. S., & Folstein, M. F. (1993). Population-based norms for the mini-mental state examination by age and education level, *JAMA, 18,* 2386–2391.

D'Ath, P., Katona, P., Mullan, E., Evans, S., & Katona, C. (1994). Screening, detection and management of depression in elderly primary care attenders. I: The acceptability and performance of the 15 item Geriatric Depression Scale and the development of shorter versions. *Family Practice, 11*(3), 260–266.

DePaulo, J. R., Folstein, M. F., & Gordon, B. (1980). Psychiatric screening on a neurological ward. *Psychological Medicine, 10*, 125–132.

Fillenbaum, G., Heyman, A., Willians, K., Prosnitz, B., & Burchett, B. (1990). Sensitivity and specificity of standardized screens of cognitive impairment and dementia among elderly Black and White community residents. *Journal of Clinical Epidemiology, 43*, 651–660.

Fisher, J., & Corcoran, K. (1994). *Measures for clinical practice: A sourcebook* (2nd ed.). New York: Free Press.

Fisher, G. L., & Harrison, T. C. (2000). *Substance abuse: Information for school counselors, social workers, therapists, and counselors.* Needham Heights, MA: Allyn & Bacon.

Folstein, M. F., Folstein, S. E., & McHugh, P. R. (1975). Mini-mental state: A practical method for grading the cognitive state of patients for the clinician. *Journal of Psychiatric Research, 12*, 189–198.

Franklin, C., & Jordan, C. (1992). Teaching students to perform assessment. *The Journal of Social Work Education, 28*(2), 222–241.

Garb, H. N. (1998). *Studying the clinician: Judgment research and psychological assessment.* Washington, DC: American Psychological Association.

Garrison C. Z., Addy A., Jackson K. L., McKeown R., & Waller J. L. (1991). The CES-D as a screen for depression and other psychiatric disorders in adolescents. *Journal of the American Academy of Child and Adolescent Psychiatry, 30*, 636–641.

Germain, C., & Gitterman, A. (1986). The life model approach to social work practice revisted. In F. Turner, (Ed.), *Social work treatment* (pp. 00–00). New York: Free Press.

Gjerde P. F., Block J., & Block J. H. (1988). Depressive symptoms and personality during late adolescence. *Journal of Abnormal Psychology, 97*, 475–486.

Hamilton, M. (1967). Development of a rating scale for primary depressive illness. *British Journal of Social and Clinical Psyhology, 6*, 278–296.

Hare, R., (1991). *Manual for the revised psychopathy checklist.* Toronto: Multihealth Systems.

Hathaway, S. R. & McKinley, J.C. Minnesota Multiphasic Personality Inventory. Minneapolis, MN: The University of Minnesota.

Hemphill, J. F., Hare, R., & Wong, S. (1998). Psychopathy and recidivism: A review. *Legal Criminologist Psychologist, 3*, 139–70.

Karls, J. M., & Wandrei, K. E. (1994). PIE as a new tool for more effective case management. In J. M. Karls & K. E. Wandrei (Eds.), *Person-in-environment system: The PIE classification system for social functioning problems* (pp. 151–157). Washington, DC: NASW Press.

Kessler, R. C., McGonagle, K. A., Zhao, S., Nelson, C. B., Hughes, M., Eshleman, S., Whittchen, H. U., & Kendler, K. S. (1994). Lifetime and 12 month prevalence of DSM III-R psychiatric disorders in the United States. *Archives of General Psychiatry, 51*, 8–19.

Kutchins, H., & Kirk, S. A. (1997). *Making us crazy: DSM: The psychiatric bible and the creation of mental disorders.* New York: Free Press.

Lambert, M. J., & Finch, A. E. (1999). The Outcome Questionnaire. In M. E. Maruish (Ed.), *The use of psychological testing for treatment planning and outcome assessment* (pp. 00–00). Mahwah, NJ: Erlbaum.

Lambert, M. J., Hansen, N. B., & Finch, A. E. (2001). Patient-focused research: Using patient outcome data to enhance treatment effects. *Journal of Consulting and Clinical Psychology, 69,* 147–149.

Launer, L. J., Dinkgreve, M. A., Jonker, C., Hooijer, C., & Lindeboom, J. (1993). Are age and education independent correlates of the Mini-Mental State Exam performance of community-dwelling elderly? *Journal of Gerontology, 48,* 271–277.

Lawton, M. P., & Brody, E. M. (1969). Assessment of older people: Self-maintaining and instrumental activities of daily living. *Gerontologist, 9,* 179–186.

Lezak, M. D. (1995). *Neuropsychological assessment* (3rd ed.). New York: Oxford University Press.

Mattaini, M. A. (1990). Contextual behavioral analysis in the assessment process. *Families in Society, 7*(4), 236–245.

Mattaini, M. A., & Kirk, S. A. (1991). Assessing assessment in social work. *Social Work, 36*(3), 260–266. National Assn. of Social Workers, US.

Mayfield, D., McLeod, G., & Hall, P. (1994). The CAGE questionnaire: Validation of a new measure. *American Journal of Psychiatry, 131,* 1121–1123.

McAllister, L. W. (1996). *A practical guide to California Psychological Inventory interpretation.* Palo Alto, CA: Consulting Psychologist Press.

Millon, T. (1997). *The Millon inventories: Clinical and personality assessment.* New York: Guilford.

Munson, C. E. (2000). *The mental health diagnostic desk reference.* Binghamton, NY: Haworth Press.

Murden, R. A., McRae, T. D., Kaner, S., & Bucknam, M. E. (1991). Mini-Mental State Exam scores with education in Blacks and Whites. *Journal of the American Geriatrics Society, 43,* 138–145.

O'Neil, J. V. (1999). Profession dominates in mental health. *NASW NEWS, 44*(6). The National Association of Social Workers. Washington, DC.: NASW Press.

National Institute on Alcoholism and Addiction. (1994). *Alcohol Health & Research World (AHRW), Vol. 18, No. 3, 1994.*

Neimeyer, R. A., & Raskin, J. D. (2000). *Constructions of disorder: Meaning-making frameworks for psychotherapy.* Washington, DC: American Psychological Association.

Prescott, C. A., McArdle, J. J., Hishinuma, E. S., Johnson, R. C., Miyamoto, R. H., Andrade, N., Edman, J. L., Makini, G. K., Nahulu, L. B., Yuen, N. Y., & Carlton, B. S. (1998). Prediction of major depression and dysthymia from CES-D scores among ethnic minority adolescents. *Journal of the American Academy of Child & Adolescent Psychiatry, 37*(5), 495–503.

Radloff, L. S. (1977). The CES-D scale: A new self-report depression scale for research in the general population. *Applied Psychological Measurement, 1,* 385–401.

Radloff, L. S., & Rae, D. S., (1981). Components of the sex difference in depression. *Residential Community Mental Health, 2,* 111–137.

Radloff, L. S., & Terri, L. (1986). Use of the Center for Epidemiological Studies-Depression Scale with older adults. *Clinical Gerontologist, 5,* 119–136.

Rodwell, M. K. (1987). Naturalistic inquiry: An alternative model for social work assessment. *Social Service Review, 61,* 231–246.

Saleeby, D. (1992). Biology's challenge to social work: Embodying the person-in-environment perspective. *Social Work, 37*(2), 112–118.

SAMSA. (1997). *National household survey on drug abuse: Main findings, 4/99.* Washington, DC.

Selzer M. L. (1971). The Michigan alcoholism screening test: The quest for a new diagnostic instrument. *American Journal of Psychiatry, 127,* 89–94.

Simon, C. E., McNeil, J. S., Franklin, C., & Cooperman, A. (1991). Treatment of schizophrenia: Another view: Response. *Families in Society, 72*(7), 436–438.

Spielberger, C. D. (1983). *Manual for the State-Trait Anxiety Inventory.* Palo Alto, CA: Consulting Psychologists Press.

Sullivan, J. T., Sykora, K., Schneiderman, J., Naranjo, C. A., & Sellers, E. M. (1989). Assessment of alcohol withdrawal: The revised Clinical Institute Withdrawal Assessment for Alcohol scale (CIWA-AR). *British Journal of Addiction, 84,* 1353–1357.

Vigilante, F. W., & Mailick, M. D. (1988). Needs-resource evaluation in the assessment process. *Social Work, 33*(2), 101–104.

Yesavage, J. A., Brink, T. L., Rose, T. L., Lum, O., Huang, V., Adey, M., & Leirer, V. O. (1983). Development and validation of a geriatric depression screening scale: A preliminary report. *Journal of Psychiatric Research, 17,* 37–49.

Widiger, T. A., & Clark, L. A. (2000). Toward DSM V and the classification of psychopathology. *Psychological Bulletin, 126,* 946–963.

Wood, J. M., Garb, H. N., Lilienfeld, S. O., & Nezworski, T. M. (2002). Clinical assessment. *Annual Review of Psychology, 53,* 519–543.

CHAPTER 8

Family Systems

Cynthia Franklin, Laura Hopson, and Christine Ten Barge

Social workers are frequently consulted to help with problems confronting families and marriages. This chapter provides several methods for conducting a family assessment and summarizes key concepts and issues to consider in the evaluation of family systems. Selected assessment and developmental frameworks for understanding the normative characteristics of families are reviewed and summarized, as well as methods that may be used as techniques for gathering information on families. A family assessment illustrating how to formulate and write up a family assessment is included. Finally, some guidelines for moving from assessment to intervention are discussed.

KEY CONCEPTS AND ISSUES OF FAMILY SYSTEMS

The focus of family practice has been on the assessment and treatment of families as a system. This grounding in systems theory helps us to understand a family as a whole, functioning entity. A family system is made up of a group of individuals who are interconnected and interdependent. These individuals are related to each other in a stable manner over time, and each individual's behavior influences the behavior of the others. Thus, mutual causality of interactions can be assumed (Buckley, 1967). All the members interrelate; together they create interactive and reactive behavioral sequences, which may be viewed as a family drama, dance, or game.

Thinking about families from a systems perspective focuses our attention on the way the family functions as an entity, rather than on the individual behavior or attributes of one of its members. Systems theorists have often used the description, "The whole is greater than the sum of its parts." Wholeness or "whole systems" functioning means that the family system is not just the sum of its parts viewed separately, but that the family members' interactions produce a unique type of behavior pattern all its own (Foley, 1989; Grotevant & Carlson, 1989). These interactions are often referred to as systemic patterns. We cannot truly understand a family's systemic functioning until we understand how all the parts function together to make up the behavior of the whole.

The converse is also true: we cannot understand the individual behavior of a family member unless we understand how that behavior relates to the functioning of the whole family. For example, we cannot understand the behavior of a child experiencing separation anxiety unless we also understand how these behaviors relate to the functioning of the family. The child's family may have experienced a disruption or recent loss (such as death or divorce). The mother herself may be depressed, and the child's anxious and clinging behavior may be a response to the distress of the mother. It may also be the child's way of protecting the mother; the anxious and avoidant behavior of the child may serve to pull a distant and conflicted parental relationship together by allowing the couple to mutually focus on the behavior of the child.

As another example, the passive and persistently nonassertive behavior of a female client cannot be understood outside the context of her relationship with a live-in lover. It may be that the lover is an assertive, take-charge person and prefers to be in control of the direction of their relationship. At the same time, the female may encourage this type of relationship through her passiveness and lack of assertiveness. Their relationship therefore is one of complimentarity, so it may be necessary to change the behavior of the male to change the behavior of the female, and vice versa. The consequence of changing one without changing the other would throw the couple system out of balance. It is also true, however, that change may be produced in the couple system by changing the behavior of either person.

Family researchers and practitioners developed several models for helping us understand and evaluate how families function and change. Several family systems models emerged: structural, strategic, behavioral/functional, psychodynamic/transgenerational, experiential, and communication. Other more-recent, strengths-based models have also been developed, such as the postmodern; brief, solution focused, narrative models, feminist, and multicultural perspectives. A comprehensive discussion of these models is beyond the scope of this chapter. The models have been reviewed in textbooks on family treatment and therapy. Please see Franklin & Jordan (1999) for a review.

In recent years, family practitioners have expanded their emphasis on assessing family systems to understanding broader ecological systems such as the school, and neighborhood (Franklin & Jordan, 2002).

The family in context is the main concern of family practitioners. Although systems theory is the most widely used theory in family assessment and practice, postmodern approaches, feminist, multicultural, narrative therapy, and brief solution focused therapy have become popular alternatives for the practice of family therapy. These newer approaches developed in reaction to traditional systems models; each model disavows allegiance to the family systems theory (Franklin & Jordan, 2002).

Brief, solution focused therapy, for example, does not emphasize understanding problems as a basis for assessing and helping families. Instead, the practitioner moves to assess exceptions to the problems and to co-construct with the client a set of goals and new behaviors. In the narrative model, the social worker assesses the restraining aspects of the client's narrative construction of the self and helps the client to challenge constraining and oppressive narratives that have been internalized from societal discourses.

Assessing families from postmodern viewpoints emphasizes the constructed nature of reality and the need for collaborative relationships between client and therapist. Postmodern family therapists examine sociocultural issues, such as how client problems and beliefs become socially constructed, the need for empowerment of marginalized clients, the political nature of therapy, and a need for social justice (Franklin & Jordan, 2002). The postmodern perspective appears to prefer qualitative methods to quantitative methods because of their emphasis on individuality and context. Standardized methods and any approach to assessment that seeks to categorize and marginalize is not believed to be very helpful to clients.

Multicultural perspectives emphasize race and culture and how these issues affect the presenting problems of clients. Multicultural, postmodern, narrative, and solution focused practices share an emphasis on nonpathological, antidiagnostic approaches to client assessment. Instead, these models have a functionalist and contextual orientation to assessment. These family assessors share similar beliefs to those discussed in Chapter 10 concerning the assessment and measurement of multicultural clients. Normative approaches to assessment may not be the best way to describe clients or to help them solve their problems. Contextual methods that are congruent with the clients' culture and unique context are the best way to assess clients of any background. Clinicians should use multiple methods and always include the opinions and viewpoints of the clients involved in the assessment. The strengths and resources of the family are always at the forefront of assessments.

In summary, family therapists practice from the perspective that problems must be understood as resulting from the relationship patterns in a family and broader ecological system. Understanding individual family members without understanding the whole family system and other systems would be like trying to understand a concert by listening to the instruments one by one. All the instruments synchronized with their own unique chords, rhythms, and arrangements is what makes the music. Similarly, the way families synchronize as a group accounts for the functional and dysfunctional behavior patterns of their members.

Practicing therapists often use a combination of traditional systems theory, postmodern, and solution focused approaches when assessing families. Integrationism and technical eclecticism are the preferred ways to practice family therapy (Franklin & Jordan, 2002). In this chapter we will selectively borrow relevant concepts across family therapy models.

From a family systems perspective, several qualities of family functioning are important to evaluate in a family assessment. The list of qualities briefly described below is not comprehensive; it does not include every possible aspect of family life that can be considered in an assessment. Rather, the qualities mentioned are practical guidelines for practitioners to use when conducting a family assessment.

Family Strengths

Strengths encompass both individual and environmental factors. The individual factors are often referred to as *resilience*, whereas the environmental factors are referred to as *protective factors*. Some examples of resilience include social skills and competencies, and the abilities to set goals and have a future orientation. Protective factors include characteristics of the environment, such as having a caring family or other adults, safe schools, and parental monitoring. A strengths perspective assumes that clients who come for help are more than their problems and circumstances dictate. All clients have competencies, knowledge, hidden resources, and resilience that may be used to reverse the misfortunes of their life struggles. Therapists practicing from a strengths perspective are convinced that clients have aspirations, motivation, untapped goals, and spiritual fortitude that they can muster against the impossible odds of their disabilities and social environment. Clients have self-determination and are able to resist and shape their environments and can utilize hidden resources within their environments (Franklin, 2002)

Many popular and effective approaches to martial and family therapy (including the brief, solution focused; narrative; and multisystemic models) employ the idea of utilizing client strengths in therapy. This idea can be traced back to the early foundations of the profession in strategic/structural models through, concepts like the utilization principal of Milton Erickson (Franklin & Jordan, 1999). Psychotherapy research indicates that positive belief and expectation for client change is a prerequisite for effective therapy, regardless of the model practiced. Practicing from a strengths perspective incorporates a value system that encompasses beliefs in the dignity and worth of individuals, their self-determination, and the transformative power of humans and human relationships. Regardless of the model used, practicing with clients from a strengths perspective means viewing them through a humanistic lens that assumes *all clients can grow and change* (Franklin, 2002). The importance of assessing client strengths is illustrated in a case study published by Franklin (2002). See box 8.1.

Box 8.1
The importance of a strengths based assessment
A CASE STUDY

Venetia is a sixteen-year-old African-American female. She has a son, Charles, age four months. Venetia dropped out of high school after she was five months pregnant. Prior to dropping out, she was in trouble with school authorities for skipping school and failing several of her classes. Her teachers suspected that Venetia was using drugs and said that she was known to "hang out" with some of the older gang boys. Venetia was ordered to see a therapist at the student assistance program at the school. She saw the therapist only once before quitting school. During a home visit, the school's truant officer encountered an elderly woman who said she was Venetia's grandmother and that Venetia no longer lived with her but was staying with her boyfriend. She did not know the address.

Venetia currently lives with her maternal aunt in public housing in a small one-bedroom apartment in an extremely poor, ethnic minority neighborhood. Her aunt has limited resources but offers Venetia and her son a place to live. Venetia's mother has a crack addiction and lives down the street with her maternal grandmother. Venetia sees her mother and her grandmother approximately twice a week. Her grandmother's eyesight is failing and she is also hard of hearing and can offer little support to Venetia. Venetia's father is in prison for murder and armed robbery, and she has not seen him in over eight years. Venetia anticipates that he may get parole in a few years. The baby's father is an African-American man named Charles who is approximately eight to ten years older than Venetia. After her pregnancy, Charles disappeared, though Venetia has not seen him since three months prior to her son's birth.

Adding Strengths to the Case

Venetia is attractive, verbal, and intelligent—slender, introverted girl who liked arts and math in school. She was a good to average student (earning Bs and Cs) until one year before she became pregnant. Venetia liked music and sang in the school choir for two years. She had several friends and one best friend, Latisha. Together, they sang in the church choir at the African-Zion Baptist Church. When Venetia was thirteen, she went on tour with the choir and performed in several African-American churches across the south. Venetia's childhood dream is to be in a singing group with her soul sister, Latisha (who is also a pregnant and parenting mom who attends an alternative school to finish her education). Venetia stopped taking drugs when she found out she was pregnant. Since Venetia had her baby, her aunt and mother have spoken and been in each other's house for the first time in ten years. Venetia's father writes from prison three to four times a year and, in his latest letter, he encouraged Venetia to finish high school and not to let her motherhood stop her from singing in the choir. Venetia says she wants to finish her education and get more instruction in music. She has an interest in attending the alternative school where Latisha is enrolled. The school offers childcare and special groups for pregnant and parenting teens.

SOURCE: C. Franklin. (2002). Becoming a strengths fact finder. *AAMFT Magazine*. Washington, DC: The American Association of Marital and Family Therapists.

Ethnicity, Culture, and Gender

Social workers recognize the importance of social variables, such as a client's ethnic background, culture, and gender. These socially derived experiences shape who a person becomes and also set into motion a host of societal expectations, limitations, and stereotypes with which the person is confronted. The behaviors, expectations, and prescribed roles that emerge from one's social class, ethnicity, culture, and gender roles are sometimes outside a person's awareness; at other times a client's awareness of these viewpoints may restrict or oppress the client so that he or she feels that he or she has limited options. For example, after facing incidences of discrimination in trying to find housing in middle-class areas, an African-American may feel that his or her options have been limited because of his or her color. The African-American may further transfer these feelings to other areas of his or her life or even have similar experiences that validate these social realities.

As another example, a woman may experience depression because she feels trapped in a unhappy marriage with a domineering husband. She may be unaware, however, that the gender roles that each of them plays are partly responsible for this dilemma. Both she and her husband have internalized culturally prescribed roles for how men and women are to behave in relationship to one another. She wants more intimacy, and he has difficulty sharing feelings, for example.

As a part of the assessment process, the practitioner assesses a person's culture, ethnicity, and social class and becomes aware of both the social oppression and strengths that such experiences offer a client. To understand a client's culture and ethnic experiences, it is important to use interpersonal skills and cultural sensitivity to form a helping relationship with a client (Grier, Morris, & Taylor, 2001). Some strategies that can facilitate the relationship-building and assessment process include:

1. Remaining open and nonjudgmental to alternative life styles. Clearly communicate to clients that you know there are many different ways of living and doing things. Cite examples and initiate conversation into an area so that the client will feel comfortable talking to you about his or her family and life situation.

2. Disclose patterns and ways of doing things in your family and culture and ask the client to describe how things are handled in his or her family and culture. A comparison and contrast sort of conversation may facilitate information exchange and mutual understanding.

3. Ask the question, "How do you do that in your family or culture?" Or, "What does this mean in your culture?"

4. Be self-aware and explore possible cultural biases with a supervisor.

5. Ask and accept feedback from the client about your level of cultural knowledge and sensitivity. Tell clients what you are thinking and ask them to comment on whether your thoughts and beliefs are accurate from their viewpoint.

Family Structure

Family structure relates to the way family members organize themselves into interactional patterns (Minuchin, 1974; Minuchin & Fishman, 1982). It also includes the family constellation, which describes the nature of the family (e.g., single parent, intact family), and the number of its members. For example, a recently divorced father is depressed over his divorce and fears that it will damage his two teenage sons and complicate his already strained relationship with them. The father attempts to form a blended family in which the father and his two children cohabitate with the father's new consort. The following structural interactional pattern emerges. The father doesn't enforce the rules because he is used to a mother figure assuming the discipline of the children. When the consort therefore attempts to step in and enforce the rules, the children resist the discipline because she is not "our mother." The consort and the children get into a "screaming match," and then the father becomes involved and tries to negotiate. The children refuse to obey the father because he is siding with the consort against them. This angers the father, who threatens the children with a severe punishment (taking their transportation away) but then changes his mind after further argument, in exchange for the boys' half-hearted compliance. By this time, however, everybody is mad at everybody else, including the father and the consort.

If this type of structural interactional pattern occurs over time, it becomes well rehearsed and well known. This behavior pattern involves every member of the family and composes part of the structural, interactional sequences of the family system. Such interactional sequences are circular in nature, rather than linear. Systems explanations for human behavior are contextual; no simple, linear cause-and-effect relationships exist. That is to say that A and B coexist and cause each other, rather than A causing B or B causing A (Goldenberg & Goldenberg, 1990). In this example, it is impossible to identify a simple cause-and-effect relationship for the dysfunctional pattern of this family. Causes and effects feed into one another to produce complex and interactive behavioral chains (such as, consort looks to father to intervene with children, consort intervenes, father reacts to screaming, children resist, father chastises children, children comply, father backs down, consort looks to father to intervene, etc.). For questions that you may use to assess family structure, see the section on interviewing in this chapter and review the information on circular questions in appendix 8A.

Subsystems

Subsystems are smaller parts of the systemic arrangement of the family and important to the organization of the family (Aponte & Van Duesen, 1981; Minuchin, 1974). The main subsystems in a family are the couple subsystem, parental subsystem, sibling subsystem, and parent-child subsystem (Janzen & Harris, 1986). Each subsystem in the family should be evaluated carefully to see if it is carrying out its own appropriate function. For example, the couple subsystem should be evaluated to see if the two individuals involved are having a satisfactory relationship that is mutually beneficial. The couple subsystem is one of the most important because it provides for the direction and health of the family (Beavers & Hampson, 1990). Two individuals join (couple subsystem) to form a family, and it is important for each to accommodate the other in a complimentary way. For example, the unconditional giving of "pleasing behaviors" to one another is important to marital adjustment and satisfaction (Stuart, 1980). At the same time, the couple must keep their individual autonomy so that they can act independently and continue their own individual development. A healthy couple subsystem is *sine qua non* for a healthy family organization (Beavers & Hampson, 1990; Janzen & Harris, 1986). For this reason, practitioners may choose to evaluate the couple subsystem separately from the other subsystems in a family assessment. Social workers may talk to the couple privately about issues related to their personal relationship (e.g., time spent together, quarrels, sex life, financial management, etc.).

The parental subsystem should also be evaluated to see how the couple is handling parenting responsibilities. Do they have adequate parenting skills and social support necessary to be effective parents? In a healthy parental subsystem, the parents lead the family and hold most of the power (Beavers & Hampson, 1990; Brock & Barnard, 1988). The notion of a hierarchy of the subsystems becomes extremely important to well-functioning families; parents must maintain their adult roles and appropriate control of the direction of the family (Haley, 1990; Minuchin, 1974).

Hierarchy across generations (parents and children, parents and grandparents) must be maintained in a functional family system. The parental subsystem works out complementary ways of handling the demands of parenting and the roles between and across the generations. The availability of such social supports as mother's and father's day out, child care, nurturing extended family relationships, and supportive interactions with other parents help parents to fulfill their parenting responsibilities without becoming exhausted, frustrated, and lost.

The sibling subsystem should be evaluated to see how the siblings get along together. What is the nature of their relationship? Is the relationship conflicted, competitive, approving, or similar to that of best friends? In a healthy family, there are strong emotional bonds between individuals within the sibling subsystem, and they share information and commonalities that are unique to that bond (Brock & Barnard, 1988). The parent-child subsystem should also be explored. How do the children get along with their parents? Are their any prolonged parent-child coalitions, in which a child and parent form a power alliance against another parent or another child?

It is important for subsystems to maintain their own unique roles, identities, and boundaries. Some examples of subsystem dysfunction that social workers frequently encounter in their work with families include 1) child taking sides with one parent against another parent; 2) children providing ongoing nurturing, emotional support, and parenting to a parent; 3) parents being overly intrusive into the private lives of their children; 4) parents asking their children to take sides in an argument between them; 5) adults in one generation forming a prolonged coalition with a member of another generation against particular family members (say, parent and grandparent against a spouse or grandparent and grandchild against parents); 6) parents refusing to interact with or negotiate with their children; 7) children shutting themselves off from guidance, interactions, and relationships with their parents; and 8) parents forming a prolonged coalition against a child, or children forming a prolonged coalition against their parents.

Such breakdowns in the integrity and interactions between subsystems are common in dysfunctional families. See figure 8.1 for a visual representation of the family system and its various subsystems, and some of the important roles that the different subsystems fulfill.

Boundaries

Boundaries are the demarcations that distinguish one system or subsystem from another (Minuchin, 1974). The terms *disengagement* or *enmeshment* describe boundary traits or specific situational interactions of a family. They usually describe a family trait that defines specific characteristics concerning the structure, communication, and interpersonal involvement of family members (Brock & Barnard, 1988). Boundaries can be rigid, and tightly drawn, resulting in *disengagement*, or loose and diffuse, resulting in *enmeshment* within families.

Members of disengaged families are uninvolved with one another and tend to be self-absorbed. These families have low cohesion, appear to lack appropriate bonding, and are therefore slow to respond to the emotional needs of family members. In fact, it may take a serious crisis before members of these families will come to the aid of one another; even then, they may resent the demands placed on them by the others. These families value individual freedom and personal autonomy. They are highly tolerant of differences among family members, and their members are oftentimes more involved with people outside their own family.

Figure 8.1   Family Systems

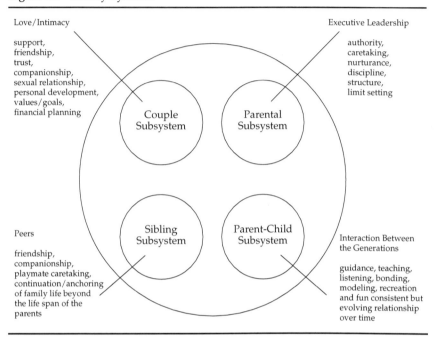

Love/Intimacy

support,
friendship,
trust,
companionship,
sexual relationship,
personal development,
values/goals,
financial planning

Executive Leadership

authority,
caretaking,
nurturance,
discipline,
structure,
limit setting

Couple
Subsystem

Parental
Subsystem

Peers

friendship,
companionship,
playmate caretaking,
continuation/anchoring
of family life beyond
the life span of the
parents

Sibling
Subsystem

Parent-Child
Subsystem

Interaction Between
the Generations

guidance, teaching,
listening, bonding,
modeling, recreation
and fun consistent but
evolving relationship
over time

Enmeshment is overinvolvement and a lack of appropriate boundaries in a family. Enmeshed families usually have high cohesion and family loyalty. These families demand consensus from their members and are
intolerant of them having views that differ from the family norms. In the
extreme example of this type of family, individual autonomy and growth
are stifled. Enmeshed families are family absorbed and not open to outsiders. They may have many family secrets, hidden agendas, and secret
power alliances within the family. Because enmeshed families are invested in keeping an image of agreement and alliance, they are often resistant to exploring conflict and possible differences that may exist between the members.

Some family therapists believe that when the transactions within a
family system cause a family to take on the characteristics of either extreme (disengagement or enmeshment), the family becomes dysfunctional (Olson, 1985). Other family therapists believe there is more of a
continuum, and that families relate in competent or less-competent ways,
depending on degrees of cohesion and their ability to maintain clear
boundaries (Beavers & Voller, 1983).

Regardless of a practitioner's theoretical views, if a family tends to
have rigid boundaries, communication across the subsystems may be extremely difficult, resulting in impaired relationship functioning similar to

that described in problems 6 through 8 in "Subsystems," above. Conversely, if boundaries are too loose in a family, there may be inappropriate transactions between subsystems, resulting in the kinds of interactions described in problems 1 through 5 in "Subsystems," above.

In assessing characteristics of families, it is critical to consider the many cultural variations in family functioning. No behavior pattern should be considered dysfunctional if it is culturally prescribed or satisfactory and functional for those involved (Minuchin, 1974; Olson et al., 1985), which means it is the responsibility of the practitioner to find out what cultural considerations occupy the family spaces. See Chapter 10 for descriptions of different ethnic and cultural patterns within families. Families in each different ethnic and cultural community have unique ways of thinking and behaving. These patterns are normative for that particular culture, and families should be assessed from the perspective of that culture. The ethnographic assessment methods described in Chapter 5 offer suggestions for how to gain an inside understanding of cultural variations within families.

Homeostasis, Information, and Feedback

Family systems are dynamic systems, constantly changing, simultaneously pursuing their goals, and responding to outside information. Family homeostasis is the self-regulating mechanism of a family system, the proclivity for members of a family to maintain a steady state in their relationships (Janzen & Harris, 1986). Families develop recurring patterns of interaction that maintain the stability of the family system (Becvar & Becvar, 1988). Thus, family therapists have observed that if a disturbed child is removed from the family system, another child in that family will develop disturbed behaviors. In such a family system, the child's disturbed behavior is believed to serve as a homeostatic mechanism. It may be that the child's parents have a severe marital conflict that would lead to divorce, but they rely on the misbehavior of the child to keep them focused on a common goal that keeps the family together.

All systems seek to maintain themselves, and they regulate the flow of information from inside and outside of the system to this end. Family systems that allow a free flow of information are known as open systems; those that restrict the flow of information are known as closed systems. Families with *open systems* are often highly visible in the community and are involved in numerous civic and recreational activities. Families with *closed systems* are more exclusionary and totally rely on their internal resources to sustain them.

Regulation of information by a system occurs through *feedback loops*, circular mechanisms that return to its input information about the system's output, to correct and ultimately manage the system's functioning

(Goldenberg & Goldenberg, 1990). Feedback provides information that helps a system guard against too much fluctuation and govern itself in a way that will promote its longevity. Negative or attenuating feedback is self-corrective and allows for the deviation in a system to be corrected, so that the system can maintain its steady state (Constantine, 1986). An example of a negative feedback mechanism in a family is a battering husband's plea for forgiveness. By pleading for forgiveness and promising to never hit his wife again, the husband may convince the wife to give the marriage another try, thus returning the system to its former steady state.

Positive or amplifying feedback does the opposite; it accelerates the deviation in a system. If the woman in our previous example comes to a battered women's shelter and insists that unless her husband gets help, she will end the marriage, the system will not be allowed to return to its former steady state, and further change in the system will be initiated. Positive feedback forces the system to change; the ultimate outcome of positive feedback if unregulated may be the destruction of the system (divorce).

From the systems perspective, for example, an affair may be seen as a positive feedback loop and the reconciliation of the married couple and discontinuation of the affair a negative feedback loop. Both positive and negative feedback processes operate at the same time, to regulate the flow of information, change, and homeostasis in a family system. Questions that help social workers track the circular feedback sequences in a family system are known as *circular questions*. This interviewing technique and examples of questions used to elicit systemic information are described in the section on interviewing methods later in this chapter.

Communication and Relationships

From a family systems view, all behavior in the family is relational in its etiology. Pathological behavior does not exist within the internal processes of one of the family members, but in the relationships between the members and in the social context. This view of pathology is ecological in perspective, and the focus is shifted from healing pathology in the individual to correcting dysfunctional relationships. The focus of a family assessment, therefore, is to understand the nature of relationships in the family.

Social workers must gain an understanding of the health of dyads and triads in the family. Dyadic relationships function most harmoniously when those involved function in a complementary pattern rather than a symmetrical one. Complementary patterns denote reciprocal interaction and inequality of responses. Symmetrical patterns are equal and may lead to competition (Watzlawick, Beavin, & Jackson, 1967).

For example, in a couple's relationship, one may be assertive and domineering while the other is passive and submissive. When they disagree, the submissive partner may defer to the more assertive one. Such reciprocal interaction is characterized as complementary. Another couple may both be assertive and, during disagreements, they may find themselves in an argument over who is right. The second couple's relationship is symmetrical, and although it is more equal, it is also more at risk for escalations, quarrels, and competition.

Triadic relationships in families are especially important to observe. In family systems, the triad (triangle) is believed to be the basic building block of family relationships (Bowen, 1978). Triangulation is a common occurrence and happens when any two members of a family experience too much stress between them. These two members may pull a third member into their relationship, thus regulating the stress between them. Another way to think about a triad is in terms of its ability to defocus conflict. An example of this process, known as detouring, is when parents focus on a child's behavior instead of their own issues (Minuchin, 1974). Family relational processes often consist of a series of interlocking triangles that may extend across generations and that lend stability to the system but also cause family dysfunction (Bowen, 1978). Social workers assessing such processes must evaluate the nature of these triangles to understand the network of relationships within the family system.

Communication is important to the competent functioning of family systems. For communication to be effective between family members, it must be open, direct, clear, and congruent at different levels, such as the tone and content of one's message. People communicate at three basic levels: verbal, nonverbal, and metacommunication. Verbal communication refers to the words and content of the message; nonverbal communication refers to the body posture and subtle innuendoes sent with a message; and, metacommunication (communication about communication) refers to the context of the communication, such as voice tone, tenor, and timing (Janzen & Harris, 1986).

In most dysfunctional families, members have difficulty communicating with one another. It is common to observe members of these families sending messages through a third party (e.g., the daughter tells the father why the mother is mad at him). Dysfunctional families also withhold information or send confusing and doublebinding messages to one another. Here is an example of a doublebinding message: A mother says to her daughter that she can confide in the mother about her relationship with her boyfriend (content level), and that she will be accepting and not upset (voice rising sharply and arms crossed at nonverbal level) if she confides that she has chosen to have sex with the boyfriend.

Rules and Myths

Families are rule-governed systems and rules define the relationship agreements between family members (Janzen & Harris, 1986). Some rules are explicit and clearly stated (such as, This family goes to church every

Sunday). Other rules are implicit or covert and may not be as clearly stated. For example, it may be an implicit rule that a family does not talk about sex in front of members of the opposite sex, or that the family does not discuss grandpa's drinking problem at all. Rules dictate much of the family members' behavior toward one another.

Family myths, like rules, contribute considerably to a family's behavior. Myths, here, are family members' shared beliefs and expectations concerning one another (Janzen & Harris, 1986). A family may develop a type of shared mythical reality concerning the behavior of one of its members. For example, the highly successful, artistic son of a conventional, enmeshed family may receive the label "queer" or "deviant." He may be viewed by the family as inadequate, even though he wins a scholarship to study art at a prestigious university and later establishes a successful art gallery. Such an inadequate view of an obviously creative and successful young man is a family myth that serves an important function in that family.

Problem Solving, Negotiation, and Decision Making

Related to communication is the art of problem solving. Functional family systems have good problem-solving skills. They do not get lost in the process or stuck in a power struggle. Effective families are able to brainstorm for solutions and come to agreement about how to proceed to solve a problem. Families that can effectively solve problems may have special times to meet to discuss problems and come up with solutions (such as a weekly family gripe session). They may also have a way to monitor the progress of the proposed solutions, such as a daily report card or a meeting to discuss outcomes (Dinkmeyer & McKay, 1983).

Like problem solving, negotiation is important to the functioning of family systems. Couples in particular must learn to negotiate roles and power between them and model these behaviors to their children. The adage goes, "The two shall be one," but the ultimate task may be to negotiate *which one*. Families work out different ways to negotiate for the things that each member wants. For example, some couples work out relationship agreements in which one member exchanges something for something else. In this bargaining type of relationship the wife may be willing to do the husband's laundry if he washes her car, or each may care for the children one night in exchange for a free night out. These are sometimes referred to as *quid pro quo* relationships (Stuart, 1980). Other families take a more giving attitude in which members go out of their way to please each other. Members of these types of families behave similarly toward one another. Some families have difficulty negotiating their relationships; the result may be endless and relentless power struggles and conflict.

Decision making, like negotiation, is central to the functioning of a family system. Who makes the decisions, and how are critical determinants made to the way the family operates. Equally important is who appoints the decision maker. Observing the pattern of decision making is important to understanding a family. In some families, for instance, the major decisions are made by one person, such as the father. In other families, decisions are made in an egalitarian, democratic fashion. In most families, the patterns of decision making shifts from situation to situation or role to role. For example, the mother may be responsible for making the major decisions about the home, and the father, the finances. Some families may delegate decision making to the members most proficient in those tasks, while others may rigidly follow the terms established in their family of origin. Some families have difficulty deciding who is going to make the decisions and how they are going to be made. These families may argue over decisions or shift responsibility for making the decisions from one person to another in a chaotic manner. As part of a family assessment, social workers need to become acquainted with the problem-solving and negotiation skills, as well as the decision-making processes of the family.

Individual Dynamics and Biological Systems

Thus far, this review of major concepts for understanding families has focused on families as a social system. In keeping with the holistic view of systems theory, social workers also need to assess psychological and biological competencies and vulnerabilities of families (Brill, 1988; Hepworth & Larsen, 1989; Johnson, 1987; Simon, McNeil, Franklin, & Cooperman, 1991). There is increasing evidence that major mental disorders like schizophrenia and major depression have biological determinants that may be biochemical. In addition, there is other evidence suggesting genetic links and biological vulnerabilities for problems such as attention deficit hyperactivity disorder and alcoholism. It is impossible for social workers to effectively treat such disorders in families until interventions in the biological system are made. Family assessments need to identify or rule out psychological or biological dysfunctions.

Teamwork and collaboration with medical professionals need to be a routine part of a family assessment for high-risk families. For example, a family brings a hyperactive child with severe behavior problems to a social worker for treatment. In this case, there is a repeated family history of alcoholism, mood disorders, and psychotic reactions. As a part of a good social work assessment, the social worker should refer and consult with medical professionals to establish a proper diagnosis and identify the appropriate combination of medical and family interventions for the child and family. See Chapters 6 and 7 for examples of questions for assessing the individual and biological aspects of children and adults.

Thus far in this chapter, we have summarized some major concepts important for understanding how families function as a system and family assessment considerations. Next we will review developmental frameworks and empirical assessment models that will help us to better understand the normative characteristics of families.

DEVELOPMENTAL LIFE CYCLE STAGES OF FAMILIES

Developmental frameworks for understanding families have emerged from research and theoretical explorations of the passage of families through life cycle stages, and from therapeutic work with them. In this section we will discuss the life cycle stages of families as depicted by Carter and McGoldrick (1988).

Families, like individuals, are believed to pass through developmental life cycle stages. Each life cycle stage is believed to have its own accompanying set of tasks to be accomplished if families are to make successful transitions from one stage to the next. When families consult social workers for help, it tends to be during periods of difficult transition. It is, therefore, important for family practitioners to evaluate where families are in their life cycle and to be cognizant of any difficulties that these families may be experiencing in accomplishing the tasks that are essential at different points in their life cycle development.

Family cohesion and the ability to maintain family "get togethers" and rituals are important to the adjustment of families throughout the life cycle. Life cycle transitions sometimes require families to renegotiate rituals to maintain these important family connections. For example, when an adult child moves away from home, the family may need to establish a new tradition of spending Christmas together. Tables 8.1, 8.2, and 8.3 present schemas for understanding family life cycle development. Table 8.1 describes the normal life cycle development of an intact nuclear family; tables 8.2 and 8.3 show the additional tasks that must occur in a divorced, single-parent, or blended family.

Evidenced-Based Assessment Models

To accurately assess a family system, practitioners must develop an internal baseline or standard from which to evaluate normative or healthy characteristics of families, keeping in mind the existence of cultural issues and their impact on family systems. In this section, we will discuss empirically derived family assessment models. These models, based on systems theory, demonstrate how families work and develop over their life cycles, giving us the perspective to judge when families are working well and when they are not. Evidenced-based assessment models are derived from research on the classification and assessment of family functioning, as well as clinical work with families.

Table 8.1 Life Cycle Stages for Intact Majority American Families

Family Life Cycle Stage	Emotional Process of Transition	Developmental Tasks
1. Leaving home: single young adults	Accepting emotional and financial responsibility for self	a. Differentiating self in relation to family of origin b. Developing intimate peer relationships c. Establishing self through work and financial independence
2. The joining of families through marriage: the new couple	Committing to new system	a. Forming marital system b. Realigning relationships with extended families and friends to include spouse
3. Families with young children	Accepting new members into the system	a. Adjusting marital system to make space for child(ren) b. Joining in child-rearing, financial, and household tasks c. Realigning relationships with extended family to include parenting and grandparenting roles
4. Families with adolescents	Increasing flexibility of family boundaries to include children's independence and grandparents' frailties	a. Shifting parent-child relationships to permit adolescent to move in and out of system b. Refocusing on mid-life marital and career issues c. Beginning shift toward joint caring for older generation
5. Launching children and moving on	Accepting a multitude of exits from and entries into the family system	a. Renegotiating marital system as a dyad b. Developing adult-to-adult relationships between grown children and their parents c. Realigning relationships to include in-laws and grandchildren d. Dealing with disabilities and death of great grandparents
6. Families in later life	Accepting the shifting of generational roles	a. Maintaining own and couple functioning and interests in face of physiological decline; exploration of new familial and social role options b. Supporting a more central role of middle generation c. Making room in the system for the wisdom and experience of the elderly, supporting the older generation without overfunctioning for them d. Dealing with loss of spouse, siblings, and other peers, and preparation for own death; life review and integration

SOURCE: B. Carter & M. McGoldrick. (1988). *The changing family lifecycle: A framework for family therapy* (2nd ed., p. 15). New York: Gardner.

Table 8.2   Dislocations in the Family Life Cycle Requiring Additional Steps to Restabilize and Proceed Developmentally

Phase	Emotional Process of Transition	Developmental Tasks
Divorce		
1. The decision to divorce	Accepting inability to resolve marital tensions sufficiently to continue relationship	Accepting one's own part in the failure of the marriage
2. Planning the breakup of the system	Supporting viable arrangements for all parts of the system	a. Working cooperatively on problems of custody, visitation, and finances b. Dealing with extended family about the divorce
3. Separation	a. Willingness to continue cooperative coparental relationship and joint financial support of children b. Working on resolution of attachment to spouse	a. Mourning loss of intact family b. Restructuring marital and parent-child relationships and finances; adaptation to living apart c. Realigning of relationships with extended family; staying connected with spouse's extended family
4. The divorce	Working further on emotional divorce: overcoming hurt, anger, guilt, etc.	a. Mourning loss of intact family; giving up fantasies of reunion b. Retrieving hopes, dreams, expectations from marriage c. Staying connected with extended families
Postdivorce family		
Custodial single parent	Willing to maintain financial responsibilities, continue parental contact with ex-spouse, and support contact of children with ex-spouse and his or her family	a. Making flexible visitation arrangements with ex-spouse and his or her family b. Rebuilding own financial resources c. Rebuilding own social network
Noncustodial single parent	Willing to maintain parental contact with ex-spouse and support custodial parent's relationship with children	a. Finding ways to continue effective parenting relationship with children b. Maintaining financial responsibilities to ex-spouse and children c. Rebuilding own social network

SOURCE: B. Carter & M. McGoldrick. (1988). *The changing family lifecycle: A framework for family therapy* (2nd ed., p. 22). New York: Gardner.

Table 8.3 Remarried Family Formation

Step	Prerequisite Attitude	Developmental Issues
1. Entering the new relationship	Recovery from loss of first marriage (adequate "emotional divorce")	Recommitting to marriage, to forming a family, and dealing with complexity and ambiguity
2. Conceptualizing and planning new marriage and family	a. Acceptance of one's own fears and those of new spouse and children about remarriage and forming a stepfamily b. Acceptance of need for time and patience to adjust to complexity and ambiguity of: (i) Multiple new roles; (ii) Boundaries of space, time, membership, and authority; and (iii) Affective issues of guilt, loyalty conflicts, desire for mutuality, and unresolvable past hurts	a. Working on openness in the new relationships to avoid pseudomutality b. Planning for maintenance of cooperative financial and co-parental relationships with ex-spouses c. Planning to help children deal with fears, loyalty conflicts, and membership in two systems d. Realigning relationships with extended family to include new spouse and children e. Planning maintenance of connections for children with extended family of ex-spouse(s)
3. Remarriage and reconstruction of family	a. Final resolution of attachment to previous spouse and ideal of "intact" family b. Acceptance of a different model of family with permeable boundaries	a. Restructuring family boundaries to allow for inclusion of new spouse-stepparent b. Realigning relationships and financial arrangements throughout subsystems to permit interweaving of several systems c. Making room for relationships of all children with biological (noncustodial) parents, grandparents, and other extended family d. Sharing memories and histories to enhance stepfamily integration

SOURCE: B. Carter & M. McGoldrick. (1988). *The changing family lifecycle: A framework for family therapy* (2nd ed., p. 24). New York: Gardner.

Olson Circumplex Family Model

The Circumplex Model is derived from systems theory. It provides a classification schema for understanding marital and family functioning, which provides a typology of family functioning along three important dimensions: cohesion (emotional bonding), adaptability/flexibility (degree of change in family rites and structure), and communication (facilitative dimension). The communication dimension is important for establishing appropriate levels of the other two dimensions. Through research on over 1,000 families over the last decade, Olson and colleagues (1985) have developed a number of empirically derived family inventories that measure these three dimensions of family life. Family assessment instruments, including the Family Satisfaction Inventory and the Family Crisis Oriented Personal Evaluation Scales (F-COPES), have been developed for the model.

The most famous of these self-report measures is the Family Adaptability and Cohesion Scale (FACES III), which measures the first two dimensions of the Circumplex Model: cohesion and adaptability/flexibility. Recall that this measure was introduced and evaluated in Chapter 4. The third dimension, communication, can be assessed using other inventories developed by the authors (such as the Parent and Adolescent Communication Form). FACES III is a twenty-item, normative-based, paper-and-pencil, self-report inventory that operationalizes the Circumplex Model. The original Circumplex Model posits a curvilinear understanding of family functioning that emphasizes the need for balance in family relationships. Families that fall along extreme dimensions of functioning in cohesion, adaptability/flexibility, or communication are believed to be at risk for dysfunction. Those that fall into balanced or midrange dimensions are believed to be better adjusted.

For example, in the cohesion dimension, families characterized at the two extremes of enmeshed or disengaged are both considered at risk for dysfunction, whereas those characterized as balanced between the these two extremes are considered to function well. The same idea applies to the adaptability/flexibility (change) dimension. Families characterized at the extremes of chaotic (too much flexibility and random change) or rigid (not enough flexibility and change) are at risk for dysfunction; those characterized as balanced between these dimensions function well (Olson, 1986; Olson, Sprenkle, & Russel, 1979).

FACES III categorizes families into sixteen types, from lowest to highest on four categories each of the cohesion and adaptability dimensions (see figure 8.2). They form a helpful typology for understanding how various families function regarding their cohesion and adaptability/flexibility. FACES III also provides a reference for understanding what types of families may have dysfunctional characteristics; the ones falling into the extreme dimensions on the model (such as the chaotically disengaged, chaotically enmeshed) tend to have greater dysfunction. The real key to family functioning, however, is not in the classification per se but in the amount of family life satisfaction experienced by the family members participating in the various family types. If individuals in the family are satisfied with a chaotic or rigid family structure, the type is considered to be functional for the individuals involved in that type of relational patterns. Fortunately, the FACES III instrument provides a way for family

Figure 8.2   FACES III

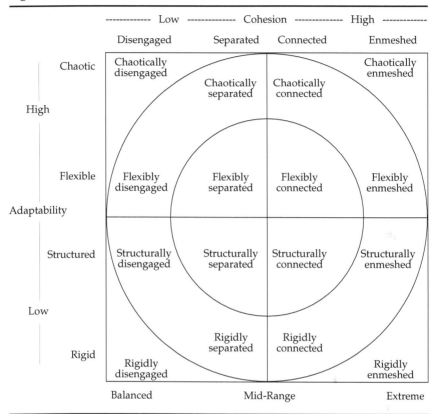

SOURCE: D. H. Olson. (1986). Circumplex Model VII: Validation studies and FACES III. *Family Processes*, 26, 337–351.

practitioners to calculate a family satisfaction score that makes it possible to determine the amount of family satisfaction derived by family members, thereby adding to the clinical utility of the model for a wider variety of families from different cultures.

Thomas and Olson (1993) found considerable research support for the curvilinear Circumplex Model, using the Clinical Rating Scale (CRS) with sixty clinical families and sixty control families. Less support has been found for the self-report measure FACES III (Green, Harris, Forte, & Robinson, 1991). In response to criticisms concerning the validity of the FACES III measure, Olson and colleagues reconceptualized the Circumplex Model as a 3-D-Circumplex Model. The 3-D model is linear, and the FACES III, when used in conjunction with this model, is believed to provide a valid assessment of family functioning (Olson, 1991). Practitioners are instructed by the researchers and developers of the instrument to use the 3-D model for their clinical assessments.

Figure 8.3 provides a graphic depiction of the linear scoring of FACES III on the 3-D Circumplex Model. The 3-D model, like the curvilinear model, measures only the cohesion and adaptability dimensions of the Circumplex Model. Each is measured on an eight-point continuum, ranging from low cohesion (disengaged) to high cohesion (very connected) and from low adaptability (rigid) to high adaptability (very flexible). With the 3-D model, high scores on cohesion and adaptability are conceptualized as measuring balanced family types: low scores on these two dimensions indicate extreme family types. Franklin and Streeter (1993) found support for the full 3-D Circumplex Model but found that the adaptability dimension lacked validity; they questioned whether the introduction of the 3-D model had been an improvement.

Another recent study, by Thomas and Zechowski (2000), challenged the validity of the FACES III as a means to operationalize the curvilinear dimension of the Circumplex Model constructs. The authors cite numerous studies to support their conclusions that two central concepts of the model—cohesion and adaptability—appear to be linear rather than curvilinear in relating to family functioning. Thomas and Zechowski note that the Clinical Rating Scale (CRS), rather than FACES, should be used to test the central hypotheses of the model, which include:

1. Direct effects of cohesion and adaptability on family functioning

2. Direct effects of communication on cohesion and adaptability

3. Indirect effect of communication on family functioning through its facilitation of cohesion and adaptability

4. Orthogonal relationship between cohesion and adaptability

They concluded that the direct relationship between cohesion and family functioning, the communication and cohesion, and the communication and adaptability were supported, but not the direct relationship between adaptability and family functioning. And, they found that, instead of an orthogonal relationship (independent of one another) between cohesion and adaptability, these were significantly correlated.

This recent test of the Circumplex Model using the CRS implies that therapists should help families raise levels of communication to promote healthy family cohesion. This is consistent with other popular models of marital and family therapy, such as Emotionally Focused Marital Therapy, Integrative Couple Therapy, and Functional Family Therapy.

To respond to the criticisms of the previous FACES measures, Olson and colleagues recently developed the FACES IV hoping to contribute a reliable and valid, self-report measure that will assess the Circumplex Model. A copy of the items of the FACES IV measure may be obtained from Dr. Olson at the University of Minnesota, Department of Family Social Sciences. Similar to its predecessors, FACES IV is a self-administered,

Figure 8.3 Three Dimensional (3-D) Circumplex Model

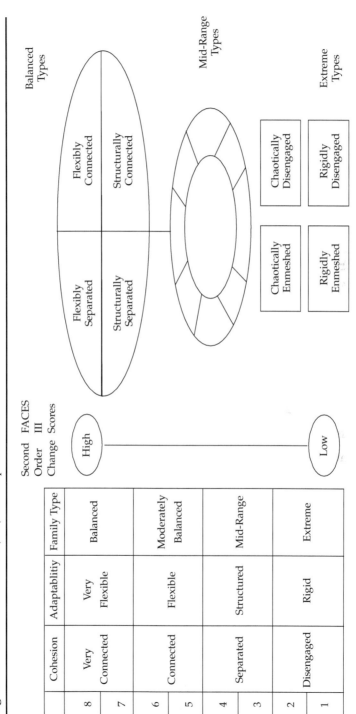

SOURCE: D. H. Olson & J. Tiesel. (1991), *FACES III: Linear scoring and interpretation*. St. Paul: University of Minnesota, Family Social Science.

pencil-and-paper, rapid assessment instrument. The current measure contains twenty-four items, measured on a five-point Likert scale, to assess four dimensions (chaotic, disengaged, enmeshed, and rigid) representing the extremes of the Circumplex Model. The constructs cohesion (enmeshed, disengaged) and flexibility (chaotic, rigid) are inferred from the four subscales as being the higher order dimensions of those four subscales (Franklin, Streeter, & Springer, 2001).

Previous empirical research showed that attempts to change the response format of the measure to enhance its ability to capture the extremes of the model failed to demonstrate an advantage. For this reason, the FACES IV follows the same rationale and response format as previous versions of the measure, except that the items are worded in an extreme manner in an effort to assess dysfunction in the families who fell into the upper extremes of the model. Franklin et al. (2001) however, showed in a subsequent validity study that the FACES IV continues to have difficulty with its validity and reliability. Practitioners should currently use the FACES II or the linear version of the FACES III until Olson is able to resolve these difficulties.

Beavers Systems Model

The Beavers Systems Model, originally called the Beavers Timberlawn Family Evaluation Scales, developed over a twenty-five-year period from clinical observations of both dysfunctional and healthy, competent families in treatment and research settings. From this work, three assessment instruments have been developed: the Beavers Interactional Scales, the Family Competence and Style Scales, and the Self-Report Family Inventory. The first two scales are observational clinical rating scales. The third is a self-report instrument completed by family members (Beavers & Hampson, 1990; Olson & Tiesel, 1993).

The Beavers Systems Model (Beavers, 1981, 1982; Beavers & Hampson, 1990; Beavers & Voller, 1983) integrates family systems theory with developmental theory and is widely used in clinical practice. It seeks to understand the health and competence of families in relationship to their ability to produce healthy and competent children. This model classifies families on the axes of family competence and family style. The competence axis classifies families into types that fall along a continuum according to their level of functioning: optimal, adequate, midrange, borderline, and severely disturbed. The style axis classifies families according to their quality of interaction: centripetal and centrifugal. Centripetal families turn inward and seek pleasure and gratification from within the family. Centrifugal families turn outward and seek fulfillment in relationships outside the family. Both family competence and style converge to produce levels of family functioning, which are believed to have implications for the types of difficulties children may have, as defined by psychiatric categories. Figure 8.4 is a visual representation of the Beavers Systems Model.

The areas of family life used to obtain an assessment of the family competence and style dimensions on the Beavers Systems Model as described by Beavers (1982) are shown in figure 8.5. When the two dimensions of the Beavers Systems, family competence and family style, are combined, nine distinct family groups are diagramatically defined, based on clinical observation and empirical research. Three of these groups are considered functional, whereas six are problematic and require clinical intervention (Beavers & Hampson, 2000). See figure 8.6 for a description of the characteristics of each grouping.

Development of the model, as with all assessment models, is ongoing. The recent introduction of a self-report version of the family assessment instrument has added to the clinical utility of the model. The Self-Report Family Inventory (SFI) measures two dimensions of family functioning.

McMaster Family Model

The McMaster Family Model (Epstein, Baldwin, & Bishop, 1982) is another widely used family assessment model that evolved out of clinical practice. The model was developed over a fifteen-year period with families at the Brown University and Butler Hospital Family Research Program. This model assesses whole-systems functioning of the family and evaluates family structure, organization, and transactional patterns that distinguish healthy from unhealthy families. Two assessment instruments have emerged from this work: the McMaster Clinical Rating Scale and a self-report family measure, the McMaster Family Assessment Device (FAD), version three.

These scales assess seven dimensions of family functioning: 1) problem solving, 2) communication, 3) roles, 4) affective responses, 5) affective involvement, 6) behavior control, and 7) overall family functioning. They subscales assess the following dimensions:

Family problem solving—How families solve both instrumental (e.g., financial) and affective (e.g., social support and nurturance) problems. Families are assessed to be most effective when they follow these seven steps in their problem-solving efforts:

1. Problem identification

2. Communication of the problem to the appropriate family members

3. Development of a plan and subsequent alternatives (brain storming)

4. Commitment to a plan

Figure 8.4   Beavers Systems Model

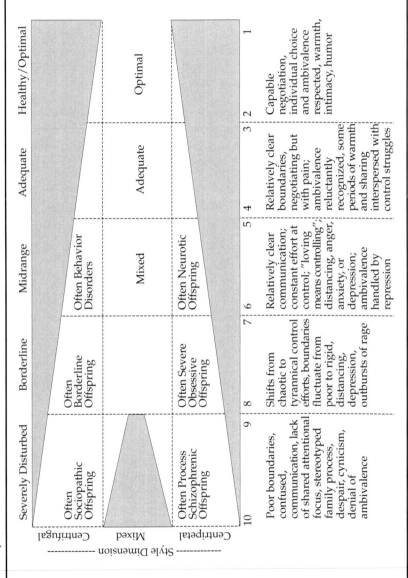

Figure 8.5   Assessing Family Competence and Style Dimensions, Beavers System Model

---

I. Structure of the family
   A. Overt power: chaotic vs. egalitarian
   B. Parental coalition: parent-child coalitions vs. strong parental coalition
   C. Closeness: indistinct boundaries vs. close, distinct boundaries
II. Mythology: congruent vs. incongruent reality perception of the family
III. Goal-directed negotiation: efficient vs. inefficient problem solving
IV. Autonomy
   A. Clarity of expression: directness of expression of thoughts and feelings, from less clear to clear
   B. Responsibility: voicing responsibility for personal actions, from taking responsibility to taking no responsibility
   C. Permeability: open vs. unreceptive to statements of others.
V. Family affect
   A. Range of feelings: broad range vs. limited range of feelings
   B. Mood and tone: open and optimistic vs. cynical and pessimistic
   C. Unresolvable conflict: chronic underlying conflict vs. ability to resolve conflict
   D. Empathy: empathic vs. inconsiderate of individual feelings
VI. Global health pathology scale: optimal/adaptive (1) vs. severely dysfunctional (10)
VII. Family style
   A. Dependency needs: discouraged/ignored vs. encouraged
   B. Adult conflict: quite open vs. indirect, covert, hidden
   C. Proximity: all members give and expect lots of room between members vs. all members stay physically close with much touching
   D. Social presentation: try hard to appear well behaved and to make a good impression vs. seem unconcerned with appearances and social approval
   E. Expression of closeness: consistently emphasize that they are close vs. deny that they are close
   F. Assertive/aggressive qualities: discourage aggressive or disruptive behavior and expressions vs. solicit or encourage assertive, even aggressive behavior and expressions
   G. Expression of feelings: express positive feelings more often vs. express negative feelings more often
   H. Global centripetal/centrifugal style: total inward oriented vs. total outward oriented

---

5. Action on the plan
6. Accountability and monitoring of the action
7. Outcome evaluation

Families are assessed to be least effective in their problem solving if they cannot accomplish step one.

Figure 8.6   Beavers Systems Model of Family Functioning Dimensions of Competence and Style Characteristics of Nine Family Groupings

---

GROUP 1. Optimal families
Optimal families serve as the model for effective functioning. The families have a systems orientation, with equality, respect, group problem-solving skills, individuation, and clear boundaries. Conflicts are easily and quickly resolved.

GROUP 2. Adequate families
Adequate families are more control oriented than systems oriented, attempting to resolve conflict with fear and intimidation. Although this type of parental control exerting more overt power tends to achieve results, these families have less intimacy and trust and there is greater role stereotyping and greater power differentiation.

GROUPS 3, 4, & 5. Midrange families
In midrange families, the children tend to be more vulnerable and parents susceptible to psychological problems. The families are very concerned with power and control, and negotiating of discipline is not allowed. These families do not have boundary problems, scapegoating is a common method, favorite children apparent, hostility, blame, and attack are frequent responses to familial conflict.

GROUPS 6 & 7. Borderline families
Borderline families present with frequent ineffective struggles to maintain power. Parents express anger openly, and children learn manipulation early. Chaotic is used to describe the often-stormy and intense battles for dominance.

GROUPS 8 & 9. Severely dysfunctional families
Severely dysfunctional families have almost total breakdown of communication, which means a limited ability to resolve conflict. Family members lack a shared focus, children are often seen as emotionally delayed. There is an insistence within the family system to maintain togetherness and extreme loyalty.

Communication—Families with effective communication use a clear, direct style. Those with the least effective communication have a masked, indirect style. For example, a husband saying, "It really bothers me when you don't call before you come home if you are going to be late," versus not speaking to his wife all evening, because she was late.

Roles—How the family assigns instrumental, affective, and mixed-dimension (e.g., system maintenance, teaching independent living skills) role functions and handles accountability for those functions. Families are assessed to have effective role assignments when all the necessary family functions have been clearly allocated to appropriate family members and some form of monitoring and accountability takes place. Least effective role functioning occurs when the necessary family functions are not addressed or accountability for those functions is not maintained.

Affective responsiveness—How families respond to crises and the degree to which emotional responses are aimed at the well-being of family members. Families are assessed to have appropriate affective responses when they can demonstrate a full range of emotional responses that are consistent in degree and congruent with the context. Families are least effective when the type and severity of emotional responsiveness is incongruent with the context.

Affective involvement—A range of emotional involvement, from absence of involvement to symbiotic involvement. Families are assessed to be most effective when they express empathic involvement and least effective when they express an absence of involvement.

Behavior control—A range of styles from rigid to chaotic. Control of behavior is assessed in three areas:

1. Dangerous or threatening situations
2. Meeting and expressing family members needs and drives such as eating, sleeping, sex
3. Monitoring interpersonal socializing both within and outside the family

Flexible behavior control is assessed to be most effective and chaotic least effective.

Although there has been some debate over the past couple of years about whether the FAD scoring procedures should be reorganized to reflect higher-order factors from self-report measures (Ridenour, Daley, & Reich, 2000), Miller, Ryan, Keitner, Bishop, and Epstein (2000b) argue that the overall ecological validity of the scale, with the backing of numerous studies, suggests an absence in the utility for higher-order factors. In addition, Miller et al. (2000a) suggest that the most important issue regarding any scale is its clinical utility and validity, which the FAD has demonstrated repeatedly.

Moos Family Environment Scales

The Moos Family Environment Scales (FES) (Moos & Moos, 1986; Moos & Spinrad, 1984) evolved from research on social climates, the unique personality or attributes of social environments. The FES is a self-report measure that assesses whole-family functioning and is compatible with social and systems ecological theory. It has been widely used in both clinical research and practice and has been demonstrated to be an effective outcome measure. The FES evaluates families' perceptions of their social or interpersonal climate along three dimensions: interpersonal relationships, personal growth, and systems maintenance. Each of these dimensions is made up of subscales that evaluate diverse areas of family functioning:

Relationship dimensions—The first three dimensions measured by the FES assess how involved people are in their family and how openly they express both positive and negative feelings in a bipolar dimension of cohesion versus conflict, and then in a unipolar dimension of organization versus control.

The **Cohesion subscale** measures the degree of commitment, help, and support family members provide for one another (such as, the way they support one another, the amount of energy they put into what they do at home, and how much feeling of togetherness there is in the family).

The **Expressiveness subscale** taps the extent to which family members are encouraged to act openly and to express their feelings directly (e.g., how openly family members talk around home, how freely they discuss their personal problems, and how often they just pick up and go if they feel like doing something on the spur of the moment).

The **Conflict subscale** measures the amount of openly expressed anger, aggression, and conflict among family members (such as, the frequency of fights, whether family members sometimes get so angry that they throw things, and how often they criticize each other).

Personal growth dimensions—The Personal Growth, or Goal Orientation, subscales make up another set of FES dimensions. This set focuses on the family's goals by tapping the major ways in which a family encourages or inhibits personal growth.

The **Independence subscale** measures the extent to which family members are assertive, self-sufficient, and make their own decisions (e.g., how strongly family members are encouraged to be independent, how much they think things out for themselves, and how freely they come and go in the family).

The **Achievement Orientation (AO) subscale** taps the extent to which activities, such as school and work, are cast into an achievement-oriented or competitive framework (such as, how important they feel it is to do their best and to get ahead, and how much they believe in competition and "may the best man win").

The **Intellectual-Cultural Orientation (CO) subscale** assesses the degree of interest in political, social, intellectual, and cultural activities (e.g., how often family members talk about political or social problems, how often they go to the library, and how much they like music, art, and literature).

The **Active-Recreational Orientation subscale** taps the extent of participation in social and recreational activities (such as, how often friends come over for dinner or to visit, how often family members go out, and how often family members go to movies, sports events, camping, etc.).

The **Moral-Religious subscale** measures the degree of emphasis on ethical and religious issues and values (e.g., how frequently family members attend church, synagogue, or Sunday School; how strict their ideas are about what is right and wrong; and how much they believe there are some things that just must be taken on faith).

Systems maintenance dimensions—The last set of dimensions measured by the FES assesses the family's emphasis on clear organization, structure, rules, and procedures in running family life.

The Organization subscale measures the importance of clear organization and structure in planning family activities and responsibilities (such as, how carefully activities are planned, how neat and orderly family members are, and how clearly each person's duties are defined).

The Control subscale assesses the extent to which set rules and procedures are used to run family life (such as, how much one family member makes the decisions, how set the ways of doing things are at home, and how much emphasis is on following rules in the family).

Even though the FES is one of the most popular environmental measures in clinical and family research, Chipuer and Villegas (2001) and others have found a potential problem with using the three-factor structure of the FES across different groups of respondents. In particular, their study of wives' and husbands' responses to the perceptions of their family environment did not support the Moos and Moos (1986) three-factor model. Rather, they found evidence supporting a two-factor solution—cohesion versus conflict and an organization versus control dimension. They recommend using the two-factor second-order solution when comparing perceptions of spouses, and to provide the best fit across data for wives and husbands (Boake & Salmon, 1983; Chipuer & Villegas, 2001).

Family Assessment Measure

The Family Assessment Measure (FAM) (Skinner, Steinhauer, & Sitarenios, 2000) is based on the Process Model of Family Functioning. That model describes how to conduct family assessments based on seven dimensions: affective involvement, control, task accomplishment, role performance, communication, affective expression, and values and norms. Each of these dimensions is measured at three levels: whole family systems, dyadic relationships, and individual functioning.

Affective involvement—Assesses how much interest and concern are shown by family members. There are five types: 1) uninvolved, 2) interest and devoid of feeling, 3) narcissistic, 4) empathic, and 5) enmeshed.

Control—Assesses how family members influence each other's behavior—their techniques and strategies. These include 1) rigidity, 2) flexibility, 3) laissez-faire, and 4) chaotic.

Task accomplishment—Assesses three types of family tasks, which are defined in a cultural context: 1) basic tasks, 2) developmental tasks, and 3) crisis tasks.

Role performance—Is tied to task accomplishment and assesses three distinct operations: each family members' assigned role; the agreement of each family member to accept his or her role; actually enacting those roles and behaviors.

Communication—Assesses how the affective role performance and tasks are accomplished. Three forms of communication are assessed: affective, instrumental, and neutral.

Affective expression—Assesses the content, intensity, and timing of affective expression. This is considered the most important form of communication for the family system in how it expresses itself.

Values and norms—Assesses basic family processes, in terms of values and norms. The focus is on whether the family rules are explicit or implicit, how free family members are to determine and express their own attitudes, and whether the family values and norms are consistent with those in the society at large.

The FAM, following twenty years of work in developing the measure, has four self-report components, including the General scale, which has fifty items and nine subcales; the Dyadic relationship scales with forty-two items and seven subcales; the self-rating scale with forty-two items and seven subcales; and the brief FAMS with fourteen items.

ASSESSMENT METHODS

Now we will discuss some frequently used methods of family assessment. First, it is important to point out that the assessment models discussed in the previous section, including standardized observational measures and self-report inventories, are all empirically derived methods of assessment. (See Chapter 4 for a discussion of standardized measures.) Those standardized measures represent the state of the art in objective assessment of families; practitioners are urged to become skillful in one or more of the models and learn how to administer and score the various assessment measures. But, we should not exclusively rely on these models or measures, because many other methods for assessing family functioning exist (Holman, 1983; Jacob & Tennenbaum, 1988). As discussed throughout this text, it is important for practitioners to use multiple methods of assessment. Some of the other methods—ones that are consistent with the types of assessment methods summarized in Chapter 3 on quantitative assessment and Chapter 5 on qualitative assessment—will be covered in this section. Specifically, interviewing techniques; family task observations; family goal recording; graphic problem-oriented, standardized measures; and specific methods for assessing family strengths, are briefly reviewed. The assessment methods presented here are not comprehensive but provide practitioners with several useful techniques for collecting assessment information on families.

Figure 8.7   Clinical Guidelines for Using the Family Assessment Measurement
(FAM)

---

1) According to the authors, this is a good instrument for obtaining an overall
   index of family functioning, especially in time-limited situations (Skinner
   et al., 2000)
2) This instrument helps to pinpoint gaps in the assessment
3) This instrument helps identify areas of confusion where family members'
   perception of a situation is quite different
4) This instrument provides an independent and objective validation of the
   clinical assessment
5) This instrument identifies a starting point for circular questioning
6) This instrument allows the nonverbal members of the family a forum for
   expressing themselves
7) This instrument provides good visual representation of the strengths and
   weaknesses of the family
8) This instrument helps both the therapist and family members define
   treatment goals
9) This instrument shows a quantitative measure of change in response to
   treatment

Interviewing Techniques

Social workers frequently rely on talking with family members as
their primary means of gathering assessment information. Interviewing
is one of the most-important social work practice skills to acquire (Compton & Galaway, 1989; Garrett, 1991). Throughout this chapter, several examples of questions are provided to guide the social worker through the
interview and to aid in gathering pertinent information concerning family process and behavior. Family members may be interviewed together
or apart, depending on the type of information the social worker is seeking. For example, in exploring problems such as family roles or rules,
everyone may be included because such issues affect the entire family;
however, only the parents would be interviewed in exploring problems
occurring in the couple's sexual relationship.

Regardless of how many family members are interviewed at one
time, the social worker should remember that the members being interviewed are a part of the larger family system. In essence, when interviewing families, social workers always have two clients: the family as a
system and the individual members of that system (Schulman, 1992).
This makes interviewing families complex and calls the social worker to
engage all family members, observe their interactions, and assess the
family at different levels. For example, the social worker may need to assess the behavior of an individual family member, such as the eight-year-old boy named Chad who has disruptive behavior. Chad started rocking

back and forth on a chair in the social worker's office, distracting his parents from the meeting. The social worker may recognize not also the disruptive behavior but also assess a parental subsystem interaction—the parenting skills deficits of the parents who are unable to set appropriate limits on the boy's behavior. In addition, the social worker may note a systems level interaction—that Chad's behavior of jumping on the chair started immediately after the parents made critical remarks about his poor school performance and compared it to the superior performance of a twelve-year-old brother, Chip.

The following interactional sequence is then observed. The father yells for the boy to stop his behavior of jumping on the chair (parent-child subsystem interaction). The older brother, Chip, joins in the interaction by calling Chad stupid for acting the way he does (sibling subsystem interaction and parent-child coalition). The social worker observes this interaction so that she can see the interactional functioning. The mother intervenes and tells Chip not to call his brother stupid (parental subsystem interaction). She also tells the father not to raise his voice to Chad (parent-child coalition). The father tells the mother to stop interfering in his discipline and states that she is too easy on Chad (parental subsystem interaction). At the same time, Chad jumps out of the chair, sits in another chair near the mother, and begins to pick a fight with his older brother. They exchange a few putdowns (sibling subsystem interaction). Chip asks the parents to stop Chad from picking on him (parent-child subsystem interaction). The parents then unite and tell Chad to stop picking on Chip, and the mother states that they both owe each other an apology (parental subsystem interaction). Chip says angrily, "You always take up for Chad" and pouts, refusing to apologize (parent-child subsystem interaction). Chad goes and sits away from the family in the chair in which he was rocking back and forth before he moved to taunt his brother (individual member interaction).

Both parents turn to the social worker and deny that they give preferential treatment to one child over the other. Chip shakes his head no. The father looks at the social worker and says that it is difficult to have peace in this family when Chad throws such fits. The mother agrees that there is much tension in the family but adds that it is not all Chad's fault. The father adds that Chad wears his feelings on his sleeve and does not cooperate. Chad starts rocking the chair again (systems/contextual level). In such a scenario, the social worker uses the face-to-face interview to observe the multiple interactions of the family. Interviewing in this context requires expert observation skills and the ability to engage the family verbally. It might be helpful, at this point, to refer back to the assessment protocol in Chapter 1 and review some of the important information on family functioning that may be gathered during a comprehensive assessment.

As has been emphasized throughout this chapter, it is important to assess the family as a system and to understand how all the members' separate behaviors fit together into the complex, circular behavioral chain known as systemic functioning. One interviewing technique that helps to assess the complexities of how families work as systems is known as circular questioning. Circular questions provide a structure for eliciting information from various family members about the transactions and operations embedded in the family system. The structure of circular questions is nonthreatening to the family because the questions generally ask family members to comment on the family process from the viewpoint of a different family member. Thus a father might be asked to comment on how he believes a son is responding to the behavior of the mother, or a sister might be asked how she believes her brother might be feeling in response to his mother.

Circular questions can be divided into categories of information-eliciting probes. O'Brien and Bruggen (1985) have offered five categories for organizing different types of circular questions:

1. **Relationship to others.** These questions may refer to the relationship between two people in a family. For example, "How do your mom and dad solve disagreements between them?"

2. **Relationship to events in family life.** These questions refer to how people organize meanings around events or time. "When mom comes home late from work, what does dad do?"

3. **Ranking behavior within the family.** Actual or hypothetical situations can be used. Examples include: "Who is most strict, your mother or your father?" "Pretend for a moment that I am a magic fairy with the powers to send you on a vacation to an adventurous island; who in your family would you take with you?"

4. **Relationships to time.** Both events in time and specific points in time may be used. Examples include: "How was your husband different before you moved to this city?" "How were things different between you a year ago?"

5. **Eliciting information from the perspective of the silent member.** This may include members not present at family sessions or those who will not talk. Examples include: "If your father were here in the session, what do you think he might say about your family?" "If your brother were to answer my question, what do you think he might say?"

Fleuridas, Nelson, and Rosenthal (1986) offer a more-detailed categorization for understanding different types of circular questions. as presented in appendix 8A. The ethnographic interviewing covered in Chapter 5 also provides important interviewing techniques for gathering information from the insider perspective of a family system.

Family Task Observations

Observations of family members undertaking structured tasks provides an important way for social workers to observe and assess family functioning. Such tasks as playing a game, planning a vacation, solving a problem, and making a decision have been used. As an example of making a decision, families may be asked to decide what is their main issue in therapy. They are asked to come to this decision while being observed by the social worker from the corner of the room or through a one-way mirror. Observing families in such a task allows the social worker to view many aspects of family functioning, such as roles, power, communication, and decision-making processes.

Enactment is a structured family task in which the family is instructed to role-play or act out a previous situation in the family. For example, a couple who complains that they argue about how to spend their free time on weekends might be asked to reconstruct or re-enact the argument in the office while the practitioner observes. As another example, a wife who complains that she cannot talk to her husband might be instructed to tell her husband those feelings now in the session and to talk to him about them. Enactments help social workers understand both the strengths and weaknesses of family process and provide meaningful information on which the social workers may base their interventions.

Family sculpting is an experiential task in which an individual family member is asked to place other family members in stationary positions that would represent what the family is like from that individual's perception. The individual is instructed to place himself or herself among the family members. Significant therapeutic information is believed to emerge from the sculpting. For example, a woman sculpting her family placed herself on the floor with her husband's foot on top of her. From a family sculpture, social workers can assess such family dynamics as power, cohesion, affective responses, coalitions, and triangles. The experiential aspects of the sculpture also serve as a powerful tool that may help family members to gain insight into the interactions in their own family.

Family Goal Recording

Family goal recording (FGR) was adapted from goal attainment scaling, a method of assessment and measurement that has been used in over 150 mental health settings since 1968 (Fleuridas, Rosenthal, Leigh, & Leigh, 1990). Goal attainment scaling was summarized in Chapter 3. Fleuridas et al. (1990) developed the FGR method at the University of

Iowa, Marriage and Family Clinic. They conceptualized this method as being contextually relevant and possessing sensitivity to the uniqueness of each client's or program's needs. FGR, like the goal attainment method, provides a therapeutic tool for helping social workers select and define desirable outcome goals for clients. It further provides a scaling and weighing system in which these outcomes may be measured relative to the degree of change achieved toward the desired goals, and weighted according to the importance of the problem to the family.

The scaling system requires social workers to solicit information from families that will help to objectively and quantifiably understand the current base rate of a presenting problem(s). When the base rate of presenting problems is defined, the social worker and family determine a desired, achievable level of change within a given period. They also determine levels of change if the situation were to deteriorate during this time period. For example, a family agrees that one of their problems is that there are verbal arguments involving everyone in the household at least three or four times a week. This serves as the base rate for the problem the family is seeking to change. The family may agree that if they could decrease these arguments to one or less a week, this would be their desired level of positive change. They may also agree that if the situation at home were to deteriorate, if they increased their arguments to five or more a week, for example, the family might split up as a result of their persistent fighting. Social workers guide family members in defining outcome goals such as these for each presenting problem. Outcome goals would be scaled between +1 and –1. In such a mathematical system, the base rate is 0.00. See appendix 8B for an example of FGR provided by Fleuridas and colleagues (1990).

Because individual family members often define family difficulties differently, several goals may be established that represent the different concerns of each family member. When possible, social workers should mediate these different perceptions and help family members come to agreement concerning some goals of mutual interest. Fleuridas and colleagues (1990) suggest that goals may first be defined according to the interests of individual family members and later classified as they relate to the different subsystems or whole systems functioning within a family. See appendix 8B for an example of FGR classification schema.

Classifying goals according to the different subsystems makes it possible for family therapists to monitor how change in one part of the family system may be affecting change in another part. Assigning weights to the different goals takes this method a step further, making it possible for social workers to mathematically calculate a level of change score for each family. In this mathematical system, the goals for subsystem areas are weighted according to their significance to the family. All the cumulative weights for each area must add up to one hundred percent. Again, see appendix 8B for an example of weights that were assigned to the family goals in the example and their accompanying change rate. As shown in the example, the change score is calculated by multiplying progress or deterioration on the levels scale by the weight given to that particular goal. Readers may want to consult Fleuridas and colleagues (1990), Kiresuk and Sherman, (1968), or Kiresuk, Stelmachers, and Schultz (1982) for a more detailed explanation of this method.

To use the FGR approach, social workers must objectively identify the specific problem areas and desired level of changes. This means, for example, that if the mother of a thirteen-year-old son complains that he is slovenly and rebellious, the social worker would help the mother be more specific about what behaviors her son is actually demonstrating that make her believe that he is slovenly and rebellious. Slovenly may come to mean that the boy does not clean his room, leaves dirty dishes in the living room, and leaves his dirty underwear on the bathroom floor. Rebellious may come to mean that he doesn't help with the dishes when asked and refuses to turn off the television at his designated bedtime. When the problems are clearly defined the social worker may proceed to find a base rate of how often these behaviors occur and also determine what would connote a reasonable amount of positive change. Definitions of deterioration are also determined. Finally, the social worker can work with the family to prioritize the goals and assign the appropriate weights to each area.

FGR has been shown to be a valid and reliable method for the assessment and measurement of family functioning. Like its progenitor, goal attainment scaling, this method is believed to enhance assessment and treatment effectiveness.

Graphic Measures

Several pictorial and graphic methods for assessing family functioning have been developed by family therapists. Graphic methods were covered in Chapter 5, and the reader may want to review this material before proceeding. One of the most popular of these methods is the genogram, which was popularized through the Bowenian approach to family therapy (Bowen, 1976). The genogram provides an assessment of the family from an intergenerational context and provides a map of the family from a longitudinal perspective across three generations. Symbols are used to depict the types of family members and different aspects of family functioning. For example, a square is used to symbolize males and a circle is used to symbolize females. A horizontal line symbolizes a marriage and a vertical line, offspring. The genogram also provides a method for gathering psychosocial information from the family. Such information as the family members' cultural and ethnic backgrounds, socioeconomic status, religions, dates of marriage, dates of birth, birth order, dates of divorce, deaths, amounts of contact with and social support from family members, and other significant events such as serious illnesses, abortions, and personal tragedies may be recorded on the genogram. Some social workers also record personal information about family members, such as descriptions of personality characteristics and personal and emotional problems. The genogram can provide a wealth of assessment information, and it is not unusual for transgenerational patterns of a certain type of family difficulty to emerge. See appendix 8C for a description of symbols for use in a genogram.

Another important graphic assessment method developed by the systemic family therapists is the Film Strip (Fisch, Watzlawick, & Segal, 1982; Watzlawick, Weakland, & Fisch, 1974). The Film Strip is used to identify the sequences of behavior that occur before and after a problem behavior. The Film Strip also helps the social worker assess the full context in which the behavior occurs. In an assessment, social worker tells the family that he or she would like to see a film of their problem and then proceeds to interview the family to gather information the Film Strip. A Film Strip may be drawn on a piece of paper, blackboard, or flip chart.

Usually, the clinician draws two vertical lines with several horizontal lines making up "frames," up and down the vertical lines; when the drawing is complete, it looks like a ladder. Then the family therapist writes the problem in one of the blocks (usually near the middle) and proceeds to find out more about the context of the problem. For example, the therapist may ask, "Who was there when the problem occurred? What were they doing? Where in the house did it happen?" After the family therapist has fully identified the context of the problem and has a clear picture of what was happening at the time it occurred, the family may be asked for assistance with filling in the frames before the problem happened.

Usually, the frames are broken into blocks that represent five or ten minutes, to track the antecedents and context of a problem. For example, the therapist will ask, "What were you doing just five minutes before the problem occurred? Who was doing what and where were you in the house? Who was gone and who was present?" In this manner, the therapist may develop a clear and descriptive assessment of the behavior of the family just prior to the occurrence of the problem. When this information is recorded on the Film Strip drawing, the family therapist proceeds to track what happened after the problem occurred. Again, in gathering this information, the frames on the graphic Film Strip are used to represent small sequences of behavior of five to ten minutes.

Information is usually gathered about successive five- and tenminute increments, until there was some type of resolution to the problem or standoff in which nothing else seemed to be happening, such as when people just elected to go away from each other or forget it. The social worker should always seek to know how the event depicted in the Film Strip ended. Of course, gathering information on the Film Strip in this manner helps the social worker track a problem and provides useful information for knowing when, how, and where to make changes in the family system.

We have discussed several different methods for assessing families. All of them are useful in helping social workers learn about family functioning. It is not practical, however, for social workers to use all these methods as an assessment situation with a family, because different families may respond to some techniques better than others. For example, Ho (1986) indicates that Hispanic families may respond favorably to the genogram technique, because of their multigenerational family orientation. Individual social workers may also find a certain set of techniques more effective in helping them assess family processes. Social workers must choose among the assessment options and use knowledge of their clientele and practice wisdom to help them decide which methods to use in a family assessment. Social workers are encouraged to develop their own personal assessment outline that may guide them in practice. Chapter 3 provides guidelines for using multiple methods for assessing clients; it is important to remember these guidelines in assessing families.

Standardized Measures: Problem-Oriented Measures

Many standardized measures may be used to aid in the assessment of marital and family systems. A comprehensive discussion of these measures is beyond the scope of this chapter. Comprehensive reviews of available measures have been provided however, by Fredman and Sherman (1987), Grotevant and Carlson (1989), and Toulitas, Perlmutter, and Straus (2000). Darro et al. (1990) have also provided a helpful review of measures associated with parenting, and Corcoran and Fischer (2000) have provided a review of several rapid assessment instruments that may be used in assessing marital and family systems. You will recall from the discussion on standardized measures in Chapter 4 that several different types of standardized measures exist, ranging from global, multidimensional to specific, unidimensional problem inventories. Standardized measures are most effective when administered as part of a comprehensive clinical assessment and evaluation. Using standardized clinical measures in any other way to diagnose a client or client system is ineffective clinical practice.

This section mentions a few problem-oriented measures, to provide practitioners with an understanding of the breadth of the available standardized measures that are helpful in the assessment of families. Problem-oriented standardized measures are discussed here, because they are important to assessing clinical outcomes, and they differ from the whole system functioning measures discussed in the earlier section on empirical assessment models. In addition, social support and network measures are discussed, because they seem especially relevant to social work's approach to understanding the impact of broader systems on family functioning.

Problem-oriented measures are particularly useful, because they are more specific than whole system measures. These measures focus on a particular problem area for a family (such as parenting). They are especially useful to social work practitioners because they help assess clients at risk for a particular problem behavior and provide feedback concerning that client's improvement in this area. It may, for example, be important to learn that a family is less chaotic and enmeshed (whole systems measure), but the question our funding sources and clients may want answered is, "Does Ms. Jones know how to parent her children better?" or, "Have the violent arguments stopped?" Chapter 11 discusses in more detail how to assess change and the outcomes of clients during treatment. Problem-oriented standardized measures may help in tracking outcomes.

As our first example, several measures of parenting effectiveness are available for use in social work practice. For example, the Parenting Stress Index (PSI) is a 101-item, self-report measure that identifies families at risk for dysfunctional parenting and psychopathology. This measure is useful for screening, diagnostic assessment, and practice evaluation (Abidin, 1983). Social workers assessing families under stress and believed to be at risk for dysfunctional parenting may find this measure helpful to their assessment protocol. Another useful problem-oriented measure is the Battering Severity Index, a measure aimed at identifying women at risk of being battered. Although this measure was developed to assess at-risk behaviors in women, it may be useful in family practice insofar as battering is understood to be related to dysfunctional family dynamics as well as individual pathology. Another useful measure for assessing battering in families is the Abusive Behavior Inventory (Shepard & Campbell, 1992). This thirty-item, self-report measure has both psychological and physical abuse items. It may be completed by the victims of domestic violence or their partners. See appendix 8D for a copy of the Abusive Behavior Inventory.

Some other measures that may be helpful to social workers include those that assess the levels of stressors encountered by families. For example, the Family Inventory of Life Events and Changes (FILE) is a seventy-one-item, self-report measure that assesses the accumulation of normative and nonnormative life events and changes experienced by a family over the past year.

Social support and social network measures also have special significance to social work family practice. Social workers know a family does not exist in a vacuum, the level of capacity to solve problems inside the family is tied to the resources outside the family, and visa versa. Resolving family problems therefore is intricately tied to the social context in which the family lives. Social support resources are essential to a family's well-being. These become especially important to families who have multiple problems (Tracy & Whittaker, 1990; Wood & Geismar, 1989). See Chapter 9 for a detailed discussion on assessing families with multiple problems.

Social support resources range from emotional support to material assistance. Measures are available for several types of social support. Social support measures assess both the *perceived support* (cognitive appraisal of support) and *enacted support* (support actually given) of family members and their social network (Streeter & Franklin, 1992). For example, the Perceived Social Support Scale, a twenty-item, self-report measure, assesses the extent to which individual family members perceive that their needs are being met by their families. This scale also measures perceived support by friends (Procidano & Heller, 1983). The Inventory of Socially Supportive Behavior (Barrera, Sandler, & Ramsey, 1981) and the Social Support Behavior Scales (Vaux, 1982) both have the capacity to measure actual social support received. Social network measures one's social network identifying its strengths and weaknesses. Social networks may include one's family but also expand to neighborhood, community, friends, and work relationships. Tracy and Whittaker (1990) developed the Social Network Map, a social network measure to be used in clinical practice.

Social support and network measures are useful in understanding the broader context of the family environment. Social support has been shown to be an important predictor of individual health and well-being (Vaux, 1988). For reviews of the available social support and network measures, practitioners are directed to Vaux (1988), Barrera (1986), and Darro et al. (1990). See also Streeter and Franklin (1992) for a review of eight social support network measures that are applicable to clinical practice.

Assessing for Family Strengths

In recent years, family researchers and practitioners have been developing specific methods for assessing family strengths. Early (2001), for example, reviews several measures that have been developed to assess family strengths and have been modified for these purposes by practitioners. Gilgun (2001) has also developed the Clinical Assessment Package for Assessing Client Risks and Strengths (CASPARS). This measurement package was developed for use in children's mental health and child welfare services, such as foster care and in-home services with families. The CASPARS specifically includes two measures that relate to the family: the Family Relationships, and the Family Embeddedness in the Community scales. See box 8.2 for a list of strengths-oriented family measures.

Box 8.2
Strengths-Based Measures for Families and Children

Family Functioning Style Scale (FFSS): Measures family strengths and capabilities.
Family Support Scale (FSS): Assesses the degree to which potential sources of social support have been helpful to families.
Family Resource Scale (FRS): Measures tangible and intangible resources that are considered important for families with young children. The FRS can be used to identify areas in which the family is successfully meeting needs and for identifying goals.
Family Empowerment Scale (FES): Measures empowerment in families with children with emotional disorders.
School Success Profile (SSP): Measures protective and risk factors in the areas of neighborhood, school, friends, and family.
Social Skills Rating System (SSRS): Measures skills in children and adolescents in the areas of cooperation, assertion, responsibility, empathy, and self-control.
Clinical Assessment Package for Assessing Client Risks and Strengths (CASPARS) Five scales that measure risk and protective factors: Family Relationships, Family Embeddedness in Community, Peer Relationships, and Sexuality.

SOURCES: T. J. Early. (2001). Measures for practice with families from a strengths perspective. *Families in Society: The Journal of Contemporary Human Services, 82*(3), 225–232.
J. F. Gilgun. (2001). CASPARS: New tools for assessing client risks and strengths. Families in society. *The Journal of Contemporary Human Services 82*, 450–459.

Graybeal (2001) discusses ways that social workers can include strengths in traditional psychosocial assessments by using the ROPES interviewing approach. The acronym ROPES reminds the practitioner to consider all of the approaches indicated by the initials it contains: resources, options, possibilities, exceptions, and solutions, as follows:

Resources—Personal, family, social environment, organizational, community.

Options—Present focus, emphasis on choice, what can be accessed now? What is available and hasn't been tried or used?

Possibilities—Future focus, imagination, creativity, vision of the future, play, what have you thought of trying but haven't tried yet?

Exceptions—When is the problem not happening? When is the problem different? When is part of the hypothetical future solution occurring? How have you survived, endured, thrived?

Solutions—Focus on constructing solutions, not solving problems. What's working now? What are your successes? What are you doing that you would like to change?

The ROPES interviewing approach encourages practitioners to think about strengths in areas they already assess. For example, they assess exceptions to the problem when collecting information about presenting problems, or list resources when describing the family and social environment of clients.

The ROPES approach can also be used in the following other areas, in a traditional assessment of clients.

1. **Presenting problems**—Add exceptions, solutions, and options to your assessment.

2. **Background information**—Add resources and options to your social assessment.

3. **Goal setting**—Add exceptions, and coconstructed options and possibilites to your set of goals for the client change.

4. **Intervention plan**—Add possibilities and solutions to the set of recommendations for your assessment report.

COMPLETING A FAMILY ASSESSMENT

Following is a family assessment completed by a social worker practicing in a juvenile justice setting. The identifying information has been changed to protect the confidentiality of the clients.

Peggy Weeks, MSSW, is a social worker employed in a youth shelter for juvenile offenders. She frequently conducts family assessments to make recommendations to the court concerning youths who are brought to the shelter. Ms. Weeks employs several of the assessment methods discussed above in her data-gathering process. She usually relies on interviews with family members, family task observations, and standardized measures. The major purpose of an assessment is to make decisions about treatment. Notice that Ms. Weeks used multiple methods in her assessment; interviews, task observations, and a standardized measure guided her decision about what she would recommend to the court concerning Madie.

For example, from her family assessment information, she was able to conclude that Madie's family had many strengths. They were loving and supportive, and capable of providing the structure and guidance that Madie needed. On the other hand, the family had experienced many stressors and had some significant cross-generational conflicts that needed resolution. These stressors, however, did not appear to interfere with Mr. and Mrs. Williams' functioning as parents. Therefore, the social worker concluded that they were competent parents and able to provide a good home for Madie.

As another example, the social worker's assessment uncovered many emotional and psychological issues contributing to Madie's behavior problems. She was able to use this information to make a clinical judgment concerning what types of issues should be addressed in a treatment plan. Thus, in the recommendation section of the assessment report, Ms. Weeks outlined Madie's emotional issues (i.e., loss, depression, anger) and made suggestions that these issues be addressed in therapy. She also interpreted those emotional issues in relationship to Madie's adolescent developmental issues. She further looked at the severity of her behavior problem (e.g., running away) and inferred that Madie was going to need a fairly intensive treatment program that provided additional supports and structures, besides those her family could provide. The social worker, therefore, recommended the day treatment program as an intervention for Madie.

Clearly, the information uncovered in the assessment and written in the report was used to develop the recommendations section of the assessment report. The recommendations section is the first step toward developing a treatment plan for a client. In an appendix to Chapter 7, a more-detailed treatment plan for an assessment report further illustrates the connections between assessment and intervention. Treatment plans, however, generally flow out of and are the next step to be completed after the assessment (see Chapter 11).

The process by which Ms. Weeks used the assessment information to create her recommendations for Madie is complex; she drew on her knowledge of child development, psychopathologies, and family practice theories, as well as her clinical experiences with adjudicated youth, that is, she used her clinical expertise to infer from the assessment information and make decisions about needed treatments. All practitioners must rely on their clinical judgment when they move from assessment to intervention; this is not a completely objective nor a linear process.

Here are some guidelines for using the assessment information to construct treatment recommendations. Begin by reviewing information on the presenting problems. Focus on resolution of the presenting problems (in Madie's case, running away). Next, focus on resolving associated problems (in Madie's case, depression, and identity disturbance). Ask yourself what interventions are needed to resolve these problems. Focus on the other dimensions (i.e., developmental context of the client's life, history, family situation, etc.) and decide what is affecting the presenting problems and how it needs to be considered in the treatment process. Consider all the assessment information in terms of resolving the problems, then construct a set of recommendations.

INTEGRATED SKILLS ASSESSMENT REPORT: THE WILLIAMS FAMILY

The Williamses are an African-American family of four: Willie Joe (father), Rosie (mother), Madie (daughter), and Player (son). They reside at 1200 Wagon Wheel Drive, Austin, Texas.

The following assessment information is based on two interviews with the parents on February 7 and 9, one interview with the whole family on February 11, and two separate interviews with the daughter, Madie, while she was in detention on February 6 and 7 at the Youth Shelter of Travis County. Behavioral observations of the family carrying out a task and scores from the administration of the Family Environment Scales, a standardized measure, were also used to determine the family's overall level of functioning. All interviews took place in the shelter except for one of the parental interviews, which took place in the family home.

Presenting Problem.   Madie Williams, a fourteen-year-old female detained at the shelter for stealing two packs of cigarettes and awaiting a detention hearing, was assigned to the social worker, Peggy Weeks. On February 6, 1991, Judge Lyndon L. Roberts ordered this social worker to assess the family and be prepared to recommend placement in the best interest of Madie Williams, a juvenile.

Individual Characteristics.   Madie Williams, a fourteen-year-old, attractive, African-American female, is the older child in a family of two children. She is in the eighth grade at Johnson High School. Mrs. Williams reports that Madie has never failed a grade or had any significant academic problems. She has consistently been on the honor roll at school. There are no reports of significant behavior problems until age twelve, when Madie became openly defiant of authority and began to lie persistently and be truant from school. Mr. and Mrs. Williams also stated that Madie's "feelings are easily hurt, and that in the past she has allowed herself to be easily taken advantage of by friends just so she wouldn't lose them." Mrs. Williams believes that Madie became "depressed" about age thirteen and began stealing at about age fourteen. Madie reportedly ran away from home overnight on two occasions since age thirteen. At age fourteen, she left home with a boyfriend for five days. She was arrested, returned home, and promised not to leave again.

From reports of both parents, the onset of Madie's behavior problems at age twelve occurred when she found out from the Jeffersons, Mrs. Williams' parents; that Rosie Williams was not Madie's biological mother. This incident was reported to have happened during a family argument where some "pretty mean things were said." Madeline Jones is Madie's biological mother. Her whereabouts are unknown, and she has not been heard from since she left Madie at the age of eighteen months with her father, Mr. Williams. Less than a year after Madie found out about the identity of her biological mother, she allegedly started a fire in her grandmother's house that destroyed the house and injured her grandmother and her brother, Player.

Rosie Williams is a thirty-six-year-old, attractive, African-American female. She is both verbal and intelligent. She is stepmother to Madie, and biological mother of Player. Mrs. Williams has cared for Madie since she was eighteen months old, and she states that she "loved her like her own." Mrs. Williams works as an assistant at the Austin Library and is the primary financial support for the family. She reports that she is currently estranged from her family, the Jeffersons, in Dallas due to the fire at her parent's house, their negative comments, and their attitude toward Madie and Willie Joe. She states that those family relationships are very stressful, but she truly believes her mother and father have misjudged the situation and that the fire was started by accident due to Madie trying to hide her smoking from them. Mrs. Williams graduated from high school and attended college where she met her husband.

Willie Joe Williams is a highly articulate, attractive, thirty-five-year-old African-American male. He is the biological father of both Madie and Player. Mr. Williams graduated from high school and attended college. He played football through college and for eight years as a professional for the L. A. Bulldogs. Mr. Williams has worked only part-time outside the home in the last five years. He provides child care and attends to the needs of the family at home. He began his current job as a part-time night stocker at the H.E.B. grocery store six months ago.

Player Williams is an eleven-year-old African-American male. He is in the fifth grade at Travis Elementary School, is consistently on the honor roll, and has won several trophies for his athletic abilities in baseball. He has a speech impediment, a stutter, which his parents report he has always had. Player receives speech therapy at his school. Player reports feeling very close to his sister and being worried that she "may be in very big trouble."

Family Background/History.   Mr. and Mrs. Williams met in Dallas, Texas, nineteen years ago while attending Dallas College. They have been married for thirteen years. Mr. Williams was previously involved in a relationship with Madeline Jones in which he fathered one child, Madie, in 1977. When the child was 18 months old, Madeline Jones disappeared, leaving Madie in the care of her father, who subsequently married Rosie Jefferson very shortly thereafter. The family moved to Los Angeles, California, in 1979, after Mr. Williams was recruited out of college to play football for the L.A. Bulldogs, a semiprofessional team. Their son Player was born one year later, in 1980. Mrs. Williams worked as an assistant in a library while Mr. Williams played football for eight years. Due to numerous knee injuries, Mr. Williams was dropped from the team in December 1988, and the family moved to Dallas, Texas, where they lived with Mr. and Mrs. John Jefferson, Mrs. Williams' parents. Mr. Williams held odd jobs, mostly as a security guard, and Mrs. Williams worked at a Dallas library.

Nine months after moving in with the Jeffersons, a fire burned the house completely down. Mrs. Jefferson and Player were injured in the fire but recovered within a couple weeks. Madie was arrested, placed on probation for arson, and sent to Buckner Children's Home for two weeks. Madie appears to have been arrested because the fire was started in or near her room, and the Jeffersons very much believed that she had set the fire with a lighter later found on her person. Madie and her parents maintain that she did not start the fire on purpose, but that it did result from her smoking in her room. Relations between the Williamses and the Jeffersons deteriorated, and one year after moving to Dallas the family decided to move to Austin. Mr. Williams moved first and found a job at the AppleTree grocery store. He later took a similar job at the H.E.B. food store chain. Rosie, Madie, and Player followed three months later, after Rosie was able to get a job at the Austin library.

Social Support/Current Living Arrangements.   The Williamses live in a single-family home that they own. The home is spacious, with three bedrooms and two baths, and from the observation of the social worker, it appears tidy and well kept. Both Madie and Player have their own rooms, and the home is enriched with music, art, and literature provided by Mrs. Williams. The family home is located in a middle-class neighborhood with parks and recreational facilities. The neighborhood is well integrated ethnically, and the family reports that the neighbors are friendly with each other. Mr. and Mrs. Williams socialize with one couple in the neighborhood and know several others. Both Madie and Player state that they have friends that live on their street.

The family is very involved in the local Protestant church, and the parents state that religion is important to the family life. Mr. Williams stated the minister had been a comfort to them during this "trial with Madie" and that several people in the church had offered emotional support to them.

Both Mr. and Mrs. Williams are also involved in several civic and recreational groups. They belong to and attend meetings at the neighborhood association. Mr. Williams belongs to a black fraternity and frequently plays sports with a "few of the men" from that group. Mrs. Williams loves African art and serves on the committee of the local art museum. Both children have been active in sports; Player is especially involved in baseball and Madie in track. Family members report that they have been satisfied with the quality of their social relationships and that they like their neighborhood.

Both Mr. and Mrs. Williams have expressed a regret, however, that they were not close to their extended family members and hope that something could be done about the problem between Mrs. Williams and her parents in the future.

The family at this time has adequate financial resources and expressed no concern for their financial well-being. Mr. Williams, however, expressed a concern that he should make plans for developing a new career now that he has left football.

Results of the Family Environment Scale (FES).   The Family Environment Scale, a standardized measure, was used to assess the family's social climate as it compares with a normative group. This measure was given to each family member in the office of the social worker during a family interview on February 11. The results from this administration appear to be valid and consistent with the observations of the family made by the social worker.

According to the scores on the FES, this is a relationship-oriented family that also encourages personal growth. They also scored above average in Achievement and Support Orientation. The Family Incongruence score indicates that this is a highly congruent family; they answered fifty-two questions out of ninety exactly the same. The actual scores on the measure are included at the end of this report. Given these results, the below-average score for Madie on the Independence subscale can be explained as normal for an adolescent trying to master developmental goals of separation and individuation.

All family members' scores indicate a high degree of cohesiveness. They appear to be very committed to and supportive to each other. Their feelings of togetherness as a family are above average. Mr. Williams described his family as his "heart beat." When he said this the whole family embraced each other.

Mr. Williams and both children report an average feeling of openness; they can express their feelings openly and discuss their personal problems. Mrs. Williams, however, scored considerably below average on the Expressiveness subscale, which is consistent with her observed quieter demeanor; she was the least outspoken and did not offer any information without being asked a direct question. Mrs. Williams and both children scored below average on the Conflicts subscale, indicating a lack of aggression or fighting in the family. All members agreed that "If there's a disagreement in our family, we try hard to smooth things over and keep the peace," that they "do not fight a lot in our family," that "Family members do not get so angry that they throw things," and that "Family members do not hit each other." This family appears to show a preference for conflict avoidance and agreement. The social workers also observed these patterns during the family interview; family members were quick to come to the aid and defense of one another.

Except for the Independence subscale, this family measured above average in encouraging personal growth. The family measured well above average on the Achievement Orientation subscale. Their dedication to school and sports clearly illustrates this pattern. They all report that it is important to be the best at whatever they do, and "work before play is the rule in our family." Given these results, the below-average score for Madie on the Independence subscale may be related to her own personal turmoil over her identity and recent psychosocial stressors. It may also reflect Madie's own sense of powerlessness over the situation and her level of depression.

The family scored average on the Intellectual and Cultural Orientation subscale, which is consistent with the social worker's observations of their experience. The Williamses are very culturally aware and proud of their African heritage. They report that they have been discriminated against because of their race but continue to encourage their children to be proud of and to preserve their African heritage. Their political and social interests, however, do not go much beyond their own experiences. The average subscale measure is consistent with my own observations and conversations with them. The Williamses are heavily involved in their children's athletic activities, which is indicated in the above and well above average Active Recreational Orientation subscale measures. Mr. Williams reports that he is Madie's trainer for track.

The Williamses range from average to well above average on the Moral-Religious Emphasis subscale. The family attends church on a regular basis and reports that they say prayers, believe that sin will be punished, and that there is a heaven and hell.

This family is highly organized and structured. Their activities and responsibilities are planned and clear. The social worker's observation while in their home on one occasion is consistent with these outcomes. Their home is neat and orderly, as are their persons. When Mr. Williams observed his daughter being escorted from detention to the courtroom, his first comment to her was, "Baby, look at your hair—why didn't you comb it?"

The measures on the Control subscale also fell into the well above average range. Mr. Williams, who is clearly the head of the house, scored above average on this subscale. The score appears to reflect both his cultural and religious beliefs concerning the gender roles of men in a family. All family members agreed that Mr. Williams makes most of the final decisions. They agreed that there are set ways of doing things at home and that there is a strong emphasis on following rules in the family.

Recommendation to the Court.   The recommendation of this social worker is that Madie be returned to her family. They are able to and have in the past provided needed support and structure for her. Madie's decline can be traced directly to several major events in her life: at the age of ten she and her family moved from Los Angeles, California, to Dallas,

Texas, a major disruption requiring a great deal of adjustment. At this time Madie also discovered that Rosie Williams was not her biological mother, causing a major shift in her self-image and in their relationship. She subsequently developed several behavior problems. Next her grandparents' house burned down, injuring her grandmother and her brother. Madie was arrested, charged with arson, placed on probation, and briefly removed from her home when she was sent to the Buckner Children's Home. These events confirmed Madie's distorted beliefs that the Jeffersons were correct, "she wasn't good enough to be Rosie's daughter." To complicate matters, Madie entered adolescence at this time.

It is believed that Madie may suffer from depression associated with these stressors. Madie will benefit from weekly, individual, long-term counseling and family counseling. She needs a safe place to explore and talk about her feelings of loss at suddenly becoming a stepchild, anger toward her parents for keeping her ignorant of her biological mother, anger about the events that occurred in Dallas, and shame over her behavior in the last two years. It is believed that the family also needs help in adjusting to their stresses, their extended family conflicts, and the issues regarding Madie's runaways, stealing, and identity problems. To facilitate Madie's adjustment in the home, it is also recommended that she attend a day treatment program for not less than six months so that she may receive the extra support and the structure needed to resolve her difficulties. She can do this best with the loving support of her family.

Table 8.4   FES Raw Scores on Subscales

	Mother	Father	Daughter	Son
Relationship Dimensions				
Cohesion (C)	9	8	8	9
Expressiveness (Ex)	3	5	6	5
Conflict (Con)	1	4	2	1
Personal Growth Dimensions				
Independence (Ind)	5	8	4	7
Achievement Orientation (AO)	7	9	7	6
Intellectual-Cultural Orientation (ICO)	7	9	9	7
Achievement-Recreational (ARO)	8	7	7	8
Moral-Religious Emphasis (MRE)	7	6	5	6
System Maintenance Dimensions				
Organization (Org)	8	5	7	7
Control (Ctl)	5	8	7	7
Family Incongruence Score: 13.66				

Table 8.5   FES Raw Scores on Subscales

	Mrs. Williams	Mr. Williams	Madie	Player
C	90	80	80	90
Ex	30	50	60	50
Con	10	40	20	10
Ind	50	80	40	70
AO	70	90	70	60
ICO	70	90	90	70
ARO	80	70	70	80
MRE	70	60	50	60
Org	80	50	70	70
Ctl	50	80	70	70

Figure 8.8   FES Scores Graphed

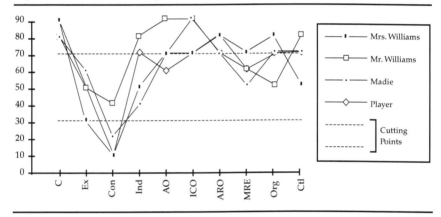

SUMMARY

This chapter has reviewed some of the important literature from the field of family assessment. Its goal was to help social work practitioners develop knowledge that will aid in their assessment of families. In particular, the chapter explored the understandings of family functioning from a systems perspective. Several concepts from the family systems literature were defined and explained in relation to their significance to the assessment of families. Selected stage developmental models were also covered.

Five empirical models, the Beavers Systems Models, the Olson Circumplex Family Model, the McMaster Family Assessment Model, the Moos Family Environment Scales, and the Family Assessment Measure were summarized. In addition, the chapter described five different types of methods for assessment and measurement that may be used in a social worker's assessment of a family system. Interviewing techniques, family task observations, family goal recording, two graphic methods, and problem-oriented standardized measures were discussed.

The chapter also presented a family assessment write-up to show how these methods may be combined to develope a family assessment. Finally, the chapter discussed how one moves from gathering assessment information to prescribing intervention methods to help the client.

STUDY QUESTIONS

1. Describe five key characteristics of family systems.
2. Explain how whole systems measuerment instruments help family practitioners.
3. Develop a family genogram on yourself or a friend.
4. Where are you presently in the family life cycle and what will be the next stage of development for you and your family?

REFERENCES

Abidin, R. R. (1983). *Parenting stress index manual*. Charlottesville, VA: Pediatric Psychology Press.

Aponte, H., & Van Deusen, J. M. (1981). Structural family therapy. In A. S. Gurman & D. P. Knirsken (Eds.), *Handbook of family therapy* (pp. 45–72). New York: Brunner/Mazel.

Barrera, M., Jr. (1986). Distinctions between social support concepts, measures, and models. *American Journal of Community Psychology, 14*, 413–416.

Barrera, M., Jr., Sandler, I. N., & Ramsey, T. B. (1981). Preliminary development of a scale of social support: Studies on college students. *American Journal of Community Psychology, 9*, 435–447.

Beavers, W. R. (1981). A systems model of family for family therapists. *Journal of Marital and Family Therapy, 7*, 229–307.

Beavers, W. R. (1982). Healthy, midrange, and severely dysfunctional families. In F. Walsh (Ed.), *Normal family processes* (pp. 00–00). New York: Guilford.

Beavers, W. R., & Hampson, R. B. (1990). *Successful families: Assessment and intervention*. New York: Norton.

Beavers, W. R., & Hampson, R. B. (2000). The Beavers Systems Model of family functioning. *Journal of Family Therapy, 22*(2), 128–133.

Beavers, W. R., & Voller, M. N. (1983). Family models: Comparing the Olson circumplex model with the Beavers systems model. *Family Models, 22*, 85–98.

Becvar, D. S., & Becvar, R. J. (1988). *Family therapy: A systemic integration*. Needham Heights, MA: Allyn & Bacon.

Boake, C., & Salmon, P. G. (1983). Demographic correlates and factor structure of the Family Environment Scale. *Journal of Clinical Psychology, 39*(1), 95–100.

Bowen, M. (1976). Theory in the practice of psychotherapy. In P. J. Guerin (Ed.), *Family therapy: Theory and practice* (pp. 24–90). New York: Gardner.

Bowen, M. (1978). *Family therapy in clinical practice.* New York: Aronson.

Brill, N. (1988). *Working with people* (3rd ed.). New York: Longman.

Brock, G. W., & Barnard, C. P. (1988). *Procedures in family therapy.* Needham Heights, MA: Allyn & Bacon.

Buckley, W. (1967). *Sociology and modern systems theory.* Englewood Cliffs, NJ: Prentice Hall.

Carter, B., & McGoldrick, M. (1988). *The changing family lifecycle: A framework for therapy* (2nd ed.). New York: Gardner.

Chipuer, H. M., & Villegas, T. (2001). Comparing the second-order factor structure of the Family Environment Scale across husbands' and wives' perceptions of their family environment. *Family Process, 40*(2), 187–199.

Compton, B., & Galaway, B. (1989). *Social work process* (4th ed.). Belmont, CA: Wadsworth.

Constantine, L. L. (1986). *Family paradigms: The practice of theory in family therapy.* New York: Guilford.

Corcoran, K., & Fischer, J. (2000). *Measures for clinical practice* (3rd ed.). New York: Free Press.

Darro, D., Abrahams, N., Casey, K., Rose, S., McCurdy, K., & Brown, L. (1990). *Parent program evaluation manual.* Chicago: National Committee for Prevention of Child Abuse.

Dinkmeyer, D., & McKay, G. D. (1983). *Systematic training for effective parenting: The parents' guide.* St. Paul, MN: American Guidance Service.

Early, T. J. (2001). Measures for practice with families from a strengths perspective. *Families in Society: The Journal of Contemporary Human Services, 82*(3), 225–232.

Early, T., & GlenMaye, L. F. (2000). Valuing families: Social work practice with families from a strengths perspective. *Social Work, 45,* 118–130.

Epstein, N. B., Baldwin, L. M., & Bishop, D. S. (1982). *McMaster family assessment device (FAD) manual (version 3).* Providence, RI: Brown University/Butler Hospital Family Research Program.

Epstein, N. B., Baldwin, L. M., & Bishop, D., (1983). The McMaster family assessment device. *Journal of Marital and Family Therapy, 9*(2), 171–180.

Epstein, N. B., Bishop, D. S., & Baldwin, L. M. (1982). McMaster Model of Family Functioning: A view of the normal family. In F. Walsh (Ed). *Normal family processes. Guilford family therapy series* (pp. 115–141). New York: Guilford.

Fisch, R., Watzlawick, P., & Segal, L. (1982). *The tactics of change.* San Francisco: Jossey-Bass.

Fleuridas, C., Nelson, T. S., & Rosenthal, D. M. (1986). The evolution of circular questions: Training family therapists. *Journal of Marital and Family Therapy, 12*(2), 113–127.

Fleuridas, C., Rosenthal, D. M., Leigh, E. K., & Leigh, T. E. (1990). Family goal recording: An adaption of goal attainment scaling for enhancing family therapy assessment. *Journal of Marital and Family Therapy, 16*(4), 389–406.

Foley, V. D. (1989). Family therapy. In R. J. Corsini & D. Welding (Eds.), *Current psychotherapies* (4th ed., pp. 455–502). Itasca, IL: Peacock.

Franklin, C. (2002). Becoming a strengths fact finder. *AAMFT Magazine*. Washington, DC.: The American Association of Marital and Family Therapists.

Franklin, C., & Jordan, C. (1999). *Family practice: Brief systems methods for social work*. Pacific Grove, CA: Brooks/Cole.

Franklin, C., & Jordan, C. (2002). Effective family therapy: Guidelines for practice. In A. R. Roberts & G. J. Greene (Eds.), *Social workers desk reference* (pp. 256–262). New York: Oxford University Press.

Franklin, C., & Streeter, C. L. (1993). Validity of the 3-D circumplex model for family assessment. *Research on Social Work Practice, 3*(3), 258–275.

Franklin, C., Streeter, C. L., & Springer, D. W. (2001). Validity of the FACES IV family assessment measure. *Research on Social Work Practice, 11*(5), 576–596.

Fredman, N., & Sherman, R. (1987). *Handbook of measurements for marital and family therapy*. New York: Brunner/Mazel.

Garrett, A. (1991). *Interviewing: Its principles and methods* (3rd ed.). Milwaukee, WI: Family Service America.

Gilgun, J. F. (2001). CASPARS: New Tools for Assessing Client Risks and Strengths. *Families in Society: The Journal of Contemporary Human Services, 82*, 450–459.

Goldenberg, I., & Goldenberg, H. (1990). *Family therapy: An overview*. Pacific Grove, CA: Brooks/Cole.

Graybeal, C. (2001). Strengths-based social work assessment: Transforming the dominant paradigm. *Families in Society: The Journal of Contemporary Human Services, 82*(3), 233–242.

Green, R. G., Harris, R. N., Forte, J. A., & Robinson, M. (1991). Evaluating FACES III and the circumplex model: 2,440 families. *Family Process, 30*, 55–73.

Grier, R., Morris, L., & Taylor, L. (2001). Assessment strategies for school-based mental health counseling. *Journal of School Health, 71*, 467–469.

Grotevant, H. D., & Carlson, C. I. (1989). *Family assessment: A guide to methods and measures*. New York: Guilford.

Haley, J. (1990). *Problem solving therapy*. San Francisco: Jossey-Bass.

Hepworth, D. H., & Larsen, J. A. (1989). *Direct social work practice* (3rd ed.). Belmont, CA: Wadsworth.

Ho, M. (1986). *Family therapy with ethnic minorities*. Newbury Park, CA: Sage.

Holman, A. M. (1983). *Family assessment: Tools for understanding and intervention*. Beverly Hills, CA: Sage.

Jacob, T., & Tennenbaum, D. L. (1988). *Family assessment: Rationale, methods, and future directions*. New York: Plenum.

Janzen, C., & Harris, O. (1986). *Family treatment in social work practice* (2nd ed.). Itasca, IL: Peacock.

Johnson, H. C. (1987). Biologically based deficit in the identified patent: Indications for psychoeducational strategies. *Journal of Marital and Family Therapy, 13*(4), 337–348.

Kiresuk, T. J., & Sherman, R. E. (1968). Goal attainment scaling: A general method for evaluating community mental health programs. *Community Mental Health Journal, 4*, 443–453.

Kiresuk, T. J., Stelmachers, E. T., & Schultz, S. K. (1982). Quality assurance and goal attainment scaling. *Professional Psychology, 13*, 145–1522.

Miller, I. W., Ryan, C. E., Keitner, G. I., Bishop, D. S., & Epstein, N. B. (2000a). Factor analyses of the family assessment device, by Ridenour, Daley, & Reich. *Family Process, 39*(1), 141–145.

Miller, I. W., Ryan, C. E., Keitner, G. I., Bishop, D. S., & Epstein, N. B. (2000b). Why fix what isn't broken? A rejoiner to Ridenour, Daley. *Family Process, 39*(3), 381–385.

Minuchin, S. (1974). *Families and family therapy.* Cambridge: Harvard University Press.

Minuchin, S., & Fishman, H. C. (1982). *Family therapy techniques.* Cambridge: Harvard University Press.

Moos, R. H., & Moos, B. S. (1986). *Family environment scale manual* (2nd ed.). Palo Alto, CA: Consulting Psychologist Press.

Moos, R. H., & Spinrad, S. (1984). *The social climate scales: An annotated bibliography.* Palo Alto, CA: Consulting Psychologist Press.

O'Brien, C., & Bruggen, P. (1985). Our personal and professional lives: Learning positive connotation and circular questioning. *Family Process, 24*, 311–322.

Olson, D. H. (1985). Commentary: Struggling with congruence across theoretical models and methods. *Family Process, 24*, 203–207.

Olson, D. H. (1986). Circumplex model VII: Validation studies and FACES III. *Family Process, 26*, 337–351.

Olson, D. H. (1991). Commentary: Three-dimensional (3-D) circumplex model and revised scoring of FACES III. *Family Process, 30*, 74–79.

Olson, D. H., McCubbing, H. I., Barnes, H., Larsen, A., Muxen, M., & Wilson, M. (1985). *Family inventories: Inventories in a national survey of families across the family life cycle* (rev. ed.). St. Paul: University of Minnesota, Family Social Science.

Olson, D. H., Sprenkle, D. H., & Russel, C. S. (1979). Circumplex model of marital and family systems: Cohesion and adaptability dimensions, family types and clinical applications. *Family Process, 18*(1), 3–28.

Olson, D. H., & Tiesel, J. (1993). *FACES III: Linear scoring and interpretation.* St. Paul: University of Minnesota, Family Social Science.

Pardeck, J. T. (2000). Clinical instruments for assessing and measuring family health. *Family Therapy, 27*(3), 178–187.

Procidano, M., & Heller, K. (1983). Measures of perceived social support from friends and from family: Three validational studies. *American Journal of Community Psychology, 11*, 1–24.

Ridenour, T. A., Daley, J. G., & Reich, W. (2000). Further evidence that the family assessment device should be reorganized: Response to Miller and colleagues. *Family Process, 39*(3), 375–381.

Schulman, L. (1992). *The skills of helping individuals and groups.* Itasca, IL: Peacock.

Shepard, M., & Campbell, J. A. (1992). The abusive behavior inventory: A measure of psychological and physical abuse. *Journal of Interpersonal Violence, 7*(3), 291–305.

Simon, C. E., McNeil, J. S., Franklin, C., & Cooperman, A. (1991). The family and schizophrenia: Toward a psychoeducational approach. *Families in Society, 72*(6), 323–334.

Skinner, H., Steinhauer, P., & Sitarenios, G. (2000). Family Assessment Measure (FAM) and process model of family functioning. *Journal of Family Therapy, 22*(2), 190–210.

Streeter, C. L., & Franklin, C. (1992). Defining and measuring social support: Guidelines for social work practitioners. *Research on Social Work Practice, 42*(1), 81–98.

Stuart, R. B. (1980). *Helping couples change: A social learning approach to marital therapy.* Champaign, IL: Research Press.

Thomas, V., & Lewis, R. A. (1999). Observational couple assessment: A cross-model comparison. *Journal of Family Therapy, 99, 21*(1), 78–96.

Thomas, V., & Olson, D. H. (1993). Problem families and the Circumplex Model: Observational assessment using the clinical rating scale (CRS). *Journal of Marital and Family Therapy, 19*(2), 159–175.

Thomas, V., & Zechowski, T. J. (2000). A test of the circumplex model of marital and family systems using the clinical rating scale. *Journal of Marital and Family Therapy, 26*(4), 523–534.

Tiesel, J. W., & Olson, D. H. (1992). Preventing family problems: Troubling trends and promising opportunities. *Family Relations: Journal of Applied Family & Child Studies, 41*(4), 198–403.

Toulitas, J., Permutter, B. F., & Straus, M. A. (2000). *Handbook of family measurement techniques.* Thousand Oaks, CA: Sage.

Tracy, E. M., & Whittaker, J. K. (1990). The social network map: Assessing social support in clinical practice. *Families in Society, 71*(8), 461–470.

Vaux, A. (1982). *Measures of three levels of social support: Resources, behaviors and feelings.* Unpublished manuscript.

Vaux, A. (1988). *Social support: Theory, research and intervention.* New York: Praeger.

Watzlawick, P., Beavin, J. H., & Jackson, D. D. (1967). *Pragmatics of human communication.* New York: Norton.

Wood, K. M., & Geismar, L. L. (1989). *Families at risk: Treating the multiproblem family.* New York: Human Science Press.

Watzlawick, P., Weakland, J., & Fisch, R. (1974). Change: Principles of problem formation and problem resolution. New York: Norton.

Assessing Families Who Are Multistressed

Catheleen Jordan, Ski Hunter, Joan Rycraft, and Vikki Vandiver

Chapter 9 addresses families involved with oppressive situations, multiple systems, and environmental stress. Reviewed here are families of gay and lesbian persons, families experiencing child maltreatment, and families experiencing health problems. All of these diverse populations experience external stressors that impinge on their lives.

GAY AND LESBIAN FAMILIES

Gay and lesbian families are defined as including at least one lesbian or gay adult or two or more adults with a same-sex orientation who are rearing a child. The current knowledge focuses on couples' friendship and on lesbian and gay couples with children (Allen & Demo, 1995). The following section provides a brief overview of these two important areas.

Friendships and Couples

Although they are members of families of origin and extended families, gay and lesbian persons claim other families composed of friends and partners. These families, also called "created families" (Weinstock, 1998) or "chosen families" (Weston, 1997), develop through voluntary choice and love. Although they are the major support system for most gay and lesbian persons, racial and ethnic group members may not place as much value on others who are outside their biological families (D'Augelli & Garnets, 1995). Families of choice typically provide benefits that families of origins do: protection, socialization, belongingness, a source for self-esteem, and a sense of identity (Matthews & Lease, 2000).

After self-identifying as lesbian, gay, or bisexual (LGB) and establishing friendships with LGB persons, individuals usually begin to seek involvement in same-sex or bisexual linkups. This reflects the desire to be linked with someone of the same sex as well as a deepening commitment to a new identity (Savin-Williams, 1998). Gay and lesbian couples include persons who are emotional and usually sexual partners. Partners are also most likely the central focus of one's chosen family (James & Murphy, 1998).

Gay and lesbian couples are diverse. For example, some persons participate in more than one couple link at a time and make a distinction between primary and nonprimary links (Hostetler & Coher, 1997). Some couples may participate in a public "marriage" and some in a private commitment ceremony. Some couple members wear rings or show their commitment in other ways or in no way. Variable close-couple configurations exist, including partners who commit to each other but do not live with each other, partners who see themselves as a couple but who have more than one significant partner, or partners who coexist with heterosexual marriages (James & Murphy, 1998). Shernoff (1995) reported that the diverse patterns in gay couples include those who are: 1) sexually exclusive, 2) primarily sexually exclusive, 3) sexually nonexclusive but in an unacknowledged, open relationship, 4) sexually nonexclusive but in an acknowledged, open relationship, and 5) linked with nonsexual lovers.

Given the diversity among same-sex couples, asking couples to define their configuration is the best way to know what it is (Hostetler & Coher, 1997). Another source of diversity is what gay and lesbian couples call themselves, such as "lovers" or "partners." It is also best to ask each individual couple what they prefer to call themselves (Berger, 1990).

Satisfaction and Other Positive Characteristics of Same-Sex Couples.   Being in a couple provides benefits for gay and lesbian persons including increased self-esteem and a sense of well-being (Wayment & Peplau, 1995). Many studies also reported no discrepancies between lesbian and gay couples and heterosexual couples in *quality* (Kurdek, 1994, 1995a); *closeness, adjustments* (Kurdek, 1995); or *satisfaction* (e.g., Kurdek, 1994). In some studies, gay and lesbian couples experienced higher levels of functioning than did heterosexual couples (Kurdek, 1995). Lesbian couples in particular also reported higher levels of cohesion, adaptability, equality, and satisfaction than did heterosexual couples (Rosenbluth & Steil, 1995).

Bryant and Demian (1994) reported that, compared to gay men, more lesbians rated the quality of their link at the highest level (47% vs. 36%). Lesbian couples, when compared to gay couples, also reported stronger liking for their partner; greater satisfaction, trust, and shared decision making; stronger intrinsic desire for involvement in their link; and less external motivations for involvement in their link (Kurdek, 1988). Several studies also showed that satisfaction was higher in lesbian couples than in gay couples because of the higher value lesbians attributed to their links or to the rewards attained from them (Kurdek, 1991). Kurdek (1988) thought that the high ratings of lesbians for interpersonal factors such as caring and sensitivity to the needs and feelings of their partners might also partly account for their higher satisfaction levels.

Duration of Same-Sex Links. Without marriage and divorce records on lesbian and gay couples, the longevity of most of their links is not determinable (Peplau, 1993). From the few studies that have reported on longevity, the best information on breakup rates comes from the Blumstein and Schwartz (1983) landmark study of 3,574 married couples, 642 cohabiting couples, 957 gay couples, and 772 lesbian couples. When the survey began, all groups had comparable expectations of staying together; over 18 months, 1 one in 5 couples broke up. The percentage of breakups by group were highest among lesbian couples (22%), compared to gay (16%), cohabiting heterosexual (17%), and married heterosexual couples (4%). Several other studies also reported a higher rate of breakups for lesbian couples. The Teichner poll (Results, 1989) reported a median duration of 2.5 years for gay couples compared to 1.8 years for lesbian couples. Weinberg, Williams, and Pryor (1994) also found that lesbian linkups were shorter in duration than other linkups (heterosexual, bisexual, and gay). Kurdek (1997) reported that over a 5-year period, breakup rates were comparable to those found by Blumstein and Schwartz (1983): 7% for heterosexual couples, 14% for gay couples, and 16% for lesbian couples. Kurdek (1997) also pointed out, however, that over the 5 years of study, 86% of gay couples and 84% of lesbian couples were still together. Several studies found lesbian and gay couples together 10 years or longer (e.g., Berger, 1982/1996). Older lesbian and gay persons reported in anecdotal accounts linkups of 20 to 30 years duration or longer (Clunis & Green, 2000).

Breakups of Couples. Every couple is vulnerable to an eventual breakup; and internal, interpersonal, and external factors may play a role in any breakup. Internal factors such as personality and maturity and interpersonal factors such as sexual incompatibility and arguments about money can contribute to difficulties for any couple. External factors, that is, those in the wider social context beyond the individual and interpersonal contexts, also can affect all couples (Kitzinger & Coyle, 1995). An example of such a factor would be the intrusion of work responsibilities. Lesbian and gay couples, however, face additional, unique external challenges to their links.

External Challenges. There are many external challenges to gay and lesbian couples including *heterosexism*. Lesbian and gay couples exist in a climate of heterosexism, defined as "the ideological system that denies, denigrates, and stigmatizes any nonheterosexual form of behavior, identity, relationship, or community" (Herek, 1995, p. 321). Society condemns the love the couple members have for each other, their sexuality, and their partnerships (Kitzinger & Coyle, 1995). If the couple expresses affection openly, they risk harassment ranging from minor, but humiliating, insults such as name-calling to threats of death (James & Murphy, 1998). Except for registration of domestic partnerships in a few locales, these couples can obtain no legal status (D'Augelli & Garnets, 1995). They also cannot receive the benefits that heterosexual couples enjoy such as the institutional policies of insurance regulations, inheritance laws, tax regulations, and hospital visitations (Bryant & Demian, 1994; Greene, 1997; Huston & Schwartz, 1995).

Lack of support from families and heterosexual friends is a second external challenge. A married heterosexual couple can usually count on congratulations, blessings, presents, and other tangible and intangible support from families and friends, beginning at the time they declare themselves as a serious couple. Lesbian and gay couples rarely receive anything close to the same degree of support. If they announce their partnership to their families, the reaction is often one of overt hostility (Bryant & Demian, 1994). Instead of celebrating the link, families often deny or trivialize it (Serovich, Skeen, Walters, & Robinson, 1993). Lesbian couples in most racial and ethnic communities experience a collusion of silence, ambivalence, and denial (Greene & Boyd-Franklin, 1996). If a lesbian or gay couple is in trouble, neither families nor heterosexual friends are likely to encourage the couple to work out the problems (Greene, 1997).

Hindrances in lesbian and gay communities pose another external challenge. Though friendships and support provided by the lesbian and gay community are valuable resources for couples (Weston, 1997), the community can also pose a threat to them. Couples in the San Francisco sample studied by Weinberg et al. (1994) did not view the lesbian and gay community as promoting long-term linkups. In Meyer's (1990) study of gay couples, many men reported that they limited contact with bars and other aspects of the gay community because the primary support available is for individuals not couples. Blumstein and Schwartz (1983) observed that the more a lesbian couple was involved in the community, the more often they broke up because of the availability of alternative partners.

Consequences of External Obstacles for Couples.   The external obstacles discussed above can create internal difficulties for lesbian and gay couples that interfere with if not destroy happiness. Hiding and passing and internalization of negative beliefs and images are two behaviors that contribute to such dilfficulties.

Hiding and passing is one strategy used by couples. Many lesbian and gay couples make no public disclosures because of anticipated hostile responses. Instead, they engage in various subterfuges to hide their links such as not talking about their personal life, introducing partners as "friends," changing pronouns when talking about with whom they did things over the weekend, talking as if going out on heterosexual dates, inventing (if not acquiring) a fiance or spouse, and sleeping in different rooms when parents visit (Kitzinger & Coyle, 1995). Although hiding may not affect a couple's satisfaction directly (e.g., Eldridge & Gilbert, 1990), it is an endless struggle for the couple members to do it.

Caron and Ulin (1997) found that relationship quality was higher when both partners were open about their link, especially with their families of origin. There also were positive effects on couple satisfaction when families took such actions as asking the partner to family events and accepting the display of affection between the partners. Closeting exceedingly limits the potential social support available from one's family as well as from friends and work associates. In response the couple may intensify their dependency on each other (Patterson & Schwartz, 1994). Isolation from other lesbian and gay persons also means that there are no models to observe for alternate and more satisfying couple behaviors and maintenance. Partners can also experience a sense of unreality about their couple status because the link is only real to them (Patterson & Schwartz, 1994).

Negative cultural beliefs and images saturate the lives of lesbian and gay persons. They may be internalized to the point that couples conjecture that they cannot form enduring, happy linkups or that their linkups do not compare favorably to heterosexual linkups (Bryant & Demian, 1994). Same-gender couples also may play out negative expectations (Bryant & Demian, 1994) and experience guilt, fear, self-hatred, hatred of the partner, failing satisfaction, and painful endings (Murphy, 1994).

Some of the same external factors delineated here can be obstacles with similar consequences in gay and lesbian families with children. A brief summary of these families, their children, and the challenges they face is presented below.

Lesbian and Gay Couples with Children

Many lesbian and gay persons create and maintain a family life with children; however, it is impossible to know the number of such families (as well as of couples without children). Recent estimates suggest a range from two to eight million in the United States (Hare, 1994). These rates could result in four to fourteen million children being raised in same-sex households (Patterson, 1995).

Formerly, most children of gay or lesbian parents probably resulted from heterosexual unions, that is, the parents today probably married, had children, and later divorced. Today there are more options such as foster care, adoption, surrogacy, and donor sperm insemination (McLeod & Crawford, 1998). For example, in the context of a same-gender linkup, lesbians may conceive children with donor sperm contributed by a friend, relative, or acquaintance or by an unknown person through a sperm bank. Lesbians might also conceive a child through planned sexual intercourse with a consenting male who may or may not play a part in the child's upbringing. Gay men may become fathers to children through sexual intercourse with a woman with whom they have agreed to share the parenting role. This could mean entering a parenting arrangement with a lesbian friend who gives birth to a child conceived with the gay man's sperm. Alternatively, arrangements could be made that include a lesbian and a gay man or a lesbian couple and a gay couple who agree to joint biological or custodial parenting. Gay men may also use paid surrogacy arrangements, but this route can often entail legal and moral dilemmas (McLeod & Crawford, 1998).

Lesbian and gay persons may also become parents through adoption or foster care (Patterson, 1992). However, state foster care and adoption policies, regulations, and practices often either forbid or discourage gay and lesbian parenting or at least accord it low priority (Leiter, 1997). The exception may involve the placement of adolescents identified as gay or lesbian with gay or lesbian couples; however, the agencies' motives for this are ambiguous. Do they do this to provide support and role models for the child or to avoid placing any adolescent not identified as gay or lesbian in these homes. Even if successful with the foster home or adoptive course, a gay or lesbian couple cannot officially enter such an arrangement. Instead, the partners must negotiate which partner will be the foster or adoptive parent of record (Appleby & Anastas, 1998).

Although lesbian and gay couples experience many issues that heterosexual couples experience when pursuing options to have children, they face an additional set of issues because of their sexual orientation. This variable does not affect everything, but what it does affect can lead to different types of stressors for gay and lesbian families.

Stressors.   To bear and rear children, gay and lesbian persons must overcome many obstacles, the overriding obstacle being heterosexism. Gay and lesbian persons experience no validation for their families because of disapproval of their sexual orientation and coupling. They face beliefs that they should have no association with children and that they are unfit to raise children. Further, their children, if they do raise them, will be psychologically and socially maladjusted; will suffer social stigmatization (Matthews & Lease, 2000); will be negatively affected in the development of their gender identity; or will turn out as gay or lesbian themselves (Shapiro, 1996). On a practical and economic level, the parents cannot procure insurance or file income tax as a family, and their children cannot receive Social Security benefits from both parents. In many states, lesbian and gay sexual partners violate laws and are highly vulnerable to negative outcomes in courts if there is a challenge to the custody of their children (Segal-Sklar, 1996). Because of these and many other outcomes of the heterosexist ideology, gay and lesbian persons may come to believe themselves that they are not fit for parenting (Matthews & Lease, 2000).

Once a lesbian couple decides to have a child, the issue arises about which partner will become pregnant and what will be the role of the partner who does not. The next big issue is how to achieve a pregnancy: The heterosexual sex way? The gay-friend donor way? The medical system way? For this last option, one hopes to find affirming health care providers, but this may not be an easy thing to do in many parts of the country. If a couple uses assisted insemination, other questions arise: Will the sperm donor be anonymous? Is there any future possibility of legal or social connection with the donor? Gay men are unlikely to experience these kinds of issues because they know the women giving birth; however, as noted earlier, there can be difficulties associated with paid surrogacy arrangements (Shernoff, 1996).

For gay and lesbian persons who have custody of their children, one of the biggest stressors they experience is the fear that because of their social orientation, they will lose custody of or contact with their children (Bigner, 1996). This is a realistic fear as many gay and lesbian parents are denied visitation with or custody of their biological children (Patterson, 1992). In many jurisdictions, court decisions have awarded custody to the heterosexual parent or even to other persons in the extended family such as biological grandparents (Hartman, 1996).

If custody is granted to a gay or lesbian parent, there may be a requirement that the parent not live with a same-sex partner or associate in any way with other gay or lesbian persons (McLeod & Crawford, 1998). In some states, if a mother sharing a household with a lesbian partner does not receive custody of her children, she may be permitted visitation but only outside her home and no where else in the presence of the partner (Segal-Sklar, 1996).

The general assumption underlying much of the decision-making process regarding custody is that gay and lesbian parents have adverse effects on the social and psychological development of their children (Patterson, 1992). The related judicial assumption is that the best interests of a child require being reared by heterosexual parents instead of by gay or lesbian parents. As a greater number of lesbian and gay persons have had children, however, and as national attention to this phenomenon has increased, there has been more variation in court decisions. Cohn reported in 1995 that although five state supreme courts ruled against a gay or lesbian parent, eight other state supreme courts ruled against automatic denial of custody to a gay or lesbian parent. In other words, some judges now take the stance that same-sex sexual orientation alone does not necessarily render a parent unfit to raise children (Rosenblum, 1991). The National Association of Social Workers (NASW), the American Psychological Association (APA), and other professional and human services organizations and associations likewise support the position that a person's sexual orientation should have no effect on child custody cases or in determining whether a person qualifies to be a foster or adoptive parent (Benkov, 1994). This line of thinking has resulted from consistent research findings that the developmental outcomes for children reared by lesbian or gay parents are as good or better when compared to children reared in comparable heterosexual households.

All studies to date also have found that lesbian and gay persons function just as well as parents as their heterosexual counterparts (Tasker & Golombok, 1997). Compared to heterosexual mothers, lesbian mothers are as knowledgeable about effective parenting skills, and they demonstrate equal abilities to identify critical issues in child care situations and to formulate suitable solutions to the problems encountered with their children. Similarly, the parenting styles and attitudes of gay fathers are more similar than different from those of nongay fathers (Bigner & Jacobson, 1992). No discrepancies in these two father groups occurred in the extent of involvement in their children's activities or in the recreational activities provided for their children. Further, there are no differences in intimacy with children or in problem solving regarding childrearing issues (Bigner & Jacobson, 1992).

Disclosures to the Children and to Others.   Because of the fear of losing custody and of other potential harms, gay and lesbian parents may keep their sexual orientation secret (Patterson & Chan, 1996). Fredriksen (1999) found that three fourths of the gay and lesbian persons with children she studied had experienced harassment because of their sexual orientation: verbal (88%), emotional (50%), physical (9%), and sexual (9%). Parents want to protect their children as well from possible discrimination because they have parents with a same-sex orientation. Yet, secrecy can be a stressor and contribute to relationship difficulties especially if partners disagree about the need for secrecy. It can limit support from others as well as leave a family with no one with whom to share celebrations with (Matthews & Lease, 2000).

The available research also suggests that there is an association between psychological health and openness regarding one's sexual orientation (Rand, Graham, & Rawlings, 1982). Rand found a positive link between a lesbian mother's sense of psychological well-being and the extent to which she is accepting of and open about her lesbian identity. Secrecy with the children limits both intimacy between parents and children (Rohrbaugh, 1992) and openness in addressing family issues (Patterson & Chan, 1996).

Partners who wish to disclose their link to children may have to negotiate how and when to do it (Bigner, 1996). When they do make the disclosure, it is a complex and delicate task because it may entail discussing the children's origins and include such issues as alternative insemination or why they do not have a dad or mom (Segal-Sklar, 1996). If a partner enters a family where the other partner already has children, the presence, role, and meaning of the new same-sex partner also requires explanation. Many gay, lesbian, and bisexual parents who do not live with or have custody of their biological children may also face disclosure issues, such as tempering the reactions of the custodial parent or members of the child's extended family who can have influence on the continuation of contact with the child (Appleby & Anastas, 1998).

How do children react to the knowledge of their parent's sexual orientation? The reactions of most children are positive (Bigner, 1996); they respond with a sense of protectiveness toward their parents (O'Connell, 1993). They may indicate that the information makes no difference or that they already knew it (Turner, Scadden, & Harris, 1990). Even so, this does not mean that the children will have no questions. Generally, children will need continued discussion (Patterson, 1992).

Other children may react with distress, anxiety, anger, and sorrow and may make deprecating statements to the parents. However, it is unlikely that this will be the only response, or an enduring one. Other issues such as divorce can also influence negative responses (Appleby & Anastas, 1998). The ages of the children also may make a difference. Children first told of their parents' gay or lesbian sexual orientation in early adolescence, as opposed to at younger or older ages, may have a more difficult time adjusting (Patterson, 1992). Moreover, those who came from heterosexual marriages and are now living with lesbian and gay parents may suddenly worry about being seen as different by their peers (Hargaden & Llewellin, 1996). Adolescents do not like to feel different, and the disclosure of the parents' stigmatized sexual identity may lead to these negative feelings (O'Connell, 1993). Cramer (1986) reported that, compared to younger children of lesbian mothers who rarely recalled facing harassment from peers, adolescent children were more likely to receive negative messages from peers concerning their parents' sexual orientation. Older children who will likely make their own decisions about disclosure concerning their parents may decide against it because they do not want to risk being singled out by peers (Matthews & Lease, 2000).

Some parents may caution their children to keep their sexual orientation secret (Crawford, 1987). Yet, even if the children want to keep the information to themselves, the secrecy can then create anxiety about discovery for the children (Baptiste, 1987; Crawford, 1987). The parents as well may fear that the children will accidentally reveal the information or out them (Segal-Sklar, 1996).

Parents also have to decide if they will disclose to a variety of people involved in a child's life such as medical staff, child care workers, school officials, and the children's peers and parents. How open will they be both as a family and as gay or lesbian parents when dealing with these individuals and groups? Are they going to cross out "Father" or "Mother" on forms and put in "Other Mother" or "Other Father" or "Parent/Parent"? (Segal-Sklar, 1996). Fredriksen (1999) found that most parents were open in at least some settings: 51% were out to all coworkers, 58% to medical service providers, 65% to school personnel and 34% to neighbors. Parents must also make endless decisions in ordinary encounters out in the world. For example, how will they talk about who is the mother or the father of their child if someone inquires? (Martin, 1993).

The Coparent.   The coparent in a gay or lesbian family is the nonbiological parent of a child born into a lesbian link or the nonadoptive parent in a gay or lesbian couple. The presence of this person can provide both support and stress. For lesbian mothers, a partner who is a coparent can provide considerable support as a full partner with a child born or adopted into their link. In contrast, with blended families, or those in which a partner takes a parenting role in a relationship with a person who was already a parent, there can be more variation in the coparent's role (Appleby & Anastas, 1998). Coparents in gay male relationships also provide benefits; for example, inclusion of gay father's partners and the quality of the partner's relationships with the children is associated with happiness with family life.

However, the presence of a coparent can be a unique stressor because usually only one person is the legal parent or parent of record. It is the coparent who has no legal rights regarding a child. Rarely are both parents' names included on the birth certificate. It is also rare for the nonbiological parent to win the right to adopt the child (Segal-Sklar, 1996). If the partners break up, there is no legal protection of the link between the nonbiological, or nonlegal, parent and the child. If a custody fight ensues with the biological mother, the nonlegal mother has no grounds for a case. If the biological parent becomes incapacitated or dies, custody may be granted to the biological father, to other relatives, or to the state (Segal-Sklar, 1996).

If the couple wants several children, one solution is that parents can take turns in childbearing (Appleby & Anastas, 1998). Another solution is for the coparent to adopt a child born to or adopted by the other (Shernoff, 1996), but this legal recourse, or second-parent adoption, has been granted in only a few states. This solution may more often be successful when pregnancy happened through donor insemination and the biological father was unknown or when there was a legal adoption in which both biological parents relinquished rights to the child.

It is prudent for parents to seek assistance from legal advocacy groups. Practitioners also need to know both the legal status of LGB families in their community and state as well as attorneys who are themselves knowledgeable and affirmative. The web page for the National Gay and Lesbian Task Force (www.ngltf.org) provides a starting point for an overview of state laws and assistance in reaching LGB-affirmative lawyers and lawmakers (Matthews & Lease, 2000).

Ambiguity of Parenting Models.   A lack of parenting models for gay and lesbian families may create difficulties. In particular, having a family with one legal parent and a coparent with no legal rights can make the definition of parenting roles for a couple ambiguous (Patterson, 1995). What are the parents of the same gender to be called? Will "mom" refer only to the birth mother? Will the names be the same inside and outside the home? Will the child use only one surname or both? (Appleby & Anastas, 1998).

A benefit for these families is that there is the opportunity to create new parenting models (Weston, 1994). Because society does not recognize these families, it is especially important for them to develop rituals, traditions, and ways to celebrate their family successes, whatever model they choose to use.

Less Support from Family of Origin, Formal Systems, and the Gay/ Lesbian Community.   Even when one's family of origin is somewhat accepting or tolerant of one's sexual orientation and even of the couple relationship, reactions may change if the couple decides to raise children. Members of one's family of origin learn and act on the myths about psychological and social difficulties the children may experience (Matthews & Lease, 2000). Gay and lesbian parents also face many health care, legal, financial, social, and emotional hurdles, including lack of support from formalized support systems that assist heterosexual couples during parenthood (Patterson, 1995). Further, gay and lesbian families usually receive less support from their community than do heterosexual families partly because the lesbian and gay community is not as structured around children as the heterosexual community is. In a comparison of lesbian and heterosexual parents, Stiglitz (1990) discovered that when heterosexual mothers experienced the arrival of a child they felt more integrated into the community and more satisfied with emotional support from family, whereas lesbian mothers felt more isolated or more like a separate family. Not being able to reach out to support systems can be especially isolating for lesbian and gay individuals or couples who are first-time parents. However, because of the increase of lesbian and gay couples who are parents, support systems for them are expanding (Scrivner & Eldridge, 1995).

Impact on Children. The children of gay and lesbian parents do not differ from children of heterosexual parents in overall social (interpersonal relations) or psychological adjustment (emotional health) (Golombok & Tasker, 1996). They may experience greater acceptance of their sexuality, greater empathy for others, and greater tolerance of alternative viewpoints (Patterson, 1992). They are also no more likely to be gay than are children of heterosexual parents nor do they differ in gender identity, gender role behavior, or sexual orientation (Golombok & Tasker, 1996). The children of lesbian parents do not lack male role models. In fact, they are more likely to have contact with their fathers than are children of divorced heterosexual mothers. They also have more male friends and relatives involved in their lives than do children of heterosexual mothers (Golombok, Spener, & Rutter, 1983). Greene, Mandel, Hotvedt, Gray, and Smith (1986) found no differences in the ways that lesbian and heterosexual mothers rated the social skills and popularity of their children; moreover, the children did not rate themselves differently in their popularity among peers whether with the same or the other sex. As indicated earlier, adolescent children may experience a difficult adjustment to their parents' sexual orientation, but altogether, the children of gay and lesbian parents do not experience the expected downfalls heterosexist beliefs suggest.

Assessment Tools for Families of Gay and Lesbian Persons. Appropriate measures for this population evaluate individual issues and characteristics, such as self-esteem, social skills, and social support; also relevant are measures of the quality family relationship and satisfaction (see Table 9.1).

Table 9.1 Assessment Tools for Families of Gay and Lesbian Persons

MEASURES FOR INDIVIDUALS	MEASURES FOR COUPLES/FAMILIES
Index of Self-Esteem	Index of Marital Satisfaction
Social Support Inventory	Index of Family Relationship
Loneliness	Child's Attitude toward Parent
Beck Depression Inventory	Parent's Attitude toward Child

CHILD MALTREATMENT IN FAMILIES

Child maltreatment is a pervasive problem in our society and is experienced by families of all races, income status, beliefs, and structure. Causal indicators include individual characteristics of parents and children, familial factors, community environment, culture, and societal values (Pecora, Whittaker, Maluccio, & Barth, 2000). The most commonly recognized form of child maltreatment is familial abuse and neglect. Nearly three million incidents of child maltreatment are reported annually to child protection agencies. Following evidentiary investigation, just under one million of these reports are confirmed (U.S. Department of Health and Human Services, 1999). This section reviews types of maltreatment, risk assessment, and cultural sensitivity.

Types of Maltreatment

The four major types of familial child maltreatment include physical abuse, sexual abuse, physical neglect, and psychological maltreatment. Although states have varying definitions of specific categories of child maltreatment, the universal definition is found in the Federal Child Abuse and Prevention and Treatment Act of 1974 (PL 93-237):

> the physical or mental injury, sexual abuse, negligent treatment of a child under the age of eighteen by a person who is responsible for the child's welfare under circumstances which would indicate that the child's health or welfare is harmed or threatened thereby.

There are several perspectives on the etiology of child maltreatment that should be used to inform assessment strategies. These perspectives cover the range of specific personality traits of caregivers, social factors such as attitudes toward violence and living conditions, child characteristics, and parent-child interaction. Based on the findings of numerous studies, Pecora et al. (2000) note specific parent, child, and family causal factors identified across the different types of child maltreatment (see Table 9.2).

Child maltreatment is a complex phenomenon requiring a multidimensional assessment to determine appropriate interventions; singularly, the various perspectives individually fail to adequately address the cause of child maltreatment. The more contemporary theoretical framework is based on an ecological perspective that views the cause of child maltreatment as multifaceted and as resulting from the interface of parent and child traits and relationships, environmental stressors, cultural beliefs and practices, and societal norms (Belsky, 1980; Belsky & Vondura, 1989).

Families experiencing child maltreatment typically come to the attention of child protective services (CPS) agencies. If the report of alleged

Table 9.2   Types of Child Maltreatment

Physical Abuse	*Sexual Abuse*
Children with disabilities Premature births Children with behavioral problems Domestic violence Marital conflict Parental history of maltreatment Family social isolation Low income Lack of social supports Lack of knowledge of child development Parental substance abuse	Parental substance abuse Family violence Parental history of maltreatment Low income Low educational level of mother Stepfather in the home Absent or ill mother Weak bonds with mother Social isolation Few friends during childhood
Psychological Maltreatment	*Neglect*
Parental substance abuse Parental history of maltreatment Lack of parenting skills Adolescent parent Social isolation	Loneliness Social isolation Disorganization Lack of social supports Apathy Family size Parental substance abuse Low income Low education

abuse or neglect is determined to warrant intervention, an initial assessment will be conducted. The purpose of this initial assessment is to verify if child maltreatment has occurred and, if so, the likelihood that it may happen again, who was involved in the maltreatment, and what should happen as a result of the maltreatment. This initial assessment of child maltreatment has three possible outcomes: the report is considered unsubstantiated if there is no evidence that abuse or neglect occurred; the report is ruled inconclusive, meaning that although there are indicators that maltreatment has occurred, the evidence is lacking and statements cannot be corroborated; or the report is substantiated based on strong evidence that the maltreatment occurred or the caregiver admits to the abuse or neglect (Wiehe, 1992).

The primary mandate of child protection agencies is to ensure no further harm to children who are reported as alleged victims of child abuse and neglect. Child protection agencies use a systematic collection of data to determine the degree of potential harm to a child at some future point in time (Doueck, English, DePanfilis, & Moote, 1993). Across the nation the prevailing approach is to combine practice wisdom and risk assessment instruments to create a risk assessment model. In addition to predicting risk of potential maltreatment, these models assist in prioritizing cases (English & Pecora, 1994; Fanshel, Finch, & Grundy, 1994; Jagannathan & Camasso, 1996), and in developing individualized treatment plans based on individual case levels of risk (English & Pecora, 1994). The risk assessment model provides a framework for case assessment, and documentation and is used as the foundation for case planning and service delivery.

Risk Assessment

Pecora et al. (2000) classify the various risk assessment models into four types: matrix, empirical predictor, family assessment scales, and the Child At Risk Field (CARF). The matrix model was one of the first types developed. It uses a table of 16 to 32 factors relating to severity of potential risk to the child. The empirical predictor model focuses on the identification of the small set of risk factors most predictive of child maltreatment. The family assessment scales use behaviorally anchored scales to assess child and family functioning levels and identify areas of concern. CARF is based on the ecological approach and uses open-ended questions and anchored scales to identify risk indicators present in the case.

Although a number of evaluative studies have been conducted on the various types of risk assessment models, the debate continues regarding their accuracy, validity, and predictability. Critics of currently used risk assessment models find that workers receive little training on their use (English, Aubin, Fine, & Pecora, 1993; Gelles, 1996; Wald & Woolverton, 1990). Additionally, factors included on many risk assessment instruments neither predict nor correlate with future abuse and neglect (Lyons, Doueck, & Wodarski, 1996), and they do not have significant predictive validity (English et al., 1993). Throughout the studies, methodological problems have also been documented on risk assessment including small sample sizes, ungeneralizable findings, and threatened statistical conclusion validity (DePanfilis, 1995). Other weaknesses noted are a lack of cultural sensitivity (English et al., 1993) and a predominant focus on deficits rather than on a family's strengths (Wald & Woolverton, 1990). Recognizing the potential utility of these models for improving child protection practices and outcomes, child welfare scholars and practitioners have issued a call for more empirical validation of these approaches (Lyons et al., 1996).

Morton (1998) questions responding to all child maltreatment reports and assessments. He posits that the criminal justice model should be used in those instances where facts substantiate violation of criminal statutes.

However, he also argues that a safety or risk-of-harm standard would focus on the child rather than on "who did what to whom," thus determining which families are in need of services without labeling them with the stigma of child maltreatment. This more positive approach is based on the premise that "use of the strengths perspective rather than the deficit model reframes the nature of the intervention relationship from an involuntary one to a partnership with the child and family" (Holder & Lund, 1995, p. 21).

Following this approach, many child protection agencies have developed a safety assessment to determine the appropriate intervention for those children and families who have been identified as needing services. The safety assessment identifies the strengths of individuals and of the family as a whole that may help protect the child from future harm. In addition, the safety assessment determines areas in which supportive services are needed to ensure continued safety of the child. These safety assessments are in the initial stages and have yet to be evaluated for accurate outcomes.

Further, there are increased mandates for greater accountability and results in the child welfare system's response to child maltreatment. To meet these demands, it is crucial that the system develop an effective assessment framework for interventions with families experiencing child maltreatment. In response, the Child Welfare League of America, with support from the Edna McConnell Clark Foundation, has proposed the development of an "assessment tool kit" that would include the following: screening tools, safety assessment tools, risk assessment tools, and tools and processes that identify family connections, resources, and capacity to care for children (Day, 1999). LeVine and Sallee (1999) suggest that assessments of families engaged in the child welfare system include the family life cycle, the stage of family development, identification of internal and external stressors, a critical analysis of present functioning, and the strengths and challenges of the family members.

Cultural Sensitivity

A major challenge to the development of a comprehensive assessment package is the assurance of cultural sensitivity. According to Lewis-Fernandez and Kleinman (1995), culture should be viewed as a dynamic process influenced by differences in gender, ethnicity, age, class, and race. Building on this definition, Canino and Spurlock (2000) make a cogent plea for the "in-depth understanding of patients' lives, their family myths, and cultural mores—essential if we hope to help troubled children and adolescents" (p. viii).

Although children and families of color have always been disproportionately represented in reports of child maltreatment, Caucasians predominate the child protection workforce. To address cultural sensitivity it is essential that Caucasian practitioners in particular have a keen cultural self-awareness and awareness of others' cultures. A culturally sensitive assessment of families experiencing child maltreatment should take into account cultural influences on the following areas: 1) expectations of child development and behavior; 2) attitudes toward health practices; 3) childrearing practices (sex education, sex roles and expectations, discipline, and social skills development); and 4) family history (role of the extended family, family values, level of acculturation and adaptation to the community, and religion) (Canino & Spurlock, 2000).

A comprehensive, culturally sensitive assessment is crucial to appropriate interventions and positive outcomes for families experiencing child maltreatment. Practitioners in all fields of practice who provide services to abused and neglected children and their families should be familiar with and have access to a cadre of empirically tested assessment tools. Although a number of such tools are currently available, in the field of child protection there is great need for improved assessment instruments and models.

Assessment Tools for Use with Child Maltreatment

Table 9.3 describes the most commonly used tools for assessing child maltreatment. Measures described address issues including risk assessment, program evaluation, and family strengths.

HEALTH PROBLEMS: SUBSTANCE ABUSE, HIV, AND BRAIN INJURY

In the current health care system, families are not always recognized as part of the network of care when a major illness, disease, or injury occurs. The result is that many families are multistressed by the physical complication of the disease and the psychological effects the illness has on the family interactions. This section will survey three health problems that affect many families: substance abuse (alcohol), HIV, and brain injury. These health problems will be examined from the perspective of scope (or epidemiology) of the problem, issues, and interventions.

Substance Abuse

Alcohol abuse has long-range stressful effects on marital relations, marital status, childrearing, and the health of women. In the area of marital relations, numerous studies have documented that the risk of marital violence is higher among men who drink excessively than among moderate drinkers. Murphy and O'Farrell (1997) found greater marital vio-

Table 9.3   Assessment Tools for Families at Risk of Child Maltreatment

Assessment Tools

Abidin, R. R. (1990). *Parenting stress index* (3rd ed.). Charlottesville, VA: Pediatric Psychology Press. This index contains 101 items covering both parent and child domains of stress separate from general life stressors.

Magura, S., Moses, B. S., & Jones, M. J. (1987). *Assessing risk and measuring change in families: The family risk scales.* Washington, DC: Child Welfare League of America. These scales are standardized and measure a child's risk of entering substitute care. It consists of 26 individual scales that apply to a full range of risk situations that bring families into the child welfare system.

Magura, S., & Moses, B. S. (1986). *Outcome measures for child welfare services.* Washington, DC: Child Welfare League of America. This package includes several instruments for assessing individuals and families dealing with child abuse and neglect.

Milner, J. S. (1986). *The child abuse potential inventory: Manual* (2nd ed.). Webster, NC. Pystec is a 160-item self-report instrument designed to identify an individual's potential for physical abuse.

Parenting program evaluation manual published by the National Committee for Prevention of Child Abuse. The manual contains information on over 50 instruments that can be used in the assessment of individuals and families experiencing child abuse and neglect. Prevent Child Abuse, 200 S. Michigan Avenue, 17th floor, Chicago, IL 60604-2404.

Parent-child conflict tactics scale designed by Straus, Hamby, Finkelhor, Moore, & Runyan (1998). The scale is used to measure psychological maltreatment, neglect, and physical and sexual abuse.

Straus, M. A., Hamby, S. L., Finkelhor, D., Moore, O. W., & Runyan, D. (1998). Identification of child maltreatment with the Parent-Child Conflict Tactics Scale. *Child Abuse & Neglect, 22*(4), 249–270.

The family activities inventory: A tool for assessing family strengths developed by the Children's Division of the American Humane Association. This inventory is a strengths-based inventory of parenting skills, beliefs, and practices designed for home visitation services to parent of children (birth through age three). American Humane Association, 63 Inverness Drive E, Englewood, CO 80112-5117.

lence among episodic drinkers than among those who drank steadily. They concluded that the marital relationships of episodic drinkers were marked by significant levels of negativity and coercion, whereas those of steady drinkers were characterized by less negativity and by increasing stability in proportion to the level of drinking. Wakefield, Williams, Yost, and Patterson (1996) state that alcoholic women have more marital difficulties than do women in the general population. More often than alcoholic men, alcoholic women report marital difficulties as a cause for their drinking. However, using measures of marital functioning, couples with an alcoholic wife were more satisfied with each other and themselves in their core functioning than were couples with an alcoholic husband.

Marital status can also be a risk factor for alcoholism. Research has suggested that women who become separated or divorced from a spouse increase their alcohol consumption (Fecaces, Harford, Williams, & Hanna, 1999; Wakefield et al., 1996). Findings from national cross-section surveys indicate that married persons drink less than those who are either separated, divorced, or single and that moving from single to married status is associated with a time-specific decrease in alcohol consumption in situations where alcohol use is a problem, or where child-rearing or positive parenting is at risk. There is a fairly substantial body of research that describes the potential negative side effects on children's lives when parents have alcohol or drug problems. These include physical exposure (e.g., prenatal exposure), impact on development, disrupted family contexts and environments, and psychological/physical harms.

One overlooked group may be mothers. The reported effects of parental alcohol and drug problems in children's lives have been largely based on studies of fathers' substance abuse. Mothers still provide the dominant child care, and their alcohol or drug (AOD) problems may have more direct adverse consequences for children than those of fathers. Miller, Smyth, and Mudar (1999) found that mothers with current or past alcohol or drug problems are more punitive toward their children. Mothers' histories of partner violence and parental violence also predicted higher levels of mother-to-child punitiveness. Violence and AOD problems frequently coexist.

The extent to which women's increased aggression and violence toward their children as a result of AOD problems can cause for following:

- immediate crises that emerge in homes where such violence is prevalent
- long-term consequences for children of abuse and violence
- potential for violent behaviors to be repeated across generations
- violent victimization experiences that present one pathway for the development of alcohol and drug problems later in children's lives

Women's health as well is compromised by excess alcohol consumption. Recent research on the impact of alcohol on women indicates that women's bodies are more biologically vulnerable to the effects of alcohol than are men's. Some of the factors are poor nutrition, differences in metabolism, a pattern of more continuous drinking as compared to binge drinking, body weight or body water, hormonal factors, genetic factors, and use of contraception. Additionally, women who experience alcohol dependence or abuse are more likely to suffer from anemia.

In recent years, there has been much controversy over whether alcoholism should be classified as a physical disease or as a socially determined behavior. There are numerous ways in which the learning environment affects the development and treatment of alcoholism. Therefore, setting the question of whether alcoholism is a disease or not may be less important for treatment than helping people with alcohol problems and their families learn about drinking behaviors in order to change them.

Until this debate is resolved, there are some identified treatment interventions that can help a stressed family deal with an alcohol problem. Much of the intervention research emphasizes the importance of equipping couples and parents with skills and problem-solving techniques to decrease the risk of violent victimization toward family members, particulary children. Evidence suggests that directive, cognitive, and action-oriented treatment approaches are useful.

HIV

At the end of 1996, the World Health Organization (WHO) estimated that, worldwide, 2.5 million adults and 1 million children had AIDS and that about 22 million people were infected with HIV. The ratio of men to women who are infected is estimated to be 6 to 1, but the number of infected women is growing 4 times faster than the number of infected men. After infection with HIV, AIDS is estimated to develop in 8 to 11 years, although this time frame is gradually increasing because of early implementation of treatment (Kaplan & Sadock, 1998).

When a family member is diagnosed with HIV, a myriad of issues emerge—parenting dilemmas, declining health status, socioeconomic challenges, and feelings of guilt and grief. The stresses are enormous when a family member has been diagnosed with HIV, but they are magnified when children are involved. Research reveals that HIV-infected people are now living longer and caring for children at the same time. Thus, the number of children with at least one infected parent is likely to continue to grow (Schuster et al., 2000). This parent is likely to be the mother. Because the HIV epidemic is spreading at a faster rate among women than men (especially young women) and because it is spreading faster among heterosexual than among gay men, we may see an increase in the percentage of HIV-infected mothers who are caring for their children. In one study (Schuster et al., 2000), 26% of women younger than 30 years had conceived children after being diagnosed with HIV.

With regard to health status, women who are HIV infected may suffer more from secondary illnesses associated with HIV than do men. For example, in contrast to the effects of the virus in men, constituted primarily by cancer-related disease processes (e.g., Kaposi's Sarcoma), HIV in women causes organ-specific effects including pelvic inflammatory disease (PID), endometriosis, uterine tumors, cervical cancer, vaginal candidiasis, and higher incidences of some conditions like simple urinary tract infections, and human papillomavirus infection (HPV) (Gabriel, 1996). With all this said, women also tend to be offered less aggressive treatment than men even when they are symptomatic (Crystal & Schlosser, 1999).

The socioeconomic challenges for HIV-infected parents are significant and contribute to family stress. Practical concerns revolve around employment, medical benefits, life insurance, career plans, burial, and child and pet placement. Families will experience a range of emotional stresses in response to the HIV infection. For example, a spouse or lover may feel guilt about possibly having infected the partner. The ill individual may experience anger toward the partner for possibly having been infected by him or her. Families may also experience anticipatory grief, whereas the ill relative may be going through issues of unresolved grief that are likely to intensify depressive and anxious symptoms.

Intervention research has identified two key areas of support for the HIV-infected individual and his or her family members: support groups and psychotherapy groups. Members of a support group can provide the ill individual with emotional support as well as problem-solving advice for financial, medical and estate planning, living arrangements, and medical care and child care issues. Psychotherapy groups help the family and ill relative work on issues of self-blame, self-esteem, and death. The ill individual's significant others may benefit from the attention of a therapist in coping with the illness and the impending loss of a friend or family member. Overall, family members, lovers, and close friends are often important allies in treatment.

Brain Injury

Each year, an estimated 50,000 to 70,000 Americans sustain brain injuries serious enough to leave significant impairments. Epidemiological data report that the vast majority of brain injuries occur in males, with most studies suggesting a two- or three-to-one, male to female ratio. The peak incidence for brain injury is between fifteen and twenty-four years of age. The majority of brain injuries are nonpenetrating, or closed, injuries in which the substance of the brain has not been violated by a foreign object. Motor vehicular accidents account for most injuries (50% to 60%), followed by assaults (10% to 15%) and sports or recreational events (10%). In terms of mental health needs, estimates suggest that between 20% and 60% of (TBI) survivors suffer from a major depressive episode (Brown, Fann, & Grant, 1994). Post-TBI symptoms of anxiety occur in 18% to 60% of injured individuals; patterns of substance abuse and dependence have been investigated with incidence rates of 28% to 32%. Common problems reported by survivors of brain injury are impaired social relations, feelings of estrangement and isolation, difficulty accepting physical and lifestyle changes and difficulty accepting loss of control or competence in day-to-day decision making. Most individuals with severe brain injury require ongoing care and supervision and are thus dependent on their families to meet their daily needs. Unfortunately, most families are not equipped to care for a member with a severe brain injury. Brain injury results in cognitive deficits and behavioral and emotional changes that lead to problems the family must deal with on a daily basis. Families generally have little knowledge about the effects of brain injury, how to manage the associated problems, or how to care for individuals with brain injury (Rosenthal & Hutchins, 1991). Stress results from role adjustments, long-term caretaking responsibilities, and financial burdens (Williams, 1991). In addition, dealing with the brain-injured person's "former self," and feeling trapped and isolated contribute to stress levels.

In general, family stress following brain injury revolves around three areas: isolation, quality of life, and health status. With regard to isolation, studies have shown that friends and relatives may rally around the family in the early stages of recovery but tend to withdraw support and contact over time (Bond, 1983). Clinical experience suggests that outpatient psychological care may be offered to people in the early stages of recovery, but family members may not be ready to receive this form of support at that time. Several years after injury, when problems are finally recognized, relatives may not know how to request services or may be ineligible for them because of insurance or other financial restraints (Gervasio & Kreutzer, 1997).

The compromised quality of life for families who have experienced a family member's brain injury is well known in the rehabilitation community. The caretaking duties of the family can last a lifetime, as many brain injury survivors do not return to an independent lifestyle. Shrinking social networks or and fewer opportunities for respite and leisure activities ultimately place a great burden on the primary caretakers and compromise the quality of life for the entire family unit.

The emotional and physical health status of the family caregiver can be as compromised as that of the survivor after TBI. Hall and colleagues (1994) report an increase in depression, anxiety, use of tranquilizers, alcohol use, and mental health counseling among members who have a relative with traumatic brain injury. In a 15-year longitudinal study by Thomsen (1984) of long-term survivors of brain injury, relatives of people with TBI apparently had a high rate of distress many years postinjury, regardless of injury severity.

Intervention research has identified two areas of support for the family with a brain-injured individual: education and hopefulness. Providing adequate information to families is an important component of successful rehabilitation. Better educating of family members has the potential to encouraging realistic expectations and to promoting effective coping. The goal of family education is to enable the family to reach the competency needed to seek out resources and services. Miller and Borden (1992) argue that education intervention should focus on reducing distress, facilitating coping skills, and promoting the use of social networks to mobilize resources of social and emotional support.

With regard to hopefulness, family members desire honesty from professionals but have a negative response to pessimism. Generally, families stress that health care professionals need to understand the patient's and family's worldview to be able to provide effective care. Families prefer the sharing of probabilities to authoritative (and often inaccurate) predictions that, in turn, further erode the family's trust in getting knowledgeable assistance when they access professional services.

Assessment Methods for Health Problems

Typical problems of this population include stress, substance abuse, and caregiver burden. Table 9.4 lists state of the art measures for assessing health problems (available in Corcoran & Fischer, 2000).

CASE EXAMPLE: INTEGRATIVE SKILLS ASSESSMENT PROTOCOL

Identifying Information

Name: Emily Parker
Date of Birth: 3/16/92
Address: 1201 Fair Avenue, Oakdale
Phone: 555.765.4321 (home), 555.211.1098
People living in the home:

Emily Parker	Client	Female	10 y.o.	Anglo	4th grader
Brad Hunt	Brother	Male	6 y.o.	Anglo	1st grader
Susan Blake	Mother	Female	30 y.o.	Anglo	Secretary
Renee Lewis	Mother's Partner	Female	36 y.o.	Anglo	Cook
Eddie Cantrell	Renee's Son	Male	12 y.o.	Anglo	6th grader
Jessica Cantrell	Renee's Daughter	Female	6 y.o.	Anglo	1st grader

Table 9.4   Assessment Measures for Health Problems

Stress-Arousal (Mackay & Cox)
Adult Health Concerns (Spoth & Dush)
Alcohol Outcomes (Leigh & Stacy)
Drug Abuse (Skinner)
Caregiver Burden (Zarit, Reever, & Bach-Peterson)
Chronic Pain (Jacob, Kerns, Rosenberg, & Haythornthwaite)
Willingness to Care (Abell)

Family income: The family income is between $2,000 and $3,000 per month depending on the collection of child support from fathers. Some months, the child support checks are delayed or remain uncollected. *Presenting problem:* Emily is crying uncontrollably at times, both at home and at school. The teacher complains that Emily sometimes becomes so upset that she must go to the nurse's office. When asked why she is crying, Emily says that she's just sad and doesn't know why. Recently, Emily has begun having nightmares and has expressed anxiety about being separated from her mother. She is having "stomachaches" and does not always want to eat at school. *Previous counseling:* There has been none for Emily, but her mother and her mother's partner, Renee, have attended counseling as a couple. In addition, Emily's mother, Susan, reports that she is being treated for bipolar disorder and that both she and Renee have sought counseling separately for substance abuse issues. *Source of data:* In-office assessment visit with Emily and her mother. Additional information was obtained from the other children in the home, the pediatrician, the school nurse, teachers, and the school counselor.

Nature of Presenting Problem.   In the six months since school started, the teacher has observed a decline in Emily's schoolwork. She says that Emily seems tired and unfocused; she says that Emily is listless in class and often prefers sitting with her (the teacher) during recess instead of playing with the other children. At times, when she looks into the classroom, the teacher sees Emily sitting at her desk with her head down, crying softly. At these times, the teacher tries to comfort Emily, but she says that Emily is not always consolable. If the crying becomes distracting for the class, the teacher sends Emily to the nurse's office. Some days, Emily asks to go to the nurse's office because she has a stomachache. The teacher is not sure if Emily has a real stomachache or if something else is bothering her. The teacher worries that Emily is not getting enough rest or that something unusual is happening at home. She has called Emily's mother to report these concerns.

Emily's mother reports similar behavior at home. She says that Emily seems to be having trouble sleeping—that Emily goes to sleep at around 9 pm but that she is often awake again around midnight for an hour or more. She comes to her mother in the night and asks her mother to sleep with her. Emily's mother usually just takes Emily back to bed and spends a few minutes with her before returning to her own bed. She says that on many mornings Emily is so tired that she is hard to wake up for school. Emily tells her mother that she "can't think" at school. She expresses worry about her schoolwork, saying that she is too tired to do her homework and that it is boring anyway. About the stomachaches, Emily says that she has them after she eats. She cannot tell what causes them, but sometimes she skips lunch at school to avoid having a stomachache afterward. Emily's mother thinks that because Emily goes all day without eating, her stomach is upset by dinner, too. Often Emily eats very little of what is prepared for her.

Emily's mother reports, too, that Emily cries for no apparent reason. When she arrives home from work, she will find Emily on her bed crying. When she asks Emily what is wrong, Emily says that she doesn't know. Her mother reports that she spends extra time to console Emily, but she admits that the problem is not improving. Emily's brother and the other children in the home are beginning to ask what is wrong with her. Emily has been asked by her mom if the other children are mean or if things are going badly at school, but Emily always responds no, and that she is just sad. Until now, Emily's mother has regarded this problem as a "phase." She says that Emily has always been a sensitive child and that she has always cried easily if teased or in trouble. However, this spontaneous crying is new. She says that she took Emily to the pediatrician a week ago to see if anything was wrong physically. After a full checkup, the doctor could not find anything seriously wrong, though he did prescribe some medication for Emily's stomachaches.

Emily's teacher reports that Emily has many friends at school. She says that Emily is generally easygoing. In fact, she believes that, at times, Emily does not stand up for herself, that she will allow other girls to take advantage of her rather than cause a conflict. Nevertheless, Emily plays appropriately and displays appropriate empathy and social skills among her peers. The teacher added that Emily's early performance in class was much better than her current work. The teacher believes that this decline is the result of whatever stress Emily is enduring and not the result of increasing difficulty of the work. She believes that Emily is capable of performing well in school.

The school nurse reports that when Emily comes to her office, she is often too busy to devote much individual time to her. On those occasions, Emily just lies on a cot for a while and cries. After about thirty minutes, she will get up, clean her face, and return to class. If the nurse has the time, they talk together about what is happening in the classroom and at home. Emily says everything is all right, but she does complain of stomachaches. The school nurse says that she contacted Emily's mother to report the stomachaches and that her mother agreed to bring some antacid tablets to school to see if these would alleviate the symptoms. The nurse expresses concern that Emily is under stress that she is unable to talk about. She contacted the school counselor about her concerns just this week.

The school counselor says that she has met with Emily only once so far, but she has observed her in class on two occasions. She plans to see her weekly during the next several weeks to see if Emily is appropriate for group work.

Emily demonstrates several strengths. Despite her lack of sleep, her stomachaches, and her tearfulness, she is able to maintain a B average. In addition, she has many friends whom she claims to enjoy. Her mother seems genuinely concerned for her and says that she will work with the school to help Emily overcome her difficulties.

The school prioritizes the problems (with 1 being the most severe) in the following order: 1) excessive crying or sadness, 2) time away from the classroom and in the nurse's office, 3) inability to focus on schoolwork. Emily's mother prioritizes the problems similarly: (1) sadness, (2) being unable to sleep, (3) stomachaches.

Client Intrapersonal Issues. *Cognitive functioning:* Emily's school achievement tests indicate that she is capable of high classroom achievement. She consistently scores in the 90th percentile in language and math. Neither her pediatrician nor her mother reports any type of cognitive developmental delay. In fact, she has always made mostly A's in school. Her cumulative file reveals that she might be eligible for the talented and gifted program if her performance in fourth grade is good enough. According to her mother, Emily achieved most developmental milestones ahead of schedule; for example, she was able at one year old to say two- and three-word sentences. The teacher reports that Emily is capable of working independently in all subjects and that she will help her classmates with their work if she has finished her own. Sometimes she even works ahead in math, though she has stopped doing that lately.

Emotional functioning: During the assessment visit, Emily was attentive and polite. She sat very close to her mother, seeming rather shy, but she answered all questions directed to her clearly and without hesitation. She displayed no disturbance or inappropriate affect. When asked why she had been crying so much, she just looked at the floor and shrugged. She said that her stomach is better, so she thinks the medicine is helping. At one point, she mentioned that she did not want her mother to worry about her.

Behavioral functioning: Emily's mother reports that Emily has always been easy to discipline and easy to direct. She says that Emily does her homework without prompting and that she helps out with her younger brother and with Renee's daughter, Jessica, by helping them get dressed and by playing with them while her mother cooks dinner. At those rare times when Emily needs correction, her mother reports that she is always remorseful and worried that she has been "bad." Emily's mother says that Emily may, in fact, be "too good," that is, more responsible than is typical of her age. Until now, however, Emily has never displayed any problems coping with her responsibilities. Emily expresses some worry that if she continues to cry at school, the other children may not want to play with her. Someone has already called her a "baby."

Physiologic functioning: Emily's medical records reveal basically normal development. Emily is in the 50th percentile for height and the 75th percentile for weight, which is not unusual for girls this age. Her immunizations are up-to-date, and she currently takes only Nexium to help settle her stomach. Her illness history is not remarkable, although she did have a broken arm that required setting when she was five years old. The injury was caused from falling out of a tree, and her arm seems to have healed without incident. Emily has had only chickenpox and minor colds and infections that have responded to conservative medical intervention. Emily's fine motor skills appear to be advanced in that she writes in cursive exclusively and legibly. She is not as adept with gross motor skills. Never an athlete, Emily is awkward in sports and prefers to avoid them; she has not even learned to ride a bike. Her mother reports that Emily prefers writing and drawing to being outside. She has attributed this to the tree accident, believing that Emily fears getting hurt again. The PE teacher reports that Emily is never chosen first in team sports but that she does participate, and she is typically chosen early because the children like her. She says that Emily's awkwardness in gross motor skills would likely disappear with more activity in sports.

Developmental considerations: All developmental milestones have been achieved within normal time ranges; some have been reached early, such as speech and fine motor development. Emily's birth history reveals that she was delivered spontaneously and without complications at thirty-nine weeks gestation and weighed seven pounds, four ounces.

Client Interpersonal Issues: Family.   Emily resides in a three-bedroom apartment with her mother, her younger brother, her mother's partner, and the partner's two children. The boys sleep in one room, the girls in another, and the mothers in a third. Emily's mother reports that she finished high school in a small town and married her high school sweetheart, Emily's father, Van Parker. She says that they were already separated when Emily was born two years later. She says that she and Van were too young to be married and that they argued all the time. She sought counseling at this time and was referred to a psychiatrist who diagnosed her with bipolar disorder. In the last ten years, she has been hospitalized three times with symptoms from this disorder—once when Emily was a baby, again when Emily was three, and again when Emily was five. Mr. Parker does not see Emily regularly; but his paycheck is garnished for child support, and his parents see Emily for two weeks each summer. They live on a farm, and Emily seems happy to go there to visit.

She is already worrying, however, about having to go this summer, saying that she does not want to leave her mother.

Emily's mother says that she left the small town after her first "breakdown" in order to get away from her former husband and her own family. She moved to Oakdale because she thought that she would have better opportunities for work. She has worked as a clerk and is now a secretary for a home mortgage company. She and Emily lived alone, until they met Barry Blake whom Emily's mother married when Emily was almost two. Emily's mother admits that she married for security but quickly found that life with Barry was anything but secure. They fought physically and drank heavily in their time together; she was hospitalized once during this time for depression and alcohol abuse. She finally moved away from Barry when Emily was five, but she says that he continued to harass her until her new boyfriend, Mr. Hunt, threatened him one evening. She and Mr. Hunt dated for only a short time before she discovered that she was pregnant with her second child, Blake. At this time, she sent Emily to live with her paternal grandparents and spent about six weeks in a private psychiatric hospital.

Since Emily's mother never married Mr. Hunt, she became the single mother of two children. About three years ago, she met Renee Lewis and fell in love. They moved in together after dating for two months. Apparently, all of the children get along well, and both women love all the children as their own. Even so, Emily's mohter admits that things are not perfect. She says that Ms. Lewis also has a history of emotional problems and that they argue and fight physically at times. She says that she is concerned about Ms. Lewis's drug and alcohol problems but that she is able to control her own impulses with alcohol because she can see that drinking makes the fights worse. Recently, she and Ms. Lewis have talked about separating; however, they are dependent on one another financially and for help with the children. Ms. Lewis is able to be home when the children come home from school, and Emily's mother is able to stay with them at night while Ms. Lewis works. Their combined income barely meets all of the expenses.

Emily's younger brother, Brad, is healthy and developing normally, although he is not as advanced as Emily. He struggles with reading in first grade but remains on level. Teachers report that he is easily frustrated with schoolwork and sometimes demonstrates angry, even somewhat aggressive, behavior toward classmates. They add, however, that he responds well to discipline and shows some remorse for his actions. If he continues to struggle with reading and language, teachers say that they will ask the school diagnostician to test him for possible learning disabilities. When asked about his sister, Brad openly admits that he loves her and thinks she is a good big sister.

The other children in the home, Eddie and Jessica, attend the same school. They do not display major difficulties, though Eddie has been diagnosed with ADHD, and Jessica is described as shy. Teachers say that Eddie can be difficult to control if he is not taking his medication and that they often must remind his mother to send his medication to school. Without the medication, Eddie cannot focus on work and he finds it hard to sit still in class. Jessica displays no symptoms of ADHD. Instead, she seems overly quiet, often avoiding other children. She prefers to play with one person at a time and seems overwhelmed by rambunctious playground activities. Since school has started, though, she is showing increasing tolerance for the active school environment. Teachers believe that she will achieve normally in school, even if she remains somewhat socially immature. All of the children speak of one another as if they are siblings, and all speak highly of Emily. Jessica notes that Emily is sad much of the time. She says this makes her sad, too.

Emily's mother and Ms. Lewis evenly divide parenting responsibilities. Even though Ms. Lewis works on weekends, she works in the evenings and devotes much of her day to activities with the children. All of the children express affection for both women, yet all of the children report that the two women fight a lot. Emily's mother admits that the stress of her job, her finances, the children, her own struggles with mental health, and her fights with Ms. Lewis interfere with her ability to parent well. She is close to Emily, and she tries to provide security for her, but she worries that Emily's crying may be the result of their tumultuous homelife.

Client Interpersonal Issues: School. Emily says that she likes school. She enjoys learning about new things and thinks that she is a good student. The school counselor reports that she has observed Emily on two occasions. On the first occasion, she noticed that Emily worked independently and easily on her schoolwork. She seemed focused and confident. On finishing her work, she sat at her desk reading a book until the class was ready to move on to the next assignment. From this observation, the counselor found Emily to be bright and mature.

The second observation was surprising to the counselor. She said that Emily was simply staring at her paper, making no attempt to work the problems. As she sat at her desk, Emily began to cry, tears slipping over her cheeks. Eventually, she put her head on the desk and began to sob. When the teacher came to her, Emily spoke with the teacher briefly before getting up to go to the nurse's office. The counselor walked to the nurse's office with Emily, patting her her on the back and asking her what was wrong. Emily just replied that she did not know. The counselor thinks that Emily is a bright child who copes well in general with schoolwork and with peers, but she finds Emily's tearfulness disturbing and, perhaps, an indication of deeper problems either emotionally or at home.

Client Interpersonal Issues: Peers.   Emily says that she has lots of friends. She can name three "best" friends, but she adds that she likes other people, too. Teachers confirm that Emily plays well with other children and often assumes the role of peacemaker in disputes. They say that she enjoys the quieter play of girls but that she will participate with large group activities of boys and girls on the playground. The teachers also say that some children rely on Emily to help them with their work, and Emily is willing and able to provide this support.

Context and Social Support Networks.   This family is isolated from the support of extended family. Neither partner maintains close contact with her own parents and siblings. Emily's mother has sought some help from her family, but she says that they do not approve of her lifestyle and will not acknowledge Ms. Lewis as her partner. She says that she has never met Ms. Lewis's family. Because of their busy schedules, they also do not have a large network of friends. They have met some people in the apartment complex; and these neighbors have, at times, intervened in their fights, sometimes taking the children away from the conflict. Overall, however, they do not have a well-defined social network.

Both women have friends and acquaintances at work, but Emily's mother is not "out" at work. Her friends there believe that Ms. Lewis is simply a roommate who helps with expenses. Ms. Lewis's friends at work are aware of the nature of the relationship, but they do not socialize with the couple.

Emily's mother expresses her desire to make this family work, but she admits that she is tired of the conflict and that she is not sure she can continue with things as they are. She loves Ms. Lewis's children, but she says that even the burden of extra children makes her life harder. She has no plan for supporting herself and her children without the help and financial resources Ms. Lewis provides. She worries that she may have another "breakdown" if her life does not improve.

Measurement.   *Family functioning:* Administer the Hudson Index of Family Relations (Hudson, 1982) to assess overall family function and an anger diary to monitor parental fighting.

Individual functioning: 1) Design a daily log for Emily's mother and her teachers to determine the triggers for Emily's crying episodes, when they occur, and how long they last. 2) Design a similar log to track stomach problems, noting what Emily eats and what occurs before each stomachache, to determine whether the attacks are related to food or to emotions. 3) Administer the Child Depression Scale to determine the level of Emily's depression.

BOX 9.1
Treatment Plan: Emily Parker

Problem: Crying, stomachaches, and parental fighting

Definitions: Child crying at home and at school, complaints of stomachaches that interfere with schoolwork, parents' disagreements that escalate to yelling and screaming

Goals: 1. To reduce parental fights
2. To reduce child's depression, associated symptom of crying, and stomachaches

Objectives:	Interventions:
1. Parents learn anger control	1. Teach parents anger management and conflict resolution
2. a. Reduce child depression b. Reduce tearful episodes c. Eliminate stomachaches	2. Cognitive therapy for depression

Diagnosis: 296.2 Major Depressive Disorder

SUMMARY

Chapter 9 discussed families who are multistressed by external sources: gay and lesbian families, families experiencing child maltreatment, and families with health problems. For gay and lesbian families, the couple's friendship and couples with children were the two assessment areas reviewed. Families experiencing child maltreatment have been categorized according to type of maltreatment: physical, sexual, or psychological, or physical neglect abuse. Important areas for assessment for this group are risk assessment and cultural sensitivity. Three types of health problems families experience also were reviewed, including substance abuse, HIV, and brain injury. Each problem was reviewed in terms of its scope, relevant issues, and intervention research.

Assessment techniques were suggested in each of the three areas. Measurement is similar for these families as for families described in preceding chapters. Finally, a case example was presented using the integrative skills assessment protocol and treatment plan presented earlier in the text.

STUDY QUESTIONS

1. Discuss the assessment issues for the multistressed family populations presented in this chapter. What are the similarities and differences in assessment method for each of the three groups presented here?

Chapter 9 Assessing Families Who Are Multistressed

2. Consider the case of Emily, presented at the end of this chapter. Suppose her mother had divorced and moved in with a male partner. How would the assessment have been different?

3. Chose a family you know that is experiencing one of the problems described in the chapter and write an assessment using the integrative skills assessment protocol. Design a comprehensive measurement and treatment plan. Describe any difficulties you encountered.

REFERENCES

Allen, K. R., & Demo, D. H. (1995). The families of lesbians and gay men: A new frontier family research. *Journal of Marriage and the Family, 57,* 111–127.

Appleby, G. A., & Anastas, J. W. (1998). *Not just a passing phase: Social work with gay, lesbian, and bisexual people.* New York: Columbia University Press.

Baptiste, D. A., Jr. (1987). Psychotherapy with gay/lesbian couples and their children in "stepfamilies": A challenge for marriage and family therapists. *Journal of Homosexuality, 14,* 223–238.

Belsky, J. (1980). Child maltreatment: An ecological integration. *American Psychologist, 35,* 320–335.

Belsky, J., & Vondura, J. (1989). Lessons from child abuse: The determinants of parenting. In D. Cicchetti, & V. Carlson (Eds.), *Child maltreatment: Theory and research on the causes and consequences of child abuse and neglect* (pp. 153–202). New York: Cambridge University Press.

Benkov, L. (1994). *Reinventing the family: The emerging story of lesbian and gay partners.* New York: Crown.

Berger, R. M. (1982/1996). *Gay and gray: The older homosexual man* (2nd ed.). Binghamton, NY: Haworth.

Berger, R. M. (1990). Men together: Understanding the gay couple. *Journal of Homosexuality, 19,* 31–49.

Bigner, J. (1996). Working with gay fathers. In J. Laird & R. Green (Eds.), *Lesbians and gays in couples and families* (pp. 370–403). San Francisco: Jossey-Bass.

Bigner, J. J., & Jacobson, R. B. (1992). Adult responses to child behavior and attitudes toward fathering: Gay and nongay fathers. *Journal of Homosexuality, 23,* 99–112.

Blumstein, P., & Schwartz, P. (1983). *American couples.* New York: William Morrow.

Bond, M. (1983). Effects on the family system. In M. Rosenthal, E. Griffith, M. Bond, & J. P. Miller (Eds.), *Rehabilitation of the head injured adult.* Philadelphia: F. A. Davis.

Brown, S. J., Fann, J. R., & Grant, I. (1994). Postconcussional disorder: Time to acknowledge a common source of neurobehavioral morbidity. *Journal of Neuropsychiatry and Clinical Neurosciences, 6,* 15–22.

Bryant, S., & Demian (1994). Relationship characteristics of American gay and lesbian couples: Findings from a national survey. *Journal of Gay and Lesbian Social Services, 1,* 101–117.

Canino, I. A., & Spurlock, J. (2000). *Culturally diverse children and adolescents: Assessment, diagnosis, and treatment* (2nd ed). New York: Guilford.

Caron, S. L., & Ulin, M. (1997). Closeting and the quality of lesbian relationships. *Families in Society: The Journal of Contemporary Human Services, 78,* 413–419.

Clunis, D. M., & Green, G. D. (2000). *Lesbian couples: A guide to creating healthy relations* (2nd ed.). Seattle, WA: Seal.

Cohn, D. (1995, May). Courts send mixed messages in custody cases. *Washington Post, p. 87.*

Corcoran, K. & Fischer, J. (2000). *Measures for clinical practice: A sourcebook* (3rd ed., Vols. 1 & 2). New York: The Free Press.

Cramer, D. (1986). Gay parents and their children: A review of research and practical implications. *Journal of Counseling and Development, 64,* 504–507.

Crawford, S. (1987). Lesbian families: Psychosocial stress and the family-building process. In Boston Lesbian Psychologies Collective (Eds.), *Lesbian psychologies* (pp. 195–214). Urbana: University of Illinois Press.

Crystal, S., & Schlosser, L. (1999). The HIV-mental health challenge. In A. V. Horwitz & T. L. Scheid (Eds.), *A handbook for the study of mental health* (pp. 526–549). New York: Cambridge University Press.

D'Augelli, A. R., & Garnets, L. D. (1995). Lesbian, gay, and bisexual communities. In A. R. D'Augelli & C. J. Patterson (Eds.), *Lesbians, gay, and bisexual identitiesover the lifespan* (pp. 293–320). New York: Oxford University Press.

Day, P. (1999). Rethinking assessment in an evolving child welfare system. *Protecting Children, 15*(3/4), 19–20.

DePanfilis, D. (1995). *The epidemiology of child maltreatment recurrences.* Unpublished doctoral dissertation, University of Maryland.

Doueck, H. J., English D. J., DePanfilis, D., & Moote, G. T. (1993). Decision-making in child protective services. *Social Service Review, 65,* 112–132.

Eldridge, N. S., & Gilbert, L. A. (1990). Correlates of relationship satisfaction in lesbian couples. *Psychology of Women Quarterly, 14,* 43–62.

English, D. J., Aubin, S. W., Fine. D., & Pecora, P. J. (1993). *Improving the accuracy and cultural sensitivity of risk assessment in child abuse and neglect cases.* Seattle, WA: University of Washington, School of Social Work.

English, D. J., & Pecora, P. J. (1994). Risk assessment as a practice method in child protective services. *Child Welfare, 73,* 451–473.

Fanshel, D., Finch, S. J., Grundy, J. F. (1994). Testing the measurement properties of risk assessment instruments in child protective services. *Child Abuse & Neglect, 18,* 1073–1084.

Fecaces, M., Harford, T., Williams, G., & Hanna, E. (1999). Alcohol consumption and divorce rates in the United States. *Journal of Studies of Alcohol, 60,* 647–652.

Fredriksen, K. I. (1999). Family caregiving responsibilities among lesbian and gay men. *Social Work, 44,* 142–155.

Gabriel, M. (1996). Aids trauma and support group therapy. New York: Simon & Schuster.

Gelles, R. J. (1996). *The book of David: How preserving families can cost children's lives.* New York: Basic Books.

Gervasio, A., & Kreutzer, J. (1997). Kinship and family members' psychological distress after brain injury: A large sample study. *Journal of Head Trauma Rehabiliatation, 12*(3), 14–26.

Golombok, S., Spener, A., & Rutter, M. (1983). Children in lesbian and single-parent households: Psychosexual and psychiatric appraisal. *Journal of Child Psychology, 24*, 551–572.

Golombok, S., & Tasker, F. (1996). Do parents influence the sexual orientation of their children? Findings from a longitudinal study of lesbian families. *Developmental Psychology, 32*, 3–11.

Greene, B. (Ed.) (1997). *Ethnic and cultural diversity among lesbians and gay men.* Thousand Oaks, CA: Sage.

Greene, B., & Boyd-Franklin, N. (1996). African American lesbians: Issues in couples therapy. In R. Green, J. G. Mandel, M. E. Hotvedt, J. Gray, & L. Smith (1986). Lesbian mothers and their children: A comparison with solo parent heterosexual mothers and their children. *Archives of Sexual Behavior, 15*, 167–184.

Greene, R., Mandel, J. G., Hotvedt, M. E., Gray, J., & Smith, L. (1986). Lesbian mothers and their children: A comparison with solo parent heterosexual mothers and their children. *Archives of Sexual Behavior, 15*, 167–184.

Hall, K., Karazmark, P., Stevens, M., Englander, J., O'Hare, P., & Wright, J. (1994). Family stressors in traumatic brain injury: A two year follow-up. *Archives of Physical Medicine Rehabilitation, 75*, 876–884.

Hargaden, H., & Llewellin, S. (1996). Lesbian and gay parenting issues. In D. Davies & C. Neal (Eds.), *Pink therapy: A guide for counselors and therapists working with LGB clients* (pp. 116–130). Philadelphia: Open University Press.

Hare, J. (1994). Concerns and issues faced by families headed by a lesbian couple. *Families in Society, 75*, 27–35.

Hartman, A. (1996). Social policy as a context for lesbian and gay families: The political is personal. In J. Laird & R. J. Green (Eds.), *Lesbians and gays in couples and families* (pp. 69–850). San Francisco: Jossey-Bass.

Holder, W., & Lund, T. R. (1995). Translating risks to positive outcomes: Outcome-oriented case management from risk assessment information. *The APSAC Advisor, 8*(4), 20–24.

Hostetler, A. J., & Coher, B. J. (1997). Partnership, singlehood, and the lesbian and gay life course: A research agenda. *Journal of Gay, Lesbian, and Bisexual Identity, 2*, 199–230.

Hudson, W. (1982). *The clinical measurement package: A field manual.* Chicago: Dorsey.

Jagannathan, R., & Camasso, M. J. (1996). Risk assessment in child protective services: A canonical analysis of the case management function. *Child Abuse & Neglect, 20*, 599–612.

James, S. E., & Murphy, B. C. (1998). Gay and lesbian relationships in a changing social context. In C. J. Patterson & A. R. D'Augelli (Eds.), *Lesbian, gay, and bi-*

sexual identities in families: Psychological perspectives (pp. 99–121). New York: Oxford University Press.

Kaplan, H., & Sadock, B. (1998). *Synopsis of psychiatry* (8th ed.). Baltimore: Williams & Wilkins.

Kitzinger, C., & Coyle, A. (1995). Lesbian and gay couples: Speaking of difference. *The Psychologist, 8,* 64–69.

Kurdek, L. A. (1988). Perceived social support in gays and lesbians in cohabiting relationships. *Journal of Personality and Social Psychology, 54,* 504–509.

Kurdek, L. A. (1991). Correlates of relationship satisfaction in cohabiting gay and lesbian couples: Integration of contextual, investment, and problem-solving models. *Journal of Personality and Social Psychology, 61,* 910–922.

Kurdek, L. A. (1994). The nature and correlates of relationship quality in gay, lesbian, and heterosexual cohabiting couples: A test of the contextual, investment, and discrepancy models. In B. Greene & G. M. Herek (Eds.), *Lesbian and gay psychology: Theory, research, and clinical applications* (pp. 133–135). Thousand Oaks, CA: Sage.

Kurdek, L. A. (1995). Developing changes in relationship quality in gay and lesbian cohabiting couples. *Developmental Psychology, 31,* 86–94.

Kurdek, L. A. (1997). Relation between neuroticism and dimensions of relationship commitment: Evidence from gay, lesbian, and heterosexual couples. *Journal of Family Psychology, 11,* 109–124.

Leiter, R. A. (1997). *National survey of state laws.* Detroit, MI: Gale Research.

LeVine, E. S., & Sallee, A. L. (1999). *Child welfare: Clinical theory and practice.* Dubuque, IA: Eddie Bowers.

Lewis-Fernandez, R., & Kleinman, A. (1995). Cultural psychiatry: Theoretical, clinical, and research issues. *Psychiatric Clinics of North America, 18*(3), 433–448.

Lyons, P., Doueck, H. J., & Wodarski, J. S. (1996). Risk assessment for child protective services: A review of the empirical literature on instrument performance. *Social Work Research, 20,* 143–155.

Martin, A. (1993). *The lesbian and gay parenting handbook.* New York: Harper-Collins.

Matthews, C. R., & Lease, S. H. (2000). Focus on lesbian, gay, and bisexual families. In R. M. Perez, K. A. DeBord, & K. J. Bieschke (Eds.), *Handbook of counseling and psychotherapy with lesbian, gay, and bisexual clients* (pp. 249–273). Washington, DC: American Psychological Association.

McAllister, T. (1997). Evaluation of brain injury related behavioral disturbances in community mental health centers. *Community Mental Health Journal, 33*(4), 341–358.

McLeod, A., & Crawford, I. (1998). The postmodern family: An examination of the psychosocial and legal perspectives of gay and lesbian parenting. In G. M. Herek (Ed.), *Stigma and sexual orientation: Understanding prejudice against lesbians, gay men, and bisexuals* (pp. 211–222). Thousand Oaks, CA: Sage.

Meyer, J. (1990). Guess who's coming to dinner this time? A study of gay intimate relationships and the support for those relationships. *Marriage & Family Review, 14,* 59–82.

Miller, F. E., & Borden, W. (1992). Family caregivers of persons with neuropsychiatric illness: A stress and coping perspective. In S. C. Yudofsky & R. E. Hales (Eds.), *The American psychiatric press textbook of neuropsychiatry* (2nd ed.). Washington, DC: American Psychiatric Press.

Miller, B., Smyth, W., & Mudar, P. (1999). Mother's alcohol and other drug problems and their punitiveness toward their children. *Journal of Studies of Alcohol, 60*, 632–642.

Murphy, B. C. (1994). Difference and diversity: Gay and lesbian couples. *Social Services for Gay and Lesbian Couples, 1*, 5–31.

Murphy, C. M., & O'Farrell, T. J. (1997). Couple communication patterns of maritally aggressive and nonaggressive male alcoholics. *Journal of Studies of Alcohol, 58*, 83–90.

O'Connell, A. (1993). Voices from the heart: The developmental impact of a mother's lesbianism on her adolescent children. *Smith College Studies in Social Work, 63*, 281–299.

Patterson, C. J. (1992). Children of lesbian and gay men. *Journal of Sex Research, 30*, 62–69.

Patterson, C. J. (1995). Lesbian mothers, gay fathers, and their children. In A. R. D'Augelli & C. J. Patterson (Eds.), *Lesbian, gay, and bisexual identities over the lifespan: Psychological perspectives* (pp. 262–290). Oxford: Oxford University Press.

Patterson, C. J., & Chan, R. W. (1996). Gay fathers and their children. In R. P. Cabaj & T. S. Stein (Eds.), *Textbook of homosexuality and mental health* (pp. 371–393). Washington, DC: American Psychiatric Press.

Patterson, D. G., & Schwartz, P. (1994). The social construction of conflict in intimate same-sex couples. In D. D. Cahn (Ed.), *Conflict in personal relationships* (pp. 3–26). Hillsdale, NJ: Erlbaum.

Pecora, P. J., Whittaker, J. K., Maluccio, A. N., & Barth, R. P. (2000). *The child welfare challenge* (2nd ed.). New York: Aldine de Gruyter.

Peplau, L. A. (1993). Lesbian and gay relationships. In L. D. Garnets & D. C. Kimmel (Eds.), *Psychological perspectives on lesbian & gay male experiences* (pp. 395–419). New York: Columbia University Press.

Rand, C., Graham, D. L., & Rawlings, E. (1982). Psychological health and factors the court seeks to control in lesbian mother custody trials. *Journal of Homosexuality, 8*, 27–39.

Results of Poll. (1989, June 6). *San Francisco Examiner*, p. A-19.

Rosenblum, D. M. (1991). Custody rights of gay and lesbian parents. *Villanova Law Review, 36*, 1665–1696.

Rosenbluth, S. C., & Steil, J. M. (1995). Predictors of intimacy for women in heterosexual and homosexual couples. *Journal of Social and Personal Relationships, 12*, 163–175.

Rosenthal, M., & Hutchins, B. (1991). Interdisciplinary family education in head injury rehabilitation. In M. Williams & T. Kay (Eds.), *Head injury: A family matter*. Baltimore: Paul H. Brookes Publishing.

Savin-Williams, R. C. (1998). ". . . and then I became gay": Young men's stories. New York: Routledge.

Schuster, M., Kanouse, D., Morton, S., Bozzette, S., Miu, A., Scott, G., & Shapiro, M. (2000). HIV-infected parents and their children in the United States. American Journal of Public Health, 90(7), 1074–1081.

Scrivner, R., & Eldridge, N. S. (1995). Lesbian and gay family psychology. In R. H. Mikesell & D. D. Lusterman (Eds.), Integrating family therapy: Handbook of family psychology and systems theory (pp. 327–345). Washington, DC: American Psychological Association.

Segal-Sklar, S. (1996). Lesbian parenting: Radical or retrograde? In K. Jay (Ed.), Dyke life: A celebration of the lesbian experience (pp. 174–191). New York: Basic Books.

Serovich, J. M., Skeen, P., Walters, L. H., & Robinson, B. E. (1993). In-law relationships when a child is homosexual. Journal of Homosexuality, 26, 57–75.

Shapiro, J. (1996). Custody and conduct: How the law fails lesbian and gay parents and their children. Indiana Law Journal, 71, 623–621.

Shernoff, M. (1995). Male couples and their relationship styles. Journal of Gay & Lesbian Social Services, 2, 43–57.

Shernoff, M. (1996). Gay men choosing to be fathers. In M. Shernoff (Ed.), Human services for gay people: Clinical and community practice (pp. 41–54). Binghamton, NY: Harrington Park.

Stiglitz, E. (1990). Caught between two worlds: The impact of a child on a lesbian couple's relationship. Women & Therapy, 10, 99–116.

Tasker, F. L., & Golombok, S. (1997). Growing up in a lesbian family: Effects on child development. New York: Guilford.

Thomsen, I. V. (1984). Late outcome of very severe blunt head trauma: A 10-15 year second follow-up. Journal of Neurosurgical Psychiatry, 47, 260–268.

Turner, P. H., Scadden, L., & Harris, M. B. (1990). Parenting in gay and lesbian families. Journal of Gay and Lesbian Psychotherapy, 1, 55–66.

U.S. Department of Health and Human Services, Administration on Children, Youth and Families. (1999). Child maltreatment in 1997: Reports from the states to the National Child Abuse and Neglect Data System. Washington, DC: U.S. Government Printing Office.

Wakefield, P., Williams, R., Yost, E., & Patterson, K. (1996). Couple therapy for alcoholism—A cognitive behavioral treatment manual. New York: Guilford.

Wald, M. S., & Woolverton, M. (1990). Risk assessment: The emperors new clothes. Child Welfare, 69, 483–511.

Wayment, H., & Peplau, L. A. (1995). Social support and well-being among lesbian and heterosexual women: A structural modeling approach. Personality and Social Psychology Bulletin, 21, 1189–1199.

Weinberg, M. S., Williams, C. J., & Pryor, D. W. (1994). Dual attraction: Understanding bisexuality. New York: Oxford University Press.

Weinstock, J. S. (1998). Lesbian, gay, bisexual, and transgendered friendships in adulthood. In C. J. Patterson & A. R. D'Augelli (Eds.), *Lesbian, gay, and bisexual identities in families: Psychological perspectives* (pp. 122–153). New York: Oxford University Press.

Weston, K. (1994). Building gay families: In G. Handlel & G. G. Whitechurch (Eds.), *The psychosocial interior of the family* (4th ed., pp. 525–533). New York: Aldine de Gruyter.

Weston, K. (1997). *Families we choose* (2nd ed.). NY: Columbia University.

Wiehe, V. R. (1992). *Working with child abuse and neglect.* Itasca, IL: Peacock.

Williams, J. M. (1991). Family support. In M. Williams & T. Kay (Eds.), *Head injury: A family matter* (pp. 00–00). Baltimore: Paul H. Brookes Publishing.

CHAPTER 10

Multicultural Assessment

Dorie J. Gilbert

Diverse value orientations, life experiences, and worldviews are all implicit within the term *multiculturalism*. In our increasingly multicultural society, social work practitioners are challenged to demonstrate an understanding of how factors like race/ethnicity, gender, sexual orientation, age, and differing physical and mental abilities affect our practice with clients. This chapter focuses on the influence of race/ethnicity or ethnocultural factors on a client's assessment. Wong (2000) aptly notes that as practitioners are asked more frequently to evaluate clients who are of different ethnic, cultural, or language backgrounds than themselves, they are "finding few resources to aid them" (p. 43). Culture does affect the assessment process; however, the ethnocentrism of the U.S. majority culture has created a situation in which our assessment procedures and measurement instruments have not fully considered culturally based ways of thinking, feeling, and behaving that may be outside of the majority (Eurocentric) cultural perspective. Zayas, Torres, Malcolm, and DesRosiers (1996) have identified four elements of culturally sensitive practice: 1) being aware of the existence of differences, 2) having knowledge of the client's culture, 3) distinguishing between culture and pathology in assessment, and 4) taking culture into account in therapy. These criteria accurately reflect the importance of culturally competent assessment, without which, well-intentioned practitioners are acting unethically (Dana, 2000; Devore & Schlesinger, 1996).

This chapter covers the limitations of many assessment methods with four groups (American Indians/Alaska Natives, African Americans/ Blacks, Hispanics/Latinos, and Asian Americans) and provides an overview of ethnic-sensitive assessment strategies. Numerous ethnic groups now live in the United States, and it is impossible to cover all of these different groups in one chapter; it is fair to say that many of the multicultural assessment issues for the groups covered also apply to other groups. Finally, this chapter includes a tabular guide for identifying specific measures, by ethnicity, that are recommended for use with ethnic-minority clients. A case study illustrates a culturally grounded assessment approach.

BACKGROUND ON ETHNIC-MINORITY CLIENTS

Racial/ethnic trends in the U.S. point to a society that is increasing in ethnic diversity and developing a growing awareness of ethnic identity. By the year 2025, racial and ethnic minorities will represent nearly 38% of the population (U.S. Bureau of the Census, 1998). At the same time, many Whites are gaining increased understanding of their ethnic heritage as it may be linked to Italian-American or Irish-American heritage, for example (Waters, 2001), and thereby are creating a new entity in the history of American ethnic groups, referred to as Euro-Americans (Rubin, 2001). As Lum (2000) notes, ethnic groups who are able to blend into the White-dominated society of Anglo-Saxon and European groups have successfully assimilated into the mainstream of American society and power. However, the color factor has been a barrier to African Americans, Latino Americans, Asian Americans, and Native Americans. Thus, groups of color, while increasing in numbers, remain a minority due to a lack of economic, political, and social power (Feagin & Feagin, 1999; Lum, 2000). The social, rather than biological, construction of race in our society means that most ethnic-minority individuals continue to contend with societal stigma and negative outcomes perpetuated by a biased majority culture. The basic demographic, sociocultural experiences of the four groups discussed in this chapter are outlined below, along with a brief discussion of relevant group-related factors that contribute to group-level differences and may influence a client's clinical presentation at assessment. A comprehensive description of the four groups addressed here is beyond the scope of this chapter. Practitioners are advised to consult other works for detailed discussions of histories, cultural norms and practices, and salient intragroup differences for each broad group and its corresponding subgroups.

American Indians and Alaska Natives

The term *Native Americans* that is used to describe this group can be extended to include all descendants of the pre-Columbian inhabitants of North America, including American Indian, Alaska Native, and Canadian and Mexican Indian people. There is an enormous amount of diversity both within and between each of these subgroups. The land, language, religion, and culture of Native peoples were nearly destroyed by the colonialization practice of the Europeans (McDonnell, 1991; Snipp, 1989). Today, American Indians number just over 2 million, less than 1% of the U.S. population; but they are one of the fastest growing groups within the United States due to increased birthrates, decreased infant mortality rates, and a greater willingness to report American Indian ancestry (McLemore & Romo, 1998). There are more than 550 federally recognized American Indian tribes and Alaska Native village groups in the United States (Reference Encyclopedia of the American Indian, 2000). Native peoples remain one of the most disadvantaged groups in the United States (Russell, 1998). Data from the Indian Health Service (IHS) indicate that native persons primarily seek professional psychological services primarily for substance abuse, anxiety, depression, and adjustment-related problems, which can be associated with a historical trauma response to the genocide of native peoples (Brave Heart, 2000). For example, Griffin-Pierce (1997) notes that there can be stress-related responsiveness when Navajo people are distanced from sacred tribal lands.

Native cultural values, which should be viewed as strengths, often conflict with those of the majority culture. Weaver and White (1997) describe values and norms associated with traditional native culture, including, but not limited to: a deep respect for people, especially elders; generosity and sharing beyond the family unit; a collective identity strongly linked to family, clan, and nation; cooperativeness among people along with a valuing of individual responsibility; harmony with nature and a continuous rather than linear worldview; noninterference, particularly the reluctance to interfere in someone else's life; and religion or spirituality, which may play an important role in development and rites of passage.

African American/Blacks

African Americans make up 13% of the U.S. population. While the term *African American* accurately reflects those individuals who descended from slaves in this country, many prefer the term *Black*, which is sometimes used interchangeably with African American. However, the term Black more accurately reflects the various ethnic subgroups, such as Caribbean immigrants who compose a particular subgroup of African Americans.

The more than 33 million individuals constituting this group include people with roots in the West Indies, South America, Africa, and Caribbean, and many have Native American, White, or Latino/ancestors (Feagin & Feagin, 1999). In addition, the number of immigrants from African countries is increasing with the largest groups being from Nigeria and Ghana (Healy, 1995).

In addition to country of origin, this group varies substantially in terms of income, education, employment, and geographic location. Yet, for most U.S. Blacks the unemployment rate has remained twice as high as that for Whites (Tienda & Stier, 1996; Wilson, 1996), and African Americans continue to lag behind Whites in areas such as income level, adequate housing, and educational opportunities. Twenty-one percent of

African Americans report no usual source of medical care and generally use clinic or emergency room care (Flack et al., 1995). As is the case for Native peoples, many current problems of American Blacks can be traced to the historical trauma resulting from slavery and the persistent societal oppression.

A major strength of this group is the ability to compete and survive in both mainstream and African-American communities, (Davis, 2000). A common cultural value among U.S. Blacks is an "Africentric" worldview that is rooted in and incongruous with the dominant Eurocentric culture (Asante, 1988). Africentric based cultural norms have been described as holistic, emotionally vital, interdependent, and oriented toward collective survival. They differ from Eurocentric views that are characterized by an emphasis on "knowing" rather than on emotional experiences, a focus on personal responsibility versus independence, and valuing of individualism versus collectivism, and an assumption of personal control over one's environment.

Hispanic/Latino Americans

Hispanic is an ethnocultural label for a heterogeneous constituency comprised of people from Mexican, Dominican, Puerto-Rican, and Cuban descent as well as of individuals from Central and South America. Mexican Americans, who reside primarily in the western and southwestern United States, constitute the largest and fastest growing subgroup of Hispanics. Among Mexican Americans, approximately 45% are age twenty or younger (Guinn, 1998). The actual number of Hispanics in the United States is probably larger than official data indicate due to undocumented immigrants who are missed by the census. Hispanics are characterized by strong identification with and attachment to families, that are generally a strong, cohesive support. However, Hispanics (mostly Mexican Americans) have been found to have higher rates of frequent heavy drinking and higher rates of alcohol problems than either Blacks or Whites (Gilbert & Cervantes, 1986) with this rate increasing over the past decade (Caetano & Kaskutas, 1996). Among Mexican Americans, women tend to report more depressive symptoms and more psychological distress in general than do men (Harman & Arbona, 1991). This gender difference is stronger in English-speaking Mexican Americans than among their Spanish-speaking counterparts (Golding & Karno, 1988).

Findings suggest that Hispanics have similar rates of psychiatric disorders as non-Hispanic Whites (Hough et al., 1987), but, as a group, they underuse the mental health care system (O'Sullivan & Lasso, 1992). Hispanics may not view counselors as credible sources of help (Ponce & Atkinson, 1989), and some have different expectations for the content and process of counseling with Hispanic counselors versus Anglo counselors.

According to Guinn (1998), studies of health conceptions of Mexican Americans in the Southwest reveal salient cultural beliefs that can be traced to both a traditional Mexican belief in supernatural sanctions and a tendency toward fatalistic acceptance. For example, the cause of an illness may be believed to be beyond realm of human forces. Although Catholicism is relatively common among this group, many Hispanics may simultaneously practice other forms of religion or healing, such as spiritism in Puerto Rico and santeria in Cuba (Comas-Diaz, 1981; Fuller-Torrey, 1986), and healers may play roles similar to psychotherapists (Fuller-Torrey, 1986). Less acculturated Mexican Americans, who are the least likely to seek mental health care, might view psychiatric symptoms as indicative of physical health problems and may tend to seek care from a general practitioner.

Asian and Pacific Islander Americans

One of the fastest growing racial-ethnic groups in the United States, Asian and Pacific Islander Americans are expected to account for nearly 6.2% of the U.S. population by the year 2025. Currently, they constitute about 3% of the population and reside primarily in California, New York, and Hawaii. This group represents an extremely diverse ethnic backgrounds, including Japanese, Chinese, Filipinos, Koreans, Vietnamese, Hmong, Laotians, Cambodians (now Kampucheans), Asian Indians, native Hawaiians, Samoans, Tongans, Fijians, and Chamorros (Guamanians). There are multiple and complex reasons for the diversity among the subgroups of Asian and Pacific Islander Americans, and practitioners should be able to recognize the distinctions among the various groups and subgroups in order to ensure appropriate assessments (Fong & Mokuau, 1996). In addition, immigrants and refugees are a growing population within this group with vast differences among the incoming subgroups. For example, new immigrants from India and Pakistan are more highly educated in contrast to immigrants from Vietnam, Cambodia, and Thailand who tend to have less formal education, fewer job skills, and higher unemployment and poverty rates (Du Phuoc Long, 1996).

Similar to other ethnic-minority groups, Asian Americans and Pacific Islanders are more group oriented than self-oriented (Fong & Mokuau, 1996) and have histories of discrimination and continued oppression in this country. As a group, they have been labeled a "model minority," which has harmed members of the group as a whole. This label masks the socioeconomic struggles among some of the subgroups and inaccurately portrays the group as having no problems, thereby causing the plight of many subgroup members to go unrecognized. For example, native Hawaiians are known to have disproportionately high rates of cancer, diseases of the heart, and diabetes mellitus (Mokuau, 1990). Moreover, women make up 51% of the Asian- and Pacific Islander-American population and may experience culture-related mental health problems, and the National Minority Health Organization notes that Asian-American women have the highest rates of suicide among all American women.

CONSIDERATIONS IN ASSESSING ETHNIC-MINORITY CLIENTS

The concepts of "emic" and "etic" functioning underlie the notion of culturally competent assessment practice. Some aspects of functioning are unique to the client's culture (emic); others are common across many cultures (etic). Eurocentric (or majority) culture assumes an etic position, and this may be detrimental or inappropriate for members of ethnic minority groups. Within our multicultural society, when practitioners approach assessment from the assumption that all individuals should be treated the same (e.g., with the same assessment instruments, the same assumptions about mental health), they are likely to misdiagnose clients who do not identify with mainstream culture. The special concerns about assessing ethnic-minority clients center around three main issues: 1) practitioners' bias and/or lack of awareness of cultural differences, 2) reliance on stereotypes or overgeneralizations for assessment strategies, and 3) culturally biased measurement and assessment instruments.

1. Practitioners' bias and/or lack of awareness of cultural differences

Practitioners bring to their work particular biases that derive from their personal backgrounds and characteristics, as well as from their training in a specific institutional system (Pedersen, 1997). The dominant cultural standards (i.e., White, middle-class, heterosexual, male) have tended to result in more diagnoses of mental disorders and pathology among those who are outside the dominant culture than within it (Kutchins & Kirk, 1997).

The literature contains numerous examples of misdiagnoses and differential assessment outcomes that place ethnic-minority clients in disadvantaged positions. Most of the research findings have focused on the biased assessment of African Americans/Blacks that has occurred for decades. For example, Abramowitz and Murray (1983) noted evidence that more symptoms are prescribed to Black than to White patients, Blacks receive more severe diagnostic labels than Whites, and Blacks receive more than their share of schizophrenic and paranoid diagnosis. More recently, Flack et al. (1995) found that diagnostic testing is used less frequently with African-American clients even when insurance is present. Further, African-American men are sometimes subjected to an assumed and unverified history of drug abuse during assessments and intake procedures (Uomoto & Wong, 2000). In the area of neuropsychology, Uomoto and Wong (2000) express concern that "patients from certain ethnic backgrounds who may be exhibiting common behavioral/cognitive sequelae of certain types of brain injuries, such as restlessness, agitation, or disinhibition following frontal lobe damage, may be suspected of having premorbid personality problems" (p. 163). Oppenheimer (1992) discusses how Latino clients who believe in the supernatural and believe that fate or a deceased person is in control of their lives may be diagnosed as psychotic. Other research suggests that older Caribbean people might use terms for emotional distress that differ from those found in standard screening instruments (Abas, Phillips, Richards, Carter, & Levy 1996). These examples highlight the need for practitioners to be aware of cultural differences that can affect the assessment process.

Practitioners must first be aware of their own cultural orientation in order to understand how they may potentially impose their own values or worldviews on others. Pedersen (1997) observes that when people, particularly Euro-Americans, are asked to describe their culture, the question may be difficult to answer. Thus, engagement in a self-assessment process is the first step toward cultural competence (Dubois & Miley, 1996; Pedersen, 1997; Pinderhughes, 1989). Social workers from both the majority as well as minority cultures should first conduct self-assessments to determine their own cultural orientation and how their culture and values may interact with clients from diverse backgrounds. Pedersen and Ivey (1993) suggest that ignoring the influence of our own and others' culturally learned assumptions "is a little like speeding in a car down a busy street without having your hands on the steering wheel" (p. 1). Thus, self-assessment is a tool by which practitioners can ensure more accurate analysis and understand culturally learned meanings behind their own and others' behavior. In addition, it is important to note that ethnic-minority practitioners also face challenges with internalized oppression and horizontal prejudices and may have a "cultural blind spot," whereby they perceive those who share their cultural identity as just like themselves and ignore the uniqueness of clients (Pinderhughes, 1989).

2. Reliance on stereotypes or overgeneralizations for assessment strategies

A common mistake made by practitioners in their attempt to master culturally sensitive assessment is to apply stereotypes and overgeneralizations about a client's ethnic/racial group during the assessment process. For example, a practitioner conducting an assessment with an Asian-American female client may notice the client's quiet, withdrawn behavior and assume that this is a "normal" demeanor of Asian-American women. The practitioner therefore may not explore other reasons for the observed behavior nor investigate the specific beliefs and norms of the client's subgroup (i.e., Chinese, Filipino, etc.). An erroneous assumption made by some practitioners in assessing ethnic-minority clients is that racial/ethic status is the equivalent construct of culture, a concept Trimble (1995) refers to as *ethnic glossing*. Although this glossing may be acceptable for broad classifications and policy making, Oetting, Swaim, and Chiarella (1998) warn against equating culture with racial/ethnic status:

> Professionals need to use special care in defining what is meant by culture in different contexts and situations. Culture can, under certain circumstances, still serve to define at least some of the characteristic attitudes, beliefs, and behaviors of a group of people that share a commonly perceived cultural identity. The extent to which a person conforms to those culturally determined behaviors, however, depends on both cultural identity and the level of identification with that culture. (p. 132)

Oetting and colleagues (1998) define *culture identity* as a person's affiliation with a specific group, for example a person's membership in an ethnic group. In contrast, *cultural identification* is a personal trait; it is the extent to which individuals view themselves as involved with an identifiable group along with their investment or stake in that particular culture. Thus, the first step in any assessment involves determining the client's ethnic-group schematicity, or the extent to which the client's culture, derives from his or her ethnic group (Gilbert-Martinez, 1996). There is substantial intragroup differences among the four major groups addressed here. Cultural orientations will vary within each of the ethnic-minority groups, particularly as an increasing number of people identify with multiple ethnicities or choose not to be defined by racial/ethnic categories at all.

Furthermore, in addition to cultural orientation that centers around racial/ethnic status, individuals within any group will differ with regard to a number of other variables (class, gender, age, religion, recency of immigration, sexual orientation, educational level, etc.), all of which challenges the myopic notion of the monolithic group. Each client is unique and must be encountered without prejudgment and assumptions. Considering the range of cultural orientations, practitioners should first determine the level of acculturation (Dana, 1993, 1998) and identity attitudes to assess the cultural orientation of clients.

Acculturation is defined as the "adaptation of language, identity, behavior patterns, and preferences to those of the host/majority society" (Lum, 2000, p. 231) and affects each client's cultural identity differently. A good example is the use of the term *Hispanic* to describe a large, ethnically diverse group of people who differ regarding a number of demographic variables. However, Hispanic groups are often aggregated when examining drinking patterns, for example. Epstein, Botvin, and Diaz (2001) examined the roles of Hispanic group identification (Puerto Rican versus Dominican) and gender in alcohol use among inner-city youth. Sixth and seventh graders in twenty-two New York City schools who identified themselves as Puerto Rican or Dominican completed self-report questionnaires at two assessments. The questionnaires showed that Dominican adolescents generally engaged in more alcohol use than Puerto Rican adolescents. Gender also played a role in drinking patterns for Dominican adolescents. Specifically, Dominican boys reported greater use than Dominican girls, but use was similar across gender for Puerto Rican adolescents. These findings highlight the importance of considering Hispanic group and gender when examining adolescent drinking. Moreover, the above study underscores the need to consider multiple variables, not just broad categories of race/ethnicity, in assessment of clients.

3) Culturally biased measurement and assessment instruments

Selection of assessment measures and strategies must also be done within the context of cultural norms and values. Although most practitioners embrace the valuing of diversity, they also fall prey to conformity in their adherence to dominant cultural standards and the judgment of what constitutes an objective assessment. Standardized measures are usually the first choice for social work practitioners in conducting assessments; however, most of these measures have been constructed based on the majority culture and with little attention to the values, attitudes, and life experiences of individuals from nonmainstream cultures. As society becomes more diverse, there is a recognized shortage of cross-culturally validated assessment instruments.

While standardized measures may pass the test of high reliability and stability, they can be culturally biased when used with ethnic-minority groups (Aponte & Crouch, 1995; Dana, 1993, 1998; Paniagua, 1994). Jones (1996) states that the bias inherent in standardized measures is multifacted: the content of the items constituting the measure; the administration of the measure by a person unfamiliar with the language, behavior, or culture of the person being given the measure; and the validation and norming of measures without consideration of diverse cultures. Paniagua (1994) ranks measurement instruments based on the level of cultural bias. Highly biased instruments include clinical interviews, such as the mental status examination; trait measures; self-report psychopathology measures (i.e., Minnesota Multiphasic Personality Inventory (MMPI, MMPI2) and Beck Depression Inventory [BDI]); and the Rorschach test (Dana, 1993). For example, compared to the BDI, the Center for Epidemiologic Studies Depression (CES-D) Scale contained a number of items that were more likely to be endorsed by Chinese Americans regardless of their level of depression. In another example, Reid et al. (1998) explored the extent to which the ADHD Rating Scale-IV (School Version) differed across male Caucasian and African-American 5 to 18-year-old students. Teachers rated African-American students higher on all symptoms across age groups, and analyses indicated that the scale does not perform identically across groups.

Similarly, the *DSM-IV* has been criticized for its lack of cultural validity and absence of commitment to culturally sensitive assessments (Dana, 1998; Kutchins & Kirk, 1997). In an effort to improve the measure, Mezzich et al. (1999) outlines significant changes to the *DSM-IV*, including an introductory statement about cultural considerations for the use of diagnostic categories and criteria, a glossary of culture-bound syndromes and idioms of distress, and an outline for a cultural formulation. Because the *DSM-IV* is commonly used, social workers must commit to incorporating the guidelines presented by the cultural formulation. These include the consideration of cultural identity, cultural explanations of illness, cultural factors and psychosocial environment, and cultural factors in the clinical relationship. Brave Heart (2000) presents a detailed discussion of how to incorporate the cultural formulation guidelines with American Indians (specifically the Lakota tribe), and a similar strategy should be employed with other ethnic-minority groups.

Despite the significant changes to the *DSM-IV* however, several authors also point to the need for further contextualization of illness, diagnosis, and care (Dana, 1998; Kutchins & Kirk, 1997; Mezzich et al., 1999). Furthermore, the *DSM-IV* does not include disorders resulting from oppression (Akbar, 1991) and does not explicitly label oppression-induced conditions (Dana, 1998). Fabrega (1992) recommends including a cultural axis among several possible avenues to resolve the conflict between disease and cultural viewpoints. Dana (1998) notes that "in the absence of basic DSM changes, assessment of culturally diverse groups, therapeutic assessment, and assessment as a precursor to interventions by psychologists [and other counseling practitioners] could become increasingly medicalized under managed mental health auspices with implications for quality of care" (p. 7).

With such noted disappointments in the culturally-appropriate utility of both the *DSM-IV* and commonly used standardized instruments, practitioners will undoubtedly feel caught between two conflicting professional demands when conducting assessments. On one hand, practitioners are accountable to institutionalized mental health guidelines that specify the use of standardized and widely used measurement tools and diagnostic procedures. On the other hand, practitioners are required to conduct culturally competent assessments for clients who may not be appropriately served—and may even be harmed—by such "objective" measures and procedures. So, how are we to proceed in resolving this assessment dilemma? The recent assessment literature points to three new directions as alternative or mixed models of assessment with ethnic-minority clients: assessment of cultural identity, assessment of acculturative stress and responses to oppression, and the use of pictorial tests.

RECOMMENDED ALTERNATIVES FOR MULTICULTURAL ASSESSMENT PRACTICE

Table 10.1 includes a selected list of measures for the four ethnic groups covered in this chapter and information on how to obtain those

Table 10.1 Selected List of Measures for Four Ethnic Groups

Racial/Ethnic Group	Measure	Measure Characteristics	Reliability/Validity	Where to obtain
American Indians/ Alaska Natives	**Cultural Involvement and Detachment Anxiety Scale (CIDAQ)** Promising measure for examining culturally related anxiety in American Indian and Alaska Natives, particularly in college counseling and behavioral health care centers	Scale contains 3 factors measuring anxiety about (1) social involvement w/National American and cultural knowledge, (2) economic issues, and (3) social involvement with majority culture	High levels of item-total reliability, internal consistency, and convergent and divergent validity. Cronbach's alpha .92 for total scale.	Daniel W. McNeil Dept. of Psychology West Virginia University, Anxiety, Psychophysiology, and Pain Research Laboratory P. O. Box 6040 Morgantown, WV 26506-6040 Email: dmmcneil@wvu.edu
	Native American Addictions Severity Index (ASI) Adult Version Customized for Native Americans; assesses chemical dependency and behavioral health concerns	The ASI (developed by S. M. Manson) is a comprehensive survey-type questionnaire that assesses a range of areas that could be affected by respondent's substance abuse (legal status, employment, family and social relationships, etc.)	The ASI has been found to be reliable and valid over the past 12 years across various populations. The Native American version is available for both adults and adolescents.	Computerized programs: Accurate Assessments 1823 Harney Street, Suite 101 Omaha, NE 68102 (402) 341-8880 (800) 324-7966

Figure 10.1   Selected List of Measures for Four Ethnic Groups—*(continued)*

Racial/Ethnic Group	Measure	Measure Characteristics	Reliability/Validity	Where to obtain
	Tribe-Specific Thematic Apperception-Type (TAT) Tests Developed by Dana, (1982) to assess emotional themes, conflicts, and concerns unique to Lakota culture.	Tests use picture story techniques; assessors and interpreters should be familiar with specific culture, history, philosophy, healing practices, and language of the population.	In the absence of adequate validity research for most standardized instruments with American Indians/Alaska Natives, local adaptations of TAT tests can provide valuable emic-based alternatives (Allen, 1998).	Richard H. Dana, Ph.D. Regional Research Institute Portland State University P. O. Box 751 Portland, OR 97207 (503) 725-4040
African Americans/ Blacks	**Optimal Extended Self-Esteem Scales (OESES)** Instruments for assessing the extended self concepts for African Americans' racial/cultural identity and values based on Africentric principles.	Separate scales are developed for children, adolescents, and adults. Items on each scale vary according to developmental level.	Cronbach alpha coefficients were .82 and .76 for the OESES-Adolescent and the Rosenberg Self-Esteem, respectively ($n = 95$ males and 95 females adolescents).	Seward E. Hamilton, Jr. Ph.D. Gore Education Complex-Building–C, #305 Dept. of Psychology Florida A & M University Tallahassee, FL 32307

Figure 10.1 Selected List of Measures for Four Ethnic Groups—(*continued*)

Racial/Ethnic Group	Measure	Measure Characteristics	Reliability/Validity	Where to obtain
	Index of Psychological Well-Being among African Americans A 23-item index constructed from 40 items in the National Survey of Black Americans interview schedule.	Factors analysis revealed 7 factors: 10 happiness, self-esteem (positive), blame for bad job, self-esteem (negative), economic well-being, role performance, and interpersonal relations.	Reliability coefficients for the scale range from .59 to .70.	Anderson Franklin, Ph.D. Psychology Dept. The City College of New York Convent Ave. @ 138th Street New York, NY 10031 Ajfcc@cunyvn.cuny.edu
	The Perceived Racial Stress and Coping Apperception Test (PRSCAT) Designed to elicit child and adult conceptualizations of race-related stressors and the racial coping strategies available to cope with those stressors.	The PRSCAT consists of 5 picture cards for which the respondent tells a story and offers an explanation of what he/she would do. Responses are coded from 0 to 4 depending on the intensity of the racial conflict expressed by the respondent.	Interrater reliability coefficients for racial conflict ratings and racial coping strategies were .83 and .75 respectively.	Deborah J. Johnson, Ph.D. Dept. of Child and Family Studies 1430 Linden Drive University of Wisconsin-Madison Madison, WI 53706 (608) 263-4066

Figure 10.1   Selected List of Measures for Four Ethnic Groups—*(continued)*

Racial/Ethnic Group	Measure	Measure Characteristics	Reliability/Validity	Where to obtain
	Scale for Racial Socialization for Adolescents (SORS-A) (Stevenson, 1994) A 45-item scale designed to assess the degree of acceptance of racial-socialization attitudes and race-related messages of childrearing within African-American culture.	The SORS-A has 4 sub-scales: spiritual and religious coping, extended family caring, cultural pride reinforcement, and racism awareness teaching.	Initially normed with 236 inner-city African American adolescents, the SORS-A has fair reliability with an alpha of .75 for the total scale. Factors analyses suggest racial socialization has 2 dimensions: proactive and protective, regarding adolescents' perceptions of racial socialization.	Dr. Howard C. Stevenson, Jr. University of Pennsylvania Graduate School of Education, School, Community and Child Psychology 3700 Walnut St., Philadelphia, PA 19104
Hispanic/Latino Americans	**Children's Health Locus of Control** A 20-item measure that has been suggested as appropriate for cross-cultural use with Mexican-American youth.	Scale determines the extent to which respondent believes that one has control over the status of one's health, ranging from belief in self-control (Internal), control by someone more powerful (Powerful Other) or uncontrollable factors (Chance).	Two studies by Guinn (1998) using the scale with Mexican-American youth reported alpha reliabilities of .76 for Internal, .72 for Powerful Others, and .80 for Chance (Study 1, 1997) and .78 for Internal, .75 for Powerful Others, and .81 for Chance (Study 2).	Parcel, G., & Meyer, M. (1978). Development of an instrument to measure children's health locus of control. *Health Education Monographs, 6,* 149–159.

Figure 10.1   Selected List of Measures for Four Ethnic Groups—(*continued*)

Racial/Ethnic Group	Measure	Measure Characteristics	Reliability/Validity	Where to obtain
	Spanish Version Expectations About Counseling Questionnaire (EAC-B) Based on research documenting the relationship between ethnicity and counseling expectations and counseling Hispanics' unmet expectations of counselors and the counseling process.	Questionnaire is composed of 53 items constituting 17 scales grouped into 4 general expectance factors: personal commitment, facilitative conditions, counselor expertise, and nurturance.	All scales correlated above .60, the criterion proposed for translated instruments. Results suggest that the Spanish version of the EAC-B is a reliable and valid translation for students and nonstudents from a variety of Hispanic populations.	Robin A. Buhrke School of Education 312 Merrick University of Miami Coral Gables, FL 33124
	Simpatica Scale (SS) The SS is a 17-item scale developed to measure the concept of simpatia, the Hispanic cultural script that denotes the general tendency to avoid interpersonal conflict.	The concept of simpatica is often cited as potentially important for Hispanics in drug treatment.	SS has good construct validity and good internal consistency with alpha of .80 for the overall scale.	Dr. James D. Griffith Institute of Behavioral Research Texas Christian College Fort Worth, TX 76129

Figure 10.1   Selected List of Measures for Four Ethnic Groups—*(continued)*

Racial/Ethnic Group	Measure	Measure Characteristics	Reliability/Validity	Where to obtain
Asian Americans/ Pacific Islander Americans	**Hawaiian Culture Scale-Adolescent Version** To assess the degree to which adolescents know of, believe in, value, and practice elements of traditional Hawaiian culture and to delineate the biological (i.e., blood quantum) and sociocultural factors shaping ethnic identification.	The 50-item inventory (7 subscales) measures the source of learning the Hawaiian way of life, how much the maintaining of Hawaiian beliefs is valued, Hawaiian blood quantum, and specific cultural traditions.	Cronbach alpha ranged from .82 to .96 for Hawaiian adolescents and from .76 to .96 for non-Hawaiian adolescents. These coefficients indicate satisfactory internal consistency.	Earl S. Hishinuma, Dept. of Psychiatry, Native Hawaiian Mental Health Research Development Program, 1356 Lusitana St., 4th Floor, John A Burns School of Medicine University of Hawaii at Manoa, Honolulu, HI 96813 earlhish@aol.com
	Suinn-Lew Asian Self-Identity Acculturation Scale (SL-ASIAS) To assess self-identity and level of acculturation among Asian Americans.	Scale has been used in conjunction with MMPI-2 with Asian Americans; less acculturated Asian Americans scored in the most disturbed direction on MMPI-2.	Researcher reported Cronbach's alpha for internal consistency of .88 and .91 from two studies. Scale has been widely used in the last 10 years in spite of limited research.	Suinn, R. M., Rikard-Figueroa, K., Lew, S., & Vigil, P. (1987) The Suinn–Lew Self-Identity Acculturation Scale: Concurrent and factorial validation. *Educational and Psychological Measurement, 52,* 1041–1046.

Figure 10.1   Selected List of Measures for Four Ethnic Groups—*(continued)*

Racial/Ethnic Group	Measure	Measure Characteristics	Reliability/Validity	Where to obtain
Cross-cultural measures for Ethnic Minority Children and Families	**Kaufman Assessment Battery for Children (K-ABC)** (Kaufman, 1983) and **Kaufman Adolescent and Adult Intelligence Test (KAIT)** (Kaufman & Kaufman, 1993).	K-ABC is an individually administered assessment battery that measures achievement and intelligence in children. The KAIT is designed to assess cognitive functioning and may be useful when working with culturally diverse persons 11–85. (Russo & Lewis, 1999).	Research suggests that the measure is useful for Mexican-American assessment and may be useful for general cross-cultural assessment. Scales are currently undergoing revisions and norming with widely diverse populations.	American Guidance Service 4201 Woodland Rd. Circle Pines, MN 55014-1796 1-800-328-2560

Figure 10.1 Selected List of Measures for Four Ethnic Groups—*(continued)*

Racial/Ethnic Group	Measure	Measure Characteristics	Reliability/Validity	Where to obtain
	The **Dominic** (Valla, Bergeron, Berube, & Gaudet, 1994; Valla, Bergeron, Bidaut-Russell, St. Georges, & Gaudet, 1997) is a cartoon-based questionnaire designed to study the mental health status of children age six to eleven.	Drawings convey situations based on symptoms of 7 more prevalent diagnoses in the *DSM-III-R* Axis I: Attention Deficit Hyperactivity Disorder (ADHD), Conduct Disorder (CD), Oppositional Defiant Disorder (ODD), Major Depressive Disorder/ Dysthymia (MDD), Separation Anxiety Disorder (SAD), Over-Anxious Disorder (OAD), and Simple Phobia (SPh).	The Dominic/Dominique character was designed to be interpreted as either a boy or a girl and also includes racially appropriate pictures of the characters. Internal consistency for each of the subscales ranged from .62 to .88 (Valla et al., 1994).	Jean-Pierre Valla, Ph.D. Hospital Riviere-des-Prairies 7070 Boulevrad Perras Montreal, Quebex H1E 1A4 Canada (514) 323-7260, ext. 2281 Fax (514) 323-4163 Jpvalla@sympatico.ca

Figure 10.1   Selected List of Measures for Four Ethnic Groups—*(continued)*

Racial/Ethnic Group	Measure	Measure Characteristics	Reliability/Validity	Where to obtain
	Family Pressures Scale-Ethnic (FPRES-E) (McCubbin, Thompson, & Elver, 2000) is a 64-item measure designed to be inclusive of pressures related to the life experiences of families of color.	Adapted from the Family Inventory of Life Events and Changes, this scale obtains an index of the severity of culturally sensitive pressure in the family system, especially in Native-American families, including families of Hawaiian descent.	The FPRES-E has excellent internal consistency with an alpha of .92. Scale was normed on 174 families of Native Hawaiian ancestry and was found to be the strongest predictor of family distress among this study population.	In H. I. McCubbin, A. I. Thompson, & M. A. McCubbin (1996). *Family assessment: Resiliency, coping, and adaptation: Inventories for research and practice.* Madison: University of Wisconsin, 227–236. The book provides instructions for permission to use the instrument.
	Multigroup Ethnic Identity Measure (MEIM) (Phinney, 1992) Designed to measure ethnic identity, particularly among adolescents across multiple ethnic groups.		The MEIM has good internal consistency with alphas above .80 for subscales across a range of ethnic groups. There is evidence of some degree of concurrent validity between the MEIM and the Rosenberg Self-Esteem Inv. for Minority Students.	Jean S. Phinney, Ph.D. Department of Psychology California State University Los Angeles, CA 90032

measures. The measures presented reflect the four recommended alternatives discussed below.

Alternative I: Use of Revised Tests and Newly Devised Ethnic Specific Tests

Revised tests are instruments that have been developed and validated to tap the emic-based cultural contexts of mental health issues; they include translations of commonly used tests. Examples include the Chinese Depression Symptom Scale and the Vietnamese adaptation of the MMPI-2 (Tran, 1996). Whenever possible, tests that have been normed on the client's ethnic population should be used in assessments; however, such tests are few and far between and their development lags behind revisions of the original test. As Okazaki and Sue (2000) note, "often, by the time individual researchers have conducted cross-cultural adaptation studies with a given assessment instrument, the revised version of the same instrument may well be under development" (p. 278).

On the other hand, some researchers question whether or not the areas of needed assessment are the same for Euro-Americans as they are for ethnic-minority groups. For example, traditional psychology assesses such attributes as IQ, cognitive functioning, personality, and achievement. However, Africentric theorists challenge the appropriateness of such measures to understand African-Americans' behaviors and functioning. Instead, these researchers recommend perceptions of racism, responses to racism, acculturation, identity development and formulation, and self-consciousness as crucial constructs to be assessed with African-American clients. The *Handbook of Tests and Measurements for Black Populations* contains more than one hundred instruments and approaches for assessing Black clients (Jones, 1996). Some of the tests represent traditional constructs such as self-esteem, stress, coping, and social support (e.g. Optimal Extended Self-Esteem Scale); whereas other measures are unique to assessing the impact of societal oppression on psychological functioning (e.g., Scale for Racial Socialization for Adolescents). Another example of culture-specific constructs for assessment included in Table 1 is the Simpatia Scale. This was developed to measure the concept of simpatia, the Hispanic cultural script that denotes the general tendency to avoid interpersonal conflict.

Advocating that both traditional and ethnic-based constructs are important, Lindsey (1998) argues that "we have to create African-American norms for the existing instruments being used . . . at the same time, we must continue to develop instruments from the Africentric perspective" (p. 46). More research is needed toward establishing psychometric properties for ethnic-based, revised, standardized norms and newly devised, ethnic-specific measures; some of this work is underway. Noting that Asian Americans have been severely underrepresented in validation studies, Okazaki and Sue (2000) advocate for test revisions with cross-cultural validation with Asian Americans and other heterogeneous groups. They cite the recent publication of the Hmong adaptation of the MMPI-2 (Dienard, Butcher, Thas, Vang, & Hang, 1996) as an example of collaborative test development between mainstream (majority culture) test developers and ethnic-minority researchers.

Alternative 2: Assessment of Cultural/Ethnic Identity, Acculturation, and Acculturative Stress as Moderators of Standardized Tests

In discussing the development of the Hawaiian Culture Scale, Hishinuma et al. (2000) note that the first step in discerning the role of ethnicity is to develop valid measures; the second step is to determine the association of ethnic constructs with indicators of psychological adjustment. There is some evidence that ethnic-identity measures offer some assistance in interpreting problematic standardized instruments. Dana (1998) recommends that, as a first step toward culturally competent assessment, practitioners should assess the client's cultural identity as a moderator variable and that appropriate measures for this should be administered as part of the assessment interview with the client. Accordingly, an increasing number of such scales are appearing in the assessment literature.

Dana (1998) suggests that measures used to examine the client's "culture self" can provide critical information on clients' cultural identity and it also may be a precondition for mental, physical, and spiritual well-being (p. 8). In a study to identify the relationship between reference-group labels and characteristics of personality such as self-esteem and social competence, Rotheram-Borus (1990) identified reference labels as mainstream, bicultural, and ethnically identified. He studied 330 Black, Hispanic, Asian, and White high school students to determine the extent to which subjects identified with the dominant culture. The study showed that reference group labels were consistently associated with differences in ethnic group values, attitudes, and behaviors. Thus, understanding the cultural orientation of the client, beyond racial/ethnic categorizing, is a crucial step toward culturally competent assessment. Among those scales measuring cultural orientation, Walters's (1999) Urban American Indian Identity Scale (UAIIS) measures four dimensions of identity attitudes: internalization, marginalization, externalization, and actualization.

Acculturation (low to high) has been studied extensively among ethnic-minority populations and has mental health implications. For example, acculturation has been linked to anxiety responding in American Indian and Alaska Natives (McNeil, Kee, & Zvolensky, 1999). Moreover, a growing body of assessment research focuses on the inclusion of acculturative stress as part of a holistic assessment procedure with ethnic-minority clients. Indeed, researchers report that some native peoples experience clinical levels of stress-related responsivity (termed *intergenerational posttraumatic stress disorder*) that is associated with decades of cultural abuses against native peoples (Choney, Berryhill-Paapke, & Robbins, 1995).

A number of scales are designed to explore the level of acculturation of ethnic minorities. The Native American Cultural Involvement and Detachment Anxiety Questionnaire (CIDAQ) was developed by McNeil et al. (2000) to assess acculturation anxiety in American Indian and Alaska Natives. The Acculturative Stress Scale (Williams-Flournoy & Anderson, 1996) is designed to assess the degree of psychological discomfort experienced by African Americans assimilating into an unfamiliar cultural environment. For information on some cultural-specific rapid assessment instruments in the area of cultural identity and acculturation, Corcoran and Fischer's (2000) most recent volumes of *Measures for Clinical Practice: A Sourcebook* now contain new scales and material, including the Acculturation Rating Scale for Mexican-Americans-II, the Scale of Racial Socialization-Adolescent Version, the Orthogonal Cultural Identification Scale, and the Multigroup Ethnic Identity Scale.

Alternative 3: Use of Thematic Apperception Type Tests

There has been increased debate about whether projective measures are inherently based on Eurocentric assumptions and should thus be summarily dismissed with ethnic-minority clients, or whether there is some value in emic-based adaptations (Allen,1998; Dana, 1998; Okazaki & Sue, 1995). With respect to American Indians and Alaska Natives, Allen recommends that, in the absence of adequate validity research for most standardized tests, adaptations of TAT-type tests can provide valuable emic-based alternatives; however, those available are in various states of development.

Several picture story tests have been developed over the years targeting various Indian tribes, including Inupaiq people (Parker, 1964), Lakota adults (Dana, 1982), Hispanic children (Malgady, Costantino, & Rogler, 1984), and African-American children and adults (Johnson, 1996). When depictions are created to cultural specifications, these tests hold promising possibilities for emic-based assessments. The Tell-Me-A-Story-Test (TEMAS) measure, when used with Eurocentric-structured stimuli can be very biased; however, French (1997) has used the Draw-A-Person (D-A-P) and a modified Thematic Apperception Test (TAT) for bibliotherapy with American-Indian children. Costantino and colleagues also have established reliable and valid scoring systems for their emic-based picture story techniques with Hispanic, Black, Asian, and White children (Allen, 1998; Dana, 1998).

Dana (1982) developed Lakota-specific cards with some interpretative guidelines for picture story assessments in order to tap emotional responses, conflicts, and social themes and concerns unique to Lakota culture. Johnson (1996) developed the Perceived Racial Stress and Coping Apperception Test (PRSCAT). This projective test is designed to elicit child and adult conceptualizations of race-related stressors and the racial coping strategy available to cope with those stressors. Although still in a development phase, one of the most important findings from her use of the scale is reflected in the perceptions of children as young as five years old, who not only perceived racial conflicts in the cards but were able to articulate racial coping strategies used to address the perceived conflict.

When assessing mental health outcomes, picture-type assessments may be more appropriate for some use or for mixed assessment use with children of color. For example, Murphy et al. (2000) reports that the pictorial approach (using the Dominic mental health assessment measure) may be more effective than a written version in assessing anxiety and depression in children. The Dominic (Valla et al., 1994; Valla et al., 1997) is a cartoon-based questionnaire designed to study the mental health status of children aged six to eleven. The drawings convey situations based on symptoms of the seven prevalent diagnoses in the *DSM-III-R* Axis I: Attention Deficit Hyperactivity Disorder (ADHD), Conduct Disorder (CD), Oppositional Defiant Disorder (ODD), Major Depressive Disorder/Dysthymia (MDD), Separation Anxiety Disorder (SAD), Over-Anxious Disorder (OAD), and Simple Phobia (SPh). Children are shown a series of ninety-seven cartoon drawings. In eighty-nine of these, a child, Dominic, is depicted exhibiting ninety-five symptoms covering sixty-two of the sixty-six *DSM-III-R* criteria included in these diagnoses. Mixed in with these are eight pictures of a smiling Dominic enjoying various activities. Children are asked to respond yes they are like Dominic or no they are not. The Dominic/Dominique character was designed to be interpreted as either a boy or a girl and also includes racially appropriate pictures of the characters.

Alternative 4: Qualitative Assessment and Triangulated Assessment Approaches

Paniagua (1994) suggests that the least-biased assessment approaches involve self-monitoring (client's own records of thoughts, behaviors, feelings, etc.) and self-report individualized rating scales, which can accurately capture a client's interpretations and beliefs about behavior. Culture-specific measures, such as life histories and interviews, can be used to elicit assessment information (Dana, 1993). Mapping technique is especially appropriate for those minority families with language barriers, and it is more visual and activity oriented (Jordan & Franklin, 1995).

In addition, whenever possible, more than one assessment strategy should be used. Often this requires combining qualitative and quantitative assessment techniques or using multiple standardized instruments. For example, practitioners working with a Native population at the Eagle Lodge Behavioral Health Treatment Center utilize extensive psychosocial qualitative assessment interviews in conjunction with the Traumatic Symptoms Inventory Index. Stephens, Kiger, Karnes, and Whorton (1999) advise that a single test also will not suffice when assessing economically and culturally diverse children for academic giftedness. The researchers used the Culture-Fair Intelligence Test, the Raven Standard Progressive Matrices, and the Naglieri Nonverbal Abilities Test to assess 189 third through eighth graders who attended a rural elementary school and who were underrepresented in gifted student programs. Together the three tests identified 26 students who merited additional consideration for gifted programs.

Combining measures can also be useful when assessing mental health in ethnic-minority groups. Multiple screenings was used to determine that the Center for Epidemiologic Studies—Depression Scale (CES-D), a 10-item scale that takes about 2 minutes to administer, is a useful tool for identifying Puerto Rican patients in need of in-depth mental health evaluation in a primary care setting. To assess convergent validity, Robison, Gruman, Gaztambide, and Blank (2002) compared multiple versions of four depression screening tools (Center for Epidemiologic Studies—Depression Scale [CES-D], Geriatric Depression Scale, Yale 1-question screen, and PRIME-MD 2-question screen) to the Composite International Diagnostic Interview (CIDI), the World Health Organization's diagnostic interview, that has been validated in adult Latino populations. The study involved 303 Puerto Rican primary care patients age 50 and older who completed all screens and the CIDI in a face-to-face interview. Between 34% and 61% of patients screened positive for depression, depending on the measure, with 12% meeting Mental Disorders-IV (*DSM-IV*) criteria for major depression (CIDI). The researchers report that the 10-item CES-D worked best to identify major depression in this population, with a sensitivity of 84% and specificity of 64% using a cutpoint of 3 (instead of the conventional cutpoint of 4), which is recommended for optimal sensitivity and specificity.

SUMMARY

Social work practitioners are encouraged to probe, question, and make changes in any cases where there is a possibility that standardized assessment techniques may not be culturally appropriate for a client assessment. Once an individual is labeled with an invalid assessment or inaccurate pathological diagnosis, intervention and evaluation of the client's progress are no longer valid. In addition to the above-recommended alternatives, social work practitioners are encouraged to utilize Jordan and Franklin's Integrative Skills Assessment Protocol, a detailed guide for conducting a comprehensive assessment framework (see Chapter 1). This protocol focuses on assessing the client within an environmental context and utilizes an integrative assessment approach that borrows from a number of assessment models. General guidelines from this protocol are used for presenting the following case study.

Brief Assessment Case Study

Client Identifying Information.   Client Demographics: Janet is a 19-year-old, African-American female attending a small community college in a large, predominantly Euro-American metropolitan area about an hour away from her hometown community, an inner-city urban environment.

Nature of Presenting Problem.   Although Janet had a successful first semester in the community college, during the beginning of her second semester she begins to have difficulty passing her exams and feels that she is "falling apart at the seams." Janet is torn between wanting to be more involved with her family and "just moving on" with her life, which she defines as getting an education and getting away from her inner-city upbringing. Her boyfriend, whom she has dated for the past five months, is supportive but feels that Janet's recent problems with her schoolwork will pass and that she is "trying too hard to prove herself" in her new college environment.

Family and Social History.   Janet is from a lower-middle-class, urban background. Janet's parents divorced when she was thirteen, and she and her brother lived with her mother but had regular contact with their father. Janet's parents never really got along; their difficulties were often associated with her father's periodic bouts with unemployment in the construction business. Janet's mother is a nurse. After the divorce, Janet's brother, Derek, began having problems at home and at school. He became defiant with his mother, started skipping school, and has spent some time in jail for possession of marijuana. Over the past year, Janet has drifted away from her family. Janet was extremely frustrated with "not being able to get through" to her brother. Janet's parents are also very concerned about Derek but as Janet put it, "they are caught up in their own problems" from the divorce. For the past seven months, Janet has worked part-time at a popular chain restaurant, which is where she met Sam, her boyfriend. Janet has not made many friends at her college.

Ethnic Considerations.   Janet comes from an inner-city neighborhood, but she has not been part of that community for nearly a year. Janet came from a predominantly African-American community and has not had very much exposure to a large, predominantly Euro-American metropolitan school or community. Considering her ethnicity and nonmainstream background, it is necessary to assess Janet's preference for the host/majority society.

Measurement.   Two standardized clinical measures and two ethnocultural measures were administered to Janet during the initial intake. As recommended in this chapter, the first step in multicultural assessment strategy is to access the cultural orientation of clients and their level of acculturation by identifying attitudes.

Measure: Ethnic-group schemasticity (Gilbert-Martinez, 1996). This 10-item scale, based on Phinney's (1992) Multiethnic Identity, assesses ethnic-group schemasticity or the degree of identification with one's ethnic group. This scale has been normed on female and male African-American students in predominantly Euro-American college environments. Sample scale items: "Of all the things about me, my ethnicity is most important"; "I don't try to become friends with people from other ethnic groups." Janet scored 30, reflecting a moderately high level of ethnic group schematicity. Because Janet is strongly ethnic group schematic, it is possible that she might be experiencing what Cross (1987) calls the "encounter stage," in which one experiences significant racial incongruity with the majority culture for the first time.

Two standardized clinical scales were used to assess Janet's anxiety level and her degree of psychological splitting.

Measure: Clinical Anxiety Scale (Thyer, 1992): This 25-item scale measures the amount, degree, or severity of clinical anxiety. Sample scale items: "I feel afraid without good reason"; "I feel generally anxious." Janet scored 40, which exceeds the clinical cutting score of 30, indicating that that she is experiencing anxiety in the clinical range.

Measure: Splitting Scale (Gerson, 1984): This 14-item scale assesses symptoms of splitting, the psychological defense mechanism used to keep ambivalence at bay. This scale has been normed on female and male psychology students as well as on a sample from an urban health clinic; it has moderate to good reliability and validity. Sample scale items: "When I'm with someone really terrific, I feel dumb"; "I often feel I can't put the different parts of my personality together so that there is one 'me.' " Janet scored 60, reflecting moderately high characterological use of splitting.

Measure: The Acculturative Stress Scale (Williams-Flournoy & Anderson, 1996). This is a 9-item scale that assesses the psychological stress resulting from the day-to-day clash of values, beliefs, and lifestyles of the majority culture and of African Americans. Sample questions: "It's difficult to really trust someone if they're from a different racial background"; "I feel especially nervous going into a room full of people if I am going to be the only one of my racial group." Janet scored a 40, well above the mean score (20) for samples on which the scale was normed.

Moving From Assessment to Intervention

The intervention selected for Janet should address each of the concerns identified in the assessment, with specific attention to the high score on the acculturative stress scale and to the presence of acculturative stress, anxiety, and splitting. Given Janet's ethnic considerations and the timing of the onset of her anxiety, it appears acculturative stress plays a substantial role in her presenting problem; treatment should include intervention to reduce acculturative stress. Treatment also should involve community and school-based resources that would help Janet feel more connected to her ethnic background and repair her sense of disconnection with her identity. It would be important to acknowledge and to address the discomfort and stress associated with loss of identity. Because extended family and peer groups buffer the impact of acculturative stress (Williams-Flournoy & Anderson, 1996), one goal of the intervention would be to help Janet reconnect with family and community. Once acculturative stress is reduced, effects would be expected in the areas of clinical anxiety and characterological splitting. In addition, reduction in acculturative stress should allow Janet to concentrate on her schooling and career plans without the interference of extreme stress and anxiety.

STUDY QUESTIONS

1. How has the ethnocentrism of the U.S. culture affected assessment procedures and measurement instruments for non-majority (ethnic-minority) clients?

2. The special concerns about assessing ethnic minority clients center around three main issues. List and define these three issues.

3. Discuss some of the criticisms about the *DSM-IV* with respect to assessing ethnic minority clients.

4. The chapter states that "practitioners feel caught between two conflicting professional demands for conducting assessments. Explain these two conflicting professional demands.

5. Discuss the recommended alternative or "mixed models" for multicultural assessment. List alternative models applied in the case study?

REFERENCES

Abas, M., Phillips, C., Richards, M., Carter, J., & Levy, R. (1996). Initial development of a new culture-specific screen for emotional distress in older Caribbean people. *International Journal of Geriatric Psychiatry, 11*(12), 1097–1103.

Abramowitz, S. S., & Murray, J. (1983). Race effects in psychology. In R. M. Crystal & R. J. Alston (1991). Ethnicity and culture in rehabilitation counseling: The perspectives of three prominent counselor educators. *Rehabilitation Education, 5*(3), 209–214.

Akbar, N. (1991). Mental disorder among African Americans. In R. L. Jones (Ed.), *Black psychology* (3rd ed., pp. 339–351). Berkeley, CA: Cobb & Henry.

Allen, J. (1998). Personality assessment with American Indian and Alaska Natives: Instrument considerations and service delivery style. *Journal of Personality Assessment, 70*(1), 17–42.

Aponte, J. F., & Crouch, R. T. (1995). The changing ethnic profile of the United States. In J. F. Aponte, R. Y. Rivers, & J. Wohl, (Eds.), *Psychological interventions and cultural diversity* (pp. 1–18). Boston: Allyn & Bacon.

Asante, M. K. (1998). *Afrocentricity.* Trenton, NJ: Africa World Press.

Brave Heart, M. Y. H. (2000). Clinical social work assessment with Native clients. In R. Fong and S. Furuto (Eds.), *Culturally competent practice: Skills, interventions, and evaluations* (pp. 163–195). Boston: Allyn & Bacon.

Caetano, R., & Kaskutas, L. A. (1996). Changes in drinking problems among Whites, Blacks, and Hispanics: 1984–1992. *Substance Use and Misuses, 31*(11 & 12), 1547–1571.

Choney, S. K., Berryhill-Paapke, E., & Robbins, R. R. (1995). The acculturation of American Indians: Developing frameworks for research and practice. In J. G. Ponterotto, J. M. Casas, L. A. Suzuki, & C. M. Alexander (Eds.), *Handbook of multicultural counseling* (pp. 73–92). Thousand Oaks, CA: Sage.

Comas-Diaz, L. (1981). Puerto-Rican espiritismo and psychotherapy. *American Journal of Orthopsychitary, 51*, 636–645.

Corcoran, K., & Fischer, J. (2000). *Measures for clinical practice: A sourcebook* (3rd ed., Vols. 1 & 2). New York: The Free Press.

Cross, W. E. (1987). A two-factor theory of black identity: Implications for the study of identity development in minority children (pp. 117–133). In J. Phinney & M. J. Rotheram (Eds.), *Children's ethnic socilaization: Pluralism and Development* (pp. 113–117). Newbury Park, CA: Sage.

Dana, R. H. (1982). *Picture-story cards for Sioux/Plains Indians.* Fayetteville: University of Arkansas.

Dana, R. H. (1993). *Multicultural assessment perpsectives for professional psychology.* Needham Heights, MA: Allyn & Bacon.

Dana, R. H. (1998). *Understanding cultural identity in intervention and assessment.* Multicultural aspects of Counseling Series, Vol. 9. Thousand Oaks, CA: Sage.

Dana, R. (Ed.). (2000). *Handbook of cross-cultural and multicultural personality assessment*. Mahwah, NJ: Erlbaum.

Davis, E. (2000). Evaluation skills with African American individuals and families: Three approaches. In R. Fong and S. Furuto (Eds.), *Culturally competent practice: Skills, interventions, and evaluations* (pp. 343–354). Boston: Allyn & Bacon.

Devore, W., & Schlesinger, E. G. (1996). *Ethnic-sensitive social work practice* (4th ed.). Boston: Allyn & Bacon.

Dienard, A., Butcher, J. N., Thao, U.D., Vang, S. H. M., & Hang, K. (1996). Development of a Hmong translation of the MMPI-2. In J. N. Butcher (Ed.), *International adaptations of the MMPI-2* (pp. 194–205). Minneapolis: University of Minnesota Press.

DuBois, B., & Miley, K. (1996). *Social work: An empowering profession* (2nd ed.). Boston: Allyn & Bacon.

Du Phuoc Long, P. (with L. Ricard). (1996). *The dream shattered: Vietnamese gangs in America*. Boston: Northeastern University Press.

Epstein, J. A., Botvin, G. J., & Diaz, T. (2001). Alcohol use among Dominican and Puerto Rican adolescents residing in New York City: Role of Hispanic group and gender. *Journal of Developmental & Behavioral Pediatrics, 22*(2), 113–118.

Fabrega, H., Jr. (1992) Commentary. Diagnosis interminable: Toward a culturally sensitive DSM-IV. *Journal of Nervous and Mental Disease, 180*, 5–7.

Feagin, J. R., & Feagin, C. B. (1999). *Racial and ethnic relations* (6th ed.). Upper Saddle River, NJ: Prentice Hall.

Flack, J. M., Amaro, H., Jenkins, W., Kunitz, S., Levy, J., Mixon, M., & Yu, E. (1995). Epidemiology of minority health. *Health Psychology, 14*(7), 592–600.

Fong, R., & Mokuau, N. (1996). Not simply "Asian Americans": Periodical literature review on Asians and Pacific Islanders. In P. L. Ewalt, E. M. Freeman, S. A. Kirk, & D. L. Poole (Eds.), *Multicultural issues in social work* (pp. 269–281). Washington, DC: NASW Press.

French, L. (1997). *Counseling Native Americans*. Lanham, MD: University Press of America.

Fuller-Torrey, E. (1986). *Witchdoctors and psychiatrists: The common roots of psychtherapy and its future*. Northdale, NJ: Jason Aronson.

Gerson, M-J. (1984). Splitting: The development of a measure. *Journal of Clinical Psychology, 40*, 157–162.

Gilbert, M. J., & Cervantes, R. C. (1986). Patterns and practices of alcohol use among Mexican-Americans: A comprehensive review. *Hispanic Journal of Behavioral Sciences, 8*, 1–60.

Gilbert-Martinez, D. J. (1996). *A multivariate analysis to explore personality correlates of stigma vulnerability: Implications for social work practice with vulnerable populations*. Ann Arbor, MI: UMI Publications.

Golding, J. M., & Karno, M. (1988). Gender differences in depressive symptoms among Mexican American and non-Hispanic Whites. *Hispanic Journal of Behavioral Sciences, 10*, 1–9.

Griffin-Pierce, T. (1997). When I am lonely the mountains call me: The impact of sacred geography on Navajo psychological well being. *American Indian and Alaska Native Mental Health Research, 7,* 1–10.

Guinn, B. (1998). Acculturation and health locus of control among Mexican American adolescents. *Hispanic Journal of Behavioral Sciences, 20,* 492–499.

Harman, M. J., & Arbona, C. (1991). Psychological adjustment among Hispanic adult children of alcoholics: An exploratory study. *Hispanic Journal of Behavioral Sciences, 13,* 105–112.

Healy, J. F. (1995). *Race, ethnicity, gender, and class: The sociology of group conflict and change.* Thousand Oaks, CA: Pine Forge Press.

Hishinuma, E. S., Andrade, N. N., Johnson, R. C., McArdle, J. J., Miyamoto, R. H., Nahulu, L. B., Makini, G. K., Yuen, N. Y. C., Nishimura, S. T., McDermott, J. F., Waldron, J. A., Luke, K. N., & Yates, A. (2000). Psychometric properties of the Hawaiian Culture Scale-Adolescent Version. *Psychological Assessment, 12*(2), 140–157.

Hough, R. L., Landsverk, J. A., Karno, M., Burnam, M. A., Timbers, D. M., Escobar, J. I., & Reiger, D. A. (1987). Utilization of health and mental health services by Los Angeles Mexican Americans. *Journal of Operational Psychiatry, 14,* 42–51.

Johnson, D. J. (1996). The perceived racial stress and coping apperception test. In R. L. Jones, (Ed.), *Handbook of tests and measurements for Black populations* (pp. 231–244). Hampton, VA: Cobb & Henry.

Jones, R. L. (1996). *Handbook of tests and measurements for Black populations* (Vols. 1 & 2). Hampton, VA: Cobb & Henry.

Jordan, C., & Franklin, C. (1995). *Clinical assessment for social workers: Quantitative and qualitative methods.* Chicago: Lyceum Books.

Kaufman, A. S., & Kaufman, N. L. (1983). *The Kaufman Assessment Battery for Children.* Circle Pines, MN: American Guidance Service.

Kaufman, A. S., & Kaufman, N. L. (1993). *The Kaufman Adolescent and Adult Intelligence Test.* Circle Pines, MN: American Guidance Service.

Kutchins, H., & Kirk, S. A. (1997). *Making us crazy: DSM: The psychiatric bible and the creation of mental disorders.* New York: Free Press.

Lindsey, M. L. (1998). Culturally competent assessment of African American clients. *Journal of Personality Assessment, 70*(1) 43–53.

Lum, D. (2000). *Social work practice and people of color: A process-stage approach.* (4th ed.). Pacific Grove, CA: Brooks/Cole.

Malgady, R. G., Costantino, G., & Rogler, L. H. (1984). Development of thematic apperception test (TEMAS) for urban Hispanic children. *Journal of Consulting and Clinical Psychology, 52,* 986–996.

McCubbin H. I., Thompson, A., & Elver K. (2000). Family pressures scale ethnic (FPRESE). In K. Corcoran & J. Fischer (Eds.), *Measures for clinical practice: A sourcebook* (3rd ed., 2 Vols., pp. 338–341). NY, Free Press.

McDonnell, J. A. (1991). *The dispossession of the American Indian, 1887–1934.* Bloomington: Indiana University Press.

McLemore, S. D., & Romo, H. D. (1998). *Racial and ethnic relations in America.* Boston: Allyn & Bacon.

McNeil, D. W., Kee, M., & Zvolensky, M. J. (1999). Culturally related anxiety and ethnic identity in Navajo college students. *Cultural Diversity and Ethnic Minority Psychology, 5,* 56–64.

McNeil, D. W., Porter, C. A., Zvolensky, M. J., Chaney, J. M., & Kee, M. (2000). Assessment of culturally related anxiety in American Indian and Alaska Natives. *Behavior Therapy, 31,* 301–325.

Mezzich, J. E., Kirmayer, L. J., Kleinman, A., Fabrega, H., Parron, D. L., Good, B. J., Lin, K., & Manson, S. M. (1999). The place of culture in DSM-IV. *Journal of Nervous and Mental Disease, 187*(18), 457–464.

Mokuau, N. (1990). The impoverishment of native Hawaiians and the social work challenge. *Health and Social Work, 15,* 235–242.

Murphy, D. A., Cantwell, C., Jordan, D. D., Lee, M., Cooley-Quille, M. R., & Lahey, B. B. (2000). Test-retest reliability of Dominic anxiety and depression items among young children. *Journal of Psychopathology and Behavioral Assessment, 22*(3), 257–270.

Oetting, E. R., Swaim, R. C., & Chiarella, M. C. (1998). Factor structure and invariance of the orthogonal cultural identification scale among American Indian and Mexican American youth. *Hispanic Journal of Behavioral Sciences, 20,* 131–154.

Okazaki, S., & Sue, S. (1995). Methodological issues in assessment research with ethnic minorities. *Psychological Assessment, 7,* 367–376.

Okazaki, S., & Sue, S. (2000). Implications of test revisions for assessment with Asian Americans. *Psychological Assessment, 12*(3), 272–280.

Oppenheimer, M. (1992). Alma's bedside ghost: Or the importance of culturally similarity. *Hispanic Journal of Behavioral Sciences, 14,* 496–501.

O'Sullivan, M. J., & Lasso, B. (1992). Community mental health services for Hispanics: A test of the culture compatibility hypothesis. *Hispanic Journal of Behavioral Sciences, 14*(4), 455–468.

Paniagua, F.A. (1994). *Assessing and treating culturally diverse clients: A practical guide.* Multicultural aspects of counseling series, Vol. 4. Thousand Oaks, CA: Sage.

Parcel, G., & Meyer, M. (1978). Development of an instrument to measure children's health locus of control. *Health Education Monographs, 6,* 149–159.

Pedersen, P. B. (1997). *Culture-centered counseling interventions: Striving for accuracy.* Thousand Oaks, CA: Sage.

Pedersen, P. B., & Ivey, A. (1993). *Culture-centered counseling and interviewing skills: A practical guide.* Westport, CT: Praeger.

Phinney, J. S. (1992). The multigroup ethnic identity measure: A new scale for use with diverse groups. *Journal of Adolescent Research, 7,* 156–176.

Pinderhughes, E. (1989). *Understanding race, ethnicity, and power: The key to efficacy in clinical practice.* New York: Free Press.

Ponce, F. Q., & Atkinson, D. R. (1989). Mexican-American acculturation, counselor ethnicity, counseling style, and perceived counselor credibility. *Journal of Counseling Psychology, 36*, 203–208.

Reid, R., DuPaul, G. J., Power, T. J., Anastopoulos, A. D., Rogers-Adkinson, D., Noll, M., & Riccio, C. (1998). Assessing culturally-different students for attention deficit hyperactivity disorder using behavior rating scales. *Journal of Abnormal Child Psychology, 26*(3), 187–198.

Robison, J., Gruman, C., Gaztambide, S., & Blank, K. (2002). Screening for depression in middle-aged and older Puerto Rican primary care patients. *Journals of Gerontology*. Series A, Biological Sciences & Medical Sciences. Vol 57A(5), M308–M314.

Rubin A. (2001). Is this a white country or what? In M. L. Andersen & P. H. Collins (Eds)., *Race, class, and gender: An anthology* (4th ed., pp. 430–438). Belmont, CA: Wadsworth.

Russell, C. (1998). *Racial and ethnic diversity: Asians, Blacks, Hispanics, Native Americans, and Whites*. Ithaca, NY: New Strategist.

Russo, S. A., & Lewis, J. E. (1999). The cross-cultural applications of the KAIT: Case studies with three differentially acculturated women. *Cultural Diversity and Ethnic Minority Psychology, 5*(1), 76–85.

Snipp, M. C. (1989). *American Indians: The first of this land*. New York: Russell Sage Foundation.

Stephens, K., Kiger, L., Karnes, F. A., & Whorton, J. E. (1999). Use of nonverbal measures of intelligence in identification of culturally diverse gifted students in rural areas. *Perceptual and Motor Skills, 88*, 793–796.

Stevenson, H. C., Jr., (1994). Validation of the Scale of Racial Socialization for African-American adolescents: Steps toward multidimensionality. *Journal of Black Psychology, 20*, 445–468.

Suinn, R. M., Rickard-Figueroa, K., Lew, S., & Vigil, P. (1987). The Suinn-Lew Self-Identity Acculturation Scale: Concurrent and factional validation. *Educational and Psychological Measurement, 52*, 1041–1046.

Thyer, B. A. (1992). Clinical Anxiety Scale (CAS). In W. W. Hudson (Ed.), *The Walmyr Assessment Scale Sconing manual*. Temple, AZ: Walmyr Publishing Co.

Tienda, M., & Stier, H. (1996). Generating labor market inequality: Employment opportunities and the accumulation of disadvantage. *Social Problems, 43*(2), 147–165.

Tran, B. N. (1996). Vietnamese translation and adaptation of the MMPI-2. In J. N. Butcher (Ed.), *International adaptation of the MMPI-2* (pp. 175–193). Minneapolis: University of Minnesota Press.

Trimble, J. E. (1995). Toward an understanding of ethnicity and ethnic identity, and their relationship with drug use research. In G. J. Botrin, S. Schinke, & M. A., Orlandi (Eds.), *Drug use prevention with multiethnic youth* (pp. 00–00). Thousand Oaks, CA: Sage.

Uomoto, J. M., & Wong, T.M. (2000). Multicultural perspectives on the neuropsychology of brain injury assessment and rehabilitation. In E. Fletcher-Janzen, T.

L. Strickland, & C. R. Reynolds (Eds.), *Handbook of cross-cultural neuropsychology* (pp. 169–184). New York: Plenum.

U.S. Bureau of the Census. (1998). *Statistical abstract of the United States 1998* (118th ed.). Washington, DC: U.S. Department of Commerce, Economics, and Statistical Administration.

Valla, J. P., Bergeron, L., Berube, H, & Gaudet, N. (1994). A structured pictorial questionnaire to assess DSM-III-R based diagnoses in children (6–11): Development, validity and reliability. *Journal of Child Psychology, 22,* 404–423.

Valla, J. P., Bergeron, L., Bidaut-Russell, M., St.-Georges, M., & Gaudet, N. (1997). Reliability of the Dominic-R: A young child mental health questionnaire combining visual and auditory stimuli. *Journal of Child Psychology and Psychiatry, 38*(6), 717–724.

Walters, K. (1999). Urban American Indian identity attitudes and acculturation styles. *Journal of Human Behavior in the Social Environment, 2*(1/2), 163–178.

Waters M. C. (2001). Optional ethnicities: For whites only? In M. L. Andersen & P. H. Collins (Eds.), *Race, class, and gender: An anthology* (4th ed., pp. 430–438). Belmont, CA: Wadsworth.

Weaver, H., & White, B. (1997). The Native American family circle: Roots of resiliency. *Journal of Family Social Work, 2*(1), 67–79.

Williams-Flournoy, D. F., & Andersen, L. P. (1996). The Acculturative Stress Scale: Preliminary findings. In R. L. Jones (Ed.), *Handbook of tests and measurements for Black populations* (pp. 351–358). Hampton, VA: Cobb & Henry.

Wilson, W. J. (1996). *When work disappears: The world of the new urban poor.* New York: Knopf.

Wong (2000). Neuropsychological assessment and intervention with Asian Americans. In E. Fletcher-Janzen, T. L. Strickland, & C. R. Reynolds (Eds.), *Handbook of cross-cultural neuropsychology* (pp. 43–53). New York: Plenum.

Zayas, L. H., Torres, L. R., Malcolm, J., & DesRosiers, F. S. (1996). Clinicians' definitions of ethnically sensitive therapy. *Professional Psychology: Research and Practice, 27,* 78–82.

CHAPTER 11

Linking Assessment to Outcome Evaluation Using Single System and Group Research Designs

Bruce A. Thyer and Laura L. Myers

The social work profession has long paid attention to the importance of conducting empirical evaluations of the outcomes of clinical services. For example, over eighty years ago one of the founders of social casework, Mary Richmond (1917/1935), claimed that "Special efforts should be made to ascertain whether abnormal manifestations are *increasing* or *decreasing* in number and intensity, as this often has a practical bearing on the management of the case" (p. 435). Individual clinical social workers are concerned with evaluating the outcomes of their own practice with clients, not only to help build on the evidence-based foundations of social work knowledge but also to use feedback in continuing work with clients, small groups, couples, or families. This is why, for example, the *Code of Ethics* of the National Association of Social Workers (NASW) mandates that:

> Social workers should monitor and evaluate policies, the implementation of programs, and practice interventions. Social workers should promote and facilitate evaluation and research to contribute to the development of knowledge. Social workers should . . . fully use evaluation and research evidence in their professional practice." (NASW, 1996, p. 20)

Relatedly, the *NASW Standards for the Practice of Clinical Social Work* clearly states that "Clinical social workers shall have . . . knowledge about and skills in using research to evaluate the effectiveness of a service" (NASW, 1989, p. 7). The *NASW Standards for School Social Work Services* further claims that "All school social work programs, new or long standing, should be evaluated on an ongoing basis to determine their relevance, effectiveness, efficiency, and contributions to the process of educating children" (NASW, 1992, p. 16).

Empirical research on the outcomes of clinical services can be roughly divided into two major categories. *Efficacy studies* are tightly designed experimental investigations, usually using carefully screened clients meeting certain inclusion criteria; specially trained and supervised therapists; interventions delivered in accordance with a treatment manual or other structured protocol; and the repeated administration of reliable and valid outcome measures. *Effectiveness studies* are investigations that attempt to replicate the positive findings obtained through prior efficacy studies in practice contexts in contexts that more closely approximate the real world of clinical services. Effectiveness studies involve the type of heterogeneous clientele seen at community mental health agencies (as opposed to volunteers treated at specialized university-based clinics); clients with multiple diagnoses (as opposed to only one); more complex problems (such as serious mental disorders complicated by psychosocial difficulties such as abuse or poverty); naturally occurring treatment groups (clients with similar problems seen at two different agencies using differing interventions, as opposed to being randomly assigned to different treatment conditions); and the more usually encountered clinicians (most often with a master's degree, as opposed to a doctorate in medicine, psychology, or social work).

It is a particular strength of the clinical social work profession, which is the largest provider of mental health services in the United States, that the bulk of our practitioners are engaged in agency-based practice in public or not-for-profit private agencies. Thus we are ideally positioned to collaborate with other disciplines in the design and conduct of effectiveness research. This has been noted by Mullen (1995):

> Social work has no more important use of research methods than assessment of the consequences of practice and policy choices . . . small scale, agency-based studies are worthwhile if they succeed in placing interest in effectiveness at the center of agency practice and when they create a critical alliance between practitioners and researchers. (pp. 282–283)

Katherine Ell, past executive director of the Institute for the Advancement of Social Work and Research, has similarly pointed out that "Studies are needed on the effectiveness of psychosocial intervention, including interventions previously tested under ideal controlled conditions, in real-world health care systems" (Ell, 1996, p. 589).

If social work is to continue to enjoy substantial amounts of financial support from local, state, and federal sources, it is imperative that we be able to demonstrate, *with legitimate data that are credible to others*, that we are genuinely capable of helping the clients we serve. Similarly, clinical social workers whose services are reimbursed via third-party payers are under considerable pressure to empirically document client changes. Among some managed care firms, actual reimbursement can be contingent on the clinical social worker being able to provide such information.

Evaluating the outcomes of clinical social work services can be considered a specialized form of research inquiry. It is so specialized that some have argued that outcome studies should not be considered research at all, given their focus on individual clients or specific programmatic services, and given the traditional construction of research as an effort to build theory and to contribute to generalizable knowledge. One may construe evaluation studies as either a legitimate component of the larger field of scientific research or as a more limited role best described by terms such as a quality assurance study, clinical evaluation, or outcome assessment. However, the field of evaluation, clinical or programmatic, does make use of the same methods of inquiry as mainstream scientific investigations. The clinical social worker attempting to undertake an empirical evaluation of services should be thoroughly familiar with and comfortable in using these methods. But fear not: the actual design and conduct of evaluation studies is not as complex and intimidating as it may appear, and the balance of this chapter will attempt to bare out this claim.

Evaluating the outcomes of clinical social work generally makes use of two major forms of inquiry—the general methods known as *single system designs* and the general methods known as *group designs*. Both rely on certain fundamental prerequisites: 1) The clinical social worker must have available a practical, reliable, inexpensive, and valid *outcome measure* which can be used to evaluate results. 2) It must be possible to administer this outcome measure with clients on at least two, and ideally more, occasions.

If you can accomplish the above, with some modest efforts you can be well on your way to designing empirical evaluations of the results of clinical social work practice. This may include practice conducted on a variety of levels, such as one-to-one therapy, group work, marital or family counseling, or the treatment of couples. In principle and in fact these methods also can be used in the design and conduct of social work outcome studies of organizational, community, and policy practice as well; but such endeavors are outside the scope of the present chapter. We will now review the basic principles of the design and conduct of single system designs, as used in the evaluation of clinical social work. This will be followed by a similar explication of using simple group designs for the same purpose.

THE DESIGN AND CONDUCT OF SINGLE SYSTEM DESIGN

Elsewhere in this text we have reviewed the factors involved in selecting reliable and valid quantitative and qualitative outcome measures for use in clinical assessment. We also have presented the distinction between assessment and screening measures suitable to arriving at, perhaps, a formal diagnosis of a mental disorder or other baseline or pretreatment assessment of client status or functioning. Throughout we have encouraged the use of measures that are sensitive to the types of important changes in client functioning that may occur during clinical social work. Please note that the application of the methods of single system designs (SSDs) may be undertaken within the context of virtually any model of social work assessment and treatment. If you anticipate your clinical services to be affecting client functioning in meaningful ways, then SSDs can be useful ways to document this. In general:

Axiom 1: If something exists (e.g., a client problem or strength), it is potentially measurable.

Axiom 2: If you measure client functioning, you are in a better position to treat client functioning.

Axiom 3: If you measure client functioning, you are in a better position to evaluate clinical outcomes.

The above three simple principles can be called Thyer's Axioms, which are an extension and somewhat of a softening of my late and respected friend Walter Hudson's "First Axioms of Treatment," which created quite a stir when they were first published (see Hudson, 1978, and subsequent commentaries in later issues of the same journal). Actually there is now some preliminary evidence supporting the hypothesis that the clients of social workers who evaluate their practice using single system research designs (SSRDs) have more improved clinical outcomes that those enjoyed by clients whose social workers *do not* use SSRDs to evaluate their practice (see Faul, McMurtry, & Hudson, 2001; Slomin-Nevo & Anson, 1998).

Within the context of SSDs, the clinical social worker attempts to empirically measure client functioning repeatedly over time. This can be done before, during, and/or after intervention. Measures taken before formal treatment begins can be called a *baseline* of client functioning. How many measures are enough to constitute a credible baseline? There is no simple answer to this. One is better than none; two are better than one; at least three are necessary to ascertain a real trend in the data (because any two data points can be linked to form a straight line); four are better than three; and so forth. Ideally, baseline data, if graphed, should seem to appear relatively stable when looked at by you and your colleagues. Stable means that one would answer no to the questions "Are the data clearly increasing?" or "Are the data clearly decreasing?" This is a rather conservative test, because it requires fairly unambiguous trends in your data to be detected visually.

Data can also be gathered during the course of actual clinical social work intervention; such data is labeled the *treatment phase*. Data collected after treatment has been discontinued is called the *follow-up phase*.

The experimental logic behind SSDs is relatively simple. The baseline data phase is an operational manifestation of the hoary (but most certainly valid) social work precept—*begin where the client is*. If your outcome measure is carefully selected to be reliable and valid, you may be able to augment your clinical judgment that the client is getting worse, getting better, or staying the same during this assessment process. You may, therefore, be able to go to your supervisor or managed care utilization reviewer, and, in addition to your personal and professional powers of suasion, be able to display a graph justifying the need for intervention.

Next, continue the process of assessment/measurement during treatment using the same methods and measures as you employed during the baseline. If you get immediate and dramatic improvements, this too is good and is consistent with the hypothesis that your intervention caused these improvements. Note the careful wording here: "consistent with the hypothesis that treatment caused these improvements." This is a more cautious and conservative interpretation than claiming "My services *caused* the client to improve." In most circumstances, your clinical assessment of outcomes may justify the former conclusion, but it is a very rare practice situation indeed that enables you to embrace the latter. Some examples of using SSDs to evaluate the outcome of clinical social work will be used to illustrate the scope and flexibility of these evaluation methods.

The A-B Design

The A-B design is among the simplest forms of SSD and involves the social worker taking baseline measure of client functioning before and during intervention. This approach was used by second year MSW student Krista Barker in her practicum setting at a vocational rehabilitation program for persons with disabilities. One client, John (a pseudonym), was a 23-year-old African-American man with moderate mental retardation and a seizure disorder. While in the program, John displayed numerous inappropriate behaviors such as taunting peers, throwing objects, threatening violence, demonstrating physical aggression against staff and peers, and making inappropriate sexual advances. The severity and frequency of John's inappropriate behavior were placing him in danger of imminent discharge from the vocational rehabilitation program.

Krista developed a way to reliably observe and count John's inappropriate behavior; she did this for five consecutive work days. She then implemented a simple reward program wherein John could earn reinforcers (augmented opportunities for socialization) based on appropriate behavior. This plan was used over the next seven days and seemed to result in a considerable reduction in John's inappropriate behavior (see Figure 1). The data in Figure 1 suggest, but cannot be said to prove, that the reward program Krista developed *caused* the improvements in John's behavior. There are too many other explanations that could account for these changes. However, the data certainly suggests, and at the very least reveals, that the plan did not seem to result in any exacerbation of inap-

Figure 11.1   Daily Number of Aggressive Behaviors Displayed by John.
Reproduced from Barker and Thyer (2000, p. 40) with permission

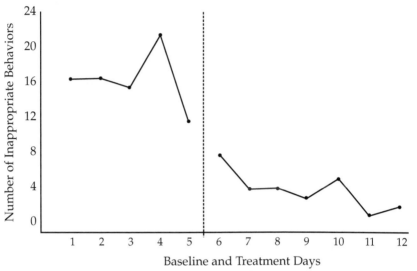

Baseline and Treatment Days
Total Number of Inappropriate Behaviors From 9:00AM - 2:00PM
Daily number of aggressive behaviors displayed by John

propriate behavior. The agency staff were very impressed with the apparent results of Krista's program, which, it should be noted, focused on
strengthening positive behaviors via rewards and made no use of punishment. Barker and Thyer (2000) provide addition details about this
case.

The A-B-A Design

The A-B-A design is simply the continued collection of data after social work intervention is discontinued. This approach was used by social
work student Susan Massa at a senior citizens' center, which served a
daily hot meal at lunchtime. In Florida in the late 1980s, there was no law
requiring safety belt use among automobile drivers, and Susan wanted to
see if she could get senior citizens to use their safety belts more frequently. She developed a reliable method of using independent observers
stationed outside the senior citizens' center parking lot to record the over-
the-shoulder use of safety belts by exiting drivers. This was baselined for
seven consecutive days (the first A phase). The intervention consisted of
having an MSW student stand at the exit to the parking lot after lunch
and display to the departing elderly drivers an 11 x 14 inch printed sign

reading *Please Buckle Up—I Care* on side one and *Thanks for Buckling Up!* on side two. The observer displayed side one to unbuckled exiting drivers, and flipped the sign to side two if they were seen to buckle up. Only side two was displayed if the driver was already buckled as he or she left. Independent observers collected data on safety belt use while this intervention was implemented for two weeks (the B phase). Use of the sign was then halted, but data continued to be collected for another six consecutive days (the second A phase).

The data from this A-B-A study are depicted in Figure 2 (see Thyer, Thyer, & Massa, 1991). The baseline data showed that on average about 42% of the exiting drivers were using their safety belts. This increased to about 60% during the intervention phase and dropped to about 48% during the second A phase. The first A phase data are fairly stable, and the magnitude of the change between the first A phase and the B phase suggests that a real change occurred—certainly an 18% increase in safety belt use is a meaningful one. The immediate decline in belt use after the intervention was halted favors the hypothesis that the display of the promoting sign actually *caused* more frequent safety belt use. Further, because we see *two* changes in the outcome measure coincident corresponding to the introduction and removal of the intervention, the A-B-A design can be a methodologically stronger SSD than the A-B design alone, which allows only one such possible shift in the data. Herein is the experimental logic behind the stronger SSDs, that is, those that may permit *causal inferences*.

Figure 11.2   Daily Percentages of Observed Safety Belt Use. Reproduced from Thyer, Thyer, and Massa (1991, p. 128) with permission.

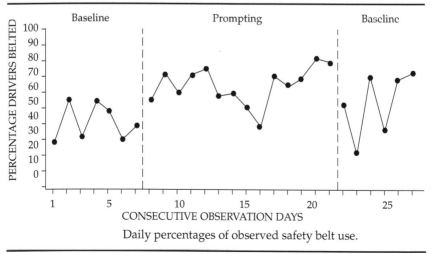

Daily percentages of observed safety belt use.

Faced with an A-B design like Krista Barker's described above, the skeptic could claim that something else may have happened at the same time treatment was implemented and that the observed changes were due to this other factor and not to the introduction of social work intervention. Indeed, the skeptic is correct to raise this reasonable caveat. However, when faced with the results of the A-B-A design used by Susan Massa, the skeptic would have to argue for *two, successive, coincidental changes*—one that just happened to occur when treatment began, and the second that just happened to occur when treatment was halted! Here one's skepticism must begin to weaken. Perhaps, just perhaps, social work intervention really *did* cause the observed changes. What seems more plausible? Either there is a real functional relationship between social work and outcomes, or there is no such relationship; it is merely a coincidence. Of course such a judgment needs to take into account the nature of the client problem/situation, its duration and severity, and the quality and magnitude of any observed changes. Nevertheless, you can appreciate the logic at work. You will appreciate it even more with the next design.

The A-B-A-B Design

By now you have figured out where this is going. The A-B-A-B design involves the collection of reliable and valid data over a first baseline phase, then during an initial treatment phase, then over a second baseline phase during which treatment is halted, and then during a second treatment phase when treatment is reinstated. A clear example of this type of design was used at an elementary school to evaluate a simple intervention designed to reduce school violence. Prior to the school opening at 8:45 am, arriving children went to a playground for free play. One to three teachers' aids monitored the playground, which contained over 220 kids. Playground violence was common—interpersonal physical aggression, property abuse, and so forth. A reliable and valid way to measure violent acts was developed, and baseline assessments were gathered for twelve mornings (first A phase). The first intervention period involved the introduction of organized games that were mediated by the teachers' aids and had a brief time-out contingency for particularly dangerous behaviors; this was implemented for seven days (first B phase). This was followed by four days of baseline conditions (second A phase), and then six days of the same intervention (second B phase). The data are depicted in Figure 3. The average number of violent acts observed during the first A phase was 212; during the first B phase, 91; during second A phase, 191; and during the second B phase, 97. The clarity of the data argue very strongly in favor of the hypothesis that introducing structured games actually *caused* the observed reductions in violence and aggression. The

Figure 11.3   Frequency of Incidents Recorded during the 20-min Morning Observation Periods on the Play Group. Reproduced from Murphy, Hutchison, and Bailey (1983, p. 33) with permission.

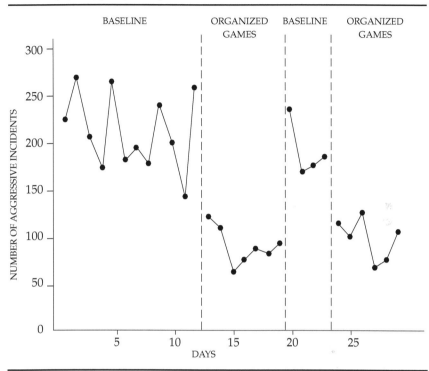

skeptic would be very hard-pressed to plausibly argue that anything *except* the psychosocial intervention was causally responsible for these changes because there are three, consecutive alterations in the data clearly associated with the introduction or removal of the intervention. This is quite compelling visually, so much so that there is no need to use inferential statistics to help the reader make a conclusion. The data almost "hit you between the eyes" (pun intended). Given the paucity of intervention research that actually tries to reduce school violence (as opposed to simply study it using descriptive or correlational methods), this study by Murphy, Hutchison and Bailey (1983) is all the more compelling, despite the elegant simplicity of its research design.

Single system research designs have been used by social workers to evaluate their practice since the late 1960s, and examples of clinical assessment and evaluation using these methods have been published in every major social work journal (see Thyer & Thyer, 1992). Mainstream social work research textbooks include these methods as a viable and practical approach to clinical assessment (e.g., Royse, Thyer, Padgett, & Logan, 2000; Rubin & Babbie, 2000; Thyer 2001a, 2001b), and they can be creatively employed in the evaluation of social work practice that is derived from all theoretical orientations. Although originating in the traditions of quantitative research that emphasizes reliable, valid, and objective measurement of clinical phenomena and other aspects of clients' lives, SSDs lend themselves very nicely to integration with qualitative research methods. For example, they are readily integrated with narrative case histories as a research method. They are also well positioned to be of use in the evaluation of community, organizational, and other forms of macro social work practice (Thyer, 1998), as well as of use in clinical supervision (Artelt & Thyer, 1998).

THE DESIGN AND CONDUCT OF GROUP RESEARCH DESIGN

You have undoubtedly been exposed to the general principles behind the design and conduct of group research designs, also called nomothetic research designs. Rather than relying on many consecutive measurements taken from one or from a very small number of clients (as in single system designs), group designs typically rely on very few (usually two or three) repetitions of measurement on larger groups of clients.

Group designs typically use inferential statistics such as t tests, analysis of variance, or chi square assessments to aid the practitioner-researcher in making reliable judgements as to whether change has really occurred. Single system designs usually rely on the visual inspection of graphically presented data to infer the existence of reliable changes in client functioning. Each approach has its strengths and limitations, indications, and contraindications. If you are employed in an agency where relatively few clients with a particular problem appear seeking assistance, it will be very difficult to conduct a credible group research design to evaluate the outcomes of social work services. In such circumstances single-system designs may be applicable. If, on the other hand, you have access to large numbers of clients and/or multiple repeated measurement of client functioning is not possible, then a nomothetic approach would be the way to go. It is definitely not the case that one method is intrinsically superior to the other.

The inferential statistical methods used to evaluate changes in average scores for group designs are very good at detecting reliable, but very small, effects, especially if your sample sizes are large. This is good if you spend a lot of time studying interventions of modest to minimal effectiveness. Making inferences about changes through visual inspection of graphically presented data is not very good for detecting small (but reliable and statistically significant) changes. This means you could potentially overlook an intervention that is only modestly effective and learn only about treatments that produce whopping effects. Claiming that an effect is present when it is not (for all practical purposes) is known in research as a Type I error. This kind of error is more likely using inferential statistics. Claiming that an effect is not present, when it really is (although it is a really small change) is labeled a Type II error and is more likely using visual analysis of data. The authors tend to side with those who claim that in the field of evaluation research, committing a Type II error is less damaging to good science than a Type I error: you learning about fewer (weaker) interventions, but those that you end up studying are only those that are quite powerful. This is an arguable point, and as it is not central to this chapter it will not be pursued any further.

Nomothetic designs used in evaluation research can be hierarchically ranked in terms of their strength or potential for yielding internally valid conclusions. One common system is to categorize them as *pre-experimental, quasi-experimental,* and the truly *experimental* group designs (see Royse et al., 2000; Thyer, 2001a), and this convention will be followed here.

Pre-Experimental Group Research Designs

Perhaps the simplest outcome study used in clinical assessment is the *posttest only group design,* wherein a group of clients are formally assessed after they receive a social work intervention. Consider the following scenario: In our hometown once or twice a year an entreprenurial hypnotist (let us call him Professor Marvel) rents a hotel meeting room and offers a one-session smoking cessation program involving so-called group hypnosis. He takes out a large advertisement in the local paper, charges a modest fee, packs the room with his gullible clients, and does his group hypnosis. He might even sell "booster" treatments on cassette tapes for an extra charge. Even if a small number of clients are unhappy at the end of the evening's session and demand their fees back, Professor Marvel does well enough out of this night's work to make a profitable living.

It is conceivable for a clinical social worker to attend one of Marvel's hypnotic workshops and, as clients exit the meeting room at the end of the session, to distribute a stamped, self-addressed postcard asking participants to mail it in a month to the social worker, perhaps anonymously, indicating whether or not they are smoking. The outcome measure can be the percentage still smoking. Assuming that all clients accepted the postcard, returned it after one month, and reported their smoking behavior honestly, this would be an instructive evaluation of Professor Marvel's hypnosis workshops. If 100% claimed that a month later they were still smoking, we could be fairly sure that Marvel's intervention was not really helpful in quitting smoking. If 100% claimed that they were not smoking, this would be evidence corroborative (but not conclusive) of Marvel's claim to be able to help people quit smoking. In the arcane symbolism of group designs, this study could be labeled an X-O study, with X representing exposure to the intervention and O representing some reliable and valid assessment of client function.

A realistic example of the X-O design was undertaken by Myers and Rittner (1999, 2001), who used a convenience sample of about 100 adults who had been raised in a traditional, old-fashioned orphanage. Many years after these people had left the orphanage, Myers and Rittner contacted them and asked them to complete some standardized assessments about their psychosocial functioning, including such issues as family and interpersonal relationships, educational attainments, employment history, emotional/mental disorders, quality of life, life satisfaction, and so on. In this way, the social workers were able to determine that these adults who had been raised in an orphange enjoyed fairly positive lives, with generally good incomes, interpersonal relationships, life satisfaction, educational attainments, and quality of life.

A stronger form of pre-experimental group design systematically assesses client functioning before social work intervention, and then again using similar methods after social work treatment. This design can be diagramed as an O-X-O design. A recent example that illustrates the use of this design in the evaluation of clinical practice was conducted by MSW student Wendi Schwartz, who was interning at a psychiatric hospital in Atlanta, GA. Wendi was assigned to a partial hospitalization program, wherein depressed or substance-abusing clients spend 9:00 am to 3:00 pm, Monday through Friday, in a structured hospital setting, receiving psychotherapy, group work, family therapy, vocational services, and other interventions. Partial hospitalization is much less expensive than inpatient treatment. Wendi found that there were very few studies that had examined the outcomes of partial hospitalization services. She was able to work with her field instructor and hospital administrators and administer to all newly admitted, depressed patients a rapid assessment instrument called the *Generalized Contentment Scale* (GCS), which is a measure of depression. Then, just before discharge, Wendi asked the patients to complete the GCS again. During the course of her internship, Wendi obtained admission and discharge GCS scores from a total of nine clients, finding that the mean score at admission was about 60, and the discharge score averaged 43.

A *t* test found this reduction (lower scores mean less depression) to be statistically significantly different. Did Wendi show that partial hospitalization *caused* these clients to improve? By no means. There are too many alternative explanations for these improved scores to permit her to draw such a conclusion. However, these data are *consistent with* the hypothesis that the program is effective; the data are also consistent with the hypothesis that the clients are not getting worse. Most psychiatric programs lack even this minimal level of evaluation data, and in this limited sense, Wendi's study was a useful undertaking in programmatic assessment. More details can be found in Schwartz and Thyer (2000).

Quasi-Experimental Group Research Designs

The quasi-experimental group research designs are characterized by their use of some sort of control group, that is, a number of people who receive no social work treatment, alternative social work or other treatment method, or (more rarely) placebo social work treatment. The logic being that if improvements are seen in a group of clients who receive an active social work intervention, and no changes or only small effects are seen in the control group, one has tentative evidence (evidence consistent with the hypothesis) that social work *caused* improvements.

Victor Aeby and his social worker spouse, Tracey Carpenter-Aeby, conducted a quasi-experimental evaluation of alternative schooling provided to disruptive middle and high school youth. These authors wanted to compare the results of a standard alternative school program to the regular alternative school *combined with* an intensive family intervention component. In lieu of complete suspension (with its deleterious academic effects), behaviorally disruptive youth are placed in a alternative schools (AS) that provide a much more structured and disciplined school environment. The standard AS program was provided to 95 youth during the 1994–1995 school year, and the same AS program *plus* a program of intensive family involvement was provided to 120 youth during the 1995–1996 school year. Victor and Tracey wanted to test the hypothesis that augmenting AS with intensive family work (largely provided by the AS school social worker) would help the kids make greater academic and disciplinary gains than those achieved through the standard AS program. Outcome measures included standardized measures of self-esteem, depression, locus-of-control (all assessed before and after AS) academic grades, and school attendance achieved. These areas were assessed in the home school during the terms before and during the terms after placement in the AS. This design is a bit more complicated to diagram and looks like this:

	1994–1995	1995–1996
Year 1 (standard AS program)	O-X-O	
Year 2 (standard AS with intensive family involvement)		O-Y-O

The X refers to the standard program, and Y refers to the standard program plus intensive family involvement. The dashed line separating the two groups means that they were not constructed using *random assign-*

ment (more on this later). Obviously the school administration could not preselect or randomly assign school-age kids to the AS in given years, hence the mandated use of a nonrandom comparison group. Inferential statistics were used to look at group scores both before and after the youths' entry into the AS program (within group changes) and also between the two groups at the beginning and end of the program (between group changes). Although the overall results were mixed, students who received the AS program with added family involvement demonstrated greater improvements in locus-of-control, grades, and attendance; a smaller proportion of kids dropped out of school as well. Aeby, Manning, Thyer, and Carpenter-Aeby (1999) can be consulted to learn more details about this quasi-experimental study.

Social worker Betsy Vonk used a very similar design to compare the clinical outcomes at a student counseling center. Betsy was employed at this center and arranged for all college students seeking counseling services to complete the *Symptom Checklist 90* (SCL 90), a rapid assessment instrument that measures multiple psychiatric symptoms like anxiety and depression. In the normal course of the center's operation, not all students seeking counseling could be immediately accommodated and were instead placed on a waiting list. Some time later they were recontacted, readministered the SCL 90, and scheduled for counseling. All clients were then readministered the SCL 90 when counseling was terminated. This structure lent itself to the naturalistic construction of the following quasi-experimental group design:

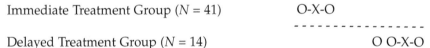

Immediate Treatment Group ($N = 41$)   O-X-O

Delayed Treatment Group ($N = 14$)   O O-X-O

Here both groups of college students received the same treatment (counseling provided by licensed mental health professionals, including clinical social workers), but the second group received delayed treatment. This delay was noncontrived, having been dictated by the exigencies of agency resources and staff availability. Inferential statistics were used to examine pre- versus posttreatment mean scores on various psychiatric symptoms both within the groups over time and between the groups at pre- and posttreatment. On the initial assessment, the groups had essentially equivalent levels of symptoms. After counseling, the immediate treatment group's symptoms were greatly reduced. However, after a time, when the delayed treatment group was reassessed (not having had any formal treatment), their scores were found to have not changed. When the delayed treatment group subsequently received counseling, they improved to an extent similar to those seen among the immediate treatment group. This creative study produced data consistent with the hypothesis that the services at the counseling center were followed by symptomatic improvements among the students and that these improvements were unlikely due to the simple passage of time, because the delayed treatment group experienced no change between their first and second evaluations. Given the very few published studies empirically evaluating the clinical outcomes of college-based student counseling centers, Betsy Vonk's study was a very useful contribution to the literature (see Vonk & Thyer, 1999 for more details).

Experimental Group Research Designs

True experiments involve the random assignment of clients to differing conditions, a new social work intervention, to standard care, to some other alternative service, to placebo treatment, or to no treatment whatsoever. There are considerably fewer opportunities to conduct genuine experimental group research designs to evaluate clinical social work practice, but occasionally circumstances do permit their use. True experiments have much higher levels of *internal validity*, allowing stronger inferences about whether social work treatment *caused* any observed improvements. This is why our research textbooks stress their value.

Clinical social worker Rufus Larkin was employed as an elementary school social worker, and a large number of behaviorally disruptive kids were referred to him each year. He used a structured group work treatment program using cognitive behavioral methods to try to help these kids. Rufus could not always accommodate his referrals immediately, and he had to place some kids on a waiting list before he could place them in a new group. In order to be fair to all the kids, Rufus tossed a coin to determine which kids got into group intervention immediately, and which began group work later. This process naturally generated a genuinely random waiting list comparison group and enabled him to develop the following experimental design:

Immediate Treatment Group (*N* = 31)	R O-X-O-O
Delayed Treatment Group (*N* = 21)	R-O-O-X-O

The R represented the group that was developed using random assignment. The O's indicated some type of standardized assessment, and X stood for the group enrolled in cognitive behavioral group therapy. The outcome measures included student self-control, self-esteem, and reliable assessments of in-class behavior; and the data were examined using inferential statistics. The results provided answers to the following questions: "Did kids who got group work have improved self-esteem, self-control, and behavior?" Yes. "Were these improvements due to simply being assessed?" No. "Were these improvements *caused* by the group work?" Yes. "Were these improvements maintained over a fairly long period of time after the social work intervention was completed?" Yes. The clinical social worker who can provide data-based answers to such questions is indeed in an enviable position. Larkin and Thyer (1999) provide more details about this experimental evaluation of clinical social work practice.

If you can use random assignment to create sufficiently large groups (greater than about 20), a pretreatment assessment is not really necessary to be fairly sure that the groups are equivalent. Some genuine experiments make use of an approach called a *Posttest-Only Control Group Design* to evaluate the outcomes of social work. Social worker Kelly Canady did this to see if he could promote voting behavior among low-income African-American residents of a small Georgia community. A couple of months prior to the presidential election of 1988, Kelly went to the voting office and obtained the names and addresses on mailing labels for all registered voters in the poorest voting precinct in his town. This precinct contained a large number of public housing projects and was over 90% African American. Kelly random picked 400 voters from this list of 2,500 names and randomly assigned each to one of four different experimental conditions. Those assigned to Group 1 received a letter signed by the local chairs of the Democratic and Republican parties, urging the citizen to be sure to vote in the upcoming presidential election. They got this letter about 3 days before the election. Those assigned to Group 2 got the same letter twice, about a week before, and again about three days before, the election. Those assigned to Group 3 got the letter three times—two weeks, one week, and a few days before the election. Voters randomly assigned to Group 4 got no reminder letters.

Kelly hypothesized that a higher proportion of those receiving the letter would vote, relative to those who did not get the letter and that the more letters a voter received, the more likely he or she would be to vote. After the election, Kelly went back to the voting registrar's office and got a print out of who among his 400 voters actually voted (This information did not reflect how they voted, but simply if they actually cast a ballot. This information is open to the public). He was able to use simple inferential statistics to see if the groups reliably differed in terms of the proportion that voted. This elegant experimental strategy can be diagrammed as follows:

Group 1 (1 letter)	R	W	O
Group 2 (2 letters)	R	X	O
Group 3 (3 letters)	R	Y	O
Group 4 (no letter)	R		O

Again, the R refers to that the group formed on the basis of random assignment, the W, X, or Y refers to the experimental treatment condition, and the gap in the 4th group's diagram signifies no intervention. Would you be interested in the results? Read Canady and Thyer (1990) to find out!

As demonstrated in the above examples, clinical social workers have a wide array of pre-experimental, quasi-experimental, and experimental group research designs that can be used to evaluate the outcomes of practice. Practicality and internal validity are almost inversely proportional to each other. The designs that are easiest to implement in real-life practice are usually the weakest ones you can undertake. Those possessing the higher levels of internal validity are usually too difficult to implement in agency-based or private practice settings.

WHAT ABOUT EXTERNAL VALIDITY?

You also have no doubt been exposed to the concept of *external validity*, which refers to the extent that a researcher (or reader of a research study) can generalize the findings of a given study to similar clients or groups. There are two basic methods by which external validity of a given study may be demonstrated. The first approach (the most widely taught, but paradoxically all too rarely employed) involves obtaining a sample of clients that is genuinely representative of the larger universe of individual with similar problems. The method used to approximate a representative sample involves *randomly* choosing a subset of clients to participate from the larger sample of such persons. As you know from your research training, a randomly chosen sample can be confidently viewed as legitimately representative of the larger group from which they were chosen. Therefore, a finding from a truly randomly selected sample of clients can be legitimately generalizable. For example, consider determining the average age of all clients currently receiving services at your agency, about 4,000 of them (this is a BIG agency). You could manually extract the information from every chart. However, this would be a lot of unnecessary work because you could obtain virtually the same result by randomly sampling a much small subset of charts from your entire set of patient records, perhaps as few as a couple of hundred records. There are some handy tables found in some research books (e.g., Royse et al., 2001) that tell you what size sample you need to randomly select from a given population to have a fairly accurate estimate of the real statistic you are interested in. Using the same statistical logic, based on elementary probability theory, if you find through using a suitably rigorous research design that a randomly selected sample of clients genuinely benefits much more from Treatment A than from Treatment B, you may infer that Treatment A is very likely better than Treatment B for the others in the universe of clients you sampled from. Thus, all things being equal (cost, social validity, ethical appropriateness), Treatment A should be offered in lieu of Treatment B to members of that group. So far so good, but here is where we come up abruptly against the practical realities of agency-based clinical research: we can almost never obtain a randomly chosen sample of clients from the larger universe of clients we wish to generalize to.

The truth of the matter is that field research usually employs convenience samples of clients, that is, persons chosen on the basis of their availability, ability, and willingness to provide informed consent, among other qualities. Even client groups obtained through some approximation of random sampling are usually compromised because of patient mortality (dropping out of the study), inability to locate clients posttreatment or at follow-up, refusal to continue participation in the study, or other detrimental developments. As soon as *any* of your initially randomly selected clients begin dropping out of your study for any reason, the representativeness of your sample becomes compromised and external validity becomes suspect.

Therefore, our advice to the clinical social worker evaluating his or her own practice and to the novice program evaluator valiantly trying to determine if clients being seen at his or her agency are getting better is simply this: Accept from the outset that your findings may well end up *not* being generalizable and that you are *not* capable of conducting a study with strong external validity. This is unfortunate when measuring your study against the idealized canons of ivory tower science, but it need not be a source of embarrassment so long as you are modest in your initial goals. Don't claim that you are going to see if assertive community treatment for persons with bipolar disorder is better than, say, interpersonal psychotherapy for such persons, *as a general rule*. It is ill advised to conduct such a study to yield generalizable knowledge applicable to all persons meeting the *DSM* criteria for bipolar disorder. Instead be more modest in your aspirations: "Do the clients seen at *our* agency do better with assertive community treatment compared to those of our clients receiving interpersonal psychotherapy?" Note the subtle distinction. You *can* accomplish the latter goal at your agency, whereas it is extremely unlikely that with your modest resources you would be able to satisfactorily answer the former question. It is perfectly legitimate and desirable to find out if *your* clients are getting better and to leave the development of generalizable knowledge to others better equipped via training and resources. It is unfortunate that many clinical social workers, imbued with the mistaken notion that the only scientifically acceptable finding is one obtained from a randomly selected sample, abandon any efforts at empirically evaluating the outcomes of their work because the findings may not be generalizable. Remember, that small scale, locally conducted, unfunded, less-than-perfectly-designed evaluation studies *are* an exceedingly valuable undertaking. They should not be dismissed by sherry-sipping academics comfortably housed in ivory towers.

But how will the profession ever develop generalizable knowledge, you may ask. The answer is through a process called *replication*. Replication can be accomplished in many ways. Let's say that Dr. Faust at the

XYZ agency made the following finding: drug-abusing clients randomly assigned to receive reinforcers, contingent on submitting drug-free urine screens, were more abstinent than clients who submitted similar urine specimens but did not get reinforcement for abstinence. This finding can be replicated by Dr. Faust at the same agency at a later time, using a different group of similar clients. If the same result emerges, then our confidence in this approach to treating drug abusers is somewhat strengthened. Or, Dr. Faust can try and replicate his study at another agency with similar clients. Or other researchers at different agencies (perhaps in different parts of the country), independent of Dr. Faust can use this approach and see if they obtain similar outcomes. Or other independent researchers at different agencies in other parts of the country can try and replicate Faust's findings with differing clients. If the effect was first obtained only using samples of men, try to see if it holds up using samples of women. If it was first demonstrated with White clients, see if similar results are found in samples of African Americans or Hispanics.

You can see the value in this approach: science via creeping incrementalism it could be called. Rather than conducting one massive study that controls for all possible threats to internal and external validity, more limited investigations can approach solving a given problem in a more piecemeal manner. Such lofty aspirations are not for most agency-based clinical social workers who are concerned not with building the edifice of scientific knowledge but rather with obtaining credible data regarding the outcome of their own efforts. This too is a noble endeavor and should not be dismissed as trivial. Indeed, localized efforts by clinical social workers can be argued to be more relevant to practice and evaluation concerns than grandiose megastudies.

SUMMARY

The social work profession has a long history of recognizing the importance of clinical practice evaluation. The two major forms of inquiry for evaluating social work outcomes are single system designs and group designs. Using single system designs, the clinician measures a single client's (or small groups of clients') functioning before, during, and after intervention; whereas group designs use inferential statistics to look at outcomes on larger groups of clients. Different models of each design are reviewed and the issues of external validity, and generalizability of results are discussed.

STUDY QUESTIONS

1. Think of a client you have seen in your field placement. Design a single system study to evaluate client outcomes. Include problem, measurement, and goal/objective. Present expected findings on a graph.

2. Now consider your field placement agency. Design a group study to help the agency look at its client outcomes. What design would be best? What measures? What would you expect to find?

3. Considering both of the above examples, speak to the issue of generalizability (external validity). How could you improve the external validity of your designs?

REFERENCES

Aeby, V. G., Manning, B. H., Thyer, B. A., & Carpenter-Aeby, T. (1999). Comparing outcomes of an alternative school program offered with and without intensive family involvement. *The School Community Journal, 9*, 17–32.

Artelt, T., & Thyer, B. A. (1998). Empirical approaches to social work supervision. In J. S. Wodarski & B. A. Thyer (Eds.), *Handbook of empirical social work practice: Volume II, psychosocial problems and practice issues* (pp. 413–431). New York: Wiley.

Barker, K. L., & Thyer, B. A. (2000). Differential reinforcement of other behavior in the treatment of inappropriate behavior and aggression in an adult with mental retardation at a vocational center. *Scandinavian Journal of Behaviour Therapy, 29*, 37–42.

Canady, K., & Thyer, B. A. (1990). Promoting voting behavior among low-income black voters using reminder letters: An experimental investigation. *Journal of Sociology and Social Welfare, 17*(4), 109–116.

Ell, K. (1996). Social work research and health care policy and practice: A psychosocial research agenda. *Social Work, 41*, 583–592.

Faul, A. C., McMurtry, S. L., & Hudson, W. W. (2001). Can empirical clinical practice techniques improve social work outcomes? *Research on Social Work Practice, 11*, 277–299.

Hudson, W. (1978). First axioms of treatment. *Social work, 23*(1), 65.

Larkin, R., & Thyer, B. A. (1999). Evaluating cognitive-behavioral group counseling to improve elementary school students' self-esteem, self-control, and classroom behavior. *Behavioral Interventions, 14*, 147–161.

Mullen, E. J. (1995). A review of *research methods for generalist social work. Social Work, 40*, 282–283.

Murphy, H. A., Hutchison, J. M., & Bailey, J. S. (1983). Behavioral school psychology goes outdoors: The effect of organized games on playground aggression. *Journal of Applied Behavior Analysis, 16*, 29–35.

Myers, L. L., & Rittner, B. (1999). Family functioning and satisfaction of former residents of a non-therapeutic residential care facility: An exploratory study. *Journal of Family Social Work, 3*(3), 53–68.

Myers, L. L., & Rittner, B. (2001). Adult psychosocial functioning of children raised in an orphanage. *Residential Treatment for Children and Youth, 18*(4), 3–21.

National Association of Social Workers. (1989). *NASW standards for the practice of clinical social work.* Washington, DC: Author.

National Association of Social Workers. (1992). *NASW standards for school social work services.* Washington, DC: Author.

National Association of Social Workers. (1996). *Code of ethics.* Washington, DC: Author.

Richmond, M. (1935) (Original work published in 1917). *Social diagnosis.* New York: Russell Sage Foundation.

Royse, D., Thyer, B. A., Padgett, D. K., & Logan, T. K. (2000). *Program evaluation: An introduction.* Belmont, CA: Brooks/Cole.

Rubin, A., & Babbie, E. (2000). *Research methods for social work* (3rd ed.). Pacific Grove, CA: Brooks/Cole.

Schwartz, W. L., & Thyer, B. A. (2000). Partial hospitalization treatment for clinical depression: A pilot evaluation. *Journal of Human Behavior in the Social Environment, 3*(2), 13–21.

Slomin-Nevo, V., & Anson, Y. (1998). Evaluating practice: Does it improve treatment outcome? *Social Work Research, 22,* 66–74.

Thyer, B. A. (1998). Promoting research on community practice: Using single-system research designs. In R. H. MacNair (Ed.), *Research strategies in community practice* (pp. 101–113). Binghamton, NY: Haworth.

Thyer, B. A. (2001a). Single system designs. In B. A. Thyer (Ed.), *The handbook of social work research methods* (pp. 239–262). Thousand Oaks, CA: Sage.

Thyer, B. A. (2001b). Single system designs. In R. M. Grinnell (Ed.), *Social work research and evaluation: Quantitative and qualitative approaches* (pp. 455–480). Itasca, IL: F. E. Peacock.

Thyer, B. A., & Thyer, K. B. (1992). Single system research designs in social work practice: A bibliography from 1965–1990. *Research on Social Work Practice, 2,* 99–116.

Thyer, B. A., Thyer, K. B., & Massa, S. (1991). Behavioral analysis and therapy in the field of gerontology. In P. K. H. Kim (Ed.), *Serving the elderly: Skills for practice* (pp. 117–135). New York: Aldine de Gruyter.

Vonk, E. M., & Thyer, B. A. (1999). Evaluating the effectiveness of short-term treatment at a university counseling center. *Journal of Clinical Psychology, 55,* 1095–1106.

Cassata History Questionnaire

Date: _____

General Information:

Name: _____   Age: _____

Address: _____   Soc. Sec. # _____

City: _____   Zip: _____

Home phone: _____   Work phone: _____

Ethnic background: __White   __American Indian   __Black

                     __Oriental   __Hispanic   __Other, specify

Sex: __Male   __Female

Educational History:

School last attended: _____

Highest grade completed: _____   Grade average: _____

Are you interested in school now?   __Yes   __No

If not enrolled in school, how long have you been out?   __months

Check reason(s) you left school:

___   Failing

___   Learning problems

___   Suspended for aggressive behavior (ex., fighting, hitting teachers, vandalism, etc.)

___   Truancy

___   Ran away

___   Drug/alcohol problem

___   Pregnancy

___   Took a full time job

___   Couldn't get along with school authorities (ex., argued with teachers or principal)

___   Family problems

___   Got in trouble with police (ex., was arrested for stealing, drug possession, etc.

Other (please specify) _____

Starting with elementary school, how many schools have you attended in your lifetime?

__(give number)

How did you hear about Cassata? _____

Why do you want to enroll in Cassata? _____

Employment History:

Are you working?   ___Yes   ___No

Where: _____   How long? _____

How many hours a week do you usually work? _____

What shift or work schedule do your work? _____

Past Employment

Employer	From/To	Reason for leaving
1.		
2.		
3.		

Family History:

MOTHER: ___living ___deceased   If deceased give your age at time of death. ___

Mother's name: _____   Age: _____

Address: _____   Home phone: _____

Occupation: _____   Work phone: _____

Circle highest grade completed by Mother:

Grade School:	1	2	3	4	5	6	7	8
High School:	1	2	3	4				
College:	1	2	3	4				
Graduate School:	1	2	3	4				

Marital Status of Mother:

___Married   ___Separated   ___Common law
___Single   ___Divorced   ___Widowed

Write in number of times your Mother has been married? _____

FATHER: ___living ___deceased   If deceased give your age at time of death. ___

Father's name: _____   Age: _____

Address: _____   Home phone: _____

Occupation: _____   Work phone: _____

Circle highest grade completed by Father:

Grade School:	1	2	3	4	5	6	7	8
High School:	1	2	3	4				
College:	1	2	3	4				
Graduate School:	1	2	3	4				

Marital Status of Father:

___Married   ___Separated   ___Common law
___Single   ___Divorced   ___Widowed

Write in number of times your Father has been married? _____

Your parents are currently:

__Married   __Separated   __Divorced   __Never been married

SIBLINGS:

Number of brothers: _____   Ages: _____
Number of sisters: _____   Ages: _____

PERSONAL INFORMATION

Rate your ability to get along with other people. *Circle* one:

1. *Poor*   2. *Fair*   3. *Not sure*   4. *Good*   5. *Excellent*

What is the current state of your health? *Circle* one:

1. *Poor*   2. *Fair*   3. *Not sure*   4. *Good*   5. *Excellent*

Do you have any medical or physical disabilities?   __Yes   __No
If yes, please specify: _____

CASSATA believes in helping people deal with problems that keep them from accomplishing their goal of finishing school.

Check those which apply to you:

___ Low self-image	___ Afraid
___ Inconsiderate of others	___ Nervous
___ Authority problems	___ Withdrawal
___ Lead others into trouble	___ Concentration difficulties
___ Easily led into trouble by others	___ Sad
___ Aggravate others	___ Suicidal attempt
___ Easily angered	___ Strange thoughts
___ Stealing	___ Hear voices
___ Alcohol or drug problem	___ Learning difficulties
___ Lying	___ Family problems
___ Fronting (always putting on an act)	___ Aggressive behavior (fighting, property destruction, etc.)

With whom have you lived most of your life?

___ Both parents	___ Mother and Stepdad
___ Mother	___ Father and Stepmom
___ Father	___ Grandparents

If other, please specify: _____

What are your goals in life?

_____

_____

Where do you want to be in five years? (career, school, other)

_____

_____

List current activities, interests and hobbies:

_____

_____

Financial Information

CASSATA has scholarships available to students who qualify. Documentation of income will be required to prove eligibility. *Check* all that apply to you and your family:

___ AFDC recipient
___ Food stamp recipient
___ Supplemental Security income recipient
___ Foster child
___ Employed full time for last six months
Number of family members who live with you _____
What is your gross family income per year? (Include income of all family members) _____
Other income: _____

Present living arrangement:

Where do you live now?

___ With both parents   ___ With Mother
___ With Father   ___ With Mother and Stepdad
___ With Father and Stepmom   ___ With grandparents
___ Live independently and support self

Treatment/Counseling History:

I have received counseling and/or treatment for a drug-alcohol problem.
___ Yes ___ No

Please check one of the following:

___ I *was* in the hospital for treatment for a drug-alcohol problem.
___ I *was not* in the hospital for treatment for a drug-alcohol problem.
I have sought help from a professional person about my emotions (ex., depression, fear, suicide, anger).   ___Yes ___No

Please check one of the following:

___ I *was* in the hospital for treatment of my emotions.
___ I *was not* in the hospital for treatment of my emotions.
I have been to family counseling.   ___Yes ___No
I have been counseled or tutored for a learning problem.   ___Yes ___No
I have been told I have an attention problem (attention deficit disorder, hyperactivity) by a doctor or therapist.   ___Yes ___No
I have been in some type of counseling or treatment. (Please check the one that is true for you):
___Not at all ___1 time ___2–3 times ___4 times ___5 times or more

Check the one that is true for you:

I feel that my participation in counseling or treatment

__ made me worse
__ didn't help at all
__ helped a little
__ helped me alot
__ helped me to make a complete change

Please list the doctors or therapists you have seen and dates:
(Please begin with the most recent)

Agency seen for counseling   *Name of Doctor or Therapist*   *Dates seen:*

Sample Biofeedback Profile

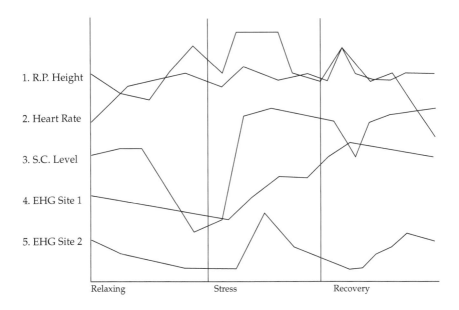

1. R.P. Height

2. Heart Rate

3. S.C. Level

4. EHG Site 1

5. EHG Site 2

| Relaxing | Stress | Recovery |

Brief Psychophysiological Stress Analysis (PSA)

Individual Tested: I. M. Stressed   Testing Date: 26 July 1989   Time: 10:18
Plethysmograph Site: left forefinger   EMG Site 1: right trap
SCL Site: left middle finger   EMG Site 2: forehead

    This procedure sampled levels of physiological activity during a brief guided relaxation condition, in response to the stress of a short test, and for a second guided relaxation condition. Each condition was approximately one minute in duration and consisted of five ten-second periods.

    A photoelectric plethysmograph was used to detect the peripheral blood volume pulse. Changes in pulse height (PH) indicate changes in peripheral blood flow. Increases in PH generally correspond to vasodilatation, and decreases to vasoconstriction. The PH units are relative and have no absolute value. A peripheral vasoconstriction change index (PCI) is calculated that represents the change in PH relative to the mean PH for the initial relaxation condition. In the presence of stable or increasing cardiac output, increasing PCI values (i.e., lower PH) indicates an increase in peripheral resistance. The actual relationship between changes in PH or PCI values and peripheral resistance cannot be assumed to be linear.

The interval between pulse wave peaks is equivalent to the interbeat interval (IBI) of the cardiac cycle. Heart rate (HR) is derived from IBI using the formula HR=(1/mean IBI) x 60. Because PCI and heart rate are derived from PH and IBI respectively, standard deviation values are provided only for the latter. Electrodermal activity (EDA) and muscle activity(EMG) from two sites were also measured.

An analysis of the PSA results should take into account the initial level for each measure, the magnitude of the response of each measure to the stress of the short test, and the extent to which each measure returns to the starting level. This procedure was designed specifically to be used as part of an initial work-up or as a screening device. An extended evaluation should be considered for individuals showing high initial levels, minimal recovery, or atypical patterns such as a general decrease in arousal across the three conditions. The latter pattern is usually associated with high arousal relating to the testing procedure that overwhelms the modest stress of the short test.

PHYSIOLOGICAL MEASURES:

PCI	peripheral vasoconstriction change index
HEART RATE	beats per minute
EDR	Electrodermal activity in micrOmhos
EMG	muscle activity in microvolts
PULSE HEIGHT	peripheral blood volume pulse in relative units
IBI	interbeat interval of cardiac cycle in seconds

SOURCE: BRIEF PSA version 2. Released by Biobehavioral Associates for MEDAC 3000.

Sample Report of Psychological Examination

Referral Background

Bart Jackson is an eight-year-old 2nd grader at Central Elementary School. His parents asked that I do an assessment with him in conjunction with one I was conducting with his six-year-old sister, Sister, following disclosure of a sexual abuse episode involving Sister and two young male cousins. Bart had been the one to report the sexual episode to his mother.

In two history-taking interviews, Mr. and Mrs. Jackson indicated a number of concerns about Bart independent of the current family crisis situation. They reported Bart is teased at school because of his clear preference for playing with girl toys, particularly Barbie dolls and My Little Ponies. They indicated that Bart has a number of fears and phobias, including a fear of flying, and Mr. Jackson indicated that he also had numerous fears and phobias as a child and even at times as an adult. They mentioned Bart's recent commentary about his sister's scars (from removal of moles on her back and chest) which led to a discussion of his undescended testicle, which was surgically corrected when he was 18 months of age; soon thereafter in the bath, Bart reportedly was interested in finding the scar from such a surgery on his own body. Because of his fears, preference for girls' toys, and concerns about his body, they have at times suspected he has anxieties about his own masculinity. Mr. and Mrs. Jackson also mentioned that Bart tries very hard to please and is greatly upset whenever he is accused of being wrong about something. Whatever may happen, he will insist, "It wasn't my fault!"

Personality Factors:

On the various measures that tap more directly into psychological status, including the drawing tasks, Rorschach, and Thematic Apperception Test (TAT), Bart showed how hard he works to use his excellent cognitive abilities to master his anxieties. His drawing was extremely carefully done, showed small figures with unusual detail, and took a great deal of time to complete. While he drew he asked me if I had asked his sister to draw, and he told me she drew very well.

In general, he has a good beginning array of defenses, including rationalization, intellectualization, and some forms of sublimation; he did not rely heavily on the more immature defenses of denial and avoidance. Bart's intense but cautious approach, his keen attention to detail, and the complex responses he offered to the Rorschach all suggest, however, that he probably already has some obsessional tendencies in his thought process, and his conscience seems still to be rather punitive.

Bart told me he liked the Rorschach. He gave complex responses that showed he has a very intense inner life and is gifted (and burdened) with tremendous psychological "charge." He feels things very intensely, which makes his achievement of a reasonably effective array of psychological defenses all the more impressive. He tends to be introverted and attempts to deal with stress and feelings internally. His ability to carefully organize complicated precepts by uniting different areas of the blot showed his good conceptual potential as well as his reliance on an inner fantasy life for gratification. Several of his responses suggested considerable creativity as well.

At the time of this assessment, however, Bart was experiencing considerable psychological upheaval, shown in abundant evidence of his fear and anxiety. The fears and anxieties came out particularly vividly in his responses involving human or human-like areas of the blots. For example, to Card II he responded, "It looks like two ghosts dancing; they're coming out of a fire." When I asked him why they seemed to be ghosts, he told me, "Nothing can dance in fire; it would have to be dead." On Card VI he saw two men tied together on a pole while fire burned beneath them, and on Card III he saw "two naked ladies dancing, they look naked to me at least, see the boobs?, they're cracking coconuts on the floor, and the milk is dripping on the floor, see the puddle?" Bart also showed his preoccupation with sexual issues; on the same card, he saw two Indian girls attached to each other like Siamese twins, and he reported they were French kissing. Turning it upside down, he saw two other girls "bop-bop-bop-bopping their butts together." His Rorschach responses suggested that when he cannot manage emotional stresses intellectually, he can become flooded with affect.

At eight, most children see "good form" percepts about 85 percent of the time; Bart gave "good form" responses only about 60 percent of the time. Of some additional concern is the fact that Bart scored quite high on a constellation of Rorschach scores that have been shown in research to be correlated with suicidal ideation in children and adolescents. Bart had six of the total of eight such Rorschach indicators, and his mother did indicate on her CBCL that Bart sometimes had talked about killing himself.

On the TAT, Bart gave unusually lengthy and richly detailed stories. One in particular seemed to me to represent the "bind" Bart may feel he is in at the moment, and how isolated he may feel within the family.

> Card 1. Ok there was this boy named Jeremy. And he asked his little sister if she'd play with him; he didn't have anyone to play with. His little sister said No, and uh . . . his little sister said Yes, and she was playing dolls, and he started playing dolls, they were playing paper dolls, and he was bending the arm backward and forward, she screamed at him "You can't play with me; you're about to break my doll" and so he went and asked his big brother if he'd play with him, and he said "Ok but I'm reading, but ok" and they were playing, and he almost broke one of his toys, and his brother said he didn't

want to play with him anymore. He asked his mother if she'd play with him and she said no, go to your father. His father was reading the newspaper, and he touched the typewriter and it went "ping" and his father yelled at him and said "GO PLAY WITH OUR LITTLE SISTER." And he ran to his room and cried and cried and cried and he sat down in his chair at his desk, see he sat down, and everybody came and said "I know why he's crying (teasing tone)" [Why?] He was lonely. So later on, a few weeks, months later his father came home and said he found a friend for him, and you'll have to go outside, he's out there, and outside he didn't see anything, but there was a box out there, and he opened the box and there was a little puppy dog in it. The end. [Ok Bart, what's this?] A crayon box? [No, it's a violin] Ok it's a violin and he's practicing.

Bart had particular difficulty with sexual and aggressive themes, especially when they also seemed to touch on body-damage issues. When I offered him TAT Card 8M (which shows an adolescent boy looking straight out of the picture; the barrel of a rifle is visible at one side, and in the background is the dim scene of a surgical operation, like a reverie-image) he asked "Can I try a different one?" When I offered Card 13MF as an alternative (it shows a young man standing with downcast head buried in his arm while behind him is a figure of a woman lying in bed) he had great difficulty choosing, and then he chose the latter and gave a story which showed his great difficulty dealing with sexual and aggressive themes without getting confused, fearful, and disorganized:

There's a guy, and he's married to a lady, and they went to sleep and they had a horrible, the wife had a horrible dream that Freddie Kruger came and killed her, and she woke up and the real Freddie Kruger was there and he came and killed her. She was naked, laying there. When the man woke up she was dead. Next day he had a dream Freddie Kruger tried to kill him, but he woke up. [You've never seen a Freddie Kruger movie?] Uhuh, but I know whatever people dream, when they wake up it comes true. And he saw Freddie Kruger; he took Kung Fu so he kinda did Kung Fu on him and chopped his head off. I mean not his head, chopped his arm off. And out of his head, a big hole was in his head, opened up, and all these hands came out and tore off his face, and this bloody stuff was coming out of his eyeballs. [That's in this picture?] No he was crying when she died. And he got killed, he wasn't really killed but he come back from the grave, that's in Part IV.

However, some of Bart's TAT stories showed that he still retains hope that things will work out all right. Even when it seems at first in his stories that characters are in terrible difficulty, Bart sometimes resolved things with the infusion of good luck, magic, or a caring adult who understood what needs to be done to make them better.

Computer-Generated Millon Clinical Multiaxial Inventory Narrative

MCMI narratives have been normed on patients experiencing either genuine emotional discomforts or social difficulties and who are currently engaged in the early phases of assessment or psychotherapy. Respondents who do not fit this normative population or who have inappropriately taken the MCMI for nonclinical purposes may have distorted reports. Based on theoretical inferences and probabilistic data from actuarial research, MCMI report statements cannot be judged definite and must be viewed as only one facet of a comprehensive psychological assessment. The report should be appraised in conjunction with other clinical data such as current life circumstances, observed behavior, biographic history, interview responses, and information from other tests. To avoid possible misconstrual or misuse, computer-based test interpretations should be evaluated by mental health clinicians who are thoroughly trained in recognizing the strengths and limitations of psychological test data. This report should not be shown to patients or their relatives.

This female patient showed no unusual characterological or test-taking attitudes that may have distorted her MCMI results.

Axis II: Personality Patterns

The following pertains to the enduring and pervasive characterological traits of this woman that underlie her personal and interpersonal difficulties. Rather than focus on currently distinct but essentially transitory symptoms, this section concentrates on her habitual, maladaptive methods of relating, behaving, thinking, and feeling.

There is evidence of a moderate level of pathology in the overall personality structure of this woman. She is likely to have a checkered history of disappointments in her personal and family relationships. Deficits in her social attainments may be notable, as is a tendency to precipitate self-defeating vicious circles. Earlier hopes for herself may have met with frustrating setbacks, and efforts to achieve a consistent niche in life may have failed. Although she is frequently able

SOURCE: MCMI copyright 1976, 1981 by Theodore Millon. All rights reserved. Scored by National Computer Systems, P.O. Box 1294, Minneapolis, Minnesota 55440

to function on a satisfactory ambulatory basis, she may evidence a persistent emotional discontrol with periodic psychotic episodes.

This woman has been typified by a social undependability and a tendency to exploitation, capriciousness and irresponsible behavior, a glib social style, the persistent seeking of excitement, and frequent seductive and self-dramatizing behavior. Interpersonal relationships are characteristically shallow or tense, and she appears indifferent to the welfare of others. Praise and approval are actively solicited by immature and histrionic demands for attention. She is easily excited and quickly bored. Although willing to expend effort to achieve something for herself, she is difficult and resistant about carrying out what others ask of her Intolerance of inactivity and an inability to delay gratification are associated with her impulsiveness, short-sighted hedonism, and her minimal regard for the consequences of her behavior, which may lead to difficulties with legal authorities.

Her judgment is typically undependable and highly erratic, and her surface affability is often punctuated with abrupt and angry outbursts. She may appear charming to casual acquaintances, but those with more enduring relationships with her are likely to see her testy, irritable, flippant, and manipulating side. Notable also is that her energies may be devoted to clever deceptions designed to seduce others into supporting her immature or irresponsible excesses. An exploitive pattern, often characterized by a history of disregarded agreements may be seen in her family and work settings. She will typically offer only fleeting and superficial displays of affection in return for meeting her demands. Her inability to sustain meaningful and trustworthy relationships with others may have recently disrupted her characteristically unruffled composure. Current difficulties may stem from family problems or legal entanglements resulting from impulsive and immature behavior. These difficulties are likely to shake her illusion of omnipotence only briefly. Accustomed to viewing herself as the center of attention and an admired figure in a select group, she will not likely tolerate a lessened role for too long.

Her habitual exploitation of others and careless disregard for social conventions may not be overtly hostile or malicious in intent. Rather, they appear to derive from her attitude of omnipotent self-assurance and her indifference to the rights of those she uses to enhance and indulge her desires. Only when her manipulative skills falter, as when she may be faced with legal difficulties or disruptive family tensions, is she likely to recognize her personal deficiencies. During these times, her moods may range from giddy elation to desperate unhappiness to being caustic and vindictive. Troubled by mounting and inescapable evidence of inadequacy and failure, she may not only disown these objectionable traits, but project them onto her accusers. This not only absolves her of fault, but justifies her resentment and anger, at least in her own eyes.

Axis I: Clinical Syndromes

The following distinctive clinical disorders are notable. They may be of brief duration, arise in response to external precipitants, and accentuate the more persistent features of her basic personality.

This woman feels apprehensive and restless and may complain of distressful phobias, recurrent indecisiveness over picayune matters, and acute physical discomforts such as insomnia, muscular tightness, headaches, tremors, and cold sweating.

These symptoms are an extension of her basic personality style although she has recently felt subjected to unjust social condemnation or the constraints of a routine and boring life pattern. Unable to tolerate humiliation and failure or withstand the restraints of tiresome pursuits, she may act out somewhat irresponsibly or unconventionally, with periodic outbursts of hostility.

Noteworthy Responses

The following statements were answered by the patient in the direction noted in the parentheses. These items suggest specific problem areas that may deserve further inquiry on the part of the clinician.

Health Preoccupation

73. I have a very tight feeling in the pit of my stomach every few days or so (T)

Interpersonal Alienation

No items.

Emotional Discontrol

No items.

Self-Destructive Potential

54. I have begun to feel like a failure in recent weeks (T).

Parallel *DSM-III* Multiaxial Diagnoses

Although the diagnostic criteria utilized in the MCMI differ somewhat from those in the *DSM-III*, there are sufficient parallels to recommend consideration of the following assignments. More definitive judgment should draw upon biographic observation, and interview data in addition to self-report inventories such as the MCMI.

Axis I: Clinical Syndrome:

The major complaints and behaviors of the patient parallel the following Axis I diagnoses, listed in order of their clinical significance and salience.

300.02 Generalized Anxiety Disorder

Axis II: Personality Disorder:

A deeply ingrained and pervasive pattern of maladaptive functioning underlies the Axis I clinical syndrome picture. The following personality diagnoses parallel the most salient features that characterize the individual.

301.89 Mixed Personality; histrionic, antisocial and borderline traits (provisional; rule out paranoid traits).

Course:

The major personality features described previously reflect long-term or chronic traits that are likely to have persisted for several years prior to the present assessment.

The clinical syndromes described previously tend to be relatively transient, waxing and waning in their prominence and intensity depending on the presence of environmental stress.

Axis IV: Psychological Stressors

The report on personality traits and current symptomatology suggest the following complicating factors may be exacerbating the present emotional state. They are listed in order of probable applicability. The listings should be viewed as a guide for further investigation by the clinician and should not be assumed to be definite factors in the case.

Recent life changes.

Family tensions; work upsets; authority difficulties.

Severity of Disturbance:

On the basis of the test data it may be reasonably assumed that the patient is experiencing a moderately severe mental disorder. Further professional study is justified to assess the appropriateness of clinical care.

Therapeutic Implications

The following considerations are likely to be of greater utility and accuracy during early treatment planning than in later management phases.

This patient is not likely to have sought therapy voluntarily and may be convinced that, if let alone, self-resolutions will suffice. If treatment was self-motivated, it probably followed a period of prolonged and unaccustomed social humiliations or achievement failures. Complaints are likely to take the form of vague feelings of boredom, restlessness, and discontent. Her tendency to avoid major problems by wandering from one superficial topic to another or to dramatize minor issues should be monitored and prevented. She may view the therapist in the early stages of treatment as a person possessing extraordinary powers. This enthusiasm will be short-lived because she is likely to become extremely uncomfortable following intensive therapeutic probing. Treatment may be best geared to short-term goals, such as re-established psychic balance and strengthening previously adequate coping behaviors.

Narrative Assessment Report

Identifying Data and Background Information

Juanita Crosby is a thirty-eight-year-old working-class female of Hispanic origin. She is of average height and build, and her weight appears normal. She appears to be of average intelligence and is verbal. Juanita dropped out of high school to get married but later obtained her GED. She is in her second marriage and has four children: son Jose, age fourteen; daughter Julia, age twelve; daughter Monica, age seven; and son Peter Jr., age four. The two oldest children are by a previous marriage and the two youngest by her present marriage. The client is a waitress at a local bar and grill, where she works rotating shifts that may vary from month to month. She is currently working mostly weekends and evening shifts. Her husband, Pete, an Anglo male, works at a local factory on the "graveyard" shift (11:00 P.M. to 7:00 A.M.). The client wants help but is extremely reluctant to come to the Mental Health Center (MHC) because she fears that her family will find out and will only serve to confirm their belief that she is "crazy." She expressed similar fears regarding people at her place of employment finding out. She also stated that she would not be "locked up" and she knew that "Doctors at the MHC like to lock people up."

Presenting Problem

Juanita was referred to a social worker at the local community mental health center by her priest, to whom she had confided that she was subject to intense "fits" in which she screamed at her children and threw things at her husband; sometimes she needed to be physically restrained by her family. The client reported that for approximately the last two years, these fits happened about every three to five weeks and lasted several hours. The client further reported that the frequency of the fits had remained fairly constant but the intensity had grown considerably worse, especially in the past six months. The client stated she did not understand these fits or why she was getting worse. The social worker identified these fits as fits of rage, and the client agreed with this description. From the report of the client, in the last fit of rage, which occurred about one month ago, she actually smashed several pieces of furniture and dishes in their home before she gained control of herself. Her husband and she usually engage in a "big fight"

SOURCE: Franklin, C. (1993). *Case Assessment*. Unpublished manuscript, University of Texas, School of Social Work, Austin.

about one of these fits of rage. The client stated that these big fights could be about almost anything (e.g., money, sex, the children). When asked by the social worker what the big fights are mostly about, however, the client responded "keeping the house."

The social worker identified the following context for a fit of rage to happen Juanita comes home from work and the chores are not done, "Pete's beer cans are on the floor and table in the living room." She is "fed up" with doing the work. She cleans up and goes to bed around 2:00 A.M. without eating or relaxing. Juanita described herself as having a "fitful" sleep, tossing and turning. She gets up about 6:00 or 6:30 A.M. to help get the children off to school. Pete arrives home around 7:30 or 7:45 A.M. She gives him a "mean stare." He asks where his breakfast is? She says, "Fix your own. I am tired of waiting on you hand and foot." They start arguing, and he will go to bed. She mops and does various chores throughout the day. The children arrive home around 3:00 P.M., and Pete gets up right before she goes to work. They either don't speak or "light into each other." When they "light into each other a fit will usually come on." According to the client, Sunday is the "big fight day" at their house.

At least once every two months the fights between the client and her husband end in them exchanging physical blows with their hand and fists, and she has also struck her husband with other physical objects such as a lamp. She stated, however, that he did not "hit her back" with anything except his hands on most occasions and usually was "acting in self-defense." The client admitted on at least one occasion pulling a weapon, a butcher knife, on her husband, but she stated her oldest child became involved, telling her to put the knife down. The client then reportedly became ambivalent about using the knife, and the husband was able to take it out of her hand.

When asked by the social worker, the client admitted that the children were present many times during the "fits of rage" and sometimes became involved by siding with one of the parents, usually the father, when the arguments between she and her husband were intense. This was especially true of the two oldest children. Most of the time, though, the children had learned to run off to their rooms and lock their doors when she begins to "rant and rave." She would scream such things at them as, "did you do your homework" and "look at this messy house." She also would call them names like "stupid," "dumb ass," and "lazy," along with many other obscenities. Juanita further admitted that during one of her episodes of rage she stood one of the children, the seven-year old daughter Monica, in the corner of the room and screamed vulgarities such as, "you no good mother fucker" for at least twenty minutes. The child reportedly hovered in the corner and begged, "please don't hurt me mommy." This incident raises a great concern for the social worker that the client's behavior may be out of control in relation to her family members. The incident with Monica occurred about one month ago and has been a major precipitant for the client to seek help. She denies ever striking the children or using physical force against them.

The client reported that she believes her fits have caused "her family to hate her." She has overheard her children referring to her as "crazy mommy." Her husband also would not talk to her for several days after one of these incidents and has threatened to leave her but has never followed through on his threats. The social worker noticed that the client herself appears to feel very guilty and ashamed following one of the episodes and tries hard to make up with her children and husband. She reports being "extra nice." Juanita does not know what brings on these fits of rage and was unable to identify any specific insights regarding her severe behavior problems. Detailed questioning by the social worker, however, revealed that the last episode was apparently associated with the client "sneaking a few drinks" of whiskey from a bottle she kept hidden from her husband in the trunk of her car. The client denied that her rages occurred every time she drank the whiskey, which was about two or three times a week or whenever she felt "bad at Pete." She also denied getting drunk.

Process Recording

Worker: Teyla Haas	Client: Sarah Duncan	Date of Session: 2/19/93
	Shareka and Roderick Trotter	
Date turned in: 2/23/92	Place: Their home, East Austin	

Client System (including age/sex/ethnicity): Sarah Duncan: African American woman, late 60s; Shareka Trotter: African American girl, five years old; Roderick Trotter: African American boy, eight years old.

Present Problem: Adoption.

Goals for the Session: Explain my role, the lifebooks, and the process of adoption. Also, begin lifebooks and start to build rapport.

Content	Worker's Feelings	Analytical Comments	FI/Liaison Comments
ME: How long have Shareka and Roderick lived with you?	Feeling comfortable		
SARAH: I have taken care of them almost their whole life. Let's see, they have lived with me for about three years, but when they was little, I always lived real close to them and took care of them. Their mother—she treat them real bad.			

SOURCE: Haas, Tayla. (1993). Process Recording. University of Texas at Austin, School of Social Work.

Content	Worker's Feelings	Analytical Comments	FI/Liaison Comments
ME: Yes, that is what I heard.			A response such as "she treated them real bad?"—a minimal encouragement would have been appropriate. However, Sarah did go on to provide specifics.
SARAH: She used to throw them up against the wall all the time, and she would tie them up and gas them up.	Feeling uncomfortable and somewhat sad.		
ME: What does "gas them up" mean?	Feeling confused about what "gas them up" meant.		Nice pursuit.
SARAH: She would turn on the gas on the stove and leave it on, to try to kill them. Then, I would come in and find them. I take them home with me after that and take care of them.	Feeling sad about this child abuse, but feeling glad that she felt comfortable enough to talk to me about this.	This sounds like a situation that could cause Sarah to feel afraid, angry, or sad. I was wondering what her emotions were about this. I also wanted to attend to her feelings because this sounded like a very painful event for her.	Nice sensitivity on your part.
ME: How did you feel about this?			
SARAH: I felt real sad. I still do. It's just not right.			
ME: I can see the sadness on your face as you talk about this. You look like this is very painful for you.	I feel sad because she looked so hurt. Her facial expression displayed a great deal of pain.		

Content	Worker's Feelings	Analytical Comments	FI/Liaison Comments
SARAH: It is, very painful. Roderick, he don't want to see his mother no more. I used to take him to visit her, but he would always say, Granny, I don't want to go. So I wouldn't make him. Sometimes, I try to talk to him about the way his mother treated him, but he won't talk about it. He won't talk to the people at Day-Glo about it either.			
ME: It sounds like he has a lot of hurt and anger toward his mother.	Feeling sad.		
SARAH: Yes, a lot of anger. He has had such a hard life, so has Shareka. I try not to be too hard on them. Their mother, she used lots of drugs when she had them—lots of drugs. That is why they hyper like they are right now.	I was glad that she seemed to be very understanding of Shareka and Roderick.	I wanted to communicate this to her.	
ME: I think that Shareka and Roderick are very lucky to have a grandmother as kind and understanding as you to take care of them.			

Case Study on Ethnic Identity

The Dream

Linda was upset. The houseparent told the social worker at the Home that Linda seemed distracted, out of sorts, and "not her usual cheerful, well organized self" that morning. Before school she requested an interview later in the day with the social worker because she had something "very important" to discuss, so it was no surprise when Linda appeared mid-afternoon in the clinical director's office, having left school early. But the purpose of Linda's session was a surprise. She wanted to talk about a dream she had had the previous night—a very disturbing dream, like none she had had before, or at least none that she remembered. In fact, she had taken time to write the dream down during a lull at school, so that she would not forget any part of it (although at this time she felt it was unforgettably seared in her brain).

This was the dream:

It all started the summer before (according to Linda's dream). She met a nice boy at the beach. The other kids at the Home, the houseparents, the directory, really liked her new boyfriend. The couple went everywhere together, and she felt the "world smiling" on them as they fell in love. Although she knew that she was going to miss the Home, with the staff's blessing she decided to marry him in the fall. It was a happy marriage, with Linda learning to cook, keep house, and do "wifely" things. Everything was wonderful except she knew that her family would not approve of him, so she put off telling them of the marriage. Then she discovered she was pregnant. From the beginning she had mixed feelings about the pregnancy and found herself sad and happy at the same time. The husband seemed completely happy, but she just couldn't seem to reconcile herself to the approaching birth. The crux of the dream came when she was about six months pregnant and showing quite a bit. It was early in the morning and her young husband had gone to work. She went into the bathroom to wash up and began thinking about how she was going to be forced to tell her parents. A feeling of overwhelming depression swamped her and she began to cry bitter tears. She raised her eyes to the mirror to look at her swollen body and tearstreaked face. As she confronted her image in the mirror, she suddenly realized why she was reluctant to tell her folks and what was so sad about the pregnancy. In the mirror her skin was white—she was white and the boy she had married in her

SOURCE: Williams, B. E. (1987) Looking for Linda: Identity in black and white. Child Welfare, 60(3), 207–216.

dream was black. The child she carried would not belong to either race (as she perceived it) and would have no home. She cried for her "bastard baby" (her words) and for herself with her white face. She knew then that she was "white" and that there was no home for her, either. In fact, at the point she even repudiated the love her black husband professed for her. Linda woke up sobbing, depressed, and alarmed. The dream was so vivid she examined her flat stomach and tried to figure out who and where her husband was. Dragging herself out of bed she went to the bathroom mirror (the same one in her dream) to examine herself. With disbelief and still groggy from sleep, she stared at the black face reflected.

Background Case Material

Linda was a seventeen-year-old black girl who had been a resident of the Home for almost two years at the time of the dream. In school she was a senior, approaching graduation and facing termination of current living arrangements. The residents were welcome to stay in placement during the summer following high school graduation, working and saving money for a start in the "adult" world. They had to make plans to leave by mid-August. Linda was a ward of the court and the state juvenile justice system, which had agreed to continue monetary support for placement until that time. She had been in the care of various agencies since childhood, but with the advent of her seventeenth birthday, she was essentially free to go where she wanted.

There had been no contact with the family, in spite of repeated attempts on the director's part to encourage their participation. Linda reported that distance was the reason they would not come. As near as could be ascertained by the staff, they had written two letters during her stay. She was encouraged to call them at Christmas and again when she was approaching graduation. There was no response. The question arose as to how welcome she would be should she return to her hometown to work. She made the decision to remain in the vicinity.

Linda first came to the attention of the authorities on a dependent and neglect charge against the parents. The family lived in a border where Mexican Americans constituted the majority of the citizens. Black families were few and far between and black foster families practically nonexistent. So, although things were never really satisfactory, she was left in her own home for some years with a white caseworker keeping close tabs on the situation. Linda became very fond of her child welfare worker, who seemed to be the only bright spot in her existence. The worker dearly loved Linda and constantly took her on outings. The contrast with her neglectful and abusing mother was stark.

At school Linda did well with her white teachers. Because she was very bright and verbal, as well as frequently being the only black child in the classroom, she attracted the attention of well-meaning teachers who gave her a lot of time and attention. Many hours after school and on weekends were spent in various activities to which school personnel invited her. All of her role models were white, and it was obvious that she was not participating in what little black community there was. And no one wanted her to. She had become everyone's pet project, and they were accepting her as "one of us" and not perceiving her as a member of the black community. It was almost as though her daily brief periods at home were interludes in her real life in the white world.

When she grew to adolescence and went out of the neighborhood school into a central high school, she knew well how to navigate the white world. Although the opportunity for a choice of black friends broadened considerable, Linda chose not to associate with them, making friends among the "liberal" white teenagers. Her caseworker resigned, and another took her place. The new worker had heard such good things about Linda—what a rewarding case she was and what progress she was making under child welfare auspices—that she was immediately favorable. Linda never felt as close to her as the initial one, but apparently made the transition smoothly.

At fifteen Linda made her first "mistake." In solidly with the middle-class white teenagers who were trying their wings and their parents' patience, she began to experiment with drugs. Although she really didn't like drugs, she bought, sold, and used with the best of them. And they were caught. The other children were given probation and placed in the custody of their parents. Linda was sent to the detention center by shocked child welfare workers who had "done their best." Once at the receiving center, however, the workers could not forget what an exemplary child she had been and pleaded for treatment rather than a detention facility. The decision was "a child in need of supervision," rather than a psychiatric or juvenile delinquency case. Removing her from the home community seemed to offer the best solution, and she was sent across the state to a residential facility that had an excellent track record in the care of adolescents.

Linda was only the second black girl in the history of the Home. Welcomed with open arms by the staff, she immediately became a favorite. Likable, intelligent, friendly, and apparently happy to be there, her winning ways made the other girls appear surly. The staff was concerned that she might not be happy at the neighborhood high school, which had been integrated by means of crosstown busing. Fear of "contamination" by the discontented black students in that population prompted the decision to take her downtown every day to the central high school. A good socioeconomic mix, this was the only "naturally" integrated school in town. She was encouraged (as were all the children) to make friends and bring them home for supper or other activities at the Home. She did make friends—all white—and also soon had several white teachers whom she really liked. The staff was happy; Linda seemed to have settled in.

It should be noted that the staff of the facility was without exception white. A training site for the local state university graduate school of social work, even the social work interns were white. The board members, the physicians who furnished medical care, and the benefactors of the nonprofit institution were white, as was the surrounding neighborhood. How well Linda fit and what a credit she was to the Home always pleased the staff. Not so the two black boys in one of the boys' cottages. By comparison, they were always into some devilment and maintained close ties with their "irresponsible families." It seemed as if every time they went home for a visit, they came back obstreperous. Linda, however, always spent her holidays with a staff member and conducted herself with both liveliness and good manners.

Discussion

Black psychiatrists Grier and Cobbs (1968) have denied the existence of positive self-esteem among blacks, while Foster and Perry (1982) point out that the prevailing view of blacks has been that they suffer from negative self-esteem manifested in feeling of self-hate and a lack of self-actualizing behavior. Oppressive social and economic conditions, racism, and discrimination, in combination with an attempt to identify with the values of the dominant white society, have contributed in a large measure to this negative self-image. Undeniably, color is a tag that is difficult to dispense with. Blacks become members of a highly visible victim group, thus lacking an inconspicuous avenue of escape from their disempowered status (Maguire, 1980). Pinderhughes (1976) emphasized that the most severely victimized adopt values of autonomy and isolation as a defense against the stresses that overwhelm them. Their autonomy is not based on growth and self-actualization, however, but on a feeling that they have been abandoned, are now alone and cannot expect help from anyone. One of the best-known defenses against powerlessness is that of identifying with the aggressor (Pinderhughes, 1979).

It does not take a complicated analysis of Linda's dream to recognize a psyche under stress. Stehno (1982) writes that the minority child's sense of well-being is developed in interaction with the inner, nurturing environment before he or she is directly confronted with the hostile wider society. This forms patterns of close involvement, including frequent interactions among and exchange of help with kin (McAdoo, 1982). Social workers must realize that individuals do not learn their coping behaviors or their mores, social drives, or values from the larger society. Children learn a particular culture and a particular moral system only from those people with whom they have close contact and who exhibit that culture in frequent relationships with them (Washington, 1982). Perceptual experiences, shared symbols, oral traditions, feelings and sentiments that make up ethnicity are learned and constitute the individual's nurturing environment (Davis, 1948).

What is the result when that nurturing environment is not that of the child's own family, or not even within the appropriate ethnic group? Linda, though remaining in her own home until age fifteen, was separated psychologically from her cultural heritage much earlier. A review of her childhood reveals only essentially negative relationships with a broader black community. Every helping or positive relationship was established with the white community. At no time in her seventeen years did Linda become involved with a warm, caring, or powerful black role model. All power and all goodness appeared to be vested in the majority-controlled systems with which she interacted—child welfare, juvenile justice, the Home.

Linda's family and ethnic group became merely shadow persons, existing in the background of the satisfying world that stroked her. Her lack of interest in and contact with them during her placement contrasted strikingly with the attachment and identification the other children, both black and white, had with their origins. And this was encouraged by those helping her. She was a satisfying case, quickly picking up the required behavior, excelling in the prescribed ways, warmly attached to her caseworkers and teachers, apprenciative of and seemingly satisfied with the living arrangements at the Home. The houseparents particularly enjoyed having her because they did not have to compete with her family, who stayed out of their way, literally and psychologically. Each step away from a cultural identity earned her points. However, the color of her skin remained the same. Clark's assertion (1965) never was more true than in Linda's case: "It is still the white man's society that governs the Negro's image of himself."

Linda's dream brought to consciousness her dilemma. She was a creature of both worlds and citizen of neither. The "bastard child" within her was tragically not welcome in her family and her dual black-white identity would not serve her well in the wider world to which she was going. Her poignant cry to the caseworker, "Don't you understand? I looked in the mirror and I was white!" chilled her listener.

Hilson Adolescent Profile

Hilson Research Inc.   HAP Narrative Report
HILSON ADOLESCENT PROFILE

Age 16

Agency 0555-2	Date 09/18/87	Case 72	Sex -M-	Race -0-

Introduction

This report is intended to be used as an aid in evaluating an adolescent's emotional adjustment, social skills, and behavioral patterns. These results are also designed to provide information to support classification, treatment, and case disposition decisions. While the HAP is not intended to be used as a sole source for making such decisions, it has been developed with the purpose of providing relevant data for further evaluation.

Test Response Style—Validity Measure

This adolescent has not been entirely candid about his feeling and behaviors. He has favored socially acceptable responses, showing a tendency to deny minor faults or shortcomings to which his peers more readily admit. He has presented himself as a somewhat wary, guarded individual with an overriding need to be seen in a positive light. This test-taking strategy of attempting to portray himself as virtuous in all areas may have made the results of this test less valid, especially in areas where apparent emotional adjustment may be due to the denial of problems rather than to their nonexistence. Limited insight and strong concern for appearances are indicated for this adolescent.

"Acting-Out" Behavior Measures: Specific "External" Behavior

He may be a habitual user of alcohol. He describes himself as a social drinker with a good alcohol tolerance. There may be a tendency for this person to use alcohol in an attempt to avoid painful feelings. A careful evaluation of his item endorsements and drinking habits is suggested.

This person may be a habitual user of drugs and has endorsed more drug-related items than have his peers. He is likely to use marijuana on a regular basis

437

and may also use other substances such as cocaine. A history of frequent drug usage and/or drug dependence is indicated. Similar adolescents find they are comfortable within a subculture that accepts the use of drugs as a routine part of life. The extent of this adolescent's drug involvement should be carefully evaluated.

Compared with others tested, this individual endorsed some items suggestive of antisocial attitudes and/or behavior. He may feel misunderstood by others and may participate in activities that deviate from social norms. Some conflicts with authority and difficulty accepting criticism may also be evident. If internalized conflicts are not reported on this test, insight regarding his behavior may be limited, making this individual a questionable candidate for success in traditional psychotherapy. A careful evaluation of items endorsed in this area is suggested to determine the extent of difficulty he experiences in adhering to society's rules and regulations.

Attitudes and Temperament

This individual has endorsed items indicative of risk-taking or "thrill-seeking" behavior. He may seek a sustained level of excitement through a variety of experiences in a pattern similar to those of substance abusers. He may have some difficulty controlling behaviors requiring moderation (such as eating, drinking, gambling, or smoking). This adolescent may also have some detached, skeptical, or antisocial views about his position in society. He may feel that life is usually unfair and that self-serving motives are most appropriate.

Interpersonal Adjustment Measures

A serious pattern of family conflicts is indicated. This adolescent shows evidence of an unhappy, perhaps disruptive, childhood, as well as alienation from family members and/or relatives. Although some alienation is recognized as a normal feature of adolescent growth, this individual displays significant homelife conflicts compared with peers. He may view his home situation as intolerable and a history of running away or other "acting out" behavior may be evident. A thorough evaluation of current relationships with family members is advised. If possible, the family should be involved in any treatment program developed for this individual. Family counseling/therapy may be considered as a useful treatment intervention.

At least one item was endorsed indicating he may have been physically abused. It is advised that this be verified in follow-up interviews with this individual and/or his family.

Endorsements suggested this individual may be experiencing some social/sexual adjustment difficulties. Although he may view himself as sexually knowledgeable and/or experienced, this adolescent may also have endorsed items suggesting difficulties with the opposite sex. There may be signs of social discomfort with peers, and item endorsements on this scale should be carefully evaluated for evidence of social/sexual problems.

Internalized Conflict Measures

This adolescent has endorsed specific items indicating suicide has been considered and/or attempted. A thorough clinical evaluation is recommended to assess current suicide potential.

Item endorsements show similarities to the responses of individuals who suffer from psychoses or serious emotional disturbances. Unusual or bizarre thinking may be apparent at times. Because this adolescent has responded positively to items not usually endorsed by his peers, it is suggested that the item endorsements in this area be verified in a clinical interview.

This individual has endorsed items suggestive of auditory hallucinations and/or referential thinking. These should be examined more closely in follow-up interviews.

Summary Statement

Overall, these test results suggest the presence of behavioral problems and/or serious emotional adjustment difficulties. Compared with his peers, this adolescent has significantly elevated scores falling outside the average range (see above report). Follow-up interviews and treatment interviews are recommended.

HAP CRITICAL ITEMS FOR FOLLOW-UP EVALUATION

The following endorsed item(s) may provide useful leads for follow-up interviews and/or further investigations. Because individual items may have been endorsed in error, they should not be used alone as a basis for making decisions and should be verified by the tested individual and/or by outside sources.

Alcohol and/or Drug Use

5. I like to drink a six-pack of beer, or have 4 or 5 mixed drinks. (T)
31. I have smoked marijuana without other people around. (T)
96. There have been times when I had trouble knowing what I was doing or what was going on around me. (T)
146. I go drinking with my friends at least once a week. (T)
157. I could easily drink a six-pack of beer, or four or five drinks. (T)
168. Sometimes I need a drink in order to relax. (T)
238. There have been times when I smoked marijuana three or four days a week. (T)
241. Some people, who do not know me really well, have said that I sometimes drink too much. (T)
244. I once sold a small quantity of drugs to a friend. (T)
248. I have tried cocaine more than once. (T)
264. I have used unprescribed pills to keep me going or to keep me calm. (T)
277. I have tried PCP (angel dust) or LSD to see what it was like. (T)
284. I have smoked marijuana more than two times in a week. (T)

Family Conflicts

60. I have some enemies in my family. (T)
69. I have run away from home more than once. (T)
77. I have run away from home and stayed out overnight. (T)
235. I often have arguments with one or both of my parents. (T)
288. I have been physically abused in my life. (T)

School Adjustment Difficulties

11. I have been suspended from school. (T)
58. In my last year at school, I failed more than one subject. (T)
121. I have had trouble being passed on to the next grade in school. (T)
257. I once had to repeat a grade in school. (T)
280. I have had to go to summer school to make up a failed course. (T)

Trouble with the Law/Society

160. I have been involved in a stolen car incident. (T)
171. I was arrested over a minor incident. (T)
295. More than once I have taken small items from a store without paying. (T)
304. I have been out with friends when they wrote on walls or damaged some property. (T)

Temperament

172. I used to have a really bad temper. (T)
252. When I become angry, I like to punch something.

Depression/Suicide Potential

39. I have thought about killing myself. (T)
104. Someone in my family has tried to kill him/herself. (T)
126. I have tried to kill myself more than once. (T)
154. When I feel blue or depressed, I often stay in bed all day. (T)
204. I have seriously considered ending my own life. (T)
215. There have been times when I have thought a lot about ways to kill myself. (T)

Health/Anxiety/Phobic Symptoms

108. I often have one of these: headaches, backaches, or neckaches. (T)
134. I usually get off a very crowded train or bus to wait for one less crowded. (T)
270. Sometimes, without warning, I have at least one of these: fast heart beat, dizziness, feeling faint or fast breathing. (T)

Counseling/Medication History

41. I have had counseling or therapy for a problem. (T)
84. I have attended a drug rehabilitation program. (T)

Social/Sexual Adjustment

23. I have a close friend and we can talk about almost anything. (F)
247. I have had sexual experience with someone at least 5 years older than I am. (T)

Unusual Suspicions/Thoughts

33. Someone has tried to poison me. (T)
132. I sometimes hear voices that others around me do not hear. (T)
213. I have sometimes heard voices that have tried to tell me what to do. (T)
236. I have special mental powers that few others know about. (T)

Critical Item total = 46

SOURCE: Hilson Research, Kew Gardens.

Psychological Testing Instruments for Children & Adolescents

Infant Development Scales

Brazelton Neonatal Behavioral Assessment Scales
1. Neurological intactness
2. Interactive behavior
   (a). Motor control (putting thumb in mouth)
   (b). Remaining calm and alert in response to stimuli (bell or light)
3. Responsiveness to the examiner and need for stimulation

Bayley Scales of Infant Development
1. Mental abilities (memory, learning, problem solving)
2. Motor skills
3. Social behaviors (social orientation, fearfulness, and cooperation)

Gesell Development Schedules
1. Fine and gross motor behavior
2. Language behavior
3. Adaptive behavior (eye-hand coordination, imitation, and object recovery)
4. Personal-social behavior (reaction to persons, initiative, independence, play responses)

Denver Developmental Screening Test
(Can be administered by a person with limited training, screening test to indicate if more in-depth testing is needed.)
1. Developmental delays
2. Problems in personal/social, fine motor/adaptive, language, and gross motor skills

Intelligence Tests for Preschool and School-Age Children

Stanford-Binet
(Used with both preschool and school-age, usually administered to children between 2-8 years old. Disadvantage is that it gives only an overall score, doesn't address specific strengths and weaknesses. May not be good for bilingual/bicultural children.)

1. Vision
2. Eye-hand coordination
3. Hearing
4. Speech

Wechsler Scales consist of:
Wechsler Preschool and Primary Scale of Intelligence (WPPSI) and Wechsler Intelligence Scale for Children-Revised (WISC-R). Most widely used to test cognitive functioning of school-age children. These scales include six verbal and six performance subtests.

System of Multicultural Pluralistic Assessment (SOMPA)
This test is based on the WISC-R, and takes into account a child's handicapping condition and sociocultural background.

Special Abilities Tests

Bender Visual Motor Gestalt Test
1. Visual perceptual skills
2. Eye-hand coordination

Peabody Picture Vocabulary Test
(Originally designed to be used with persons who are nonverbal, mentally retarded, and/or have cerebral palsy.)

Detroit Test of Learning Aptitude
1. Auditory and visual memory
2. Concentration

Testing for Mental Retardation

(An IQ score below 70 indicates that a client may be mentally retarded. However, a low IQ score by itself is not sufficient for diagnosis. The client's adaptive score must also be measured. The following three instruments measure adaptive behavior.)

Vineland Social Maturity Scale

American Association on Mental Deficiency's (AAMD) Adaptive Behavior Scales

Adaptive Behavior Inventory for Children

Personality Tests

I. Objective tests, designed to determine predominant personality traits or behavior:

Minnesota Multiphasic Personality Inventory (MMPI)
(can be used with adults and adolescents)

Personality Inventory for Children (PIC)

II. Projective tests give clients a stimulus, such as a picture to respond to—responses indicate problem areas.

Rorschach Test

Holtzman Inkblot Technique

Thematic Apperception Test (TAT)

Children's Apperception Test (CAT)

Michigan Picture Test

Task of Emotional Development Test

Blacky Pictures

Make-a-picture-story Test

SOURCE: Sheafor, B., Horejsi, C., & Horejsi, G. (1988). *Techniques and guidelines for social work practice*. Newton, MA: Allyn & Bacon.

Multiaxial Assessment with the *DSM-IV-TR*

Axis I: Clinical Disorders

- Disorders usually first diagnosed in infancy, childhood, or adolescence (excluding mental retardation, which is diagnosed on Axis II).
- Dementia, delirium, amnestic, and other cognitive disorders
- Mental disorders resulting from a general medical condition; for example, CNS infections
- Substance-related disorders
- Mood disorders
- Anxiety disorders: panic attack, agoraphobia, PTSD
- Somatoform disorders: somatoform disorder, conversion disorder
- Factitious disorders (intentional production of physical or psychological symptoms)
- Dissociative disorders: amnesia, dissociative fugue, MPD
- Sexual and gender identity disorders
- Eating disorders
- Sleep disorders
- Impulse control disorders not elsewhere classified
- Adjustment disorders (in response to an identifiable psychosocial stressor)
- Other conditions that may be a focus of clinical attention

Axis II: Personality Disorders and Mental Retardation

- Paranoid personality disorder
- Schizoid personality disorder
- Schizotypal personality disorder
- Antisocial personality disorder
- Borderline personality disorder
- Narcissistic personality disorder
- Mental retardation
- Avoidant personality disorder
- Dependent personality disorder
- Obsessive-compulsive personality disorder
- Personality disorder not otherwise specified

Axis III: General Medical Condition

Must be diagnosed by a physician

Axis IV: Psychosocial and Environmental Problems

(Usually problems that have occurred during the past year)

- Problems with priority support system
- Problems related to the social environment
- Educational problems
- Occupational problems
- Housing problems
- Economic problems
- Problems with access to health care services
- Problems related to interaction with the legal system/crime
- Other psychosocial or environmental problems

Axis V: Global Assessment of Functioning (GAF) Scale

Measurement of level of current functioning and measurement of highest level of functioning during past year. Anchored scale, 0-100

Schizophrenia and Other Psychotic Disorders from the *DSM-IV-TR*

A. Essential features are a mixture of characteristic signs and symptoms (positive and negative) that have been present for a significant time during a one-month period (less if successfully treated), with some signs of a disorder persisting for at least six months
   1. Positive symptoms reflect an excess or distortion of normal functions (such as delusions, hallucinations, disorganized speech, grossly disorganized or catatonic behavior)
   2. Negative symptoms reflect a diminution or loss of normal functions (such as affective flattening in the fluency and productivity of thought and speech (alogia), in the initiation of goal-directed behavior)
B. Diagnostic Criteria
   1. Characteristic symptoms (two or more for most of one month)
      a. delusions
      b. hallucinations
      c. disorganized speech (such as, frequent derailment or incoherence)
      d. grossly disorganized or catatonic behavior
      e. Negative symptoms (that is, flattened affect, alogia, or avolition)
   2. Social/occupational dysfunction
   3. Duration—signs of disturbance for at least six months
   4. Schizoaffective and mood disorder ruled out
   5. Not resulting from substance/general medical condition

Schizophrenia subtypes

A. Paranoid type
   1. Preoccupation with one or more delusions or frequent auditory hallucinations
   2. None of the following is prominent: disorganized speech, disorganized or catatonic, or flat or inappropriate affect
B. Disorganized type (old Hebephrenic)
   1. All of the following are prominent
      a. Disorganized speech
      b. Disorganized behavior
      c. Flat or inappropriate affect

C. Catatonic type
  1. Marked by psychomotor disturbance; at least two of the following:
     a. Motoric inability as evidenced by catalepsy (waxy flexibility) or stupor
     b. Excessive purposeless motor activity
     c. Extreme negativism (motiveless resistance to all instructions) or mutism
     d. Peculiarities of voluntary movement as evidenced by posturing, stereo-
        typed movements, prominent mannerism, or prominent grimacing
     e. Echolalia (parroting) and echopraxia (parroting movements)
D. Undifferentiated type
E. Residual type
   Specifiers:
   Episodic with interepisode residual symptoms
   (With prominent negative symptoms)
   Episodic with no interepisode residual symptoms
   Continuous (with prominent negative symptoms)
   Single episode in partial remission (with prominent negative symptoms)
   Single episode in full remission
   Other or unspecified pattern

Schizophreniform Disorder

A. Identical to schizophrenia, but of less than six months duration

Schizoaffective disorder

A. An uninterrupted period of illness during which, at some time, there is either
   a major depressive episode, a manic episode, or a mixed episode concurrent
   with symptoms that meet criterion A for schizophrenia

Delusional Disorder

A. Essential feature is the presence of one or more nonbizarre delusions that per-
   sist for at least one month
B. Diagnostic Criteria
   1. Nonbizarre delusions for at least one month duration
   2. Criterion A for schizophrenia has never been met
   3. Apart from the impact of the delusion(s), or its ramifications, functioning is
      not markedly impaired and behavior is not obviously odd or bizarre
   4. If mood episodes have occurred concurrently with delusions, their total
      duration has been brief relative to the duration of the delusional periods
   5. Not due to substance abuse effects
C. Subtypes
   1. Erotomania-delusions that another person, usually of a higher status, is in
      love with the individual
   2. Grandiose-delusions of inflated worth, power, knowledge, identity, or of a
      special relationship to a deity or famous person
   3. Jealous-delusions that individual's sexual partner is unfaithful

4. Persecutory-delusions that the person (or someone to whom the person is close) is being malevolently treated in some way
5. Somatic-delusions that the person has some physical or general mental condition
6. Mixed-characteristics of one or more of the above but none predominates
D. Unspecified
Bi-polar disorders from *DSM-IV-TR*

Major Depressive Episode

A. Essential feature is a period of at least two weeks during which there is either depressed mood or loss of interest or pleasure in nearly all activities
B. Diagnostic criteria
1. Five or more of the following for two weeks:
   a. Depressed mood most of the day, nearly every day
   b. Markedly diminished interest or pleasure in all, or almost all, activities most of the day, nearly every day
   c. Significant weight loss or gain (5% of body weight) or decrease or increase in appetite nearly every day
   d. Insomnia or hypersomnia nearly every day
   e. Psychomotor retardation or agitation nearly every day
   f. Feelings of worthlessness or excessive or inappropriate guilt
   g. Diminished ability to concentrate or think, or indecisiveness
   h. Recurrent thoughts of death, recurrent suicidal ideation with or without a plan
2. Symptoms cause clinically significant distress or impairment in social, occupational, or other important areas of functioning
3. Symptoms are not resulting from the direct physiological effects of a substance or a medical condition (for example, hypothyroidism)
4. Is not bereavement

Manic Episode

A. Essential feature is defined by a distinct period during which there is an abnormally elevated, expansive, or irritable mood, lasting at least one week
B. Diagnostic criteria
1. Distinct period of abnormally and persistently elevated, expansive, or irritable mood of at least one week duration
2. During the period of disturbance, three or more of the following, four if the mood is only irritable:
   a. Inflated self-esteem or grandiosity
   b. Decreased need for sleep
   c. More talkative than usual or pressure to keep talking
   d. Flight of ideas or subjective experience that thoughts are racing
   e. Distractibility
   f. Increase in goal-directed activity (socially, occupationally, sexually) or psychomotor agitation

     g. Excessive involvement in pleasurable activities that have a high potential for painful consequences (spending, business ventures)

3. Does not meet criteria for a mixed episode
4. Mood disturbance is sufficiently severe to impair functioning or necessitate hospitalization
5. Symptoms not resulting from direct physiological effects of a substance or medical condition (for example, hyperthyroidism)

Mixed Episode

A. Essential feature is characterized by a period of at least one week in which the criteria are met for both a manic and major depressive episode. Rapidly alternating moods (sadness, irritability, euphoria) accompanied by manic and major depressive symptoms
B. Diagnostic Criteria
    1. Criteria met for both a manic episode and a major depressive episode (except for duration less than one week, in contrast to two weeks)
    2. Mood disturbance is sufficiently severe to cause marked impairment in functioning
    3. Symptoms not a result of direct physiological effects of a substance or a medical condition

Hypomania Episode

A. Essential feature is a distinct period during which there is an abnormal and persistently elevated, expansive, or irritable mood that lasts at least four days
B. Diagnostic criteria
    1. Distinct period (at least four days) in which there is persistently elevated, expansive, or irritable mood
    2. During period of the mood disturbance, three of the following, or four if only irritable:
        a. Inflated self-esteem or grandiosity
        b. Decreased need for sleep
        c. More talkative than usual or pressure to keep talking
        d. Flight of ideas or subjective experience that thoughts are racing
        e. Distractibility
        f. Increase in goal-directed activity (socially, occupationally, sexually) or psychomotor agitation
        g. Excessive involvement in pleasurable activities that have a high potential for painful consequences (spending, business ventures)
    3. Episode is associated with an unequivocal change in functioning that is uncharacteristic of the person
    4. Disturbance in mood is observable by others
    5. Episode is not severe enough to cause marked impairment in social or occupational functioning or to require hospitalization, and there are no psychotic features
    6. Symptoms do not result from the direct physiological effects of a substance or medical condition

Serious Neurological and Cognitive Impairments from *DSM-IV-TR*

Delirium

Disturbance in consciousness and changes in cognition that occurs over a short period of time. Rule out dementia, may change throughout the day. May come on over one to three days, or suddenly. More common in elderly, and children are very prone to development. Differential diagnosis—Dementia alone; Delirium superimposed on Dementia; or Delirium alone.

Grouped according to etiology.

General Medical Condition—hypoglycemia, stroke, encephalitis etc.). Substanced-induced (e.g., cannabis, cocaine, hallucinogens, diazepam, alcohol withdrawl, etc.).
Multiple Etiologies—(such as viral encephalitis and alcohol withdrawl).
NOS

No single psychological variable can account for on-set of delirium but sleep and sensory deprivation have been implicated. The elderly and those recovering from surgeries (10-15%) and burn patients (30%) often experience.

Prodromal symptoms: restlessness, anxiety, irritability, and sleep disruption. Short onset after these symptoms appear.

Mental Status Tests for Delirium: Count backwards from 20. Draw the face of a clock (constructional tasks deficits); name objects (tests for dysnomia); write a sentence (tests for dysgraphia). Dysgraphia is one of the most sensitive indicators of delirium but can occur in other disorders too, such as dementia. Be aware of emotional responses to the confusion and delirium. EEG is either slowed or rapid.

Questions to ask in looking for medical and substance-induced concerns:

Is there a history of alcohol or drug usage?
Is the patient showing signs of sympathetic nervous system activity, such as rapid heart, increased blood pressure, sweating?
Does the person have high blood pressure?
Are there chest pains or other signs of cardiac distress?
Is there a history of insulin-dependent diabetes?
Is there a history of hypoglycemia?
Is there a history of pulmonary disease?

Dementia

Multiple cognitive deficits that include impairment in memory. Experience aphasia—deterioration in language; apraxia—impaired abilities at motor activities. Agnosia—failure to recognize objects. Executive functioning—plan, sequence, monitor, and execute complex behaviors. Differential diagnosis—delirium, amnesia, mental retardation, schizophrenia, major depressive disorder. Can be understood as cortical and subcortical. Cortical involves cerebral cortex—amnesia, aphasia, apraxia and agnosia (that is, Alzheimer's disease). Subcortical involves grey and deep-white matter structures—basal ganglia, thalamus, brain stem nuclei, and frontal lobe projections of these structures. Subcortical disrupts arousal, attention, motivation, rate of information processing. Clinically observed as psychomotor retardation, defective recall, poor abstraction and strategy formation, and mood and personality alterations such as depression or apathy.

Grouped according to etiology.

Alzheimer's type
Vascular
General medical condition—Parkinson's disease, syphilis, brain tumors, HIV infection; Huntington's disease; Picks disease; Cruetzfeldt-Jacobs diseases, head injury, etc.).
Substance Induced
Multiple Etiologies
NOS

Differentiating Dementia syndrome of depression (pseudodementia) from primary dementia

Shorter referral times for depression
History of mood disorder
More depressed mood and delusions in depression
More behavioral deterioration in patients with primary dementia
Sleep disturbance is more severe and involves early morning awakenings.

Anxiety Disorders

Panic attack (term not codable—uses panic disorder)

A. Essential feature is a discrete period of intense fear or discomfort that is accompanied by at least four of thirteen somatic or cognitive symptoms. Attack has a sudden onset and builds to a peak rapidly (usually ten minutes or less) and is often accompanied by a sense of imminent danger or impending doom and an urge to escape.
B. Diagnostic Criteria (four or more of the following)
    1. Palpitations, pounding heart, or accelerated heart rate
    2. Sweating
    3. Trembling or shaking
    4. Sensations of shortness of breath or smothering
    5. Feeling of choking
    6. Chest pain or discomfort
    7. Nausea or abdominal distress
    8. Feeling dizzy, unsteady, lightheaded, or faint
    9. Derealization (feeling of unreality) or depersonalization (being detached from one's self)
    10. Fear of losing control or going crazy
    11. Fear of dying
    12. Paresthesias (numbness or tingling sensations)
    13. Chills or hot flashes

Agoraphobia (not codable—code specific disorder in which it occurs)

A. Essential feature is anxiety about being in places or situations from which escape might be difficult (or embarrassing) or in which help might not be available in the event of a panic attack or panic-like symptoms.
B. Diagnostic Criteria
   1. Anxiety about being in places or situations from which escape may be difficult if an attack occurs. Typically involves a cluster of symptoms that include being outside of the home alone, in a crowd or standing in line, being on a bridge, traveling in a bus, train, or automobile.
   2. The situations are avoided (such as, travel) or else endured with marked distress or anxiety about having an attack.
   3. Anxiety or avoidance is not better accounted for by another mental disorder; for example, social phobia.

Panic Disorder without Agoraphobia

A. Essential feature is the presence of recurrent, unexpected panic attacks followed by at least one month of persistent concern about having another panic attack, worry about the possible consequences of the attacks, or a significant behavioral change related to the attacks.
B. Diagnostic Criteria
   1. Both a and b
      a. Recurrent unexpected panic attacks
      b. At least one or more of the attacks has been followed by one month or more of the following
         i. Persistent concern about having additional attacks
         ii. Worry about implications or consequences (e.g., going crazy, having heart attack, losing control)
         iii. Significant change in behavior related to the attacks
   2. Absence of agoraphobia
   3. Not the result of physiological effects of a substance or a medical condition
   4. Other diagnoses ruled out

Panic Disorder with Agoraphobia

A. Essential feature is the presence of recurrent, unexpected panic attacks followed by at least one month of persistent concern about having another panic attack, worry about the possible consequences of the attacks, or a significant behavioral change related to the attacks.
B. Diagnostic Criteria
   1. Both a and b
      a. Recurrent unexpected panic attacks
      b. At least one or more of the attacks has been followed by one month or more of the following
         i. Persistent concern about having additional attacks
         ii. Worry about implications or consequences (e.g., going crazy, having heart attack, losing control)
         iii. Significant change in behavior related to the attacks

2. Presence of agoraphobia
3. Not the result of physiological effects of a substance or a medical condition
4. Other diagnoses ruled out

Obsessive-Compulsive Disorder

A. Essential features are recurrent obsessions or compulsions that are severe enough to be time-consuming (that is, that take more than an hour a day) or cause marked distress or significant impairment. Obsessions are persistent ideas, thoughts, impulses, or images. Compulsions are repetitive behaviors.
B. Diagnostic Criteria—either obsessions or compulsions.
   1. Obsessions
      a. Recurrent and persistent thoughts, impulses, or images that are experienced at some time during the disturbance, as intrusive and inappropriate and that cause marked anxiety or distress
      b. The thoughts, impulses, or images are not simply excessive worries about real-life problems
      c. The person attempts to ignore or suppress or neutralize with some other thought or action
      d. The person recognizes that the obsessions are products of his or her own mind (not thought insertion as in schizophrenia)
   2. Compulsions
      a. Repetitive behaviors (such as, hand washing) or mental acts (such as, praying, counting) that the person feels driven to perform in response to an obsession, or according to rules that must be rigidly applied.
      b. The behaviors or mental acts are aimed at preventing or reducing distress or preventing some dreaded event or situation
C. At some point during the course of the disorder, the person has recognized that the obsessions or compulsions are excessive or unreasonable.
D. They cause marked distress, are time-consuming, or significantly interfere with the person's normal routine, occupational functioning, or social relationships.

Posttraumatic Stress Disorder

A. Essential feature is the development of characteristic symptoms following exposure to an extreme traumatic stress or involving direct personal experience of an event that involves actual or threatened death or serious injury, or other threat to one's physical integrity. This includes witnessing an event that involves death, injury, or a threat to the physical integrity of another person; learning about unexpected or violent death, serious harm, or threat of death or injury experienced by a family member or other close associate.
B. Diagnostic Criteria
   1. Both of the following present:
      a. The person experienced, witnessed, or was confronted with an event or events that involved actual or threatened death or serious injury, or threat to the physical integrity of self or others
      b. The person's response involved intense fear, helplessness, or horror

2. The traumatic event is persistently re-experienced in one or more of the following ways:
   a. Recurrent and intrusive distressing recollections of the event, including images, thoughts, or perceptions
   b. Recurrent distressing dreams of the event
   c. Acting or feeling as if the traumatic event were reoccuring (flashbacks, illusions, hallucinations, etc.)
   d. Intense psychological distress at exposure to internal or external cues that symbolize or resemble an aspect of the event
   e. Physiological reactivity on exposure to internal or external cues that symbolize or resemble an aspect of the event
3. Persistent avoidance of stimuli associated with the trauma and numbing of general responsiveness (not present before the trauma), as indicated by three or more of the following:
   a. Efforts to avoid thoughts, feelings, or conversations associated with the trauma
   b. Efforts to avoid activities, places, or people that arouse recollections of the trauma
   c. Inability to recall an important aspect of the trauma
   d. Markedly diminished interest or participation in significant activities
   e. Feelings of detachment or estrangement from others
   f. Restricted range of affect (for example, unable to have love feelings)
   g. Sense of foreshortened future (for example, does not expect to have a career, marriage, normal life span)
4. Persistent symptoms of increased arousal (two or more of below)
   a. Difficulty falling or staying asleep
   b. Irritability or outbursts of anger
   c. Difficulty concentrating
   d. Hypervigilance
   e. Exaggerated startle response
5. At least one month duration of symptoms
6. Causes significant distress and functional impairment
   Specify if:
   Acute: Symptoms less than 3 months
   Chronic: Symptoms 3 months or longer
   With delayed Onset: Symptoms begin at least six months after the stressor

Differential Diagnosis in Panic Disorders

Generalized anxiety
Depressive disorders
Schizophrenia
Depersonalization disorder
Somatoform disorder
Personality disorders
Hyper- and Hypothyrodism

Mitral valve prolapse (also acts as precursor to Panic Disorder)
Cardiac arrhythmias
Coronary insufficiency
Hypoglycemia
True vertigo
Drug and alcohol withdrawl

Important Differential Diagnosis in Obsessive Compulsive Disorders

Schizophrenia
Other anxiety and depression

SOURCE: DSM-IV-TR

The Scales of MMPI II Measure

Scales

Validity and Clinical Scales

VRIN–Variable Response Inconsistency

TRIN–True Response Inconsistency
F–Infrequency
FB–Back F
FP–Infrequency-Psychopathology
L–Lie
K–Correction
S–Superlative Self-Presentation
?–Cannot Say
1 Hs–Hypochondriasis
2 D–Depression
3 Hy–Conversion Hysteria
4 Pd–Psychopathic Deviate
5 Mf–Masculinity-Femininity
6 Pa–Paranoia
7 Pt–Psychasthenia
8 Sc–Schizophrenia
9 Ma–Hypomania
0 Si–Social Introversion

Superlative Self-Presentation Subscales

(Forensic Report only)

S1–Beliefs in Human Goodness
S2–Serenity
S3–Contentment with Life
S4–Patience and Denial of Irritability and Anger
S5–Denial of Moral Flaws

Supplementary Scales

(Extended Score Report, Interpretive Reports, and Personnel Adjustment Rating)

A–Anxiety
R–Repression
Es–Ego Strength
Do–Dominance
Re–Social Responsibility
Mt–College Maladjustment
PK–PTSD/Keane
MDS–Marital Distress
Ho–Hostility
O-H–Overcontrolled Hostility
MAC-R–MacAndrew-Revised
AAS–Addiction Admission
APS–Addiction Potential
GM–Gender Role–Masculine
GF–Gender Role–Feminine

PSY-5 Scales—part of the Supplementary Scales

(Extended Score Report only)

AGGR–Aggressiveness
PSYC–Psychoticism
DISC–Disconstraint
NEGE–Negative Emotionality/ Neuroticism
INTR–Introversion/Low Positive Emotionality

Content Scales
(Extended Score Report, Interpretive
Reports, Criminal Justice and
Correctional Report, and Personnel
Adjustment Rating)

ANX–Anxiety
FRS–Fears
OBS–Obsessiveness
DEP–Depression
HEA–Health Concerns
BIZ–Bizarre Mentation
ANG–Anger
CYN–Cynicism
ASP–Antisocial Practices
TPA–Type A
LSE–Low Self-Esteem
SOD–Social Discomfort
FAM–Family Problems
WRK–Work Interference
TRT–Negative Treatment Indicators

Content Component Scales
(Extended Score Report, Interpretive
Reports, and Personnel Adjust-
ment Rating)

FRS1–Fears: Generalized Fearfulness
FRS2–Fears: Multiple Fears
DEP1–Depression: Lack of Drive
DEP2–Depression: Dysphoria
DEP3–Depression: Self-Depreciation
DEP4–Depression: Suicidal Ideation
HEA1–Health Concerns: Gastroin-
testinal Symptoms
HEA2–Health Concerns: Neurologi-
cal Symptoms
HEA3–Health Concerns: General
Health Concerns
BIZ1–Bizarre Mentation: Psychotic
Symptomatology
BIZ2–Bizarre Mentation: Schizotypal
Characteristics
ANG1–Anger: Explosive Behavior
ANG2–Anger: Irritability
CYN1–Cynicism: Misanthropic
Beliefs

**Clinical Subscales—Harris-Lingoes
and Social Introversion Subscales**
(Extended Score Report, Interpretive
Reports, and Personnel Adjustment Rating)

D1–Subjective Depression
D2–Psychomotor Retardation
D3–Physical Malfunction
D4–Mental Dullness
D5–Brooding
Hy1–Denial of Social Anxiety
Hy2–Need for Affection
Hy3–Lassitude-Malaise
Hy4–Somatic Complaints
Hy5–Inhibition of Aggression
Ma1–Amorality
Ma2–Psychomotor Acceleration
Ma3–Imperturbability
Ma4–Ego Inflation
Pa1–Persecutory Ideas
Pa2–Poignancy
Pa3–Naiveté
Pd1–Familial Discord

**Clinical Subscales—Harris-Lingoes
and Social Introversion Subscales
(Cont.)**
Pd2–Authority Problems
Pd3–Social Imperturbability
Pd4–Social Alienation
Pd5–Self-Alienation
Sc1–Social Alienation
Sc2–Emotional Alienation
Sc3–Lack of Ego Mastery-Cognitive
Sc4–Lack of Ego Mastery-Conative
Sc5–Lack of Ego Mastery-Defective
Inhibition
Sc6–Bizarre Sensory Experiences
Si1–Shyness/Self-Consciousness
Si2–Social Avoidance
Si3–Alienation–Self and Others

CYN2–Cynicism: Interpersonal Suspiciousness ASP1–Antisocial Practices: Antisocial Attitudes ASP2–Antisocial Practices: Antisocial Behavior TPA1–Type A: Impatience TPA2–Type A: Competitive Drive LSE1–Low Self-Esteem: Self-Doubt LSE2–Low Self-Esteem: Submissiveness SOD1–Social Discomfort: Introversion SOD2–Social Discomfort: Shyness FAM1–Family Problems: Family Discord FAM2–Family Problems: Familial Alienation TRT1–Negative Treatment Indicators: Low Motivation TRT2–Negative Treatment Indicators: Inability to Disclose	
SOURCE: NCS, Pearson Inc. NCS Assessments®, MMPI II-A, registered Trademark of the University of Minnesota	

Examples of Circular Questions

I. Problem: Definition Questions: Whenever possible, ask for a description of the specific behaviors which are perceived to be problematic.

  A. *Present*
- What is the problem in the family now?
- What concerns bring you into therapy now? or: What concerns bring you here now?
- What is the main concern of the family now?
- What problems do the other children have?
- For children: What changes would you like in your family?

    1. Difference
- How is this different than before?
- Has this always been true?

    2. Agreement/Disagreement
- Who agrees with you that this is the problem?

    3. Explanation/Meaning
- What is your explanation for that?
- What does his behavior mean to you?

  B. *Past*
- What was the problem in the family then?

    1. Difference
- How is that different from now?

    2. Agreement/Disagreement
- How is that different from now?
- Who agrees with Dad that this was the major concern of the family then?

    3. Explanation/Meaning
- What is your explanation for that?
- What do you believe was the significance of that?

SOURCE: Fleuridas, C., Nelson, T. S., & Rosenthal, D. M. (1986). The evolution of circular questions: Training family therapists. *Journal of Marital and Family Therapy, 12*(2), 113–127.

C. *Future/Hypothetical*
  • What would be the problem in the family if things were to continue as they are?

  1. Difference
    • How would that be different than it is now?

  2. Agreement/Disagreement
    • Do you agree, Mom?

  3. Explanation/Meaning
    • If this were to happen, how would you explain it?
    • What purpose would that serve?

II. Sequence-of-Interaction Questions: Focus on interactional behaviors.

General Examples	*Specific Examples*
A. Present	
• Who does what when?	• Ask Daughter: When Mom tries to get Sister to eat (to solve or prevent the presenting problem) and she refuses, what does Dad do? Then what does Mom do? What does Brother do? And what does Sister do? Then what happens?
• Then what happens?	
• What next?	
• Where is she when this happens?	
• What does she do?	
• Then what do they do?	
• Who notices first?	• When Mom and Brother are fighting, what does Dad do?
• What does he respond?	• Does Dad get involved in that fight or stay out of it? Describe what happens.
• When he does not do that (problem definition), what happens?	• When Dad doesn't get involved in their fights, what happens? How does Mom react when Dad doesn't get involved and fight with Brother?
1. Difference	
• Has it always been this way?	• Has Brother always behaved in this manner?
2. Agreement/Disagreement	
• Who agrees with you that this is how it happens?	• Who agrees with you that Mom yells at Dad every time he stomps out of the house?
3. Explanation/Meaning	
• What is your explanation for this?	• How do you explain Dad's tendency to leave home often?
• What does this mean to you?	• What does Dad's behavior mean to you?

General Examples	Specific Examples
B. Past	
• Who did what then?	• What did Dad do on those
• What solutions were tried?	days when Brother used to
	push Mom around?
	• What did Dad do?
1. Difference	• How was Dad's behavior dif-
• How was it different?	ferent? Describe what he used
• When was it different	to do?
• What else was different then?	• When did he do this? How
• How does that differ from	often?
how it is now?	• When did he change?
• Was it then more or less than	• How did Dad respond to the
it is now?	earlier situation? Then what
	happened?
	• How does that differ from
	how he responds now?
	• Was he gone more or less of-
	ten then he is now?
2. Agreement/Disagreement	• Who agrees with Mom that
• Who agrees with you?	Dad is more involved in the
	fights now?
3. Explanation/Meaning	• How do you explain this re-
• How do you explain this	cent involvement?
change?	• What does it mean to you that
• What does this change (or	day after day, year after year,
lack of change) mean to you?	things between the two of you
	have not changed?
C. Future/Hypothetical	
• What would she do differently	• What do you think Mom
if he did (not) do this?	would do if Dad were to ig-
	nore Brother?
	• What will Dad do with
	brother when Mom begins to
	work nights?
1. Difference	• How would your parents' re-
• How would it be different if	lationship be different if
he were to do this?	Mom were to return to
	school?
2. Agreement/Disagreement	• Do you think Mom would
• Who would agree with you	agree that they would proba-
that this is probably what	bly get a divorce if she were
would happen?	to return to school?

General Examples	*Specific Examples*
3. Explanation/Meaning • Tell me why you believe this would happen? • How do you think your wife would explain it? • What would this mean to you?	• Dad, why do you think your daughter and wife both agree that a divorce is likely should your wife return to work? • What would a divorce between your parents mean to you?

Family Goal Recording

PRESENTING PROBLEMS OR CONCERNS		GENERAL CHANGES DESIRED
Mom:	"Main concern is Ed. . . ." (10-yr-old son)	That he "like himself," have more confidence in his work (school, home)
	"Poor self-concept"	Keep his room clean without being told
	"In trouble at school," often fighting with other children	
	"Sloppy," his room "a pig's pen" (*Note*: they raised hogs on their farm)	
	Kids fight daily: "agitation is continuous "	
Dad:	Ed's social functioning worries him	"He must learn to get along better than others"
	"Poor self-concept . . . speaks derogatorily" about himself and others—"nasty statements"	
Ed: (10 yrs.)	His sisters pick on him (call him "fatty"), fights	That his sisters "quit picking" on him
	"Nothing else needs to change"	
Claire: (8 yrs.)	Mom yells too much	Get mom not to scream at us
Sara: (8 yrs.)	Ed "is a bully . . . calls us dirty names "	"For Ed to be nice to us"
Dad:	Ed's room is filthy—"he never picks it up until I come down there with a shovel, angry as hell, and help him"	At least clear a path from the door to his bed"
Mom:	. . .	"And bring up wet sheets in the morning" (NOTE: Ed wets his bed 2–4 x/wk.)

SOURCE: Fleuridas, C., Rosenthal, D. M., Leigh, E. K., & Leigh, T. E. (1990). Family goal recording: An adaptation of goal attainment scaling for enhancing family therapy and assessment. *Journal of Marital and Family Therapy, 16*(4), 389–406.

Worksheet #2: Classify Presenting Problems and Changes

Record how many times they see a specific problem occurring in a specific time frame; how often it would be reasonable for the behavior to occur (a reasonable optimal change desired); and how often they think this behavior would be exhibited if things were to become much worse.

WEIGHT %	PROBLEMS OR CONCERNS	WEIGHT %	DESIRED CHANGE	DETERIORATION
	CHILD RELATED:			
50%	A. Ed's self-esteem: he speaks negatively about himself: 2x/day	33%	Negative statement about self = 2x/wk (more positive)	Suicide attempt or physically harm self
	B. Ed's school fights/social troubles with teacher: 2x/day; trouble with principal: 1x/week	33%	Okay to be in trouble w/teacher 1x/wk, w/principal 1x/yr	Expulsion from school for the rest of the year
	C. Fights among children; Ed: "6x/day," Sara: "3x/day," parents: "continuous"	17%	2x/day	Fights increase in violence; teasing continues to be constant but "meaner"
	D. Ed's room: always a mess	17%	Ed brings up dirty dishes, clothes, & sheets: 4x/wk	Ed leaves his mess elsewhere in the home daily
		100%		
	PARENT RELATED:			
40%	A. Private time for parents' apx. 1x/mo (w/o children "butting in")	40%	2x/wk, one of which is out of the home	No planned time alone for 3 months
	B. Mom screams at kids 1x/day	20%	1x/wk	4x/day
	C. Dad makes no effort to spend time with Ed (positive time)	40%	Dad initiates activities w/Ed 1x/wk (e.g., baseball, swimming, walks)	Dad & Ed have no verbal exchange in a month
		100%		
	FAMILY RELATED:			
10%	A. Family "get-togethers" at most 1x/mo, including meals	100%	1x/wk	None in three months

(BEHAVIORAL CHANGE EVALUATION)
CHILD SUBSYSTEM GOAL AREAS

OUTCOME STATUS	LEVEL	A ED'S SELF ESTEEM WEIGHT (33%)	B ED'S SOCIAL RELATIONS WEIGHT (33%)	C CHILDREN FIGHT WEIGHT (17%)	D ED'S ROOM WEIGHT (17%)
OPTIMAL	1.00	Negative self-statements only 2x/wkØ	1x/wk trouble w/ teacher; 1x/yr trouble w/principal≠ÆØ	Fight w/sisters 2x/wk	Dishes, clothes, & sheets brought up 4x/ wk 2x/wk
	0.75	1x/every other day			
	0.50	1x/day (7x/wk)	5x/wk/teacher; 1x/every other wk/principal	2x/day	1x/wk
	0.25	3x/every two days			1x/mo
PRESENT BASE RATE	0.00	2x/day (14x/wk)	Hostile w/children at school: 2x/day trouble w/teacher 1x/wk w/principal	4x/day (only verbal)	Room always messy (unless dad cleans it . . .)
	-0.25	5x/day or statements more nasty or negative		Fights increase	
	-0.50	5x/day plus more negative	4x/day/teacher 2x/wk/principal	All interaction are negative, or occasional fights are physical	3–4 x/wk other rooms of house
	-0.75	Threats to harm self; only negative statements, depression	Physically harms another child		

OUTCOME STATUS	LEVEL	A ED'S SELF ESTEEM WEIGHT (33%)	B ED'S SOCIAL RELATIONS WEIGHT (33%)	C CHILDREN FIGHT WEIGHT (17%)	D ED'S ROOM WEIGHT (17%)
DETERIORATION	-1.00	Attempts suicide or harms self	Expulsion from school for rest of year due to hostility w/children	Physical fights daily	1x/day Ed leaves his trash & stuff in the rest of the home
FORMULA:		Level A: _____ x Weight A: _____	Level B: _____ x Weight B: _____	Level C: _____ x Weight C: _____	Level D: _____ x Weight D: _____
1ST ASSESSMENT		= Score A: _____	= Score B: _____	= Score C: _____	= Score D: _____
2ND ASSESSMENT		A: .75 X .33 = .2475	B: .33	C: -.25 X .17 = -.0425	D: .25 X .17 = .0425
3RD ASSESSMENT		A: .75 X .33 = .2475	B: .33	C: 0	D: .25 X .17 = .0425
4TH ASSESSMENT		A: 1.0 X .33 = .33	B: .33	C: 0	D: .75 X .17 = .1275

TOTALS $\neq$ =.5775   Æ =.62 $\emptyset$ =.7875 = % of child subsystem goals attained

(BEHAVIORAL CHANGE EVALUATION)
PARENT SUBSYSTEM GOAL AREAS:

OUTCOME STATUS	LEVEL	A PRIVATE TIME FOR PARENTS WEIGHT (40%)	B MOM SCREAMS AT CHILDREN WEIGHT (20%)	C DAD SPENDS TIME W/ED WEIGHT (40%)	D WEIGHT (%)
OPTIMAL	1.00	Parents spend time alone together 2x/wk (one of which is out of the house)	At most 1x/wk	Dad initiates activities w/Ed 1x/wk	
	0.75	1x/wk out			
	0.50	2x/mo out, maintaining 1x/wk in home≠	1x/every other day	1x/month	
	0.25	2x/mo. out w/no home time, or in-home time alone increases w/o out of home		1x/3 mo	
PRESENT BASE	0.00	1x/mo/alone (at most) out of the home (1hr/ wk in home)	1x/day (never physical)	Dad makes no effort to spend positive time with Ed	
	−0.25				
	−0.50	1x/two months	2x/day or physically abusive once		
	2-0.75				
DETERIORATION	−1.00	No time at all alone in 3/mos (planned time)	4x/day &/or regular physical abuse	No verbal contact between Dad and Ed	

OUTCOME STATUS	LEVEL	A PRIVATE TIME FOR PARENTS WEIGHT (40%)	B MOM SCREAMS AT CHILDREN WEIGHT (20%)	C DAD SPENDS TIME W/ED WEIGHT (40%)	D WEIGHT (%)
FORMULA:		Level A: _____	Level B: _____	Level C: _____	Level D: _____
		x Weight A: _____	x Weight B: _____	x Weight C: _____	x Weight D: _____
		= Score A: _____	= Score B: _____	= Score C: _____	= Score D: _____
1ST ASSESSMENT					
2ND ASSESSMENT		A: .50 x .40 = .20	B: .50 x .20 = .10	C: .50 x .40 = .20	D:
3RD ASSESSMENT		A: 1.0 x 4.0 = .40	B: .80 x .20 = .16	C: .25 x .40 = .10	D:
4TH ASSESSMENT		A: 1.0 x 4.0 = .40	B: .90 x .20 = .18	C: .25 x .40 = .10	D:

TOTALS ≠ = .50   Æ = .66   Ø = .68 = 68% of parent subsystem goals attained

APPENDIX 8C

Genogram Symbols

I. Symbols for genogram assessment

  A. Symbols to describe basic family membership and structure (include on genogram significant others who lived with or cared for family members—place them on the right side of the genogram with a notation about who they are.)

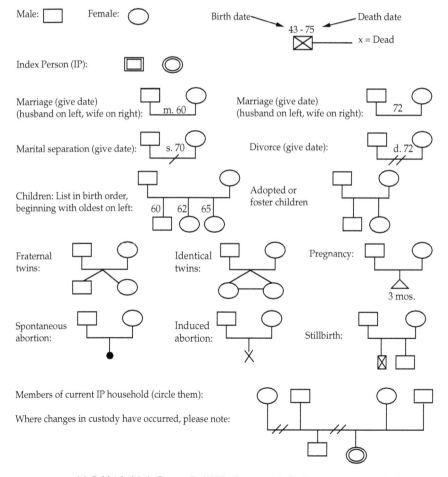

ADAPTED FROM: McGoldrick, M, & Gerson, R. (1985). *Genograms in family assessment.* New York: W. W. Norton.

B. Family interaction patterns. The following symbols are optional. The clinician may prefer to note them on a separate sheet. They are among the least precise information on the genogram, but may be key indicators of relationship patterns the clinician wants to remember:

Very close relationship: Conflictual relationship:

Distant relationship: Estranged or cut off (give dates if possible):

Fused and conflictual:

C. Medical history. Because the genogram is meant to be an orienting map of the family, there is room to indicate only the most important factors. Thus, list only major or chronic illnesses and problems. Include dates in parentheses where feasible or applicable. Use DSM categories or recognized abbreviations where available (e.g., cancer [CA]; stroke [CVA]).

D. Other family information of special importance may also be noted on the genogram:
   1) Ethnic background and migration date
   2) Religion or religious change
   3) Education
   4) Occupation or unemployment
   5) Military service
   6) Retirement
   7) Trouble with the law
   8) Physical abuse or incest
   9) Obesity
   10) Alcohol or drug abuse (symbol =)
   11) Smoking
   12) Dates when family members left home: LH 74
   13) Current location of family members

Other key information: critical events, changes in the family structure since the genogram was made, hypotheses, and other notations of major family issues or changes. These notations should always be dated and kept to a minimum, since every extra piece of information of a genogram complicates it and therefore diminishes its reliability.

Abusive Behavior Inventory Partner Form

Here is a list of behaviors that many women report have been used by their partners or former partners. We would like you to estimate how often these behaviors occurred during the six months prior to your beginning this program. Your answers are strictly confidential.

CIRCLE a number of each of the items listed below to show your closest estimate of how often it happened in your relationship with your partner or former partner during the *six months* before he started the program.

1 = Never
2 = Rarely
3 = Occasionally
4 = Frequently
5 = Very frequently

1. Call you names and/or criticized you.	1 2 3 4 5
2. Tried to keep you from doing something you wanted to do (example: going out with friends, going to meetings).	1 2 3 4 5
3. Gave you angry stares or looks.	1 2 3 4 5
4. Prevented you from having money for your own use.	1 2 3 4 5
5. Ended a discussion with you and made the decision himself.	1 2 3 4 5
6. Threatened to hit or throw something at you.	1 2 3 4 5
7. Pushed, grabbed, or shoved you.	1 2 3 4 5
8. Put down your family or friends.	1 2 3 4 5
9. Accused you of paying too much attention to someone or something else.	1 2 3 4 5
10. Put you on an allowance.	1 2 3 4 5
11. Used your children to threaten you (example: told you that you would lose custody, said he would leave town with the children).	1 2 3 4 5
12. Became very upset with you because dinner, housework, or laundry was not ready when he wanted it or done the way he thought it should be done.	1 2 3 4 5

SOURCE: Shepard, C. E., & Campbell, J. A. (1991). *The Abusive Behavior Inventory*, Deluth, MN: University of Minnesota at Deluth, School of Social Work.

13. Said things to scare you (example: told you something
    "bad" would happen, threatened to commit suicide).   1 2 3 4 5
14. Slapped, hit, or punched you.   1 2 3 4 5
15. Made you do something humiliating or degrading (exam-
    ple: begging for forgiveness, having to ask his permission
    to use the car or do something).   1 2 3 4 5
16. Checked up on you (example: listened to your phone calls,
    checked the mileage on your car, called you repeatedly at
    work).   1 2 3 4 5
17. Drove recklessly when you were in the car.   1 2 3 4 5
18. Pressured you to have sex in a way that you didn't like or
    want.   1 2 3 4 5
19. Refused to do housework or child care.   1 2 3 4 5
20. Threatened you with a knife, gun, or other weapon.   1 2 3 4 5
21. Spanked you.   1 2 3 4 5
22. Told you that you were a bad parent.   1 2 3 4 5
23. Stopped you or tried to stop you from going to work or
    school.   1 2 3 4 5
24. Threw, hit, kicked, or smashed something.   1 2 3 4 5
25. Kicked you.   1 2 3 4 5
26. Physically forced you to have sex.   1 2 3 4 5
27. Threw you around.   1 2 3 4 5
28. Physically attacked the sexual parts of your body.   1 2 3 4 5
29. Choked or strangled you.   1 2 3 4 5
30. Used a knife, gun, or other weapon against you.   1 2 3 4 5

Index